RFID

RFID

APPLICATIONS, SECURITY, AND PRIVACY

Edited by

Simson Garfinkel
Beth Rosenberg

✦Addison-Wesley

Upper Saddle River, NJ • Boston • San Francisco
New York • Toronto • Montreal • London • Munich • Paris • Madrid
Capetown • Sydney • Tokyo • Singapore • Mexico City

Many of the designations used by manufacturers and sellers to distinguish their products are claimed as trademarks. Where those designations appear in this book, and the publisher was aware of a trademark claim, the designations have been printed with initial capital letters or in all capitals.

The authors and publisher have taken care in the preparation of this book, but make no expressed or implied warranty of any kind and assume no responsibility for errors or omissions. No liability is assumed for incidental or consequential damages in connection with or arising out of the use of the information or programs contained herein.

The publisher offers excellent discounts on this book when ordered in quantity for bulk purchases or special sales, which may include electronic versions and/or custom covers and content particular to your business, training goals, marketing focus, and branding interests. For more information, please contact:

> U.S. Corporate and Government Sales
> (800) 382-3419
> corpsales@pearsontechgroup.com

For sales outside the U.S., please contact:

> International Sales
> international@pearsoned.com

Visit us on the Web: www.awprofessional.com

Library of Congress Cataloging-in-Publication Data
Garfinkel, Simson.
  RFID : applications, security, and privacy / Simson Garfinkel and Beth Rosenberg, editors.
      p. cm.
    Includes index.
    ISBN 0-321-29096-8 (alk. paper)
  1. Inventory control—Automation. 2. Radio frequency identification systems. 3. Privacy, Right of—United States. I. Rosenberg, Beth
  II. Title.
  TS160.G37 2005
  658.5'14—dc22
                                                            2005006610

ISBN 0-321-29096-8
Text printed in the United States on recycled paper at Courier in Westford, Massachusetts.
First printing, July 2005

CONTENTS

Chapter 2   Understanding RFID Technology 15
Simson Garfinkel, Henry Holtzman

Chapter 3   A History of the EPC 37
Sanjay Sarma

FOREWORD

Radio frequency identification (RFID) is the first important technology of the twenty-first century. That's an awesome responsibility. The first important technology of the twentieth century, radio, had a profound impact: Its descendents included television, computers, and even air travel. Big, fundamental technologies do that—they are the first steps onto a new continent of possibility. What follows are decades of exploration and discovery, much of it entirely unexpected and initially unbelievable.

RFID is important because it enables machines to perceive. Machine perception is common in science fiction, where sentient robots walk and talk as a matter of course, but it is rare and primitive in everyday life. Airport faucets struggle to sense people impatiently waiting to wash their hands, bar code scanners frequently fail to beep, and home burglar alarms have trouble distinguishing between pets and intruders. During the next few decades, RFID will help change all that: It will usher in a new wave of computing in which devices can effectively sense and interpret the world around them.

RFID, as its name suggests, is the means of identification. Later, related technologies will piggyback on RFID infrastructure to provide data about things like temperature, pressure, and wear. Warehouses will sense whether they are low on stock or overstocked; airports will find and route luggage automatically; cars will know whether their tires are about to blow; homes will know if lights are left on, doors are unlocked, or windows are open. Because of RFID, we are entering what Paul Saffo has called "The Sensor Age." In the nineteenth century, machines could do; in the twentieth century, they could think; in the twenty-first century, they will perceive.

For some, this is a Utopian vision. For others, it sounds like hell. As usual, the reality will be somewhere in between. To dispense with Utopia first: One thing is certain about the future—it won't ever be perfect. RFID will not cure war, end hunger, or eliminate all waste. But it may help sustain our world, increase our standard of living, raise the efficiency of our economy, and enhance the quality of our lives. At its very best, it may improve healthcare by making pharmaceutical distribution more efficient and accurate; it may lead to more recycling by providing automatic sorting of garbage; and by improving the efficiency of government and business alike, it could contribute to lower prices and, maybe, reduced taxes. These are real benefits, of real value both to individual lives and to the human race as a whole. And this is just what we see today; there will be other benefits too, as yet unimagined. The technologies of the twentieth century—television, radio, computing, and so on—brought comparable advantages. Major technologies often start out as luxuries, indulgences, or conveniences and then, because they reshape society, become essential.

On the other side of the debate are those who think RFID means instant doom. Another certainty is that the world will not end in our lifetime. (Noam Chomsky jokes that this is the safest prediction to make because if you are wrong, no one will be around to notice.) All new technologies merit diligence. RFID is no different. Its risks must be measured, and where appropriate, we should be cautious. But not all risks are equal, and some must be dismissed to improve the debate.

First, RFID is not the work of the Devil. The Devil, by all accounts, is a supernatural being with inhuman powers: He doesn't need RFID. Second, RFID is not part of a plot by evil corporate interests intent on spying on everyone. A corporation, in contrast to the Devil, is a group of human beings with human powers, not evil villains who conspire against their customers. The people who work at corporations are interested in RFID because they think it will help them build a better business, not because they are secretly out to get us. Third, RFID is not about to give rise to a whole new class of totalitarianism. While dictators and oppressors *are* out to get us—or at least some of us—they have regrettably managed very well over the centuries without RFID. Dictators will use whatever they can to work their evil, but whether or not they succeed in the future probably has little to do with new technology.

Once these dramatic exaggerations are excluded, we are left with some important, serious, and reasonable questions. How can we know when and how RFID is being used? How can we make sure it is not misused? How can we exercise choice over how it affects us personally? How do we ensure that it is safe?

This book is an important contribution to the ongoing effort to find the answers. My friend and colleague, Sanjay Sarma, says, "Writing is the highest form of thought." It follows that reading allows us to hold other people's thoughts up to the light for closer examination. We can test their logic, measure their assumptions, and check their sources. Written argument has a vulnerability that is not found in sound bites, speeches, or journalism where it is too easy to gloss and gild and misrepresent. A written idea is a naked idea.

I do not agree with everything that is written here, but I welcome every word. RFID is too important for there to be no public debate or for a debate that is badly informed, sensationalized, or manipulated. It is an inevitable technology, and its impact will be felt for generations. We are at the start of a new century, the beginning of our adventure in machine perception, and the dawning of the Sensor Age. Now is the perfect time to wonder.

—*Kevin Ashton*
  cofounder and former executive director, Auto-ID Center
  vice president, ThingMagic Corporation
  February 2005

PREFACE

There's a school bus stopped outside a middle school in Spring, Texas, a wealthy suburb on the northern edge of Houston's metropolitan sprawl. Inside the bus, several well dressed and obviously well-off children stand in the aisle waiting to get off. Sandra Martinez, a 10-year-old with a thick brown braid and a charcoal gray blazer, pauses while she takes her ID card, hanging from a lanyard around her neck, and presses it against the large gray panel mounted on the big padded barrier that divides the stairwell from the passenger compartment.

The panel beeps.

Sandra descends the school bus steps and the next student fumbles for her ID card. Meanwhile, a computer onboard the bus is hard at work. First the computer takes a geospatial reading from the Global Positioning System receiver that's mounted inside the bus. Next, the computer, using an onboard digital cell phone, sends to Spring Independent School District the precise time and location that Martinez left the bus. This information is made instantly available on a Web site where it can be accessed by Martinez's parents, the school administration, or anyone else with the appropriate access codes. The purpose of the system, which was installed at a cost of $180,000, is to let parents know precisely when and where their children get on or off the school bus. "If it works one time, finding a student who has been kidnapped, then the system has paid for itself," Brian Weisinger, the head of transportation for the Spring district, told the *New York Times*.[1]

No student has ever been kidnapped in Spring, Texas.

---

1. Richtel, M. "In Texas, 28,000 Students Test an Electronic Eye." *The New York Times*. November 17, 2004. p. A1.

A slightly different student tracking system is in use at the Enterprise Charter School in Buffalo, New York. There, a pair of kiosks that were purchased at a cost of $40,000 read ID tags as students enter and exit the building. Mark Walter, head of technology for the Buffalo school, told the *New York Times* that initially, the system failed to register some students, but now it works pretty well. Advocates of the technology say that it just might be expanded—for example, with readers placed on individual classroom doors to see if students are attending their classes.

Some students, of course, invariably forget their tags at home or lose them. Some might even purposely throw them away. Even for these students, technology has an answer: In late 2004, the U.S. Food and Drug Administration approved for general use a tiny radio tag that can be implanted under the skin. Similar technology has been used to track household pets since the 1990s.

Meanwhile, the U.S. State Department is discussing the prospect of issuing passports that carry a tiny RFID chip that includes 64 kilobytes of memory and alas can be covertly read at a distance of 30 feet by anyone with a suitable reader and a good antenna.[2] The State Department says that there's no need to worry: The data on the chip will reportedly be encrypted, so anybody who reads it will read only gibberish.

The RFID Controversy and the Technology That Fuels It

Radio Frequency Identification, better known as RFID, is fast becoming one of the most controversial technologies of our era.

Proponents of RFID say that the tiny tags, made of silicon chips and radio antennas, can stamp out counterfeit drugs, fight terrorism, and at the same time help Wal-Mart keep its shelves stocked. They say that widespread adoption of RFID will allow companies to improve efficiency, cut costs, and offer dramatic new products and services to their customers. Most proponents scoff that the technology has a downside at all—other than perhaps the cost of the tags, and the cost of tags is dropping quickly.

But RFID has many critics. The most vocal are privacy activists who argue that the technology's unprecedented ability to track the movements of individually

---

2. Wald, M.L. "New High-Tech Passports Raise Snooping Concerns." *The New York Times.* November 26, 2004.

serialized objects could be turned around and used to track the people carrying those objects. They worry that the RFID readers across the nation could report back to a single global network that could be used by the government as a kind of roving geographical wiretap.

Many critics argue that RFID is a threat not just to individuals but to corporations and governments as well. In a few years, RFID readers at warehouse doors will allow companies to inventory the contents of cartons without opening them. But without the proper controls, the technology could also facilitate industrial espionage by giving competitors unprecedented access to a company's inventory. And once you begin thinking about RFID as an offensive technology, a lot of possibilities start emerging. Just as toll roads can use RFID to read E-ZPass tags and automatically debit drivers' accounts, a bomb with a built-in RFID reader could wait patiently in the roadway until it senses the tag of a particular individual drives above, and then detonate. Want to falsely implicate someone in a crime? Just clone one of that person's RFID tags and then arrange for it to pass by a particular reader just minutes before a murder.

The book you are holding is the first of its kind to explore the wide range of security and privacy issues that are being raised by RFID technology. It is the first book to bring together advocates and opponents from across the RFID spectrum. In its pages you will find chapters from companies that are producing RFID readers; from companies that are busy putting products with embedded RFID-tags on their shelves; and from the very privacy activists who are trying to stop them. Bringing together this diverse group of individuals and organizations has taken a lot of time and work. The result is the most balanced and accurate discussion you will find of RFID technology and its attendant controversy anywhere on the planet.

RFID: What Is It?

As its name implies, the term RFID is generally used to describe any technology that uses radio signals to identify specific objects. In practice, this means any technology that transmits specific identifying numbers using radio. Electronic Article Surveillance (EAS) systems, used by many clothing and music stores to set off an alarm when a shoplifter steals an item, are not RFID because the EAS tags do not have individual codes or serial numbers that can be read remotely. The Mobil Speedpass system used to pay for gas *is* an RFID system: Each Speedpass tag contains a unique serial number that is used to identify the tag's owner.

Each RFID tag consists of a silicon chip, an antenna, and some kind of housing. The tags come in sizes as large as a paperback book and smaller than a grain of rice. So-called active tags contain batteries, while passive tags are powered directly by the radio frequencies used to read them. The reading range of a tag depends on many factors, including on the tag's electronics, its antenna, the reader, the radio frequencies used, and decisions made at the time the system is deployed. It is therefore inaccurate to state a "typical tag's" read range without first specifying what kind of tag you are using. (I explain these technical issues and others in Chapter 2, Understanding RFID Technology.)

Already, RFID technology is broadly deployed within the United States. Between the "proximity cards" used to unlock many office doors and the automobile "immobilizer chips" built into many modern car keys, it's estimated that roughly 40 million Americans carry some form of RFID device in their pocket every day. I have two: Last year MIT started putting RFID chips into the school's identity cards, and there is a Philips immobilizer chip inside the black case of my Honda Pilot car keys. Don't think you have an immobilizer chip? Look at Figure 1—you might be surprised.

Many of today's media accounts of RFID aren't about these proprietary devices or RFID in general but about the standardized Electronic Product Code (EPC) chips that were developed by the Auto-ID Center and are now being overseen

Figure 1   The Immobilizer is built into the housing of the auto key.
(Image reprinted courtesy of Texas Instruments Inc.)

by EPCglobal, a trade organization. RFID systems have been around for more than thirty years, opening office doors and tagging laboratory animals, but when the EPC was introduced, these systems were too expensive for mass deployment. By standardizing on a simple chip design and over-the-air protocol, EPC is able to take advantage of mass production's efficiencies.

EPC tags are designed to replace today's ubiquitous Universal Product Code (UPC) bar codes, except instead of identifying the maker and kind of product, the 96-bit EPC code will give every package of razors, box of pancake mix, and pair of sneakers its own unique serial number. The tags, which operate in the unlicensed radio spectrum between 868MHz and 965MHz, can be read at a distance of many feet and through paper, fabric, and some plastics. And although the tags can cost as much as 40 cents today, when they are purchased by the millions, the cost rapidly decreases to 10 cents per tag or less. (Sanjay Sarma, one of the founders of the Auto-ID center, explains the birth of the Auto-ID center and the EPC in Chapter 3, A History of the EPC.)

RFID Comes of Age

I had my first experience with RFID technology in January 1984. I was a freshman at the Massachusetts Institute of Technology and had just taken a job at one of MIT's new biology labs. For added security, the lab had installed a keyless entry system. The lab gave me a thick blue card to put in my wallet. To get into the secure area, all I had to do was wave my wallet in front of a special reader. Within a few days I learned that I could just bump against the reader, leaving my wallet in my pocket. It was very cool and high tech and allegedly very secure.

After a few weeks in my wallet, the top layer of the card's plastic was starting to peel away. And a few days after I quit that job, I ripped open the card to see how it worked. Underneath the laminate, I found a printed circuit board, a chip that was the size of a postage stamp, and a dozen or so metal pads, some of them shorted together with a dab of solder.

It was immediately clear that my card's serial number was determined by which pads were soldered together and which had been left open. My ID number had been canceled when I resigned, but in theory I could have changed my card's ID to someone else's simply by making or breaking a few connections on the card. I never tested this hypothesis, but there is no reason it shouldn't have worked. (Twenty years later, the security of many proximity card systems has only marginally improved; Jonathan Westhues explores other ways of subverting the security of proximity cards in Chapter 19, Hacking the Prox Card.)

I promptly forgot about RFID for the next ten years. Then, in 1994, my editor at *Wired Magazine* asked me to write a brief article about ID chips that were being injected into cats and dogs. I called the chip manufacturer and learned that the technology was being used for far more. Some firms were using RFID to track the movement of gas cylinders; other companies were using it to follow the paths of tools at job sites. A few nursing homes were even experimenting with tagged bracelets that could automatically set off alarms when Alzheimer patients wandered out the back door.

A few months later I learned that highway authorities from Massachusetts and New York to California were in the final stages of testing RFID-based Electronic Toll Collection (ETC) systems for a variety of highways and bridges. The tags, which could be read at speeds of 100 miles per hour, would cut traffic jams and the resulting levels of smog at toll booths. But it was also clear that the new ETC systems would create a huge database recording the precise time and location of every toll crossing by every tagged car.

The planners of those early RFID systems said that it was important to establish policies that would prevent toll-crossing information from being used for purposes unrelated to traffic management. But such policies were never adopted. These days ETC databases are routinely used by law enforcement agencies to track the movement of suspect cars—and by both divorce lawyers and labor lawyers to track the movements of people under investigation. I spoke with these technologists in the 1990s: None of them wanted to create a ubiquitous surveillance system that would permanently record the movements of cars on the highways and make that information available to anybody with a subpoena. Yet somehow, that's the system we got.

Newspaper and magazine stories about RFID frequently present the technology as one that forces us to make tradeoffs and compromises. Almost always, RFID is portrayed as promising some new convenience or security feature, but in return, consumers must be willing to give up a little privacy to reap these benefits.

ETC is perhaps the best example of this tradeoff. With an E-ZPass tag, you can speed through the toll booths on the George Washington Bridge, but that nasty divorce attorney will be able to get a blow-by-blow record of every time you entered and left Manhattan for the past year.

But making E-ZPass a combination toll payment and surveillance system was a conscious choice on the part of the engineers who designed the system and the highway administrators who approved it. Instead of broadcasting a serial number that's used to debit an account, the creators of E-ZPass could have adopted a more complex over-the-air protocol based on anonymous digital cash. Such a system would actually have been more secure—that is, more resistant to various kinds of cloning, fraud and abuse—than the account-based systems in a growing number of states. But as near as I have been able to determine, the system based on digital cash was never seriously considered.

The question of whether or not the nation's ETC system should preserve privacy or be a tool of surveillance should have been a subject of public debate. But it wasn't. Instead, policy was determined by a small number of technologists and administrators with virtually no input from either the public or elected officials.

In Massachusetts, for instance, when the Massachusetts Turnpike Authority (MTA) issued its request for proposal to contractors interested in supplying the ETC technology to the state, the RFP mandated that respondents propose only account-based systems similar to New York's E-ZPass. (Not surprisingly, a Boston-area company called ATCom, which had a system based on anonymous digital cash, cried foul, arguing that it had been frozen out of the bidding process because it had a technology that preserved privacy!)

John Judge was the MTA official responsible for the decision. When I called him to ask about the RFP, he told me in 1997, "Privacy is a non-issue."

> I think that is the experience nationwide, as least as it relates to electronic toll collection. Privacy has not been an issue that has emerged nationally. I think that [is] principally because it is a voluntary system. If you are of a mind where you might be concerned about privacy issues, you just don't have to join the program, and can use the traditional toll collection methods. I don't think that it is any more an issue than credit cards.[3]

Did John Judge and other MTA administrators not hear an outcry from an enraged electorate because the electorate simply wasn't informed about any decisions? Wide-scale public notification of the system's design happened only after contracts were signed, equipment was installed, and administrators were trying to accelerate the public's adoption of Massachusetts' "FastLane" technology. At that point it was too late to challenge the system's underlying design. Instead, consumers were simply given a "take it or leave it" choice for the convenient but admittedly invasive technology.

---

3. Interview with John Judge, June 27, 1997. Reported in Garfinkel, S. *Database Nation: The Death of Privacy in the 21st Century*, O'Reilly & Associates, 2000.

RFID Is Different

For the record, John Judge was wrong. The privacy and security considerations of RFID systems are profoundly more complex than those associated with credit cards.

For starters, radio waves are both invisible and penetrating. I cannot read your credit card if it is in your pocket, but I can read a proximity card or even an RFID-enabled credit card in that same place. Every E-ZPass or FastLane tag has a small battery that lasts for five years or so; without significantly increasing costs, each E-ZPass tag could have been equipped with a tiny speaker that would "beep" whenever the tag was read. Because it is not, there is no simple way for users of E-ZPass and the like to audit the system for themselves. Are there hidden E-ZPass readers scattered around New York City or Washington, D.C.? If each E-ZPass tag had a tiny speaker, it would be a simple matter to find out about unpublicized reader deployments.

The choice between using RFID-based payment systems on the highway and abstaining from them is profoundly different from the choice between using cash and using credit in another important way. Whether you buy your lunch with cash or a credit card, the length of the overall transaction is about the same. With RFID this is not the case. At Boston's Logan Airport on a typical weekday night, you might wait in line for 10 minutes or longer to make it through the tolls. But if you're willing to give up your privacy, you can sail through the FastLane electronic toll lane at 100 miles per hour—well, at 40 miles per hour, at least. So unlike people who buy their lunch with cash, people who try to travel the highways with cash end up paying a considerable penalty for the privilege of preserving their privacy.

It's probably too late to change a toll payment system used by Connecticut, Maine, Massachusetts, New Jersey, New York, Pennsylvania, and a growing number of other states. Today's highway regulators aren't interested in experimenting with new RFID systems; they're interested in seeing a single system deployed throughout the United States so that drivers can travel coast-to-coast without reaching for their coins. Once a technological direction is embarked upon, it is very difficult to start making incompatible choices.

This is not to say that privacy on the highway is lost. We can still have the privacy of our toll crossings; we just can't assure that privacy through technical means. But states or the federal government could pass legislation, if there were political will, to set a high threshold for protecting toll-crossing information. Such legislation could make RFID-collected toll crossing information "off limits" for use in divorce proceedings, for instance, much in the way that the Video Privacy Protection Act of 1988 (18 U.S.C. §2710) made videotape rental records off limits. (The VPPA, better known as the Bork Bill, was passed after Judge Bork's video rental records were obtained by Washington, D.C.'s *City Paper.* The bill sped through Congress soon afterwards—allegedly because lawmakers were worried that their own video rental records might be similarly obtained and published.) RFID-protection legislation could set standards that needed to be followed for the protection of the information, and it could establish a "data retention" policy that required RFID-collected information to be destroyed after six months.

Our lawmakers could pass such legislation. All that it takes is the political will. (Stephanie Perrin and Jonathan Weinberg explore global and national privacy regulations and discuss how those regulations apply or could be applied to RFID in Chapter 4, RFID and Global Privacy Policy, and Chapter 5, RFID, Privacy, and Regulation, respectively.)

Alternatively, privacy protections can be built directly into RFID technology itself. The EPC standard, for instance, supports a "kill" command that makes it possible to permanently disable tags after they are no longer needed. If tags might be needed for some kind of post-sale use—for example, enabling a product return—it might be possible to remove the tag's antenna so that the reader needs to be in physical contact with the device. Yet another approach is the so-called RFID blocker tag that jams all RFID transmissions within a sphere around the holder—think of this as a kind of "sphere of privacy." (Ari Jules, one of the co-inventors of the blocker tag, explores these and other technological solutions to the RFID privacy problem in Chapter 21, Technological Approaches to the RFID Privacy Problem.)

RFID Is Not Different

But on a deeper level, John Judge was right—just not for the reason that he thought. Privacy on the highways is a non-issue because the right to anonymous travel had already been considered at the dawn of the automobile and rejected.

Horses and buggies didn't have to be registered, but soon after motorized vehicles were introduced, they were required to display license plates in every state of the United States. The explicit purpose of the plates was to make every car different and, by so doing, eliminate anonymity.

These days, the technology for reading and automatically recognizing license plates has been virtually perfected. RFID-based systems are more accurate than optical license plate readers: They can read when the car is moving at a higher speed, and they are not affected by mud, rain, or fog. But the fundamental question of anonymous travel on the roads has already been resolved in the negative: Americans don't have it—at least not if they want to drive their own cars.

And here, RFID promoters maintain, is the fundamental problem with discussing the technology in a vacuum: Practically without exception, every threat to privacy that could conceivably be caused by RFID can already be accomplished through some combination of other technologies. The cat is already out of the bag! What the RFID industry really needs to do, noted Canadian computer columnist Peter de Jager argues in Chapter 30, Experimenting on Humans Using Alien Technology, is to stop scaring the public with frightening scenarios and product names and instead clearly articulate to the public the advantage that will come from the technology—be that advantage improved customer service, lower costs, or decreased fraud.

Such thinking might be dangerous, however. Privacy activists like Beth Givens (Chapter 29, Activists: Communicating with Consumers, Speaking Truth to Policy Makers) argue that before we deploy this technology, we should more carefully assess its impact—something that really hasn't been done to date. Although it is true that stores can use store loyalty cards, credit cards, and even face-recognition technology to track people and their purchases, it may be that the increased accuracy of an RFID tag hidden in your clothing or buried in the sole of your shoe fundamentally changes the kinds of applications that stores and other businesses are willing to deploy.

RFID and the Public's Right to Know

Whether RFID presents a doomsday scenario or not, I believe that at the very least, we have a right to know when we are being monitored by radio frequency devices. Because radio waves are invisible and penetrating, RFID has the potential to be a uniquely covert technology. I can't tell if there is an RFID tag buried in the sole of my shoe. I can't see if a store's RFID reader is silently and invisibly inventorying the clothes on my body.

Philips Semiconductors, one of the worldwide leaders in RFID, claims that it has shipped more than a billion RFID devices worldwide. This astonishing figure was announced by Mario Rivas, the company's executive vice president for communications, at the MIT RFID Privacy Workshop.

Many people in the audience were visibly shocked when Rivas made his statement. After all, RFID is usually presented in the popular press as a fledgling technology that is still being tried out, not as a mature technology that has a solid role in the worldwide marketplace. But over the past ten years, RFID has made stunning gains. Indeed, Mark Roberti, editor of the *RFID Journal*, estimates that between 20 and 50 million Americans carry an RFID chip in their pockets every day, either in a proximity card used for entering buildings and garages or in an automobile key with an immobilizer chip molded into the key's plastic handle.

One way to make the invisible visible is through the use of regulations and laws. Two years ago, I called on the RFID industry to adopt an RFID consumer "Bill of Rights"[4] in which the industry would pledge to refrain from nefarious practices such as hiding RFID chips in clothing or other consumer products without notification, having secret RFID readers, and giving consumers the option of having chips killed in products that they purchase. Other policy suggestions included in this book are in a Privacy Rights Clearinghouse position paper (Appendix A), a position paper from the Electronic Frontier Foundation (Appendix B), and Japan's METI Draft Guidelines on the use of RFID (Appendix C).

Some of these proposals are actually in the "Guidelines on EPC for Consumer Products"[5] (Appendix E), which that are on the Web site of EPCglobal, the internal consortium that is overseeing the allocation of RFID serial numbers used in many consumer products. But the guidelines are considerably watered down from what others and I have proposed. For example, EPC guidelines say that consumers should have the right to know if an EPC RFID tag is inside a product that is purchased, but they don't have a right to know about the presence of readers in a store or other public place. Instead of giving consumers the right to have a tag removed or deactivated (killed), the guidelines instead say that consumers have to be told whether or not they have such a right. Instead of giving consumers a right to know what the RFID information is being used for, the policies simply call for companies to publish their policies regarding "Record Use, Retention, and Security" on their Web sites.

About This Book

This book is an outgrowth of a workshop on RFID Privacy issues that I organized at the Massachusetts Institute of Technology in the fall of 2003. That conference, sponsored by MIT's Computer Science and Artificial Intelligence Laboratory and by the MIT Media Lab, brought together roughly 200 researchers, developers, reporters, and students from around the world. We gathered on Saturday, November 15, 2003, to hear presentations from 15 technologists and privacy activists. For many, it was the first time coming face to

---

4. www.technologyreview.com/articles/02/10/garfinkel1002.asp
5. www.epcglobalinc.org/public_policy/public_policy_guidelines.html

face with the other side for serious discussions. You can find videotapes of those presentations, together with presenters' slides and papers, on the conference Web site at www.rfidprivacy.us.

This book takes up where the conference left off. Since we met in Cambridge, RFID has gone from the headlines to the loading docks and the store shelves. We are living in the future. Nevertheless, many of us are still thinking about RFID using the language of the past.

Although discussion on some form of RFID technology seems to be in the newspaper every day, surprisingly few books on RFID technology are available. Our hope with this book is to give you a good overview of RFID applications, the underlying technology, and the public policy debate.

Organization of This Book

This book is divided into 5 parts; it includes 32 chapters and 6 appendixes:

Part I, Principles, examines the history, underlying technology, and public policy debates that affect RFID technology in general.

Chapter 1, Automatic Identification and Data Collection: What the Future Holds, by Dan Mullen and Bert Moore, looks at the past, present, and future of Automatic Identification and Data Collection technologies, from the bar code to advanced RFID systems. Dan Mullen is president of AIM Global, the Association for Automatic Identification and Mobility. I met him when I was serving on the Auto-ID Center's outside public policy committee. Bert Moore is director of IDAT Consulting & Education, a technology-agnostic, vendor-independent firm that helps companies understand, evaluate, select, and implement automatic identification and data collection (AIDC) solutions. Think of this chapter as the RFID industry's position paper on what can be done with the technology.

Chapter 2, Understanding RFID Technology, by Henry Holtzman and me, is a brief tutorial on how RFID systems work. Henry Holtzman is Research Scientist at the MIT Media Laboratory and the founder of Presto Technologies, which developed an RFID-based payment system back in the go-go 1990s. My contributions to this chapter are based, in part, on Matt Reynolds's presentation at the RFID Privacy Workshop, which Henry and I organized in the fall of 2003. In this chapter, you'll learn the theoretical range at which RFID devices can be read. You'll learn of some basic RFID applications that aren't covered elsewhere in this book.

Chapter 3, A History of the EPC, by Sanjay Sarma, looks specifically at the history and development of the Electronic Product Code and the Auto-ID center. Sanjay Sarma is the cofounder of the Auto-ID center; we are honored to have his personal perspective on the history of what may be the twenty-first century's most important commercial code.

Chapter 4, RFID and Global Privacy Policy, by Stephanie Perrin, introduces the reader to various international conventions and national laws on data protection and shows how those rules are likely to affect the deployment and use of RFID systems. Based in Montreal, Stephanie Perrin is a recipient of the Electronic Frontier Foundation's Pioneer Award for her role as a global privacy advocate. These days she spends her time consulting on various privacy issues to the Canadian government and global corporations.

Chapter 5, RFID, Privacy, and Regulation, by Jonathan Weinberg, explores how U.S. law might respond to RFID technology. Jonathan Weinberg, a professor of law at Wayne State University, has written extensively about privacy and Internet law and regulation.

Chapter 6, RFID and the United States Regulatory Landscape, by Doug Campbell, is an in-depth examination of how RFID technology is likely to be regulated by the U.S. federal bureaucracy. In this chapter, Doug Campbell looks at issues such as government access to stored data, the impact on health, impact on labor regulations, and ways various actors are likely to respond to changing frameworks.

Chapter 7, RFID and Authenticity of Goods, by Marlena Erdos, explores uses of RFID tags in product authenticity. The chapter looks at the interaction of authentication of tags and the authentication of goods and at other related authentication issues. Marlena Erdos is an expert in secure distributed computing systems having architected, designed, and implemented them for well over a decade. Recent interests (and work assignments) have led her into analysis and design of secure RFID-based systems.

Chapter 8, Location and Identity: A Brief History, by Michael R. Curry, explores the evolution of "location" as a concept throughout the ages. Written by Michael Curry, an associate professor at the University of California, Los Angeles, department of geography, this chapter spans 3,000 years of history and asks whether or not the "time-honored" ways of identifying places and things are in fact far more complicated than the notion that everything has a place and every event takes place at a particular time. It's certainly the only chapter in this book to discuss both Aristotle and Lee Harvey Oswald.

Chapter 9, Interaction Design for Visible Wireless, by Chris Noessel, Simona Brusa Pasque, and Jason Tester, looks at techniques for making RFID and other wireless technology visible to nontechnical users. The trio of designers began working with RFID while attending the Interaction Design Institute Ivrea in Italy. Noessel has gone on to a job in research. Brusa Pasque is pursuing studies in industrial design in Milan. Tester is working with the Institute for the Future in Palo Alto, California.

Part II, Applications, looks at specific consumer-facing RFID applications that have been or are about to be fielded.

Chapter 10, RFID Payments at ExxonMobil, looks at one of the most successful RFID deployments to date: the Speedpass payment system developed by Mobil in the 1990s. Based on an interview that I conducted with Speedpass inventor Joe Giordano in the summer of 2003, this chapter details the deployment problems and eventual triumphs of the world's largest RFID payment system.

Chapter 11, Transforming the Battlefield with RFID, explores the reasoning behind the so-called RFID Mandate issued by the Defense Logistic Agency of the U.S. Department of Defense. Written by Nicholas Tsougas, a retired Naval Logistics Officer and technical lead for emerging technologies working at the U.S. DoD Automatic Identification Technology (AIT) Office, the chapter recaps a bit of military history showing the importance of logistics—and explaining why the DLA hopes that RFID can make the U.S. military the most efficient military in the world.

Chapter 12, RFID in the Pharmacy: Q&A with CVS, profiles one of the nation's largest pharmacy chains and discusses how that chain is actively piloting RFID. Unlike other companies deploying RFID, CVS decided to start with item-level tagging in the pharmacy and move slowly back though the supply chain to progressively larger items. Based on interviews I conducted at CVS in the summer of 2004, this chapter explores part of the RFID equation that is often overlooked in press accounts.

Chapter 13, RFID in Healthcare, looks at a variety of RFID applications with medical purposes developed by Intel Labs. This chapter is filled with ideas, mock-ups, demos, and a very real acknowledgement of the challenges faced in moving these product ideas to market. It's a fun chapter written by Ken Fishkin, a researcher at Intel Research Seattle and an Affiliate Professor of Computer Science at University of Washington, and Jay Lundell, Senior Researcher in the Proactive Health Group at Intel Research.

Chapter 14, Wireless Tracking in the Library: Benefits, Threats, and Responsibilities, by Lori Bowen Ayre, explores the benefits, threats, and responsibilities of libraries and librarians when RFID technology is deployed into the world of the public and private libraries. Ayre is the principal of Galecia Group, a small group of technologists who have left the corporate world to provide technical assistance to libraries and related organizations. Ayre notes that even though some libraries have been using RFID technology since the 1990s, very few have come to terms with what RFID means for potential eavesdropping and surveillance on patrons.

Chapter 15, Tracking Livestock with RFID, by Clint Peck, takes us to the farm and cattle ranch, where numbered and coded plastic ear tags and steel clips now adorn practically every cow. In the coming years, these tags will increasingly have RFID tags in them, in part to help trace the movement of diseases such as bovine spongiform encephalopathy (BSE) through the food system. Clint Peck is a Senior Editor for *Beef* magazine; I met him when he interviewed me for an article on RFID that he wrote for his publication. We liked the article so much that we asked him to expand it for this book.

Part III, Threats, gathers in one place the potential threats to privacy and security caused by RFID and other current wireless technologies.

Chapter 16, RFID: The Doomsday Scenario, by Katherine Albrecht, addresses what many privacy activists say is the largest looming threat of pervasive RFID systems: that the ubiquitous network we build and deploy will be used to deny people their civil liberties and enable the emergence of a totalitarian government. Although this might once have seemed like the product of hyperactive imagination, in these post-9/11 days of the USA PATRIOT Act and "Total Information Awareness," the idea that such a network might be used inappropriately by overly enthusiastic intelligence officers and law enforcement agents doesn't seem so far off the mark. Katherine Albrecht is one of the leading activists fighting RFID. Her amazing ability to find the industry's missteps and then heavily publicize them has earned her a reputation for truth and accuracy that her opponents have tried hard to discredit but have failed. Katherine is also the person who is responsible for getting me interested in RFID technology.

Chapter 17, Multiple Scenarios for Private-Sector Use of RFID, by Ari Schwartz and Paula Bruening, follows Albrecht's chapter by imagining ways that the RFID debate could play itself out. Ari Schwartz is Associate Director of the Center for Democracy and Technology (CDT); Paula Bruening is CDT's Staff Counsel. Their organization's mission, working to promote democratic values and constitutional liberties in the digital age, may depend on very minor decisions that are made regarding the design and deployment of RFID technology.

Chapter 18, Would Macy's Scan Gimbels?: Competitive Intelligence and RFID, by Ross Stapleton-Gray, examines a very real threat of RFID in the supply chain that its advocates have been slow to acknowledge: the threat of economic espionage. There's probably no better person to write this chapter than Ross Stapleton-Gray, whom I met in the 1990s when he was the Central Intelligence Agency's delegate to the annual Computers, Freedom and Privacy Conference. His specialty is open source data collection, looking at ways of knitting together an information mosaic from lots of small pieces that individuals and organizations let slip out. For him and people like him, RFID is a gold mine. Tags can be read covertly, at a great distance, and without leaving any trace. Alternatively, a spy from Wal-Mart could walk down the aisles of a Best Buy with an RFID scanner in a backpack. And an activist could program his backpack scanner to "kill" the tags as they are found. I believe that manufacturers haven't addressed these issues because they don't have good answers. Most of them aren't even thinking about the problems.

Chapter 19, Hacking the Prox Card, details the adventures of Jonathan Westhues, who built a proximity card cloner for his senior project while he was an undergraduate at the University of Waterloo. Westhues's cloner is like a tape recorder that listens to the squawk that a prox card makes when it is stimulated with a radio frequency beam and then plays it back on demand. It's quite the tool: Just by standing next to somebody, you can record that person's card's signature. Although there is an easy way to defeat this sort of attack, as Westhues notes, most proximity cards don't employ the solution.

Chapter 20, Bluejacked!, by Pius Uzamere II, Ricardo A. Garcia, and me, shows how the same privacy and security mistakes made with RFID are simultaneously being made in the field of Bluetooth, another allegedly short-range wireless communications standard. This chapter helps readers understand which security and privacy issues are inherent to RFID and which are simply the result of poor system design.

Part IV, Technical Solutions, presents a variety of technical solutions for addressing the privacy problems caused by RFID that were detailed in Part III.

Chapter 21, Technological Approaches to the RFID Privacy Problem, by Ari Juels, a Principal Research Scientist at RSA Laboratories, is a detailed exploration of the main approaches that have been proposed for dealing with the problems of covert tag reading and data aggregation.

Chapter 22, Randomization: Another Approach to Robust RFID Security, by Michael R. Arneson and William Bandy, explores an alternative to the code space and Object Naming Service developed by EPCglobal for managing the

RFID code space. Instead of giving every object a version number, a manager number, a product number, and a serial number, Arneson and Bandy argue that it would be more secure and privacy friendly to simply give every tag a unique code. Suppliers would then give retailers a list of which codes were shipped. Given the large number of 96-bit codes that are possible, it is very unlikely that two codes would ever be used for the same purpose.

Chapter 23, Killing, Recoding, and Beyond, by Ross Stapleton-Gray, David Molnar, and David Wagner, is a critical look at the "kill" feature that was built into the EPC standard as a privacy-enhancing feature. The trio's conclusion: There are many cases in which killing is not a workable solution; thus, other privacy-protecting features need to be developed. Killing may be "kill in a biblical sense," to quote Sanjay Sarma, but it isn't effective.

Part V, Stakeholder Perspectives, presents specific points-of-view of companies, consumer groups, and whole countries.

Chapter 24, Texas Instruments: Lessons from Successful RFID Applications, by Bill Allen, presents the Texas Instruments' side of the RFID story. In this chapter Allen addresses issue of electronic toll collection systems, wireless payment systems, and anti-theft systems. A major RFID supplier, Texas Instruments explains that issues of trust and security aren't restricted to the technology; they also apply to the organizations that are deploying the technology. For this reason, purely technical solutions to the privacy problem advocated by some might not be sufficient. On the other hand, we must be careful that the appeal to policy controls doesn't cloud the importance of having strong technical underpinnings that provide for security and privacy.

Chapter 25, Gemplus: Smart Cards and Wireless Cards, by Christophe Mourtel, is a mini-tutorial on the capabilities and recommended roles of small computational devices commonly used in smart card or RFID applications. Mourtel is a hardware security expert in the security technology department at Gemplus, one of the world's smart card leaders. Mourtel is in charge of the contactless product security and electromagnetic analysis of side channel broadcasts. With large amounts of storage and increasing amounts of processing capabilities being deployed in RFID devices, the information contained in this chapter will increasingly be relevant to all RFID designers and users.

Chapter 26, NCR: RFID in Retail, by NCR's RFID evangelist Dan White, takes an unflinching look at the "holy grail" of RFID applications in the supermarket: automatic checkout. As the findings presented here and at the RFID conference make clear, we're years away from RFID-based checkout. Naïve implementations in which shoppers simply put items into a cart or drop them into their pockets are sure not to work.

Chapter 27, P&G: RFID and Privacy in the Supply Chain, by Sandy Hughes, looks inside one of the world's largest so-called consumer product goods (CPG) companies. "The P&G employee mantra is 'The Consumer Is Boss.' We strive to win consumers at 'the first moment of truth' (e.g., the retail shelf) and at 'the second moment of truth' (e.g., when they actually use the product)," writes Hughes, Procter & Gamble chief privacy officer. Increasingly, the third moment of truth is when consumers find out Procter & Gamble is doing, or not doing, with their personal information.

Chapter 28, Citizens: Getting at Our Real Concerns, by Robert Ellis Smith and Mikhail Zolikoff, looks at a variety of consumer threats and shows how they can be addressed by consumers who take privacy and activism into their own hands. Smith is the founder and publisher of *Privacy Journal*, which has been documenting the impact of information processing technology on privacy, liberty, and freedom for more than thirty years. Zolikoff is a graduate student at the Gerald R. Ford School of Public Policy at the University of Michigan.

Chapter 29, Activists: Communicating with Consumers, Speaking Truth to Policy Makers, by Beth Givens, discusses the issues faced by activists attempting to educate the public and policy makers about privacy issues that have a strong technical bent. This is a job in which Givens has found herself for more than a decade, when she started in California educating citizens about their consumer rights with a grant made possible from a settlement with Pacific Telephone. These days she heads the Privacy Rights Clearinghouse (www.privacyrights.org) and has served on numerous privacy advisory committees.

Chapter 30, Experimenting on Humans Using Alien Technology, by Peter de Jager, discusses what may well be the biggest threat to RFID deployment: heavy-handed and poorly thought-out public relations and communications on the part of RFID vendors and proponents. Peter de Jager is a consultant and motivational speaker who specializes in institutional change; before embracing the change, he helped prepare the world to conquer the Y2K problem. His point in this chapter is simple: RFID vendors had better start being a whole lot more media savvy and public friendly or they might get regulated out of existence.

Chapter 31, Asia: Billions Awaken to RFID, by Bimal Sareen, explores how "Asia, home to more than 50 percent of humankind, is waking up to RFID." We don't hear much about Asian RFID adoption in the United States, but in Asia, developments are moving forward with gusto. The real question facing this development, writes Sareen, the founding president of the RFID Association of India and founder and CEO of AVAANA, is whether or not privacy will be part of Asia's RFID equation or whether those doing the deployments will think that privacy is something that Asia cannot afford. Complicating the equation is the question about the nature of privacy and data protection: Are these inherently Western notions or notions of a world that has experienced the information revolution? Probably the most important thing that Sareen teaches us is that it's a mistake to group all of Asia into just one or two markets: Each of Asia's countries is likely to have a significantly different reaction to RFID's promise and potential threats.

Chapter 32, Latin America: Wireless Privacy, Corporations, and the Struggle for Development, combines Jennifer Torres-Wernicke's personal observations from living in El Salvador with research about the state of privacy and wireless communications in Central and South America. Among other things, Torres-Wernicke notes that poor data handling practices are setting up Latin America, or at least El Salvador, for a wave of identity theft incidents as soon as the criminals become sophisticated enough. Torres-Wernicke is the CISO of an important Central American financial institution.

The **Appendixes** present material that has been published elsewhere but is included here for completeness.

Appendix A, Position Statement on the Use of RFID on Consumer Products, is a paper signed by 39 organizations and individuals (including me) that calls for putting on the brakes and performing a detailed technology assessment before product-level RFID technology is incorporated in consumer products. This paper uses the term "RFID," but it mostly concerns itself with the Electronic Product Code.

Appendix B, RFID and the Construction of Privacy: Why Mandatory Kill Is Necessary, is a position paper from The Electronic Frontier Foundation. Like the previous position statement, this paper is concerned mostly with the Electronic Product Code.

Appendix C, Guidelines for Privacy Protection on Electronic Tags of Japan, translated by Takato Natsui, professor of law at Meiji University, recounts the June 8, 2004, guidelines passed by Japan's Ministry of Internal Affairs and Telecommunications (MIT) and Japan's Ministry of Economy, Trade and Industry (METI). This document is a "private translation" that Takato Natsui did for this book and is not an official translation performed by or for either government ministry.

Appendix D, Adapting Fair Information Practices to Low-Cost RFID Systems, is my paper presenting the RFID Bill of Rights, a set of five principles outlining one way to ensure consumer privacy, security, and choice, and still provide for the use of RFID in a variety of situations. Unlike other RFID guidelines presented in Part V, the RFID Bill of Rights can be equally applied to all RFID systems.

Appendix E, Guidelines on EPC for Consumer Products, presents the official guidelines of EPCglobal for the way EPC tags should be deployed on packaged goods like razors, bras, and bars of soap. The guidelines are similar to those in the RFID Bill of Rights and stress that consumers should have notice that EPC tags are present, consumers should be told that they have the choice to discard the tag if they wish, consumers need to be educated, and companies need to make clear their data-retention policies for data that EPC tags produce. But it's important to remember that these guidelines are just that—guidelines. In the absence of regulation, these guidelines may be followed or ignored as companies see fit.

Appendix F, Realizing the Mandate: RFID at Wal-Mart, is based on a series of interviews conducted with Gus Whitcomb, Wal-Mart's then-director of corporate communications, in the fall of 2004. Wal-Mart's push to have its suppliers equip their pallets and cartons with EPC tags has been one of the primary forces moving RFID from the laboratory into the supply chain. Because of its scale and visibility, Wal-Mart's experience with RFID will have reverberations well beyond the company's store shelves and suppliers.

Expect the Unexpected

If there is one thing that's clear about this new world of RFID, it's that there are both big changes ahead and surprises in store. As more researchers, developers, and entrepreneurs turn their attention to RFID, we're sure to see developments that couldn't have been anticipated. Many of the truths about RFID that have been accepted as gospel are sure to be disproved, or at least qualified.

For example, as this book was going to press, a team of researchers announced that they had reverse-engineered the secret encryption algorithm used by the Mobil Speedpass. What's more, the team had built a hardware-based key cracker that allows them to clone a Speedpass tag. They even used their system to purchase gas at an unsuspecting Mobil station! You can read about it at http://rfid-analysis.org.

Meanwhile, a school in northern California that had been testing an RFID-based system for automatically taking attendance was forced to pull out the system after parents protested. "Our children are not inventory," wrote two parents, Mike and Dawn Cantrall, in a letter to their school district in Sutter.[6]

---

6. Bailey, Eric. "School's electronic tracking zapped," *Los Angeles Times*. Reprinted in the *Boston Globe*, March 6, 2005. A20.

Many people feel that we are on the cusp of a massive RFID deployment. But if proper attention isn't paid to issues of privacy and security, the resulting public backlash could delay or even cripple the industry's plans. Just a few high-profile snafus could set developments back years. In order to make progress, those seeking to promote RFID technology will need to act with responsibility and transparency.

ACKNOWLEDGMENTS

A book of this size and scope requires the work of dozens of people. The danger in trying to list them all is that someone invariably is left out. Nevertheless, I will try.

These acknowledgements are personal and somewhat longwinded. Before I start, I wish to express my deepest thanks to each and every one of the chapter contributors. The strength of this book is the broad range of experience and expertise that we have brought together in a single volume. Even if I had been foolish enough to try to write this book without help, it is a task that I simply could not have accomplished. My thanks go to all of my collaborators. Thank you all!

But indeed, it was never my plan to write or even edit a book about RFID. In early April 2002, I learned that I had been accepted into the doctoral program at the Massachusetts Institute of Technology, with classes starting in September 2002. At that time, my primary goal was to find a research project, write a dissertation, and graduate. The last time I was a graduate student, back in 1990, a book project that I started effectively prevented me from continuing in the program.

My resolve started to falter just a few days later, when I attended a conference for Privacy Activists hosted by Robert Smith and *Privacy Journal* on April 12. There I met Katherine Albrecht, who was all fired up about RFID. Katherine, who had cut her teeth on consumer issues by opposing supermarket loyalty cards, had somehow invited herself into a sponsor meeting of the MIT Auto-ID Center a few weeks earlier. She saw RFID as something much more dangerous than any loyalty card could ever be: not just a way for tracking a person's individual purchases, but for tracking a person's movements through space, a way for examining people remotely and determining what they were wearing, and where it had been bought. "I don't want someone who is standing next to me to know what kind of bra I'm wearing," she told me, voicing fear that someone might covertly read an EPC tag that had been embedded in her clothing for inventory management. It was a quotation that I would use again and again.

Speaking with Katherine and the other activists at the workshop, I thought that one of the best ways for privacy activists to make a difference in an area that was dominated by billion-dollar corporations would be to establish "rules of use" or "best practices" for the appropriate use of RFID technology. I had previously written a "Smartcard Holder's Bill of Rights" and a "Video Surveillance Bill of Rights," so that idea of writing an "RFID Bill of Rights" seemed quite natural.

The following week, on April 19, MIT Professor Ron Rivest invited me to join a meeting of his Cryptography and Information Security Seminar. At that meeting, Sanjay Sarma spoke about the low-cost RFID system that he had developed at the Auto-ID Center—the center that he cofounded just a few years before. At the end of the meeting, I suggested once again that we could easily apply the Fair Information Practices developed more than thirty years before to the emerging field of RFID. Elaborating on the idea that I put forth at Bob Smith's conference, I said, "no secret databases" could become "no covert readers" and "no hidden tags."

That July, I received an invitation from Scott Lederer at University of California at Berkeley's Group for User Interface Research to speak at a workshop on privacy issues at the Ubicomp2002 conference in Sweden. The RFID issue was still on my mind, so I suggested to him that I could write a paper on the RFID Bill of Rights. Sanjay Sarma graciously agreed to help me with some technical aspects of the paper and then funded my trip to speak at the Ubicomp conference. The paper was submitted to the workshop and is reprinted here in Appendix D.

When I told my editor Herb Brody at *Technology Review* about all of the work I was doing in RFID, he suggested that I write about the Bill of Rights for my monthly column. This was quite a challenge because the monthly column allowed me only 850 words. But Herb is a great editor and we got the whole thing to fit.

As a result of these publications, many people sent me questions about RFID technology. It was clear that the technology was quickly transitioning from the laboratory to the marketplace—or at least to the marketplace of ideas. People wanted to know how much storage was on the tags, whether they used encryption, or even simple passwords. I found myself having to ask questions of engineers so that I could answer them for journalists.

On October 15, 2002, I was invited to a meeting of the RFID Privacy Working Group at ThingMagic with Ravi Pappu, Sanjay Sarma, Ari Juels, Steve Weis, and Ron Rivest. It was here that I first met Ravi and Ari—and the meeting blossomed into an incredibly productive working relationship on this topic. Here at last were people who knew all of the technical answers!

That November, I was invited to join the Auto-ID Center's Public Policy Advisory Council. Through my work on this Council, I became more acquainted with a variety of RFID public policy issues. I also had a chance to meet Jill Friedman-Wilson, Douglas Campbell, Alex Allan, Natsui Takato, Herbert Burket, Becky Burry, and Elliot Maxwell, who was the Committee's chair. The Committee discussions proved to be incredibly valuable both to its members and to the Auto-ID center, and it is a shame that EPCglobal decided to suspend its support for the Committee when it took over the reins of EPC development.

In any event, my work on the Committee and the continuing media attention to RFID policy—and especially to privacy issues—convinced me that it would be useful to have a day-long workshop examining these issues. In August 2003, I met with my longtime friend Henry Holtzman and we decided to hold a workshop at MIT to discuss these issues. Deciding that there was no time to lose, we conceived the workshop, obtained a venue and funding, solicited speakers, publicized the event, and held the workshop in less than three months! More than 200 people from around the world attended the event, which received international media attention. Along with Henry and me, the organizing committee consisted of Kevin Ashton, Ari Juels, Ron Rivest, Sanjay Sarma, and Stephen Weis. Ravi Pappu also provided us with great assistance. And we are indebted to Lissa Natkin and Rodney Brooks at the Computer Science and Artificial Intelligence Laboratory, and to Walter Bender at the MIT Media Laboratory, which jointly sponsored the event.

Many people at the workshop suggested that we simply record the proceedings in a book. I didn't think that this would be the best use of our time or resources. After all, the proceedings were already published on the Conference Web site (www.rfidprivacy.us/2003). Many of the papers presented at the workshop could have been improved based on feedback that the authors received. What's more, many organizations that I had wanted to participate at the workshop hadn't been able to do so because of scheduling considerations. I decided that if we were to do a book, it would have to be done with considerably more forethought.

During the summer of 2003, I attended the USENIX Security Conference in Washington, D.C. At that conference, my good friend Radia Perlman introduced me to Mary Franz, her editor at Addison-Wesley. The three of us had dinner together, during which Mary asked if I would be interested in writing a book for her at Addison-Wesley. I told her that I couldn't consider a book: I was working on my Ph.D. thesis!

But after the terrific response that we got from the Privacy Workshop, I called Mary and told her that I might be interested in editing a book of contributions on the topic of RFID privacy and security. Over the following weeks I put together a book proposal and got a variety of authors who tentatively committed to writing a chapter for the book. During this time, I received specific encouragement from David Alexander, Ken Fishkin, Beth Givens, Sandy Hughes, Peter de Jager, Ari Juels, Dan Mullen, Bimal Sareen, Robert Ellis Smith, Ross Stapleton-Gray, Christophe Mourtel, Natsui Takato, Jennifer Torres-Wernicke, and Dan White, all of whom said that they would be interested in participating in the project. Confident that I would be able to deliver a few more chapters on my own, I signed a contract, promising to deliver a book of approximately 15 chapters and 300 pages "no later than August 15."

My, how things change.

Editing a book of contributed chapters is lot like eating a box of chocolates: There's always a huge incentive to take just one more. Throughout the spring and summer of 2004, I kept running into people or topics that would make good chapters. We also realized that there were a number of holes and reached out to some of the major players in the RFID field, including ExxonMobil and Wal-Mart. After much negotiation, we were able to arrange contributions from both of these organizations. A special thanks to J. Donald Turk at ExxonMobil and Gus Whitcomb at Wal-Mart for their help. Kim Novino at Bridgeman Communications was instrumental in working with Texas Instruments RFid (note the capitalization!) systems to participate in the project. I ran into Ari Schwartz at a conference and was able to convince him to participate with his chapter on multiple future scenarios.

Despite her whirlwind schedule, Katherine Albrecht was able to make time to write her chapter. Perhaps more important, she worked with Mary Franz, Addison-Wesley's legal department, and me to help us adopt a contributor's agreement that was far more contributor friendly.

Around this time, I invited Michael Curry to contribute his unique vantage point in a chapter. Michael, whom I had met several years ago at a conference on privacy in upstate New York, said that he was very busy but would try. We are grateful to have his contribution.

Karen Schiff at Tufts introduced me to Marlena Erdos, who graciously agreed to write the much-needed chapter on authentication and authorization issues.

A big breakthrough during this time was Elliot Maxwell's invitation that I attend an RFID seminar that IDC put on in Boston. There I had a chance to meet Jack DeAlmo from CVS and learned of Nicholas Tsougas from Defense Logistics Agency. Both of them graciously agreed to participate in the book project.

A surprising number of individuals were stricken with health or family problems while we were working on this project. Peter de Jager had open heart surgery, Doug Campbell was hit by a car, and Mary Franz suffered the loss of her mother. Our hearts went out to these individuals and their families.

We would also like to thank Ingo Heinicke, for giving us permission to reprint his table on Bluetooth profiles from www.skyynet.de.

Kevin Fu at MIT and Steven Shafer provided a technical review on all of the book chapters—a massive job. The Bluetooth chapter was additionally reviewed by Collin R. Mulliner. The chapter on authentication was additionally reviewed by Ivan Milman, Ron Williams, Bob Blakley, Brenda Kelly, and Lenny Foner. Our thanks go to all of our reviewers for finding numerous small errors that slipped through our editorial process. Any errors that remain are the faults of the editorial team, not the authors.

In November 2004, Catherine B. Nolan at Addison-Wesley joined our editorial team, taking over for Mary Franz. Catherine has been a fabulous editor and our champion at Addison-Wesley.

At Addison-Wesley this book was copyedited and typeset by Techne Group. Noreen Regina provided administrative support. Marketing plans were put together by Chanda Leary-Cotu and Marie McKinley.

Once again, I am both honored and amazed that so many people could take the time to contribute chapters to this book. This project never would have happened had you all not been so generous.

Finally, I wish to thank Beth Rosenberg, who agreed to co-coordinate and co-edit this project—a project that started big and then continued to grow and grow. Truthfully, I would not have signed the contract with Addison-Wesley had Beth not agreed to be my co-editor. And what did she get for her promise? Hundreds of hours obsessing over details, communicating with authors, editing first and second drafts, and tirelessly banning the multitude of references to "Big Brother" and George Orwell's *1984* that were littered through the original submissions. This book is as much a product of her effort as it is mine.

Again, a heartfelt "thanks" to all of you.

—*Simson Garfinkel*
Belmont, MA
May 2005

Part I
PRINCIPLES

Chapter 1

Automatic Identification and Data Collection: What the Future Holds

Dan Mullen[1]
Bert Moore[2]

Introduction

Many of us don't remember a time before the automatic identification and data collection (AIDC) technologies we take for granted came into common use. Scanners at checkout counters read product bar codes and, when the database is properly configured, can alert us to sale prices even if the item itself isn't specially marked. The magnetic stripe on the credit or debit card we use to pay for our purchase is another AIDC technology. And we notice the electronic article surveillance (EAS) tag on items only when a clerk forgets to remove it or deactivate it properly. Yet all of these technologies have helped make life far more convenient and—equally important—have improved industrial and retail distribution processes, which help keep costs down and productivity up.

The next "new" technological innovation to help streamline the supply chain is radio frequency identification (RFID). But is RFID really new?

---

1. Dan Mullen is the president of AIM Global, the Association for Automatic Identification and Mobility.
2. Bert Moore is director of IDAT Consulting & Education, a technology-agnostic, vendor-independent firm that helps companies understand, evaluate, select, and implement AIDC solutions.

A Brief History of AIDC

Several AIDC technologies, including RFID, have histories dating back to the 1930s and 1940s. Today, many of us use RFID without even knowing about it.

One notable RFID application is the "smart key" used as a security feature in many newer cars. The car's door and ignition locks read an RFID transponder (tag or chip) in the key. If it doesn't have the right code, the lock won't work. Far more common but far less recognized as RFID technology is the remote control garage door opener. The remote control is actually an active RFID transponder that sends a unique signal to the receiver in the garage, telling it to open or close the door.

Other AIDC technologies, including optical character recognition (OCR) and magnetic ink character recognition (MICR), have found places in everyday life. But the bar code, magnetic stripe, and, increasingly, RFID are the most pervasive.

Bar Codes

The bar code is the newest of the three common technologies. The first bar code patent was issued in 1949, and the first major application of bar code technology was a rail car tracking system (using multicolored bar codes and early color television cameras) that was implemented in the late 1960s. The system worked well until the bar codes became excessively dirty or worn, and the technology was subsequently abandoned. Some older rail cars still have remnants of their multicolored bar code labels.

There were many attempts in the 1960s and early 1970s to create a usable bar code for item identification. Early bar codes were circular, either like the spokes of a wheel or in a bull's-eye pattern. The first practical bar code that could be scanned in any orientation was a bull's-eye pattern, readable by a single scan line no matter how it was positioned. Linear bar codes, the ones in use today, became more practical in the late 1960s, in part, because of the new bar code scanners, the predecessors of today's supermarket scanners, that produced multiple scanning lines at various angles so that they could more easily read bar codes in various orientations.

It was not until 1972, with the introduction of the universal product code (UPC), the now-familiar symbol on virtually every retail product, that bar codes became more than an experiment. Ironically, as late as 1976, a respected business magazine ran an article titled "UPC: The Supermarket Scanner That Failed."[3]

---

3. *Business Week*, March 22, 1976, p. 52b.

Magnetic Stripes and MICR

Magnetic stripe has its origins in dictating machines and wire recorders (wire was used before metalized plastics were available for "tape" recorders) sold in the 1930s and 1940s. Other than to go from analog to digital encoding, this technology has not changed fundamentally. The recording head produces a magnetic field that creates a magnetic pattern on the recording medium. When this is run past the reading head, the magnetic pattern produces an electrical signal that reproduces the original signal.

Magnetic stripe is widely used on credit and debit cards as well as on "stored-value" cards, which are used in lieu of cash for transit tickets, prepaid phone cards, and cards that can be used in vending machines, video games, and other "coin-operated" equipment.

Many organizations also use magnetic stripe cards for employee ID (automated time and attendance) and access control.

In the 1960s, the American Banking Association adopted both magnetic stripe and MICR to expedite processing of financial transactions. Currently, the only significant use of MICRs is on bank checks. MICR relies on a specific and limited character set, printed in magnetic ink, to produce a code that both humans and machines can reliably read.

The MICR font is odd looking because each character is designed to produce a unique pattern of magnetic fields in six zones when it's read. It is these unique patterns, not the shape of the characters, that the reader recognizes.

Radio Frequency Identification

The British pioneered RFID during World War II to identify their own aircraft returning from sorties over occupied Europe. Early radar systems could spot an incoming aircraft but not determine its type. But with the transponders in RAF planes, RFID could differentiate Allied from enemy aircraft. In fact, this is essentially the same kind of friend-or-foe (FoF) system still used today.

In the late 1960s, the U.S. Government began using RFID to tag and monitor nuclear and other hazardous materials.

In 1972, the same year as the first deployment of UPC, Schlage Electronics (now Westinghouse) developed an RFID card for access control. In 1977, Los Alamos Scientific Laboratories transferred its technology to the public sector, which encouraged a number of companies to explore new uses of RFID.

Along with garage door openers, an early major use of RFID was animal identi-fication. Livestock could be tagged or collared, for example, to control access to feeding stations at feedlots. Meanwhile, companion animals could be implanted with RFID tags for identification purposes.

Interestingly, RFID animal tagging has become important enough for the International Standards Organization (ISO) to develop the animal ID stan-dards ISO 11784 and ISO 11785.

Today, RFID is used for automatic toll collection; access control (personnel and vehicle); security (automobile); equipment tracking (railroad rolling stock); pay-ment at gas pumps, fast food establishments, and other retail outlets; and a wide range of other applications. Additionally, an entire committee inside the ISO (ISO/IEC JHC1/SC31/WG4) is responsible for international RFID standards.

The "Industry" That Isn't

It's important to recognize that the AIDC industry is not monolithic. That is, companies—and indeed individuals in those companies—do not necessarily share the same vision of its future. In the aggregate, however, technological innovations, economic conditions, world events, governmental regulations, and market pressures all combine to determine the direction of the industry. In this respect, AIDC is no different from any other industry.

The AIDC industry as a whole focuses on providing products and services that improve business efficiencies, streamline processes, and improve daily life.

Our nearly ubiquitous credit and ATM cards are an example of an AIDC tech-nology at work. Automated highway toll collection, supermarket and retail checkout scanning, identification and tracking of blood products for transfu-sions, the symbols and scanners used by overnight express services to track par-cels, and bedside use of mobile computers and bar codes in hospitals are all examples of AIDC that are in the public view and benefit the public directly.

Behind the scenes, however, are thousands of applications in which AIDC is used to identify, track, or manage products and processes to improve efficiency in manufacturing and distribution. These applications benefit the public indi-rectly by ensuring that the right products arrive at the right destination in the right quantities to serve customer needs.

Managing all of this information takes tremendous effort. "Wouldn't it be nice," someone thought, "if people and items could identify themselves directly to computer systems and be able to communicate critical data automatically?"

Thus was born the idea of an "Internet of Things," in which items themselves can communicate to host computer systems or, if necessary, can carry all the information necessary to process the item.

It's important to note that neither version of this vision includes monitoring individuals. Instead, each envisions computer-readable documents that can communicate required information, such as passport or pilot license information, when presented at a border crossing or airport.

The Interconnected World

The world is becoming increasingly interconnected, and we, the public, are becoming increasingly dependent on that interconnection.

The growth of multinational companies and the rising number of complex international trading relationships have created the need to exchange vast amounts of data to better manage processes and products in a wide range of social, political, and geographic environments.

Current global conditions, with escalating threats of terrorism, have also fueled the need to gather and disseminate information more quickly and efficiently. It's equally important to protect sensitive or critical information in secured areas and computer systems from attack by terrorists and intrusion by spies or malicious individuals and organizations.

Reliance on existing telecommunications systems—whether landline, cellular, or satellite—has been seen as a limitation in these efforts. A terrorist act that targets the power or telecommunications grids can bring down even the most sophisticated systems. And it's abundantly clear that the Internet itself is the source of many of today's threats.

On a more mundane and practical note, the data communications requirements to exchange such huge volumes of data could overwhelm existing systems. Thus, again, the idea that individuals or items can carry their own data has become increasingly desirable.

Clear and Present Benefits

The following sections review some key AIDC applications and the areas in which they provide benefits. The list below is by no means comprehensive; current applications of AIDC are so varied and pervasive that it's nearly impossible to catalog all of them.

Manufacturing

Manufacturing is a complex task. It requires that the right materials arrive at the right station and receive the right process—and that the manufacturing process itself is done correctly. Bar codes, RFID, and vision systems have long been used in manufacturing to identify items or batches of items, direct processes, and ensure product quality.

In some cases, AIDC aids in such seemingly simple tasks as ensuring that the right label goes on a product or that a box contains everything it should. In other cases, AIDC is put through such complex uses as tracking an item through every workstation and recording every tool that performed an operation on it. This information can be used to quickly identify potential problems and correct them before they show up in the product.

Hand tools and jigs are also identified and tracked with AIDC tags. Many of these are specialized tools that cost thousands of dollars, and one of them may be the only one of its kind on site. Tool checkout that uses AIDC employee ID badges has saved companies tens of thousands of dollars annually in "lost" tools and has helped boost productivity.

Distribution and Inventory

Maintaining an accurate inventory is critical to any operation. Cycle counting everything in a warehouse has always been a necessary but loathsome task. A properly designed and implemented AIDC program, however, can eliminate the need for physical cycle counting, saving companies hundreds of employee hours and days of down time.

Making accurate inventories also ensures that orders can be filled quickly and correctly with a minimum of "safety" stock. This process, too, keeps costs down.

On a different note, during "Operation Iraqi Freedom" the U.S. Department of Defense (DoD) used passive RFID to identify shipping units stored inside metal cargo containers that were themselves equipped with active RFID tags. Getting the right material to the right place at the right time is far more "mission critical" to the DoD than it is to most users of RFID—and with much higher stakes. The DoD's experience in 1991's "Operation Desert Storm" demonstrated that shipping massive quantities of materiel to an operational theatre was of no use if it could not be quickly and easily identified and located. Thus, the DoD issued a mandate to its 30,000 suppliers: All shipments to the DoD must be RFID-tagged. This move dwarfed the number of affected suppliers under the combined mandates of retailers in the United States and Europe.

Retail

AIDC has proven to be extremely useful in maintaining adequate stock levels in distribution of "perishable" goods such as food or fashion. The ability to automatically record sales, check inventories, and replenish or order additional stock reduces the amount of inventory and waste in the system while helping to assure shoppers fresh (or current) products on the shelves.

RFID tags, used as both "smart labels" and EAS systems, have been proven to reduce theft at the store level as well as product diversions in the supply chain. Loss prevention directly benefits consumers by minimizing costs and improving selection.

Document Tracking

Whether for an x-ray from a hospital's radiology department or evidence in a criminal trial, bar codes have been used for years to identify and track critical documents. They also have been used to inventory the files in law offices and to identify and track financial instruments and insurance policies.

Because paper is still so pervasive in today's society, identifying the location and use of important documentation has greatly assisted firms in effectively managing theirsources.

Security

Access to secure areas is already being controlled through the use of a variety of AIDC technologies. Bar codes, RFID, and biometrics are the leading technologies used. Given recent lapses in security at U.S. governmental facilities, one can expect greater use of AIDC for internal security and asset tracking, not just access control.

With the mounting concerns about national security, the U.S. government is beginning to require biometrically enabled passports and visas to identify the bearers and verify the documents' authenticity. The use of RFID in such documents helps prevent counterfeits; RFID, unlike holograms and other security features, is extremely difficult to duplicate.

Overseas shipping facilities and cargo containers are increasingly being secured by the use of AIDC technology to prevent the importation of chemical or biological weapons.

Food Supplies

Recent outbreaks of "mad cow" disease, hepatitis, and other food-borne illnesses have focused international attention on the need to maintain better records on the world's food supply.

Agencies are using both RFID and bar codes to maintain a data history of animals and food products in various parts of the world. This use will undoubtedly increase as the public and governments become more sensitized to food safety concerns.

In the United Kingdom, for example, companies are already required to be able to trace an individual package of meat in the supermarket back to the original animal and to document that animal's heritage and feed history.

Healthcare

In a medical emergency, minutes—even seconds—can make the difference between life and death. An individual brought unconscious to an emergency room cannot supply healthcare providers with the critical information they may need to save his or her life. But a "smart card" containing a patient's complete identification, including medical insurance, blood type, allergies, and critical medical history, could speak for the patient in life-threatening situations.

The healthcare sector is just now taking up AIDC technology, with significant opportunities for increased efficiency and patient safety. Today, many healthcare providers use AIDC in routine treatment, especially for patient identification and automatic recording or updating of records on procedures, medications, and outcomes.

Bar codes and RFID can also be used throughout the medical supply chain to maintain adequate inventories at a facility, ensure the authenticity of medications and medical devices, and give healthcare professionals more time to focus on patients rather than paperwork.

Future Applications

The need to gather and exchange information about people, products, and processes has increased exponentially since the introduction of the original UPC symbol in 1972. But many new opportunities to use AIDC are just now being implemented or developed:

Sensor-Enabled RFID

One of the more promising new RFID applications is RFID tags that contain sensors to measure temperature, humidity, shock, and other environmental conditions. Sensor-enabled RFID provides us the ability to remotely monitor a product's condition—in some cases, even when the product is inside a sealed freight container.

Semi-passive tags can maintain a record of these conditions; passive tags can report conditions only when interrogated. The latter are beginning to be used in limited applications today.

One growing use of sensor-enabled RFID tags is for monitoring refrigerated food storage. Because these tags do not require wiring, they can be placed in an optimal location, depending on the current need. And they can be easily moved to another location when needs change.

Another recent use of these prototype systems has been to monitor the curing process of structural concrete, then record that history on a tag embedded within the item.

Extremely short-range ultrawide band (UWB) tags have demonstrated their use inside freight containers. These signals can be picked up and transmitted to a remote host system.

Pharmaceutical Authenticity

Drug counterfeiting has become a global problem. Although the number of drugs affected is relatively small, the consequences of administering a compromised pharmaceutical can be catastrophic.

An initiative is already under way to develop systems that will provide a pedigree for all packaging levels of pharmaceutical products, then track them through the supply chain. Each package would be uniquely identified and tracked, and individuals working along the supply chain would have to assume responsibility for the validity of accompanying data. Any delay in transportation or discrepancy in serial numbers would trigger an immediate alert and physical inspection.

Product Authenticity

While counterfeit products usually do not pose a life-threatening problem, they are finding their way into the supply chain every day. One major manufacturer discovered that a significant percentage of its own products, sold in its flagship store, were counterfeit. Customers deserve assurance that they're getting what they pay for, whether it's fashion or software.

Counterfeits cost companies money in a number of ways, including lost sales and refunds paid out on counterfeit returns, in turn affecting consumer prices.

Intelligent Items

Some visionaries foresee a day when every retail item contains a unique serial number in an RFID tag to provide product authentication, automated inventory and checkout, and information for product recall and shrinkage control.

In a few cases, having the RFID tag active following purchase could offer consumers real benefits: Warrantee information can be stored on the tag for expensive electronics or appliances, assuring customers of warrantee repairs whether they've registered the product or not.

Prescription drugs with RFID labels could communicate with a "smart medicine cabinet" not only to remind patients to take a specific medication at a specific time but also to dispense the right medication(s) and notify a healthcare provider if they're not being taken. While this may seem to hint of "Big Brother," it could allow elderly patients to live independently rather than move to a managed care facility.

Data Exchange

One of AIDC technology's most overlooked benefits over the past 30 or so years has nothing to do with the technologies used. It has to do with the standardization of data.

Many analysts claim that the greatest benefit produced by the introduction of the UPC code was the standardization of product codes. Previously, product numbers could vary from a few digits to 30 or more alphanumeric characters (and this practice persists in some industries today) with no indication of who assigned the number. In other words, dozens of products from different manufacturers could theoretically have the same product number. This was a nightmare for retailers and distributors that often had to rely on manual methods or create their own codes to avoid confusion.

By providing a unique, fixed-length identity for the vendor and product, the UPC code ensured that databases could be developed to accurately and economically identify and track products.

Although it is a common notion that "memory is cheap," the truth is "programming is expensive." Translating product attributes from different suppliers and distributors is a costly and time-consuming programming chore.

Standardization of product attributes, including many descriptive fields, is a necessary outgrowth of RFID's use in modern identification and data communications systems.

Standardizing data will enable smoother exchange of data among trading partners, eliminate ordering errors based on different descriptions, reduce waste (of product, money, and time), and improve operating efficiencies.

Conclusions

AIDC technologies and their application are becoming increasingly interdependent. In other words, it's possible to leverage one application into another for increased benefit.

An employee ID badge, for example, can serve as a "cash card" for work sites. It can also be used for access control, equipment and tool checkout, automated time-and-attendance recording, security, in an emergency, help in pinpointing the location of missing workers.

In all cases, the intelligent deployment of technology is required. Organizations in the analysis and adoption phase of any AIDC project must fully understand the business process or outcome before considering any automation technology. To paraphrase healthcare's pharmaceutical credo: The right technology should be used for the right application, in the right way, for the right reasons.

Chapter 2

Understanding RFID Technology

Simson Garfinkel
Henry Holtzman[1]

Introduction

This chapter presents a technical introduction to the RFID, the Electronic Product Code (EPC), and the Object Name Service (ONS). It then looks at two specific RFID applications that have been fielded over the past ten years.

RFID Technology

Most histories of RFID trace the technology back to the radio-based identification system used by Allied bombers during World War II. Because bombers could be shot down by German anti-aircraft artillery, they had a strong incentive to fly bombing missions at night because planes were harder for gunners on the ground to target and shoot down. Of course, the Germans also took advantage of the cover that darkness provided. Early Identification Friend or Foe (IFF) systems made it possible for Allied fighters and anti-aircraft systems to distinguish their own returning bombers from aircraft sent by the enemy. These systems, and their descendants today, send coded identification signals by radio: An aircraft that sends the correct signal is deemed to be a friend, and the rest are foe. Thus, radio frequency identification was born.

---

1. Henry Holtzman is a research scientist at the MIT Media Laboratory and the founder of Presto Technologies.

Shortly after the war, an engineer named Harry Stockman realized that it is possible to power a mobile transmitter completely from the strength of a received radio signal. His published paper "Communication by Means of Reflected Power" in the Proceedings of the IRE[2] introduced the concept of passive RFID systems.

Work on RFID systems as we know them began in earnest in the 1970s. In 1972, Kriofsky and Kaplan filed a patent application for an "inductively coupled transmitter-responder arrangement."[3] This system used separate coils for receiving power and transmitting the return signal. In 1979, Beigel filed a new application for an "identification device" that combined the two antennas; many consider his application by to be the landmark RFID application because it emphasized the potentially small size of RFID devices.[4]

In the 1970s, a group of scientists at the Lawrence Livermore Laboratory (LLL) realized that a handheld receiver stimulated by RF power could send back a coded radio signal. Such a system could be connected to a simple computer and used to control access to a secure facility. They developed this system for controlling access to sensitive materials at nuclear weapons sites.

Today we would call this Livermore system an example of security through obscurity: What made the system secure was that nobody else had a radio capable of receiving the stimulating radio signal and sending back the properly coded response. But at the time it was one of the most secure access control systems available. The scientists left LLL a few years later and created their own company to commercialize the technology. This system ultimately became one of the first building entry systems based on proximity technology and the first commercial use of RFID.

The Elements of an RFID System

RFID systems fundamentally consist of four elements: the RFID tags themselves, the RFID readers, the antennas and choice of radio characteristics, and the computer network (if any) that is used to connect the readers.[5]

---

2. Harry Stockman, "Communication by Means of Reflected Power," Proceedings of the IRE, pp. 1196–1204, October 1948.
3. Kriofsky, T.A., Kaplan, L.M.: 1975. U.S. Patent No. 3859624
4. Beigel, M. 1982. U.S. Patent No. 4333072
5. Much of the information in this chapter draws on technical information presented in Finkenzeller, K. *RFID-Handbook, Second Edition*, Wiley & Sons, Ltd., April 2003. Translated from the third German edition by Wadding, R. www.rfid-handbook.de/english/index.html.

RFID Tags

The tag is the basic building block of RFID. Each tag consists of an antenna and a small silicon chip that contains a radio receiver, a radio modulator for sending a response back to the reader, control logic, some amount of memory, and a power system. The power system can be completely powered by the incoming RF signal, in which case the tag is known as a *passive tag*. Alternatively, the tag's power system can have a battery, in which case the tag is known as an *active tag*.

The primary advantages of active tags are their reading range and reliability. With the proper antenna on the reader and the tag, a 915MHz tag can be read from a distance of 100 feet or more. The tags also tend to be more reliable because they do not need a continuous radio signal to power their electronics.

Passive tags, on the other hand, can be much smaller and cheaper than active ones because they don't have batteries. Another advantage is their longer shelf life: Whereas an active tag's batteries may last only a few years, a passive tag could in principle be read many decades after the chip was manufactured.

Between the active and the passive tags are the *semi-passive* tags. These tags have a battery, like active tags, but still use the reader's power to transmit a message back to the RFID reader using a technique known as backscatter. These tags thus have the read reliability of an active tag but the read range of a passive tag. They also have a longer shelf life than a tag that is fully active.

Tags come in all shapes and sizes. The smallest tag that has ever been produced is the Hitachi mu-chip, which is less than 0.4mm on a side. Designed to be embedded in a piece of paper and used for tracking documents printed in an office environment, the mu-chip can be read only at a distance of a few centimeters. Of course, the mu-chip is a passive tag. With a larger antenna it could have a significantly longer reading range, but that would defeat its purpose.

Other small tags are the implantable tags the size of a grain of rice manufactured by VeriChip. Like the mu-chip, these passive tags have a very limited reading range; their intended application is to give machine-readable serial numbers to people. The company says that the chips can be used to authenticate people in high-security environments—unlike passwords, the implanted chips can't be easily shared—and in hospitals, where staff occasionally mix up patients and give them the wrong treatments. Implantable chips might also work to identify wandering Alzheimer's patients who go out without any identification or cognizance of their location or destination. We'll come back to the topic of implantable chips later in this chapter.

RFID tags can also be quite large. The semipassive RFID tag used in the Fast-Lane and E-ZPass electronic toll collection systems is the size of a paperback book and includes an antenna and a five-year battery. The battery gives the system a longer read range and also makes reads more reliable—at least until the battery dies. In practice, the instrumented toll crossings have a large light that flashes green if the tag is read successfully, red if no tag is detected, and amber or yellow if the tag cannot be read properly. When the light flashes amber, the driver is supposed to call the program's administrator and arrange to have the tag sent in for service.

RFID tags can be *promiscuous*, in which case they will communicate with any reader. Alternatively, they can be *secure*, requiring that the reader provide a password or other kind of authentication credential before the tags respond. The vast majority of RFID tags that have been deployed are promiscuous. Not only are these tags cheaper, but the systems also are much easier to manage. Systems that employ passwords or encryption codes require that the codes be distributed in advance and properly controlled. This is an exceedingly difficult management problem.

The simplest RFID chips contain only a serial number—think of this as a 64-bit or 96-bit block of read-only storage. Although the serial number can be burned into the chip by the manufacturer, it is also common for the chips to be programmed in the field by the end user. Some chips will accept only a single serial number, while other chips allow the serial number to be changed after it is burned in. More sophisticated RFID chips can contain read-write memory that can be programmed by a reader. Chips can also have sensors, an example of which is an air pressure sensor to monitor the inflation of a tire. The chips might store the results of the sensor in a piece of read-write memory or simply report the sensor's reading to the RFID reader. Chips can also have a self-destruct, or "kill" feature. This is a special code that, when received by the chip, causes the chip to no longer respond to commands. For financial applications, the full capabilities of smart cards have been combined with the wireless protocols and passive powering used in RFID. The result is a class of high-capability RFID tags also called contactless smart cards.

RFID tags can interfere with each other. When multiple tags are present in a reader's field, the reader may be unable to decipher the signals from the tags. For many applications, such as raising the gate in a parking lot, this is not a problem. The systems are optimized so that only one tag is within range at a time. However, for other applications, reading multiple tags at once is essential. For these applications, the tags need to support either an anticollision protocol or, more commonly, a singulation protocol. A singulation protocol allows a reader to determine that multiple tags are visible and to iterate through the tags, getting them to take turns responding so that each may be read without interference from the others.

Electronic Product Code (EPC) tags are a special kind of tag that follows the EPC standard developed by the MIT Auto-ID Center and is now managed by the trade organization EPCglobal. Sanjay Sarma, cofounder of the Auto-ID Center, discusses the history of the EPC standard in Chapter 3.

EPCglobal has defined a series of RFID tag "classes" and "generations" of RFID devices (see Tables 2.1 and 2.2).

Table 2.1 EPC RFID Classes

EPC Device Class	Definition	Programming
Class 0	"Read only" passive tags	Programmed by the manufacturer
Class 1	"Write-once, read-many" passive tags	Programmed by the customer; cannot be reprogrammed
Class 2	Rewritable passive tags	Reprogrammable
Class 3	Semipassive tags	
Class 4	Active tags	
Class 5	Readers	

Table 2.2 EPC RFID Chip Generations

Feature	Generation 1	Generation 2
Frequency	860–930MHz	860–960MHz
Memory capacity	64 or 96 bits	96–256 bits
Field-programmability	Yes	Yes
Reprogrammability	Class 0—read only Class 1—write once/ready many	NA
Other features	NA	Faster and more reliable reads than Generation 1 Better compliance with other global standards

Readers

The RFID reader sends a pulse of radio energy to the tag and listens for the tag's response. The tag detects this energy and sends back a response that contains the tag's serial number and possibly other information as well.

In simple RFID systems, the reader's pulse of energy functioned as an on-off switch; in more sophisticated systems, the reader's RF signal can contain commands to the tag, instructions to read or write memory that the tag contains, and even passwords.

Historically, RFID readers were designed to read only a particular kind of tag, but so-called *multimode readers* that can read many different kinds of tags are becoming increasingly popular.

RFID readers are usually on, continually transmitting radio energy and awaiting any tags that enter their field of operation. However, for some applications, this is unnecessary and could be undesirable in battery-powered devices that need to conserve energy. Thus, it is possible to configure an RFID reader so that it sends the radio pulse only in response to an external event. For example, most electronic toll collection systems have the reader constantly powered up so that every passing car will be recorded. On the other hand, RFID scanners used in veterinarian's offices are frequently equipped with triggers and power up the only when the trigger is pulled.

Like the tags themselves, RFID readers come in many sizes. The largest readers might consist of a desktop personal computer with a special card and multiple antennas connected to the card through shielded cable. Such a reader would typically have a network connection as well so that it could report tags that it reads to other computers. The smallest readers are the size of a postage stamp and are designed to be embedded in mobile telephones.

Antennas and Radio

The RFID physical layer consists of the actual radios and antennas used to couple the reader to the tag so that information can be transferred between the two.

Radio energy is measured by two fundamental characteristics: the *frequencies* at which it oscillates and the strength or *power* of those oscillations. Commercial FM broadcast stations in the United States transmit with energy at a frequency between 88MHz and 108MHz, or 1 million isolations per second. The AM spectrum, by contrast, transmits at 500,000 to 1,500,000 oscillations per second, or between 500KHz and 1500KHz. Microwave ovens cook with RF energy that vibrates 2.4 billion times each second, which is 2.4GHz.

Most RFID systems use the so-called *unlicensed spectrum*, which is a specific part of the spectrum set aside for use without a radio license. Popular bands are the low-frequency (LF) band at 125–134.2KHz, the high-frequency band at 13.56MHz, the ultrahigh-frequency (UHF) band at 915MHz (in North America; varies in other regions), and the industrial, scientific, and medical (ISM) band at 2.4GHz.

The names of the LF, HF, and UHF bands reflect the history of radio's development: Radio systems first transmitted at the lower frequencies and moved to the higher frequencies only as technology advanced. For this reason, lower-frequency radio gear was traditionally cheaper than equipment that operated at higher frequencies. Today, however, the difference in radio prices more often reflects market sizes, the cost of patents and other licenses, and the result of subsidies or cross-marketing agreements from equipment manufacturers.

Radio energy moves in waves, and each radio wave has not only a frequency but also a wavelength. The wavelength is like the distance between two wave crests on the ocean. With radio energy, the wavelength of a radio wave multiplied by its frequency is equal to the speed of light: 3×10^8 meters per second (roughly equal to 186,000 miles per second). The size of waves for each of the unlicensed bands is presented in Table 2.3.

Table 2.3 Band Frequency, Wavelength, and Classical Usage

Band	Unlicensed Frequency	Wavelength	Classical Use
LF	125–134.2KHz	2,400 meters	Animal tagging and keyless entry
HF	13.56MHz	22 meters	
UHF	865.5–867.6MHz (Europe) 915MHz (U.S.) 950–956MHz (Japan)	32.8 centimeters	Smart cards, logistics, and item management
ISM	2.4GHz	12.5 centimeters	Item management

Building proximity cards, automobile immobilizer chips, and implantable RFID ampoules tend to operate in the LF band. The FDA has adopted the HF band for RFID systems used for prescription drugs. The EPC system operates in the HF and UHF bands, although early deployments are favoring the UHF band.

When analyzing the energy that is radiated from an antenna, electrical engineers divide the field into two parts: the *near field*, which is the part of radiation that is within a small number of wavelengths of the antenna, and the *far field*, which is the energy that is radiated beyond the near field. Because the wavelength of LF and HF devices tends to be much larger than the ranges at which

RFID systems typically operate, these systems operate in the near field, while UFH and ISM systems operate in the far field.

As with most radio systems, the larger the antenna on the reader and the tag, the better an RFID system will work because large antennas are generally more efficient at transmitting and receiving radio power than are small antennas. Thus, a large antenna on the reader means that more power can be sent to the RFID tag and more of the tag's emitted energy can be collected and analyzed. A large antenna on the tag means that more of the power can be collected and used to power the chip. Likewise, a large antenna on the chip means that more power can be transmitted back to the reader.

The Network

Most RFID tags transmit a number and nothing more. So what does a typical reader do with a typical 96-bit number like 79,228,162,514,264,337,593, 543,950,335?[6] In most cases, the reader sends it to a computer.

What the computer does with the RFID code depends on the application. With an access-control system, the computer might look to see if the RFID number is present on a list of numbers that's allowed access to a particular door or location. If the number is present, the computer might energize a solenoid that would unlock the door. In the case of the Mobil Speedpass system, the tag's serial number and its response to the random challenge that was generated by the reader are sent over Mobil's payment network. If the challenge response matches the token, Mobil's computers approve the user of the customer's credit-card number to complete the transaction.

With the EPC, the serial number will be sent to a network of computers that make up the Object Name Service (ONS), a large distributed database that will track a variety of pieces of information about objects that have been assigned EPC codes. The database consists of both central "root" servers and distributed servers at each company that creates products labeled with EPC tags. Given any EPC code, the root servers would tell a computer which company's servers to go to, and then the company's servers would explain what the EPC code means. The overall design of the ONS is similar to that of another distributed database, the Domain Name System (DNS), which maps Internet hostnames to Internet Protocol (IP) addresses. In fact, VeriSign, the company that has the contract to run the global DNS, was also awarded the contract by EPC-global to run the ONS.[7]

---

6. This number is actually $2^{96}-1$, the largest number that can be represented with an unsigned 96-bit integer.
7. "VeriSign to Run EPC Directory," *RFID Journal*, January 13, 2004. www.rfidjournal .com/article/articleview/735/1/1.

Here's how it might work. A computer at Wal-Mart that receives an EPC code would send that code to one of the ONS root servers and learn that the particular code space is operated by a manager at Gillette. The computer might then query the ONS server operated by Gillette and learn that the code is for a box of Mach3 razors, which was manufactured on a particular date and is authorized for sale in the United States.

Coupling, Range, and Penetration

As mentioned previously, active and passive RFID systems have very different reading ranges. With batteries and high-gain antennas, active RFID systems have ranges roughly equivalent to those of any other system operating under the rules for unlicensed radio systems. In the United States, for example, an unlicensed system can transmit with up to 1 watt of power; under these conditions, a signal can be received over a mile if directional antennas are used and there are no obstructions.

Coupling

While it is possible to build RFID systems such that both the tag and reader contain a radio transmitter and a radio receiver, this method of operation is ideal only for active systems attempting to communicate over the longest distances. Because placing and powering a transmitter on the tag is an expensive proposition, passive tag systems are usually chosen for applications that are extremely sensitive to the cost of the tag. Either the passive tag will have to have some form of energy storage, for example a capacitor, to provide power when the reader stops transmitting and starts receiving or the reader must always transmit, meaning the tag has to reply on a different frequency.

Instead, passive RFID systems typically couple the transmitter to the receiver with either *load modulation* or *backscatter*, depending on whether the tags are operating in the near or far field of the reader, respectively.

In the near field, a tag couples with a reader via electromagnetic inductance. The antennas of both the reader and the tag are formed as coils, using many turns of small gauge wire. The current in the reader's coil creates a magnetic field. This field, in turn, induces a current in the coil of the tag. A transformer works by the same principle, and in essence the coils of the reader and tag together form a transformer. The reader communicates with the tag by modulating a carrier wave, which it does by varying the amplitude, phase, or frequency of the carrier, depending on the design of the RFID system in question. This modulation can be directly detected as current changes in the coil of the tag. The tag communicates with the reader by varying how much it loads its antenna. This in turn affects the voltage across the reader's antenna. By switching the load on and off rapidly, the tag can establish its own carrier frequency (really a subcarrier) that the tag can in turn modulate to communicate its reply.

Tags that operate in the far field (UHF and ISM bands) couple with their readers using backscatter. Backscatter results when an electromagnetic wave hits a surface and some of energy of that wave is reflected back to the transmitter, and it is one of the fundamental physics behind RADAR. The amount of energy reflected depends on how well the surface resonates with the frequency of the electromagnetic wave. RFID tags that use backscatter to reply to their readers have antennas that are designed to resonate well with the carrier put out by the reader. The tag can throw a switch that changes the resonant properties of its antenna so that it reflects poorly instead, thus creating a pattern in its backscatter that is detected at the reader. The return communication is encoded in the backscatter pattern.

There is a third, less common type of coupling between reader and tag: *electrostatic coupling*. With electrostatic coupling, the reader and tag antennas are charged plates. Adding electrons to the plate on the reader will push electrons off the plate onto the tag, and vice versa. The plate area determines range with electrostatic coupling. An advantage to electrostatic coupled systems is that the antenna patches can be printed with conductive ink, making their design very flexible and inexpensive.

Reading Range of Passive RFID Systems

Passive systems operate under far more limiting circumstances. To be read, a passive RFID tag must be provided with sufficient power to both run the electronics and generate a return signal that the reader can detect. Thus, the read range of a passive system depends on

- Pr: The reader transmitter power (typically 1 watt)
- Sr: The reader receiver sensitivity (typically -80dBm or 10^{-11} watts)
- Gr: The reader antenna gain (typically 6dBi)
- Gt: The tag antenna gain (1dBi is an omnidirectional antenna)
- Pt: The tag's power requirement (typically 100 microwatts or -10dBm)
- Et: The tag modulator efficiency (typically -20dB)[8]

A system can be limited either by the power available to power the tag or by the reader's ability to detect the tag's transmissions. Since the goal of RFID systems

---

8. This example was presented by Matthew Reynolds of ThingMagic at the MIT Privacy Workshop in November 2003.

is to make the chips as cheap as possible, lots of money can be invested into readers to make them very sensitive. Thus, a well-designed RFID system will be limited by the power available to the tag.

The power available to the tag, Pt, is given by the formula:

$$Pt = \frac{Pr \times Gr \times Gt \times \lambda}{(4\pi)^2 \ d^2}$$

Where λ is the wavelength of the radio waves used by the system.

Crunching the numbers for a 915MHz system, d_{max} = 5.8 meters. In other words, 19.4 feet is the greatest distance that a typical EPC tag can be read by a reader with the parameters given previously. On the other hand, if someone could build a tag that could be powered with only 1 microwatt—100 times better than is possible today—d_{max} would increase to 194 meters. However, the return signal would have energy of –99dBm because the RFID tag would be transmitting its limited amount of power in all directions. A signal at –99dBm is on the edge of what can be detected with even the best amplifier and radio available today. (The noise power in 50 ohms at 500KHz is –109dBm; with a practical receiver that has an NF of 3dB, the power of noise is raised to –106dBm. Distinguishing a –99dBm signal from a –106dBm noise floor requires a receiver that has a signal-to-noise ratio of just 7dB.)

One way to improve the reading range of such a system is to use a larger antenna that can collect more power from the tag. For example, a proximity card system manufactured by Indala (www.indala.com) has a read range of eight inches with the company's lowest-cost reader, but that range jumps to 24 inches with the company's more expensive reader that has a larger antenna and more expensive electronics. Researchers at the MIT Computer Science and Artificial Intelligence Laboratory (CSAIL) have created a one-of-a-kind reader with a very large antenna that can read cards more than four feet away. Although greater reading ranges are theoretically possible, background noise and other real-world factors make it difficult to construct readers with significantly longer range.

Penetration, Screening, and Shielding

The calculations in the previous section assume that both the RFID reader and the tag are in a vacuum. This is rarely the case, of course. Most tags are read through the air, but sometimes there is intervening material, such as water, plastics, cans, or people. As with all radio signals, the range of an RFID system is dramatically affected by the environment through which the radio signals travel.

Two of the most potent barriers for radio signals in the HF and UHF regions of the spectrum are water and metal, and they can profound impacts on RFID in typical operations. For example, cardboard is normally transparent to radio waves. But if a cardboard box picks up moisture, the water in the cardboard will attenuate the radio signal from an RFID reader, perhaps to the point that the RFID tag inside the box will not receive enough power to send back a response.

Metal blocks radio waves, so there's no hope of reading a tag inside a can. What about a tag that's on a can? The answer depends on where the reader is in relationship to the tag and the can, how far away the tag is from the can, and even what kind of antenna is built into the tag. In some cases, the can will block the radio waves, but in other cases, the can will focus the waves and make it easier to read the tag. This is especially a possibility if several cans are packed tightly together, as might be the case on a supermarket shelf.

Another phenomenon to be considered is dielectric coupling. Dielectric coupling can take place between antennas and dielectric materials like cardboard or, in some cases, the human body. Using this coupling will result in detuning the antenna, which will make the antenna less efficient and, consequently, will decrease read range. This is why some proximity cards can be read if they are in a wallet but can't be read if that wallet is in a person's pocket. In other cases, two proximity cards placed next to each other can cause mutual interference because of this kind of coupling.

If the intention is to shield an RFID tag against an RFID reader, it is quite easy to do. A single layer of aluminum foil is sufficient to shield most low-power RF devices. For RFID, aluminum needs to be only 27 microns thick, according to Matthew Reynolds at ThingMagic (www.thingmagic.com), to effectively shield a tag. And just 1mm of dilute salt water (also a conductor) provides similar protection.

All of this math and physics have caused some interesting reflections by journalists. In *Wired News,* for instance, Mark Baard wrote this technically accurate lead for his article about the MIT RFID Privacy Workshop:

> You may need to read the following sentence twice: Aluminum foil hats will block the signals emitted by the radio tags that will replace bar-code labels on consumer goods.

That is, of course, if you place your tin-foil hat between the radio tag and the device trying to read its signal.[9]

RFID Applications

In this section, we look at a few specific applications of RFID technology that have been deployed and see how the technical underpinnings of the technology have a direct impact on the applications.

Supply Chain Visibility and Inventory Management

The largest use of RFID anticipated within the next ten years is in tags to track the movement of consumer product goods from the manufacturer to the point of sale.

The international manufacture and movement of goods is a huge business. Many items sold in the United States are actually manufactured in China, loaded into containers, sent by truck to a port, and then shipped on a freighter to a port in the United States. Once in the country, the containers are sent to distribution points where they are unloaded, repackaged onto trucks, and sent to stores such as Wal-Mart, where their contents are unloaded, put on store shelves, and sold to consumers.

At least, that's the way that the process is supposed to work. In practice, many things can go wrong. For example, boxes that are supposed to be loaded into one container can be accidentally loaded into another one and sent to the wrong customer. Product can be lost in port for days—or weeks—or sent to the wrong distribution center. Boxes can be lost in distribution centers or, even worse, sent to a store and then misplaced in a storage room. As a result, a product could be out of stock on the store shelves, which means that a customer who wants to buy a particular razor or battery won't be able to do so. The number and cost of lost sales can add up.

Equally troublesome for companies like Gillette are product counterfeiting and product diversion. This problem starts in China, where a look-alike product can be manufactured in "bandit" factories. (Sometimes a bandit factory is authorized to make genuine goods but creates extra product that it doesn't report to the U.S. company.) Legitimate product with packaging in Chinese and designed to be sold

---

9. Baard, M. "Is RFID Technology Easy to Foil?" *Wired News*, November 18, 2003. www.wired.com/news/privacy/0,1848,61264,00.html.

in Hong Kong or Taiwan at a low price can be sent to New York and sold on the so-called gray market in which the intermediaries reap big profits and the American consumers get their razors or batteries at a lower price, but the brand owner misses out on the higher profits that are supposed to result from U.S. sales. And sometimes there is just out-and-out theft: Cases of product disappear out of "sealed" containers or "fall off" the back of trucks.

Finally there is shoplifting, increasingly an activity of organized gangs who empty stores of dozens or hundreds of packages of razors or batteries at a clip. Sometimes insiders facilitate shoplifting and receive a commission or cut from the perpetrators. Shoplifting causes many problems, of which the actual theft is just one. Consumers who see shoplifting taking place feel uncomfortable and may not return to the store. Shoplifting also results in out-of-stock conditions that are not detected by the store's inventory management system because the items were never actually sold.

It is into this supply chain that RFID is likely to make the largest impact over the next decade. If every package of razors or batteries manufactured in China had its own embedded and individually serialized RFID tag, it would be possible to track it as it moves through the entire supply chain. RFID readers at the factory would verify that the cases left the factory and got onto the truck. RFID readers built into the shipping container would verify that the products left the truck and were put in the container. RFID readers in the U.S. port could verify that every package coming into the country contained product that was both legitimate and licensed for sale in the United States. Readers at the distribution center would record the arrival of every package and note which packages went to which stores. In those stores, RFID readers would be on every shelf. They would keep track of which product was in the back rooms and which was on the store shelves.

RFID readers on store shelves would give stores a degree of visibility that today can only be dreamed of. For starters, they would pick up when product was mis-shelved—perhaps when a consumer picked up a box of razors, had a change of heart, and put it down on another shelf a few minutes later. The tags could detect "out-of-stock" conditions caused by theft. It would even be possible to have the system generate an alert when there is a suspicious removal of product, such as the simultaneous removal of 12 razor packages, and put a notation on the surveillance video.

Once this RFID infrastructure is deployed, it could be used for additional purposes. For example, a special light-sensing RFID tag might detect if the container was opened between the times that it left a port in China and arrived at a port in San Francisco; such containers could be subject to extra scrutiny by the Department of Homeland Security or simply rejected out of hand. The Customs Service, meanwhile, could automatically impound and destroy any products that did not have RFID serial numbers from an approved list of "genuine merchandise" or any products that had been manufactured for another market.

In theory, RFID is great. When a product is made, the tags can be applied in a way that they can't be removed. (Checkpoint, for example, has developed a series of RFID tags that are on the back of designer clothing labels.) RFID lets a retailer see what's inside a pallet or carton without actually opening it. RFID eliminates counterfeiting. RFID eliminates the problems that result when people mistype product numbers or mis-scan optical barcodes. Lost shipments can be automatically tracked or traced. In addition, companies can get better visibility into their operations by simply adding more RFID readers: A reader on a forklift, for instance, would make it possible to figure out precisely how many packages per hour a forklift operator is moving and would probably make it possible to pinpoint specifically which forklift operator was responsible for skewering an expensive case of HP printers. (Assuming, of course, that the forklift operator's union consented to this degree of worker monitoring.)

That's the theory. In practice, those trying to deploy RFID into the supply chain have discovered many problems. As we'll see in later chapters, although it's possible to read 75 or more tags per second, it has been remarkably difficult to design systems that can read 100% of the cases on a pallet, let alone all of the individual cartons inside a case. Metal and water inside the packaging add to the difficulty of reading. Readers sometimes interfere with each other. One of the greatest problems has been the cost of the tags themselves; the tags could even cost more money than they would possibly save.

There are other problems, as well. Most organizations deploying RFID assume that serial numbers on tags can't be counterfeit (they can) and that they can't be read by competitors (they can). So U.S. Customs needs more than a read-only list of all the valid RFID tags allowed to enter the country: It also needs to cross items off the list when they come into the country. A read-write database system is dramatically more difficult to operate than one that is read-only. As for the competitive intelligence problem, it's one that is addressed in Chapter 18, Would Macy's Scan Gimbels?: Competitive Intelligence and RFID, so we won't dwell on it here. Suffice it to say that there are a lot of opportunities for competitors to snoop on each other. As evidenced by Appendix F, Realizing the Mandate: RFID at Wal-Mart, many organizations haven't even considered this possibility.

Implants

Perhaps no single application of RFID technology has generated more controversy than the implantation of RFID chips into people.

Implantable RFID transponders are typically small glass cylinders approximately 2 or 3mm wide and between 1 and 1.5cm long. Inside the glass cylinder are a microchip, a coiled antenna, and a capacitor for energy storage. Microchips are typically implanted under the skin of the arm (in human beings) or the back of the neck (in laboratory animals) with a 12-gauge needle.[10] Someone with proper training can implant a device in less than 20 seconds.

Implantable RFID chips are typically read through use of an intense magnetic field operating at a radio frequency of 100KHz to 15MHz. The alternating magnetic field induces a current in the transponder's coil, which in turns powers the chip. Stimulated in this manner, the chip transmits a low-power response that is then detected on a different radio frequency by the reader.

On October 14, 2004, an article titled "Identity Chip Planted Under Skin Approved for Use in Health Care"[11] ran on the front page of the *New York Times* and many other publications. The photograph beneath the headline showed a human index finger and, on top of the clearly visible fingerprint, a tiny glass cylinder containing an RFID chip and antenna manufactured by Applied Digital.

What readers of the *New York Times* may not have realized is that the technology is more than 20 years old. In 1986, four inventors had filed a series of patent applications for a Syringe-Implantable Identification Transponder. Despite being abandoned three times, the patent was finally refiled in 1991 and issued in 1993.[12] According to the patent, the system was designed for the identification of horses. The patent was assigned to Destron/Identification Devices Inc. and Hughes Aircraft. One of the early uses, according to Troyk, was for tracking fish passing through dams on the Colorado River. Patent applications filed by other inventors anticipated RFID devices augmented with sensors to report back information such as body temperature.

In the mid-1990s, implantable chips were initially marketed to scientists seeking to keep track of laboratory animals and to zoos that wanted a way to track exotic animals. Soon they were being marketed to veterinarians and animal shelters that wanted a way to identify pets that were stray but had been previously owned. According to an article in the January 1997 issue of *Pet Bird Magazine:*

---

10. Much of the technical information in this section is from Troyk, P. "Injectable Electronic Identification, Monitoring and Stimulation Systems," *Annual Review of Biomedical Engineering,* 1999.01:177–209.

11. Feder, B.J., and Zeller, Jr., T. "Identity Chip Planted Under Skin Approved for Use in Health Care," *The New York Times,* October 14, 2004. A1.

12. Taylor V., Koturov D., Bradin J., Loeb, G.E. 1993. U.S. Patent No. 5211129.

"Loss of a beloved pet or valued bird is a painful experience. However, there are some measures you can take to help find or identify your bird if this happens to you. One of these is the use of a microchip, a tiny device which can be inserted into your pet by means of a simple injection. Bird breeders and pet owners across the country are implanting microchips in their birds as a means of positive identification. The chip is implanted under the skin and resides there as a small non-intrusive and foolproof method of permanently identifying a bird."[13]

A variety of incompatible chips were sold during this time, including the AVID, Destron, and Trovan, which sold items under the AVID, Home Again, and Info-PET brands, respectively. In Canada, another system called PetNet was popular. This multiplicity of players only created confusion in the industry: The Ratite industry and SeaWorld endorsed AVID, the American Kennel Club endorsed Home Again, and the American Society for the Prevention of Cruelty to Animals (ASPCA) endorsed Trovan. Trovan was also adopted by the International Union of Conservation of Nature for captive breeding programs. Although a so-called universal scanner could read any chip, such scanners were not available initially and were always more expensive than a single-mode scanner.

Simply having a chip implanted in an animal did not guarantee its recovery because the chips contained a serial number, not a name, address, or phone number. To map the serial number to an owner's name required looking up the serial number in a registry. Although all registries allowed owners to list their names, addresses, and phone numbers, some registries allowed alternative names and contact numbers to be listed. In most cases, registration required a one-time fee of $7 to $25 per chip.

Although any of these chips *could* be implanted into a person, this use was specifically prohibited by the chip manufacturers. One reason, presumably, was liability; although the chips had been tested in animals, they were not approved as medical devices. But conversations I had with chip manufacturers at this time revealed another reason that implantation was prohibited: The vendors didn't want the negative publicity that could result from having their chips implanted in human beings. To paraphrase one manufacturer's representative who spoke to me on condition of anonymity, "We are trying to stay clear of the creepy factor."

One company didn't share this view. To the contrary, Applied Digital Solutions (ADS) positively courted the creepy factor.

---

13. Highfill, C. "Microchips: An Idea Whose Time has Come," *Pet Bird Magazine*, January 1997. Archived at: www.birdsnways.com/wisdom/ww7eiii.htm.

Incorporated in May 1993, ADS is a holding company that owns other companies involved in the high-tech area. The company's two best-known products are the Digital Angel and the VeriChip. Unfortunately, these two products are frequently confused with one another.

Digital Angel is device that monitors the wearer's location using a Global Positioning System (GPS) receiver and then reports the position back to a central monitoring facility using a cellular telephone network. One version of the Digital Angel is designed to be worn around a child's wrist. Another version designed to be implanted in the chest cavity is marketed to businesspeople in South and Central American who are fearful that they might be kidnapped.

ADS's second major product is the VeriChip, an implantable RFID device that ADS markets for a variety of security, safety, and healthcare applications.

Consider security, which has long been promoted by ADS as a natural use of the technology. As it is promoted, the implanted chip is the ultimate security device: an unforgeable identification number that cannot be lost or stolen. Each VeriChip has a unique serial number. The serial numbers are programmed into the computer that controls access to a building or a set of confidential files, and if the person whose hand waves in front of a reader has an approved serial number, the computer grants access. This application is so transparent and so easy to understand that it is not just promoted by VeriChip, it's also a staple of science fiction, having appeared in works such as Arthur C. Clark's *3001* and the 1995 Sylvester Stallone movie, *Judge Dredd*. Perhaps because of the high-tech appeal, the Attorney General of Mexico recently had himself and 16 people in his office implanted with the VeriChip to gain access to sensitive areas and files in the country's fight against organized crime.[14]

A second application that is promoted for the VeriChip is for tracking patients and medical records. Once again, the advantage of the chip is that, unlike a dog tag, it cannot be lost. Alzheimer patients often become disoriented and wander off, sometimes after taking off all their clothes (dissatisfaction with clothes is another symptom of the disease). A study of caregivers in Massachusetts found that 69 percent of wandering cases are associated with severe consequences, with 3 percent (24 out of 700) of them resulting in a lengthy search that ends with the death of the patient. In theory, an implanted RFID chip interacting with a long-range reader could be used to lock the door or sound an alarm if an Alzheimer patient approached it. When a patient is recovered, the chip could be used to find contact information for the patient, much as with the chips that are implanted in dogs and cats.

---

14. Greene, T.C. "Anti-RFID Outfit Deflates Mexican VeriChip Hype," *The Register*, November 30, 2004. www.theregister.co.uk/2004/11/30/mexican_verichip_hype.

The serial number on the implanted chip can also be used as an index into medical records. ADS operates a "Global VeriChip Subscriber Registry" that reportedly will act as a password-protected centralized database of medical records for any VeriChip user. The company is also promoting VeriChip as a payment system. The Baja Beach Club in Barcelona, Spain, has given its patrons the option of having a chip implanted in their hands so that they can pay for drinks.[15] So far 35 patrons have signed up for the service.[16]

According to the company's 2003 Annual Report: [17]

> "VeriChip … can be used in a variety of security, financial, personal identification/safety and other applications.… About the size of a grain of rice, each VeriChip product contains a unique verification number. Utilizing our proprietary external RFID scanner, radio frequency energy passes through the skin energizing the dormant VeriChip, which then emits a radio frequency signal transmitting the verification number contained in the VeriChip. VeriChip technology is produced under patent registrations #6,400,338 and #5,211,129.
>
> This technology is owned by Digital Angel Corporation and licensed to VeriChip Corporation under an exclusive product and technology license with a remaining term until March 2013."
>
> On October 22, 2002, the US Food and Drug Administration issued a ruling that the VeriChip is not a regulated device. As a result, the FDA reasoned, the FDA had no say as to whether or not people could implant the device in their bodies for financial and personal identification purposes—just in the same way, presumably, that the FDA has no say on whether or not people pierce their ears to wear earrings. After receiving this approval ADS began aggressively marketing its device not just for these applications, but apparently also as for linking to a database of medical records. On November 8, 2002, the company "received a letter from the FDA, based upon correspondence from us to the FDA, warning us not to market VeriChip for medical applications."

15. Gossett, S. "Paying for Drinks with the Wave of the Hand," *WorldNetDaily.com*, April 14, 2004. http://worldnetdaily.com/news/article.asp?ARTICLE_ID=38038.
16. Crawley, A. "FDA Clears VeriChip for Medical Applications in the United States," *findBiometrics.com*, October 14, 2004. www.findbiometrics.com/Pages/feature%20articles/verichip-fda.html.
17. "Annual Report Pursuant to Section 13 or 15(d) of the Securities Exchange Act of 1934, For the fiscal year ended December 31, 2003," Applied Digital Solutions, Inc. March 15, 2004, amended on March 16, 2004, May 21, 2004, and September 24, 2004. http://www.sec.gov/Archives/edgar/data/924642/000114420404015032/v06849_10ka.txt.

The annual report continues:

> "Examples of personal identification and safety applications are control of authorized access to government installations and private-sector buildings, nuclear power plants, national research laboratories, correctional facilities and sensitive transportation resources. VeriChip is able to function as a stand-alone, tamper-proof personal verification technology or it can operate in conjunction with other security technologies such as standard identification badges and advanced biometric devices (for example, retina scanners, thumbprint readers or face recognition devices). The use of VeriChip as a means for secure access can also be extended to include a range of consumer products such as personal computers, laptop computers, cars, cell phones and even access into homes and apartments.
>
> Financial applications include VeriChip being used as a personal verification technology that could help prevent fraudulent access to banking, especially via automated teller machines, and credit card accounts. VeriChip's tamper-proof, personal verification technology can provide banking and credit card customers with the added protection of knowing their account could not be accessed unless they themselves initiated and were physically present during the transaction. VeriChip can also be used in identity theft protection."

In October 2004, the FDA ruled that the serial number inside the VeriChip could be linked to healthcare information. It's important to note that the FDA has never actually ruled on the safety of the VeriChip device itself. The FDA's ruling gave ADS the green light to move forward on its attempts to market the VeriChip to the healthcare arena. Quoting once again from the company's annual report:

> "Examples of the healthcare information applications for VeriChip include, among others:
>
> - Implanted medical device identification
> - Emergency access to patient-supplied health information
> - Portable medical records access including insurance information
> - In-hospital patient identification
> - Medical facility connectivity via patient
> - Disease/treatment management of at-risk populations (such as vaccination history)"

Evaluating VeriChip's security claims is remarkably difficult; the company has surprisingly little technical information on its Web site.

VeriChip and Mark of the Beast

The Revelations of St. John the Divine, popularly known as the Book of Revelation or The Apocalypse, is the final book of the Christian Bible. The book tells the story of the end of the world, including the final battle between good and evil. According to Revelations, God wins this final battle and restores peace to the world.

Revelations is relevant to discussions of RFID, and especially the VeriChip, because of three verses that discuss the Beast from the Earth. The Beast is introduced in Revelations 13:11; the sections relevant to a discussion of RFID are verses 13:16, 13:17, and 13:18:

- **Revelations 13:16:** And he causeth all, both small and great, rich and poor, free and bond, to receive a mark in their right hand, or in their foreheads.
- **Revelations 13:17:** And that no man might buy or sell, save he that had the mark, or the name of the beast, or the number of his name.
- **Revelations 13:18:** Here is wisdom. Let him that hath understanding count the number of the beast: for it is the number of a man; and his number is Six hundred threescore and six.

When bar codes were introduced in the 1970s, some Christians were opposed to the technology, noting that the UPC bar code could be considered to be some kind of "mark" that was being used to buy and sell. Credit cards were similarly attacked—especially in the late 1990s run-up to the change of the millennium—on the grounds that they enabled people to use numbers to buy and sell and that this could be considered a fulfillment of the visions of Revelations. To those who held this belief, the VeriChip, an electronic mark that is received in a hand, is an even closer fulfillment.

Whether or not the Beast's mark is a VeriChip or a credit card number is beyond the scope of this chapter. What's important, though, is that a number of individuals *believe* that RFID may be an instrument of Beast—that is, of the Devil—and have decided to fight against it for that reason. As Peter de Jager argues in Chapter 30, whether or not you personally subscribe to this viewpoint, it is important to remember that other people do and that their opinions must be considered when and if this technology is deployed.

Conclusions

ADS representatives declined requests to submit a chapter to this volume or to be interviewed for this chapter. Nevertheless, many of the claims made by ADS can be evaluated in the context of RFID technology in general. The first important point is that just as the chip can be easily implanted with a 12-gauge needle, it can be easily removed with a penknife or a machete, provided that the person removing the device is not concerned about any damage that may be done to the surrounding tissue. It thus seems advisable that the chip not be used for guarding access to high-security areas unless a secondary form of identification is used; otherwise, an attacker could simply hack off a person's arm, recover the chip, and implant it in him or herself.

In fact, it may not be necessary to engage in such gruesome exploits. If the ADS annual report on file with the U.S. Securities and Exchange Commission is without error, the VeriChip transmits a simple serial number when it is stimulated with an RF beam and does not participate in a challenge-response protocol. Therefore, the chip can be cloned or otherwise hacked by someone using technology described in Chapter 19, Hacking the Prox Card.

VeriChip says that its chip might be usable in deterring identity theft, but this claim is unsubstantiated. One of the mechanisms fueling identity theft is the use of unchangeable identifiers such as Social Security numbers as keys into online databanks. Once a person's VeriChip number is compromised, presumably the same sort of access could take place. For example, a home computer running a financial application might be equipped with a VeriChip reader to guard against unauthorized access, but if this number is transmitted to a remote Web site, it would be very difficult for the remote Web site to distinguish between a number that had been read by the scanner and one that had been typed on the computer's keyboard and then sent over the Internet through use of a hacked device driver.

Although RFID devices have been used for identifying laboratory animals and livestock for nearly 20 years, no one is experienced in using these devices in an adversarial environment against an active attacker. Just as numerous privacy and security problems surfaced when Microsoft's Internet Explorer made its transition from the laboratory to the marketplace, we are likely to find numerous problems with the VeriChip and the computational infrastructure on which the identification system depends.

Chapter 3
A History of the EPC

Sanjay Sarma[1]

Introduction

Although the concept of radio frequency identification (RFID) is not new, the term RFID has been in use for only a couple of decades.[2] In the 1980s and 1990s, long after the early use of RFID during World War II, innovations in RF circuitry enabled passive RFID tags (tags without batteries, which scavenge power from the reader's field) to provide enough range to become viable. Today, RFID tags are seemingly everywhere: in toll passes, card-keys, automobile keys, payment systems (like the Mobil Speedpass system), and animal identification.

What has changed is the emergence of the Electronic Product Code (EPC) system, which is a suite of standards and technologies that weaves basic RFID into a standardized scheme for keeping track of material in the supply chain. The EPC was created at MIT by a few researchers involved in a research project called the Distributed Intelligent Systems Center (DISC). Later, this research effort morphed to fulfill a growing need in the retail supply chain and became the Auto-ID Center. This chapter presents a brief history of the Auto-ID Center, talking mostly about the technology, the industry, and the adoption of the EPC system.

The Beginning

My own first, forgettable, brush with RFID occurred in the early 1990s when I was a graduate student at Berkeley. At that time, I was interested in identifying

---

1. Sanjay Sarma is a professor at MIT and a cofounder of the Auto-ID Center.
2. For additional information, see Landt, J. "Shrouds of Time: The History of RFID." www.aimglobal.org/technologies/rfid/resources/shrouds_of_time.pdf.

and locating work-pieces for manufacturing automation. I had looked at RFID as a possible positioning device in automation and rejected it as being far too imprecise and expensive. Little did I realize then that our paths would cross again!

The Distributed Intelligent Systems Center

A colleague at MIT, David Brock, reintroduced me to RFID. At the Artificial Intelligence (AI) Labs, David had spent a great deal of time thinking about the problem of artificial perception in robotics. He wrote a white paper at the AI lab wondering why an RFID tag couldn't be used as a marker to identify objects rather than recognize the object from scratch. He suggested using a unique number to identify the object and using the network to download an almost unlimited amount of information about the object.

David charged into my office one day in the beginning of 1998 and described this idea to me. As a roboticist myself, I found it aesthetically appealing. However, my earlier worries persisted. For true ubiquity, cost would be the barrier. Yet I was intrigued enough that I invited David to join my group, and we founded the DISC.

The bug that David infected me with was the idea of ubiquitous RFID—*let's put it everywhere*. We could use it in the supply chain, we could use it in robots and machines to replace computer vision, and we could use it to track food, drugs, and cattle. But in all these applications, the high costs of tags were a huge stumbling block. High costs initiated a vicious cycle: The higher the costs, the lower the adoption; the lower the adoption, the higher the costs. Over the next several months, we met several times to talk about the idea and co-opted another colleague, Sunny Siu, to join us in our brainstorming sessions. We became aware of similar thinking that had been going on in the Media Lab at MIT and by Nick Negraponte in the early 1990s.

The seeding idea was a numbering scheme. Over time, we decided the structure of the number, and we named it the EPC. The EPC would have four fields:

- Version number
- Manufacturer number
- Product number
- Serial number

The EPC was to point to a database. The obvious thing to do was to use XML to represent the data about an object. We called this language Physical Markup Language (PML). Dan Engels was finishing a Ph.D. in the Department of Electrical Engineering and Computer Science at that time, and David, Dan, and I spent a great deal of time looking at a number of approaches for describing physical objects and distributing the information, including many emerging representations and schemes like the Resource Description Framework (RDF) and Information and Content Exchange (ICE).

The missing piece was how to map the EPC to the IP address of the database. In our brainstorming sessions, a student, Eric Nygren, suggested simply co-opting the Domain Name System (DNS). We called this new system the Object Name System (ONS), and Joe Foley, another student, implemented the first prototype. Then we hacked into the controls of an old microwave oven and installed an RFID reader in it. We then attached RFID tags to a few microwave-ready meals. Joe and I created a Web page to provide cooking instructions in the form of Physical Markup Language (PML). When a food packet was inserted into the microwave oven, the oven would read the tag, locate the server using ONS, download PML cooking instructions, and automatically cook the food. This would be our first and most enduring demonstration. Seeing this, the head of the Department of Mechanical Engineering at MIT, Professor Nam Suh, contributed $100,000 from the department to support this fledgling effort. This gave us the breathing room to incubate our effort.

In early 1999, it occurred to me that the way to get the RFID industry out of its vicious cycle would be to inject it with minimalism. This would become the overriding theme that would drive the progress of the Auto-ID Center. In time we would develop low-cost tags by making the chip extremely small, making the protocols extremely simple, developing simple network ideas built on existing standards, developing new ways to package extremely small chips, developing minimalist data standards on the chip, and so on. That theme of minimalism would be a harder vision to sell than I had expected. Sell it we did, though, and it has led to the creation of the EPC network.

Meanwhile, at Procter & Gamble

The EPC revolution would not have taken off had a fateful meeting not taken place in early 1999, when Dave and I met Kevin Ashton, then a brand manager for Oil of Olay with Procter & Gamble in London. Before we met Kevin, I expected that ubiquitous RFID tags would first find application in the front end of the supply chain, which consists of factories and automation systems. Here I was wrong. For a few years, Kevin had been struggling with a problem that plagues the retail industry: out-of-stocks. It turns out that fast-selling items are out of stock about 10 percent of the time in a typical retail store. This problem can mean billions of dollars of lost revenue, not to mention dissatisfied customers who could switch brands and stores. Kevin's idea was simple: tags on all retail items, readers on all retail shelves, and a system that would proactively inform the retailer and the manufacturer of shrinkage and stock-outs. Kevin had spent the last year trying to get the RFID industry interested in low-cost tags. Unfortunately, instead of receiving support from RFID vendors, Kevin, like David and me, had been given a list of reasons why his approach simply would not work. At our first meeting, in 1999, we knew that there was a resonance of vision. Kevin's passion for the possibilities of RFID in the retail supply chain sealed the deal; we had a new application area. The Auto-ID Center was therefore, the confluence of two independent streams: DISC technology and Procter & Gamble's and Gillette's struggles with retail.

A Mini-Lecture: The Supply Chain

To understand the growth of the EPC, it is important to understand the problems of the supply chain. The *extended supply chain* starts in a mine or on a farm, and it ends in either a recycling plant or in a trash can. In between, material is transported from stage to stage, it is combined or separated, it is modified or processed, and it changes hands from one owner to another. When material changes hands heading downstream, money goes upstream, and each entity makes a profit for adding value to the evolving work piece.

The term *logistics* usually refers to the handling of material and the aggregation and deaggregation into and from bulk for transportation. The term *supply chain* (as opposed to extended supply chain) usually refers to the management of materials in the chain from the factory to the consumers' hands. The retail industry is analogous to routers in the Internet. Retailers route material as efficiently as possible from the suppliers to customers in stores. Their efficiency determines the cost to the customer, the profitability of the retailer, and the sales of the supplier.

At each stage in the chain, uncertainties, losses, and errors of estimation cause inefficiencies. Carrying too much inventory is bad because it results in billions of dollars of locked-up capital, high carrying costs, obsolescence, problems with quality and freshness, and theft. Having too little inventory results in empty store shelves, a problem that plagues the retail industry worldwide to the tune of billions of dollars. Unfortunately, difficulties in counting inventory cause the pendulum to swing precipitously between too much inventory and too little inventory in a phenomenon called the bullwhip effect. First described by Forrester, an MIT professor who also invented key components of early computers, the bullwhip effect is inevitable in any dynamic chain like the supply chain. Simply put, even if demand at the end of the chain is nearly constant, small ripples multiply upstream and create tremendous variations in demand.

The secret to walking the tightrope between these two problems is accurate measurement of inventory. Bar codes were conceived as a way to measure inventory, and to a large extent, they did help. However, bar codes are essentially line-of-sight in their operation and require manual manipulation. The result is that every scan of a bar code has a hidden cost associated with it; in fact, UPC bar codes are often scanned only once in their life-times, at checkout. To a large extent, inventory is still guessed at, often incorrectly. In a study of a retailer by a Harvard group, up to 65 percent of all inventory records were inaccurate. This is where RFID tags come in. RFID tags permit one to count inventory without line-of-sight. The tags permit better, faster, cheaper, and more frequent inventory measurement. This measurement, in turn, enables more efficient change of hands between commercial entities, better traceability of goods, better protection from theft and other malfeasance, and most important, a more stable tightrope walk between the two ills of the supply chain: too much inventory and too little inventory. Together, these benefits are worth, potentially, billions of dollars to companies and to society.

As our research into RFID began, I wanted to be sure that this was the case. We had already been introduced to the problems of stock-outs. Was that the tip of the iceberg? In 2000, my student Yogesh Joshi and I studied the bullwhip effect and the effect of inventory visibility on this debilitating phenomenon.[3] What we found was startling. By making inventory visible to trading partners across the supply chain by using RFID, we could, at least in theory, almost completely eliminate the bullwhip effect. Armed with this profound insight, we plunged into the RFID world in search of our elusive goal of ubiquitous, inexpensive RFID tagging. We knew there was value there.

The Auto-ID Center

In 1999, David, Sunny, and I met Alan Haberman, who is frequently called the "father of the bar code." Alan was on the original CEO committee that took bar code technology and made it the ubiquitous, standardized symbol of retail commerce that it is today. In the process, that committee created the Uniform Code Council (UCC), which administers the UPC bar code in the United States. Its sister organization, EAN International, administers the bar code for the rest of the world.

Back in the 1970s, MIT Chairman Howard Johnson had put together a cross-disciplinary group of young professors to evaluate the Symbol Selection

---

3. Joshi, Y. "Information Visibility and Its Effect on Supply Chain Dynamics," M.S. Thesis, Department of Mechanical Engineering, MIT. June 2000.

committee's bar code choices.[4] They had agreed with the process and the final selection and suggested that the chosen technology would stand for 25 years but had expected that the bar code would then be overtaken by a new technology. And so it was coming to pass!

Alan, then a member of the UCC Board of Governors (BoG) , was in the middle of a search for the proper research organization to for a successor technology to bar code ID techniques. The search was on behalf of the UCC's current CEO Tom Rittenhouse and the Board of Governors, Ironically, it was just shy of 25 years since the first bar code scan across a checkout. During that time bar codes had truly become ubiquitous: today more than five billion bar codes are scanned daily around the world, according to informed estimates.

Alan was also the chairman of an ISO committee on RFID standards, and he was interested in our starting a research effort to enable low-cost, ubiquitous RFID tagging. He, like us, was frustrated by the high costs of RFID tags and the lack of technical progress. During a one-hour lunch, our group struck an agreement: We would morph DISC into a new center based at MIT with funding from the UCC. Alan, David Brock, Sunny Siu, and I then had a series of conversations with MIT staff. Two people on the staff, Fritz Kokesh and Carol Carr, played a major role in laying out the financial and organizational structure of the new center. The center would be driven by end users rather than vendors, and its mission would be to enable the proliferation of low-cost passive RFID tags in the supply chain. All we needed now was money! So we then evangelized a number of companies, Procter & Gamble and Gillette being the first targets of our campaign.

The Auto-ID Center was launched on September 30, 1999, during the twenty-fifth anniversary celebration for the bar code at the Smithsonian Museum in Washington, D.C. In addition to the UCC, we had support from two founding sponsors: Gillette and Procter & Gamble. Steve David, the CIO of P&G, Allan Boath of Gillette, and Tom Rittenhouse of the UCC presented checks to Professor Nam Suh. The organization of the lab gradually fell into place. Alan Haberman would be the chairman of the board of end-user sponsors. (About a year later, Alan stepped down as chairman and Dick Cantwell of Gillette took over. Dick would play a very important role in the coming years.) Sunny Siu became research director of the lab because it was very important for us to emphasize the centrality of the Internet in this effort. (Sunny left MIT in 2001, and I took over as Research Director. I became the chairman of research a year later as the center grew.) Kevin Ashton became executive director to operate the lab. P&G graciously offered to cover Kevin's

---

4. Haberman, A. (ed.) *25 Years Behind Bars*. Harvard University Wertheim Publications Committee. Cambridge: Harvard University Press, 2001.

salary in this role. Kevin and I would work closely to hold the effort together as we navigated difficult, sometimes hostile waters. We received a great deal of support from Alan and Dick in overcoming fundamental technical and industrial barriers that would appear in our way.

The first order of business was enabling inexpensive RFID tagging. This was no minor challenge—tags cost more than a dollar at the time, and we were already being ridiculed for our assertions. The entire RFID industry was locked in a high-margin, low-volume cycle. Our objective was to break that cycle. No one even thought low-cost tags possible, with the exception of Noel Eberhardt of Indala, a division of Motorola Corporation. Noel had invented Bistatix electrostatic tags. Bistatix tags used a cheap antenna, and the chips were very small. Noel believed that they could be manufactured for about a nickel.

The Cheap Tag

It would become clear in the months after we met Noel that Bistatix tags would not provide us the read range necessary to meet the requirements of the supply chain. Yet Noel had given us a glimmer of hope. Other attractive possibilities at that time included nonsilicon tags using polymer circuits and an innovative chipless RFID technology developed by Rich Fletcher and Neil Gershenfeld at the MIT Media Lab. Over the six months following my first meeting with Noel, I plunged myself into an in-depth analysis of the manufacturing of RFID tags. I looked at the circuitry on the chip, the manufacturing issues related to the digital and analog portions, the separation of the chip from the wafer, the thinning of the wafer, the handling of the dies, the attachment of the die to the antenna, the manufacture of the antenna, and the attachment of the assembly to a package. I even attended a two-day course on paper manufacturing in Canada! My conclusion was that Bistatix, polymer tags, and chipless tags were not likely to solve the RFID problem in the near term. Instead, I felt that it would be better to return to silicon electromagnetic tags and find a way to make them work. I developed a two-pronged strategy to address this challenge.

First, I recognized that the primary and most rigid component of tag cost was chip cost, which in turn is largely proportional to chip area. We would therefore have to spend a great deal of effort minimizing the complexity of the state machine and the memory required on the chip. We would do this, ironically, by developing simpler, lower-weight protocols that, while reducing cost, were also applicable to a larger range of applications.[5] For example, earlier versions of RFID tags used complex anticollision techniques, supported large, complex

---

5. Swamy, G. and Sarma, S. "Manufacturing Cost Simulations for Low Cost RFID Systems." 2003. www.autoidlabs.org/whitepapers/mit-autoid-wh017.pdf.

memory structures, and included encryption. By contrast, we insisted on reducing the memory on the tag to a simple license plate, and we simplified the anti-collision to simpler tree-walking or Aloha-like variants. We eliminated encryption from the simplest tags because there was no memory to protect! In doing so, we had to address a number of issues ranging from digital signal processing to semiconductor manufacturing issues. This minimalist approach succeeded in reducing the size of the chip, and since cost is roughly proportional to size, it permitted us to reduce cost. Minimalist chips also had additional benefits that propelled the EPC movement. Smaller chips consume less power, increasing the possible range of the tag. A minimalist approach also enabled easier, lower-level standards that could be used by more applications.

Second, we took the earlier work of the DISC and turned it to an advantage for lower-costs tags. In DISC, we had in effect proposed putting much of the data and intelligence associated with tagged items, which had hitherto resided on the RFID tags themselves, on the network instead. In much the same way as a license plate on a car can be used to find the traffic tickets associated with that car, the EPC made it possible to refer to data associated with that tag without burdening the tag with extra memory. The ONS would be used to find the authoritative owner of the original data associated with an EPC tag. PML would store data about the tag on a server called the PML Server.

By February 2000, this two-pronged strategy had become more solid. I presented it at the Second Auto-ID Sponsor Meeting and called it the "cheap chip manifesto." The strategy was clear, but a lot of questions remained:

- Who would design the protocol?
- How would small chips be packaged?
- Who would make these chips?
- Who would make the tags?
- How would we drive adoption?

Yet our sponsors had faith in us, and the die was cast. If this strategy didn't work, we would go bust. My career was certainly on the line. From here on, we were on a mission to flesh out the strategy and bring about broad adoption.

"Low-Cost" RFID Protocols

By 2000, it was becoming clear to us that the RF protocols used to communicate between readers and tags were somewhat bloated. The bloat occurred in part because there was no incentive for making the chip small until we made that a popular idea. Also, others hadn't tried to leverage the network or take advantage of recent advances in chip design or communication theory. In 2000,

Sunny Siu and his student Ching Law published a paper describing a series of ultra-simple tree-walking protocols that permitted the fast and efficient inventorying of a field of tags. These protocols were so simple and so efficient that we wondered why they weren't being used. We would find out later that others were thinking along similar lines. However, we were completely unsuccessful in persuading bigger tag manufacturers to adopt these approaches. A few tag companies did join the Auto-ID Center, but although the engineers who attended our meetings were intrigued, they were unable to persuade their companies to take the plunge.

At the end of 2000, I met Jeff Jacobsen and Roger Stewart of Alien Technology, a startup company based in California. Jeff and Roger immediately saw the value of what we were saying, having independently come to the same conclusions we had. They committed to developing a new protocol based entirely on a minimalist approach—the smaller the better—and what followed was a period of fruitful and enjoyable brainstorming. Roger, along with his colleagues Kurt Carrender, John Price, Dr. Stephen Smith, and John Rollins of Alien, spent a great deal of time with Dan Engels, Matt Reynolds of MIT, and me, developing what would eventually become the Class I UHF protocol published by the Auto-ID Center. We were also helped by a number of people from other companies, like Leigh Turner of Rafsec. Alien committed to making chips to this protocol and continues to manufacture them to this date. Later, Dan, Professor Peter Cole of Adelaide, Australia, and researchers from Philips created the Class I HF protocol. In 2002, Matrics, a startup company that had independently created a very efficient tree-walking protocol, worked with the center to create a more secure, more efficient version of its old protocol, which we published as the Class 0 UHF protocol. Matrics also committed to manufacturing chips to this protocol, which it continues to sell today.

As we developed tag protocols, we simultaneously needed to consider the various frequencies involved in different countries and the different protocols that we needed to read. Which protocol should people buy readers for? Which frequency? These questions were proving surprisingly paralyzing to early adopters. Our view was that we should support all frequencies and all protocols. The best way to solve the problem was by building a single reader that could handle all the protocols and frequencies. At that time, *software-defined radio* had begun to gain acceptance as an alternative to hardware radio. CPU speeds were beginning to make this, the ultimate in flexibility, a reality. Kevin knew the engineers of a small MIT spinoff called ThingMagic, one of whom was Matt Reynolds, who had just graduated. We contracted ThingMagic to build a single "agile reader" that could put all the uncertainty to rest. ThingMagic published a design for an agile reader that also had a bill of materials of less than one hundred dollars. With one fell swoop, we were able to quiet all the uncertainty about reader hardware and frequencies. Now, it was possible to invest in fixed infrastructure that would absorb any future changes in protocols.

"Low-Cost" Manufacturing

One of the challenges we faced with our approach was this: We could make the chips smaller to save silicon cost, but smaller chips are much more difficult to pick up and handle. In fact, when chips become smaller than about $1mm^2$, electrostatic forces become so significant, and precision requirements so high, that the traditional robots used to pick and place these chips in their packaging become uneconomical. In other words, what we might save in silicon costs we would more than expend in expensive manufacturing processes. Manufacturing challenges like these were major roadblocks in the strategy we stated in February 2000. Others questions that were plaguing us were:

- How would we test 100,000 chips per wafer?
- How would these chips be separated from each other on the wafer without wasting a great deal of silicon in the gaps (streets) required to saw the chips from the wafer?
- How would these chips be attached to the antennae?

Over the course of 2000, we came up with what we thought were feasible answers to these questions. First, we said that in the future, small chips would be packaged not by robotics, but by massive parallel assembly. At that time, I speculated that a process in which chips would be "vibrated into place" would be the way of the future. I said that RFID tags need not be tested in the wafer because they could always be tested wirelessly. I said that chips could be separated by etching and thinning rather than by sawing to make the streets an order of magnitude thinner. I summarized these thoughts in a whitepaper that was received with a bit of pessimism and even hostility. While these ideas were seemingly sensible, how were we to get them to reality? We were, after all, at an academic institute.

Here too, we found excellent partners in companies like Alien Technology. Alien had developed a process for delivering chips using fluidic flow rather than vibration as I had suggested, which nevertheless enabled massively parallel, inexpensive assembly of ultrasmall chips into RFID packaging. Alien was also the first company to support us in our claim that low-cost tags were possible with volume.

Other companies like Rafsec Corporation also played a big part in the gelling of this approach. Rafsec had developed an inexpensive technology for manufacturing antennae, and it announced a relationship with Alien. Now, we had the prospects of a complete tag. Later, Philips confirmed my view that vibration too was a viable technology and said it had discovered that Philips itself had used vibrational techniques in other component assembly. My student Kashif Khan wrote his Ph.D. on vibration-based techniques and published it in 2003.

The Software and the Network

Handling the hardware questions was just one aspect of the EPC challenge. The other was software. Our goal was to remove data from the tag and manipulate the data on the network. As I mentioned before, the first version of the ONS was written by my student Joe Foley in the late 1990s.

Around that time, it also became obvious to me that we needed a software-architecture to handle RFID data in a scalable, sensible way. RFID data comes fast and furious and needs to be absorbed, filtered, and interpreted for local action. At the same time, the readers themselves interfere with each other, and this interference needs to be controlled. Dan Engels and I had written many papers about this problem, which we had predicted to be one of the major challenges in RFID. My student Jim Waldrop spent a great deal of time thinking about this problem, and we came up with a concept similar to the neuron and nervous system. We called our version the Savant. The Savant would get data as input, then filter, smooth, and interpret it and pass on a digested form of the data to a higher-level Savant. There would be a layer of Savants talking to readers at the edge, a layer of Savants one level up, aggregating from lower-level Savants, and perhaps the highest-level Savant aggregating all this information. Each Savant would be equipped with rules to deal with information as appropriate for its level.

Embedded in this design is the principle of *locality of reference*. The basic idea is that the closer you are to an event in space and time, the more the information is useful to you. Consider news of a theft in a company. It is of limited value to the CEO because the CEO is too far away, geographically and organizationally, to act on it. It is of use to the store clerk, though, perhaps because the clerk can apprehend the thief. Similarly, the same news is useless to the store clerk if it comes a day late. For these reasons, a centralized approach to RFID data would just not work. The Savant hierarchy decentralizes the decision process. It permits immediate decisions to be made at lower levels and presents digested information to higher levels at a stage of abstraction that is useful there.

With the launch of the field trial, which I will describe later, it became obvious that student-written software would not scale. Instead, we needed to develop a body of freeware that could be used and improved and adopted by number of people to get the RFID adoption off the ground. But who would do this?

Larger companies weren't willing to invest in this concept, and the field trial was moving ahead. At this point, I hired OATSystems, a tiny consulting company consisting of MIT graduates, to write the industrial versions of the ONS and Savant freeware and standards and to deploy them in the field trial. These efforts turned out to be surprisingly successful. Prasad Putta, Sridhar Ramachandran, and Gabriel Nasser played key roles. ONS and Savant were downloaded from our Web site hundreds of times, and more important, they were very successful in driving the field trial and early adoption. The invention of an RFID foundation proved to be critical—there was a prevailing, and completely incorrect, perception that RFID systems could be managed exactly like bar code systems. We were able to seed the creation of a whole new and entirely necessary industry by creating the Savant System. Another company that was supportive and generous in the development of this new way of thinking was Sun Microsystems, which provided not only moral support and technical guidance but also the voice of its senior executives. Scott McNealy, the CEO of Sun, was a vocal supporter of the Auto-ID Center.

Privacy

RFID is one of those technologies that naturally raise privacy concerns. The fear is justified to some extent. For one thing, passive RFID tags are often confused with Hollywood staples like global positioning system (GPS)-based tracking devices, wireless sensors, and electronic recorders, which have been the bane of many secret agents in movies. Of course, today, passive tags have such poor communication performance and such severe cost pressures that they are a poor choice for an antagonist seeking to invade one's privacy. The cell phone in your pocket and the toll pass in your car offer better opportunities to invade your privacy. Yet, if one assumes that tags have long range, privacy fears are understandable. What if someone could read the contents of your pocket and conclude that you are on a particular medication? What if this happened during an interview?

Fortunately, privacy concerns were very much on our minds from the beginning. Kevin did the community a great service by talking about privacy as early as 2000. Even in 1999, David Brock, Joe Foley, Sunny Siu, and I talked about turning pieces of the EPC off to protect privacy. In those meetings, which were held in the Given Lounge of the Lab for Manufacturing and Productivity at MIT, we also discussed ways to modify the ONS to provide more anonymity. In 2001, a major retailer surprised us all by insisting that we provided an electronic means for turning the EPC tag off within the protocol. Essentially, burning a fuse within the circuit could do this. By and large, the companies I have worked with have surprised me pleasantly with their proactive support for our research in the area of privacy.

Through 2001, Dan Engels, Peter Cole, and I spent a great deal of time thinking about the technical issues around privacy. Turning the chip off gave the consumer control and choice, but it also eliminated possible downstream benefits like recycling. Was there a better way? Our thinking was solidified further by some work we did with Professor Ronald Rivest and his student Steve Weis. We published a couple of papers, listed all the scenarios that we could think of by which RFID tags could be misused (assuming conservatively that tags could be read from a far greater range than they can now), and came up with several ways to address these problems.[6] Unfortunately, many of these solutions come at a higher cost. However, I feel confident that giving consumers the choice to kill tags protects them in every scenario I can think of.

Separately, Kevin established a distinguished panel of independent public policy experts to advise on matters related to privacy and social impacts of RFID tags. This panel, led by Elliot Maxwell, studied the problem from a number of angles and gave us invaluable guidance not only on where tags were today but also on where they could be in the future. One member of this panel was Simson Garfinkel, an MIT student who published the RFID "Bill of Rights" (Appendix D).

Ironically, questions about privacy started hitting the press after we had completed most of this analysis. While much of the writing was balanced, some of it was based on technically infeasible propositions. The stories sometimes did not recognize the physical limits of RFID tags, the technical issues we had studied, the scenarios we had analyzed, and the policies we had *already* published. Instead, they speculated on somewhat unrealistic scenarios like someone reading the contents of a home from a satellite or an RFID reader keeping track of a person's whereabouts. It is certainly the case that RF technology can be misused—indeed, any technology can. However, the EPC effort must not be painted with the same brush; it is defined to be inexpensive and therefore destined to be of minimal performance. In fact, the long ranges speculated upon would be a curse for the supply chain. Imagine if, when you tried to read a pallet in front of you, you heard the voices of all the tags within a radius of a mile. Fortunately, the balanced view seems to have won; privacy is important, and the EPC has safeguards to protect the consumer.

I have always felt that one unfortunate result of the trajectory of these privacy discussions was that many real privacy issues in RFID were never discussed.

---

6. Sarma, S.E., Weis, S.A., and Engels, D.W. "Low-Cost RFID and the Electronic Product Code," Workshop on Cryptographic Hardware and Embedded Systems (CHES 2002), San Francisco, CA, August 12–15, 2002.

   Engels, D.W., Rivest, R.L., Sarma, S.E., and Weis, S.A. "Security and Privacy Aspects of Low-Cost Radio Frequency Identification Systems," accepted for publication to the First International Conference on Security in Pervasive Computing (SPC 2003), March 12–14, 2003.

EPC has survived the trial by fire, and is better for it. However, not all RFID is EPC. Consider toll passes for cars, a prime example of privacy violation. The diminishing availability of coin lanes on highways is putting greater and greater pressure on people who don't have toll passes to get them. Yet toll passes have all the characteristics that EPC tags don't: They have long range, and they can't be turned off (I put mine inside the dash to protect myself). Our defense of EPC should not be construed as a defense of all RFID. All remote sensing technology needs to be examined carefully.

Summary: The Ultimate Systems Problem

There is a great deal of interest in *systems* research in academe today. In fact, MIT now has a new Engineering Systems Division. If there was ever any doubt about the relevance or the intellectual satisfaction of this hard-to-define topic, the Auto-ID Center should put it to rest. Under one research roof, our project touched topics as diverse as communication theory, circuit design, silicon manufacturing, manufacturing automation, paper manufacturing, cryptography, networking, software engineering, control theory, databases, distributed systems, public policy, the supply chain, logistics, and business modeling. Professors, students, technology companies, and user companies from around the world coordinated their work in this multifaceted effort to solve a pressing problem in industry. The impact was real, and the investments today are real. I believe that we have barely scratched the surface though; a great deal of research remains to be done on this exciting topic and in the related field of sensor networks.

RFID also is an excellent theme on which to base a course on system design. In fact, we taught our first graduate class on RFID in 2004, and I have rarely derived as much intellectual satisfaction from a teaching assignment.

Harnessing the Juggernaut

From 1999 to 2003, the Auto-ID Center grew from one lab to six, from three sponsors to more than a hundred, and from a gleam in our eyes to today's rollouts. This incredible growth occurred first, of course, because RFID solved fundamental problems in the supply chain. In addition, we—the researchers and the participating sponsors in the Auto-ID Center—were able to overcome some fundamental technology challenges and evangelize the concept very effectively.

The Six Auto-ID Labs

In 2000, it became clear that although we were making great progress within MIT, we needed help from other labs for several reasons. First, there was focus: Other labs with expertise in areas of RFID technology and RFID applications that we were not looking at could help us expand our horizons. Second, there are geographical differences in the use of RFID. For example, the regulatory environments in North America, Europe, and Asia are different, as are the supply chains. Even the way recycling is done is different. It was with these thoughts in mind that we set out to bring other distinguished research universities into the Auto-ID orbit. The mandate to expand the universities came from the Auto-ID sponsors, and we spent the next few years growing the family.

The first university we brought in was the University of Cambridge. For some time, I had known Dr. Duncan McFarlane there as an expert on manufacturing systems. Ironically, although manufacturing automation was where we started our research into RFID, it was the one process we were *not* doing. Duncan and his staff were the ideal group to take on the task of expanding research in the impact of RFID on manufacturing. Next, I met Professor Peter Cole of the University of Adelaide, Australia. Peter is an icon in the radio frequency systems and one of the leading lights of RFID hardware. He was also a founder of ISD (now known as Tagsys), a well-known company in the RFID space. We established both these labs by 2001. In 2002, Kevin Ashton and Dick Cantwell spent a month in Japan and met Professor Jun Murai of Keio University. Jun, who is also called the father of the Internet in Japan (the first network there was called Jun-net), established an Auto-ID Center at Keio. He brought not only a great deal of credibility but also an extraordinary knowledge of DNS and security to the group. Jun was in fact instrumental in the establishment of the 950–956MHz band in Japan for RFID. Kevin also met Professor Hao Min, a leading expert in Fudan University, China. Shanghai, where Fudan is located, is rapidly becoming the silicon fab capital of the world. With his deep knowledge of this space, Hao was another excellent addition to the Auto-ID team. Finally, in the beginning of 2003, we invited an old friend, Professor Elgar Fleisch of the University of St. Gallen, Switzerland, to the Center. The lab, which was jointly hosted by the University of St. Gallen and ETH Zurich (Einstein's alma mater), did a great deal of work not only on PML but also on the initial RFID value-calculator along with Cambridge. One of the more successful outreach efforts of the Center was a value calculator written by the University of Cambridge and offered on the Auto-ID Center Web site (with help from Mark Ferguson of Cambridge).

The Evolution of the Industry

The Center tripled its sponsorship every three years or four years. Much of this increase can be attributed to the relentless evangelizing of our staff and our existing sponsors. The vision was, after all, a seductive one. As the sponsorship grew, the organization of the labs evolved. In 2000, Dick Cantwell had taken over from Alan Haberman as chairman of the board of end-user sponsors (though Alan remains a close friend and advisor of the entire effort to this day). Around the same time, the board of vendor sponsors, which we dubbed the Technology Board, was growing bigger and contributing actively to the effort. Dirk Heyman of Sun became the chairman of the Technology Board. (Dirk later moved to Gillette, where he continues to work on RFID.)

In 2001, Wal-Mart joined the Auto-ID Center, and this move would prove to be a very important event. For a company renown for its innovative but grounded attitude to join a research effort meant that the research was getting close to practicality.

A second turning point was the field trial, which was the brainchild of Steve David of Procter & Gamble. Although I had misgivings about the organizational challenges of running such a large effort from a university, Steve's idea turned out to be a masterstroke. Wal-Mart chaired this self-organized effort, and through it, we learned the practicalities of RFID hardware and RFID software, the impact on logistics, and the impact on the economics of the supply chain. In the end, the field trial lasted two years and spanned eight states, ten cities, and 40 companies. The trial gave our emerging research a strong veneer of realism—something other research projects can only dream about. Much of the credit for the successful operation of the field trial goes to Silvio Albano, who was loaned to the Center by the Gillette Corporation to operate the field trial, and to Dan Engels, who was the technical lead. Kevin Ashton pushed for the eventual goal of item-level tagging, which we managed to get to in the field trial.

The third important event related to adoption was Gillette's order for 500 million tags placed in November 2002. The vendor that received this order was Alien Technology. Dick Cantwell, who was at that time also the chairman of the end-user sponsors' board at the Auto-ID Center, announced this order to a packed group of sponsors at our sponsors meetings. After taking over the Gillette effort from Allan Boath in 2000, Dick had passionately argued the benefits of EPC in reducing shrinkage and stock-outs in the supply chain. By placing this order, Dick was announcing three things:

- EPC technology had arrived in the real world.
- Gillette was willing to place a bet on its value.
- The race for extracting value from RFID was now on.

Executives like Dick Cantwell and Steve David play an unheralded role in moving American Corporations forward.

The final, and perhaps most powerful, step in the gathering momentum behind RFID was the Wal-Mart "mandate" announced in the middle of 2003. Linda Dillman, CIO of Wal-Mart, announced that starting in 2005, the retailer would require its top 100 suppliers to ship all cases and pallets of a few SKUs to a distribution center in Texas. Starting there from there, the expansion would encompass the entire supply chain. Nothing riveted attention more than the largest corporation on the planet making an announcement of this magnitude. (For additional information on this topic, see Appendix F.) To clarify matters even more, the Department of Defense (DoD) then followed suit, announcing a mandate of its own. Today, similar announcements from Target, Tesco, Metro, and other retailers around the world are further underlining the inevitability of the EPC.

The Creation of EPCglobal

By January 2002, the Auto-ID Center was outgrowing the confines of universities. The research was becoming more applied, and the commercial demands, like the sale of EPC numbers, were exceeding the capacity of universities. Despite the success that we were having in drawing in more companies, the need for a spin-off was apparent. In January 2002, I met Carol Carr and Tom Henneberry of the Office of Sponsored Programs at MIT to consider a number of alternatives. Should we create a new not-for-profit entity? A for-profit one? Would MIT invest and try to make money? Subsequent meetings with Professor Rohan Abeyaratne, the new head of the Mechanical Engineering Department; Dean Tom Magnanti; and Lita Nelson, the head of MIT's Technology Licensing Office made it clear to me that MIT was willing to take, and even insistent about taking, an extraordinarily generous approach to this spin-off. It wanted to create a not-for-profit organization to further EPC technology in the interests of society and the world.

Later that year, Mike DiYeso, Steve Brown, and Bernie Hogan of the Uniform Code Council traveled to MIT for a series of meetings with Kevin, Carol Carr, Tom Henneberry, Lita Nelson, and me. The UCC offered to run the EPC Network and to create a new not-for-profit group to do so. This was an ideal outcome, given that the UCC was an early sponsor of the Center and a successful not-for-profit standards body. We worked out a licensing agreement from MIT to this new entity, which we named EPCglobal. EPCglobal was a joint venture of the UCC and its sister organization, EAN. (UCC and EAN have now formally merged to form GS1.) Lita hammered out these agreements, and MIT licensed its technology free. Kevin and Lita had the excellent idea of putting a provision in the licensing agreement that the technology would not be used to tag human beings except in two scenarios: defense and hospitals. EPCglobal and the Auto-ID Center also agreed to continue a relationship wherein the center would be funded in exchange for ongoing research.

To prepare for the transition, I had already packaged the standards development process into two self-administered groups called the Hardware Action Group and the Software Action Group. Dan Engels led the Hardware Action Group, and Bruce Delagi of Sun headed up the Software Action Group. I had written an early document describing how the standards process might work, based on the W3C process. EPCglobal also created a public policy group of its own and took on the policy created by the Center. To aid the new organization, Tom Scharfeld at MIT wrote a white paper on certification, and Kevin wrote a paper on public policy. The last Auto-ID Center board meeting was held in November 2003. After that meeting, all activities other than research were transitioned to EPCglobal. A Board of Governors was created for EPCglobal, and Dick Cantwell of Gillette took over as chairman of that board. The research was to remain in the now-renamed Auto-ID Labs. Professors Elgar Fleisch and Jun Murai became the joint chairs of the new Auto-ID Labs. Dan Engels became director of research at MIT. I stepped aside as chairman of research and Kevin stepped aside as executive director of Auto-ID Center.

No transition, especially one of this magnitude, can be made without bumps in the road. The major sticking point in the transition from the Center to EPCglobal proved to be intellectual policy: EPCglobal has a unique mandate to offer royalty-free standards. We had always known that IP would be a challenge in this new space. In fact, we did a fair bit of research on intellectual policy, which Kevin summarized in a paper.[7] We had done as much as we could to avoid the minefield of intellectual policy that RFID faces. Many companies found the policy difficult to adopt, but after much negotiation, this and other similar problems seem to have been overcome. EPCglobal now has over 400 members and offices in several countries. The most recent EPCglobal meeting in Baltimore, Maryland, which was held in September 2004, had over 1,200 participants.

Conclusions

In 1999 and 2000, Kevin and I spent many evenings pondering the future and all possible outcomes for our EPC crusade. Looking back, though, I realize the

---

7. Ashton, K. "Towards an Approach to 'Intellectual Property.'" 2002. www.autoidlabs.org /whitepapers/MIT-AUTOID-EB-004.pdf.

Auto-ID Center exceeded most of my expectations. We had hit on the right formula for success: industry and academia working together. We had extremely supportive sponsors from the user and technology communities, like Gillette, Procter & Gamble, and Alien Technology. We even had, in the UCC, a respected industry body. This base gave us a great deal of license to invent and to be iconoclastic.

While many of our assertions and predictions were based on analysis and research, some were based on gut reactions. They turned into self-fulfilling prophecies because the researchers, the sponsors, and the entire community were intensely committed to them. We could ignore distractions and blind ourselves to naysayers, sometimes recklessly. Many of our predictions have come true. Some are still in progress. Others failed. For example, the mantra of minimalism and the use of the network, so difficult to convey only four years ago, are widely accepted today. We predicted that tags could be manufactured for less than five cents, which I still believe, perhaps even more confidently than before. Yet volumes are not where they need to be, and tags still cost about 20 cents. I still see this as a big step forward, given that UHF tags cost more than a dollar when we started. Where we were wrong was in assuming that item tagging was imminent. Case and pallet tagging are taking off, but the economics of item tagging are still not generally feasible.

On the other hand, RFID, and specifically the EPC form of RFID, is here to stay. It is very important to contrast RFID and the EPC and that the EPC is one way to use RFID technology—and, I will assert, a responsible and economical way. The value of the EPC to retailers is undeniable. The value to manufacturers too, in my analysis, is significant. The challenge will be in modifying business processes to extract this value.

The EPC will affect a number of industries. It will make baggage tracking in airlines more efficient and safe, it will make pharmaceuticals more difficult to counterfeit, it will enable the delivery of fresher food, and it will enable better management of spare parts in the automotive and aerospace industries. Semipassive and active tags will open up newer and even more exciting applications but will bring with them the very policy concerns that were mistakenly directed toward passive RFID tags. Either way, technology will continue to evolve, and as a society, we must ensure that we continue to extract the best of new technology to improve our standard of life.

Chapter 4

RFID AND GLOBAL PRIVACY POLICY

Stephanie Perrin[1]

Introduction

This chapter addresses the privacy and data protection issues presented by RFID, largely in view of existing human rights policy and constitutional protection, data protection law, and fair information practices. As described in other chapters, RFID poses privacy problems that are arguably the most fundamental we have encountered in many years. If so few people understand how the telephone signaling system works and so many make uninformed decisions about such issues as caller ID or data retention, how will the public be able to make educated decisions about a sophisticated technology like RFID? In this new world of machine-to-machine (M2M) communications, it is not even clear that the paradigms on which we rest our interpretations of privacy are adequate. This chapter examines some new ways of defining privacy in North America, Europe, and elsewhere.

Privacy and consumer advocates are calling for regulation, codes of best practice, and technological fixes that give them back a measure of control over RFIDs. They are trying to slow down the rollout of these transformative technologies so that the public can get involved in the dialogue. That call for discussion and policy development is not being heeded in a coherent way, and although the Data Commissioners of Europe, through the Data Protection Working Party, are studying the topic and will likely issue a report in 2005[2], there is as yet no formal

---

1. Stephanie Perrin is a recipient of the Electronic Frontier Foundation Pioneer Award for her role as a global privacy advocate.
2. RFID was on the Workplan of the Article 29 Group, a working party of data commissioners that is constituted under the European Directive 95/46. http://europa.eu.int/comm /internal_market/privacy/workingroup/wp2004/wpdocs04_en.htm. A call for comment on the issue, closing on March 31, 2005, was issued in late winter 2005.

guidance from regulators. This chapter sketches out a few realistic scenarios and looks at what the existing law, policy, and best practice might say about privacy protection. Although the core concepts are similar, the diversity in the detail of the various laws precludes our providing anything more than highlights, and certainly this chapter should be considered a policy discussion, not legal advice.

Definitions of Privacy

In a global context, "privacy" is understood in different ways by different individuals, across many cultures and sectors. Each author in this volume may well refer to privacy in a slightly different way. This chapter fleshes out some of the meanings.

Privacy has traditionally been discussed along two vectors:

- As a fundamental human right, including the right to be free from unreasonable search and seizure or intrusion
- As protection of personal information

The principal data protection instruments referred to in this chapter are the European Data Protection Directive 95/46/EC (1995), which sets the mandatory standards for the legislative framework in each European member state; the Canadian Personal Information Protection and Electronic Documents Act (PIPEDA) (2000), which does the same thing for Canada and its provinces; and the OECD Guidelines Governing the Protection of Privacy and Transborder Flows of Personal Data (1980), which underpin much of the U.S. privacy law. Various definitions of personal information exist within global legislation and other instruments, and the subtleties of these definitions could make a big difference when applied to RFID.

Definitions of Personal Information

The following are definitions related to personal information:

- **European Directive 95/46/EC: Personal Data.**[3] "Shall mean any information relating to an identified or identifiable natural person

---

3. Directive 95/46/EC of the European Parliament and of the Council of 24 October 1995, on the protection of individuals with regard to the processing of personal data and on the free movement of such data.

('data subject'); an identifiable person is one who can be identified, directly or indirectly, in particular by reference to an identification number or to one or more factors specific to his physical, physiological, mental, economic, cultural, or social identity…"; also

- **Processing of Personal Data.** "Shall mean any operation or set of operations which is performed upon personal data, whether or not by automatic means, such as collection, recording, organization, storage, adaptation or alteration, retrieval, consultation, use, disclosure by transmission, dissemination or otherwise making available, alignment or combination, blocking, erasure or destruction."
- **Personal Information Protection and Electronic Documents Act (PIPEDA) (Canada).** "Personal information" is defined as "information about an identifiable individual, but does not include the name, title, or business address or telephone number of an employee of an organization."
- **OECD Guidelines.** Personal data is defined as "any information relating to an identified or identifiable individual (data subject)."
- **Safe Harbor Arrangement: Personal Data.** "Personal data and personal information are data about an identified or identifiable individual that are within the scope of the Directive, received by a U.S. organization from the European Union, and recorded in any form".

History of Current Privacy Paradigm

In the 1970s, fears about loss of privacy focused on large, centrally held databases containing files about named or numbered individuals. People conceptualized the threat in terms of information in a file. As the Web and its attendant search engines have developed, we have only slightly modified our thinking about personal information or personally identifiable information and the way it is kept. The concept of personal information being dangerous when held centrally in a "file" is rather quaint, given the power of today's networks and search engines.

Now there are holes in this conceptual framework. On one hand, if RFIDs contribute information about individuals to large databases, the link with the individuals is often not specific enough for some of these definitions to be useful. On the other hand, if the feed from an RFID is not considered personal information because it is not linked to a name or an identifying number, it can still be combined with other data to provide personal information. PIPEDA expressly addresses this hole by defining personal information as "information about an identifiable individual" without specifying who identifies that individual, or how. This anticipates a world where data is agglomerated, crumb by crumb, from a host of different data holders, until sufficient attributes are present to re-identify the individual associated with the data-stream.[4]

University of Texas Professor, Dr. David Phillips described the problem in his article "Privacy Policy and PETS".[5] In his introduction to the problem of disambiguating the notion of privacy, he says:

> "We may identify at least four relatively distinct types of privacy concern and label them, for the sake of convenience, 'freedom from intrusion', 'negotiating the public/private divide', 'identity management' and 'surveillance'. Each way of thinking and talking about privacy will favor particular definitions of, and solutions to, the privacy problem. Obviously, these concerns are interrelated."

Phillips places the traditional definition of privacy, stated by privacy advocate Dr. Alan Westin, as individuals' right "to control, edit, manage, and delete information about them[selves] and decide when, how, and to what extent information is communicated to others" within Identity Management.[6] However, the problem of "surveillance" and its meaning appears to encompass the larger societal privacy threats posed by RFIDs:

> "In its idealized form, panoptic surveillance individualizes each member of the population, and permits the observations and recording of each individual's activities, then collates these individual observations across the population. From these conglomerated observations, statistical norms are produced relating to any of a multitude of characteristics. These norms are then applied back to the subjected individuals, who are categorized and perhaps acted upon, either with gratification or punishment, according to their relation to the produced norm."

RFID is a transformative technology because it brings about the potential for constant individual identification and the automatic sorting of individuals, named or otherwise, into groups. "Group privacy" is a newer concept, but one that will be increasingly important in a world of M2M communications. Who goes to Starbucks? RFIDS will make it easy to know when we all carry tagged loyalty cards.

---

4. www.privcom.gc.ca/legislation/02_06_01_01_e.asp
5. In *New Media and Society*, vol.6 (6): 691–706. London, Thousand Oaks, CA, and New Delhi: 2004.
6. Phillips, D. *Privacy Policy and PETS*, 693–695, citing Westin, A., *Privacy and Freedom*, New York: Atheneum, 1967

Fear of a Central Database

Work on the privacy framework in the 1960s was stimulated by a vision popular among IT specialists and government officials—that of a central database of citizen information. In the generation since then, we have averted our eyes from the rampant proliferation of databases such as those held by credit reporting bureaus, banks, insurance companies, major retailers, and information management companies such as Axciom and LexisNexis. The growth of these disparate databases has been well documented in *Database Nation.*[7] In 2005 these databases have grown into what we feared in the 1960s: the specter of an all-knowing, all-seeing, central database. However, it is manifesting not as one database but as many different databases interlinked around the globe. Governments that spent the equivalent of billions of dollars making sure records were not linked through single numbers, like the Social Insurance Number in Canada, are once more looking at ways to facilitate searching between interoperable platforms and linking data reliably to particular individuals—ostensibly in the name of fighting organized crime and terror.

People still react negatively to the loss of control over their own personal information, believing they have a right to present their unique face to the world, in their own terms. This may be in denial of the facts of the twenty-first century, as has been pointed out by various commentators, perhaps most infamously by Scott McNealy, the CEO of Sun Microsystems, when he said, "You have zero privacy anyway, get over it."[8]

In previous generations, when bankers dealt with a customer for a loan, they based their decision primarily on personal knowledge of the individual and the forms that the individuals filled out. Today neither the human being requesting the loan nor the bank manager has much influence on the decision. Databases, predictive software programs, and inexpensive telecommunications have facilitated a world where decisions are made remotely by machines fed an ever-increasing stream of data, with little human intervention. Everyone banks, but very few know about the companies that manage their financial transactional data and the relationship between those data processors and the state.

From a policy perspective, it is not clear that society and democracies have yet adjusted to this current scenario. People do not fully understand how the information infrastructure works, and the high levels of concern for privacy that we see in virtually all the polling data[9] demonstrate strongly contradictory behavior. While few people are actively protecting their privacy, the level of concern

---

7. Garfinkel, S. *Database Nation: The Death of Privacy in the 21ˢᵗ Century.* Sebastapol, CA.: O'Reilly, 2000.

8. www.wired.com/news/politics/0,1283,17538,00.html

is rising every year, leading to a profoundly unstable situation such that a scandal in the press could precipitate sudden change in consumer behavior. In fact, this scandal hit in February 2005 when it became publicly known that Choice-Point, one of the largest and most successful data brokers in the world, with 64 billion files, sold personal information to a criminal ring of ID thieves posing as small businesses. This scandal has prompted calls for legislation, Congressional hearings, complaints to the Federal Trade Commission, private actions, and investigations from State Attorneys General.[10]

Now RFID bring to us an "Internet of things," on which objects talk about their owners or handlers, thus feeding powerful new databases. Industry proponents protest that the chips are not big enough to be intelligent, but the chips' "chatter," even if it is only in monosyllables, brings to a new level a world in which humans hold increasingly less power and information holds increasingly more. In discussions about "trust" and "security", the emphasis is on building trusted systems. But does this mean we no longer trust humans?

Mapping the RFID Discovery Process

Consider the following "real-life" RFID applications:

- Alice has an employee badge, which contains her employee ID number and a set of building access privileges.
- Bob, a patient, has an implant containing data on his health conditions, medication, and identity.
- Carol's dog Rover has a pet-tracking tag, which gives Carol's name, address, and phone number or a number that is matched in a database to that same personal information.
- Dora's leather jacket has a manufacturer's tag, which contains a unique product number that is linked to the date of purchase.
- Ed buys a packet of razor blades, whose tag has product, price, and retail destination information on it.

---

9. For a view of the evolution of privacy concern, see Alan Westin's work in association with Harris Interactive, as described on the Privacy and American Business Web site, www.pandab.org. Although the surveys are proprietary, Dr. Westin has written about them since the early 1990s, and he said of the recent survey results described at the Privacy and American Business conference in Washington in June 2004, and at the Ottawa University conference "The Concealed I" March 4, 2005 that concerns continue to rise and self-professed privacy fundamentalists now stand at 37% of the U.S. population.

10. The latest news on the ChoicePoint scandals can be found at the Electronic Privacy Information Center's Choicepoint page www.epic.org. Robert O'Harrow Jr.'s book, *No Place to Hide* (New York: Free Press, 2005), contains useful updates on the database industry in the post-911 environment.

- Fred works with a shipping container that is used and reused to transport frozen dinners. The container's tag is identified with the manufacturing plant ID, store destination, contents, and date the container is filled.

The first three applications contain explicitly personal information. Every time these tags are read, personal information is emitted. The reader's ability to detect the presence of a tag is an indicator that an identifiable individual is at that geographical location at a precise moment.

Carol's dog's tag is a good example of personal tracking by proxy. If Carol is the only one who walks Rover, readers that track the dog tag will have a reliable record of her movements. Assuming Rover is not in the habit of rambling around on his own, his information becomes tracked one-to-one with Carol's, regardless of what personal information or numbering is contained in the tag.

In Dora's case, the tag in her jacket will, over time, become associated with Dora, the individual who wears it. If she is wearing the jacket as she walks past a reader every morning to enter a building, she will soon build up a profile of pseudonymous information, with the pseudonym being the unique identifier of the jacket. Identify Dora once, and the entire record of comings and goings becomes transparent. Associate the RFID with an image from a video camera, and the jacket and Dora become reliably linked with a visual image. These facts contradict the argument that RFID will be anonymous. If she buys a coffee each morning, readers in the coffee shop will know her by her jacket tag.

Unless we make a point of regularly trading our clothes, wallets, and favorite possessions with others in order to foil the system, RFID-tagged personal possessions will soon be reliable authenticators of identity because of their close association with unique individuals.

Ed's RFID-enabled package of razor blades has become the subject of numerous press stories. The activist group Consumers Against Supermarket Privacy Invasion and Numbering (CASPIAN)[11] found that a manufacturer was using hidden cameras activated by the RFID chips as merchandise left the shelf. The experiment was discovered in both in Britain, where a store filmed customers to deter shoplifting, and in the United States, where a chip was being used as a prototype for inventory tracking.

Fred's reusable container is the often-cited example of an almost totally innocuous use of RFID that will save a lot of time and money in inventory control and shipping, with few implications for personal privacy. However if the crate is read in context with other chipped devices (e.g., Fred's employee card, the

---

11. See www.spychips.com.

truck that he is assigned to drive on this shift, individually tagged articles and tools such as a trolley he is assigned for work), the threat of employee surveillance is very real.

Such crates might be candidates for high-end, rewriteable chips, and if they could register every time they were touched by specific employees, as part of an apparently innocuous time-tracking control system (useful for controlling melting and warming, in the case of frozen and refrigerated food handling), there are implications for the humans involved. For example, tool inventory control is a major cost for many service industries, so tools that remember where they have been and what they did there may become hot sellers. The value of tool tracking may be considered to be higher than the dignity of the workmen who use the tools.

To date, the public discussion on privacy issues has not focused on employee surveillance and tracking. But particularly in Europe, where unions are stronger than in the United States, it promises to be an issue.

Functions and Responsibilities for Chips, Readers, and Owners

In the ontology of data protection law and policy, the RFID itself may be a storage device containing an individual's personal information (e.g., a shopper card number, employee number, or the identity of a dog's owner). It also can be a personal information-emitting device if, when illuminated by a transmitter receiver, it broadcasts such information. Depending on the uniqueness of its own number or product code, it may also become a numeric identifier reliably associated with a human being, not just an item of merchandise; the number of a breast implant, for instance, or a pacemaker, soon might be more reliable as a numeric identifier of an individual than the current U.S. Social Security number.

An RFID reader is simultaneously a data-collection instrument, promiscuously gathering information from each RFID that responds to its broadcast, and a transmitter or broadcaster of information, as it sends its data through the information network. The databases connected to these networks hold, use, and disclose the gathered information. Here the information may be used for wholly different purposes than those envisaged by the party that installed the RFID device and these new uses are likely not apparent to the carrier of the device. We cover these aspects later in the chapter as we discuss the application of data protection law.

Privacy as a Fundamental Human Right

To date, public discussion of privacy and RFID has been at a superficial level, focusing on the effective range of readers and the ability to disable the tags. This limited scope mirrors the discussion of privacy in North America, which has been similarly focused on opt-in versus opt-out and "notice and choice." This discussion not only understates the subtleties of data protection, it also misses more fundamental issues about individual rights.

The annual report "Privacy and Human Rights," published by the Electronic Privacy Information Center[12] in cooperation with Privacy International,[13] details the constitutional privacy and data protection statutes of over 80 countries. Although countries approach privacy differently, the United Nations' Universal Declaration of Human Rights enunciates the fundamental right to privacy in the following sections:[14]

PREAMBLE

"Whereas recognition of the inherent dignity and of the equal and inalienable rights of all members of the human family is the foundation of freedom, justice and peace in the world…"

Does the right to dignity stated in the Preamble include the right not to have your possessions, wallet, vehicle, or your person equipped with a device that can be read without your knowledge or consent?

Article 12.

No one shall be subjected to arbitrary interference with his privacy, family, home or correspondence, nor to attacks upon his honour and reputation. Everyone has the right to the protection of the law against such interference or attacks.

What is "arbitrary interference"? Can one make the argument that intelligent devices interfere with this right to enjoy home, family, and correspondence in peace? When our currency, computer technology, clothes, and appliances all sport communicating devices that tag and track us, does it seem plausible that

---

12. The PHR report for 2004 is available online at www.epic.org.
13. www.privacyinternational.org
14. www.un.org/Overview/rights.html

this article has been violated? What law would protect us from interference and from attacks based on faulty data from our possessions and devices?

Article 13.

"Everyone has the right to freedom of movement and residence within the borders of each state."

Does freedom of movement mean anonymous movement and assembly, free from tracking devices? Does it imply the right to travel on trains or subways without having to use RFID-enabled tickets or passes that respond to every reader they encounter on the trip? Does it mean that public spaces cannot be wired with readers to track and analyze us?

Article 17.

"(1) Everyone has the right to own property alone as well as in association with others.
(2) No one shall be arbitrarily deprived of his property."

What does the right to own property imply? Until recently, it was nearly impossible for those selling goods to put strings on them, to have the goods report back whether in fact they were being used according to warranty requirements, to determine whether lending or copying policies were being respected, or to have the goods identify themselves to facilitate recall. These "strings" are potentially feasible with RFID, and the liability and theft issues will reduce the possibility that these features will be turned off. How many consumers are willing to forego warranty protections to have a little privacy?

In recent years, we have seen the ownership of computer software change in subtle ways to the point that we now really only license the software for a few years. We are in such dynamic contact with the licensor for security and technical updates that the software may be useless after the license expires. Could the same transformation of ownership be rolled out for other types of goods? We can envisage such Faustian bargains being offered in the near future; certainly the health industry is already interested in RFID-enabling prescription drugs to ensure expiry date accuracy, track repeats, facilitate recall, limit liability, and address a host of other public policy issues such as prescription drug abuse. If the only way a patient can be sure her antidepressants are the real thing and not cheap counterfeits is to accept them in a smart, sealed, authenticated container, she will have bargained away her health privacy to be read by whoever scans her purse.

Article 18.

"Everyone has the right to freedom of thought, conscience and religion; this right includes freedom to change his religion or belief, and freedom, either alone or in community with others and in public or private, to manifest his religion or belief in teaching, practice, worship and observance."

Article 18 provides the right to practice freedom of religion worldwide. In Canada, religious freedom is protected by the Charter of Rights and Freedoms, and recent cases before the Canadian Supreme Court suggest that recourse to the Charter over RFID use may be successful.[15] In the United States, the Constitution provides such protection, and it will not be long before a case arises involving RFID—many Christian sects have already identified RFID as the "mark of the beast" identified in the Book of Revelation. Whether or not a suit would be successful, it certainly must be heard; developers of the bar code even inserted the number 666 into the standard, so the argument has been made easy for believers in this particular chapter of the Christian Bible. The point that religious groups are raising is lost on many in the technology community: human beings have a right to live their lives without intermediation by material things. In many religions, the material world is construed as a barrier between humans and the spiritual world. People with this viewpoint do not want talking possessions, regardless of how convenient these are to retailers.

The U.N. Declaration is high level and over 50 years old. Nevertheless, the sooner RFID proponents recognize that individual autonomy, freedom of movement, human dignity, and religious expression are all threatened by widespread deployment of this otherwise extremely useful technology, the sooner we will have a fruitful discussion. In North America. we have spent the past 15 years painstakingly removing asbestos and urea-formaldehyde insulation materials from buildings after the risks to humans were discovered. We don't want to be spending the next 20 removing RFID from the communications architecture we are busy building today after people decide they want their material possessions to remain mute and unable to participate in controlling their lives.

---

15. A recent case claiming the right to put up ceremonial huts on the balconies of apartment buildings was successful (see Syndicat Northcrest v. Amselem, www.lexum.umontreal.ca/csc-scc /en/rec/html/2004scc047.wpd.html); a case is pending concerning the Sikh practice of carrying ceremonial daggers, even in public schools (see www.canlii.org/qc/jug/qccs/2002 /2002qccs12551.html). Currently, the Ontario Superior Court is hearing a case concerning the right to refuse to provide a picture in the motor vehicle license database. These cases illustrate the success of religious freedom cases under the Charter—the last involving a Christian who cites arguments based on the book of Revelation.

Constitutional Rights

The member states of the European Union have for some time been required to respect the European Convention on Human Rights (ECHR) or face being taken to the European Court of Human Rights. Each country that has ratified the Convention has also put in place its own legislation, which in many cases is stronger and more specific than the Convention's.

A recently enacted law in the United Kingdom provides that all U.K. legislation must respect the ECHR. Some of the new member states of the European Union, such as Poland and Latvia, have new constitutions that go further because they were drafted in the light of recent experience in which human rights were not respected. The Polish constitution[16] is a good example and would no doubt provide grounds for a challenge of compulsory RFID in matters that fall under its domain. Poland is also an interesting example of the specific issues that arise in cultural context because of the emphasis on labor and union rights, a legacy of the important role the labor movement played in bringing down the Communist regime.

Most discussion of RFID privacy issues in the EU directive has concerned consumers, but employees will in fact be subject to surveillance and tracking through RFID badges and ubiquitous readers as well as throughput tracking reported by the goods themselves. In Europe, works councils have been successful in disabling such surveillance mechanisms in earlier incarnations of the technology, and Courts have supported the privacy rights of workers.

The passage in December 2000 of the Charter of Fundamental Rights of the European Union[17] restates in law the basic concepts found in the Convention on Human Rights in the sections on "Dignity" and "Freedoms." The EU also included the right to legislated data protection with oversight by an independent authority as an element in the Treaty Establishing a Constitution for Europe.[18]

But given all the analysis in our possession now, can we predict what data protection law would say about RFIDs?

---

16. See www.oefre.unibe.ch/law/icl/pl00000_.html for an English version of the Constitution of Poland.
17. www.europarl.eu.int/charter/default_en.htm
18. *Official Journal of the European Community* 169, July 18, 2003. p.1.

Privacy Through Data Protection Law and Fair Information Practices

It is hard to imagine how the right to privacy can be respected if there are no detailed rules for managing personal information. Nevertheless, privacy activists often argue that data protection law actually helps debase the fundamental human right to privacy: If we follow a mere set of rules about how data will be managed once it is collected, will we forget that not collecting data in the first place should be our goal? If personal data is never gathered, it is irrelevant how well confidentiality is managed, who may access it under what circumstances, or under what circumstances an individual might legitimately be denied access to his or her own personal information. Increasingly, European privacy experts are calling for collection limitation or data scarcity—the "forgotten principle"—to be more respected because the task of auditing and supervising the management of vast collections of data is immense.

However, the fair information practices (FIPS) on which most data protection law is based are generally recognized as just that—fair—and the privacy and civil liberties communities have been calling for RFID to be deployed only if FIPS are followed.

A Brief History of FIPS

The 1973 Report of the U.S. Health, Education and Welfare Department described the worrisome findings of an extensive review of data processing. The authors recommended that a Code of Fair Information Practices be established:

The Code of Fair Information Practices is based on five principles:

- There must be no personal-data, record-keeping systems whose very existence is a secret.
- There must be a way for a person to find out what information about the person is in a record and how it is used.
- There must be a way for a person to prevent information about the person that was obtained for one purpose from being used or made available for other purposes without the person's consent.
- There must be a way for a person to correct or amend a record of identifiable information about the person.
- Any organization creating, maintaining, using, or disseminating records of identifiable personal data must assure the reliability of the

data for their intended use and must take reasonable precautions to prevent misuse of the data.[19]

In 1980, the Organization for Economic Cooperation and Development (OECD) in Paris released its "Guidelines on the Protection of Privacy and Transborder Flows of Personal Data,"[20] which set the standard for FIPS for the next 20 years. Reaffirmed as appropriate for protecting privacy in the context of Electronic Commerce at a Ministerial Conference on Electronic Commerce in 1998, these FIPS have become the basis of many data protection laws. In Canada, they were the foundation of a national standard for the protection of personal information (CAN/CSA Q-830), which was developed by the Canadian Standards Association and became a national standard in 1996. The recent Personal Information Protection and Electronic Documents Act of Canada (2000)[21] incorporates that standard as the set of FIPS that must be met.

The Act's ten principles are:

- Accountability
- Identifying purposes
- Consent
- Collection limitation
- Limiting use, disclosure, and retention
- Accuracy
- Safeguards
- Openness
- Individual access
- Challenging compliance

Accepted as adequate data protection by the European Union for the purposes of onward transmission of EU personal data, the standard has had a significant impact on the work on Privacy Guidelines of the Asia Pacific Economic Cooperation (APEC) group.

There are of course corresponding provisions in the EU Data Protection Directive, but the document is organized differently. The Directive also differentiates certain types of data whose processing is prohibited ("sensitive" data), which includes "personal data revealing racial or ethnic origin, political opinions, religious or philosophical beliefs, trade-union membership, and the processing of data concerning health or sex life" (article 8 (1)).

---

19. See U.S. Department of Health, Education and Welfare, Secretary's Advisory Committee on Automated Personal Data Systems. Records, Computers, and Rights of Citizens viii (1973)
20. www.oecd.org/dsti/sti/it/secur/prod/PRIV-EN.HTM
21. Statutes of Canada, C 5, http://laws.justice.gc.ca/en/P-8.6/.

The following analysis of the rights under data protection law follows the structure of the ten principles of the Canadian Standard CAN/CSA Q-830, now required by law in PIPEDA,[22] and adds relevant requirements from the *EU Data Protection Directive 95/46.*[23]

Accountability

The concept of accountability is a constant in data protection law. Someone is responsible, perhaps liable, for ensuring data protection, and that person must be made available to requestors and complainants. In the European context, this person is called the "data controller". The accountable person, under the Canadian law, has a number of duties, including:

- Maintaining responsibility for information that has been transferred to third parties for processing, which must be protected through contractual means
- Implementing policies and procedures to give effect to all the principles, including training staff and developing information to explain the policies and procedures to the public

But this form of accountability is complicated when applied to RFID. When does an individual or organization cease to be accountable for the RFID—either the information contained within it or the stream of location data that it generates?

A recent Federal Court of Appeal decision in Canada[24] confirmed that the Court does view an organization as having a primary responsibility to inform individuals about the implications of a decision to accept a particular information bargain—for example, the decision to allow their name, address, and phone number to appear in the phone book and in all subsequent uses of that information resulting from that public disclosure.

Responsibility in Individual RFID Scenarios

Under current and theoretical RFID policy, who is ultimately responsible for the data in Alice's employee badge, Bob's medical implant, Dora's leather jacket, and Ed's razor blades?

---

22. Statutes of Canada, http://laws.justice.gc.ca/en/P-8.6/.
23. Many other relevant statutes could and should be included, particularly in the area of medical and financial privacy where confidentiality clauses may have a decisive impact on using RFID to contain personal information, but this narrative is complex enough.
24. Englander v. Telus, see http://decisions.fca-caf.gc.ca/fca/2004/2004fca387.shtml.

Alice's employee badge will in all likelihood remain the property of the organization she works for, not of Alice the employee, so that organization will be responsible for the information on it as well as any information it broadcasts to a reader. If the technology interoperates with every reader Alice happens to pass, would she have a valid complaint that the company was not protecting her personal information? Could the company transfer the responsibility for the card and the information on it to Alice, making it her responsibility to prevent the card from accidentally disclosing its information to a reader?

Because this form of RFID technology is passive, requiring little or no action on the part of the holder of the chip, this is a fundamental question. It is one thing for the employee to be responsible for a card that needs to be put into a slot to be read or up against a reader for a proximity contactless smart card. If the device can be read even if the employee takes no action, can the accountability be passed along to the employee? Only if the employee gets a foil-lined wallet to go with the card, I would say.

Bob's patient implant is even more problematic because the information is more likely to be sensitive, he cannot remove it or wrap it in foil, and in all likelihood, the accountable organization is a healthcare provider, hospital, or device manufacturer (such as a heart pacemaker) with which he will not have an ongoing relationship. The device may be meant to be read by a broad spectrum of future players in his healthcare relationships, so the chip is likely to interoperate with any reader in range. How can we maintain accountability here? Is Bob responsible? Suppose he is too ill to know what is going on? If the data is read by alien machines against his will and harm is done, who is liable—the chip manufacturer or the reader of the machine?

This brings us to the question of the readers. Arguably, the organization that puts the information into the RFID has already done so, presumably with the consent of the individual. From then on, the individual who has custody of the device might be considered responsible. The custodian of the RFID information (although not the lookup database) is now the individual, in the case of all the examples we listed above. (We won't complicate matters by mentioning appliances, cars and car parts, and building materials that could be associated with individuals but are durable goods that are not intrinsically personal.)

If the individual comes in range of a reader, is the operator of the network to which it is attached accountable for the information it collects? Clearly, it is, at least according to the Canadian law. It will be the responsibility of the organization, and the persons accountable within that organization, to ensure compliance with the Canadian law, or all of the FIPS. A reader must collect only the data that it is supposed to collect and that it is authorized by law, policy, or a contractual arrangement to collect.

Proponents of RFID deployment tout benign scenarios such as chips on packages and a self-checkout that scans them. What happens if the persistent RFID in Dora's leather jacket (which she has not disabled because she wants to keep the warranty) is read every time she checks out her groceries or goes through the ATM door? Who is responsible or accountable for the information gathered? The creator of the RFID, Dora, or the organization responsible for the reader?

The discussion of using kill switches and permitting opt in/opt out does not focus on this fundamental problem. If you do not opt out, are you committed to transmitting whatever information could be transmitted, to every reader that is capable of reading it? Today's Internet Web browsers follow this principle: Accept cookies once, and expect them to be read by anyone who can read them. Once you agree to have your customer information shared with other "quality companies for marketing," that information is out the barn door.

Under Canadian and European law, including the European Direct Marketing Directive, future users will need some kind of evidence of valid consent, but that consent may be loopholed if the wording is broad enough. It is doubtful this permissive approach will work for RFID, particularly where sensitive information is concerned.

As for the question of accountability, the data controller or original programmer of the RFID must ensure that the device with personal information in it is labeled with the identity of the organization that is responsible for it. The reader must be identifiable so that individuals can access their data or complain if they find their data being read without their consent.

Identifying Purposes

> The purposes for which personal information is collected shall be identified by the organization at or before the time the information is collected.[25]

This section goes on to stipulate that the individual must be able to find out the purposes, and when new purposes are identified after collection, the organization must gain new consent. The idea that purposes for collection, use, and disclosure must be specified to the individual before the information is gathered is a constant in data protection law. In some law, it is part of informed consent; in others, as in the OECD Guidelines and PIPEDA, it is a separate principle. In the Canadian law, section 5(3) states further, "An organization may collect, use,

---

25. PIPEDA

and disclose personal information only for purposes that a reasonable person would consider are appropriate in the circumstances." This is likely to spark complaints, especially when readers unrelated to the original purpose of the RFID tag are gathering information for new, unanticipated purposes. If Dora's jacket were used as a link to her identity in cash sales at a department store or if Carol's dog's ID were to be used as a proxy to identify her at a weekend rock concert, there is a good chance a court would view reliance on these linkages as opportunistic and the purpose of gathering such data for unstated purposes as something a reasonable person would not find appropriate.

Consent

> The knowledge and consent of the individual are required for the collection, use, or disclosure of personal information, except where inappropriate.[26]

Unambiguous consent is required for the legitimate processing of data under Article 7 of the Directive, unless there is a clear contract, the processing is necessary for compliance with a legal obligation, the processing is undertaken in the public interest, or the processing is necessary for the legitimate interests of the controller. Under Canadian law, consent is required for the separate actions of collection, use, and disclosure of personal information with specific exceptions under each of these actions as required for law enforcement, fraud investigation, and other legitimate reasons. These two legal regimes take different routes to permit some routine use and disclosure of personal information without the express consent of the individual. If it were not the case, business would come to a halt with the never-ending process of seeking consent.

In the context of the Internet, P3P was an attempt to automate decision making with respect to cookies, enabling an individual's Internet browser to automatically negotiate with Web sites the circumstances under which the individual would agree to accept cookies and thus potentially be tracked and identified. It was not entirely successful, although individuals set the preferences themselves and could intervene since they were operating the browser. How do we negotiate consent in the RFID scenarios, where communication may be taking place without the person's knowledge?

Alice is not in a position to give meaningful consent to the performance of her ID card. She has to carry it with her to get into work, so if it interoperates with other readers, she has no control over it.

---

26. PIPEDA; inappropriate uses are specified in Section 7.

Bob may not have a choice about whether to receive a chip either, if having one is required to check into a hospital or have his medical devices covered by his insurer. Carol may be required to put a chip in her dog's ear to comply with local bylaws. The only way for these applications to comply with the law is for the devices not to contain personal information themselves. Furthermore, there must be a way to destroy the consistent pseudonymity in order to avoid the proxy problem.

Limiting Collection

> The collection of personal information shall be limited to that which is necessary for the purposes identified by the organization. Information shall be collected by fair and lawful means.[27]

We have discussed the central problem of stopping RFID from communicating. This provision is clear, it is mandatory, and legitimate collection is dependent on having a reasonable purpose. Mechanisms to limit collection would include screening out transmissions from non-targeted chips, dumping data immediately if it is not necessary to keep it, and removing identifiers to render data nonpersonal.

The problem of group surveillance that David Phillips has described will be one of the big new issues in RFID deployment scenarios. Dr. Latanya Sweeney of Carnegie Mellon demonstrated years ago how simple it is to reidentify supposedly anonymized health records;[28] and her work and techniques will certainly be relied on to find out what we can learn from RFID reporting.

Limiting Use, Disclosure, and Retention

> Personal information shall not be used or disclosed for purposes other than those for which it was collected, except with the consent of the individual or as required by law. Personal information shall be retained only as long as necessary for the fulfillment of those purposes.[29]

Canadian law further specifies that procedures must be developed to govern the permissible retention of information and its safe destruction and disposal. If the accountability were passed to the individual carrying the RFID, the problem

---

27. PIPEDA
28. www.ncc.org.uk/technology/index.htm
29. PIPEDA

of data retention would no longer belong to the issuing organization. Similarly, if somehow the responsibility for preventing transmission from the RFID could be passed to the owner, the problem of ongoing disclosure carrying on forever could theoretically be passed to the owner.

Data protection law puts the emphasis on the responsibilities of the collector, however, so it seems unlikely that readers in an RFID architecture will be allowed to gather data indiscriminately and keep it indefinitely, regardless of whether the individuals concerned are consciously exercising their rights. There will have to be a way to purge irrelevant data from systems promptly.

Accuracy

> Personal information shall be as accurate, complete, and up-to-date as is necessary for the purposes for which it is to be used.[30]

This determination is based on the needs of the individual and the original purpose of the data capture. Writing new information to a tag that serves the purposes of the organization but not necessarily the individual would not be acceptable, even if it could be argued it was more accurate. The Directive says something slightly different in the Data Quality section:

> (d) Accurate and, where necessary, kept up to date; every reasonable step must be taken to ensure that data which are inaccurate or incomplete, having regard to the purposes for which they were collected or for which they are further processed, are erased or rectified.

Whether a tag can be hacked and the data can be altered will be of major concern for retailers and those attempting to deter theft, maintain good inventory control, and provide reliable information in areas such as medical procedures. Alice's employee badge might have limited attraction for bad actors, unless she works in a nuclear facility. Bob's patient tag will have to be extremely reliable if medical staff uses to gather information about allergies and medical emergency conditions, for example. The issues in terms of data protection will arise when individuals contest the accuracy of the information on the chip, or their registration on a reader that they claim not to have experienced.

---

30. PIPEDA

Safeguards

> Personal information shall be protected by security safeguards appropriate to the sensitivity of the information.[31]

The Directive provides detail about the security of processing in Article 17, including a requirement to ensure that processing by another party is bound by contract and that the processor acts only on instructions from the controller. Both instruments refer to "having regard to the state of the art", and the Directive goes further to state that the requirements for third-party processors must be in writing.

In our scenarios, the importance of determining who is accountable is relevant. If an organization retains responsibility for the chip in an item (or a person), it is obliged to put in writing the safeguards required for processing under either the Directive or the Canadian law. There may be further requirements to anonymize data under either the Health Insurance Portability and Accountability Act of 1996 (HIPAA) or the German legislation, in cases of medical data. The limits in the potential for such anonymization in situations of persistent pseudonymity are very real, arguing for the use of technologies other than RFID that are capable of hiding identity yet providing secure assurance of statements, such as contactless smart cards containing digital credentials[32] or digitally signed assertions.

Even without requirements for anonymization, there is a requirement to encrypt data and protect it from casual interception. The only way for an organization to escape such obligations is to transfer custody of the RFID data to the individual, a bargain consumers would be unwise to accept.

Openness

> An organization shall make readily available to individuals specific information about its policies and practices relating to the management of personal information.[33]

The Canadian law goes on to provide specific information that must be made available, such as the coordinates of the accountable officer; ways to get access

---

31. PIPEDA
32. Pioneered by Dr. David Chaum over 20 years ago, use of blind signatures is an innovation in public key cryptographic technology that promises to provide anonymity for individuals. See "Security without Identification Card Computers to make Big Brother Obsolete." www.chaum.com/articles/Security_Without_Identification.htm.
33. PIPEDA

to information; a description of data held and an account of use; information that explains policies, standards or codes; and the personal information that is made available to related organizations or subsidiaries. Similar provisions exist in the Directive, in sections IV, *Information to Be Given to the Data Subject* and IX *Notification*. Data subject rights are nearly identical to the Canadian standard, but the requirements in *Notification* go further and detail requirements to notify the supervisory authority of certain types of processing.

Article 18 states that the controller must notify an individual before carrying out "any wholly or partly automatic processing operation or set of such operations intended to serve a single purpose or several related purposes." Certain exemptions apply, but if a Data Commissioner were to insist on prior notification of RFID systems, it seems logical it could be done. It will be important to see how the Article 29 Working Group decides on this issue.

Article 19 clarifies the information that must be provided, including on proposed transfers to third countries. Article 20 stipulates that certain operations are subject to prior checking with the data protection authorities and that member states will decide which operations present specific risks and therefore require prior checking. In North America and certain Asia-Pacific countries, this act of prior checking is usually encompassed in the process of Privacy Impact Assessment (PIA). This is becoming an integral part of business process in many jurisdictions and is now increasingly mandatory. Governments are requiring PIA reports and risk analyses before granting IT funding.[34]

Individual Access

> Upon request, an individual shall be informed of the existence, use, and disclosure of his or her personal information and shall be given access to that information. An individual shall be able to challenge the accuracy and completeness of the information and have it amended as appropriate.[35]

Article 12 of the Directive provides equivalent rights, including the right to have "knowledge of the logic involved in any automatic processing of data concerning him at least in the case of the automated decisions referred to in

---

34. Further information including policy, e-learning tools, and detailed templates can be found online at www.tbs-sct.gc.ca/pubs_pol/ciopubs/pia-pefr/paip-pefr_e.asp A good model of how regulatory compliance can be rolled out is at the U.S. Census Bureau Web site, at www.census .gov/po/pia/; in this case, it is the response to the E-Government Act of 2002. Such a process could be applied to RFID deployment and expedite the required notification under data protection laws.
35. PIPEDA

Article 15." Another important right is the right not just to change incorrect data but to communicate changes to third parties who may have received incomplete or inaccurate data; this right appears in most data protection law and is a significant problem in implementation where there are distributed data systems and accountability may be in question, as is the case with RFID deployments.

It is safe to say that individual access is one of the topics in data protection policy and law that has been studied the least. The volume of requests varies enormously from jurisdiction to jurisdiction. Companies do not tend to publish the statistics of use, and they may blend formal access requests with customer service statistics. Data commissioners usually conduct inquiries in confidence, so while there may be global statistics on information requests, we do not have good country-by-country statistics on who is asking for their information, what they are getting, and what the cost of compliance is.

We do know that campaigns to access personal data have been launched in response to specific media events and privacy stories in the press, and if this happened with RFID deployment, it would be difficult to gather the data in some cases. Returning to the scenarios, if Alice wanted to ask for all the data associated with her employee card, she could do the following:

- Request a printout, explained in plain English, of what is on her card
- Request all records of her ingress and egress at building and site facilities, including parking if it were on the same card, and cafeteria access and billing
- Request all records of the sharing of her data with third parties
- Request procedural and technical documentation that would allow her to understand which readers in the wider population might be capable of reading all or parts of her card and send requests to those parties

Bob or his caregiver with power of attorney could do the same with the implanted chip, and this would be a likely scenario if any medical foul-ups caused harm to Bob. If Dora suspected that her jacket was being used to associate her with certain locations, stores, or product choices, she could first obtain a readout of the tag from the store that sold her the coat and then request all records relating to that identifier and/or her name and credit card information held by any parties she suspects might have records about her.

We have said very little about Ed and the razor blades thus far, but consumer complaints about how the system works in high-volume scenarios such as grocery checkout must be considered as a basic cost. It will not be enough to provide readers in the store or shopping baskets that show the price of goods. Consumers will want to see the records of their purchases, know with whom the information is shared and how long it is kept, and examine their store profile. Because the volume of consumer requests is erratic and highly dependent on trends such as media reports and scandals, this cost is hard to predict.

Challenging Compliance

> An individual shall be able to address a challenge concerning compliance with the above principles to the designated individual or individuals accountable for the organization's compliance.[36]

All data protection laws that mandate independent supervisory authorities provide a variant of this right. The Canadian PIPEDA is broader than most in that anyone can complain, regardless of whether their information is the subject of the complaint, so consumer groups and technical experts could file complaints under Canadian law and even take a case for damages to the Federal Court. In Europe, the actual provisions of each law differ slightly, so it is likely that a pan-European campaign of complaints organized by consumer groups would have slightly different results in each jurisdiction. Data protection authorities in Europe have the power to stop a practice and block data flows, although this power has been little used. Given that the Directive will soon be up for review again, it is likely that there will be some consumer investigation of whether the Data Protection Authorities are fulfilling their mandates.

Many organizations in the United States are working on RFID issues, but it is important to note that they are networking with global consumer organizations. The National Consumer Council of the United Kingdom, for instance, has held a colloquium on RFID (see Calling in the Chips at www.ncc .org.uk/technology/index.htm) and will be publishing a book entitled *The Glass Consumer* in early 2005. Because the council is working with Consumers International, a global network of grassroots consumer organizations, this project will have impact on consumer awareness of the issues.

Conclusions

It is impossible to predict future actions of the stakeholders in the data protection community—namely the data protection authorities, the individuals who exercise their rights, and governments that respond to issues with regulations and standards development activities. The preceding analysis gives some indication of potential arguments and interpretations that could be

---

36. PIPEDA

made. Perhaps the most useful way of summarizing the potential for develop-ments is to return to the scenarios once again and sketch out some high-risk complaints that could precipitate action.

If Alice is a member of a union, it is very likely that there will be action to find out how employee cards are being used to track and monitor employees. Large companies very often negotiate privileges for their employees, from health benefits packages to discounts on goods and services and transportation. It will be tempting to use the same card to authorize such activities, potentially yield-ing a rich stream of linked personal information.

Bob and the patient chip will be the topic of malpractice suits, religious human rights arguments, and in jurisdictions where there is funded healthcare, debates about national identity or health cards. Since most jurisdictions recognize that the health sector is significantly behind in the use of IT to cut costs and stream-line services, this is a longer-range threat, but one that is bound to command public attention.

Pet tagging devices are already deployed, and many humane societies are call-ing for mandatory tagging to facilitate locating owners of lost pets. The mad cow disease problem has prompted mandatory tagging in farm animals. Study of this phenomenon, little discussed in mainstream media, should give us clues as to how the patient chip could be used.

Clothing tagging was one of CASPIAN's first targets, and it resonates with the public. A stalking scenario involving a child would put this on the public radar; imagine that a 14-year-old athlete is tracked entering and leaving a pool and a stalker abuses access to the data stream and follows her. Of course, the same thing could happen with a video surveillance feed and facial recognition systems, but RFID, being less visible and harder to conceptualize, may frighten the population more. This will be the case if bad actors start to travel about with portable readers.

Item-level tagging is clearly the major target of consumer activists at the moment, from the standpoint of accuracy, usability, profiling, discrimination, and invasion of privacy.

The reusable container is a sleeper in the debate thus far, partly because it appears unions have not woken up to the issue and deployments have not focused on persistent goods such as tool inventories. True M2M communica-tions is a threat to workers from the perspective of job quality, surveillance, and dignity. It is likely to surface in response to the significant job cuts that most manufacturers and retailers hope to achieve through RFID deployment.

Stay tuned. This privacy debate has only just begun.

Chapter 5

RFID, Privacy, and Regulation

Jonathan Weinberg[1]

Introduction

Wal-Mart and other major retailers are demanding that their top suppliers have pilot RFID implementations in place before this book sees print. The Food and Drug Administration (FDA) has called for RFID tags on every package of prescription drugs. The State Department is implementing plans to incorporate RFID in United States passports. RFID is so hot, indeed, that some really silly proposals are in the air. One company has announced a "secure, subdermal RFID payment technology for cash and credit transactions." Consumers would have the chip implanted in the triceps area and make payments by passing a scanner over their arms.[2] The Transportation Security Agency (TSA) has talked about RFID-tagged airline boarding passes that, its officials figure, would allow security personnel to track all passengers' whereabouts, in real time, throughout every airport. In this chapter, I look at RFID's likely trajectory and diffusion, analyze the privacy threats it poses, and discuss some possible answers.

---

1. Jonathan Weinberg is a professor of law at Wayne State University. He thanks Jessica Litman and Lee Tien for their contributions to this chapter.
2. The company says that implanted devices are more "secure, tamper-proof, and loss-proof" than ordinary credit cards. Press Release, Applied Digital Solutions' CEO Announces "Veripay™" Secure, Subdermal Solution for Payment and Credit Transactions at ID World 2003 in Paris (November 21, 2003). www.adsx.com/news/2003/112103.html.

Some Current and Proposed RFID Applications

Firms and governments are planning a wide range of RFID implementations. A number of large retailers are pushing hard to implement RFID tagging in their supply chains on the case and pallet level. They believe that the ability to track cases and pallets wirelessly and automatically will give them a better picture of where manufactured items are in the supply chain and how long it takes them to get there, enabling a retailer to be more efficient in moving goods through the distribution process and making sure they're where they need to be. Retail industry analysts urge that between six and ten percent of spending on the supply chain is lost because of a lack of visibility or poor visibility in the supply chain. They believe that RFID can solve that problem.

Wal-Mart thus told its top 100 suppliers that, as of January 2005, they must include working RFID tags on each of the pallets and cases they ship to three Wal-Mart distribution centers. The company plans to expand the program to a dozen distribution centers and up to 600 stores by January 2006. In Great Britain, supermarket chain TESCO has announced ambitious plans for case- and pallet-level RFID in its supply chain. European retailing giant Metro plans an RFID rollout that by December 2005 will include 100 suppliers, 269 stores, and 8 distribution centers. In the United States, Target and Albertson's have announced their own tagging plans, and other large retailers are set to follow. The United States Department of Defense (DoD) sought to require all suppliers by January 2005 to place RFID tags on cases and pallets, if not on individual parts. Wal-Mart's push and the continuing buzz over RFID in the marketplace are causing a substantial number of corporate IT departments to begin or consider RFID pilots, even without any obvious way to get a return on their investment; they fear they'll be left behind if they don't.

The buzz over RFID isn't limited to the case and pallet level. A variety of companies have engaged in *item-level* testing of tags on a broad range of consumer goods. That is, their trials involve placing tags on individual consumer items. Benetton made plans earlier to put RFID in individual items of clothing but pulled back after a publicity firestorm; consumers expressed alarm about the prospect of walking around with their shirts speaking silently and wirelessly to networked computing devices in their paths. Other companies, however, seem undeterred. British retailer Marks & Spencer has conducted two trials of item-level RFID tags in menswear and appears committed to item-level RFID as a stock control system. A major U.S. clothing manufacturer may be planning to incorporate item-level RFID tags into its clothing in 2005.[3]

---

3. See CASPIAN, Mystery Clothing Company Plans Item-Level RFID Rollout (Sept. 23, 2004), www.spychips.com/press-releases/checkpoint.html.

Michelin has begun fleet testing for RFID for passenger and light truck tires. Each tire's unique identification number will be associated in an external database with the vehicle identification number (VIN) of the car on which it's mounted and information describing when and where the tire was made, its maximum inflation pressure, its size, and similar characteristics.[4]

New and innovative uses of RFID abound:

- Casinos are putting RFID tags in chips to block counterfeiting, identify stolen chips, and track gamblers' play.
- An Italian manufacturer has introduced a washing machine equipped to read RFID washing instruction tags in clothing.
- More than 50 million pets already have implanted RFID tags.
- Students in an Osaka, Japan, elementary school will be getting RFID chips in their schoolbags, name tags, or clothing to be read by readers installed in school entrances and exits.
- A plan to keep tabs on the elderly envisions placing RFID tags on objects in the subjects' homes and networked readers on their persons to keep track of their handling of the tagged items.

RFID tags can be implanted into people subcutaneously. The FDA has approved the implantation into human subjects of RFID tags referencing the subjects' medical records. A Spanish nightclub has gone ahead and injected RFID tags into some of its customers, who thereby got free access to the club's VIP area. Subcutaneous chipping seems to have caught on in Mexico: The country's attorney general announced this summer that he and members of his staff had been equipped with chips implanted in their arms to authenticate their access to secure office areas and to enable them to be found "anywhere inside Mexico" in the event of assault or kidnapping. (How a chip with a read range of a few inches would allow the wearer to be found anywhere in the country was left unexplained.)[5] The manufacturer's Mexican distributor had earlier announced plans to implant RFID tags in children as an antikidnapping device; searchers would place readers in "strategic locations where a search is being conducted," as well as malls, bus stations, and similar locations.

The United States General Services Administration (GSA) is said to have mandated use of RFID to help it manage information on the buildings, fleets of cars, and other products it oversees. The FDA is moving ahead with plans eventually to tag every package of prescription drugs sold in the United States

---

4. Also on the automobile front, a variety of manufacturers incorporated RFID into automobile ignition keys so that a key can identify itself to the car's antitheft system.
5. Moreover, it's safe to assume that a bureaucrat with a chip implanted in his arm would, if kidnapped, quickly find himself with only one arm.

with a unique serial number on an RFID tag to ensure that the drug is legitimate and being sold through authorized channels.

Both the European and Japanese central banks have reportedly discussed incorporating RFID tags in currency. The United States government is said to have expressed interest as well. The nominal goal here is to make counterfeiting more difficult as well as perhaps keep track of money laundering and black-market transactions.

Governments have begun to embed RFID in identification documents. A committee of the International Civil Aviation Organization has approved a recommendation that all passports and other travel documents store electronic data on "contact-less integrated circuit" chips (which is to say, RFID technology or a close relation). The United States, it appears, is moving quickly to implement that recommendation: The State Department expects newly issued U.S. passports to have RFID embedded by the end of 2005. The United States Department of Homeland Security is currently equipping trusted travelers crossing the Canadian border with RFID-enabled identification cards to be read by readers in special lanes at border crossing stations. The state of Virginia is exploring proposals for RFID-equipped driver's licenses.

Whither Item-Level Tagging?

RFID tagging of pallets and cases of consumer packaged goods seems to have unstoppable momentum. I expect to see RFID tags before long on prescription drug bottles, airline baggage, and cattle. I believe that we will soon see RFID embedded in United States passports. It's by no means clear, though, which other RFID implementations will find success in the marketplace. Most important, the overall business case for RFID tags on individual retail items seems equivocal.

To begin with, it's not clear whether the cost of RFID tags will drop sufficiently. The cost of even the least expensive tag today is more than ten cents by some accounts and forty cents by others. Industry sources have suggested that we're unlikely to see widespread distribution of item-level tags unless the price per tag drops below five cents, and we are unlikely to see tags on really cheap consumer items—say, boxes of cereal and bars of soap—unless the price per tag drops to below a penny.[6] It's hardly clear that those prices are feasible.

---

6. To make a tag for less than a penny, you'd want to print RFID circuits and memory on conventional multistation printing presses, along with the regular product packaging, using layers of conductive and nonconductive inks. That's still a long way away.

Even with sufficiently inexpensive tags, taking advantage of item-level tagging will require retailers to incur the costs of purchasing and installing reader networks, training reader operators, and putting in place back-end data systems to manage the information. Some observers estimate that hardware costs for RFID will amount to only 3 percent of the total, with software to process the huge amounts of data generated by the network making up 75 percent. The hardware and software costs associated with large-scale implementation of systems such as "smart shelves," which feature large numbers of readers and terabytes of data per day, may be prohibitive.

It's important to remember that item-level RFID is desirable for inventory control only to the extent it can generate useful information more quickly and cheaply than can currently available technologies, such as bar-code scanning. Current adopters, though, are wrestling with the fact that RFID tags are subject to considerable interference from items in the retail environment, such as fluids and metal, not to mention nylon conveyor belts and dense materials like frozen meat and chicken parts. Even in environments that can be optimized for RFID, such as distribution centers receiving arriving pallets, readers today are sometimes unable to read more than 80 percent of the tags. In the words of one industry analyst: "Every site's a little different. You can't just throw up antennae; there's a tuning aspect. This is dirty fingernail stuff."[7]

It will be even more difficult to get satisfactory read rates for RFID tags on the retail store floor, which can't be optimized for RFID readers the way a distribution center can.[8] Finally, if manufacturers use the same ultrahigh frequency (UHF) band for item-level tagging that they are now using for pallets and cases, tags will have to be relatively large, often too large to place conveniently on small consumer items.

All this suggests that while RFID for cases and pallets is here to stay, there are major obstacles in the way of the industry's dream of putting an RFID tag on everything that moves in the North American supply chain. It's unlikely that we'll see much item-level tagging within the next ten years. One analyst has suggested that it'll be 2017 before we see item-level tagging on products costing less than $10.

---

7. See Margulius, D. The Rush to RFID, *InfoWorld*. April 9, 2004. www.infoworld.com /pdf/special_report/2004/15SRrfid.pdf, at 38 (quoting Tig Gilliam, partner, IBM Business Consulting Services).

8. See Stapleton-Gray, R. Scanning the Horizon: A Skeptical View of RFIDs on the Shelves. November 13, 2003. www.stapleton-gray.com/papers/sk-20031113.PDF. Stapleton-Gray also notes disadvantages of RFID for retailers in terms of competitive marketing considerations and vulnerability to corporate espionage and counterfeit tags. At the very least, these concerns may push retailers toward closed systems and away from the relatively open Object Name Space.

It's hard to predict the ultimate penetration of RFID tags into everyday life. Tags may never become widespread on consumer goods. They may become commonplace in connection with some application not discussed in this chapter, such as access badges or credit cards. It may be that all the barriers to item-level tagging of retail goods will be overcome in the next 15 years. I'll assume, for the rest of this chapter, that RFID technology will ultimately become widespread, although not necessarily pervasive, in some facets of everyday life. Therefore, we need to consider how we should think about that from a privacy standpoint.

Understanding RFID's Privacy Threats

Privacy activists have raised alarms over RFID technology. RFID-enabled goods or documents, they point out, will disclose information about themselves, and hence about the people carrying them, wirelessly to people whom the subjects might not have chosen to inform. If an ordinary citizen is carrying items or documents equipped with RFID tags, then complete strangers can read information from those tags without any current or prior relationship with the person carrying them, indeed without having known anything about that person at all before cranking up the tag reader. The subject need not be aware that the information is being collected.

Moreover, RFID's surveillance capability follows the subject and reveals to data collectors how it moves through space. Unlike most other privacy-invasive technologies, it allows observers to learn *where* the subject is physically.[9] Indeed, not only does the profile that RFID technology helps construct contain information about where the subject is and has been, but RFID signifiers travel with the subject in the physical world, conveying information to devices that otherwise wouldn't recognize her, and that can take actions based on that information.

While RFID tags on tires seem like an effective way of ensuring that the necessary safety information stays tied to the tire, the possibilities for surveillance once a tire rolling down a highway starts broadcasting its unique ID number are plain. The privacy ramifications of tags in currency are similarly apparent. (Some reports indicate that tags for currency would have a read range of only a few millimeters so that information seekers couldn't identify currency from a distance, but details are hard to come by; the tag generally discussed in this

---

9. In some critics' eyes, as a result, RFID raises the specter of Big Brother tracking consumers much as biologists use GPS-enabled radio collars to track grizzly bears. See Fialka, J. "In a Montana Valley, Grizzlies Are Closer Than People Think," *Wall Street Journal* (Aug. 4, 2004), p. 1.

connection is Hitachi's mu-chip, which is said to have a read range of about a foot.) Even less obviously problematic uses may jeopardize consumer privacy and threaten civil liberties.

How much should we worry about RFID privacy threats? A skeptic might say that RFID privacy problems are inconsequential because passive tags have a short read range. Yet this doesn't seem reassuring. Inexpensive passive tag systems using the frequency bands now contemplated appear to have a theoretical maximum distance of up to 20 meters. That leaves room for substantial surveillance capabilities. Moreover, readers can effectively invade privacy even with even much shorter read ranges. One can embed an RFID reader, invisibly, in floor tiles, carpeting, or a doorway. A read range of only a few feet is entirely adequate to track people coming through a door.

Our skeptic might next note that the data on a tag is just a string of ones and zeros; how much will it reveal to the casual listener? One can surely write implementations in which a tag's data points to an entry in a proprietary, limited-access database; in such a case, listeners can learn the tag's meaning only if they can buy, barter, or otherwise gain entry to the database. When it comes to ordinary item-level tags on ordinary retail goods, it seems increasingly likely that manufacturers will restrict access to portions of the Object Name Service (ONS) under their own control or avoid the ONS entirely so that RFID scanning will not reveal sensitive competitive informationIt's plausible, thus, that even the ONS database will reveal only the manufacturer of a good to the casual requester and will restrict access to the rest of the information the Electronic Product Code (EPC) references.

On the other hand, access to ONS information is unlikely to stay so limited. The meaning of EPC "object class" codes, identifying the type and model of goods supplied by large manufacturers, will likely leak into the public domain. Further, different manufacturers' policies on information access will vary; as manufacturers embrace the modern reality that they can monetize consumer information by selling it to third parties, it's questionable whether the information associated with tag data will remain closely held.

Perhaps more important, if the retailer that sells you a pair of shoes records that you are the purchaser of shoes with a particular tag number and then sells that information to a third party, the buyer can associate that unique tag with you without needing access to the tag database. Finally, even without such access, the unchanging data on the tag can serve as a persistent unique identifier of the person carrying it. Without knowing anything about the meaning of data on particular tags, a person with a reader can aggregate data about a particular subject over time, if only on the level of "this is the same guy who was here making trouble last week."

One might argue that RFID's privacy threat is lessened because much of the information that readers will collect (such as shoe style, though not the shoe's serial number) will likely be visible to the naked eye in any event. Yet RFID is important from a privacy standpoint even where it only facilitates the collection of information that could otherwise be collected by analog means, automating the information collection and storage process. Imagine, after all, the movement of automobiles down a highway. There's nothing stopping a government from posting an employee to copy down license plate numbers or a camera to photograph them. That information, though, comes into being in analog format; it would be time consuming and expensive to enter it into a digital database. Even automated license plate readers have accuracy problems in some environments. As a result, the information won't in fact be entered digitally except on particular occasions when it's important and cost-effective to do so. By contrast, if a reader were positioned in the highway collecting data from RFID tags in automobile tires (with the tag data linked to automobile VINs in a separate database), the collection of the data and its inclusion in a searchable digital database would be fully automated, cheap, and easy. RFID readers, in short, automate information collection and collect the information in a format that makes its inclusion in networked databases simple. That's important, because the less it costs to collect, store, and analyze information, the more information will in fact be collected, stored, and analyzed.

Our skeptic may argue that RFID will not facilitate geographic tracking because there will not be geographically pervasive reader networks in place. If RFID use becomes widespread, though, commercial and governmental users are likely to deploy a wide range of discrete reader networks. The individual networks need not be pervasive: If there are economic and political incentives for the proprietors of those various networks to share information (and there are likely to be), the result will be the functional equivalent of a single very large network.

One final characteristic of RFID will to some extent ameliorate the privacy threat: While strangers can collect RFID data from tags on goods or documents in my possession, that data isn't *necessarily* linked to my name or other personally identifying information. In some situations, giving rise to information privacy concerns, sensitive information is born already attached to the data subject's name or other personally identifying information. Think of credit-card purchase information. RFID tag information, by contrast, while attached to the geographic location or the physical person of the target, is not necessarily attached to anyone's name or personally identifying information. The data collector may know what type of sweater I wear but still may not know my name.

That means that, in order to understand RFID privacy threats, we need to distinguish situations in which some data collector has drawn a link between my name (and other personally identifying information) and the data on an RFID tag I carry, from situations in which there is no such link. If I go into a store and buy a tagged sweater, the store can link the sweater EPC with my name and other information in its database. Assuming that the tag isn't disabled at point of sale or after, then every time I walk into the store wearing that sweater, store personnel will be able to know who I am without having to ask. If the store sells or trades the data linking my tag information with my personally identifiable information, then wherever I go, *anyone* in possession of that data can read my tag and accordingly know my name and my profile without having to ask.

In that situation, I face three (overlapping) privacy threats.

The first is profiling. A reader network can cheaply and seamlessly collect RFID information from my belongings and documents and easily add it to my profile. When an entity reads information from my tags, it will be able to add to the profile associated with my name any new characteristics associated with that RFID information (as well as the unique tag numbers themselves). This may facilitate more robust and pervasive profiling, incorporating new data signaled by tags on consumers' portable possessions, clothing, vehicles, money, and identification documents.

The second is surveillance. RFID technology locates its targets in space; if the devices attached to the reader network know who the persons carrying the tags are, an RFID reader network becomes a Panopticon geolocator. If we imagine a world in which most people carry tags easily linked to their names (an RFID-equipped driver's license would more than satisfy this criterion), a listener seeking to compile a database with the identities of nearly all of the people attending a political rally, say, would merely have to station readers at the entrance. The rest of the data collection and analysis would be automatic.

The third is action. After reading RFID tag information when I enter a geographic space and associating that information with my profile and thus my name, people or devices associated with the reader network can take actions—ranging from arresting me, on the one hand, to showing me targeted ads on the other—based on their knowledge of who I am and what I'm like.

The profiling and surveillance threats largely disappear if the listener can't make a connection between my RFID data and my name or other personally identifying information. The action threat remains, however. Even without knowing my name, the listener can associate information with my physical being in a particular location and take action based on that association, such as displaying particular advertisements, steering me to particular goods the seller thinks may be of interest, offering me differential rates, or imposing obstacles to my admission to a mall. Moreover, tag numbers can still serve as unique and semipersistent identifiers. Any listener with an RFID reader situated near a place I go can collect information over time about me (the individual, located intermittently or long term in a particular geographic space, who is associated with given unique tag numbers). That information collection over time can inform the actions I've just described.

In sum, the most serious privacy threats associated with RFID rely on the fact that the listener knows something about the target *beyond* the information available wirelessly from the tags. The listener is able to connect a tag I carry to my personally identifying information only by virtue of the fact that it has collected information about me on some separate occasion, either directly from me or from some third party who got the information from me (or from some third party who bought the information from some third party who bought the information from some third party who…). How much protection does this provide? Not as much as I'd like. As profiling accelerates in the modern world, aided by the automatic, networked collection of information through technologies like RFID, information compiled by one data collector likely will increasingly be available to others as well. The economic (and homeland security) forces pushing in that direction are powerful. As a result, information linking tag data to my personal identity may well move easily into the hands of actors who are strangers to me in any meaningful sense. This suggests, though, that data privacy restrictions aimed at preventing the collection, or sharing, of information linking tag data to personally identifying information may be an important way to limit the worst threats.

Conclusions

RFID technology, in sum, can present substantial privacy threats. It would be desirable to design RFID systems so that they don't generate these threats. If we fail to protect privacy through good technical design, we may need to address those threats through restraints on information use and sharing.

We have some time to figure this out. While we're seeing an extensive and continuing rollout of RFID technology in the retail supply chain, nearly all of that rollout is directed toward cases and pallets. Tags on cases and pallets don't present any significant privacy threat. The main privacy threat from RFID in the retail supply chain comes when tags are attached to consumer goods, on the item level; those tags leave the store attached to the item, live and serialized; and the tags are not discarded with the item's packaging.[10] Although the evidence is equivocal, widespread deployment of item-level tags is likely at least a decade away. Therefore, we have some breathing room.

It would be a mistake, on the other hand, to take no action until item-level tagging systems are fully deployed and consumers have already taken a substantial privacy hit. As systems are deployed, they create facts on the ground. As the deployment of privacy-invasive technology makes us more accustomed to privacy invasions, those privacy invasions come to seem more natural and reasonable. Further, the longer policymakers wait after such systems are deployed, the more industry players have a vested stake in the technology already on the market and can point to regulation's disruption of reasonable investment-backed expectations. In addressing RFID's privacy impacts, therefore, we need to walk the thin line between acting too quickly—imposing uninformed policies because we don't yet have a good understanding of what the technology and the marketplace will do—and acting too slowly, allowing abuses as the sand disappears from beneath our feet.

It's important to note that the tendency of simple RFID tags to communicate their data indiscriminately is not an inherent characteristic of the technology. One could design RFID tags so that tag information remained inaccessible unless the reader established through a cryptographic handshake that the tags' programmer had authorized it. While reader authentication via public key cryptography would be beyond the resources of a low-cost tag, one could design a simple-minded device that would talk only to authorized readers by enabling ordinary password protection and having the tag hold a one-way hash of the password needed to unlock its information. This would at least lessen the number of people able to read data off RFID tags, and it could block the use of tags as persistent identifiers. It would not provide robust protection; the most-often queried passwords would soon leak out. But it would be a step in the right direction.

There are other plausible technical approaches that would ameliorate the privacy threats of simple-minded RFID. A more sophisticated RFID architecture would allow tags to emit not a single, unchanging, unique ID, but a series of random pseudonyms, which could be understood only by authorized verifiers. Alternatively, devices could "deserialize" RFID tags, stripping out the unique identifiers to leave only more generic descriptions.

So far at least, though, there's been no movement by device manufacturers or standards bodies to incorporate these approaches into ordinary RFID tags.

---

10. It's true that if manufacturers deploy item-level tags that do not leave the store, consumers might still be subject to surveillance as they interact with the tags inside the store. But I see that threat as relatively minor. The technology in this context would not identify customers, facilitate profiling, or enable any meaningful action threat unless the store were able to identify customers in some entirely separate manner, such as by taking pictures using in-store cameras. Stores have in fact used RFID in conjunction with cameras in tests, but I doubt that RFID is the most important threat in that context.

That shouldn't be too surprising. The business case for RFID in the retail sup-ply chain (and indeed in most government applications) depends on keeping the tags inexpensive, yet firms can make RFID tags cheap only by making them dumb. For a tag to implement access controls, it needs to add logic gates, and that increases its size and cost. A manufacturer can't make a passive tag smart enough to handle, say, public-key encryption without completely blowing the business case for the foreseeable future.

As a result, expensive special-purpose RFID tags incorporate access controls where a particular implementation calls for it and can justify the expense. On the other hand, run-of-the-mine inexpensive passive tags—including those currently intended for use in the retail supply chain—disclose their data promiscuously to anybody with a reader. Absent government mandate, that's not likely to change.

What other means of protecting privacy can we find? EPCglobal (the trade body that stepped into the shoes of the Auto-ID Center as the standards body for RFID in the retail sales chain) has endorsed the "kill" command. Under EPCglobal's first-generation specifications, an inexpensive passive tag would be designed to respond to a password-protected command directing the tag's inte-grated circuit to disable itself. Retailers could choose to give consumers the option to have RFID tags on their purchases disabled before they left the store.

The option of killing retail tags at point of sale recognizes the different tradeoffs the technology presents at different points in the retail cycle. While goods are moving through the retail sales chain, RFID tagging can offer important inventory-control benefits, with essentially no cost in terms of con-sumer privacy. Once the good is sold to the consumer, by contrast, there is no further need for inventory control, so the tag can be disabled. EPCglobal's approach would allow consumers to maintain the functioning tag if they saw benefit in that course.

EPCglobal's approach, however, has at least one important flaw: It seems unlikely to keep most live tags off the streets. Not all manufacturers are enthu-siastic about enabling the kill capability.[11] Retailers are unlikely to want to incur the additional expense. Small retailers in particular, who may find it cheaper to continue counting inventory by hand than to invest in smart shelves or a reader network, will be reluctant to buy expensive equipment to disable the RFID tags they'll be receiving, uninvited, on their consumer packaged goods. Even if the

---

11. It's not clear to what extent major manufacturers of retail goods (who will be the firms actu-ally purchasing and affixing tags in the retail sales chain) are interested in this kill functional-ity. Some are willing to enable killable tags as an option for consumers; others are not. Those others are unwilling to give up the potential functionality of tags that continue to operate past the point of sale (facilitating returns, and the like) and believe that privacy advocates represent a minority who in the end will be unable to stop the technology's rollout.

law should require that consumers be offered a kill option, consumers may not exercise that option if disabling the tag requires more time at checkout or other inconvenience for the consumer. Consumers tend to underestimate the incremental impact on their privacy of allowing just one more set of small disclosures. And once a large number of consumer goods with unsophisticated EPC tags make it onto the streets, those tags, at least as currently imagined, will incorporate no useful privacy protections.

Are there legal restraints on information use and sharing that would protect against the most egregious threats posed by RFID in the retail sales chain? In other privacy contexts, it's common to draw the content of legal restraints on information use and sharing from Fair Information Practice principles. The Federal Trade Commission's 1998 *Privacy Online: A Report to Congress* identifies five such core principles, paraphrased here:

- Consumers should get notice of an entity's privacy policies before that entity collects any personal information from them.
- Consumers should be able to choose whether to convey the information and how it can be used or transferred.
- Consumers should be able to see the information collected about them and to contest its accuracy or completeness.
- The collector must take reasonable care that the information it maintains is accurate and secure.
- There must be some mechanism, other than the data collector's good intentions, to bring about compliance.

Principles like these, though only sporadically reflected in U.S. law, play an important role in U.S. as well as European information privacy thinking.

At least at the outset, fair information practices seem remarkably ill suited to data collection systems like simple RFID. Fair information practices work best in systems with clearly identified data collectors who have the information in the first place because the consumer has voluntarily given it to them in order to facilitate some transaction the consumer wants, and who are subject to meaningful restraints on information reuse and sharing. The architecture of unsophisticated RFID systems, though, allows anyone to be a data collector. Data collectors may be entirely unrelated to the tag's manufacturer or its intended users. Reading is undetectable, and nothing will cause consumers to know that a reader is collecting data about them. In this context, government authorities are not well positioned to regulate.

This very incongruity, though, suggests two useful approaches to RFID regulation. The first is to focus on the personal identifying information that must be linked to tag data to generate the worst privacy threats. That information is

likely to have been collected in a context amenable to regulation, and fair information practice principles could be used to address that linkage. A regulator, or
a set of industry best practices, might forbid data collectors to link tag IDs to
personally identifying information except in limited circumstances. It might
require the data collector, before linking tag IDs to personally identifying
information, to disclose the fact and purpose of the linkage to the individual
and to obtain his or her written consent. It might forbid the data collector to
disclose that linkage to third parties.[12]

A second approach would impose restrictions on tag data collection to minimize the respects in which RFID makes fair information practice principles
problematic. A regulator, for example, could prohibit the use of tag readers
except where individuals have been warned that they are present. That warning
might come, say, from a tone or light that readers are required to emit when
they draw information from RFID tags.[13]

Neither of these suggestions addresses all of the dangers presented when citizens and consumers are walking around with live, unsophisticated, serialized
tags. With respect to commercial RFID, there are simpler and more effective
alternatives.

Most important, a regulator or a set of industry best practices could require
that RFID tags attached to individual items in the retail sales chain be clearly
labeled and easily removable.[14] That would not pose an insuperable barrier for
industry; EPCglobal's current best-practice guidelines for RFID tags on consumer products "anticipate that for most products," tags will be "part of disposable packaging or . . . otherwise discardable."[15]

This approach, it is true, would force consumers to choose between privacy
protection and post-sale tag functionality. If consumers discard tags, they might
not get the benefit of a retailer's use of RFID to facilitate returns.[16] Similarly, if
consumers discard tags, recycling centers won't be able to rely on EPCs to cat-
egorize recycled items. Consumer items such as stoves and washing machines

---

12. All of these suggestions can be found in the Electronic Privacy Information Center's (EPICs)
    proposed guidelines for commercial use of RFID. See Comments of the Electronic Privacy
    Information Center to the Federal Trade Commission (July 9, 2004), in connection with the
    FTC Workshop on Radio Frequency Identification Applications and Implications for Con-
    sumers, www.epic.org/privacy/rfid/ftc-comts-070904.pdf, pp. 17–18.
13. See EPIC's guidelines, p. 15.
14. See EPIC's guidelines, p. 14. This rule might not apply if a tag were sophisticated enough to
    implement privacy protection or if it carried only a generic (not globally unique) identifier.
15. EPCGlobal, Guidelines on EPC for Consumer Products. www.epcglobalinc.org/public_policy
    /public_policy_guidelines.html (last modified Sept. 13, 2004).
16. For what it's worth, I imagine that retailers would likely take returns from consumers who
    remove but retain their tags, just as they take returns from consumers who present analogous
    documentation today.

won't be able to read tag information to get cooking or washing instructions.[17] But it's still, I think, the best approach on balance. Consumers would be able to retain tags when they choose to. Manufacturers would remain free, if they choose, to incorporate information more permanently into consumer goods via a nonwireless bar code or a generic tag not carrying a globally unique identifier. I suspect that the valuable post-sale uses of unsophisticated EPC tags will be few, in part because manufacturers' reluctance to expose tag data to the world via the ONS will make it harder for third parties to offer post-sale functionality. By contrast, the privacy-invasive uses of EPCs once goods are sold will be many—that's the direction in which economic incentives push. Allowing consumers easily to opt out, simply by tearing off RFID tags and dropping them in the trash, makes sense.

---

17. Ari Juels and his co-authors believe that the ONS architecture should facilitate the use of "blocker tags," consumer-controlled devices that could be programmed to prevent the detection of particular categories of tags in a consumer's possession. Juels, A., et al., The Blocker Tag: Selective Blocking of RFID Tags for Consumer Privacy, p. 3, available at http://theory .lcs.mit.edu/~rivest/JuelsRivestSzydlo-TheBlockerTag.pdf. All else being equal, it would plainly be better for consumers to have access to blocker tags than not. To the extent that the tags' availability would tend to relieve any pressure to find other RFID privacy solutions, though, the emphatically opt-in nature of an approach requiring that consumers maintain their own privacy protection devices is disturbing. If consumer inertia would be a problem in connection with a right to disable tags at point of sale, it would surely be a problem here.

Chapter 6

RFID AND THE UNITED STATES REGULATORY LANDSCAPE

Doug Campbell[1]

Introduction

This chapter contains thoughts on the public policy and regulatory implications of RFID technology.[2] The policy issues raised by RFID have received progressively broader discussion as increasing technical and network capabilities, and falling tag and reader prices create the conditions for its widespread adoption in commerce over the coming years. A familiar principle is at work: When a technology is still in early development, a small community of policy specialists may take note and raise concerns. But when it nears or enters broad-scale implementation, people start demanding answers. The more threatening the risks seem, the further in advance of actual deployment they tend to be debated. The time for that debate is upon us.[3]

---

1. Doug Campbell is a public policy consultant in Washington, D.C.
2. Note that "regulation" as used in the title of this chapter includes any policy-generated limitation on the use or development of technology, whether self-imposed (self-regulation) or compelled by legislation or formal administrative regulation. Within the chapter, the term carries the narrower meaning of formal administrative regulation, unless context indicates otherwise.
3. Readers not accustomed to thinking about the social implications of what seem to be business-focused scientific or technical decisions may wonder why we need to spend time on these questions. After all, in a free market, businesses are motivated to shape their products or services to serve the public by being efficient, well priced, reliable, innovative, and so forth. Can't we assume that their enlightened self-interest will result in choices that optimize the product's or service's benefits? The answer, of course, is no, since a favorable outcome depends on how "enlightened" the decision maker's self-interest is and who receives the benefits. This chapter explores these issues in the RFID context. Much of the discussion is directed to those in the business and technology communities who have little policy background but are willing to give these ideas thoughtful analysis.

To state the obvious, this book was published because advancements in RFID technology are giving new capabilities to business, individuals, and government, and some uses and implications of those technologies threaten strongly held values of others in society.

A statement that is often heard on all sides of the debate is that the success of mass-market RFID deployment, in particular, depends on public acceptance. Regardless of how successful the technical standards development turns out to be, both the adoption and functionality of RFID technology will be diminished if we do not bring together the primary interests of key public stakeholders in a usable set of policy norms that respond to consumer fears.[4] Given that this process will take time, I am convinced that it's in no one's interest to delay it.

As noted in other chapters, those norms may be self-developed and imposed (through "self-regulation") or governmentally mandated through legislation, bureaucratic regulation, or international convention. Because the process of governmental action generally takes time, self-regulatory initiatives usually are the first organized response society sees to technological policy issues, at least if business is wise. We are already seeing this in the RFID space, and many of my comments relate to the factors that influence business as it tries to grapple with questions few business leaders or technologists are trained to address. I briefly discuss the role of governmental agencies, including law enforcement, especially in the United States. I give some attention to the usual interplay between business and consumer advocates to be expected, and then make a case for EPCglobal as the most logical nongovernmental forum for the development of RFID rules of the road. I conclude with observations and a recommendation, directed not at specific policy or technical design rules but at the policy development process and the mindset that business should bring to the task.

It's important to note at the outset that there are many different applications of RFID. Broadly, they can be divided into two categories: supply chain applications and applications outside the supply chain. As noted in other chapters, RFID technology in the supply chain offers potentially huge benefits to businesses and

---

4. Not everyone agrees with the need for policy engagement now, if ever. I address some of the naysayers' points in the section on the business/consumer dialogue. Note also that the need for norms, or rules, was just confirmed from a surprising source. In recent *RFID Journal* coverage of a study by Bearing Point, 55 percent of surveyed government IT managers at federal, state, and local levels indicated "the absence of guidance from government and industry around security and privacy policies and standards was leading them to defer further RFID development." (www.rfidjournal.com/article/articleview/1267/1/1/) Neither legislation nor formal regulation is inevitable, but unless key business interests unite around technology design features and enforceable usage commitments that respond to public concerns about privacy and other issues, legislation and bureaucratic regulation will be imposed. The longer the delay, the harder it will be to optimally nce public concerns and technological and business flexibility.

their customers. For example, manufacturers will be able to track high-value items, reducing shrinkage, and increasing their speed to market; they'll also be able to accelerate and better target their product recalls. It is expected that retailers will monitor inventories in real time, enabling them to keep stocks fresh and cut transportation costs. Consumers will benefit from increased product availability and faster removal of recalled products. There's also potential for increased cost savings as efficiencies gained throughout the supply chain are passed along to the consumer.

As the RFID debate unfolds, it's important to distinguish among applications according to the issues they raise and seek to tailor policies to avoid penalizing applications that by their nature or design pose fewer or no problems in policy terms. For example, non-retail supply-chain applications will rarely implicate privacy issues as applications beyond that environment do. To blindly subject all RFID applications—supply chain and non supply chain—to the same policy rules could have an adverse effect, potentially reducing the positive benefits the technology has to offer with no countervailing benefit on the other side.

Current State of RFID Policy

The RFID policy environment is one of rapidly evolving technology. Technical barriers are falling, even as new uses for smaller and more inexpensive RFID devices are explored. . For our purposes, the new waves of RFID technology will penetrate society through the implementation of different applications, one after another, starting in the business-to-business (B2B) world of commerce (including business-to-government, as in military supply movement). Thereafter it will expand eventually into broad-scale business-to-consumer and government-to-consumer uses. As these application waves spread through society, they will intersect with societal values and occasionally generate tension, if not conflict. These intersections constitute the world of public policy, which in this context is the process by which government, or on occasion private-sector initiative,[5] limits or enables private action "for the good of all" by negotiating competing values. For an emerging technology that like RFID is expected to become ubiquitous, the task is to identify those competing *values* and forecast the technology's potentially broad *impact*, then develop alternative ways of balancing them through policy *options* that influence the design or use of the technology and make the *choices* that best serve "the public good," in its broadest sense.

---

5. Why only "on occasion"? Because the private sector is not reliably good at it, though it often takes a first crack at the challenge. Neither is government, for that matter, but government action is the default mechanism.

Policymakers and advocates have become increasingly aware that where technology and policy concerns intersect, some trade-off between the two is generally implicit: Present fears or concerns can be satisfied by strict limits on the design or use of technology but at the expense of future innovation, which is forestalled by policy restrictions. However, solutions designed to secure the absolute maximum potential of future technological evolutions usually provide little if any real response to public concerns.

The key point for business leaders and technologists to understand is that to the extent most people harbor strong feelings about privacy and other issues, they are willing to sacrifice some degree of technological progress, even some degree of personal action or prosperity, to secure those values. This is admirable, not evidence that consumers are irrational or that their empowerment can be dismissed.

The key point for privacy advocates to understand is that many people do not attach the same significance as they do to values they may be asked to give up, and they may willingly compromise social values in return for a small price break or increased convenience. This doesn't mean that they should be forced to accept a high level of security regardless of the costs.

The important point for everyone is that in a diverse society, compromise will be necessary: The rules need to provide a blend of constraints and flexibility that empower citizens to make their own choices and achieve a comfortable trade-off. By the nature of things, this should usually result in a system that contains mechanisms that those on the technological-progress end of the spectrum consider needlessly burdensome, while those who are motivated primarily by social values issues will feel the resulting protection is inadequate. Policymakers have to balance all of this and cope with the overlay of the costs vs. benefits calculus by which we traditionally analyze various regulatory proposals.

So how are these policy choices best made? By and large, the best outcomes result when all significant stakeholders are included, but often, especially in the United States, a decision of this type arises not so much from a discrete, organized event as from an ad hoc process. The initial bursts of policy development activity tend to be driven more by the announcement or rollout of technology or by some corporate misstep that achieves intense media coverage than by government fiat. Government action, or the threat of it, usually drives the concluding phases of stakeholder negotiation after media exposure focuses policymakers on real or supposed adverse technology effects. Not all stakeholders may be involved in each development, with the result that the time needed for general consensus can expand until events compel a resolution, cutting off further input. This process differs from case to case and from country to country. We are in the early stages of the RFID policy debate in every region of the world.[6]

Who are the stakeholders in the RFID debate? Because of its reach, the technology affects an unusually broad array of institutional and individual interests. They can be grouped as *individuals*, *business*, and *government*, though even within these categories, there may be differences among technology *users* and technology *suppliers*:

Individuals

Individuals are defined as follows:

- "The public" in the sense of consumers or individual users (e.g., purchasers of products at retail, users of smart toll tags, future applications such as interactive medicine cabinets or automated product warranties, or tags for pets); eventually purchasers of virtually any manufactured or processed product
- Representatives of portions of the public, whether formal or self-appointed, such as unions, advocacy groups, or membership organizations

Business

The following are business users:

- Technology users, including those focused on the movement and use of RFID-tagged items or components (supply chain, production, inventory, retail sale, etc.), such as Wal-Mart, Procter & Gamble, General Motors, United Parcel Service, Pfizer, and, potentially, those seeking information generated by the RFID system, which could include *partners* of product-focused companies, such as credit agencies, advertising and marketing companies, financial services firms, or news organizations that are unrelated to the product or to the transaction generating the information)
- Technology suppliers (such as IBM, Accenture, Texas Instruments, Hitachi, Phillips, OATSystems, Symbol Technologies, Intermec, or Alien Technology)

Included in both categories are associations of like companies.

---

6. As subsequent chapters note, to the extent the policy struggle focuses on values, such as privacy, that are more prominent in developed nations, it may have little resonance in areas of the world where these values are not deeply rooted or respected.

Government

The government category consists of:

- Users of RFID systems under their own control, for their own internal operations (the military, law enforcement, intelligence agencies, VA hospitals, customs, feeding programs, mass transit, school systems, libraries, and first responders as well as government users in foreign jurisdictions)
- Those seeking information generated by the RFID systems of others but for mission purposes other than those intended by their primary users (e.g., the Internal Revenue Service, law enforcement, intelligence, first responders, and foreign governments that would like to "piggyback" on others' RFID data collection)
- Technology regulators and agencies such as, to use U.S. examples, the Federal Communications Commission, the Department of Health and Human Services, the Federal Trade Commission, the Department of Commerce export control authorities, or regional/international bodies such as the European Commission Privacy Directorate or Internet governance bodies

I do not mean to suggest that representatives of the named government agencies, for example, need to be "at the table" for policy development. However, the process at least should include informal input from enough such participants to ensure that the policy process addresses predictable, legitimate governmental interests. In practice, the government engagement stage of debate often starts early but is not driven to action until an agency seeks to exercise regulatory authority or control, thus spurring the business community to offer concessions to forestall compulsory regulation. Note, however, that when government's goal is to gain access to the RFID-generated data of others (e.g., for law enforcement purposes), the dynamic is somewhat altered. Then civil liberties advocates assume the task of principal opposition, with business resisting primarily because of the cost, disruption, and possible technological degradation involved in complying with government's requests.

Miscellaneous

Some other actors must be mentioned, not because of their direct stake in the technology, but because of their interest in discussing issues and influencing their resolution. These include policy organizations such as think tanks and academic centers and, of course, the media. Indeed, their involvement cannot be forestalled, and it can prove very helpful to a satisfactory outcome. (Consumer advocacy groups could fit in here as well, but because they typically claim to speak for individuals, I include them in the first category of stakeholders. There's no significance in where they sit, as long as one understands the impact they have and the desirability of engaging them in the process.)

As the foregoing list of stakeholders demonstrates, the tensions among interests can appear through the simple analysis of which groups and persons will interface with RFID applications. These tensions define the "issues."

RFID Policy Issues

The following sections examine RFID policy issues, some of which are speculative at this time. It is important to note that cost or technical limitations may prevent some from developing in ways that are objectionable.

Privacy

Privacy has different implications for each constituency that it affects.

Individual

- **Personally identifiable (PI) data.** RFID systems have the potential to generate PI data in the normal course of legitimate affairs. For example, in the retail setting, they could link a name and credit card number with the RFID product identifier code number of a purchased product at the point of sale (POS);[7] This kind of practice already transpires with loyalty cards and other applications, although under controlled regulation, including consent.
- **Sensitive data.** This involves the RFID code for products such as prescription drugs, condoms, unseemly books, or currency notes that might create discomfort for the person associated with them if others know about the purchase or learn that they are in the person's possession. The data may be collected legitimately, as in POS transactions, or generated improperly, such as through a tag scan by an unethical house cleaner, or by scans on the sidewalk, on a bus, in a restaurant. Thus,

---

7. Transforming anonymous data into PI data need not involve coupling RFID data to identifiers that are *part of the transaction*. Data can also be made personally identifiable if it is linked to sufficient individual identifiers available to the collector *from other sources*, like an existing database. Thus, the public concern covers situations such as when another independently knows who the subject is, either through acquaintance or archived information, and can tie the sensitive product to that person through an independent reader scan.

privacy and security concerns can arise even where the collector does not know the subject's identity at the time.

- **Location data.** Because RFID data can be collected by readers that normally are stationary at a known location in the network, people's movements, and potentially their associations, can be tracked via a tag associated with them, just as the location of products can be tracked in a warehouse. The location-tracking issue has already surfaced in the debate over the requirement that new cell phones incorporate GPS technology that will allow emergency response officials to identify their location promptly. The surreptitious use of GPS technology by law enforcement has begun to generate litigation, and the merger of GPS and RFID applications is being tested by the Department of Defense for its logistics operations.[8] Law enforcement will undoubtedly follow the progress of these product trials closely. Indeed, Nokia recently announced a new application that would implant RFID chips in most smart phones to allow consumers, for example, to pass their phones by a reader and automatically download a coupon or complete a warranty registration (and reveal user location by reference to reader location.)[9]

- Note that the intensity of concern over the preceding three issue sets will vary depending on the kind of RFID technology employed. EPC-global's policy forbids the use of EPC-compliant devices for tracking people, except in narrow applications in the medical and armed services environments.[10] Further, it argues that the absence of PI data on EPC-compliant chips, and the difficulty of accessing the unique product identifier and making sense of it without access to the coder's remote database, should moot the PI and sensitive-data issues for its branch of the technology.

- **Implantation.** A couple of years ago, this seemed on the lower end of the list of issue priorities, but its day has come. Britain already has a thriving implantation tradition for tagging pets to facilitate return to

---

8. *RFID Journal* at http://www.rfidjournal.com/article/articleview/1458/1/1/: "Using the Iridium network of global satellites, which the DOD already uses for other communications, the tags would transmit their unique identification number, the date and time, and their current position to within 3.5 feet. That capability, according to the DLA, will change the DOD's RFID network from providing information on where shipments of equipment have been and closer to a real-time understanding of where that equipment actually is." The fact that this capability may not be feasible for mass-market product applications does not erase the concern for its use by law enforcement.

9. This is a consensual use of RFID. Opportunistic or nonconsensual applications are described in Chapter 5's insightful analysis as "action threats."

10. From an EPCglobal fact sheet:
    False Allegation: EPC technology will be used to secretly track people.
    FACT: The licensing arrangements for the EPCglobal Network specifically prohibit the use of the technology for tracking or identifying people. The only exceptions to this are military personnel and medical patients. Current specifications are focused on applications deep in the supply chain, not the tracking or identification of individuals.

their owners, and VeriChip, a U.S. company, recently announced a voluntary, paid service to implant special RFID tags the size of rice grains into customers such as key business leaders, young children (in case they are lost or kidnapped), and public officials needing quick, reliable ID verification for entry into secured areas. In July 2004, some 1,000 tags already had been deployed in humans, including 160 in Mexican law enforcement officials.[11] In October 2004, the U.S. Food and Drug Administration approved the use of implanted RFID chip capsules for the storage and retrieval of individual medical information, an application that offers benefits in healthcare settings.

If by this time you are thinking, "Big Brother," you have grasped a key emotional underpinning of many privacy advocates' opposition to the vision of an "RFID world." I believe it has enormous intuitive appeal not just to policy advocates, but to the general public as well.

Business

- Much commercially sensitive information can be revealed to competitors, other customers, or suppliers if they can intercept a business's RFID query/response signals and interpret them, do their own query as products move between secure locations, or otherwise pierce the confidentiality of the target's supply chain: its product movements, volume of component purchases, ingredient purchases, and so on.
- Some PI data can also have business implications. For example, it could reveal that a CEO carries methadone, lithium, or HIV medication or that RFID chips in a researcher's car were recently read in the parking lot of a building housing a competitor or a drug treatment clinic. Again, the same distinction between EPC and non-EPC technology as to on-chip PI data should be made here as it was under the consumer issues section.

Government

- Concerns parallel to those in "Business" on the disclosure of sensitive data (Remember, this is government-as-user, as a "public business enterprise." Government-as-Big-Brother follows shortly.)

---

11. www.4verichip.com/nws_07282004_2.htm. This document also notes the coming development by Verichip of a combination RFID/GPS tag for human implantation: "Also, VeriChip is working on an implant that will contain a Global Positioning System. Such a device would allow an individual with a scanner to pinpoint someone's position on the globe."

Integrity and Security of the System

To list issues in the order they arise in the flow of data, we have tampering with data stored in the tag; tampering with tag/product association, intercepting or altering data in transit; and tampering with data as it is stored in remote databases (concerns such as industrial espionage, criminal behavior, terrorism, evasion of responsibility or liability). Additional issues include vulnerability of system software to hacking and integrity of location-linked data where location is assumed to be generated by a stationary reader that is in fact movable. Specifically:

- Tag reading occurs when a reader submits a code to the tag, triggering a response. Questions have been raised about the ability of unauthorized readers to trigger this response and the response's ability to reveal at least certain portions of the product number ID code. Further, with respect to reprogrammable tags, the question of unauthorized alteration of the data is important.
- Transmission of the collected data from the reader over an intranet or Internet pipe to a remote database presents an opportunity for the surreptitious interception, alteration, or destruction of signals.
- The security of the "always-receiving" PI database repository from hackers and others is also critical. As recent events have shown, the vulnerability of databases containing PI cannot be taken for granted. Whether from a combination of fraud and inadequate screening standards (as with ChoicePoint's sales of sensitive data to fake businesses), or physical loss (Bank of America data tapes) or hacking (LexisNexis, California State University, DSW Shoe Warehouse, numerous others), inadequate security of databases storing PI is a weakness for which other system design or use restrictions cannot substitute.

Government Access

- **Law enforcement.** Of primary concern to many privacy advocates in this country is law enforcement's ability to gain access to collected information. The applicability and impact of existing laws regulating government action in analogous areas must be decided, as must the desirability of modeling RFID rules on them where they don't by their own terms apply; for example, the Electronic Communications Privacy Act, CALEA, and the Fourth Amendment (search and seizure), and Fifth Amendment (compelled testimony) generally. Scenarios include authorized and unauthorized monitoring of tag/reader or reader/database transmissions (including potential government requirements that companies monitor data for suspicious or potentially illegal activity), whether such data can be used in a civil or criminal proceeding, and under what circumstances.

- **Regulatory access.** Government agencies may find the capabilities of networked RFID systems attractive resources to help them carry out their regulatory missions. Thus they may attempt to regulate or co-opt deployed RFID technology applications for government purposes such as levying and collecting taxes or use fees or tariffs and customs fees by requiring access to data transmissions or to databases; or collecting business data for survey or company-specific purposes. Activities of regulatory agencies with investigative and penalty powers, such as the Federal Trade Commission, the Food and Drug Administration, or the Food Safety Inspection Service, may raise questions similar to those generated by traditional law enforcement activities.

Health Impact

- Readers emit weak electromagnetic signals. A number of readers may be operating constantly in a given space, and each query generates an additional response signal. Thus concerns have been raised about their health consequences, particularly for workers in RFID settings. There is no evidence so far that any foreseeable aggregation of these signals poses a health risk. However, it is likely that predictive calculations based on signal strength fall-off, duration, and so forth ultimately will not be a sufficient substitute for actual measured data whether for exposure or for health outcomes. Additional studies will probably be required.
- Health issues generated by implantable RFID capsules may have been satisfactorily vetted by the U.S. Food and Drug Administration in its recent approval of the VeriChip device (though the agency concedes that in some areas, such as MRI incompatibility, data isn't dispositive). However, the application is new, the technology will evolve, perhaps in ways that implicate health, and the agency has been known to approve products that later prove to pose significant health risks. This one still bears monitoring.

Labor Impact

- To the extent the penetration of RFID into the workplace eliminates or transfers jobs, it may have to be submitted to labor negotiation. In the United States, any such requirement by and large results from the terms of labor contracts entered into by employers individually. In other nations, Germany for example, national law may compel this outcome much more broadly.

Spectrum Conflicts

- Because RFID typically uses unlicensed, general-purpose slices of the spectrum under the jurisdiction of the Federal Communications Commission, an explosive increase in the volume of RFID signals in an environment may raise issues of interference with other existing and future users of that spectrum. RFID readers do emit weak signals as they detect and query chips. As for the chips themselves, although current EPC class 0 and class 1 signals pose little threat, more advanced EPC chips, particularly those that are self-powered, emit increasingly powerful, long-range signals. As these devices shrink and become more cost efficient, and thus more widely used, their signal noise, combined with that of an ever-expanding universe of readers, may become a major interference problem. There are of course many self-powered non-EPC chips already in use, though their cost and features restrict their use to specialty applications. Thus, the emissions of these devices have not to date triggered any significant interference concerns.[12]

Use of RFID Technology to Limit Product Functionality

- A tag integrated into a product component can be made part of an authentication system the manufacturer creates to control the product's operation to its advantage. For example, devices that consume supplies (e.g., printer toner or ink) or that alter or process other products (DVD burner, VCR) can be programmed to operate only in the presence of tags integrated into ink cartridges or VHS tapes that are manufactured or approved by the printer or VCR manufacturer. This forces additional costs on aftermarket suppliers or prevents the production of aftermarket alternatives completely, which of course is the application's purpose. The latter then attempt to reverse engineer the tags in order to make compatible tags of their own to affix to their products. (The general strategy has already been tried by Lexmark, among others, attempting to block reverse engineering of the software codes via copyright restrictions, though without success so far at the federal appellate level.)

---

12. See brief discussion by Blair Levin, senior former FCC official: Legg Mason, RFID (Radio Frequency Identification), *An Early Look at Potential Opportunities and Impact*, July 2004, pp. 24–25. Also, October 4, 2004, reply of FCC Chairman Michael Powell to Senator Bill Nelson, explaining the agency's role with respect to readers and tags: "The RFID systems that operate in the United States are regulated under Part 15 of the Commission's rules. As such, they operate on a license-exempt basis, but the equipment used requires compliance certification in accordance with the rules."

Government Versus Individual Context[13]

Concerns related to the government in its relations to individuals seem to stir the strongest emotions among privacy advocates.[14] The fear that government agencies use matchless technological sophistication and resources to monitor what individuals are purchasing, doing, and saying and where and with whom they're doing it is not limited to veterans of totalitarian governments. In the United States, "the land of the free," whose citizens cherish a constitution that limits government power and enshrines personal liberty, there is at the same time strong support for law enforcement and an inclination to grant it additional powers under emergency conditions or when security conditions deteriorate. As a brake on the law enforcement and intelligence[15] communities' desire to acquire capabilities to make their efforts more efficient, there is a loose but broad-based and potent collection of activists deeply suspicious of government, from civil libertarians to "patriot" groups and conservative Christian evangelists.

The claim that criminal justice and law enforcement agencies will, overtly or covertly, seek to use others' RFID data generation and collection capabilities for their own ends is not an idle one. Criminal justice and crime prevention is their job, and tracking criminals and their activities can be extremely useful. We should expect, indeed welcome, the fact that they stay abreast of technology and seek to adapt it to law enforcement and terrorism prevention needs, even as we insist on review of and limits on their investigative and prosecutorial use of technology.

---

13. Although these issues extend well beyond the province of law enforcement and intelligence activities (regulating immigration and monitoring use of federal funds by loan or welfare recipients, for example), this chapter concentrates on the former because of their profile and their emotional, motivational impact on privacy advocates.

14. Katherine Albrecht, for example, seems to consider government abuse of RFID technology her deepest concern. I am not immune to those concerns myself

15. In this country, intelligence agencies—which have more sophisticated capabilities than domestic law enforcement agencies—are prohibited from engaging in domestic surveillance, at least of citizens. However, their ability to monitor communications and movements and to digest huge volumes of information into useful databases is extraordinary. Details remain closely guarded, but the capability is increasingly visible to the public. Educated by a colorful history of zealous law enforcement predating J. Edgar Hoover, we have come to suspect there will always be "rogue offices" and "rogue agents" so devoted to their missions that they rationalize breaking the rules. Concerns about government overreaching have increased as, post-9/11, newly adopted U.S. laws erode the wall between domestic and foreign intelligence, with the CIA and others now sometimes permitted to share their data with the FBI and other domestic agencies. Further, intelligence agencies' development of capabilities to exploit mass deployment of RFID devices involves the creation of data-harvesting techniques, signal systems, analytical tools, and institutional relationships that can easily be turned to pernicious ends by changes in government, claims of national emergencies, or even failure to protect such technology from falling into unauthorized hands. Thus, including "intelligence agencies" here is not a concession to "scare tactics."

An example from Internet regulatory history is illustrative. As e-mail developed into a mass-communication technology, and Internet data exchange and Web surfing became mainstream activities, senior officials from the intelligence and law enforcement communities held personal meetings with technology leaders to request the incorporation of "back-door" government access into their products or services.[16] Reportedly, this was generally resisted, but the Department of Justice then mounted administrative and legislative initiatives seeking, for example, to incorporate into Internet service provider (ISP) pipes its Carnivore technology for monitoring e-mail transmissions in real time[17]; to relax limits on law-enforcement access to stored e-mail, and so forth.

These initiatives were met with public and Congressional criticism, resulting in review and delay of Carnivore's implementation. Nevertheless, federal justice officials immediately sensed and aggressively pursued a huge opportunity following 9/11. Politically, their initial wish list would have been a "nonstarter" under any other circumstances, but in the highly charged atmosphere of a rapid national response to terrorist attacks, the usual weighing of competing interests was compromised in the crafting of the USA Patriot Act.[18] Its history is further evidence that as long as criminals escape detection and justice, there will always be a natural push by law enforcement for ever greater powers. We can expect to see this struggle joined in the RFID environment, if it hasn't been already.[19]

---

16. This was patterned on the precedent of the Comprehensive Assistance for Law Enforcement Act (CALEA), which required telecommunications common carriers to reconfigure their systems to allow efficient tapping of voice and certain data communications in the digital age. CALEA also attempted to balance the scales by expanding certain privacy and civil liberties protections, such as the requirement that access be authorized by court order, the extension of the Electronic Communications Privacy Act to mobile phones, and limitations on the ability to use pen registers for tracking purposes or to reveal location information. 47 U.S.C. §§1001–1021. See FBI Web site at www.askcalea.com/calea.html.
17. See, for initial claims and counterclaims: www.wired.com/news/politics/0,1283,37470,00.html.
18. See EPIC analysis at www.epic.org/privacy/terrorism/usapatriot. Cf. DoJ analysis at www.lifeandliberty.gov/subs/u_myths.htm. The events of 9/11 also nurtured DARPA's Total Information Awareness project, which was proposed as a great advance in countering terrorism. Despite a Congressionally mandated May 2003 report on the plan that proposed a number of civil liberties protections to render it acceptable, the initiative was denied funding in FY 2004 appropriations legislation, except for certain counterterrorism-related functions conducted abroad or against non-U.S. citizens. www.eff.org/Privacy/TIA/20031003_conf_report.php.
19. Ann Cavoukian, Ph.D., Information and Privacy Commissioner of Ontario, observed: "Law-enforcement agencies in Canada have also thought about gaining access to RFID systems. The Ontario Provincial Police has reportedly investigated the efficacy of developing a reader that could enable them to interrogate 'any and all tags that might be attached to virtually anything,' according to Clifford Horowitz, chairman and chief executive officer of SAMSys Technologies of Richmond Hill, Ont." in *Tag, You're It: Privacy Implications of Radio Frequency Identification (RFID) Technology*, www.ipc.on.ca/docs/rfid.pdf, p. 21, citing Richard Bray, "Radio ID Tags Track Inventory," *Summit: Canada's Magazine on Public Sector Purchasing*, February 2003, p. 3. www.summitconnects.com/Articles_Columns/PDF_Documents/060108.pdf.

This debate will proceed in the halls of Congress and within the Administration, and not necessarily on the same timetable as the debate over B2C RFID applications, though perhaps giving the latter additional urgency. As it does, representatives of corporations and individual members of society alike will alert policymakers to potential threats, even as the Department of Justice and others promote a list of benefits. Though a detailed analysis of the likely arguments is beyond the scope of this chapter,[20] threshold questions to be resolved are:

- Constitutional implications: To what extent are constitutional protections against government action triggered under the First Amendment (free speech and association, including the right to anonymity in speech and in access to and the consumption of information)[21] and the Fourth Amendment (unreasonable search and seizure, including surveillance)?[22]
- Statutory implications: To what extent do relevant statutes apply that offer potential protection extending beyond the Constitution (e.g., the Electronic Communications Privacy Act)?[23] ECPA provisions governing interception of data transmissions as well as access to stored electronic communications are governed by definitions and exceptions that make questionable their usefulness for RFID data, though the definition of "electronic communication" itself is broad enough to cover it.[24]
- If it is found that current constitutional case law and statutory schemes do not provide clear answers or in fact do not apply to law enforcement applications, how should Congress respond? With a broad-based limit on the collection of RFID data without the consent of the individual or appropriate judicial process? Through the imposition of evidentiary exclusions? Should RFID data, or some subset of it, simply be made subject to ECPA? Are there differences between RFID data and e-mail transactional data, for example, that justify different rules or exceptions? To what extent should the needs of law enforcement be balanced

---

20. For a comprehensive analysis of statutory and constitutional limits on law enforcement investigative activity with respect to electronic communications generally (useful insights for analogous RFID applications) from the law enforcement perspective, see the Department of Justice's online manual at www.cybercrime.gov/s&smanual2002.htm.
21. See discussion at www.law.berkeley.edu/cenpro/samuelson/projects/privacy/RFIDWorkshop-CommentP049106.pdf, pp. 2–3.
22. While one can easily construct hypothetical scenarios in which surreptitious scanning of passive tags by law enforcement would raise Fourth Amendment issues, those concerns will be highlighted when consumer-application chips gain greater response ranges, either through more efficient passive query/response technology or via onboard power (think nanotechnology) and read-write ability that permits onboard chip storage of PI data. An additional difficulty with location tracking, in particular, is that tracked individuals would typically be in public places, arguably with no expectation of privacy. For an extensive review of location-data issues see www.epic.org/privacy/location/jwhitelocationprivacy.pdf.
23. 18 U.S.C. §2510 ff., and 18 U.S.C. §2701 ff.
24. See discussion at www.law.berkeley.edu/cenpro/samuelson/projects/privacy/RFIDWorkshop-CommentP049106.pdf.

with the needs of commercial users in the integrity and reliable operation of their systems[25] and in public confidence in those systems? To
what extent should they be required to design or open their systems to
government access, and at whose cost?

I will not venture any answers of my own other than to advocate two general
principles:

- Government action should be limited in ways that are consistent with
  statutory safeguards for other kinds of sensitive electronic data, modified where specific RFID capabilities (e.g., location tracking) may indicate a tailored approach.
- The outcome must preserve the public's confidence in, and willingness
  to accept, consumer-level RFID applications.

Business Versus Individual Context

This section's observations on the environment in which the business and consumer policy debates take place relate mainly to the United States. Differences
among nations and cultures may substantially affect outcomes in some areas, as
noted in Chapter 4, RFID and Global Privacy Policy; Chapter 31, Asia: Billions Awaken to RFID; and others.

When new technology is developed, the stakeholders who typically have first
chance to consider policy implications are business or academia, since they have
first knowledge. Next usually come advocates, who often learn of developments
that pose policy concerns before the media generates any consciousness among
the public. (Government is generally the last and in this country usually does so
at the instigation of other stakeholders. However, this does not mean they are the
last to *act* on solutions, especially in nations that have a more activist regulatory
tradition than in the United States, such as those in the European Union.)

Of course, the mentality of all stakeholders is important in helping chart a
course optimized for success. However, that of advocates is well reflected in
other chapters in this book, and I suspect I can make a contribution by focusing
on factors that often play decisive roles in business' response to public policy
challenges and examining a policy development business/consumer dialogue in
the privacy setting.

---

25. Indeed, if the government were to succeed in obtaining broad, unfettered access to RFID
    data, that fact alone could ensure public rejection of all post-sale, item-level tagging.

In general, business has an interest in seeing a desired technology taken up broadly and seamlessly into society, in the most useful form possible (hence the emphasis on open standards by EPCglobal). Savvy business leaders have recognized that this penetration will happen only to the extent the public is comfortable with the design and use of the technology as it touches them. Failures to address public expectations will result in public concern, leading either to restricted commercial success of consumer applications (as consumers reject them), to legislation and regulation of the technology, or to both.

RFID has been in use for decades. Until recently, however, RFID technology was expensive and used in applications that raised relatively few public policy concerns. The current challenge is that the development of mass-deployment, commodity-priced RFID technology is influenced by business leaders who typically lack sophistication about public policy and its impact on their activities or who have not focused their attention on its role in RFID. Most necessarily know only what their general counsel or chief communications officer tells them and have no sound instinct to guide their decisions. Given that business managers are chosen for their leadership positions not because of their public policy sensitivity but rather for their discipline, focus on profits and market share, leadership ability, creative vision, or track record, this result is understandable. As a consequence, however, whether explicitly or implicitly many corporate officials invite their staff to give policy input that is not *too* disruptive of their business opportunities and plans, and they respond with whatever decision represents the "minimum required" to get over the immediate hurdle or challenge at hand.

Policy requirements are an added cost of bringing an RFID product or application to market, and business's normal goal, of course, is to reduce costs. In the ordinary case of technology deployment, those who first step outside this typical product development comfort zone may eventually be acclaimed as progressive visionaries by the media or legislators, but their judgment is often questioned by their peers, if not by their own boards of directors. Little wonder, then, that in general, business's track record in bringing forth successful new-technology public policy on its own has been sporadic. And this even in a nation that is second to none in its devotion to unfettered markets and a light regulatory hand, an environment in which politicians of all persuasions have encouraged business to regulate itself to forestall the need for formal government intervention.

The Internet, poster child for technology deregulation and self-regulation, offers several examples. In the beginning, its evolution was driven by corporate leaders who in some cases were unusually sensitive to social values and whose devotion to the greater good materially assisted its development into the flexible, creation-enabling tool it is today. Yet it, too, has seen its fair share of messy policy battles, from spam and privacy to software compatibility, where business has needlessly fought legitimate consumer expectations. Some of these have been addressed by legislation and regulation, while others are still unresolved, though business-led initiatives such as TRUSTe have managed to play a moderately useful, continuing role.[26]

It is against this background of business's variable public-policy responses to consumer concerns that we must consider attempts by commercial stakeholders to unilaterally craft RFID design features and usage "rules of the road" that address public policy values. It is perhaps too much to argue that this business-driven process is doomed to fail because it excludes other stakeholders or because those participating in it, even if savvy, in the aggregate are not senior enough in their organizations to take the internal risks necessary to allay consumer concerns. However, a failure by senior industry management to devote the attention and money resources the task requires can add up to tall odds. These concepts can be illuminated by a concrete review of the responses typically employed by business, presented below in a point-counterpoint format.

Policy Dialogue Dynamic

The following is a general discussion, not specific to RFID. In a typical business /consumer policy debate, business leaders embrace technology, seeing its positives and negatives in business-school terms. Public policy is a nuisance they may have to negotiate along the way. On the other hand, consumers and consumer advocates may appreciate technology's benefits but look for risks to their values and for unforeseen consequences. Recognition of threats like privacy is instinctive. In privacy terms, the reflexive query is, "Would I want someone to know X? What conditions would I want to impose? What would I get in return?"[27]

Business responds to the expression of consumer concerns with:

- **Business practices and self-regulation.** "We have developed a set of industry consensus practices that adequately respond to these

---

26. Consider the absence in the United States of a general Internet privacy statute or regulation, which remains a goal of the Center for Democracy and Technology, among others. Echoes of that desire are visible in the last scenario described in Chapter 17, Multiple Scenarios for Private-Sector Use of RFID.
27. See the discussion of recent survey data in the March 8, 2005, FTC Staff Report on its RFID Workshop.

fears. By following them, we will avoid objectionable or harmful conduct without the need for government action." This is a desirable outcome in many cases, but its viability depends on the details: Does it address reasonable consumer concerns or just those CEOs think are justified; does it address them fairly—are its requirements or restrictions responsive, or just "fig leaves"; is the great majority of industry actors on board, and is there real consensus, or will companies that don't participate undermine the value of the self-regulatory structure; are there realistic means for enforcement or discipline? Too often, elements critical to a successful self-regulatory regime are absent and are not adopted until it appears legislators or regulators may act. By then it is frequently too late since the credibility of the sponsoring group has been undermined.

- **A disclaimer of intent.** "We have no plans to do anything of the kind, trust us." This is often buttressed by arguments that business has valuable brands to protect, would be foolish to alienate its customers, is highly principled and would never unilaterally alter its practices to consumers' disadvantage, and so on. However, corporate intent is not enforceable and is subject to revision because of changes in leadership, deteriorating competitive position, financial imperatives, or no reason at all. Most important, in the age of Enron, long-distance subscriber slamming, abusive loan practices, spam, and breaches of ethics in the securities and accounting industries, corporate reassurances alone may lack credibility, whether with consumers or with policymakers.

- **An enforceable promise.** In this variant of the intent statement, companies promise to follow a specific practice in such a way that it becomes enforceable by a governmental agency (in the United States, the Federal Trade Commission). Although this option is better than a mere disclaimer of intent, its adequacy also hinges on the details—as recent court cases have made clear, not just any promise or commitment will trigger FTC jurisdiction. And it suffers from the problem of outliers—companies that avoid FTC jurisdiction by simply declining to make the promise.

- **Impossibility.** The technology isn't capable of the objectionable acts, thus business couldn't transgress even if it wanted to. This factor is legitimate and must weigh heavily in any policy debate. Policy struggles often expend much time and energy seeking agreement on what is and is not possible. With technology, however, particularly in electronic communication and intelligence, many advocates have developed a gut-level feeling that will resonate with many members of the public, that (1) even if there are no *commercial* products or techniques, government organizations may have the secret capability to do so, and (2) even if it's not possible today, it probably will be within five or ten years if not sooner.[28]

For example, Jim Harper made most of these arguments in a paper published by the Competitive Enterprise Institute.[29] He sums up with, "As yet, RFID tags have seen limited deployments, so there is little real-world experience on which to ground discussions of the merits or demerits of regulation. As RFID technology comes into full use, various social forces will constrain it more suitably than would government regulation. RFID users face economic incentives and consumer preferences that will direct the technology's evolution in harmony with consumer interests. Meanwhile, consumers' easy access to defensive techniques and countertechnologies will complement existing laws that already protect privacy."

Harper's faith in the ability of natural "incentives" to harmonize business and consumer interests contrasts with an ongoing parade of corporate scandals.[30] His arguments might carry more weight in an ideal world, but we aren't there.[31] His analysis dismisses as hypothetical and unlikely the scenarios described by policy activists, while he expresses confidence business practice or technology will develop in beneficial ways. And he is content that consumers be consigned to using "work-arounds" or partially effective technological solutions such as blocker tags.[32]

These typical appeals to good intent, impossibility, or even self-regulation (unless it is substantial and is enforceable) are likely a hard sell in the general

---

28. Although because of technical limitations, early applications of the EPC technology are less likely to be surreptitiously monitored, information seekers will no doubt gain sophistication, and tags will become more capable. Even self-powered, long-range tags may become small and cheap enough to become commonplace. (See a recent article touting new analogue technology that could take us to this point in a single leap at www.rfidjournal.com/article/articleview /1263/1/1/.) There are various technologies and design features in development or under discussion that may be very useful in reducing the risk of unauthorized tag reading. However, none has yet emerged as a clear winner in terms of both effectiveness and cost/feasibility. In the end it may be that design features imposed by license grantors or government regulation restricting tag uses will be more attractive to everyone than policy solutions that rest on specific choices of proprietary technologies. Thus, based on their fears of future technology capabilities, consumer activists campaign against the deployment of tags at the consumer level, even for pilot trials, seeing them as the first step toward a surveillance society (e.g., the small firestorms around Benetton's and Gillette's RFID announcements in 2003).
29. Harper, J. "RFID Tags and Privacy: How Bar-Codes-On-Steroids Are Really a 98-Lb. Weakling," Competitive Enterprise Institute, June 21, 2004 (timed to coincide with the FTC hearing on RFID).
30. Harper seems to rely on the force of competition in the "marketplace of ideas" within a product manager's head to produce the optimal result. However, that internal marketplace of ideas is rarely competitive in the sense that bottom-line profits or market share imperatives are counterbalanced by policy concerns. Indeed, where motivation is strong and risk of discovery is deemed slight, even the potential of civil and criminal liability hasn't been sufficient.

RFID context to any stakeholder other than business itself. While some of these points are plausible and seem to demonstrate sensitivity, the history of their use in past policy battles is spotted with insincerity. They have been cited in diverse technology and science policy debates regularly and without qualification in an attempt to avoid grappling with the issues. Even many ordinary members of the public who cannot formally analyze these claims will instinctively find them hollow when they are advanced to oppose any government regulatory role. Essentially, those who would make these arguments in the RFID arena need to recognize they have been seriously eroded by their use in other policy debates, and that they are unlikely, by themselves, to satisfy the public.

Industry Leadership

Thus, my purpose in conducting this analysis is largely to help important corporate actors understand the need to move beyond the business-as-usual approach and to respond in good faith to public policy issues. Not doing so only ensures business that its efforts will be superseded sooner rather than later and that it will likely find itself pitted against "the public" in a fight that leaves it less credible, and with less room to maneuver, than if it had taken a less-self-interested tack in the beginning.

Of course, business itself rarely starts out presenting a united front on policy, given the diverse interests and cultures of corporate actors. The process of attempting private-sector consensus is important, though as we see in RFID, major differences may persist even as industry is being thrust into the debate with other stakeholders. Several trade associations have engaged on RFID issues: The Information Technology Association of America (ITAA) sponsored

31. A similar stance was taken in the June 21, 2004, FTC testimony of Robert Atkinson, then of the Progressive Policy Institute (www.ftc.gov/bcp/workshops/rfid/atkinson.pdf). While it may be premature for the FTC to act, as he argues, neither his critique of privacy advocates' claims nor his view of business as naturally benign in handling PI data is persuasive. (Does Checkpoint or LexisNexis ring a bell?) He does admit a role for government in "work[ing] with and oversee[ing] industry efforts to ensure they do implement the kinds of privacy practices envisioned by groups like EPCglobal," which is a good and viable option, depending on the details. But the thrust of the approach is a surprisingly sanguine "if it's [RFID] like past rollouts of IT, things will work out fine with little harm to privacy." Putting aside what kind of harm to privacy we should consider "little," one can only suppose PPI was an ardent supporter of the Pentagon's "Total Information Awareness" project.

32. His appeal to the tort system to constrain bad behavior seems odd for a CEI paper but isn't serious at the individual, non-class-action level, at least unless attorneys' fees become recoverable. Besides, access to the courts is not what most victims of information abuse would choose as their first option, as witness the experience of those who have suffered identity fraud. They want to see harm *prevented*, not just have an avenue to redress violations, and prevention must be the role of the RFID policy debate.

a forum in Washington, D.C., on June 15, 2004. It has also cosponsored a Bearing Point study on RFID adoption in government and has established standing committees on RFID policy and technical standards. And the National Retail Federation, taking the lead for RFID technology user companies, testified at the FTC meeting, endorsing consumer notice and choice, at least in part. However, the message also argued the sufficiency of existing laws, saying "Regulation should be considered only if evolving technology and practice fail to meet consumer expectations," and we should "wait and see how things develop."[33] Neither group at this point is positioning itself as the broad consensus forum that is needed.

Globally, and here in the United States, EPCglobal is the only organization drafting any industry guidelines or rules, though remember that it speaks only for that version of the technology covered by its licenses. Its guidelines process has not been completed, being self-described as a work in progress, though it has been useful. To succeed, EPCglobal must continue educating the key user and supplier companies, as well as the public, and it needs time, with the latter being least under its control.

If EPCglobal fails, the consequence will be marginalization of its self-regulatory policy prescriptions. Any group of stakeholders seeking to write the rules for its own activities takes a risk that its system may not last. It may succeed at first because the technology's interface with society is small. However, as it becomes more visible to the public, bumps into societal values, and attracts broad public concern, the power of *inadequate* rules weakens as the real arbiters of policy—legislators and bureaucrats—step up to the plate. These decision makers will look at the issues from the ground up, considering what industry has done as perhaps useful but in no way binding. There is reason to believe that EPCglobal's efforts may avoid this fate, though the more important question may be whether the broader community of companies producing and using RFID technology outside the EPC supply chain can somehow come together and fashion an adequate response to consumer concerns.

Options for Government Leadership

Congress

If RFID technology developers and users cannot identify in advance the main issues that will arise and fail to design policies and features and mount education efforts that satisfy the legitimate concerns of outside stakeholders in a

---

33. www.ftc.gov/bcp/workshops/rfid/duncan.pdf

timely way, the momentum will shift. The center of action in the United States will migrate to Congress, with a key supporting role by the Federal Trade Commission and contributions from other agencies as well, though that process could take a few years to mature. Foreign actors such as the EU, which often regulate on a faster timetable, could well be the first to put a stake in the ground.[34]

The policy arc in Congress would likely follow a familiar path. As the issue "ripens," members of Congress—particularly leaders and members of the House Energy and Commerce and the Senate Commerce Committees, and the House and Senate Judiciary Committees—will start jockeying for leadership. An issue will ripen as policymakers sense it is becoming viable (threatening them with loss of leadership if they don't act) because of some combination of a member's own issue interest, media attention (especially that focused on revolutionary implications of technology or on industry blunders), advocate pressure, industry pressure, home-state interest, foreign action affecting U.S. leadership, and so forth.

In the RFID setting, we can expect congressional staff to become educated about the technology and potential issues by both business and policy advocates. Staff education will help generate public statements by members of Congress and initial hearings, the latter cautious explorations of alternative futures as technology develops. The tone will generally be blended optimism and concern, coupled with a commitment to follow developments and hold additional hearings as events warrant. In the meantime, advice is sought from Executive Branch agencies such as the FTC and FCC, which have already started engaging the issues and may be asked to submit reports to Congress, particularly on technology-specific questions on which Congress itself can have little depth.

Legislation may be proposed by members opportunistically seeking positive exposure (especially in an election year) or by committee leaders who intend both to stake out a substantive position and to secure their role in future legislative developments. Following this process and its variations is not my purpose; however. My point is that legislative gestation ordinarily is complicated, resource intensive, and time consuming, especially when the technology is evolving so quickly that the facts keep changing and conclusions remain tentative. Legislation also moves more slowly, and sometimes not at all, when as now a majority that is decidedly deregulatory controls the Administration and both Houses of Congress. Under these conditions, a legislative scheme addressing

---

34. Others have noted the action of Portugal in declaring RFID data and practices subject to existing privacy rules, and the International Conference of Data Protection & Privacy Commissioners' November 2003 "Resolution on Radio-Frequency Identification" at www.privacyconference2003.org/resolutions/res5.DOC.

RFID would probably take one to four years to pass *after* committee leaders introduce legislation, which itself may not occur for another two or three years. Some wild-card factors, however, can cause the process to shift into high gear: high-profile corporate blunders or misdeeds, harm to individuals, a groundswell of grassroots activism, missteps by government that energize law-enforcement privacy issues, and the threat of foreign-developed laws or international conventions preempting the field.

Federal Trade Commission

As most stakeholders would concede at least in theory new legislation may not really be necessary for implementing the most basic RFID policy goals. The Federal Trade Commission already has broad authority to regulate unfair trade practices, which it has used on behalf of consumers to impose limitations and obligations on businesses involved in commerce with the public. It is easy to construct an appealing argument that not advising consumers of the presence of RFID tags and readers is an unfair trade practice. Likewise, a requirement might be imposed that consumers must have the opportunity to consent to the creation of personally identifiable information when it is created (which is already general data policy in the EU and may well come to govern RFID usage there as well).

However, recent history suggests that the FTC will not be inclined to exercise its authority—which is discretionary—to take these kinds of steps on its own initiative. The reasons are several:

- Companies that feel the rules go too far—and there would be many of them if the rules have teeth—will sue to overturn them in federal court, a process that normally takes at least a couple of years. In the meantime, they probably would succeed in having implementation if the rules stayed by the trial court.
- The business community would lobby Congress for relief (though this could also provide a vehicle for the passage of legislative provisions they oppose) either through legislation overturning some or all of the rules (legislation originating in the Commerce Committees, which have jurisdiction over the FTC Act) or through appropriations legislation denying the agency funding to continue the development process or to implement some or all of the rules. Both techniques are time honored.
- The degree of deference accorded independent agencies like the FTC in the past has diminished over the last 25 years, with both political parties embracing deregulation (though not necessarily equally). In the current political climate, business would find many in Congress who would publicly excoriate the agency for a heavy-handed attempt to

cripple a wonderful new technology by imposing requirements that are said to deliver little benefit to consumers.

- In practical terms, the FTC's freedom of movement is maximized when different political parties control the House, Senate, or Administration. It can then play one against the other, usually positioning its initiatives to give one party an opportunity to score political points with the media and the public by coming to the agency's defense while accusing its rival of being the servant of big business. This practice has often prevented or weakened legislation that would have overturned regulations or denied agency funding.
- The regulatory development process would start with hearings and move through three or four administrative stages with petitions for reconsideration, and so on. This is an involved, arduous and expensive task—especially in an area such as RFID, which would be expected to generate large volumes of comment—with no guarantee that any resulting regulation would be sustainable.

Given the make-up of the Commission, we should not expect to see it suddenly turn activist in the next four years. Normally, it is risk averse enough that it would press for additional, clear legislative authority before proposing to regulate broadly in an area where it has no presence.

However, it has an informal working relationship with Congress that could allow it to play a useful, even formal, role without further legislation. That role hinges on the approval of key members of Congress. This could be expressed via letter from committee leaders requesting or supporting the agency's move to start proceedings in the RFID space or even to take some broadly described action. Alternatively, it could occur through discreet consultations by which the agency could assure itself that as it moves forward it will have the support of committee leaders who can speak in its defense and oppose legislative attempts to undermine its initiative. However, it's hard to imagine the FTC announcing its intent to regulate RFID without protecting its flank via one or the other of these approaches.

Perhaps more realistic, and thus more important in the near term, is the role the FTC can play without regulating broadly in the first place. While it cannot compel a company to commit to a notice and consent scheme or force design features to meet consumer concerns, it has the power to require companies to adhere to privacy commitments they make to consumers. Thus, if a retailer pledges that no RFID data will link to personal information or that it will do so only for a narrow purpose, and violates its own pledge, the agency can order it to comply and can get judicial enforcement if necessary. Likewise, if the company assures consumers that its chips are deactivated post-purchase and they are not, it risks an enforcement action.

As noted earlier, this role is helpful but not without serious shortcomings. Problems arise from the fact that the FTC's authority is discretionary and its resources are limited. Thus, it chooses not to pursue many of the violations that are presented to it. Further, its normal enforcement course is to investigate carefully and negotiate at length a reprimand of the wrong-doer and a promise that it will sin no more. It may impose a fine that in the context of large businesses is usually nominal. For many companies, the risk to reputation is more important than any of the formal FTC sanctions. In any event, agency prosecution is not an optimal solution for such tasks as quickly stopping the hemorrhage of sensitive transactional data into unauthorized channels. This brings us to the second set of problems.

Agency prosecution of a voluntary pledge violation is not possible at all unless a company has taken affirmative steps that subject it to the jurisdiction of the law. For example, if it avoids making any statements about its privacy policies and practices, its RFID system can generate PI data that it can use as it sees fit, as long as it does not run afoul of other laws, and those are likely few and not broadly protective.[35]

The real shame under either scenario—Congress or the FTC—is that the new technology is global, and competing policy requirements among nations may hinder its deployment and increase its costs. Considerations for both international harmonization and timeliness point to policy development led by the private sector but involving a full spectrum of stakeholders, resulting in design and usage guidelines that are acceptable to governments in leading markets. An international organization like EPCglobal, under the UCC/GS1 umbrella, is ideally positioned for the task. However, if in the end it cannot manage to craft and enforce such a standard, there's little reason to expect any not-yet-conceived private-sector initiative to succeed in a time frame that will forestall a national/regional governmental splintering of RFID public policies.

Snapshot of Current Status

Let's now consider where we are on the RFID policy path: Business is still educating itself though the EPC-compliant industry segment is engaged on issues within its space. Overall, there is still considerable variance in opinion over what the real level of consumer concern is, or should be, and over what combination

---

35. ECPA governs not only government but also anyone improperly intercepting or accessing electronic data; however, its application to RFID is uncertain. It does not cover the gathering and use by an RFID user of data generated by its *own* system, which of course is the case with most planned consumer applications.

(and definition) of notice, choice, access, etc., is practical and desirable. Business RFID feasibility trials in public settings, once often problematical from a public-issues perspective, seem to be maturing, at least within the EPC community. However, outside the EPCglobal supply-chain sector, no group of companies is attempting to grapple with questions of what limits on the technology (via design features), or its uses (via codes of conduct) will be necessary to maximize public acceptance of RFID at the individual product level.

In the meantime, organizations such as the Electronic Privacy Information Center (EPIC) and Consumers Against Supermarket Privacy Invasion and Numbering (CASPIAN) have generated significant publicity for doubts about leaving the technology unregulated and criticized the design of several pilot programs in particular.[36] Indeed these two, joined by other domestic and foreign organizations on November 13, 2003, issued a policy statement acknowledging the benefits of the technology but expressing concern for its abuse and demanding implementation be delayed until a study of its implications has been performed (www.privacyrights.org/ar/RFIDposition.htm). They have been aided from time to time by corporate missteps.

In the government sector, states often lead on populist issues (e.g., California and Utah bills that made some progress during 2004 sessions). However, states generally give the federal government time to address an issue that obviously benefits from a national, if not international, resolution. Indeed, federal policymakers began considering RFID issues, chiefly privacy, with an FTC workshop on June 21, 2004, titled, "Radio Frequency IDentification: Applications and Implications for Consumers,"[37] shortly followed by a hearing on July 14, 2004, before the Subcommittee on Commerce, Trade, and Consumer Protection of the House Energy and Commerce Committee, titled, "Radio Frequency Identification (RFID) Technology: What the Future Holds for Commerce, Security, and the Consumer."[38]

Both events are milestones in the development of the policy debate in the United States. As noted earlier, neither is likely to lead to immediate formal action—a good thing considering the complexity and delicacy of the issues—but both provided opportunities for assessing the need for action and the kinds of responses that might be appropriate. The FTC Workshop was followed by the issuance of a Staff Report[39] on March 8, 2005. While mostly a useful recap of the Workshop testimony and submitted comments, the Report goes on record acknowledging consumer privacy and security concerns. Recognizing that both the technology and its applications are evolving rapidly, it does not signal an intent to enter a

---

36. Though Wal-Mart's 2004 trials, by most accounts, were well-conducted and drew respect.
37. www.ftc.gov/bcp/workshops/rfid
38. http://energycommerce.house.gov/108/Hearings/07142004hearing1337/hearing.htm
39. http://www.ftc.gov/os/2005/03/050308rfidrpt.pdf

regulatory phase. Rather, it recognizes the utility of self-regulation, at the same time observing the need for an accountability mechanism. Finally, it recommends companies strive for transparency in giving consumers notice and choice, though the choice it discusses is simply that of retaining or discarding a product RFID tag and not that of enabling the creation of PI data.[40] While this encouragement of business to respond to consumer concerns is helpful, as expected the Report reaches no conclusions and positions its "guidance" in the nature of advice rather than direction (as is proper at this stage).

In the House hearing, notable was the statement of Cliff Stearns (R-FL), chair of the House subcommittee holding the hearing, which recognized consumer privacy concerns and the potential for misuse of the system and of the data it generates.[41] Naturally, it is far too early to make forecasts based on such initial fact-finding inquiries.[42]

Policy Prescriptions

Although I have voiced opinions about the course of policy development, I have not focused on ultimate policy answers, either those I think are wisest or those I think most achievable. I will leave more detailed proposals to my co-authors who

---

40. Id., p. 21: "Based on the Workshop discussions and comments submitted from technology experts, RFID users, privacy advocates, and consumers, Commission staff agrees that industry initiatives can play an important role in addressing privacy concerns raised by certain RFID applications. The staff believes that the goal of such programs should be transparency. For example, when a retailer provides notice to consumers about the presence of RFID tags, the notice should be clear, conspicuous, and accurate. The notice should advise consumers if an RFID tag or reader is present and if the technology is being used to collect personally identifiable information about consumers. This clarity is particularly important when a disclosure concerns an unfamiliar technology, as is the case with RFID. Similarly, if a company's program provides consumers with the option of removing the RFID tag, the company's practices should make that option easy to exercise by consumers. However, given the variation in RFID applications, translating these goals into concrete steps may be challenging and should occur in a way that allows flexibility to develop the best methods to address consumer privacy concerns." (Citations omitted.) Note that though the Report states it represents staff's views and not the Commissioners', the Commission voted 5–0 to authorize its release, thus signaling its comfort with this early-stage communication of advice.
41. Senator Patrick Leahy, ranking Democrat on the Senate Judiciary Committee and one of the most knowledgeable and engaged members of Congress on technology issues, expressed interest in RFID issues in a March 2004 Georgetown University Law Center speech, "The Dawn of Micro Monitoring: Its Promise and Its Challenges to Privacy and Security." http://leahy.senate.gov/press/200403/032304.html
42. As this book went to print, the Department of Commerce also convened the second in an annual series of workshops on RFID (April 6, 2005, in Washington, D.C.). While workshops focused mostly on the evolution of the technology, there was a panel on the privacy and security issues raised by RFID. As I understand it, this workshop was for the purpose of information exchange and consensus development, and is not targeted at a regulatory role. While I was out of town and unable to attend, National Journal's Technology Daily reported: "Industry panelists chaffed at suggestions that retailers should notify buyers of RFID use, and most disagreed with the idea of allowing users to voluntarily turn off the tags." It may be that subsequent reports, and the actual panel statements, when available, will be more nuanced than suggested here.

have advanced them and comment on what I believe to be essential elements of a successful, beneficial RFID use policy. The following apply specifically to consumer applications, since that is where most of the policy heat will be generated, but are easily adapted to the B2B context:

- Information transparency. Consumers must be informed about the presence and function of RFID tags in products they purchase or rent and of those in their environment if the latter can generate personally identifiable or sensitive information. They need a similar level of knowledge about the presence of readers that can generate PI or sensitive data. A broad public education campaign will be necessary, intense at first, decreasing over time to a steady background level. This campaign will need to be mounted and funded by industry, either via individual companies or through associations.
- Individual risk management. When faced with an enormously powerful and sophisticated technology administered by organizations that are not trusted to put consumer interests above their own, consumers genuinely concerned about a business practice or product either want to have sufficient control to protect themselves or want control to be exercised by another who can be trusted to look out for them. This suggests two general options (an approach that does not fall into one of these is not likely to be viable over time):
  - User empowerment. A good RFID use policy will provide consumers choices about technology implications that are important to them *and means of effectuating those choices.* Predictably, this may require technology features that would afford the choice of disabling a tag or facilitate the individual's choice to access the RFID-generated PI that has been collected, etc. A transition phase may be appropriate here just as it is under the preceding element. After a certain level of trust has been built up over time, consumers may no longer care about some options, whereas others will have become permanent fixtures.
  - Government empowerment. As an alternative or supplement to a purely voluntary policy, consumer doubts can be addressed via governmental regulation or governmentally enforced self-regulation.
- Fulfillment of consumer expectations, the touchstone. It's not about what any of us think consumers ought to expect. Consumers, not managers, define consumer expectations. If customers expect a certain level of disclosure and learn they didn't get it, they'll get angry. If consumers are told a chip was deactivated, and learn it was only partially deactivated, credibility of the technology will suffer. And they'll get angry. A business's response should not be to ignore widespread expectations it doesn't agree with but to educate consumers to its viewpoint and, if it fails, concede.
- Policy-related performance standards. Performance is no less vital in policy than in business processes. The fact that a design feature is intended

primarily to serve a policy goal—a tag disabling capability for example—does not mean that it can be implemented satisfactorily on a "hit or miss" basis. Nor does the *adoption of a policy* prohibiting the creation of certain types of PI data complete the task. Meaningful standards must be set. Monitoring mechanisms must be implemented, and the integrity of the system must be verified periodically to ensure that it meets set targets. The alternative, at least for issues of real concern, is a kind of strict-liability, zero-tolerance approach that no commercial entity will welcome.

▪ Enforceability, the Achilles' Heel of most private-sector self-regulatory systems. The most responsive policy scheme in the world will have no value unless business complies with it. Many companies may feel their reputations are so valuable that they will adhere both to the letter and spirit of whatever code of conduct they subscribe to, though recent corporate misdoing even by icons of the U.S. economy is not reassuring. Regardless, competitive and cost pressures being what they are, others will not behave unless there is a sufficiently negative consequence attached to noncompliance. There are three main approaches:

• Pure self-regulation—rarely effective. Administering organizations usually act only on complaints rather than conduct a monitoring program, are reluctant to discipline even clear cases of transgression, conduct their actions outside the public view, and often take a long time, if not forever, to render decisions, all the while letting the bad actor continue its conduct unrestrained. Thus, these kinds of systems are most sustainable when they address issues the public is not that concerned with or address areas of activity in which the public doesn't see any good alternatives; that is, where more attractive solutions are not politically achievable or are not likely to work.[43]

---

43. It has been suggested that a business-formed nonprofit group like TRUSTe could administer business best practices or a code of conduct (www.truste.com). It is not clear how such a model would work in the RFID context. In theory, when the group withdraws its approval from a company, consumers will shun the offender's products or refuse to do business with it—a kind of boycott that presumably induces companies to toe the line. This works best when the company and the consumer are directly linked. However, the movement of products and data through a pervasive RFID environment, much of it "out of sight," detaches companies from consumers, undermining the theory, and companies will know it. For example, consider violations of privacy in a retail post-purchase or purchase-by-mail context. What if a tag or reader manufacturer is a certifying-group member, signifying that it follows certain design or use requirements, and subsequently it becomes known that it's not in compliance? The consumer has no effective way to boycott the tag or reader vendor and will not know on what products which manufacturer's tags are affixed. Do irate purchasers refuse to deal further with the retailer itself? Not likely, if it apologizes and promises to do better. Or what of the host of a database service for collecting RFID data (VeriSign has just announced such a service) that fails to adhere to the guidelines? Consumers do not deal with database companies directly, so should they refuse transactions with any other company that uses its services? This is not a realistic scenario and holds little promise as a satisfactory response to consumer RFID concerns. Intervening factors could help, such as a publicity and boycott campaign organized by advocacy groups, but reliance on a system that does not contain within itself the elements necessary for success seems problematic.

- Enforcement by a government agency of voluntary pledges—can supplement or substitute for the voluntary commitment option. This is the Federal Trade Commission option mentioned earlier. Some of the states have similar consumer protection legislation that may serve as a foundation for government enforcement.
- Private-sector leverage. In an environment in which participants depend on a license(s) by an organization holding key assets, including patents or copyright and trademark interests, that organization can condition the grant of licenses on the agreement by licensees to operate within the environment only in compliance with policy conditions it sets forth. This is particularly attractive when the organization itself represents different business and nonbusiness interests, such as vendors, users, commercial, government; and where it has the capability of including input from policy experts, consumers and advocates. This is the EPCglobal model.

- The flexibility to adapt to the evolution of mass-market RFID. Within the EPC context, the nonpowered read-only data chip for EPC product tags is the first of several chip versions of basic through advanced designs. Additional chip types coming on line now and in the future will incorporate additional capabilities already available in non-EPC limited-use specialty applications, including self-contained power, programmability, and environmental sensors, allowing use in more applications. Use policy must continue to be reviewed and adapted to keep pace with these changes.

- International application. While a patchwork of privacy and other requirements among nations may not eliminate some of the key benefits of RFID technology, differing levels of issue sensitivity among governments, and differing traditions of regulation, could slow the spread of the technology, complicate its design, limit its innovation, and increase its cost. Thus a primary goal of policy development should be to develop rules within a mechanism not sponsored by any one nation, a mechanism that can produce a widely acceptable, widely replicable result. The UCC/GS1 administration of the uniform bar code is a valuable precedent. However, governance of bar code technology, with which UCC/GS1 is familiar, has not raised RFID's breadth or depth of issues, largely because it is a more limited, noninteractive technology that traditionally has not involved the creation of personally identifiable information, except for the shopping-affinity programs. Thus, UCC/GS1 has not felt the need to insert itself into these kinds of policy issues on the bar-code side.

The Case for, and Limits of, EPCglobal Leadership

It is clear that RFID public policy will best be developed by a process that:

- Has an international character, thus allowing it to sidestep most of the jurisdictional issues that limit individual national responses, in favor of a uniform global approach
- Avoids government regulation to the extent possible[44]
- Is founded on sufficient influence over market participants that will ensure a level of compliance that approaches or exceeds that of government regulation
- Although led by the businesses with the greatest stake in the success of the technology, engages the broader policy community on the basis of respect and mutual interest
- Sets as its guiding principle the creation of public acceptance of and trust in the technology through the accommodation of legitimate social interests

Other than EPCglobal, there is no forum capable of staging such a process to address the issues and ensure the implementation of design and policy requirements in the reasonably near future. The licensing levers of EPCglobal are clearly the best ones to underpin a satisfactory self-regulatory system.

However, EPCglobal does not see itself endowed with either the mandate or resources to prescribe usage rules to address all RFID issues. Its mission is focused on supply-chain applications rather than consumer applications. True, it has issued guidelines on labeling of tags applied to individual retail products, for example, so that consumers can be informed of their presence. However, this is not because it has assumed the role of overseeing the uses to which EPC licensed products may eventually be put. Rather when tags are placed on products intended for retail sale, it is clear consumers will be interacting with them while they are still in the supply chain,

---

44. This has not been the natural instinct outside countries like the United States, but even in nations and regions with a tradition favoring government regulation, self-regulation is generally deemed preferable if it can meet the basic expectations of the public. Self-regulation possesses the benefits of quicker development and deployment, more agile response to future developments, less tendency to restrict business practices more than necessary to serve public demands, and lower business and administrative costs, among others.

Other Industry Alternatives?

No industry group is currently taking up the mantle of policy development for non-EPC RFID applications, whether within the supply chain or not. This is a serious problem for those who prefer government regulation only as a last resort and for those who are eager to see the public welcome RFID consumer-level applications.

Admittedly, to the extent RFID suppliers and users individually on their own initiative follow the EPCglobal approach of seeking design features that minimize consumer concerns, they will promote consumer acceptance of RFID and reduce the risk of government intervention. However, even those features will not address every issue, and we have to expect that many companies pursuing their own RFID technologies will have little interest in limiting their products in ways that may cost them customers, or at the users' level, in voluntarily foregoing uses of RFID products in ways that hamper their commercial activities and require them to forego profits. It can be argued that purely voluntary best business practices and codes of conduct can achieve wider coverage, but no one is currently involved in that task for post-sale consumer uses. In any event, I remain convinced that such unenforceable alternatives have little future, at least in Europe, if not in Japan and a number of other nations that already are looking at RFID policy.

So, what are the business-side options? Besides EPCglobal, the most likely pan-industry forum that could mobilize to address RFID consumer-level usage rules of the road would seem to be ITAA. It has international affiliates and is a veteran of negotiating both federal and international codes of conduct. Other organizations could set up the structure to tackle this project, but ITAA already has an RFID policy committee that could move into or spin off a broad industry-consensus function.

In the absence of any comprehensive initiative, Industry may gravitate to a piecemeal, sector-by-sector process. Deferring action until retail, financial, healthcare or other RFID applications are deployed, trade groups for each affected area of commerce can on separate timetables assess the need for rules in their lines of business, develop consensus among their members, and draw up voluntary codes that reflect their individual perspectives. This approach has potential weaknesses:

- Because it is driven by the pressure generated by applications that are about to enter the marketplace, it will in most cases lag the pace of the debate, which probably will not wait for applications to come to market;
- It prolongs the policy debate—similar issues and arguments are hashed out time after time—and not to the benefit of industry's reputation and image;

- It lacks the broad buy-in, commitment, and momentum to give government policymakers the confidence that they should continue to forebear legislating or regulating.

Or even less promisingly, no one takes up the task, perhaps because of internal dissent or organizational lack of vision or resources, and policymakers eventually turn to policy formulation hindered by a discordant barrage of lobbying from individual companies and small, special purpose coalitions. A united business community would be much more effective in staking out and achieving key goals related to the usefulness of RFID.

Though these last two may be the default scenarios, and therefore the most likely, I believe it is worth the effort to replace them with an organized, broad-based industry consensus initiative. The result will be an outcome not only more favorable to business, but more responsive to consumer concerns and more likely to be able to offer them the widest range of benefits from this revolutionary technology.

Current EPCglobal Policy

EPCglobal has at length issued privacy guidelines, posted on its Web site. They declare in favor of consumer notice and choice, a responsible step, though in very general terms leaving much flexibility with individual technology users. While there is much to be said for flexibility, especially when consumer applications are just in the testing stage, it must be carefully gauged, since it can set the stage for companies less concerned with meeting consumer expectations to push the boundaries. Security and data retention, a critical area in preventing compromises to PI data, is required to be in conformance with current law. Given gaps in current law, some of which are under current Congressional scrutiny as a result of the compromised data in the cases of ChoicePoint, Lexis-Nexis, and others, the organization may do well to look at a general but more substantive successor statement, if it isn't already doing so.

Further, it does appear that EPCglobal will monitor the adoption of the Guidelines and provide a forum in which consumers and companies can air differences. The assumption of this role, which is not at all automatic or inevitable, is constructive. It is not clear whether EPCglobal is prepared to move beyond facilitating resolution to actually imposing it if necessary. The latter option would do much to provide the "accountability" described in the FTC Staff Report's guidance for RFID policy, as well as reassure EU regulators, in particular, that the EPCglobal policy scheme within its space is a viable alternative to government mandates.

In any event, it seems the policy development process is ongoing, since the Guidelines are described as a "work in progress." This apparently refers to two developmental factors: first that companies are at differing levels of awareness, understanding, and sophistication, in some cases even with regard to their own internal interests, and the work of arriving at a firm consensus on many points should be given enough time for a real convergence, a real meeting of the minds. Second, as the features and capabilities of the technology evolve, it will be appropriate to continue reviewing and, where appropriate, adjusting the Guidelines to keep pace.

Thus the current Guidelines can be seen as a good snapshot of where the process currently stands in the predeployment stage of the technology and welcomed as a signal of the direction in which EPCglobal will be moving as events progress.

Conclusions

Technology policy development, perhaps more so in the United States than elsewhere, is less the subject of *a priori* reasoning and the consistent application of mandated principles than the product of a case-by-case clash of interests and opportunities. It is a battle for advantage among several categories of actors, all of which believe their success will benefit the larger "public good." This messy process usually results in a slow path to a working consensus. Nevertheless, such struggles evolve in ways that are generally predictable and are influenced by consistent factors internal to each stakeholder group, some of which are discussed in this chapter.

I would not venture to predict the timetable for the resolution of the unusually wide range of issues raised by RFID. But some critical elements are already taking shape, and I will posit a few points against which progress can be measured:

- In the United States, Congress and the Federal Trade Commission, the two leading candidates for generating compulsory regulation, have begun the "fact-finding" phase but are unlikely to act formally before the deployment of widespread, item-level, retail RFID applications, absent other, precipitating factors.
- The prospect of foreign regulation may force Congress and the FTC to issue regulation before product-level rollouts. Depending on the direction taken abroad, both government institutions here as well as the business community may feel it is better to act domestically than rely on an attempt to carve out "safe harbors" or exceptions, as in the case of the European Data Protection Directive.

- It is likely that the law enforcement and intelligence communities will explore access to commercial RFID systems and data with suppliers and users, if they have not done so already. This issue track may develop prior to consumer-level deployment and may advance the timetable for the larger debate.

- Consumer advocates have staked out their positions and voiced demands but will have to rely on fortuitous opportunities (e.g., business announcements or mistakes) to sustain or build momentum through media or online exposure. Of themselves, they have little leverage to push policy development forward.

- Currently, the ball is in industry's court, and among business sectors, retailers have the advantage. Their requirements will drive both the adoption of consumer-level RFID systems and their design features and capabilities. Because of their direct interface with consumers, they are the obvious candidates for making the initial commitments governing data collection and use practices, both for themselves and, via contractual leverage, for spreading those commitments to others downstream who may desire that data.

- Individual companies can continue to "wait and see," taking advantage of the deliberate pace of Congressional and FTC review, or join those seeking to better understand the concerns of consumers and working to develop flexible but meaningful enforceable standards that meet consumer expectations. As far as I am aware, within the supply chain framework, that means working within the EPCglobal framework, the only game in town.

- They should choose to enter the fray, even though they are not compelled to do so now, because their self-interest truly understood is not the evasion of reasonable commitments but the creation of trust and the intelligent acceptance, even embrace, of beneficial RFID applications by consumers. It's not likely consumer attitudes will wait until the rollout of product-level tagging. I believe they will gradually jell over the next couple of years as public awareness of the technology grows and as niche applications are deployed. As argued elsewhere in this book, consumer trust and acceptance will require education and take time to cultivate and must begin now.

- EPCglobal is gaining policy development experience. It has sited participant research laboratories around the world and has invited international corporate memberships precisely in order to give its process and prescriptions credibility in as many markets (and with as many governments) as possible. It is not the only conceivable mechanism for bringing business and other stakeholders together but is the best one available within the space it has staked out. It needs to continue and ensure funding for its policy roles and would do well to give attention to the "accountability" issue.

In closing, I understand the tension between those in business who understand the larger social role, and implications, of technology and those who are driven only by pure economic motives. I believe the former serve their companies better than the latter. I am enthralled by the potential of RFID but also wary of its abuse. I fear that those who spurn solid policy commitments in favor of silence or of insincere, artful rhetoric will end up leading us into abuses with no idea of what they're doing.[45]

I'm looking for integrity, for an attitude of statesmanship in the development of RFID policy, for a willingness to leave money on the table if the result is a technology that is more widely used and more widely accepted. I'm looking for leaders who will forego the use of enticing, even lucrative RFID applications if they don't square with ideals of fair play and fair dealing, who will refuse to abuse the great disparity in technological sophistication between ordinary consumers and modern enterprises. I am confident that in the end, it will work out well, but there's no guarantee and no substitute for hard work, for the commitment of time and resources.

I believe EPCglobal will play a constructive role, and I hope it is a critical one. Its current guidelines are useful in helping shape society's view of what responsible use of the technology means, and in convincing policymakers that self-regulation is worth considering.

The final lesson for business and technology leaders, however, remains one of political pragmatism. If history is any guide, those who engage in the debate over the substance or phrasing of any corporate or industry self-regulatory guidelines will expend much effort trying to arrive at a Solomonic decision that satisfies all the commercial interests around the table. But trying hard, working hard, and gaining industry consensus is not the measure of success. Even the

---

45. As I alluded to earlier, there is a division among business and technology leaders in their sensitivity to public values. In many past cases, those who have sought to address tensions between commerce and values have been stymied by those who are focused only on the next quarter's financial statement. Thus, voluntary corporate commitments to real standards generally have come in the United States only after industry has been put on the defensive by the media, advocates, and policymakers and adverse legislation is threatened. In part, this chain of events is necessary to force disengaged senior executives to focus on policy and to make decisions that only they can make to compromise in some way corporate ability to act (to market, to promote, to exploit every potential resource, etc.) in the service of a long-term social interest. This reluctance to commit to limitations flows not only from the natural entrepreneurial desire for complete freedom to do whatever is necessary to develop new products and services but also from the instinct that it's foolish to limit oneself if one's competitors do not similarly restrain themselves. Again, at some point, the force of public affairs events overcomes these obstacles, and either commitments are made and self-regulation begins addressing public concerns or pressure builds and results in legislation or administrative regulation. I see signs that this crisis-cratered path can be avoided in the RFID environment, and I make this explanation to encourage those who are inclined to ignore public issues to follow, for example, those who are leading EPCglobal policy development.

most widely adopted policy guidelines will not protect anyone who tries to follow them and who still manages to push the consumer "fear" button. When that button is pushed, policymakers respond.

Chapter 7

RFID AND AUTHENTICITY OF GOODS

Marlena Erdos[1]

Introduction

Many proponents of RFID claim that RFID tags ensure the authenticity of consumer goods,[2] pharmaceuticals,[3] and even documents.[4] RFID tags for product authentication are being promoted as "cost-effective to implement, while being prohibitively expensive to replicate illegally."[5]

Low-cost RFID tags emit a unique identifying number[6]—effectively the tag's "name"—when queried by an RFID reader. Given that we are concerned with product authenticity, should we believe a tag (and the good that it is attached to) simply because it claims a particular name? In this chapter, we look at what makes a tag *authenticatable*, or able to prove its identity. We examine the interaction between tag authenticity and authenticity of goods. In particular, we look at an anticounterfeiting scenario that features RFID tags as a centerpiece. We also consider authentication of readers because they are a critical component of any overall system that tries to ensure product authenticity. And we also cover the special issues that arise in authenticating *people* in a multi-enterprise supply chain.

---

1. Marlena Erdos has architected, designed, and implemented secure distributed computing systems for more than a decade.
2. Texas Instruments "Tag-it™" www.ti.com/tiris/docs/news/news_releases/90s/rel01-23-98.shtml.
3. U.S. Food and Drug Administration. Combating Counterfeit Drugs: A Report of the Food and Drug Administration, February 2004. www.fda.gov/oc/initiatives/counterfeit/report02_04.html.
4. www.compukiss.com/populartopics/travel_transhtm/article960.htm.
5. Texas Instruments "Tag-it™" www.ti.com/tiris/docs/news/news_releases/90s/rel01-23-98.shtml.
6. The number is often referred to as an electronic product code (EPC), although in reality, an EPC is in a format specified by EPCglobal Inc., a standards body creating a variety of RFID related technical specifications. www.epcglobalinc.org.

Before we discuss the authenticity of tags and goods, we need to examine a few important concepts in authentication that serve as a foundation for the rest of the chapter.[7] (Readers who have security backgrounds should feel free to go on to the following section.)

A Few Important Concepts in Authentication

For each of the following topics, I provide a bit of background before conveying the main point.

Authentication Involves Secret Data

- Background. Colloquially, authentication is simply a matter of proving that you are who you say you are. To say that an entity is authenticated merely means we have gone through a series of checking steps such that we believe the entity's claimed identity with some assurance. Authentication in itself doesn't mean that the authenticated entity has the "right" to do anything.
- Point. Authentication systems almost always involve the use of secret data, whether that data is called a *password*, *shared secret key*, or *private key*[8]. This is the fundamental concept I want to drive home for our later exploration of authentication issues in RFID.

A lot more than secrets are involved in authentication, but secret data is our main issue. The secret data is combined with some of the message data via an *algorithm* (i.e., a mathematical sequence of steps); the sender and receiver typically engage in a sequence of messages called a *protocol*, whose purpose is to transport the authentication data and also to ensure that a previous legitimate message hasn't been "replayed" by an attacker. Some additional features are usually bundled into authenticated messages, including *integrity mechanisms*, which are the cryptographic equivalent of "tamper evident packaging." Authentication systems can fail because of easy-to-guess secret data, algorithms with "back doors," and "weak" protocols.

---

7. The points below are a "quick and dirty" introduction to some (but not all) important aspects of authentication systems. Readers who are interested in learning more about authentication systems are directed to one of the many fine texts on security.
8. Certain techniques, like biometrics, don't use secret data, but these don't apply to RFID since most of the entities we want to authenticate in RFID (e.g., tags, readers, etc.) aren't biological entities.

The "Key Distribution" Problem

- Background. We'll call the secret data a *key*, and we'll call the message data that has been encrypted with the secret data, *authentication data*. We'll also call a "key" the data that a recipient will use to validate the authentication data. (In some systems, such as PKI, this decrypting key is not secret.) Let's say two parties want to communicate: How does the sender securely transfer the validating key to the recipient when the sender and recipient don't already have a secure way of communicating? This is called the Key Distribution Problem.
- Point. Distributing the key for validating authentication data that's been algorithmically combined[9] with a user's key is an outstanding problem in all authentication systems. Solutions to the Key Distribution Problem exist, but all solutions to date carry high costs for the infrastructure and administration needed to support them. Distributing validation keys is definitely an issue in RFID.

Stolen Keys and Revocation

- Background. An entity's secret data can be compromised, meaning that it's fallen (or even potentially fallen) into the wrong hands. Hence, there's a need to revoke a key just as there's a need to revoke a stolen credit card.
- Point. Dealing with the possible compromise of an entity's key is another outstanding issue in authentication systems. Current schemes for attempting to protect against compromised keys include setting early expiration dates, checking against a locally held list of known compromised keys, and calling out to a validation service. Each solution for dealing with a compromised key requires a fair bit of infrastructure; for example, performing a validation check will typically add many computing cycles and bandwidth, thus making it "expensive." In RFID, time and processing power are both at a premium.

Comment on Authentication Costs

I've mentioned that significant costs and infrastructure are involved in dealing with both the key distribution problem and compromise of an entity's key.

---

9. Shared secret algorithms (e.g., DES, AES) and PKI are technically encryption techniques. Another method commonly referred to as hashed message authentication code (HMAC) combines the secret data with message data using a type of algorithm that isn't "encryption" but yet is secure.

There's no avoiding these costs in an even moderately secure system. This is a seemingly gloomy picture but I prefer to think of it as "fact of life." Authentication is costly, but (to paraphrase a well-known saying) lack of authentication tends to be even costlier!

Authenticity of Tags and Authenticity of Goods

EPC RFID tags identify themselves but do not authenticate themselves.[10] When a reader tries to read RFID tags, it essentially calls out the tag's electronic product code (EPC), and a given tag responds only if the name is its own. However, the reader usually gives only the beginning of the tag's name. This is like the reader calling roll, but saying only, "Speak up if your name begins with H."

The problem here is that any entity—whether legitimate or not—can respond. A tag could claim that its name was the EPC equivalent of anything beginning with H, and the reader would believe it.

Why doesn't an EPC tag authenticate itself? Several reasons: First, for a tag to authenticate itself, it would have to hold secret data. And it would have to use the secret data via a mathematical algorithm[11] to provide proof of identity. The reader, too, would have to have access to the right key for each tag so that it could validate the tag's identity. Mobil Speedpass tags authenticate themselves; EPC tags don't.

Given that the tags are usually provisioned with their EPC by one party (a tag manufacturer or the manufacturer of the goods that are tagged) but are read by readers belonging to entirely distinct parties (e.g., distribution centers and retail stores), there's the matter of distributing the validation keys that are associated with each tag.

But getting the tag keys from the entity that installed them to the business partners that will later read them is not an insurmountable problem. It might cost money and time to distribute the keys needed for validation, but it is certainly feasible: For example, a file containing pairs of EPCs and their associated keys could be sent via secure e-mail or even via postal mail.

---

10. The discussion applies to the low-cost tags that are part of the EPCglobal endeavor. Other tags are being produced, but the EPCglobal tags get the most attention because their low cost makes their use economically feasible for a wide variety of supply chain and retail applications.
11. Either an encryption or keyed hash algorithm.

In this case, the problem is not key distribution but the inability of tags to use keys even if they had them.

To keep costs low, EPC tags do not contain batteries. They get their power from the RF signals that the reader emits as part of querying the tag name. As it turns out, every operation a tag must do to answer the inquiry from the reader uses up some power. Creating and validating authentication data requires a large number of operations and hence a significant amount of power.

Research is being done in creating authentication algorithms, as well as in designing devices that are especially conserving of power.[12] However, current commercial EPC tags cannot in a practical way create authentication data. Nor is there an obvious solution on the horizon to this problem of authenticating EPC tags.

Authenticity of Goods and Anticounterfeiting Measures

The manufacture and distribution of counterfeit goods is a pressing global concern. A particularly worrisome issue is the injection of counterfeit pharmaceutical goods into the supply chain. Counterfeiting is a problem everywhere, but in few other cases are lives more clearly at stake. A number of proposals suggest non-authenticatable EPC tags, along with tamper-evident packaging and operational controls (such as checking for duplicate EPC tags) to help control counterfeiting.

Injection of Counterfeit Goods into the Supply Chain: Two Scenarios

Generally, goods are packed into cases at the manufacturer, shipped to a warehouse, and then sent to a retail store. Additionally, a case of goods may be opened at the warehouse, with only some of its individual items sent to a given retail store, as needed to manage retail inventory. A case of goods may have tamper-evident packaging and also may be tagged. Each item in a case might have its own RFID tag as well.

---

12. Yüksel, K., Kaps, J.P., and Sunar, B. *Universal Hash Functions for Emerging Ultra-Low-Power Networks*. Proceeding of The Communications Networks and Distributed Systems Modeling and Simulation Conference (CNDS), San Diego, CA, January 2004.

Scenario One: RFID's Role in Anticounterfeiting

As an RFID-tagged case leaves the manufacturer, it is scanned, recording both the case's tag and the tags of the individual items inside. The manufacturer also creates a shipping notice listing the goods (and their EPC tags) and sends the shipping notice to the warehouse (perhaps through secured e-mail or even "Web Services"). The manufacturer then updates a central database that lists the EPCs associated with the shipped items. This database tracks the tags and the tagged items. So, for example, the manufacturer will mark the state of shipped items as "Sent to Warehouse," possibly with the location of the warehouse indicated as well.[13]

When the warehouse receives the goods, it scans the case and the item tags. The scanner compares the results of the scan with the shipping notice. The warehouse can thus detect whether it's received the right shipment and whether any goods have been lost or stolen en route (or added, as might happen in a deliberate attempt to harm). The warehouse also checks the central database to make sure the tags (and tagged items) are in the "right" state. In this situation, the state of each item should be "Sent to Warehouse." Any location or identity information in the database should also match the characteristics of the warehouse.

If the warehouse sees an item state that isn't "sent to warehouse," that's a red flag that something is amiss. An item state of "lost," "stolen," or "not yet shipped" might indicate that:

- The goods, while legitimate, have been incorrectly or maliciously removed from the manufacturer site. The check of the shipping notice should have detected this as well.
- The goods are not legitimate. They are counterfeits that have been tagged with EPC tags programmed with the names of legitimate goods. Writable tags make this type of counterfeiting relatively easy.

In this scenario, the tags themselves are not authenticatable. However, the use of the tags in conjunction with a database that tracks the intended state of tagged goods can alert the warehouse to possible criminal activity. A secured database provides an extra level of protection over the electronic shipping notice alone.

Scenario Two: When RFID Tags and a Database Aren't Sufficient

A trucker delivering pharmaceuticals from a manufacturer to a warehouse (or from a warehouse to a retail outlet) is in league with counterfeiters. While the

---

13. I'm using item states that make sense for the example scenario. The actual states that will be kept as part of the EPC network are being developed by the EPCIS working group of EPCglobal.

products are en route, the counterfeiters, with the trucker's cooperation, substitute bottles containing counterfeit drugs for the real ones.

To circumvent the RFID-based controls, the counterfeiters read the EPCs from each legitimate bottle and copy the EPC onto a writable tag on the new bottle. To be sure, the counterfeiters have to counterfeit the bottle and its tamper-evident packaging. But for certain high-priced pharmaceuticals, experience outside the United States has shown that it is well worth the time and expense needed to do this well.

End result: The counterfeiters have legitimate pharmaceuticals that can be sold on the black market. And the warehouse (or the retail outlet) that receives the counterfeit drugs is none the wiser because the database check on the state of each tag works out just fine.

How Authenticatable Tags Could Help

Authenticatable tags hold secret data that they use (to create authentication data) but that they never release. A tag with secret data cannot be correctly duplicated.[14] Counterfeiters simply would not be able to create tags that properly authenticate themselves to RFID readers. Even if the counterfeiters were in league with the trucker and the database of tags and tagged goods indicated that everything was OK, the recipient of the counterfeit items could know immediately that something was very wrong.

Note that each authenticatable tag must be intimately bound up with the tamper-evident packaging on its associated product so that an attempt to refill (say) a legitimate bottle with counterfeit pills destroys the tag.

Switching the Security Burden

Anticounterfeiting schemes that rely on the database of tagged items rather than the authenticity of tags have switched the security burden from the tags to the database. For the anticounterfeiting scheme described above to work properly, access to the database that contains the tags' state must be tightly and properly controlled. But how can you control access to a database in a multi-enterprise endeavor such as a supply chain?

It isn't easy: The access control system must allow many people from different companies to update tag (and product) state while denying access to unauthorized

---

14. Strictly speaking, devices that hold secret data can in fact be duplicated, but only at a prohibitively high cost in time and money.

persons. Such multi-enterprise-, or "federation-", capable systems are not yet in full commercial production, although much work is being done to develop them. We'll look at this issue—generally referred to as federation—later in the chapter.

Authentication of Readers

Authenticating Readers to Tags

Some vendors of RFID-based systems claim that their systems protect against theft and counterfeiting because their tags respond only to their readers. But if the tags are batteryless EPC tags, this claim is false. Anyone with the ability to listen to radio transmissions of tags and readers can duplicate the protocols used to read a tag and thus impersonate a legitimate reader. There's simply no good way to determine whether or not an entity is entitled to perform an action, such as read a tag, without first performing authentication of that entity.

Can readers authenticate themselves to tags even if the tags can't authenticate themselves to the readers? Currently, the answer is no. Tags can't perform even the "cheapest" types of authentication algorithms (i.e., hashed MACs).

Let's assume for argument's sake that tags can perform hashed MAC authentication. But even in that case, there are problems. Inexpensive EPC tags simply don't have the memory to store lists of reader identities and the corresponding identity validation keys. And the tags don't have the power to call out to an enterprise server to get this information from a database.

A future possibility is that a tag could hold a few reader names and their corresponding validation keys. Note that for such a tag to be read by any of hundreds of readers, these reader "identities" couldn't be unique. Multiple readers would have to have the same identity. The identity is in effect a "role," meaning that the identity describes a job function, such as "incoming stock RFID reader," rather than being a reader's unique name.

This use of reader roles would provide some measure of security: The tag would respond only to readers that could authenticate themselves into a known role. (In this case, the very fact that a reader could authenticate itself to a tag would mean that it was "authorized" to receive the tag's identifier.)

But there's no way ever to revoke a compromised reader identity and key. If an attacker had one of the reader role identities *and* its key, there would be no way to stop the attacker from being mistakenly authorized to read tags. If the compromised reader's identity and corresponding secret data were publicly disseminated, any protection against unauthorized reading of tags would be lost.

Authenticating Readers Within an Enterprise

Enterprises hope to streamline the process of tracking goods as they move through the supply chain. Using RFID readers to read tags on pallets and cases can be faster, cheaper, and more accurate than manually hand-scanning bar codes. Some intended uses for RFID readers and tags include tracking "shrink" (i.e., loss of items), noting entry and exit of items, and locating stored items in a warehouse. The important point is that many organizations will begin to rely on the data from the readers rather than data collected by humans.

Just as tags can be impersonated, so can readers. If an organization intends to rely on reader data for mission-critical applications, it must have some way to ensure that its readers are legitimate and not "rogue" entities installed by attackers (who are possibly company insiders).

A rogue reader could make you think that you've received goods that you've ordered when in fact those goods were stolen en route or simply haven't arrived. Alternatively, a rogue reader could make you believe you've received goods you never wanted.

A rogue reader operating on a more subtle level might simply not read certain EPCs, thus forcing an enterprise to go back to costly hand methods to account for incoming and outgoing stock.

Most likely, a rogue reader will be discovered—for example, when another system has to deal with the phantom goods the reader reported on. But time, effort, and money will have been wasted in the interim.

Authentication of Users Across the Supply Chain (Federation)

Authentication of users in a multi-enterprise supply chain poses some challenges that are distinct from authentication within a single enterprise.

In a supply chain, goods can "flow" in a number of ways—via trucks, rail, ship, airplane, or a combination of these. In our first supply chain scenario, personnel at the manufacturer, warehouse, and retail store looked at and also updated a central database to keep track of the "state" of the goods. In practice, it's also possible that conveyer personnel (e.g., truckers) might also be charged with tracking tasks. The upshot is that many people from many companies "touch" the database, either to read it or to both read and write it.

Here's the problem: Most existing authentication systems know only how to authenticate users who have *registered* with that system. In general, authentication systems have a registry that holds each user's login name and the validation key that is matched to a user's secret data. In a supply chain, the personnel belong to many different companies and typically are registered with only the authentication system of their employer.

An overly simple solution is to have everyone involved in the supply chain register with the authentication system used by the central tracking database. But this is highly burdensome for both the administrators of the authentication system and the users who need to view and update databases that track goods. Here's why:

Burden on System Administrators

It's highly impractical to register everyone who might need to update the tracking database. First, how does an administrator determine that a given person— for example, one who claims to be an employee of the warehouse—is the correct individual, works at the warehouse, and is entitled to view or update the database? Simply validating that a person deserves a login and access is time intensive and hence expensive.

Also, how would administrators handle employee turnover at each company that accesses the database? They would need to delete users who no longer are employees of partner companies and add users who are new employees or in new roles that would require more or less database access. While individual registration of users might work for a pilot project, it doesn't scale up to a real-life supply chain potentially involving thousands, or even tens of thousands of users.

Burden on Users

While there's a central database for tracking a given item, there will likely be many distinct databases for tracking diverse goods. A user in the supply chain might have to register with multiple authentication systems. As people who have had to "register" with multiple Web sites know, management of all of one's user names and passwords is cumbersome and error prone. Many users, in an attempt to simplify their lives, resort to tactics such as using the same password for most or all entities they communicate with or writing down names and passwords on notes attached to their computer monitors. Suffice it to say that neither of these tactics is "secure." In the case of deliberate contamination of goods, such lack of security could be catastrophic.

The Answer Is Federation

In a *federated system*, companies register with each other rather than have their users cross-register. Federated registrations occur at the corporate level via both technical means (exchange of validation keys) and legal means (contracts). Individual users no longer need to register at foreign sites that are part of the federation. Instead, when a user wishes to contact a Web page at a partner institution in the federation, the user's own institution sends identity data (and possibly role data or other attributes) to the partner.

Current federation standards (such as SAML, Shibboleth, and Liberty) accomplish this process through clever use of Web-based protocols, making the process "transparent" to the user. Current federation standards also employ secret data and, typically, public key encryption algorithms for both authentication of the communicating institutions and tamper-evident packaging of protocol messages. However, many federation issues still need to be resolved, including agreement on name formats, agreement on what attributes are sent and the meanings thereof, identity mapping procedures, and the ability to maintain accountability.

Conclusions

Authenticity of goods is a pressing problem, particularly in the pharmaceutical industry, where stolen, mislabeled, or falsified drugs could cause catastrophic results. RFID tags can be a very helpful part of an overall system that authenticates and tracks products as they move through the supply chain. But it isn't a silver bullet in the fight against counterfeit goods. Critical aspects in ensuring product authenticity go beyond the RFID tag and include ways RFID readers, databases (and other supply-chain systems), and humans are authenticated and authorized.[15]

The multi-enterprise aspect of the global supply chain makes authentication and authorization that much harder. While technology providers know how to

---

15. Another hugely important aspect of RFID and product authenticity is how an RFID tag is securely attached to the product. This topic deserves its own full discussion.

solve most of the problems from a technical standpoint, real-world operation of a secure supply chain will require not just technology but many and varied agreements among manufacturers, distributors, retailers, technology providers, and also government agencies.

Much work is being done, but much work needs to be done. In the meantime, any company that claims product authenticity because it attaches RFID tags to goods must be looked at with a jaundiced eye.

Chapter 8

LOCATION AND IDENTITY: A BRIEF HISTORY

Michael R. Curry[1]

Introduction

When we think of "location," we usually imagine something quite simple. I can determine my location with a GPS receiver, an RFID tag can signal it, or a CCTV camera can capture it. Or someone can just look up my address in a telephone book. In every case, we could from that original datum move from the initial spot to my neighborhood, my town, my state, my country, then Earth, the solar system, the Milky Way, the universe. It's all the same, all ultimately comprehensible in terms of some standard metric.

Or is it? In this chapter, I suggest that it is *not* the same, that in our everyday lives we in fact appeal to multiple and very different ways of conceptualizing location. We learn if a particular car will fit in a particular parking space, if a particular sofa is too big for a room, if something is in the wrong location not by using a tape measure, but by exposure to a series of examples or by trial and error. And even where we can in principle later quantify those judgments, we seldom rely on such measurements. Most of what we know about places and location begins and ends with habitual, everyday activity.

This is not an idle matter. The ways we define our location always have been closely related to the ways we define our identity. And the ways we understand both location and identity—human and otherwise—are connected to the technologies that we use.

---

1. Michael Curry is a professor at the University of California, Los Angeles, Department of Geography.

When we change the technologies that we use to determine and communicate our locations, by default we change how we think about our relationships to those places. Will the use of RFID and related locational technologies change our way of thinking about *ourselves*? Or is the way we think about our physical presence, planted in a physical place, too organic—too "human"—to be altered by technology?

This chapter makes these concepts clearer by laying out a brief history of the technologies of location. The evolution of these technologies has by no means followed a simple, linear trajectory; indeed, systems for determining location have typically incorporated a complex mixture of sometimes contradictory elements, each exerting a different set of forces. Against the similarly complex background of technologies used to determination identity, we shall see that seemingly minor technological changes can at times have unexpected and even major consequences. Hence, as we consider the privacy and other social, cultural, moral, and legal implications of technologies such as RFID tags, we find that the matter is by no means simple or clear-cut.

Place and Identity in a World of Habits and Symbols

If you are asked how to describe *where* or *who/what* something or someone is, it seems obvious that you are doing two different things. *Where*, or *location*, requires tools like a sextant or a GPS receiver. *What/who*, or *identity*, requires fingerprints, a botanical guide, or perhaps a gas chromatograph. But if we look back to a world in which such specialized technologies were absent—the classical world, for example—we find that the methods used to identify a person or a place were very often *identical*.

Fundamentally, this remains true today. I may identify a house, a wrench, or a friend "just by looking." If asked how I knew which house was which, I'd likely respond, "I just know what it looks like," or "I'd recognize it a mile away." The term "physiognomy" is not reserved for describing the human face: Students of the landscape sometimes use that term to refer to a scene or view, which too can have a kind of face.

This form of identification relies fundamentally on *vision*. We identify something based on its external appearance. Someone sees my face and says, "Oh, Michael Curry," or sees a mountain and says, "Mount Fuji."

Because it appears so simple, we have a tendency to imagine that visual inspection is the most fundamental form of identification and that all other means derive from it. But there is another basic way of identifying both people and places that is not bound to the visual, and that does not necessarily share vision's distanced relation with its objects. This means of identification *relies on the relationship of the body to the place or object in question.*[2]

These means of determining identity and distance hark back to two classic ways of thinking about places: the *topographic* and the *chorographic*. The topographic is concerned primarily with places insofar as a person is moving through them, describing what is seen along the way. A traveler's account is typically a topographic account of a place, wherein the experience of the traveler is as important as the description of the place traveled. In modern terms, people are describing topographic location when they discuss their commutes in terms of minutes, rather than miles.

Chorographic descriptions were first a formal way to describe large-scale climate zones and the like. Concern is with the nature of those places taken as wholes, as though seen all at once, and from the outside.[3] Chorographic descriptors speak of a place as though it is of a piece: Is this place wet or dry? Dangerous or safe?

Note that neither topographic nor chorographic description relies on technology. No maps, written lists, latitude and longitude, street addresses, or other familiar means of defining or characterizing location need be used.

But classical accounts of people and places are not merely of antiquarian interest. They illustrate a way of thinking about the world in which any discourse about places may also be a discussion of people and objects and vice versa. Is a description of New England complete without a description of New Englanders? Would a New Englander dropped on a desert island soon begin to act differently? What about a Fijian who finds himself in Harvard Square?

These questions provide a counter-example to the prevailing modern belief that people and objects are all potentially isolable and mobile, that we live in a world in which nothing has a place where it really belongs, and that we can talk about people and objects and places in ways very different from one another.

The "antiquated" notion that important interconnections exist among objects, people, and places is in fact of practical interest because it is also at the heart of much recent discussion of new locational technologies. Current discourse on

---

2. Golledge, R.G. *Wayfinding Behavior: Cognitive Mapping and Other Spatial Processes*. Baltimore: Johns Hopkins University Press. 1999.
3. Curry, M.R. "Discursive Displacement and the Seminal Ambiguity of Space and Place," in Lievrouw, L. and Livingstone, S. (eds.). *Handbook on New Media*. Beverly Hills: Sage. 2002. pp. 502–517.

the social and cultural implications of locational technologies states that *where* we live, work, and shop is important information. When we acquire such information about people, we know something important about them. Is the fact that I live at 1835 Pandora Avenue just a contingent matter, one I might change just by getting in my car? Or does it *matter* that I live at that address? Does learning my address mean learning something important about me as a person?

"Location, location, location!" chant the Realtors, and they are right. We as a society are not so disassociated from ourselves that our location doesn't matter. And the question "Where are you from?" is more than small talk—it is a way of fixing a person's place on the Earth and giving that person substance.

Locational Technologies

Ptolemy and the Development of Classified Space

The most familiar locational technology is certainly the map. But as a locational device, even a map relies on other, more basic, technologies.

The traditional way of thinking about the history of the map begins with Homer's description of the shield of Achilles:

> He made the earth upon it, and the sky, and the sea's water, and the tireless sun, and the moon waxing into her fullness, and on it all the constellations that festoon the heavens, the Pleiades and the Hyades and the strength of Orion and the Bear, whom men give also the name of the Wagon, who turns about in a fixed place and looks at Orion and she alone is never plunged in the wash of the Ocean. [4]

After Homer come the Portolan charts, used for navigation, and then Ptolemy, whose first-century A.D. development of mathematical means for the projection of a spherical earth onto a flat surface is often seen as the starting point for modern cartography.[5]

Although accounts of Ptolemy's work typically include cartographic representations based on his formulas, it is not clear that Ptolemy himself created such

---

4. Homer. *The Iliad*. Tr., Lattimore, R.A. Chicago: University of Chicago Press. 1951.
5. Ptolemy. "The Elements of Geography" in Cohen, M.R. (ed.) *A Source Book in Greek Science*. Cambridge: Harvard University Press. 1948. pp. 162–168.

maps or that they looked anything like what we commonly think of as a "map." But Ptolemy's work did seem to involve a conceptualization of the earth's surface wherein one might see any point as defined by the intersection of two lines: one horizontal and intersecting the poles and one perpendicular to it.

Aristotle had several centuries earlier pioneered the idea that one defines an object in terms of a set of *attributes*. Ptolemy's innovation was to conceptualize location in terms of neither physiognomy nor everyday activities, but rather in terms of the *intersection* of *sets* of attributes. A human is a featherless biped, the intersection of all objects that are featherless and that are bipeds; Rome is the place that is at the intersection of this line of latitude and that line of longitude.

Although Ptolemy's work still appeals to vision as the primary source of knowledge, his way of thinking, which he termed "geographic," in fact recast much of traditional thinking about location. Perhaps most important is this: In the chorographic, where the focus was on the nature of particular places, those places—and the people who occupied them—were typically described in prototypical terms. That is, one picked out a key feature or set of features and around them built a larger account of a "typical" resident. We find this in Hippocrates's *Air, Waters, Places*, an early medical work that goes to great lengths to describe who lived where and what both the people and the places were like.[6] Those who live near brackish water; those who ride horses; the residents of the steppes; something can be said about each. But they are not typified under the neat Aristotelian classification system. Rather, Hippocrates, like Homer before, describes the life of a single, prototypical individual and says of the others, "They are like him."

In Aristotle and then Ptolemy this prototypical approach is not enough. Aristotle depicts a world in which every member of a group has a set of characteristics. Ptolemy sees location as one of those characteristics. To extrapolate, in Aristotle we see the roots of information systems, whereas in Ptolemy we see the roots of geographic information systems—which are, after all, merely tabular information systems in which one or more data fields are allocated to location or to locational coordinates.

There are two things to note about this change. The first is that this move from prototypical to Aristotelian classification (the terms adopted by Bowker and Star.[7]) is, we see from contemporary studies of language, a move away from a model of language consistent with its everyday use to an idealized model that

---

6. Hippocrates (~ 400 BC). "Airs, Waters, Places" in *The Medical Works of Hippocrates*, Tr., Chadwick, J. and Mann, W.N. Oxford: Blackwell. 1950. pp. 90–111.
7. Bowker, G.C. and Star, S.L. *Sorting Things Out: Classification and Its Consequences.* Cambridge: MIT Press. 1999.

misses much that goes on in the processes of classification and identification.[8] And second, the adoption of the model adopted by Ptolemy provides the underpinnings of a way of looking at the world that gives spatial or geographical location a special status. If in one sense a geographic information system is simply an information system with columns for location, there is a sense in which those columns, after Ptolemy, come to be seen as filling a special function. They are keys that can be used to link multiple tables, and just because locational coordinates seem to be subject to exhaustive and final verification, those keys seem to have both permanence and universality. A millennium and a half after Ptolemy, this model of space, in Galileo and Newton, came to be seen as the foundation for modern science.[9,10] And the map, in two or three dimensions, came to be an everyday metaphor for this modeled and annotated space. In the process, the close connection and even similarity of the means used for identifying, classifying, and locating people, objects, and places was lost.

Getting Addressed

If the gridded map is now commonplace, so too in Western society are the address and the association of individuals with a unique address. Most Westerners take it as obvious that every person ought to have a home, and that that home should have a conventionalized address:

> My given name
> My surname
> My street number
> My street
> My town
> My region or state
> My postal code
> My country

But this form of addressing system is by no means universal. In Japan, street addresses are not laid out in numerically ascending order, and street maps typically show individual addresses on a block. Indeed, until very recently, the rural route box numbers in the United States were assigned chronologically; a new home was assigned the next number, regardless of its location.

---

8. Johnson, M. *The Body in the Mind: The Bodily Basis of Meaning, Imagination, and Reason.* Chicago: University of Chicago Press. 1987.
9. Galilei, G. *Dialogue Concerning Two New Sciences.* Tr., Crew, H. and de Salvio, A. New York: Dover. 1954.
10. Newton, I. *Newton's Philosophy of Nature: Selections from His Writings.* Tr., Thayer, H.S. New York: Hafner. 1953.

Few would attempt to identify the first occasion on which a village or road, mountain, body of water, or region was given a name; these names seem to be as old as language itself. But other elements of the common form of addressing are new indeed.

Here we can point to a series of watershed events. In Great Britain, from the sixteenth through the eighteenth centuries, the "enclosure of the commons" led to a movement of agricultural workers from a manor into individual houses.[11] The invention of the spatial and bounded nation-state, we need to remind ourselves, is only a little more than 200 years old. And in the United States, the creation of a democratic government that demanded a decennial census required some system of locating individual residences.

But street numbers have replaced house naming as an identifier only in the last 200 years. The postal code is only about 40 years old. In addition, the last 40 years have seen the rapid "rationalization" of the addressing system in the United States and elsewhere. The rush to urbanization in Europe and North America later in the nineteenth century—and the accompanying increase in anonymity—led to a decline in traditional and local knowledge as a means of identifying people and their places of residence, which in turn set the stage for this rationalization. The later introduction in the United States of rural free delivery made it a standard practice to assign a number to every house or business.[12,13]

The development of numerical street and rural route addresses, however, did not immediately lead to a universal and publicly available means for connecting individuals with addresses or to a means for determining the proximity of addresses to one another and to points of interest. In the United States, this problem was solved in part through the creation of *city directories*, which appeared as early as the Revolutionary War era. These directories became more important after the development in the middle of the nineteenth century of mass transit and the accompanying creation of new clusters of commercial enterprises around transit hubs. After the development of the telephone, telephone numbers were added to these directories and the modern "phone book" was created.

But the organization of postal delivery did not, in fact, require a cartographically organized system. This was because the postal system operated *topographically*:

---

11. Wordie, J.R. "The chronology of English enclosure, 1500–1914." *Economic History Review*, 2nd series 36. 1983. pp.483–505.
12. United States Postal Service. *History of the United States Postal Service, 1775–1993.* Washington, D.C.: The Service. 1993.
13. John, R.R. *Spreading the News: The American Postal System from Franklin to Morse.* Cambridge, Mass.: Harvard University Press. 1995.

The letter carrier walked a route that came to be habitual, populated by familiar faces and names. A route was learned by experience and did not derive from nor result in a compiled list of addresses and residents. In fact, to the extent that the United States Postal Service (USPS) had address lists, a mail carrier typically worked from a list of address ranges (deliver to numbers 199 to 599) rather than a list of the individual numbers themselves.

This means of organizing mail delivery persists, but the last 40 years have seen a series of changes that have overlain new, and in some respects contradictory, systems over that one. Central to the recasting of the address system as a *locational* one was the introduction of the postal code, or the Zone Improvement Plan (ZIP) Code in the United States. Created in the early 1960s under the Kennedy administration, the ZIP Code system divided the country into postal regions identified by five-digit numbers.[14] The first digit referred to one of ten major regions, the second two digits indicated a subregion, and the last two digits indicated the post office to which an item was to be routed and from which it was to be delivered.

This development may have been a move toward a geographical system, one integrated into the Ptolemaic system of latitude and longitude, but the address system remained traditional. This is because the ZIP Code really referred only to a point—a named, rather than geographically defined place. The point was the post office from which letter carriers operated; and changes, such as growth in population density or administrative reorganization, routinely mean that mail directed to an address must be routed through a new or different post office.

Under the ZIP Code system, the post office delivered mail using the older topographic system. And although private corporations ultimately created maps that divided the United States into ZIP Codes, they created them by drawing the route of each letter carrier within a ZIP Code and then drawing a boundary around the areas. So those boundaries were merely artificial cartographic constructs.[15] Thus, the traditional addressing system's metamorphosis into a more "modern" geographical one is still largely incomplete. And neither has it left behind other, earlier systems. Rather, the U.S. (and most other) postal systems remain embedded in a tradition within which a letter carrier learns and then walks a route.

A side effect of the ZIP Code has been the establishment of a direct marketing system. Based on the idea that "you are where you live" (YAWL), direct

---

14. Thomas, R. Jr. "Obituary: J. Edward Day, 82, Postmaster Who Brought in the Zip Code." *New York Times.* 1996. p. C19.
15. Curry, M.R. "Toward a Geography of a World Without Maps: Lessons from Ptolemy and Postal Codes," *Annals, Association of American Geographers, 95.* Forthcoming, 2005. (3)"

marketing divides the country into areas that are then characterized through a chorographic, prototypical system. For example, in the United States, mention of 90210 now brings to mind an immediate image.

Using a data-rich system and substantial computing power, these *geodemographic* systems have in a sense "reinvented the past"—a past in which identity and location were closely connected so that someone could read one from the other. The topographic and the chorographic, both ways of grasping places that can be traced to the earliest of written and oral accounts of the world, are today alive and well in the operations of the postal service and in much of everyday life.

Rethinking Identity: Beyond Traits and Names

I began this chapter with the suggestion that there are two common ways of identifying people, objects and places. One way, often termed Aristotelian (or scientific), sees identification as a process of associating characteristics or criteria with the item in question: If I know that a dog has a set of characteristics—has four legs, barks, chases cats, and so on—I can decide whether something is a dog by determining whether it has those characteristics.

A different approach, often called "prototypical classification," sees identification as operating more organically: I learn that something is a dog by being shown some typical dogs, and then I gradually learn to apply that category to more and more objects.

Both systems have their adherents, and both are widely used to determine whether something belongs in one group or another. The systems, as we know, are not utterly distinct; and as Bowker and Star have pointed out, there is a tendency to move from one to another.[16]

While both systems can be used to sort people, objects, or places into groups, they can also be used to identify individuals. A DNA strand, for example, consists of a number of sites, which are then individually identified or decoded. Working with empirical data for each site, which indicates the probability that that site will have that characteristic, it is possible to aggregate those probabilities and determine the probability that the entire strand came from a single individual. In the end, advocates of DNA analysis suggest, though each particular part of a segment may be shared by a large number of people, that when we look at an entire segment, the probability that it could belong to more than one

---

16. Ibid, 7.

person is vanishingly small. This is a fundamentally Aristotelian approach to classifying an individual. And if this approach can be used for DNA analysis, it can also be used for a range of other data, including fingerprints and those in the Bertillon system of physical measurements.[17]

When we turn to the use of Aristotelian systems for the identification of location, the system of longitude and latitude provides a good example of a way in which a classification system can be used to pinpoint a single location with great precision. This principle has been at work in most of the major radio-based navigation systems. For example, the Gee system, used in World War II, and its successor, the LORAN (Long Range Navigation) system, relied on time delays in the receipt of radio signals to determine the distance to a series of beacons, thereby determining the points of intersection of the hyperbolic surfaces defined by those distances, to establish the location of the receiving station.[18] This same principle is at work in the more recent global positioning system as well as in several of the schemes used to identify the location of cellular telephone handsets.

It is tempting to imagine that these systems somehow locate one at a particular point, that all are fundamentally embedded in an Aristotelian system wherein a location is ultimately the intersection of two locational characteristics. But modern locational systems operate within what turns out to be rather a substantial range of local variations. With respect to GPS, it is useful to keep in mind, as Laura Kurgen has suggested, that the systems tell you not where you are on the *earth*, but where you are on the *map*, with all of the contingency that that implies.[19]

When we turn to a large set of real-world classification cases, however, we face major difficulties in language, classification, and identification. And they arise whether we are considering people, objects, or places. For example, let's say we identify a person by listing a set of characteristics: height, weight, gender, eye and hair color, place and date of birth, and so on. We know that as we add characteristics or traits, the number of individuals who fit that description decreases and that at some point we will reach a set of traits that defines only one person. In fact, Latanya Sweeney has concluded, "Eighty-seven percent of the population of the United States is likely to be uniquely identified by {*5-digit ZIP, gender, date of birth*}—that is, by only three characteristics.[20]

---

17. Cole, S.A. *Suspect Identities: A History of Criminal Identification and Fingerprinting.* Cambridge: Harvard University Press. 2001.
18. Rip, M.R. and Hasik, J.M. *The Precision Revolution: GPS and the Future of Aerial Warfare.* Annapolis: Naval Institute Press. 2002.
19. Kurgan, L. "You Are Here: Information Drift." Assemblage. 1995. 25: 15–43.
20. Sweeney, L. "Replacing Personally-Identifying Information in Medical Records, the Scrub System" in Cimino J.J. (ed.). *Proceedings, Journal of the American Medical Informatics Association.* Washington, D.C.: Hanley & Belfus. 1996. pp. 333–337.

But we also know that weight and hair color often change. (Today, so too may gender.) And as Bowker and Star note in their discussion of apartheid, so may race. If a "fundamental" characteristic of an individual changes, are we speaking of the same person? How many characteristics need change before we think of that person as "someone else"?

This concept sounds abstract. But we need look no further than today's headlines to see these issues at work. What about the ongoing hunt for criminals and terrorists? At what point are we justified in believing that two people, identified by similar sets of traits, are really one and the same?

This issue is actually equally pertinent in forensic work with *places*. Intelligence services spend considerable energy attempting to determine whether two sequentially taken images of a place are identical, if time has passed between the two images, or if they are of two different locales. Is this a lab used for the production of biological weapons or just another tractor-trailer?

Some researchers have turned away from sets of traits as a means of identification, instead focusing on identifying *objects* or *tokens*—names and Social Security numbers being two of the more familiar—to identify a particular place, object, or person. Roger Clarke has suggested that the following criteria must be met if such a token is to function as an ideal means of human identification:

- Universality (every person should have one)
- Uniqueness (each person should have only one like it)
- Permanence (should not change or be changeable)
- Indispensability (an intrinsic feature of the object in question)
- Collectibility (easily available to keep)
- Storability (in manual and automated systems)
- Exclusivity (should identify a person on its own)
- Precision (should be sufficiently different from all others)
- Simplicity (recording and transmission should be easy and not error prone)
- Cost effectiveness (measuring and storing should not be unduly costly)
- Convenience (measuring and storing should not be unduly difficult)
- Acceptability (use should conform to contemporary social standards)[21]

Clarke's theories do not mention that an identification system based on Aristotelian principles can guarantee neither uniqueness nor permanency. But a name or identification number, while meeting many of these criteria, may be too loosely connected to the object in question.

---

21. Clarke, R. "Human Identification in Information Systems: Management Challenges and Public Policy Issues." *Information Technology and People.* 1994. 7 (4): 6–37.

In mass culture, these issues were raised in the story of Martin Guerre, popularized in a 1980s account and then the film.[22] The story concerns a woman whose long-absent husband returns and resumes their relationship. Questions, though, soon arise. Is this really the same man? May he not have just adopted the name? He looks different from the man that many remember. May they have forgotten? Has he changed?

The history of dress and identity (see for example Entwistle and Wilson 2001[23]) and the story of Martin Guerre suggest that identificational difficulties can arise simultaneously in Aristotelian and token-based systems. In the end, both systems are too "loose"; they are loose in the case of Martin Guerre, and they are loose in the case of street addresses or satellite imagery.

Neither a name nor a set of traits or criteria is enough to satisfy the everyday ways people think about identification in the absence of a sense that the object in question has a place within a larger and historically longer context.

On RFID

How does this knowledge of history and philosophy help us when it comes to questions raised by RFID and other location-related technologies?

Consider the following example: Someone searches my pockets and finds an RFID tag, one that came loose from an RFID-enabled library book. Your first thought might be that I had checked out the book. But what if I had found the tag lying on the ground and picked it up out of curiosity or objection to litter? What about other explanations? All we know was that the tag was in a particular place at a particular time—and this is true whether the tag is examined manually or scanned with an RFID reader.

In many cases, however, RFID tags are attached to physical objects or to their packaging, as in the case of razor blades or clothing, or the pallets on which those objects are stored and moved. Here a tag reader will tell us more: an object's physical relation to the reader or perhaps some set of map coordinates. If the object is found in the possession of an individual, we would be more likely to believe that the tag's information tells us something about that person.

But how much more can we learn from the second example? Could the person in question simply have found a discarded piece of packaging, then never found

---

22. Davis, N.Z. *The Return of Martin Guerre*. Cambridge, Mass.: Harvard University Press. 1983.
23. Entwistle, J. and Wilson, E. *Body Dressing*. Oxford: Berg. 2001.

the proper receptacle to throw it into? While we might take a person's having an empty candy bar wrapper as a sign that that person had recently eaten some candy, simple signs are inherently ambiguous, open to interpretation. The tag is, unequivocally, only a sign of itself.

But there is a growing move toward embedding tags into objects so that to separate the tag from the object would be to destroy the object. Here the tag develops a more robust and credible relationship to the object: If you can believe the tag reader, the object is where the tag is. But what can we infer merely from the fact that a person is in the presence of an object?

I have suggested above that our present concept of "identity" has been part of a long evolution, within which it has become increasingly common to imagine that we identify objects and people by somehow matching their descriptions against a set of definitions. This means of identification has been supported by the development of an information society in which the database, consisting of lists of objects or individuals and their attributes, has come to be almost ubiquitous. Anyone who patronizes a supermarket or bank, purchases an airline ticket, or uses the Internet is not exempt.

But I have also suggested that the "time-honored" ways of identifying places and things are in fact far more complex than this model suggests. For example, knowledge about particular places—what they are like, what kinds of people and activities may or may not be found there—is very often only implicit and is articulated only under limited conditions. Similarly, judgments about whether an object or person belongs to a particular category—of race, ethnicity, or gender, for example—are seldom made on the basis of a simple set of attributes. Rather, they are more likely to derive from a comparison of the object in question with some prototype, whether that prototype is conceptual or temporal.

Conclusions

The means of identification discussed in this chapter raise issues about locational technologies in general and RFID tags in particular. They suggest that the determination of identity relies far less on the appeal to solid and unambiguous facts and far more on the amassing of images and stories that seem, at least in principle, capable of being strung together into a coherent story of why we should believe that X is X.

One of our uniquely human traits is our ability make intellectual judgments out of seemingly unconnected facts. To question or discount their value would render us unable to judge or to act. At the same time, it is important to note that the increasing ability to collect such facts, and to store and retrieve them with ease, *increases the range of judgments that can be made.* Indeed, where people's everyday lives are marked by strings of such facts, the absence of such facts itself becomes a fact to be noted and explained: "Why did you stop buying wine at Ralph's?" "Why do you no longer wear that coat?" The threat of "absolute accountability," and the accompanying probability that each of us crosses paths daily with people engaged in all sorts of disreputable activities, means that the facts, or lack of them, need to be in our favor for people not to jump to negative judgments about us and act accordingly.

What would Aristotle, Homer, or Ptolemy have thought of locational technologies? What if RFID or GPS had been in use when President Kennedy was assassinated? Would Lee Harvey Oswald still have been the official "lone gunman"? What other kinds of conspiracy theories would have been manufactured and circulated? The proliferation of information about "who was where with what object" and an increasingly populous and anonymous world make RFID and similar technologies both boon and danger.

Bibliography

Beech, G., Bourin, M., and Chareille, P. *Personal Names Studies of Medieval Europe: Social Identity and Familial Structures.* Kalamazoo, MI: Medieval Institute Publications Western Michigan University. 2002.

Gelernter, D. *Mirror Worlds: Or the Day Software Puts the Universe in a Shoebox: How It Will Happen and What It Will Mean.* New York: Oxford University Press. 1992.

Gladwell, M. "Wrong Turn: How the Fight to Make America's Highways Safer Went Off Course." *New Yorker* June 11, 2001. www.gladwell.com/2001/2001 _06_11_a_crash.htm.

Tuan, Y. F. "Rootedness Versus Sense of Place." *Landscape.* 1980. 24 (1): 3–8.

Wilson, S. *The Means of Naming: A Social and Cultural History of Personal Naming in Western Europe.* London: UCL Press. 1998.

Chapter 9

INTERACTION DESIGN FOR VISIBLE WIRELESS

Chris Noessel[1]
Simona Brusa Pasque[2]
Jason Tester[3]

Introduction

In their book, *The Media Equation: How People Treat Computers, Television, and New Media Like Real People and Places,* Byron Reeves and Clifford Nass present the results of many controlled experiments from which they conclude that although people consciously know that computers, television, and other new media are *not* human, they tend to treat them as if they *are*. Reeves and Nass assert that this is because biological evolution is not keeping pace with our technological innovation: We are using Neanderthal brains to interpret our own Information Age technology. It follows that the more *human* our technology interfaces are, the more comfortable our interactions with them will be.[4]

Despite their sophistication, today's computers lack one of the most basic human skills: *recognition*, or the ability to distinguish between people. We want computers to know who we are so that they can more readily adjust to us as individuals and recognize our capabilities, preferences, privileges, and contexts. Unfortunately, systems that can be thus customized require users to identify

---

1. Chris Noessel is an an employee of Microsoft Corporation. The content of this chapter does not necessarily reflect the views or policies of Microsoft.
2. Simona Brusa Pasque is pursuing studies in industrial design in Milan.
3. Jason Tester is working with the Institute for the Future in Palo Alto, California.
4. Reeves, B. and Nass, C. The Media Equation: How People Treat Computers, Television, and New Media Like Real People and Places, Center for the Study of Language and Information Publications. 1996.

themselves, most often by providing burdensome unique user name and password pairs for every system with which they interact.

What if we could shift the "burden of recognition" to the technology itself? In many ways, wireless identification (WID) is an ideal solution to the recognition problem. WID has the benefits of being:

- A physical token. Objects equipped with WID technology reduce the cognitive load of memorized self-identification.
- Invisible. Recognition can occur subtly, minimizing the effort of self-identification.
- Noncontact. Great precision with the tagged objects is not required.
- Portable or wearable. The tagged objects are likely to be with the user at all times.

WID also solves many business problems. Businesses are information hungry: The more they know about their customers, the better they can respond to and even anticipate their needs. WID promises a low-cost, scalable, unobtrusive solution to this perpetual need for information. After all, most of the personalized devices and services customers want require individual identification, especially since many customers have already accepted the cost of being identified and have become habituated to it.

Looking beyond identification, WID technologies offer the promise of unparalleled convenience. Transactions around us can occur as if by magic, such as the ubiquitous example of scanning an entire cart of RFID-tagged groceries automatically at checkout.

The Role of Interaction Design

Of course, WID is not a perfect solution. That is what this book is about. But while other authors address privacy issues of WID from a technological viewpoint, our expertise as interaction designers leads us to ask: How do people *use* these systems? How can we best design WID systems so that all participants—in particular the end users—gain the most from their interactions with them?

A Common Vocabulary

WID does not have an industry-standard vocabulary to discuss its components. So to ensure consistency across these ideas, we have established the following vocabulary to discuss the shared generalities of RFID, Bluetooth, and Wi-Fi systems:

- Reader: Company or person who uses the Reading Device to gather IDs from tags.
- Reading Device: Device that produces the read field in which tags can be read.
- Read Field: Area of space in which the reading device can detect tags.
- Tag: Transceiver or device that sends out its ID when it is in a read field.
- Tagged Object: Object bearing the tag.
- User: Owner of the tagged object.

These terms and process are also illustrated in Figure 9.1.

Although this vocabulary is borrowed primarily from RFID, these same components are present in the other two technologies and, presumably, will be in similar future technologies.

WID technologies are attractive because they help solve both the user problem of recognition and the business problem of gathering information and providing customized services, but they can pose significant usability problems if they are *too* invisible. If we define interaction (somewhat clinically) as the set of inputs, functions, and outputs used to control a system, the core technology of WID often lacks any inherent output, or feedback. This less-than-usable solution threatens the trust of the user base and thus the longevity of the systems of which they are a part.

To remedy this problem, designers should strive to make WID systems visible in every aspect of the user experience. This key principle, along with the goal of giving users more control, underscores the ideas in this chapter.

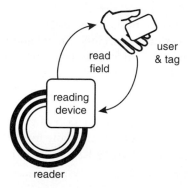

Figure 9.1 Illustration of general vocabulary related to RFID, Bluetooth, and Wi-Fi systems.

Designing and Modifying WID Systems

Taking as a starting point a user's desire for both convenience and privacy, we have documented six ideas for the design or modification of WID systems. The ideas include both broad guidelines and specific strategies. Our intent is to cleanly address consumers' right to be fully informed of any wireless control and information systems in which they participate. To this end we have deliberately set a low priority on technological and economic constraints in the following recommendations:

- Make sure users understand the location of read fields with *disclosure at read*.
- Ensure that readers understand the costs and benefits of participation with *disclosure of use*.
- Make the *read range no larger than necessary* to prevent accidental reads.
- Create *identifiable readers*.
- Use *permissions-based tags* so that users have control over who can read their tags.
- Give users *physical remedies to opt out*.

Disclosure at Read

As RFID- and other WID-enabled applications proliferate, people may not know that they own or carry devices with these tags. Even if they know what tagged devices they possess, they will likely know little about their communication ranges. Because the read fields are invisible, users won't know when they are at risk for having their actions tracked.

Despite powering many consumer applications already in everyday use, RFID is still largely unknown to the vast majority of its users. Even within the WID continuum, the technologies that power other wireless control and networking devices (e.g., infrared, radio, Wi-Fi) have broader name recognition, even if the public understands neither how the underlying technologies work nor what infrastructure is required to support them.

RFID's low level of recognition may be simply a reflection of the technology's current state of limited penetration in most consumers' daily lives. If this is the case, the more systems and controls are powered by RFID, the more users will understand and discuss the technology.

Alternatively, RFID may develop as another technology that we use in a multitude of ways and eventually take for granted, with only the slightest understanding of either its potential or its limits.

In either case, a balance will have to be struck between providing as much information disclosure as possible to protect consumers, and retaining the convenience benefits that will drive adoption of RFID systems in the first place. An apt comparison is the U.S. government's mandated nutrition labeling of prepackaged foods. This mandate revolutionized consumer understanding of food's ingredients and nutritional information and provided the public with far more information than manufacturers would likely have volunteered. While this wealth of largely numerical data has not been perfectly conveyed or interpreted, nutritional labeling has been a huge consumer victory.

As RFID and other wireless technologies are primed to enter many aspects of consumers' daily lives, the industry itself or, if necessary, a government agency would do well to overdisclose information and legitimately earn consumer trust.

Within the general principle of *disclosure at read*, we've outlined the following specific implementation strategies, which are discussed in this section:

- Create a labeling system for RFID- and other WID-enabled fields
- Create a labeling system for RFID- and other WID-tagged objects
- Indicate when a WID has been read
- Provide a device that consolidates read signals

Create a simple and standardized labeling system for RFID- and other WID-enabled fields, clearly indicating:

- The presence of a read field
- The category of WID in use (if applicable)
- The read/communication range of the WID device
- The owner of the reading device
- The categorical limitations of the reading device
- A means to obtain further information (e.g., a URL)

This labeling system (see Figures 9.2 and 9.3) should be present on the WID reading device in a place that anyone in the read field can easily see and access.

Create a simple and standardized labeling system for RFID- and other WID-tagged objects, clearly indicating:

- The presence of a tag
- The category of WID to which it responds
- The read/communication range of the tag
- A means, if any, to set personal permissions for the tag

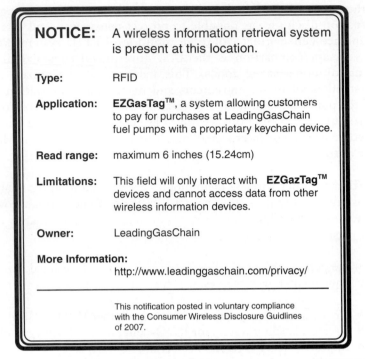

Figure 9.2   Example of a detailed RFID label.

Figure 9.3   Example of a cue for interaction.

This tag should be visible on the product or on the product packaging. Labeling by itself will not prevent applications of WID that are misleading or even invasive to consumers (see other ideas in this chapter for structural limitations on WID), but labeling will be a significant step toward full information disclosure. Examples of appropriate labeling can be seen in Figures 9.4 and 9.5. Consumers concerned about privacy would quickly learn to be wary of a WID tag or enabled device that is known to store personal data and has a long read range, just as shoppers on a diet will pause before purchasing a bag of cookies when they know the high caloric count of its contents.

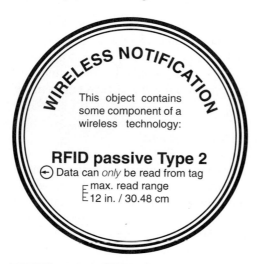

Figure 9.4   Example labeling for products.

Figure 9.5   Suggestion for alternate product labeling.

Clearly indicate when a WID tag has been read by a reading device. You can do this at the reading device or on the tag itself.

At the reading device, an unobtrusive sound or small blinking light that is clearly labeled will make the fact of the read visible. If this signal can be designed to be synchronous with the tag signal, it will form a clear, strong association for the user.

Creating a tag that identifies when it has been read would benefit consumers but would be hugely detrimental to the performance and cost of the tags. For example, a cheap, unpowered RFID tag would need to store enough energy to power a signal such as an LED or small speaker. Unfortunately, such additional technology may add enough cost to the price of each tag to make this system economically infeasible.

Provide a device that consolidates read signals.

As the proliferation of tags continues, users may be carrying dozens of tags at once on their bodies, and any notification signals would quickly degrade to noise. As an alternate approach, consumers may be able to carry a universal device aware of all WID tags in their possession, and this device would be responsible for indicating when a tag has been read. Basic indications of when a tag has been read—without elaboration as to who, where, and why—would still leave the public wanting more information about unsolicited tag reads, but even this half-disclosure would be preferable to a constant stream of silent and unknown communications.

Disclosure of Use

For all users concerned about personal privacy, a crucial question is: "How will the WID reader use the information it gathers?"

We recommend that the answer be governed by a legally binding but accessibly written privacy statement. Such a statement would protect both companies and users. Moreover, it would send the positive message that the company respects consumer privacy and the consumer's right to determine participation in the system.

Although the authors of this chapter are not lawyers, common sense argues that the privacy statement address the following concerns:

- What information are you gathering? When and how?
- Are you gathering anonymous information or information that can be associated with me uniquely? If it can be associated with me, how?

- How do you use this information? How long do you keep it?
- How do you guarantee its security?
- Do you share or sell this information with any third parties or subsidiaries? If so, why? Once this information is in the possession of a third party and out of your control, how can *I* control it?
- What happens if the company's corporate status changes, such as in a merger with a company that has a different privacy policy?
- What if I grant you permission to gather this information but change my mind later?

Additionally, answers must be placed at the point of purchase so that users may choose to opt in or out before they buy. However, this means that the information must be presented clearly and unambiguously—perhaps at the store's entrance, at customer service tables, or at every cashier station near the credit card reader. Also displayed should be some sort of "usage statement," such as "How we use the information we gather as customer feedback."

For *permissions-based tags*, users must have the option of reviewing the request to decide later; the information should be available in a take-away brochure and also easy to find on a public Web site.

Read Range

As WID technology improves, tags may be designed with a communication range that places them far outside the awareness and control of their users. It is important to make the read range no larger than necessary.

Current applications of RFID are often organized into three groups of frequency bands: low (100–500kHz), intermediate (10–15MHz), and high (850–950MHz and 2.4–5.5GHz). RFID applications using the low and intermediate bands include employee access cards, pet identification, and shopping keychain dongles. The low cost per tag is partly due to their very limited read range, usually measured in inches.

Applications in the high-frequency band require fast identification from relatively long distances, including railroad car tracking and automatic toll collection on highways and bridges. The trade-off for this speed is an expensive tag that requires a power source, requiring the tag to occupy a large footprint.

Current Limitations

Current technological limitations on WID frequency categories create a side benefit of forced restrictions on the read distances for cheap consumer RFID tags. For instance, the cheap plastic keychain dongle that automatically charges gas to a credit card fortunately works only within a very short distance.

As RFID technology improves in the coming decade, however, it is likely that cheap tags will become increasingly smaller and readable from longer distances. Generally, such exponential leaps in the power of a technology are welcomed with great enthusiasm. But such advances in RFID technology should be approached with great caution, particularly as personal, financial, and medical information is either stored on or easily referenced from RFID tags. Even if all WID readers in a given environment were made visible by *disclosure at read* and made traceable by *identifiable reader*, this would still be fertile ground for unscrupulous readings: If it *can* be done, chances are it *will* be done.

Currently, other WID technologies, including Bluetooth and Wi-Fi, also have varying limitations on their communication ranges, which may soon be greatly extended by technological advances. If current applications are indicative of future trends, Bluetooth and Wi-Fi will continue to be most effectively used in interactive devices such as computers, cell phones, and PDAs. Unlike RFID, Wi-Fi or Bluetooth-enabled devices can indicate to their users when a communication request is being made or allow users enough control to selectively or wholly block unwanted networking.

Future Restrictions

Companies offering RFID-powered services may indeed comply with voluntary, artificial restrictions on the potential of RFID technology. However, market forces might also affect such limitations, for instance, if consumers quickly learn to avoid those WID applications that use a tag too powerful for a given task.

For example, imagine that a WID technology chosen for a future bank card identifies its owner to an ATM with a wave of a wallet. Consumers might insist that the technology work within a few inches—and no further. Consumer input, combined with corporate prudence, would help engender a high degree of consumer confidence that WID applications were not silently taking over public space.

Identifiable Readers

When a WID reading device scans users' tags, the reader—which could potentially include identity thieves, police, detectives, stalkers, and marketing companies—by definition is informed of a user's proximity and at least one of the user's possessions. But with current technology, this information flow is only one way.

Additionally, read fields pass through most common materials, and even earnest attempts at *disclosure at read*, as explained earlier, may fail to allow users to find the reading device to know who is attempting to read their information.

However, a solution to this problem can be developed with the addition of two mandatory features to the technology as shown in Figure 9.6. All reading devices should be required to broadcast two pieces of data in the read field: Their own unique ID number, and their GPS location data.

Broadcasting these two essential pieces of data, combined with the registration of all the reader ID numbers in an accessible, public, and reliable online directory (similar to the WHOIS domain directory for the internet), would make the reader easily identifiable on request. This process obviously implies the creation of a regulatory body (a government agency, industry, or not-for-profit organization, such as the office for national statistics) to look after all the processes connected to the directory.

Thus, a user or watchdog group, using a portable device like a mobile phone or a PDA that would both intercept the data and access the online directory, could find out, on the spot, who or what is behind a given read field. Users could also discover exactly where the reading device is located, in case it needs to be shut down. Additionally, the GPS location data would not have to be "live" but merely set at the time the reading device was installed. Tags would automatically ignore anonymous and unlocated readers.

This technology would also make it possible for activist and watchdog organizations to develop selective blocker tags that could prevent privacy-ethics violators from reading tags.

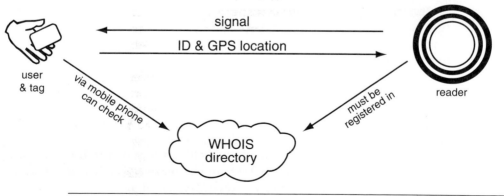

Figure 9.6   Data flow.

Permissions-Based Tags

Out of all the WID tags, RFID transceivers are the dumbest of interactors. They sit idle until they enter a read field with the right frequency, at which time they have no choice but to continually return their unique ID. Participation is binary—that is, either "all-on" or "all-off"—giving no granular control to the user who wants the benefits of participation but is concerned about privacy.

To provide this control, the WID industry should establish an independent permission service through which readers can store their read permissions on the Internet. Then, when a reading device successfully reads a tag ID in its read field, the reader is required to send the tag ID along with its own ID and GPS location (as mentioned earlier) to the service. The service looks up the user's permission list and responds. If the reader has permission, it may use the ID. If it does not have permission, it must discard the ID. If the reader ID is not on the permissions list at all, permission is denied, but the request is stored with the user's account.

The user, at his or her leisure, can visit a Web site to change existing permissions or research read requests to decide whether or not to grant permission. Since the reading device supplied its GPS location, the user can also reference a map to learn where the read field is situated.

If the number of requests becomes too cumbersome for one person to manage, other third-party services such as the Better Business Bureau can offer to check up on the privacy practices of the industry and automatically handle this task for users.

This model requires honest readers and legislation to enforce a remedy for violations but does not significantly impact the cost of the tags. When the information is more sensitive and the cost of the tags not as crucial, hardware control could be implemented.

A more secure solution would be to enable permissions at the hardware level. In this model, specialized tags equipped with technology to use the ID provided by the readers would check against internally stored permission lists to determine whether or not they respond.

Varying levels and qualities of tags might exist, each of which would grant some degree of control to users of WID-enabled products and services. The cheapest of these permission-based tags would simply have a "respond-to ID" hardwired into them. This would provide the least amount of control and security because other readers could simply emulate trusted IDs.

More expensive tags could collect and store some small amounts of data, including permission lists and read requests. However, users would need special hardware and software to allow them to read these requests and manage permissions.

Physical Remedies to Opt Out

One of the major problems generated by the invisibility of WID is that users have no way of knowing whether or not vendors are respecting their decision to opt out. Thus, WID design solutions should reassure users and return their control over the disabling process. Vendors should also provide easy physical means of disabling tags on products.

Given the different kinds of goods in which WID technology can or will soon be found, the disabling scenario can take many forms, particularly in cases in which opting out could be a *temporary* choice, such as in a user's desire to avoid illegitimate scanning while waiting for legitimate scans (e.g., warranty, authentication, or access to additional services).

The fashion industry has already started embedding tags in items for authentication purposes, so it's very likely that the phenomenon will soon expand. In this case, clothes and accessories could carry tags on the packaging or on disposable labels to be removed. Those tags that are sewn into the fabric of wearable technologies should be clearly labeled and easily removable.

The appliance and small-electronics industries also will be eager to adopt WID tags area for tags because tags will make it easier for them to access information such as warranty or service history. In these cases, the tag should be placed on the packaging on removable, scored areas or as removable stickers.

Users can either dispose of the removable tag or keep it for further use (warranty or access to additional services) associated with the object. At the point of purchase, the vendor should provide a shielded container (e.g., wallet, bag, or folder) in which the user can safely store the tag to ensure that, until the next scan, tag data won't be accessible for unauthorized reads.

In all cases, the embedded tag should be removable without aesthetic or performance impact to the object. If it is not removable, vendors should offer masking stickers that can shield the transceiver physically or provide some means in the store of testing that the shield is working.

Conclusions

WID and its various permutations appear to be moving quickly in the direction of ubiquity. Given the personal privacy risks inherent in WID, *now* is the time for consumers and consumer-friendly organizations to set the tone for developing these technologies so that both industry and end users can benefit. These six ideas we have outlined in this chapter—*disclosure at read, disclosure of use, small read range, identifiable readers, permissions-based tags, and physical remedies to opt out*—should help make users' experience with WID more visible, more controlled, and therefore more trustworthy.

References

Norman, D. *The Psychology of Everyday Things.* Basic Books. 1988.

Rechman, K., et al. *Interfacing with the Invisible Computer.* Proceedings NordiCHI 2002. pp. 213–216.

Schindler, E. "Location, Location, Location. What effect will tracking technologies like RFID and GPS have on connected businesses?" *netWorker.* 2003. 7:2. pp. 11–14.

Weiss, A. "Me and My SHADOW. RFID tags polarize the debate over privacy vs. efficiency." *netWorker.* 2003. 7:3. pp. 24–30.

Juels, A. and Pappu, R. "Squealing Euros: Privacy protection in RFID-enabled banknotes." In Wright, R. (ed.). *Financial Cryptography '03.* Springer-Verlag. 2003.

Garfinkel, S. "An RFID Bill of Rights." *Technology Review.* October 2002. p. 35.

Juels, A., Rivest, R.L., and Szydlo, M. "The Blocker Tag: Selective Blocking of RFID Tags for Consumer Privacy." In V. Atluri, ed. *8th ACM Conference on Computer and Communications Security,* ACM Press. 2003. pp. 103–111.

Part II
APPLICATIONS

Chapter 10

RFID PAYMENTS AT EXXONMOBIL

Simson Garfinkel

Introduction

M obil introduced the Speedpass[1] System in 1997 as a fast and easy way for customers to pay for their gas at Mobil's network of gas stations (Figure 10.1). The Speedpass system was soon extended to allow consumers to make purchases inside Mobil's convenience stores. Following the merger of Exxon and Mobil in 2000, the Speedpass system was extended to Exxon-branded gasoline locations as well. In 2001, ExxonMobil started trials with McDonald's (Figure 10.2), and in 2003, with Stop & Shop supermarkets, to see if the Speedpass system could let consumers purchase fast food and groceries even faster. These trials, while deemed successful, have been concluded. Today, the Speedpass system is one of the most successful RFID deployments in the world.

The Speedpass system enables consumers to use a small black plastic barrel about an inch long that hangs from a keychain and contains an RFID chip and antenna. (Other Speedpass devices are also available in a car-mounted tag and in a special version that's embedded inside certain models of Timex watches. ExxonMobil's long-term vision also includes consideration of other types of wireless devices that could be registered as Speedpass devices. One technology that is not being considered as a Speedpass device is a chip that can be implanted in a consumer's skin: ExxonMobil determined that customers simply did not find this technology "attractive."[2])

---

1. Speedpass is a registered trademark of Exxon Mobil Oil Corporation.
2. Kuykendall, L. "Special Report: The Future of Payments." *Texas Instruments RFID in the News*, March 23, 2004. www.ti.com/tiris/docs/news/in_the_news/2004/03-23.shtml.

Figure 10.1   A woman uses Speedpass to pay for gas.
(Image reprinted courtesy of Texas Instruments Inc.)

The chip inside the Speedpass device is a 134kHz device manufactured by Texas Instruments. Each chip contains a unique serial number and a secret code. This code is used in a challenge-response protocol that protects Speedpass devices from the kind of attack described in Chapter 19, Hacking the Prox Card.

Here's how the challenge-response system works: When the Speedpass reader stimulates the chip, the reader also transmits a random number. The chip takes this number, applies a mathematical operation using its secret code, and sends back both its serial number and the result. The serial number and the result are then sent back to ExxonMobil's computers, which have a list of every authorized Speedpass device and every tag's secret number. The Speedpass host computer performs the same calculation as the tag and compares the end result with the number that the tag calculated and transmitted to the reader. If the numbers match, the Speedpass device is deemed to be genuine, and the

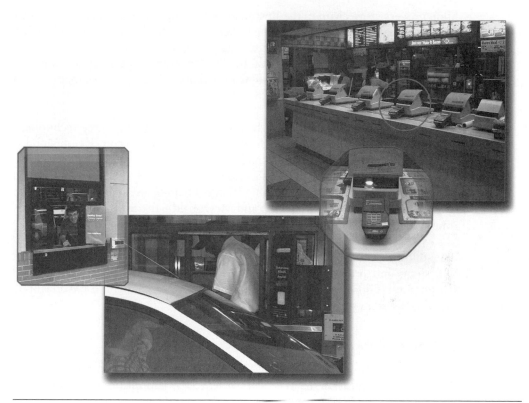

Figure 10.2 McDonald's has experimented with allowing customers to use Speedpass to pay for their meals. (Image reprinted courtesy of Texas Instruments Inc.)

Speedpass host computer takes the consumer's on-file credit card number and uses it to complete the purchase.

The Speedpass system has certainly made good on its name: By eliminating the need for consumers to root through their wallets or purses for a credit card, swipe the card through a reader, and possibly sign the resulting slip, the use of a Speedpass device cuts 30 seconds off the average pay-at-the-pump purchase transaction. By 2003, there were more than 5 million activated Speedpass devices accounting for more than 10 percent of sales at the pump.[3] In 2004, the number of activated Speedpass devices was in excess of 6 million.

And the Speedpass system isn't just for gasoline, either. In 2001, ExxonMobil started a test with McDonald's, which installed Speedpass readers in 450 of its Chicago-area restaurants.[4] In 2003, the company began a trial with the Stop &

3. McGinn, D. "I'll Help Myself." *Newsweek*, April 28, 2003. http://msnbc.msn.com/id/3070122/.

Shop grocery store chain in the Boston area. For supermarket purchases, a consumer's Speedpass device can also be linked directly to the consumer's checking account, automatically paying for the groceries out of the consumer's bank account. (When it is directly linked to the consumer's checking account, the customer needs to provide a four-digit PIN that is set up at enrollment.) Both of these tests have been concluded.

Mobil led the industry in the 1980s by introducing pay-at-the-pump technology, first for credit cards and then for debit cards. Now, once again, ExxonMobil is the trailblazer. But this time, ExxonMobil is not content merely to be copied. The Speedpass system has been so successful that ExxonMobil decided to expand the acceptance of Speedpass to enable its customers to use it at other places. In addition to the tests at Stop & Shop and McDonald's, the Speedpass system continues to expand at ExxonMobil with roughly 750 new sites added in 2004.

The following sections are part of an interview with Joe Giordano, vice president of systems and product development for Speedpass Network at Exxon Mobil Corporation. Giordano has been one of the driving forces behind ExxonMobil's Speedpass system since its inception.

Q: Where did the idea for Mobil Speedpass come from?

A: It started with a big market research study. Mobil was trying to reposition the entire organization from a sales-oriented organization to a customer-focused one. The first step was to better understand what our targeted customers wanted. Based on the results of market research done in late 1993, we learned that first and foremost we needed to be a quality and trusted brand. To differentiate ourselves from the competition, we needed to be able to deliver fast, friendly service. And we had to reward our best customers. We called the package "speed, smiles, and strokes."

In early 1994, the Speed Team, the Smiles Team, and the Strokes Team were formed. I was the leader of the Speed Team. My job was to determine what was needed to create the fastest and easiest way to get people in and out of the gas station. We started thinking of hundreds of ideas of things that we could do—perceptions that we could create to differentiate Mobil from the rest of the pack. We benchmarked with people who did things fast: quick-serve restaurants, pit crews, rental car companies with their car-pickup programs. We learned that to make processes faster and easier; we needed to study the steps of the process in detail from the consumer's perspective. We analyzed each step and looked for ways to streamline the process for our customers. We also studied technology

---

4. Brewin, B. "Exxon Mobil Plans to Extend Use of Speedpass Technology." *Computerworld*, March 18, 2002. www.computerworld.com/mobiletopics/mobile/story/0,10801,69187,00.html.

and recognized the beginnings of a trend toward the use of RFID, particularly in toll way applications. By combining RFID technology and a simplified process similar to car rental pick-up programs, where your "account was on file," we were able to create "Speedpass." We decided in 1994 to focus on the development of the Speedpass system, and we began development of the first version, which was pilot-tested initially in five stores in Austin, Texas, in 1995. A year later, in 1996, we launched an integrated market test in St. Louis at 55 locations.

Q: But why create an RFID-based payment system?

A: We focused on RFID-based technology because it enabled the elimination of several mundane steps for customers, improved reliability, and was safe and secure. In the end, we realized that customers were not just asking for speed but really wanted life to be a little bit simpler. Our customers have too many places to be and not enough time. What customers did not tell us up front, but we gleaned later, was that if it is simple, it is fast!

The goal was to create an experience that reminded the consumer of the simplicity of yesterday—where the station attendant knew who you were, how you wanted to be billed, and how you wanted to be treated—where you could wave your hand, get your gas pumped, put it on your account, and be on your way.

Q: Why not mount the tag on the car? Why put it on a keychain?

A: Using the same toll tags that were used in the toll ways was the first idea. However, the technology for toll ways doesn't work well for gas stations because the "read area" of the technology used for toll ways was quite large and made it hard to match customers with the dispenser they were using. Additionally, the cost of that technology was beyond our target. However, today, we still have a "car-tag" application, but the "key-tag" has been far and away more popular than the "car-tag." In order to understand this, you have to understand, again, that customers are interested in "simplicity," and being in control adds simplicity to their life. Control was yet another dimension of simplicity. Customers want to determine when they are paying for something. They didn't want to be read passively, essentially letting the system determine when they were paying for something. The other reason that the key tag application was more attractive to consumers comes down to the nature of buying gas; you have to get out of your car anyway. The time savings associated with having it in your window wasn't worth giving up control.

Q: When did you begin deployment?

The first step was a technology test, to make sure the technology worked. In 1994, we created a business plan and a concept. In 1995, we tested in stations in Austin, Texas, with a small set of customers and employees with the initial intent of making sure that we had a flawless operation. We knew that we had to get the technology right to be successful.

Q: What did you learn from the initial testing?

A: The biggest issue was with the car tag. The RF had to be tuned to read only one side of one pump. We spent some time getting that to work.

On the key tag side, we had only minor things to adjust. There are a million different scenarios at the pump. When you have self-service, people don't follow one specific process, but rather many different processes need to be accommodated. For example, a customer can take the nozzle out, stick it in the car, and then wave the Speedpass device. Or wave the Speedpass device and then put the nozzle in.

We had to allow for all the different scenarios—the card is rejected, the card is not rejected, but it's past the expiration date. We had to go through the process of testing those scenarios and thinking what is best for the customer and for the business and then balancing those two considerations.

In 1995, we implemented one version of the technology in Austin and tested our processes with controlled groups of customers. Then we moved into a real market test in 1996. We tested the Speedpass system in St. Louis with a marketing plan and a market wide rollout to see what kind of reception we would get.

That went so well, that test in August 1996, that by May 1997, we were able to build internal momentum to secure approval and launched half the markets in the U.S. We moved very quickly.

Q: You decided that if you were going to do it, it had to be all of the gas stations.

A: We had to have critical mass to make the program work in a given market. If we had waited for 100 percent of the locations, we would never launch anything.

Q: Does ExxonMobil own all of its service stations?

A: We have a mix of distributor-owned and franchised-dealer operations. There is a small percentage of company owned.

Q: So they had to purchase the Speedpass equipment?

A: In some form. We have different arrangements for each of those classes of trade. The distributors purchased the system outright.

Q: How did the dealers and distributors feel about spending the money?

A: They were excited about implementing the Speedpass system and therefore were willing to pay for the system. And it's quite unusual to make a decision in December and have a new technology in 1,200 sites by May. Time to market is always a concern of a "franchised" operation, as you have to allow for a "sell-in" period. To be fully sold in and implemented by May was a tremendous testament to the power of a well-implemented Speedpass initiative.

When we launched the market test in August 1996, we really pushed because in October we had our dealer convention. We went to the dealer convention with the momentum of the market test, hoping that the dealers would ask for Speedpass. And that's just what they did. They asked our management to roll out the Speedpass system. It's the best possible scenario when your dealers are asking your management to launch a new initiative.

Q: How many stations is Speedpass deployed at now?

A: 8,600 in the U.S.

Q ExxonMobil has the largest gas credit card in the industry. Did you leverage your ExxonMobil card technology for Speedpass?

A: Absolutely. That was a principle of the design and business model. We leveraged the existing point-of-sale system that we used to process credit cards and leveraged the existing settlement system as well. We viewed Speedpass as an identification system that linked to an established payment account.

Then we built a translation system. The translation system matches the identifier in the Speedpass device to the database, pulls up the customer preferences—like does the customer want a receipt or not—and then supplies the credit card number to the settlement system.

The concept of the Speedpass system was "mass customization." Of course, we don't have a lot that we can customize in the fuel-purchasing process, but we were able to personalize the payment account and automatically print or not print the customer's receipt based on each user's preference.

Q: What about security?

A: Speedpass devices are actually more secure than a credit card. Your Speedpass ID goes to the station controller, then to the satellite modem, up through the satellite provider, and to our payment system hub in Houston. It's at that point that we do the translation; only there do we turn it into a credit-card transaction. In addition to the fact that the credit card number is not present in the gas station, only in the central computer, the security algorithm mentioned above prevents counterfeiting, which is a major source of fraud with magnetic stripe-based credit card technology. Lastly, we deploy back-end systems and procedure to monitor transactions and take action if there is a possibility of a fraudulent transaction based on our business rules and fraud models.

And that whole process takes just three seconds!

Q: Was the plan always to do a general-purpose payment system?

A: No, the plan was just to differentiate our brand and make purchasing gas faster and easier for our customers.

Q: So why did you extend to the other markets?

A: We did research and the customers said they would like to use Speedpass devices everywhere—especially in these around-the-town, convenience-oriented-type purchases. Our customers said that this would be the best way to add value.

Q: But you pulled the readers out of McDonald's. Are you still moving forward on that end?

A: We are looking at a lot of different ways to move forward with other retailers. It is our vision that the Speedpass system will be available widely among many, many retailers. We are looking at the best approach to make this happen.

Q: I was told that you had this problem where valets were swapping Speedpass key fobs. How did you deal with it?

A: We implemented fraud-detection technology that's somewhat similar to what the card companies have implemented. Our initial premise was that by linking to the credit-card system, we would benefit from card companies handling the fraud issue. But we found out that there were some holes in their system.

You see, gasoline purchases are a relatively small subset of total credit card purchases, and they weren't as focused on those transactions. So we had to build our own back-end fraud system and learn what types of fraud there was out there. Now, we actually monitor transactions and determine if a given transaction has a high probability of being fraudulent. If it is, we contact the customer. If it has a very high probability of being fraudulent, we turn the tag off. This has had the effect of reducing our fraud to credit card levels, with the potential to be below credit card fraud levels due to the inherent anticounterfeit benefit of our technology. Additionally, we focused on education with our consumers.

We communicate the need for consumers to treat their Speedpass devices as they would other credit or debit cards. This message has also helped us to better manage fraud.

But the Speedpass system doesn't have most types of fraud that the credit card companies have. We don't have counterfeit fraud, which is a major if not the major source of credit card fraud. That's because it is fairly easy to duplicate a magnetic-strip card but nearly impossible to duplicate a Speedpass device. So we just don't have that kind of fraud. The only fraud we have is physical loss. However, it is still important to treat a Speedpass device like a credit card or debit card and keep it physically in your own possession.

Q: So you've had no problems with cloning?

A: None.

Q: The Web site has instructions for what to do "when you discover unauthorized purchases." Has this been a problem?

A: Whenever you have devices, people are going to lose them. It does happen. We have a system in place that manages it. Our levels of loss are consistent with card companies'.

Q: What about using a cell phone to purchase gas?

A: The Speedpass system could enable any type of device in the future, anything that customers want that is convenient, safe, and secure.

Chapter 11

TRANSFORMING THE BATTLEFIELD WITH RFID[1]

Nicholas Tsougas[2]

Introduction

There were many reasons Napoleon lost the Campaign of 1812 to Russia at the gates of Moscow. However, Napoleon lost the war not because of military errors but because of a simple miscalculation of logistics during winter—a miscalculation that Hitler made a century later in Stalingrad.

One of the reasons for the defeat of the British army in the American colonies in 1776 may have been the length of, and time involved in, replenishing the forces from a home base some 3,000 miles away. The same was true during the Russo-Japanese War in 1904 with a 4,000-mile supply line along a single-track railway through Siberia.

Many vessels arrived in France with contents completely unknown to shore personnel. One consequence was a frantic search for 81-millimeter mortar shells, needed in the hedgerow fighting, because shore troops did not know which ships carried what cargoes. They called forward a large additional quantity of these shells from England. Even when the special shipments were made, a ship-by-ship search was required to find the desperately needed munitions. Huge quantities of supplies were unloaded from ships and piled up in such disarray that they could not be identified and issued to combat forces. Ports

---

1. The conclusions and opinions expressed in this chapter are those of the author, cultivated in the freedom of expression and academic environment. They do not reflect the official position of the U.S. Government and Department of Defense.
2. Nicholas Tsougas is a retired naval logistics officer and the technical lead for emerging technologies at the U.S. Department of Defense Automatic Identification Office (AIT).

became so cluttered that identifiable supplies in the holds of other ships could not be moved ashore.

Two years after the start of the Korean War, an Army general inspected the port of Pusan. He reported that, despite prolonged hard work, one-fourth of the supply tonnage stored there had still not been sorted out. Because supply personnel did not know what these supplies were, they obviously could not issue them.

In Vietnam, 60 percent of the supplies flowed through Saigon, where the average wait for a ship to unload was 22 days. The average waiting times at two other major ports were 31 and 40 days. Understandably, inadequate unloading of the sealift added to the strain on airlift. Congestion and clogged harbors forced U.S. cargo planes to carry items normally supplied by sea vessels. Repair parts were used at an excessive rate because of greatly increased flying hours, and as a result, some critical shortages of aircraft parts developed. Airlift transported only 4 percent of the tonnage delivered to Vietnam, but that 4 percent consisted of critical items, either munitions or parts urgently needed to keep weapon systems and equipment operational.

Logistics and the Military

The definition of Logistics in the military is as follows: The science of planning and carrying out the movement and maintenance of forces. In its most comprehensive sense, logistics encompasses those aspects of military operations that deal with:

- Design and development, acquisition, storage, movement, distribution, maintenance, evacuation, and disposition of material
- Movement, evacuation, and hospitalization of personnel
- Acquisition or construction, maintenance, operation, and disposition of facilities
- Acquisition or furnishing of services[3]

Logistics is a relatively new word used to describe a very old practice: the supply, movement, and maintenance of an armed force both in peacetime and under operational conditions. Most modern militaries have an appreciation of the impact logistics can have on operational readiness, and the majority of battle plans have logistic considerations built in. During centuries of recorded military conflicts, logisticians have searched for the ability to efficiently acquire,

---

3. Joint Publication 1-02, Department of Defense Dictionary of Military and Associated Terms.

transport, and track the enormous quantity of materiel (the supplies, weapons, and equipment associated with a military force) that is required to outfit and sustain troops in the field, both at home and abroad, in peacetime and in war. For the most part, logisticians in military organizations worldwide have found that acquiring and transporting materiel and supplies proved far easier than keeping track of those items once they were acquired or moved in or around the field of battle. Adopting and adapting military logistics to the operational scenario is an essential feature for success. In fact, over the years, it appeared that Total Asset Visibility (TAV) would remain a perpetual mission for logisticians—a prize sought but never obtained in any lengthy military conflict.

Every military has long struggled with the just-in-case replenishment culture. To ensure that U.S. soldiers in the field were never caught without the food, fuel, ammunition, and other critically required supplies, distribution managers would order an excess of requirements. A lack of delivery of repair parts and general lack of status information resulted in a loss of trust and confidence in logistics systems and processes, and units were forced to improvise. A common approach is to use liaison officers and supply personnel at strategic nodes, linked by cell phones, e-mail, and homegrown databases and spreadsheets. The prioritization or diversion of cargo is done on the fly depending on who is on the ground and from what unit. As a matter of practice, if requisitioned materiel is not received within a week, the logistician reorders the item. This practice leads to inefficiency, waste, and "mountains of stuff."

Most, if not all, U.S. military logistics systems were designed for the Cold War, and they could and did track all shipments and deliveries from the United States to any overseas Port of Debarkation (POD), whether in the air and over the sea. But they lacked the full spectrum of factory-to-foxhole visibility of the supplies once they entered a theater of war. Today, the Department of Defense (DoD) has built prepositioned stocks in various areas for ammunition, fuel, weapon systems, and spare parts and has made it a practice to purchase locally wherever possible for services, fuel, water, and certain food items. Much has been contracted to outside sources, as evidenced by the continued conflict in Iraq. This trend has created additional problems in the transportation pipeline, including language barriers and customs issues. Still, scores of sustainment items must flow from the continental United States to defense logistics warehouses and forward positions. This flow is fundamentally different from the flow of commercial entities in scale, rapid requirements, and distance.

Depot-level repairable (DLR) retrograde is yet another divergence that most commercial entities do not deal with in their day-to-day operations. Retrograde is the process of collecting, retrieving, and recovering materiel and supplies and then returning them to units, depots, or prepositioned stock back in the United States to repair and eventually placed back on the shelf.

Unlike the commercial world, the military faces the problem of a lack of assured communications. Communication problems in the military are due primarily to the rapid movement of the ground troops, who are unable to stop and set up their databases and bar code scanners or RFID infrastructure to read the incoming material. Most units still skillfully do so manually, albeit slowly. This inability to communicate is cited time and again as the most pervasive weakness in military operations because the military must conduct operations in very austere environments around the world.

To modernize the force structure and address some of these problems, the DoD made some changes at the end of the first Gulf War in 1991. The logistics pipeline was clogged by thousands of duplicate requisitions and inadequately identified cargo containers. Logisticians could not find information about the status of requisitions while over 40,000 containers (20 and 40 feet long), often called the "iron mountain" in the desert, sat with their exact contents unknown. Materiel of every commodity (e.g., ammunition, food, spare parts) had been staged for a prolonged war with Iraq but never used or required in most cases. These had to be physically opened, inspected, and shipped back to the United States and into the Defense Logistics System and Service stocks.

In 1994, the DoD through an Army initiative sent a request for proposal for a TAV system. The DoD contracted for and began developing a system for tracking containers with active (battery-powered) RFID tags and other auto-identification technologies, including linear and two-dimensional bar codes, contact memory buttons, satellite global positioning systems, and optical memory card readers. The system that was developed and fielded was for active RFID tags that can respond to the signal upon interrogation from 300 feet or more. The interrogator can then identify a truck passing a depot gate or a chokepoint in the road, a container moving through a port, or a rail car arriving in a rail yard. This capability allows for nonattended tracking, reduced human error, and improved data collection on shipments where bar coding is not as robust.

The DoD has been using active RFID for more than a decade to track critical logistics shipments into and around the theatre of operations. As a result, the DoD operates the largest RFID infrastructure in the world, with over 1,500 read/write stations in over 30 countries. Containers and Air Force 463L air pallets are interrogated at various points in transit, with the information captured in an online database at the In-Transit Visibility (ITV) servers to include the Global Transportation Network (GTN). Logistics experts worldwide can then track the progress of critical supplies they ordered via automated means.

In 1996, the U.S. General Accounting Office (GAO), the investigative arm of Congress, completed a study that found that if the DoD had had the TAV system in place during the first Gulf War, it would have saved $2 billion in movement (transportation and handling costs) and tracking of materiel alone. Not a bad return on the initial $200 million investment!

In his *Defense Reform Initiative* of 1997, then Secretary of Defense William Cohen announced a comprehensive program for reforming business processes within the DoD. Specifically, it required DoD agencies to adopt the business practices their commercial sector counterparts were using to become leaner, more agile and competitive, and more compatible in the marketplace. A second initiative for the Office of the Secretary of Defense (OSD) was to revamp its oversight of DoD's Total Asset Visibility program. This came from the 105th Congress when it passed the Strom Thurmond National Defense Authorization Act for Fiscal Year 1999. A third and more critical motivation to change was OSD's management of its asset visibility program and the growing emphasis that warfighting commanders such as Central Command were placing on Joint Total Asset Visibility (JTAV) as a critical "operational imperative." A final impetus to focus additional attention on achieving JTAV came from Deputy Secretary of Defense John J. Hamre on March 23, 2000, in the form of Department of Defense Reform Initiative Directive #54 (DRID 54). In DRID 54, Hamre "directed the Services, the Defense Logistics Agency, and U.S. Transportation Command to submit annual logistics transformation plans that could be used as vehicles for obtaining resources and executing the DoD Logistics Strategic Plan goals and objectives."

The past decade has also seen the United States engaged in a revolution in military affairs of sorts in which new operational concepts of dominant maneuver, precision engagement, focused logistics, and full dimensional protection have become the new concepts for operations. Incredible advances in information technology that are shattering old paradigms and redefining businesses, economies, cultures, and militaries define this new era around the globe. Every functional area and service in the DoD is determined to apply new or emerging technologies and new business processes to overcome old challenges on the battlefield. The most significant improvement has been in the strategic movement up to and through the POD. Another major improvement is cross-command cooperation, but that is where it comes to an end for some logisticians because the information technology infrastructure has lacked the necessary interoperability. The stovepiped operations between services and commands have created barriers in communications up and down the Supply Chain.

For logisticians, emerging technologies have sparked an uprising in military logistics and a revolution in commerce with the result that DoD logistics functions are increasingly mirroring logistics processes in the civilian sector. Today, the services emphasize *velocity management, lean logistics*, and *supply chain management* as they shift their supply-based logistics systems to transportation-based systems that provide "time-definite delivery" of items on a "just-in-time" basis to consumers. This revolution in military logistics has meant exploring new and innovative ways to achieve old manually intensive objectives. Although the DoD wants to become like its commercial partners, the issue of distance to the battlefield, the challenge to provide secure and assured communications, and the thought that people are actually trying to kill other people somehow set the agency apart.

The DoD has embraced this new wave, reluctantly in some cases, and is now aggressively determined to harness every possible advantage. As the nation's military forces alter themselves to better meet today's rapidly evolving strategic environment, total asset visibility has become an *operational imperative*.

The most important reason the military decided to expand its use of RFID is the same reason civilian companies are looking at the technology: the need for asset visibility and tracking. The United States currently has about 6,000 soldiers in Afghanistan and about 130,000 military personnel involved in the war effort in Iraq. To keep the troops fully supplied, the head of the U.S. Central Command sent a memo to every branch of the military requiring "all air pallets (463L), containers, and commercial sustainment moving to/from the theater and intra-theater movements to be tagged with active RFID at origin for asset and in-transit visibility tracking." Alan Estevez, assistant deputy undersecretary of defense for supply chain integration, said:

> The way we fight wars is changing. We need to keep abreast of changes in the way that we do logistics in order to maintain the support that our forces deserve. We feel that the use of RFID technology is critical to doing that.

More recently, the commercial industry has been exploring passive RFID and the Electronic Product Code (EPC) to "maximize retail availability," and although the DoD is eager to leverage commercial best practices, it is apparent that the commercial and defense industries' objectives are somewhat different. Commercial entities are mostly concerned about such factors as "shrinkage" and "out of stock" on the shelf. While these are issues of concern, the DoD cares mostly about readiness. Whereas its commercial counterparts seek improvements in productivity and return on investment (ROI), the DoD will always focus on logistics support to the warfighter. The Department will have to introduce best commercial practices and technologies that add value to its logistics processes. Improvements in ITV, receipt processing, and inventory management, enabled by RFID, can reduce risk-averse supply behavior and can lead to reductions in inventory requirements, tighter cycle times, better utilization of cargo lift capabilities, rerouting of critical cargo, readjusted staffing requirements, and ultimately, reduced costs.

In a fully integrated distribution system, military logisticians create, capture, and use accurate and timely visibility information (i.e., internal or "inside the container," nodal, and on-demand data) via automated methods to identify assets flowing to or moving within a theater. Current information is available on demand and is updated automatically for the logistician via an end-to-end electronic automated information environment. This information provides the logistician with real-time or near-real-time nodal progression through the distribution pipeline, specific supply status and property information, and links to relevant technical and product data. Other logistics managers and automated enterprise systems can readily access this common information, some through secure portals, to support their unique management activities and efforts.

Why is the DoD pursuing passive RFID now? It has many reasons, but the most critical are:

- Eliminating human error
- Improving data accuracy and read/write capability
- Providing asset visibility and rerouting cargo
- Improving performance in rugged and harsh environments and unattended scanning
- Enabling dynamic multiblock read/write capability
- Facilitating source data collection
- Simultaneously reading and identifying multiple tags in the field
- Streamlining business processes
- Improving staff utilization
- Improving interoperability among multiple industries
- Enhancing line of site and communications
- Replacing manual procedures

In addition, the U.S. military is facing new challenges to stay ahead of potential adversaries, including:

- Rapidly moving forces on a dynamic battlefield
- Demand for better information on assets in real time or near real time
- Need for more effective management of inventory
- Need for improvement to manual business processes

"Modernize theater distribution" addresses the necessary reengineering of associated business processes and transportation methods, which are facilitated by new technological capabilities. Although recent modernization efforts focus primarily on the tactical levels of distribution, this focus is viewed as the strategic-level distribution and transportation methods along with the information processes required to link the tactical level. The DoD active and passive RFID vision complements certain aspects of an effort to completely modernize distribution (e.g., strategic and tactical-level transport processes, multinational and coalition operations, security, and accountability) via enhanced asset visibility and accurate, near-real-time transit information. This critical information will be made available for all levels of logistics management through a centralized, "network-centric" logistics information system. This will be not one system, but many standardized systems that are interoperable and that provide constant data to the warfighter. The DoD is working toward a "push" rather than "pull" concept for data utilization and retrieval because of communication connectivity, security, and other issues. This is quite different from what was proposed for the EPC network.

Currently, most DoD legacy logistics systems interact by means of distinctive system-to-system interfaces, limiting the ability to share data with other systems and requiring significant resources to maintain. Decentralized methods for storing repository data also result in high costs for system maintenance, lack of synchronization, and reliance on data that is sometimes inaccurate or out of date. This lack of interoperability poses a significant data-sharing burden and cost to the Department. The Enterprise Integrated Data Environment (EIDE), as identified and envisioned by DoD is intended to resolve significant shortcomings in the current environment. EIDE encompasses several critical capabilities, including the use of metadata and event-driven data services to form a distributed data environment.

To further enhance and fully "integrate the supply chain" in a seamless information flow between supply processes and other logistics functional areas (e.g., acquisition, supply, maintenance, transportation, and finance), the DoD has another initiative in moving toward the paperless environment. Wide Area Workflow—Receipts and Acceptance (WAWF-RA) is a secure Web-based system for electronic invoicing, receipt, and acceptance. WAWF-RA creates a virtual folder to combine the three documents required to pay a vendor: the contract, the invoice, and the receiving report. The application enables electronic submission of invoices, government inspection, and acceptance documents to support DoD's goal of moving to a paperless acquisition process. This will provide the technology for government contractors and authorized DoD personnel to generate, capture, and process receipt and payment-related documentation to include passive RFID via interactive Web-based applications. Thus, passive RFID data will flow through this portal and be provided to the warfighter.

The DoD architecture to store, manage, monitor, maintain, transmit, and access RFID and other forms of logistics data will be a secure, global network that supports and conforms with the Department of Defense Architecture Framework (DoDAF), the Global Information Grid (GIG), and the Business

Enterprise Architecture for Logistics (BEA-LOG). This network will be based on commercial best practices and fully address the unique DoD requirements, enabling the realization of a globally interoperable, network-centric architecture for the integrated management and tracking of all items in the DoD supply chain. Once developed and fully deployed, this new logistics system will be interfaced with a combat information system, such as the Logistics Common Operating Picture (LCOP), and the GIG.

The DoD RFID vision as defined offers a clear understanding of how to achieve the end state. This entails an assessment of current and emerging systems and technologies to identify shortfalls and develop a comprehensive description of requirements for the desired results. To date, most technology applications and supporting systems have been narrowly focused on specific Automatic Identification Technology (AIT), logistics activities, or sites within the distribution pipeline. This narrow focus must be expanded to create a vision that supports a comprehensive management strategy and coordinates all components, functions, processes, and information systems that support the DoD distribution supply chain. The DoD RFID road map includes:

- Sketching current business processes
- Categorizing improvement opportunities
- Scrutinizing material and data flows
- Modifying processes and infrastructure
- Describing trading partner data requirements
- Evaluating system or AIT alternatives
- Evaluating costs vs. functionality
- Selecting and defining technology and IT systems changes

There are many challenges yet to overcome before passive RFID is ready to be the wide-ranging utility to either the commercial sector or the DoD. Tag technology, particularly with respect to passive tags, is immature but gaining each day, and current capabilities are modest in most cases. Questions regarding technology standards and data formats remain; data synchronization and architectures by themselves are a huge challenge that must accompany total AIT implementation to achieve any level of success.

Full implementation and realization of active and passive RFID will minimize time spent through the typical method of inventory processing that has been followed since World War II. RFID technology will allow for the improvement of data quality, eventual item management, asset visibility, and maintenance of materiel. Furthermore, RFID will enable the DoD to improve business functions and facilitate all aspects of the DoD supply chain.

Conclusions

Despite the challenges outlined above, RFID offers great potential. In-Transit Visibility can be improved with hands-free handling, and the future holds even more possibilities as the technology evolves and becomes more capable with eventual item tagging. The vision of "smart storerooms" and "smart shelves" that automatically receive, inventory, and issue material in real time as part of a supply chain containing absolute visibility of all assets can begin to be realized as the technology matures. Just as automated systems brought increased productivity in all supply functions, RFID can provide efficiencies as tagging is integrated into our logistics business processes.

The largest benefit over time for the DoD will be the integration of RFID from acquisition to disposal to include maintenance facilities, which require by far the largest outlay of resources for the Department. Tag reads will be treated as a "transaction of record" for receipt, acceptance, close-out of requisition, and faster payment for vendors, inventory adjustments, and real-time or near-real-time updates to asset visibility systems. All of this is still predicated on the Advance Shipment Notice (ASN) or 856-type transactions within the DoD and items incoming to the distribution centers and Direct Vendor Delivery (DVD).

Improving customer confidence in the supply system is one significant benefit that can be facilitated by RFID technology. Better visibility will reduce suboptimal supply behavior by requisitioners and auto receipting will improve the rate of receipt data capture (in a timely manner). These trends will close the loop on cycle time and result in a shorter average customer wait time. Unlike in the commercial industry, the Department's readiness focus results in particularly high "stock out costs" for the military customer. The penalty for not having what the military needs when it needs it is much more severe than any consequences of supply behavior that includes overbuying and maintaining higher levels of safety stock inventory. This reality will always be the concern for the warfighter. Additionally, the current supply chain is characterized by unpredictable demand and a relative variance in service levels and performance that also leads to a number of degraders, including tenuous customer confidence, that reinforce poor supply behavior.

With the advantages outlined above, inventory managers will be able to take earlier follow-on actions (procurement) that in turn support lower inventory-level requirements and improved customer confidence. Finally, improved productivity will lead the DoD to ROI, and productivity gains that add real value to logistics processes are among of the key goals of "knowledge-enabled logistics."

Investment in RFID must benefit current and future military readiness, and that principle remains the primary focus. The DoD's vision and current policies formulate a plan that leads to integration of RFID into all logistics processes and is part of an overall logistics system to improve in-transit visibility and asset visibility.

To compound the RFID implementation, the DoD has embarked on another ambitious program to identify items via serialization. The Unique Identifier Initiative (UID) is the foundation for enabling DoD to reach established goals and objectives by enhanced total asset visibility, improved life-cycle item management and accountability, and clean financial audits. This program will initially mark items with 2D data matrix bar codes and permanently affix the data to the individual item when it meets the following criteria: $5,000 unit acquisition cost, serially managed, mission essential, controlled inventory, and consumable items or material requiring permanent identification. At this point, the DoD does not plan to affix passive RFID tags on individual items or place UID data on the tags. There may be a convergence in the future as both programs are fully fielded.

Any implementation must focus on business processes first, then integrate the systems and manage the data architecture before the implementers agonize about the particular enabler (RFID) if they are to achieve results that add value. One thing is clear: RFID is a tool of growing utility and will assume a greater role in DoD processes as the technology matures and gains prevalence in world class operations throughout commercial industry and in DoD.

In-the-box visibility will always be looked at as the savior for the DoD. Technology advances such as changing an RFID tag from passive to active read/write to provide aggregation and de-aggregation tracking can make the vision attainable today. Environmental factors tracking temperature, humidity, biological hazards, shock, light, or intrusion devices will have to be integrated with RFID to show a total picture, along with satellite and system integration to provide complete in-transit visibility and GPS.

While these factors will enhance operational security, they will always be a concern to the DoD in the battlefield. The DoD places a high value on addressing wireless LAN communication disruptions, whether they are intentional or unintentional. The proliferation of wireless devices continually challenges the DoD's ability to secure and protect these wireless transmissions of sensitive and classified information. The current DoD directives require the encryption of all information (data, voice, etc.), including unclassified, transferred to or from any wireless device to the GIG. There are many initiatives to encrypt RFID transmissions between the reader and tags, both active and passive, and to reduce emissions in the battlefield. In addition, the DoD is actively working hard to identify legitimate users via the Common Access Card (CAC), including biometrics, and to authenticate personnel including the encryption of all wireless information.

The desired end state includes end-to-end in-transit visibility for all material, from any commercial vendor or depot, through any node, to any customer, anywhere in the world; it also includes hands-free automatic receipt, inventory, real-time financial tracking, and accountability of material. The benefits of such a system would be tremendous, and the potential contribution it would provide to current and future readiness compels the DoD to employ and explore RFID tagging further as an enabler to help the Department get to the "vision" of knowing where all logistics are at any moment in the battlefield.

To fight and win future military conflicts, the DoD will have to use a net-centric capability. It cannot continue to use ad hoc approaches to developing an architecture and infrastructure in response to developments. In the future, the military will use modular packages, integrated with the combat force, capable of carrying forward and rapidly deploying combat support. RFID, both active and passive, integrated with other AITs will have the pervasive asset visibility and in-transit visibility so desperately needed. RFID is here today, and it will improve logistics when the DoD goes after that vision in the near future.

References

Engels, D.W. *Alexander the Great and the Logistics of the Macedonian Army.* Berkeley: University of California Press. 1978.

Barnett, C. *Britain and Her Army, 1509–1970: A Military, Political, and Social Survey.* New York: William Morrow. 1970.

Operation Overload, a historical analysis by the United States Army Transportation School.

General Accounting Office, GAO/NSIAD-99-40.

Cohen, W.S. (Secretary of Defense). Defense Reform Initiative Report. November 1997.

Hamre, J.J. (Deputy Secretary of Defense Department of Defense). Reform Initiative Directive #54 (DRID 54), March 23, 2000.

Chapter 12

RFID in the Pharmacy: Q&A with CVS

Simson Garfinkel
Jack DeAlmo[1]
Stephen Leng[2]
Paul McAfee[3]
Jeffrey P. Puddington[4]

Introduction

With 4,087 stores and 110,000 employees in 33 states, CVS/Pharmacy Corporation fills 10.6 percent of all drug prescriptions in the United States.

CVS is also a leader in RFID. The company initiated contact with the Auto-ID Center at MIT in late 2001 and joined the center in May 2002. CVS has also been a leader in project Jump Start, the pharmaceutical industry's first trial in RFID deployment. Jump Start will use RFID technology to track pharmaceuticals from factory to pharmacy.

When most people think of CVS, they think of the "front store"—the neighborhood convenience store that sells newspapers, chocolates, sunscreen, and nonprescription medicine from aspirin to zinc. The front of the store is clearly important, but the real financial action takes place behind the little pharmacy counter in the back of the CVS. The average price for prescription transactions

---

1. Jack DeAlmo is the vice president, Inventory Management & Merchandise Operations for CVS Corporation.
2. Stephen Leng was formerly the director of the Project Management Office for CVS Corporation.
3. Paul McAfee is lead enterprise integration architect of the Technology Office for CVS Corporation.
4. Jeffrey P. Puddington is the senior manager of Logistics Network Strategy for CVS Corporation.

in the pharmacy is seven to eight times larger than the average price customers pay in the front of the store. Not surprisingly, prescription customers are responsible for nearly 70 percent of all CVS revenues. They visit CVS stores many more times each year than do the customers who patronize only the front of the store, and they are significantly more loyal.

But it's not just CVS whose customers' purchasing habits could be further leveraged with the use of RFID. RFID deployment can benefit all sectors of the pharmaceutical industry, from corporate bottom line to end-consumer safety, by providing for the reliable tracking of legitimate drugs as they move from manufacturers through the distribution chain and into the hands of consumers.

CVS and Auto-ID

CVS is known as a leader in customer service and marketing but not in technology.

One major reason that CVS wanted to take a leadership position in RFID was to avoid what happened with the introduction of the Universal Product Code (UPC) in the 1970s and 1980s. The UPC was designed to serve the needs of the consumer product goods (CPG) industry—it was the supermarkets and the CPG suppliers that devised the UPC. But the grocery industry never considered that the UPC might have a role inside the pharmacy, so the pharmaceutical industry was forced to develop an independent bar code called the National Drug Code (NDC). Since then, grocery stores have deployed their own pharmacies. As a result, the typical box of prescription drugs today has two separate bar codes on it, and all of the back-office CVS systems have to deal with both.

When CVS contacted the Auto-ID Center at MIT to find out about the plans for RFID, the company was told that UPC would be subsumed into the EPC standard that was under development. CVS asked if the EPC would also subsume the NDC. But the Auto-ID Center had not yet addressed the role of EPC in the pharmacy: At that point, the only company at the Auto-ID Center that had pharmacy operations was Wal-Mart, and Wal-Mart was addressing other issues.

While Wal-Mart does fill a lot of prescriptions, it is by no means the dominant pharmacy retailer in the United States. By becoming involved with the Auto-ID Center, CVS could ensure that the RFID technology was developed in a way that took into account the specific privacy and security requirements of pharmacy retailing.

Consumers traditionally regard their own medical information as extraordinarily personal. Therefore, pharmacies need to be unimpeachable about the security and privacy of their customers' records. That's because many medical conditions can be inferred from the name of an individual's prescribed medication: A person prescribed AZT almost certainly has AIDS, for example. And since the passage of the U.S. Health Insurance Portability and Accountability Act of 1996 (HIPAA), healthcare-related information enjoys protection under the law.

To ensure consumer privacy, CVS sorts and handles separately the waste from its pharmacies. Printouts, empty vials, stock bottles, and other waste are put in dark blue nontranslucent bags that are returned to the company's distribution centers, where they are handled by special trash services that have signed the company's HIPAA agreement. Without these kinds of safeguards, consumers' medical privacy could be compromised by any private investigator or journalist picking through the store's trash bins!

Project Jump Start

While the standard model of using RFID to track the movement of consumer product goods was a good one, the pharmaceutical industry knew that system simply wouldn't be applicable. So Jump Start was created to test a full deployment of RFID tracking in the pharmaceutical industry, in every stop on the supply chain.

Unlike a box of Pampers, a case of Gillette Mach3 Razors, or a carton of milk, pharmaceuticals are high-value goods with extremely long shelf lives. A bottle of 500 pills might have a retail value of $1,000 and a shelf life of three or four years. What's more, pharmaceuticals are purchased and shipped all over the world. As a result, distributors and other trusted intermediaries will purchase pharmaceuticals to take advantage of not just anticipated price changes but also fluctuations in international currency exchange and interest rates. As a result, while suppliers and shippers of CPG are relatively open, the sale and movement of pharmaceuticals is confidential.

At the same time, the attention being paid to the shipment of pharmaceuticals within the United States is increasing. The Food and Drug Administration is worried about the growing threat of counterfeit drugs. The Department of Homeland Security is concerned that terrorists might try to contaminate pharmaceuticals, much in the way that Tylenol was adulterated in 1982.

Jump Start was envisioned as a full-scale trial of EPC on 10 selected drugs. The pharmaceuticals in the trial will be diverted from the primary stream at their point of manufacture and specially tagged with EPC tags. The items will then be packed into standard cases and each case given its own tag. Thus, a case with 72 bottles in it would have 73 tags.

Each case will be scanned when it leaves the manufacturer. A typical error that might be caught at this point is an order of 10+10—for example, 10 cases of 500mg tablets and 10 cases of 250 mg tablets—that gets shipped as 9+11.

When the outgoing cases are scanned, the manufacturer's computer will send an electronic shipping bill to the intended destination. That bill will probably include the 73 EPC codes as well as the lot number and expiration date of each bottle. The case will then be put on a shipping truck and sent to a distribution center (DC).

When the case arrives at the DC, it will be scanned again. Here the computer will verify that the case contains the same 72 bottles that it did when it left the manufacturer. If it doesn't, the case will be deemed tampered and sent back. If all is well, the case will be taken into the DC and put into inventory until a specific pharmacy needs to be resupplied. At that point, the case will be opened and a specific number of bottles packed into a plastic container called a "tote." A tote can hold dozens of bottles; each pharmacy typically receives five to eight totes a week.

The tote will be scanned as it leaves the DC and put on a truck. It will be scanned again when it enters the pharmacy, and the computer will verify yet again that there have been no additions, subtractions, or substitutions. The computer will also detect cloning—for instance, the same EPC tag showing up at more than one location. Bottles will be placed on shelves in the pharmacy, where their contents will be slowly dispensed over the course of a week or a month into individual prescription vials. When a bottle is empty, it will be placed in the waste stream and its EPC tag explicitly decommissioned.

That's if everything goes smoothly, of course. Naturally, sometimes things go wrong. Jump Start is designed to focus on four specific aspects of the shipping process: outdates (when a drug passes its expiration date), recalls (when a manufacturer discovers a problem and needs to get a batch back), returns, and damage. Today all of these are manual processes; RFID will automate them as well.

One place that Jump Start will not be reading RFID tags is on the delivery trucks themselves. Pharmaceuticals are typically transported by independent couriers. Ideally, each of these trucks would be equipped with a GPS-enabled RFID reader and a two-way radio, reporting the serial number and location of every tag loaded on or off the vehicle.

Currently, the cost of such a setup is considered prohibitive. That will probably change, though, as readers become less expensive or as regulations mandate geographic tracking of the items being transported.

Initially, Jump Start will be confined to bottles of 90 to 100 tablets and other kinds of pharmaceuticals that need to be broken up before being dispensed to consumers. This minimizes the chance that an RFID-labeled package would end up in consumer hands. Onto these items the manufacturer will apply a special tag that is folded in half: One side will have an adhesive pad that will stick to the package; the other side will have the RFID chip and antenna. The tag will have a perforation down the middle, making it easy for either the pharmacist or consumer to remove the tag from the product.

RFID in the Store

Unlike major retailers, which are first deploying RFID on pallets and containers, CVS is starting its RFID deployment inside the pharmacy, tagging every dispensing bottle and customer vial in its two test stores. The pharmacy shelves will be equipped with readers, as will the refrigerators and other areas. Every prescription vial will have an RFID tag, allowing the computer to track the drug acquisition and dispensation process, until the moment that the consumer picks up the prescription.

RFID is likely to have other benefits for CVS. By carefully tracking expiration dates, a pharmacy that has 50 pills that are about to expire could send them to a pharmacy that's more likely to need them—perhaps a pharmacy that has many more customers on the same prescription.

Consumers will see more benefits as RFID moves to the front of the store. Many shelves in a retail store are stocked from supplies in the back. If RFID antennas lined the shelves like contact paper, the computer could automatically alert the store's staff when the last bottle of cough syrup was taken, allowing the item to be immediately restocked. RFID readers in the stock room would eliminate the all-too-common problem of having items lost in the stock room because they were in the wrong place.

Making RFID Work: The Back End

Bringing viable RFID to CVS will require a lot of work, on both in-store hardware and back-end systems.

First, RFID technology itself must improve. Initial tests found that only 1 out of 65 RFID-tagged pallets could be read with 100 percent accuracy. Recent failure rates have dropped from 30 percent to 8 percent as experience with these systems has increased.

For example, engineers have learned that it helps to have the palette swivel as it moves past the reader. But if reading rates can't reach 100 percent consistently, other approaches will need to be tried—for example, a two-way tag inside the pallet that proxies other, hard-to-reach tags.

Next, both the cost and the footprint of the readers need to come down. Deploying a reader on every shelf of a pharmacy is prohibitive today not only because of the cost but also because of the room required for the power cables, network cables, and the readers themselves. Instead, CVS is exploring a new kind of reader that could service dozens of antennas at the same time. If this works, a single reader might be able to handle an entire pharmacy.

Back-office systems also need to be modified. CVS has over 400 applications handling data from its stores, which is typical for organizations of its size. The company is trying to migrate to a single data repository. RFID is a driver for this transition, as is the migration from its current proprietary SNA-based network to a new network based on TCP/IP.

Once that new network is deployed, CVS will start equipping its stores with secure wireless access points and wireless bar code scanners. The scanners should simplify the task of taking inventory in stores. Eventually, CVS will transition from this system to a system that takes inventory using RFID.

The following sections are from an interview with Jack DeAlmo, vice president of inventory management and merchandise operations at CVS.

Q: CVS generally isn't known as a leader on technology issues. Why did you decide to become a leader on RFID?

A: We got into RFID because we saw the reality of the value of it. We saw that it would happen. We also had the experience of the CPG (consumer product goods) companies not taking into account our needs when they devised and deployed the UPC.

Q: What are the unique requirements for pharmacies and other healthcare providers?

A: Privacy. If people [developing this technology] don't understand privacy, this thing is going to be stopped dead in its tracks. CVS needed to make sure that people understood that the needs of privacy in the pharmacy arena are completely different than in supermarkets.

Q: How so?

A: They are more sensitive. You can get upset about somebody tracking your underwear, but it is going to be completely different than the privacy problems that can crop up in a pharmacy.

In the past, people would throw prescription vials with names on them in the dumpster. That is the stuff that got us interested—and made us feel that we had to take a leading position.

We just don't lead on any technology. But we felt that the CPG companies, without pharmacy being there, would not be sensitive to our needs. We couldn't let anyone other than the pharmacy industry dictate the needs of pharmacy.

Q: While most of the industry is going with pallet-and-case-level tracking first, CVS decided to launch with item-level tracking. Why?

A: Several reasons.

First, the average prescription costs $55. There is a lot more room in there to absorb a 20-cent tag than in a box of chewing gum. We knew that it would be years before the CPG guys got around to the item level.

Second, we recognized that if we do not understand the supported needed in the store for item-level deployment, we would build the wrong RFID system. Thus, right from the beginning we diverged from what Wal-Mart and the rest of the industry was doing.

Third, we can learn from Gillette and others about pallet-level deployments; we don't *need* to do a pilot now.

Q: What are some of the other differences between your deployment and what's going on at Wal-Mart?

A: The CPG view was that everybody would share RFID information. Nobody in pharma shares this stuff. We also fall under a variety of regulatory agencies. We felt that some kind of tracking program could be mandated by Homeland Security or FDA. We felt that with Jump Start we could provide them with some useful information, and we have.

Q: *Jump Start is designed to handle outdates, recalls, returns, and damage. But aren't you handling these already?*

A: They are manually intensive work that requires the date code to be looked at by a pharmacist and a warehouse person. There is no system to manage date codes. This is a nightmarish piece of work. You can't return it to the manufacturer until it is outdated. We don't dispense a pharmaceutical if it is within 60 days of the end of its life.

Q: *The drug makers take back their outdated drugs?*

A: Yes, they do. And at the value we originally paid for it. This means that they have to pick up every bottle and they look for the exact lot number, then they go to their computer and look up the price.

In retail, everybody built their own inventory and forecasting systems. We then spent 10 years trying to glue them all together and synchronize them. The idea behind Jump Start is to build one system that works across the industry.

Q: *When did Jump Start happen?*

A: The first quarter of 2003. The next phase will be to put something in place that is real, sustainable, and deployable—something that we can build on. Get it into the supply chain and then target the FDA's 2007 deadline.

Q: *So this is not a trial? You're going to roll this out everywhere, and this is simply the start?*

A: That is our intention. We helped bring to the table the retailers and manufacturers that are fairly significant. When you have that much weight in the industry pulling in the same direction, you will have a solid process that takes into account every participant's needs.

Q: *With Jump Start you're working hard to make sure that consumers never get an RFID tag, not even a killed one. Why the concern?*

A: Because the privacy guidelines haven't been finalized, because there hasn't been privacy education for the consumer, and because there isn't a killable tag in our pilot, we decided to take a removable-tag approach. There will be a little flag on every vial. We are going to tell customers that they can rip off the flag if they choose.

We're going to notify the customer in a number of different ways. There will be signs in the store. There will be a little monograph in the bag. And there will be a label on the tag. That's for the trial. When we go into production, the RFID tag will be applied under the prescription label, and we'll use a kill command—we will kill the tag before it is placed in the customer's hands.

Q: You're going to be tagging vials before tagging pallets and cases?

A: Yes. It's precisely the opposite of what they are doing. We can meet them in the middle somewhere.

With item-level tagging, we can get the operational efficiencies in our pharmacies that CPG won't get to for 10 years. Remember, the pharmacy is 70 percent of our business. But in a typical retail store, it's only 7 percent of our footprint: 975 square feet in a 13,000-square-foot store.

Q: So the costs of deploying are much lower?

A: Exactly. We can learn everything we need by deploying this in a very small footprint. And then deploy across the front of the store when we are ready.

We've actually built and are ready to deploy an item-level tracking system for the pharmacy. We have an operational system integrated into our pharmacy practice. There is nothing hokey about it—it looks like any other set of computer screens in the pharmacy. The system associates a customer with an individual pill bottle by taking a data stream out of the pharmacy system that would normally print a label. Once the label is applied, we can track the vial anywhere in the pharmacy, from the time the pills go into the bottle to the time that the vial leaves with the customer.

Now we are waiting for FDA approval.

Q: Why does this require FDA approval?

A: We would not normally have sought it. But the FDA was investigating the issue of efficacy regarding RF on the drugs. Once we found out about that investigation, it was impossible to proceed with the FDA knowing what we were doing.

If we choose not to deploy because the number of manufacturers tagging isn't large enough until 2006, that's fine—at least we have figured it all out.

Q: You've said that RFID can help with drug compliance. How can it do that?

A: Many things affect compliance. A doctor could write five prescriptions for a patient who doesn't feel sick and the patient has only three filled. Some diseases are not obvious, like hypertension. People take their drug and say, "I feel great. I ran out of pills and don't want to take it any more."

Compliance is helped when a pharmacist can recognize such a situation; the pharmacist has a duty and a responsibility to counsel people on compliance. If you free up a pharmacist's time, that person will have more time to provide counseling.

Another reason that compliance falls down is that people come to get a prescription, it is not there, and they don't come back. RFID lets us get closer.

Way in the future—more than ten years at least—you might have smart packaging. You could read whether a patient took a pill; for example, if a blister pack is broken, that means that a pill came out. This would require a chip in the package and a reader in the house. If your 85-year-old grandmother forgets to take her meds, we could call her (or her son) and say, "Mrs. Johns, you really need to take your pills today."

That won't *ever* happen unless people are more concerned about what this technology can do for them than what it is doing to them and their privacy.

Chapter 13

RFID IN HEALTHCARE

Kenneth P. Fishkin[1]
Jay Lundell[2]

Introduction

The healthcare industry is a major component of the world economy: About 14 percent of the world's gross domestic product (GDP) is devoted to it. The intersection of RFID and healthcare is so large that it needs a book, more than a book chapter, to discuss. Given the choice between a vague overview and a selected, focused discussion, we'll choose the latter. We'll discuss two specific healthcare domains and the ways they are being affected by the RFID revolution: the hospital and home healthcare for the elderly (supporting "aging in place").

RFID has some compelling advantages that make it particularly attractive for these healthcare domains:

- Robustness. Because of the history of RFID deployment in the physically demanding environment of livestock tracking, very robust RFID tags have been developed: ones that survive high temperatures (of particular interest for the hospital domain because some RFID tags can survive sterilization) and dirt. Some in frequencies around 125kHz can even overcome mud, blood, and water, albeit at short ranges.
- Unobtrusiveness. Because RFID communication is wireless, RFID readers don't need line of sight to RFID tags, and RFID tags can be embedded behind or underneath surfaces. This is an important advantage for some healthcare applications, such as care of people with early-stage Alzheimer's or those with autism, where the presence of obvious tags is distressing and distracting.

---

1. Kenneth Fishkin is a senior research associate at Intel Research Seattle.
2. Jay Lundell is a senior researcher in the Proactive Health Department at Intel.

- Ease of Use. With care, many RFID scenarios can be designed such that the user of the RFID-tagged object need never engage in any explicit scanning action. This can be advantageous for those for whom this would be an unwelcome distraction (e.g., busy nurses and doctors) as well as those who would be unwilling or unable to perform such a special action (e.g., the patient populations mentioned above).
- Value Proposition. When RFID-tagged objects are tracked in the supply chain industry, the system cost is often dominated by the tag cost. In the healthcare domains we are focusing on here, cost concerns are less critical because these technologies can deliver services that are so highly valued. If an RFID system can prevent a patient from being mismedicated, ensure that a doctor gets the right set of tools for an operation, reduce the time spent searching for a crucial piece of hospital equipment, detect when an elder is experiencing cognitive decline, or ease the stress of a caregiver for a child with autism, the value is high enough that the greater cost of an RFID tag—compared with that of a bar code, for example—can still make the RFID system attractive.

This chapter presents some examples of how these RFID advantages are being brought to bear. Some of these examples are being deployed today, some are being tested, and others are conceptual prototypes that are years away. We hope that taken together they offer a good picture of what the RFID revolution is bringing and can bring to healthcare.

The Hospital

Within the hospital environment, we can broadly distinguish three classes of RFID applications: those designed to track people and objects around the hospital, to safeguard use of equipment, and to assist medical personnel with their jobs.

Tracking People and Objects

Hospitals are busy environments, where people and equipment often need to be found quickly. Finding a particular piece of mobile hospital equipment, a doctor or nurse with a particular expertise or knowledge, or a particular patient is often a time-critical and urgent endeavor.

Accordingly, the main application for RFID in hospitals at present is one closely aligned with supply chain management, except here the "supply" is of doctors, nurses, patients, and equipment, and the "management" consists of being able to rapidly locate them within a fixed environment (the hospital) at a particular time. For example, the U.S. Navy is partnering with Precision Dynamics to track wounded patients, and Doctor's Hospital in Dallas is partnering with Tenet Healthsystems to track newborns and ensure that they stay matched to their mothers.

Safeguarding Equipment Use

A new wave of short-range, very small RFID readers is coming online. For example, the "M1 mini" reader from SkyeTek has only a 40mm diameter (roughly that of a U.S. quarter), is only 4mm high, and weighs only 10g. Similar readers have just been announced that can be integrated into Nokia cell phones.

Readers this small have the potential to be invisibly integrated into hospital equipment, particularly hospital equipment that has items dispensed or connected into it, such as blood bags, IV drips, anesthesia lines, or medication boluses. By checking the RFID tags located on the connecting item, the equipment can ensure that the correct item is being connected at the correct time for the correct patient, reducing treatment error and helping relieve the stress on nurses. For example, Precision Dynamics is partnering with both Massachusetts General Hospital and the Georgetown University Hospital to use RFID readers to prevent mismatching on blood bags.

A similar idea, although implemented differently, lies in the arena of pill dispensing. Mismedication is a major problem in healthcare: Medication errors account for at least 7,000 deaths and at least 770,000 injuries each year.[3] Estimates are that, in the United States alone, they cause 22 percent of nursing home admissions (at a cost of $31.3 billion per year) and 10 percent of hospital admissions (at a cost of $15.2 billion per year).[4]

The pharmaceutical industry is already moving toward a standard in which RFID tags will be placed on pill bottles; the current FDA mandate is for all pill bottles to be tagged by 2007,[5] affording the industry an opportunity to develop solutions for medical compliance. When RFID readers (such as the small Skye-Tek RFID reader described earlier) are placed in the environment where medicine is kept, the system can track whether the right medications are being taken at the right time by the right person. When a system is combined with a digital scale, as has been done at Intel Research Seattle (see Figure 13.1), it can tell

---

3. Agency for Health Research and Quality, 2001. And Anonymous. "Increase in US Medication-Error Deaths between 1983 and 1993." *The Lancet*. 1998. 351:643–644.

4. http://www.epill.com/epill/statistics.html and http://www.beyond2000.com/news/jan_01/story_996.html

5. Food and Drug Administration. "Combating Counterfeit Drugs." February 18, 2004.

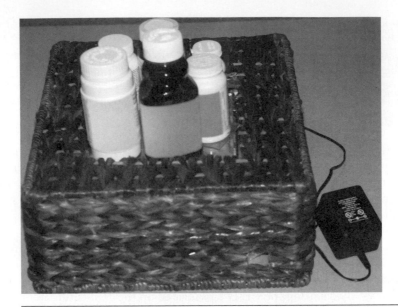

Figure 13.1   The MedPad, an RFID reader enhanced with a digital scale to detect medication taking. (Image courtesy of Kenneth Fishkin.)

both which medication was taken and how much was taken.[6] This information can be provided to a nurse, a remote caregiver, or the pill taker (other information, such as reminders or warnings, could also be displayed), thus improving the quality of the user's health and reducing the strain and uncertainty on the healthcare provider.

Assisting Medical Personnel

RFID technology can also be useful in assisting medical personnel through the course of a procedure. As part of a sensor network, RFID can infer the current state of an activity, then proactively display information, issue reminders, notify other personnel, and so forth in anticipation of the doctor's needs. At present, this is a longer-term research agenda, one being explored at several institutions, such as the Danish Centre for Pervasive Healthcare, and at Intel Research Seattle.

The preceding scenarios were examples of areas where it would be advantageous to have different pieces of medical equipment tagged. At Intel Research Seattle, the research agenda extrapolates this slightly, positing a world in which many of the objects and tools a doctor uses are RFID tagged,

---

6. Fishkin, K.P., Wang, M., and Borriello, G. "A Ubiquitous System for Medication Monitoring." Pervasive. 2004.

and interactions with them are detectable by sensor networks. In other words, a world where a computer could know which RFID-tagged objects are being used when and by whom.

In such a world, can a computer look at this sequence to infer what the doctor is doing and how the doctor is doing it? For some activities, the answer is no (e.g., when a doctor is talking with a patient, RFID tags will never know the nature or status of the conversation), but for many others, particularly activities that involve tools, we believe that the answer is yes.

As a first step in this direction, we are engaged in a pilot research project with the Anesthesiology Department of the University of Washington Medical School. The project involves having medical school students wear small RFID readers in a glove that fits under their existing latex gloves (see Figure 13.2) while they engage in simulation procedures. The glove has two antennae: one that detects

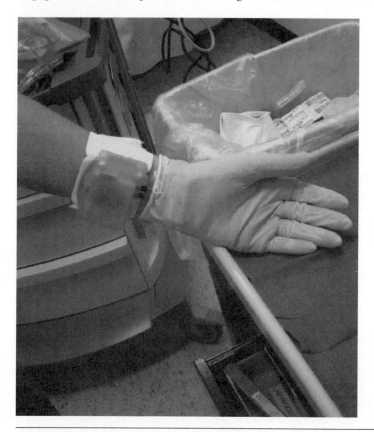

Figure 13.2   An RFID-detecting glove used in a medical simulation, under a medical student's existing latex glove. (Image courtesy of Kenneth Fishkin.)

RFID tags that come near the palm and one that detects RFID tags that come near the thumb (for objects like syringes, which never go into the palm). As the students perform procedures in response to some patient scenario in a simulation lab, the RFID reader can detect the sequence of objects used. By looking at this information, in conjunction with how long the objects are used, which hands use them, and so forth, we hope that we can assess students' performance. Did they use a different tool than an expert would have? Did they use the right tool but take too long to use it? Did they waste time getting out too many supplies or, conversely, lose time because they hadn't done enough preparatory setup? We believe we can answer questions like this by looking at the RFID traces, and these answers can be used in the short term to improve the objectivity, efficiency, and reliability of skills assessment. In the long term, if we extend the system from simply monitoring the behavior to assisting it, RFID technology can potentially be used to reduce the doctor's workload. For example, rather than simply reporting that a doctor picked up the wrong tool, the system could sound an alarm.

Home Eldercare

> "We're the Boomers! You can bet our generation will refuse to live in the places we have put our parents into." —One of many Baby Boomers we interviewed about the future of healthcare.

In healthcare circles, as well as in the popular press, it has become almost a platitude that the aging Baby Boomer population is about to dramatically change the healthcare industry. This situation is what Peter Schwartz calls an "inevitable surprise"—we know it's going to happen, we just don't fully understand how the world will change as a result. However, it's safe to assume that Boomers will begin to place a tremendous burden on the current healthcare system because of their sheer numbers. Also, members of this emerging elder cohort will demand more autonomy and independence in living style than did previous generations, just as they have throughout their lives.

Many research labs are starting to envision and prototype the future technologies that will support these elders living at home. RFID is one of the many enabling technologies that will permit elders to enjoy a high quality of life for as long as possible and can help reduce the burden on caregivers and the healthcare system.

We focus on two general areas of eldercare and describe some prototypes that have been developed to address these areas. First, caregivers will need to keep tabs on elders to make sure they are safe and functioning well. By combining secure, unobtrusive monitoring in the elders' homes with easily accessible or ambient displays that show the elders' current status to the caregiver, we can provide real-time "OKness checking." This will be important in providing independence for elders and relief and assurance for caregivers.

Second, elders will need support for specific activities that are necessary to support health and maintain quality of life. We describe a few applications in which an RFID-enabled system can help with exercise, nutrition, and social health.

Activity Monitoring and "OKness" Checking

To focus our discussion of eldercare OKness checks, consider the following representative scenario: Chester is a 90-year-old former teacher who lives alone in his New England home. Molly is his daughter who lives a few miles away. Chester is basically healthy, but he has memory problems and is quite frail. Molly must check in on him every day to make sure he is taking his medications, eating properly, getting exercise, and maintaining his hygiene. It takes a tremendous daily effort for Molly to watch over Chester and take care of her own family as well. Could technology help Molly keep track of Chester's daily activities? Is there a way that Molly can remotely determine if Chester is doing OK without having to call or drive to his house?

RFID can enable a system to provide relief to people like Molly and support to people like Chester. An RFID system has an advantage over other systems that use motion detectors and simple switch sensors. It can detect activities of much finer granularity, thus potentially providing much more accurate detection of activities. For example, a simple motion detector/switch sensor system might be able to infer that Chester is taking his medications by sensing that he has gotten out of bed, moved to the bathroom, and opened his medicine cabinet. However, it would not be able to distinguish whether Chester was brushing his teeth or taking his medications if his toothbrush and his meds reside in the medicine cabinet. If small RFID tags are placed on his toothbrush and his medicine bottle, the system can detect the difference. Furthermore, as RFID for supply chain tracking becomes more common, it may not even be necessary to place the tags on some of the household items because they will already be there.

Chester can wear an unobtrusive RFID reader that detects when he approaches an RFID-tagged object. Using inferencing techniques developed for Machine Learning applications (the same inferencing techniques discussed in the section Assisting Medical Personnel, in fact), a computer connected wirelessly to a system of RFID tags and readers can identify Chester's daily activities and notify Molly when any unexpected or potentially dangerous patterns emerge. For example, the system might learn that Chester rises every day between 7:00 and 8:00 a.m., gets dressed, takes his medications, and fixes coffee within a half hour after rising. On days when this pattern is detected, a light in Molly's house glows green. On days when this pattern varies, the light glows yellow. On days when the pattern varies considerably (such as no activity is detected by 10:00 a.m.), the light glows red and Molly's cell phone is automatically dialed to ensure that she gets the message. This saves Molly much time and effort in checking on Chester and provides Chester with relief in knowing that Molly will be notified if something goes wrong.

The system, by seeing which tagged objects come near Chester's RFID bracelet, can infer activities. For example, the system might detect the motion of the medicine cabinet door, followed by the motion of the bottle of vitamin B tablets, followed by the motion of the water glass. Like following the movements of an "invisible man," the system can accurately infer what is happening. By putting the detector in a bracelet, we give Chester complete and easy control over his privacy, as well; if Chester takes the bracelet off, the system stops recording.

Once we can accurately and unobtrusively detect activities, we can develop multiple methods to act on this information. We can use simple notifying schemes such as the "ambient lamp" described above. We can develop escalation and emergency notification strategies that will notify the appropriate people for a given situation via phone, email, pager, or other means. We can also track longer-term trends on behavior that can be provided to the elder, the family members, and medical personnel to provide information for remedial intervention.

For example, suppose Chester has been slowly decreasing in the frequency of his social interactions over the last several months. This pattern may be much too subtle for a doctor to detect via a standard office visit or even for family members. However, a tracking system might easily detect these types of subtle shifts and enable family and friends to increase their visits and phone calls. It has been shown that a decrease in social activity often precipitates a decline in overall health. This type of real-world trend analysis might be very helpful in maintaining health in the elderly.

The system described above does not yet fully exist, but Intel is on the way to developing it. In a recent study, we tagged 108 household items in an experimenter's home and had volunteers then perform daily activities in the home wearing an iGlove, an RFID reader attached to a glove worn on the volunteer's right hand, as shown in Figure 13.3. By detecting the sequences of proximity with household objects, the system was able to successfully track and identify 14 different activities.[7]

---

7. Philipose, M., Fishkin, K.P., Perkowitz, M., Patterson, D.J., Hähnel, D., Fox, D., and Kautz, H. "Inferring Multiple ADLs from Interactions with Objects." *IEEE Pervasive Magazine.* October 2004. pp. 50–57.

Figure 13.3 An RFID glove detecting daily activities (in this case, picking up the phone). (Image courtesy of Kenneth Fishkin.)

Of course, real elders couldn't be asked to wear a heavy glove like this all day. In a few years, we will be able to replace this glove with something much less obtrusive, such as a bracelet. We are currently in the planning and approval stage of deploying this technology in real homes of elders and caregivers.

Criteria for Different Types of "OKness" Systems

Automatic systems that track OKness in elders must meet some practical criteria to be effective. First, they must be cost effective. The cost of the system must be balanced against other alternatives, such as placement in a care facility or use of a full-time attendant. Second, they must meet the privacy and security requirements of the medical community as well as the needs of the family and the elder. Finally, they must be highly accurate, with a very low probability of either false alarms or failure to detect an emergency situation. Table 13.1 provides a rough comparison of three types of such systems: motion/switch, RFID, and video.

Table 13.1   Attributes of Three Types of "OKness" Systems

Type	Cost	Privacy/Security	Accuracy
Motion/switch	$	High	Low
RFID	$$	High	Moderate
Video	$$$	Low	Low

Applications for Assisting the Elderly

A system for identifying daily activities can be a launching point for numerous assistive applications. As discussed above, they can help provide safety, security, and diagnostic information for caregivers and medical professionals. Some other applications can help promote healthier lifestyles:

Exercise

Elders often fail to get enough exercise because they are not motivated or do not have the social support to help make the exercise rewarding and fun. An RFID-enabled system can detect opportune times when elders could receive encouragement from a friend to exercise. For example, an activity-tracking system could identify times of the day when the elder is inactive and proactively contact a friend to invite the elder for a walk. This system employs the elder's social support network and its knowledge of the elder's activities to provide motivation.

The system can also display activity levels to the elder to increase motivation. For example, the system might show graphs of activity levels in the home to depict trends, such as a decline in activity over time. More fine-grained analysis might show subtle changes in activity as a result of changes in diet or medications.

Nutrition

As RFID becomes more commonplace, tracking nutritional habits becomes possible. Food items might have RFID tags with nutrition information encoded. Readers in the refrigerator, microwave, or cupboard can keep track of nutrition as items are consumed and provide a daily summary of the elder's diet.

Thus, the system could suggest recipes to correct a nutritional deficit or contact the caregiver if warranted. Recent work at U.C. Berkeley,[8] for example, shows a system that looks at the supermarket purchases of a consumer and suggests similar, but mildly healthier, foods for the next supermarket visit.

Name and Face Rehearsal

It is estimated that about 50% of all adults over the age of 80 will have some type of dementia, usually observed as memory problems. Frequently, memory problems cause elders embarrassment and can cause them to avoid social situations. One remedy is to provide elders with opportunities to rehearse for social situations to reduce anxiety and improve memory performance.

Our name and face rehearsal system (see Figure 13.4) is a conceptual prototype that uses RFID-tagged photos and a reader linked to a database system.[9] This system allows the user to utilize everyday objects such as photos and mementos to trigger an interactive memory aid. When the elder places a photo at a particular spot on the table, an RFID reader underneath the table detects the photo and brings up information about the subject on a nearby TV screen. The system can provide gentle prompts to help the elder remember names and facts associated with the photos. The system could use voice recognition or simple item selection as input from the elder. This technology is currently in an early prototyping stage, and much research and development needs to be done to create a robust system.

Challenges

The scenarios presented above offer advantages to consumers, caregivers, and government, but they present a host of challenges as well.

Radio Frequency Health Issues

The hospital setting is a critical environment that contains a variety of radiation-emitting devices, including MRI units, x-ray machines, microwave sterilizers, and pacemakers. Interference concerns can prevent beneficial technologies from

8. Mankoff, J., Hsieh, G., Hung, H.C., Lee, S., and Nitao, E. "Using Low-Cost Sensing to Support Nutritional Awareness." In *Proceedings of Ubicomp 2002.*
9. Morris, M., Lundell, J., Dishman, E., and Needham, B. New perspectives on ubiquitous computing from ethnographic study of elders with cognitive decline. *Proceedings of Ubicomp 2003: Ubiquitous Computing.* pp. 227–242.

Figure 13.4   A name and face rehearsal system.
(Image courtesy of Kenneth Fishkin.)

being deployed. For example, partially because of concerns over electromagnetic interference (EMI), personal cell phones are banned in most hospital settings. However, this ban is not universal, and no comprehensive guidelines for EMI currently exist in the USA. The FDA has published several reports on EMI in hospital settings, the most comprehensive of which is "Medical Devices and EMI: The FDA perspective."[10] The agency states that it is working with several agencies to ensure that medical devices are properly shielded to minimize EMI; however, there is no mention of a ban (existing or proposed) on any EM devices that meet FCC regulations. The situation is similar in other countries, such as England[11] and Canada.[12] Although there is concern, and some evidence of EMI problems with pacemakers, electronic wheelchairs, and apnea machines, the risk seems slight with devices that have proper shielding.

However, the use of RFID in the medical setting must be taken on a case-by-case basis, and the benefit of the technology must be weighed against the possible risks, even though those risks might be small. It is safe to say that short-range RFID readers pose less of a risk than long-range readers and should be used instead of long-range readers whenever possible. RFID readers should be kept

10. www.fda.gov/cdrh/emc/persp.html
11. NHS (National Health Service) issued report DB9702, "Electromagnetic Compatibility of Medical Devices with Mobile Communications." March 1997.
12. Janice Hamilton. "Electromagnetic interference can cause hospital devices to malfunction, McGill group warns." *Canadian Medical Association Journal*. 1996. 154:373–375.

away from critical healthcare equipment and should use the lowest energy level needed to perform their function.

Standards

Electronic tagging protocols can provide much more information than was previously available. Thus, new standards must be developed for these new capabilities. Prescription drugs, for example, can be tagged with the date of manufacture, source, expiration date, recommended dosage, and side effects. In addition, RFID tags might include environmental and shipping information, such as how much heat the drug has been exposed to in transit.

The challenge to developing standards in this area lies in the end-to-end capability that RFID makes possible. Because there are potentially so many different points of contact in delivering goods such as prescription drugs, it is not clear who owns the standards process. For example, suppose a drug company wanted to add the side effects of its drugs into the data encoded into the RFID tag. Before this move is approved in the United States, the Food and Drug Administration, Federal Trade Commission, IEEE, ISO, and UCC will all want input to the specification for this extra data. Moreover, given that the pill bottle is often manufactured in, shipped through, and consumed in a variety of countries, additional international standards bodies (such as the EPC) will need a say. It is clear that it will be some time before a final standard is resolved.

However, it is important to avoid proprietary solutions to these capabilities because numerous incompatible solutions will inhibit the end-to-end tracking that is the strength of RFID tagging technology. Different proprietary solutions would likely require a variety of readers and data formats, and one could hardly expect a pharmacy or hospital to have multiple readers and multiple protocols for tracking all of the drugs it needs to process.

Privacy, Security, and HIPAA

"Have you heard the latest HIPAA joke?"
"No, what is it?"
"Knock, knock."
"Who's there?"
"I can't tell you."
—Conversation overheard at the Smart Healthcare USA conference

In 1996, Congress passed the Health Information Portability and Accountability Act. This legislation was intended primarily to provide continuity of healthcare coverage for individuals changing jobs and to simplify the administration of health insurance. But the legislation created significant protection for the *privacy* of healthcare information as well—the first national legislation in the United States.

HIPAA's Sections 261 through 264 require that the Secretary of Health and Human Services publish standards for electronic exchange, privacy, and security of health information. After two rounds of public review, a final rule known as the *Privacy Rule* was published on August 14, 2002.

The Privacy Rule protects all "individually identifiable health information" held or transmitted in any form or media, whether electronic, paper, or oral. Each healthcare provider is responsible for compliance, and these organizations have generally been conservative in applying the new rule. For example, in many waiting rooms, medical personnel will no longer announce people's last names in calling them into the doctor's office. This practice can cause confusion when multiple people with the same first name are waiting for an appointment. However, a broad interpretation of this law would classify the public announcement of a person's first and last name in a waiting room as a violation of the privacy act.

Although the rule is specific regarding intentional use or transmission of healthcare information (what can be transmitted under what circumstances), it is not as clear regarding security and unintended access. The Privacy Rule does not require that *every* risk of an incidental use or disclosure be eliminated. The healthcare entity is required to adopt reasonable safeguards and limit sharing of information to the "minimum necessary."

The Privacy Rule will impact many potential uses of RFID in the medical setting. For example, although real-time patient tracking can be very useful to hospital administration, the knowledge of where a patient is located must be restricted only to those who "need to know." A casual observer should never be able to see that certain patient is currently in MRI or undergoing radiation treatment, for example, by glancing at a computer monitor at a nurse's station.

Although any observer currently can read a medical chart or an ID bracelet to obtain patient information, the use of RFID can potentially make access to this information easier because RFID does not require physical access or line of sight to read patient information. A person could potentially use long-range RFID readers from several meters away on the other side of patient room walls to get access to private information.

Moreover, the Privacy Rule requires that patients be made aware of what type of information is disclosed. This may be problematic in the use of active tags on which information may be added or modified constantly. This is an example of tags that may have to become less "promiscuous," revealing only the appropriate information to the appropriate questioner, as discussed in other chapters.

HIPAA does not specifically deal with medical information that might be collected and used in a nonmedical setting, such as with an in-home heart rate monitor. As discussed above, there may be many uses for RFID in the home to collect medical or health information, particularly for elder caregiving. Our research has shown that elders who are faced with possible institutionalization and their caregivers are willing to sacrifice some privacy to stay at home. Nevertheless, we believe it is very important to provide elders control over the distribution of their data and to provide easy ways for them to specify who sees what types of healthcare data.

We maintain that the judicious use of RFID and other nonvisual sensor data can provide a level of security over other solutions such as video cameras and audio recordings in caring for elders. Even though some video-camera-based solutions do not send raw visual data, merely the presence of video cameras can make people more uncomfortable than nonvisual-based sensors.

As RFID applications evolve, the implications of HIPAA will become clearer. Some obvious areas for consideration and innovation are:

- Visibility of information exchange. Currently, an RFID tag gives up its information without any indication that it is being read. This may need to change for certain applications. Certain types of RFID tags may need to indicate when they are being accessed and what information is being read, and they may need to retain a history of being read. For example, a hospital patient, after waking up, may want to know who has read information from the RFID tag and what information was obtained.
- Consent. In some cases, specific consent may be required before the information contained on an RFID tag is read. Consent might come via biometric signatures, such as fingerprints or retinal ID.
- Security levels. RFID information may need to support multiple security or data access levels. This is in keeping with HIPAA's "minimum information" rule. For example, it may be necessary to restrict the information that can be accessed by an x-ray technician yet allow the patient's physician full access to the patient's data.

Other countries have directives analogous to HIPAA. For example, the European Union Privacy Directive[13] provides similar rules regarding data protection.

---

13. www.dss.state.ct.us/digital/eupriv.html

Under the terms of this directive, any nonmember state doing business in the European Union must comply with the rules. Thus, RFID companies may need to comply with privacy rules for any country in which they intend to do business.

In summary, RFID for healthcare poses many challenges to ensure safe operation in medical settings, standards and interoperability, and privacy and security. The HIPAA rule and privacy rules in other countries are just beginning to be integrated into medical practice, and many changes, clarifications, and technical advances will be required before a clear and consistent picture emerges. In the meantime, RFID innovators must keep an open dialog with the medical community on the emerging requirements for electronic storage and transmission of data. We believe that healthcare in general, and the hospital in particular, will offer many scenarios in which some of the RFID privacy techniques and policies discussed and proposed in other chapters of this book will have to be brought to bear and tested.

Conclusions

We're in the very early stages of the RFID "wave." In this chapter, we've sketched some ways that this wave could sweep through the healthcare industry. Of course, not *all* of the applications we've described here will happen: indeed, *most* of them probably will never reach a widespread deployment. However, we believe that *some* of them will, carrying with them real change and making real impact on the quality of our healthcare, whether at home or in the hospital.

We know that the healthcare industry will change dramatically over the next few years. This change will be brought about by the increasing demand for quality healthcare in the face of diminishing resources. It has been suggested that in order to cope with this demand, the current model of the medical clinic as the central health support system must change.[14] The locus of healthcare must shift to the home environment, where preventive and maintenance healthcare takes place and where informal support systems of family and friends can be utilized in lieu of scarce medical professionals.

But this shift will bring new problems in the privacy and security of healthcare information. As it becomes possible to collect more detailed information outside the clinic, the definition of "medical information" becomes blurry. Will

---

14. Dishman, E., Matthews, J.T, and Dunbar-Jacob, J. Everyday Health: Technology for Adaptive Aging. In *Technology for Adaptive Aging*, Pew, R. and Van Hemel, S. (eds). The National Academies Press. 2004. pp. 179–204.

the history of a diabetic's eating behavior collected automatically in the home be protected in the same way as the record of his last surgery? Who will set the security levels on the many different types of information that can be collected? This new potential for the collection of health information will require new policies, new security technology, and new interfaces for implementing those policies.

As Intel and many other companies continue to develop ubiquitous sensors and tags to collect biological and behavioral information, there is a need for technology developers to align with regulatory agencies in government and the medical industry to help them anticipate problems and set policy regarding this new technology. In addition, there is a need to develop new interaction paradigms and interfaces that allow patients and their physicians to control access and provide for the distribution of medical information to the right people at the right time. With RFID technology, there is great value in the ability to automatically collect information without requiring laborious and error-prone input from the user. However, there is also the potential for this largely invisible infrastructure to be misused. The question therefore is how can the interface to ubiquitous data collection and transmission be lightweight and unobtrusive yet still maintain enough visibility for informed consent and controlled access? We believe the central challenge for healthcare is not in the development of the security protocols, encryption methods, or ever smaller and more ubiquitous devices, but in the development of the policies and human-computer interfaces that will help enable the appropriate visibility, use, and control of medical information.

References

Amenta, P.S., *Histology*, 4th ed. Medical Outline Series. Norwalk, CT: Appleton & Lange. 1993. p. 138.

Baker, J.A. "The Stakes for Them—and Us." *Newsweek*. April 6, 1993. pp. 24–26.

Dishman, E., Matthews, J.T., and Dunbar-Jacob, J. Everyday Health: Technology for Adaptive Aging. In *Technology for Adaptive Aging*, Pew, R. and Van Hemel, S. (eds). The National Academies Press, 2004. pp. 179–204.

"Descriptive Geometry." *Encyclopedia Britannica*. 1986. 7:292–296.

Fishkin, K.P., Jiang, B., Philipose, M., and Roy, S. "I Sense a Disturbance in the Force: Long-range Detection of Interactions with RFID-tagged Objects." Ubicomp. 2004.

Food and Drug Administration. "Combating Counterfeit Drugs." February 18, 2004.

www.epill.com/epill/statistics.html

www.beyond2000.com/news/jan_01/story_996.html

www.hhs.gov/ocr/privacysummary.pdf

Chapter 14

Wireless Tracking in the Library: Benefits, Threats, and Responsibilities

Lori Bowen Ayre[1]

Introduction

Libraries began using RFID systems to replace their electromagnetic and bar code systems in the late 1990s. Approximately 130 libraries in North America are using RFID systems, and hundreds more are considering it.[2] The primary cost impediment is the price of each individual tag. Today, tags cost approximately 75 cents, but prices continue to fall.

Privacy concerns associated with item-level tagging are additional impediments to libraries' use of RFID tags. The problem with today's library RFID systems is that the tags contain static information that can be relatively easily read by unauthorized tag readers, allowing for privacy issues described as "tracking" and "hotlisting."

Tracking refers to the ability to follow the movement of a book (or person carrying the book) by "correlating multiple observations of the book's bar code"[3]

---

1. Lori Bowen Ayre is the principal of The Galecia Group. Her firm provides library technology consulting and project management to libraries and related organizations.
2. Molnar, D. and Wagner, D.A. Privacy and Security in Library RFID: Issues, Practices and Architectures. October 2004. Retrieved March 25, 2005, from www.cs.berkeley.edu/~dmolnar /library.pdf.
3. Ibid., 2.

or RFID tag. Hotlisting refers to the process of building a database of books and their associated tag numbers (the hotlist) and then using an unauthorized reader to determine who is checking out items on the hotlist.

Current standards (ISO 15693) apply to container-level tagging used in supply chain applications and do not address problems of tracking and hotlisting. Next-generation tags (ISO 18000) are designed for item-level tagging. The newer tags are capable of resolving many of the privacy problems of today's tags. However, no library RFID products using the new standard are currently available.

Libraries implementing RFID systems today are using tags unsuited for item-level tagging, and the cost of upgrading to newer tags when they become available is well beyond the reach of most library budgets.

This chapter addresses many of the specific issues and privacy concerns associated with RFID technology in libraries and suggests best practices in RFID-implementation for librarians. Finally, we explore the larger responsibilities of libraries in regards to RFID, public policy, privacy, and the changing world of technology.

RFID System Components and Their Effects in Libraries

An RFID system consists of three components: the tag, the reader, and the application that makes use of the data read on the tag.

Tag

Also known as a *transponder*, the tag consists of an antenna and silicon chip encapsulated in glass or plastic.[4] Tags contain a very small amount of information. For example, many tags contain only a bar code number and security bit (128 bits), but some tags contain as much as 1,024 bits of information.[5] Tags range in size from the size of a grain of rice to 2-inch squares, depending on their application. Researchers are now working on tags as small as a speck of dust.[6]

---

4. Want, R. RFID: A Key to Automating Everything. *Scientific American*. January 2004. 290(1), pp. 56–66. Retrieved July 9, 2004, from MasterFILE Premier database.

5. Boss, R.W. RFID Technology for Libraries [Monograph]. *Library Technology Reports*. November-December 2003.

6. Cavoukian, A, Ph.D. Tag, You're It: Privacy Implications of Radio Frequency Identification (RFID) Technology. Toronto, Ontario: Information and Privacy Commissioner. February 2004.

Tags can be passive, active, or semi-active (also called semi-passive). An active tag contains some type of power source on the tag, whereas the passive tags rely on the radio signal sent by the reader for power. Most RFID applications today use passive tags because they are so much cheaper to manufacture. However, the lack of power poses significant restrictions on the tag's ability to perform computations and communicate with the reader. It must be within range of the reader to function.

Semi-active tags use a battery to run the microchip's circuitry but not to communicate with the reader. Semi-active tags can rely on capacitive coupling and carbon ink for the antennas rather than the traditional inductive coupling and silver or aluminum antenna used in passive tags.

Tags operate over a range of frequencies. Passive tags can be low frequency (LF) or high frequency (HF). LF tags operate at 125kHz, are relatively expensive, and have a low read range (less than 0.5 meters). HF tags operate at 13.56MHz, have a longer read range (approximately 1 meter), and are less expensive than LF tags. Most library applications use HF tags.[7]

Tags can be read only (RO), write once read many (WORM), or read write (RW).[8] RO tags are preprogrammed with a unique number like a serial number (or perhaps eventually an ISBN number). WORM tags are preprogrammed, but additional information can be added if space permits. RW tags can be updated dynamically. Sometimes space on the RW tags is locked where permanent data is kept and the rest of the tag is writable. Most library applications use RW tags.[9]

Reader

According to Sarma et al., RFID readers or receivers are composed of a radio frequency module, a control unit and an antenna to interrogate electronic tags via radio frequency (RF) communication. Many also include an interface that communicates with an application (such as the library's circulation system).[10]

Readers can be handheld or mounted in strategic locations to ensure they can read the tags as the tags pass through an "interrogation zone." The interrogation zone is the area within which a reader can read the tag. The size of the interrogation zone varies depending on the type of tag and the power of the

7. Allied Business Intelligence. *RFID White Paper*. Oyster Bay, New York. 2002.
8. Ibid., 5.
9. Ward, D.M. March: RFID Systems. *Computers in Libraries*. March 2004. pp. 19–24.
10. Sarma, E.S., Weis, S.A., Engels. D.W. *White Paper: RFID Systems, Security & Privacy Implications*. Cambridge: Massachusetts Institute of Technology, Auto-ID Center. November 2002.

reader. Passive tags, with shorter read ranges, tend to operate within a smaller interrogation zone.[11] Most RFID readers in libraries can read tags up to 16 inches away.[12]

Readers in library RFID systems are used in the following eight ways:

- Conversion station. Where library data is written to the tags
- Staff workstation at circulation. Used to check in and check out materials.
- Patron self-checkout station. Used to check out books without staff assistance.
- Exit sensors. Verify that all books leaving the library have been checked out.
- Patron self-check-in station. Used to check in books without staff assistance.
- Bookdrop reader. Checks in books when patrons drop them in the bookdrop.
- Sorter. Automated system for returning books to proper area of library.
- Portable reader. Handheld reader for inventorying and verifying that items are shelved correctly.[13]

Application

Once the reader reads the tag, the information is passed on to an "application" that makes use of the information. Examples of library and nonlibrary applications and their uses fall into at least six categories:

- Access control (keyless entry)
- Asset tracking (self-check-in and self-checkout)
- Asset tagging and identification (inventory and shelving)
- Authentication (counterfeit prevention)
- Point-of-sale (POS) (FastTrak)
- Supply chain management (SCM) (tracking of containers, pallets, or individual items from manufacturer to retailer)

RFID is most pervasive in the supply chain management (SCM) market. ABI reports that by 2007, SCM and asset management applications will account for more than 70 percent of all transponder (tag) shipments.[14] In the SCM market,

---

11. Ibid., 10.
12. Ibid., 5.
13. Ibid., 5.
14. Ibid., 7.

items are tracked by pallet or container, not by individual item. Once the individual items are removed from the pallet, they are no longer tagged.

In contrast, library applications require that each individual item contain a tag that uniquely identifies the item (book, CD, DVD, etc). The tag contains some amount of static data (bar code number, manufacturer ID number) that is permanently affixed to the library item. This information is conveyed, via reader, to the library's security, circulation, and inventory applications.

RFID Standards

The electromagnetic spectrum on which RFID resides is regulated by local governmental bodies. Global standards "define the most efficient platform on which an industry can operate and advance".[15] The International Organization for Standardization (ISO) and EPCglobal have been very active in developing RFID standards. The AutoID Center and its commercial offshoot, EPCglobal, have also defined specifications and standards. Because most commercial applications, including library applications, use the HF, the discussion of standards is limited to HF standards.

There are two ISO standards pertinent to library RFID systems. The current standard, ISO 15693, was not designed for the item-level tracking done in libraries. Yet most library RFID tags follow this standard. ISO 15693 was designed for supply chain applications. It defines the physical characteristics, air interface, and communication protocol for RFID cards. In August 2004, a new standard, ISO 18000, designed for item-level tagging was published. It will allow for more secure communications between tag and reader.

Library RFID applications must be able to interface with the library's integrated library systems (ILS). The SIP2 protocol has made it possible for RFID products and library automation products to exchange information. Over the years, shortcomings have been identified in SIP2 and the standard has been diluted as vendors modify the protocol to suit their needs.

To address the shortcomings of SIP2, the National Information Standards Organization (NISO) convened a "standards development group with the mission of designing a protocol that would encourage interoperability among disparate circulation, interlibrary loan, self-service, and related applications." The

---

15. R. Moroz Ltd. Understanding Radio Frequency Identification (RFID) (Passive RFID). Markham, Ontario: R. Moroz Ltd. July 2004. Retrieved August 4, 2004 from www.rmoroz.com /rfid.html.

outcome of this group was the National Circulation Interchange Protocol (NCIP). NCIP was approved by NISO in 2002. No library systems vendor has yet fully implemented it.[16]

RFID in U.S. Libraries

Penetration

Richard Boss (Boss, 2003) reported that fewer than 200 RFID systems had been installed in libraries worldwide as of the middle of 2003. David Molnar (Molnar, 2004) reported that more than 130 libraries were using RFID in North America alone. As the cost of RFID tags comes down, more and more libraries are taking a closer look at the technology as a way to save staff time, reduce personnel costs, reduce staff injuries, and improve security and inventory control.

Over the past two years, increasing numbers of library conference presentations have been devoted to RFID. At the American Library Association's (ALA's) Mid-Winter Conference in San Diego, one RFID session was held. At ALA Annual in Orlando, two sessions were held. In 2003, six RFID vendors were listed on the exhibitor list for the ALA Annual Conference. By 2004, there were 13 RFID vendors at Annual.

Library Problems Addressed by RFID

Libraries are suffering from budget shortfalls as never before. With cuts to state and local governments, it is difficult for libraries to remain staffed and open. RFID is seen as a way to address the staff shortages by increasing the number of circulations that can be processed with less staff.

Self-check systems have become very popular with both patrons and staff. RFID self-check systems allow patrons to check in or check out several books at a time. Self-check systems reduce the number of staff needed at the circulation desk.

With RFID-enabled tools, inventory-related tasks can be done in a fraction of the time that it takes with bar code readers. A whole shelf of books can be read

---

16. Koppel, T. Standards in Libraries: What's Ahead: A Guide for Library Professionals About the Library Standards of Today and the Future. The Library Corporation. March 2004. Retrieved August 5, 2004, from www.tlcdelivers.com/tlc/pdf/standardswp.pdf.

with one sweep of the portable reader, which then reports which books are missing or mis-shelved. For archives handling sensitive materials, the ability to inventory items without handling them is an additional benefit.

Sorting can be accomplished automatically with RFID. For a book that is dropped into the book drop, the reader reads the tag and uses the automatic sorting system to return the book to the shelves, the stacks, or the hold area.

Reduction of repetitive stress injuries (RSIs) among staff is another reason libraries are converting to RFID system. The repetitive motion associated with checking out books using optical scanners is believed to be more problematic than with RFID-enabled scanners. It is still too early to determine whether RFID systems reduce the incidences of RSI injuries.

Security is another aspect of library operations that may be greatly improved with RFID-based security systems. Rather than purchasing additional tags for security, libraries can use a single tag for identifying items and securing them. As patrons leave the library, the tags are read to ensure that the item has been checked out. Librarians also report that they can more easily retrieve lost or hidden items using the portable readers. At the session "Tiny Tracker: The Use of RFID Technology by Libraries and Booksellers." Karen Saunders of Santa Clara City Library reported at that many DVDs were being hidden by patrons *in the library* for their own use later. Using the RFID reader, staff located these lost items and returned them to circulation.

The possibility of blocking a tag from being read with foil or by removing the tag puts into question whether RFID is truly the best approach for library security.[17] In addition, readers are already being developed that are capable of scrambling the data on tags.[18]

Cost of Implementing RFID System in Libraries

Boss (2003) estimates the cost of implementing an RFID system for a library with 40,000 items at $70,000; for a library with 100,000 items, the cost would be $166,000. However, these estimates are probably high, given that costs are continuing to fall for items such as tags (now down to 20 to 75 cents each from 85 cents) and servers (now below $5,000 from an estimated $15,000).

17. Smart, L.J. Considering RFID: Benefits, Limitations and Best Practices. *C&RL News.* January 5, 2005. 66(1).
18. Hesseldahl, A. A Hacker's Guide to RFID. *Forbes.com.* July 29, 2004. Retrieved August 6, 2004, from www.forbes.com/home/commerce/2004/07/29/cx_ah_0729rfid.html.

The actual cost to any library will depend on which RFID modules the library uses. Boss provides estimates for individual RFID components as follows:

- Exit sensor: $4,000
- Portable scanner: $4,500
- Self-checkout unit: $20,000
- Bookdrop unit: $2,500
- Exit readers: $4,000[19]

The most expensive aspect of any RFID system is the cost of purchasing tags and placing them on each item. Tags range from 20 cents to 75 cents for books. The costs go up when tags are placed on other media such as CDs, DVDs, and tapes ($1.00 to $1.50 each). Customized tags (library logo) increase the costs of each tag further.

Once a library purchases tags, it is committed to the tags and the vendor. As Molnar (2004) states, "Once a library selects an RFID system, it is unlikely that anything short of catastrophe could motivate a library to spend the money and labor required to physically upgrade the tags."

At 75 cents per tag, a 100,000-item library would spend $75,000 on tags alone. Boss estimates a laborer can install three tags per minute (new installation). The cost of programming the new tags, removing the old tags, and placing the new tags in each item makes converting or upgrading the library's RFID system highly unlikely.

Role of Librarians

RFID technology introduces an ethical dilemma for librarians. The technology allows for greatly improved services for patrons, especially in the area of self-checkout. It also allows for more efficient use of professional staff and may reduce RSIs for library workers. And yet, the technology introduces the threat of hotlisting and tracking library patrons. Librarians have taken extra steps to ensure that laws such as the USA PATRIOT Act cannot be used by government entities to invade the privacy of their patrons, but many of those same libraries are placing trackable chips on their patrons' books. Although libraries have traditionally acted to protect and defend the privacy of their patrons, some are implementing a technology before proper safeguards have been developed.

Library use of RFID technology serves to legitimize the technology in the eyes of the community. Therefore, it is incumbent on the library community to

---

19. Ibid., 5.

ensure that the technology is developed in concert with established privacy principles and that any library use of RFID follows best-practices guidelines consistent with library values.

Privacy Protections for RFID by Industry and the Government

The Privacy Act of 1974 articulates certain principles for protecting privacy. Since its passage, these principles have been applied to specific technologies and practices. Paula Bruening, staff counsel for the Center for Democracy & Technology, describes the underlying principles as follows:

- Notice. Information collection and use should be open and transparent.
- Purpose specification. Personal data should be relevant to the purposes for which it is collected.
- Use limitation. Data should be used only for the purpose for which it was collected.
- Accuracy. Personal data should be accurate, complete, and timely.
- Security. Personal data should be protected by reasonable security safeguards against risk of loss, unauthorized access, destruction, use, modification, or disclosure.
- Access. Individuals should have a right to view all information that is collected about them to correct data that is not timely, accurate, relevant, or complete.
- Accountability. Record keepers should be accountable for complying with fair information practices.[20]

Organizations such as the Center for Democracy & Technology and the Electronic Frontier Foundation[21] have joined with Consumers Against Supermarket Privacy Invasion and Numbering (CASPIAN)[22] to issue a similar position statement composed of three recommendations:

20. Bruening, P. Testimony presented at House Subcommittee on Commerce, Trade and Consumer Protection on July 14, 2004. Washington, D.C. 2004. Retrieved August 4, 2004, from www.cdt.org/testimony/20040714bruening.pdf.
21. Tien, L. RFID and Libraries: EFF Talking Points for ALA IFC. Summary of presentation to the ALA Intellectual Freedom Committee of the American Library Association at ALA Mid-Winter, San Diego, California. January 10, 2004 Retrieved from www.privacyrights.org /ar/RFID-ALA.htm.
22. Consumers Against Supermarket Privacy Invasion and Numbering (CASPIAN). *Position Statement on the Use of RFID on Consumer Products.* 2003. Available from www.privacyrights.org/ar /RFIDposition.htm.

- A formal technology assessment should be undertaken before any tags are affixed to individual consumer products.
- RFID implementation should be guided by Principles of Fair Information Practice (such as The Eight-Part Privacy Guidelines of the Organisation for Economic Co-operation and Development (OECD).
- RFID should be prohibited for certain uses.

Librarians are well aware that they are the stewards of private information about their patrons. The ALA Code of Ethics states, "We protect each library user's right to privacy and confidentiality with respect to information sought or received and resources consulted, borrowed, acquired, or transmitted."[23] Lee Tien, staff attorney for the Electronic Frontier Foundation, states, "Libraries have long been very protective of library patron privacy given that surveillance of reading and borrowing records chills the exercise of First Amendment rights."[24]

> There are currently no U.S. laws or regulations on the books that pertain to privacy or consumer rights vis-à-vis RFID despite Debra Bowen's (Senator of the 28th District of California) attempts to change that. State Senator Bowen proposed Senate Bill No. 1834, which would have added an RFID chapter to Division 8 of the Business and Professions Code. The bill would have prohibited libraries from "using RFID tags attached to circulating materials to collect information that could be used to identify a borrower unless specified conditions are satisfied.[25]

Although SB1834 did not pass the state assembly vote, it is instructive to review the guidelines Senator Bowen proposed for library use of RFID:

> A library may not use an electronic product code system that uses radio frequency identification (RFID) tags attached to circulating materials to collect, store, use, or share information that could be used to identify a borrower unless all of the following conditions are met:
>
> (a) The information is collected only to the extent permitted by law.

23. American Library Association. Code of Ethics of American Library Association. 2004. Retrieved August 5, 2004, from www.ala.org/ala/oif/statementspols/codeofethics/codeethics.htm.
24. Ibid., 21.
25. S.B. 1834. Radio Frequency Identification Systems. California Senate, 2003–2004 Regular Session. Retrieved August 4, 2004 from http://www.leginfo.ca.gov/cgi-bin/postquery?bill _number=sb_1834&sess=CUR&house=B&author=bowen

(b) The information has been voluntarily provided by the borrower for the purpose of registering to use the library's collections and services or for the purpose of borrowing an item from the library, including an item containing an RFID tag.

(c) The information is not collected at any time before the borrower actually attempts to borrow the item or at any time after the customer completes the transaction to borrow the item containing the RFID tag.

(d) The information is collected with regards only to a borrower who actually attempts to borrow the item and is in regard only to that item."[26]

Given their commitment to a "library user's right to privacy and confidentiality with respect to information sought or received," librarians and library organizations should be working closely with Senator Bowen, the Center for Democracy & Technology, the Electronic Frontier Foundation, and any other advocates of safe and responsible use of RFID technology. Instead, many libraries are quietly implementing RFID systems because of the convenience while ignoring the possible problems the technology introduces.

Best-Practices Guidelines for Library Use of RFID

Because libraries are implementing RFID systems, it is important to develop best-practices guidelines. Given the immature state of RFID implementations in libraries, guidelines are very much in flux because libraries are just now beginning to understand the implementation issues, shortfalls with the technology, and the greater privacy concerns.

For the library considering RFID, Molnar suggests that libraries ask potential vendors whether they plan to develop a system that allows for rewriting tags on every checkout and then restoring the ID at check-in. This process eliminates the problems associated with storing static data on the tags and eliminates the problems of tracking and hotlisting. The ability to write new data to the tags during circulation requires the library to use read/write tags capable of supporting all the check-ins and checkouts the item will require over its lifetime. The library will need to determine how many writes will be required and then identify a vendor that will support such a protocol.

---

26. Ibid., 25

When a library is preparing an RFP for RFID technology, Ann Cavoukian recommends including:

- The institution's obligations with respect to the notice, access, use, disclosure, retention, security ,and disposal of records
- A requirement that the institution maintain control of, and responsibility for, the RFID system at all times
- The designation of a senior staff member to be responsible for the institution's privacy obligation and its policy[27]

Incorporating and expanding on the efforts of the Berkeley Public Library, San Francisco Public Library, Cavoukian, and the Privacy Rights Clearinghouse,[28] the author proposes the following best-practices guidelines for library RFID use:

- The Library should be open about its use of RFID technology, including providing publicly available documents stating the rationale for using RFID, the objective of its use and any associated policies and procedures, and the name of the person to contact with questions.
- Signs should be posted at all facilities using RFID. The signs should inform the public that RFID technology is in use, describe the types of usage, provide a statement of protection of privacy, and explain how this technology differs from other information collection methods.
- Only authorized personnel should have access to the RFID system.
- No personal information should be stored on the RFID tag.
- Information describing the tagged item should be encrypted on the tag even if the data is limited to a bar code number.
- No static information should be contained on the tag (e.g., bar code, manufacturer number) that can be read by unauthorized readers.
- All communications between tag and reader should be encrypted via a unique encryption key.
- All RFID readers in the library should be clearly marked.
- ISO 18000 mode-2 tags rather than ISO 15693 should be used.

Educating the Public

Karen Schneider suggests that the debate concerning RFID "takes us farther into the question of what our role in society is as libraries." She further states:

---

27. Cavoukian, A., Ph.D. Guidelines for Using RFID Tags in Ontario Public Libraries. Toronto, Ontario: Information and Privacy Commissioner. June 2004.
28. Givens, B. RFID Implementation in Libraries: Some Recommendations for "Best Practices." Summary of presentation to the ALA Intellectual Freedom Committee of the American Library Association at ALA Mid-Winter, San Diego, California. January 10, 2004. Retrieved from www.privacyrights.org/ar/RFID-ALA.htm.

We have a chance here—not simply on behalf of library users and librarians, but also for society at large—to present an ethical approach to RFID and similar technologies, to actually present a framework for how to do this and preserve privacy in an increasingly non-private world. And conversely, if we don't develop best practices, I think we are acceding to an increasingly commercialized, non-private world and we're losing an opportunity to do something that we've always done very well, which is to find intellectual freedom and privacy issues in a particular technology and speak to them very clearly in a way that the public can understand.[29]

It is incumbent on librarians to educate the public about the possible abuses associated with RFID for two reasons: because libraries have an interest in using the technology and because the threat to privacy posed by "ubiquitous computing"—of which RFID is a part—is significant.

Emile Aarts, Rick Harwig, and Martin Schuurmans argue, "the ubiquitous computing generation will further expand on distribution until a huge collective network of intelligently cooperating nodes is formed." They suggest that the capacity of the Internet and the ability to connect wirelessly to the network has the effect of "moving technology into the background."[30]

Librarians can help ensure that technologies designed to be hidden in the background remain public, at least until the public understands how the technology works and has had a say about how it should be used.

One, if not *the* single most important, reason for the existence of public libraries is to promote an informed citizenry. What better time than now to actively promote education of our citizens about technologies that promise to alter our lives so dramatically.

Conclusions

RFID technology promises to change our world. It has the capability of making our personal lives and our work lives in the library more convenient. However, every new technology comes at a cost. To remediate those costs, efforts must be undertaken to guide its development and implementation.

29. Flagg, G. Should Libraries Play Tag with RFID? *American Libraries*. Chicago: American Libraries. December 2003. 34(11), 69–71.
30. Aarts, E., Harwig, R., Schuurmans, M.. Ambient Intelligence. In P.J. Denning (ed.). *The Invisible Future*. New York: McGraw Hill. 2002. pp. 235–250.

Libraries should not yet implement RFID systems. Instead, libraries should be among the entities putting pressure on government and industry organizations to develop standards, public policy, and best-practices guidelines for their use.

Libraries that choose to implement RFID technologies before policy safeguards are put in place should take extra precautions to follow evolving best-practices guidelines.

Libraries should continue to protect patrons' privacy by ensuring that they are not seen as proponents of RFID before it can be safely deployed.

Libraries should work to ensure that RFID products are manufactured and used according to well-established privacy principles. They should refuse to implement potentially unsafe RFID solutions simply because they are convenient.

Finally, libraries must be outspoken in their public education efforts related to RFID not only because they can benefit from the safe implementation of RFID systems but also because RFID represents the start of a slippery slope to ever greater loss of control over our personal information.

References

Bednarz, A. RFID Everywhere: From Amusement Parks to Blood Supplies. *Network World Fusion*. May 3, 2004. Retrieved August 4, 2004, from www.nwfusion.com/news/2004/0503widernetrfid.html.

Bednarz, A. Defense Department Goes on Offense with RFID. *Network World Fusion*. November 3, 2003. Retrieved August 4, 2004, from www.nwfusion.com/news/2003/1103forresterside.html.

Berkeley Public Library (n.d.). Berkeley Public Library: Best Practices for RFID Technology. Retrieved August 5, 2004 from http://berkeleypubliclibrary.org/BESTPRAC.pdf.

Booth-Thomas, C. The See-It-All Chip: Radio-Frequency Identification—with Track-Everything-Anywhere Capability, All the Time—Is About to Change Your Life. *Time*. 162. September 22, 2003. p. A8. Retrieved July 9, 2004, from Gale Group database.

Dorman, D. New Vendors Heating Up Radio Frequency ID Market. *American Libraries*. 33(8). September 2002. Retrieved July 9, 2004, from MasterFILE Premier database.

Dowbenko, U. (n.d.). VeriChip: RFID Microchip Implants for Humans. Retrieved July 11, 2004, from www.conspiracyplanet.com/channel .cfm?channelid=74&contentid=900.

EPC Global. Guidelines on EPC for Consumer Products. 2003. Retrieved July 11, 2004, from www.epcglobalinc.org/public_policy/public_policy_guidelines.html.

Garfinkel, S. Database Nation. Sebastopol: O'Reilly & Associates. 2001.

Garfinkel, S. An RFID Bill of Rights. *MIT Technology Review.* October 2002. Retrieved July 8, 2004, from www.simson.net/clips/2002.TR.10.RFID_Bill _Of_Rights.htm.

Landt, J., Catlin, B. Shrouds of Time: The History of RFID. Pittsburg, Pennsylvania: AIM, Inc. 2001. Retrieved August 3, 2004, from www.aimglobal.org /technologies/rfid/resources/shrouds_of_time.pdf.

McHugh, J. (2004, July). Attention, Shoppers: You Can Now Speed Straight Through Checkout Lines! *Wired 12.07 (online version).* Retrieved July 9, 2004, from www.wired.com/wired/archive/12.07/shoppers.html.

National Business Review. Japanese Children to Be RFID'd. July 8, 2004. Retrieved July 11, 2004, from www.nbr.co.nz/home/column_article.asp?id =9531&cid=5&cname=Asia+%26+Pacific.

San Francisco Public Library. RFID Implementation: Proposed Plan of Action. March 31, 2004. Retrieved August 5, 2004, from http://sfpl4.sfpl.org /librarylocations/libcomm/rfidplan040104.htm.

San Francisco Public Library. Privacy Policy. April 30, 2004. Retrieved August 5, 2004, from www.sfpl.org/librarylocations/libcomm/pdfs/privacypolicy.pdf.

Santa Clara City Library. Checkpoint RFID and the Santa Clara City Library. January 2004. Retrieved August 5, 2004, from www.library.ci.santa-clara .ca.us/rfid/checkpoint.html.

Schneider, K. RFID and Libraries: Both Sides of the Chip. Testimony presented at Committee on Energy and Utilities, California Senate, Nov. 20, 2003. Washington, D.C. 2003. Retrieved from www.senate.ca.gov/ftp/SEN /COMMITTEE/STANDING/ENERGY/_home/11-0-03karen.pdf .

Weiser, M. Ubiquitous Computing. August 16, 1993. Retrieved August 5, 2004, from www.ubiq.com/hypertext/weiser/UbiHome.html.

Chapter 15

TRACKING LIVESTOCK WITH RFID

Clint Peck[1]

Introduction

Marks of identification have been used in animal agriculture for millennia. Since the first attempts to tame and contain wild animals for human use, nearly every civilization has used hot branding and various other methods of identification (ID)—tattoos, paint marks, earmarks, tail bobs, "dewlaps" and "waddles," and other skin alterations—to prove animal ownership. Scenes on Egyptian tomb walls dating back to 2,000 B.C. depict people marking cattle with red-hot branding irons to prove animal ownership. Stone Age and Early Bronze Age cave paintings in southwestern Europe also depict branded cattle. In the Western Hemisphere, the first brands recorded under a central registry were the Three Latin Crosses of Hernán Cortéz, who landed in Mexico in 1519.

For most Americans, animal ID conjures up images of Wild West cattle ranches where brands were held as symbols of esteem equal to any knightly crest. In Spanish Texas during the days before barbed wire, brands and earmarks were registered in brand books maintained by the *ayuntamientos,* or municipal councils. After 1778, the provincial government in San Antonio maintained an official brand book for all of Spanish Texas. Today most states have a brand registry and publish lists of brands and brand owners.

While brands remain legal and necessary instruments of ID, less romantic, but certainly just as critical and practical, are the numbered and coded plastic ear tags and steel clips that adorn nearly every cow wandering our rangelands and

---

1. Clint Peck is a senior editor for *Beef Magazine.*

pastures. As animal agriculture and its associated commerce have become more structured, having means of identifying individual animals—in addition to proving herd ownership—has become a necessity. In some countries, and within regions of some countries, means of individual identification has become mandatory by law.

In November 2003, the U.S. Animal Health Association (USAHA) Livestock Identification Committee became the first quasi-governmental organization to approve the concept of a national mandatory livestock ID system. The goal of a national ID system is to facilitate traceback of all livestock within 48 hours to premise of origin. A National Identification Development Team, made up of state animal health officials, livestock industry groups, and the federal agencies, has developed a comprehensive ID plan. The plan proposes that "standardized premises" ID numbers be established for all livestock operations, market facilities, assembly points, exhibitions, and processing plants. For these purposes, "livestock" includes beef and dairy cattle, bison, horses, swine, sheep, goats, alpacas, llamas, deer, elk, poultry, and aquaculture production.

The plan calls for individual ID of cattle, swine, and small ruminants destined for interstate movement. Other food animal species would be required to be identified with unique, individual group or lot numbers, depending on species. Early estimates indicate that it will cost about $600 million to deploy an electronic tracking system throughout the U.S. livestock industry, covering cattle as well as other animals such as pigs and sheep. And it will cost up to $120 million a year to operate the system, split among livestock producers and government. The U.S. Department of Agriculture's Animal and Plant Health Inspection Service will likely maintain a centralized database to collect all ID information under the proposed system. The plan is designed to allow only government animal health officials to use the information—and only for animal disease control.

RFID technology is universally being looked at as the vehicle to accomplish the goal of ubiquitous traceback. Today, RFID devices are the most common form of electronic ID used in the U.S. cattle industry, and the button-type ear tag is the most widely used method of attaching an RFID device to the animal. The female button attachment part of the tag itself often serves as a traditional visual identification tag. Transponders for RFID in the cattle industry are passive responders, which means they possess no power source of their own. Instead, it's the charge provided by the transceiver (reader) that enables the transponder to emit a signal back to the transceiver. Electronic circuits in the transponder can be programmed as read only (RO), meaning that information contained in the chip—in this case, a unique 12-digit number—can only be read. Chips can also be programmed as read write (RW), which enables information to be added, warehoused, and transferred to them.

Central to the goal of traceback are data collection and storage systems. Traceback can be done with a laptop computer, an electronic scale head, or a handheld computer that is capable of communicating with a transceiver and accepting the information from it. Recently, several private firms that offer data collection and repository services have emerged. For a fee, they will accept either handwritten or electronically generated data tied to animal herds or individual animals within herds. This data can be analyzed and manipulated to provide various measures of animal performance. It can also provide tracking and traceback services for producers that don't wish to store and generate the myriad data that professionals trained in data analysis can provide or don't have the ability to do so.

RFID Has to Prove Itself

Livestock producers, particularly cattle ranchers, are very private about their operations. They might display, advertise, and even name their ranches after their brands. But they keep what's behind those brands very close to their chest. For example, in cow country, it's considered impolite, if not downright offensive, to ask ranchers how many cows they run or how many acres of land they own. Upon being asked the size of his spread, a rancher is likely to turn the question into his own question: "How much money do you have in the bank?" or "How much do you figure your inheritance will be?" Therefore, RFID data privacy is an area that needs to be carefully addressed.

Access to the stored ID information clearly needs to be limited before ranchers will adopt this technology. There is widespread agreement in the livestock industry that the data collected and stored in a national ID system should be used solely by animal health officials for traceback in response to animal foodborne disease outbreaks. Ranchers and cattle feeders are adamant that data held in either private databases or a national system not be accessible by meat packers, the U.S. Department of Agriculture, the Internal Revenue Service, or anyone else who could otherwise gain from, or use against the livestock producer, the information collected and shared via RFID technology.

Recent cases in Canada in which meat packers refused to buy and process cattle identified as owned by individuals belonging to a particular industry association with antagonistic views have some producers worried about ID privacy. They feel that unchecked RFID technology might make it easier to link animals with people, allowing buyers to more easily choose the suppliers they buy from. RFID in the livestock industry would certainly fail if it were used to facilitate discrimination against those who produce and manage food animals.

Ranchers also are wary of liability issues related to any form of traceback technology. For example, if a cow infected with bovine spongiform encephalopathy (BSE), or "mad cow" disease, is found "upstream" in the marketing chain, its owner might be wrongfully implicated in the transmission of the disease. In many cases, though, it's felt that the fears of discrimination and liability are the reasons the U.S. lags other major beef-producing nations in the development and operation of national RFID systems.

It can be argued that privacy concerns are among the reasons this country's food animal producers are being careful about adopting RFID technology. But livestock producers, particularly those with cattle, are moving rapidly from what's long been a mature "commodity-based" industry to a system in which their animals become "food ingredients." And as the industry evolves into increased integration between segments (e.g., cow-calf, cattle feeding, meat packing, and even retailing), the arguments against traceback using RFID become less valid.

Putting RFID to Work

Dean and Karen Wang of Baker, Montana, are family ranchers who have entered the world of RFID. In the fall of 2003, the Wangs finished tagging all of their 700+ cows with RFID. The following spring, the couple's crew tagged each calf with an RFID tag at branding, along with a "visual" that can be read from a distance, such as by someone on horseback. That calf's tag corresponds to the cow's ear tag number, possibly a number that she's carried since her birth and before the days of RFID. When the Wangs sold their calves, they had specific instructions written into the contract to be sure the buyer, an Iowa farmer-feeder, would leave the RFID tags in the calves' ears and cooperate in returning a full range of performance information. Data tracking average daily gain, the feedlot, feed efficiency, and health treatment will be fed back to the Wangs, who will correlate the information with the calves' genetics and pre-weaning management.

This practice of "data harvesting" can help the Wangs make future decisions on a specific sire (bull) genotype that they will use with their herd or even on breeding regimes for subgroups. Using the tool of expected progeny differences (EPDs), which are predictors of a bull's ability to pass on various traits such as "calving ease," they may adjust the type of bulls they purchase from seed stock producers. For example, if they identify the cows that have a history of calving difficulty, they may want to breed those cows to a bull type that (as indicated by his EPDs) tends to sire low-birthweight calves.

In the case of the Wangs, the data harvest is intended to measure end-product traits such as red meat yield and "marbling," which is an indication of better taste and increased tenderness. Therefore, the calves were tracked all the way through slaughter, where several carcass measurements that indicate carcass quality were entered into each individual's record. The latest calf crop was the fourth one for which the Wangs specified to the buyer that they wanted carcass data returned to them. In fact, for the Wangs, this process of data transfer is becoming a condition in every sales agreement. If this data transfer weren't made easier by RFID, the Wangs would find it cumbersome, if not impossible, to gather and capitalize on the information flow that began when they tagged the calves on the ranch.

Like a few dozen other Montana ranchers, the Wangs are assisted in the conceptual and physical transformation into the world of traceback and RFID by the Montana Beef Network (MBN), a program designed to help the state's cattle producers receive added value for their calves. A major MBN component involves identifying cattle that meet specific targets for beef quality and consistency. The foundation of the network is data collection and information based on the use of RFID tags. A set of records is entered into a database when the cattle are tagged with standard industry RFID ear tags provided to the MBN by Allflex Corp., a commercial RFID ear tag manufacturer. The Wangs have been in the MBN for more than six years.

RFID and Livestock Marketing

Private livestock management data includes detailed vaccination records and information on dates of weaning, health treatment, and shipping. Lisa Duffey, the MBN coordinator based in Bozeman, Montana, follows the animals through the production chain after they leave the ranch. She collects and enters the various types of performance data reported to her by cattle feeders and meat packers. It's also Duffey's job to keep the data private according to the rules established by the MBN. Those rules specify that only individuals authorized by the owner of the cattle may have access to the management records associated with an animal's RFID number.

The MBN rancher advisory committee recently hired Florida-based e-Merge Interactive to process its data. e-Merge's "CattleLog" individual animal data collection and reporting system is used for data analysis and information exchange. "The compatibility among tags and scanning systems is critical to the success of any data tracking/management program," says Duffey. While the national ID plan is still being debated, it's very likely that data recording animal movement will be stored in a central database. The information contained in the database is intended to contain only individual animal IDs and the corresponding movement data, but many producers and industry observers are worried that information from so-called secure data warehouses will leak out.

Traceback and RFID Standardization with Livestock

Most of the innovative beef production and marketing alliances springing up around the country are predicated on some kind of animal ID system. Ken Conway of Hays, Kansas, is owner and president of GeneNet, an integrated marketing alliance that's traded over 250,000 head of cattle, many "equipped" with RFID. And he says that the RFID technology he's experienced is working very well for collecting and transferring cattle performance data. Conway is working with more than 1,000 cow-calf producers, 100 feedlots, and a large number of seed stock producers throughout the United States.

"For our purposes, the RFID systems out there are working as well as conventional panel ear tags for data collection," says Conway. "Things like retention rates, readers, and software systems are good enough to make this technology look like it's the wave of the future in livestock agriculture." He knows that animal health issues like the cases of BSE discovered in Canada and the United States in 2003 are accelerating the move toward individual animal ID. But as a specialist in alliances, feedlot management, packer relationships, and retail meat marketing, Conway is interested in traceback more for animal management than for health security.

"There's no question that with all the health issues like BSE and foot-and-mouth disease around, animal ID is going to be a way of life," he says. "It's going to be dictated to us that we follow our cattle throughout the production chain. In the end, this will be a good thing for us all." But he wonders if the combination of RFID technology and producers' willingness to adopt this technology will keep pace with the ID mandates that are filtering through every aspect of the livestock business. Conway also emphasizes that the RFID-associated data collected, transferred, and stored by GeneNet can pass through a series of privacy firewalls only with the permission and acknowledgement of the cattle owner. The owners association with GeneNet is a trust-based relationship with regard to privacy issues.

"I'm not sure we're to the point yet where we can identify individual animals throughout the chain reliably and consistently, nor does everyone feel comfortable in doing so," Conway explains. "But we seem to be moving in the direction of mandatory ID very rapidly." Conway emphasizes, though that source verification—at least from an animal performance standpoint—doesn't always need to involve individual IDs. "You certainly don't have to identify your cattle individually in order to participate in GeneNet. We can use group data to provide some valuable management information."

"The larger range-calving ranching operations aren't going to find it easy to individually ID calves from birth," Conway speculates. "I'm sure, though, that they'll figure out systems to deal with the demands put on them." The likely scenario, he speculates, might be that ID tags would be applied at the ranch during branding. "Obviously the closer to birth you can get the tag on the calf, the better."

For many producers, the location of first sale, such as an auction barn or feed yard, might be the first point at which permanent RFID is applied. Conway thinks the more progressive auction yards and feed yards will begin gearing up to facilitate RFID systems. "I'm assuming that automatic ID readers will be installed in auction markets," he says. "I'm not sure who's going to pick up the tab for all this, though—I guess ultimately it will be handed back to the producer as most everyone else in the system is a margin operator."

Conway says patterns of multiple-animal ownership are going to complicate livestock traceback systems. "When you look at different scenarios, this thing could get pretty wild, especially when you see animals changing hands four or five times after they leave the ranch," says Conway. He says that's where the software systems come into the picture. He's adamant that sometime in the future, the various tag manufacturers and software and data management systems will have to standardize. "There has to be a universal system and nearly 100 percent reliable system of codes and signals that will work with most of the software systems out there," he adds. "It's a no-brainer that there must be compatibility between systems."

Auction Markets: A Critical Component

Conventional wisdom says that livestock auction markets will become central to mandatory livestock identification when it reaches the national stage. Some markets are already gearing up for that day, including one of the Heartland's largest stockyards. The crew at Joplin Regional Stockyards (JRS) in Carthage, Missouri, know they'll be called on to routinely ID cattle as a service for livestock producers and marketers. In addition to being its own "premise," JRS plans to facilitate premise establishment for a stream of consignors. But this isn't a process that begins with a flip of a switch. JRS has been evolving into ID and livestock tracking technology since 2001.

JRS has had sporadic experience handling cattle wearing an assortment of RFID tags and now uses a standard industry bar-coded panel tag to ID animals assigned to its commingled cattle sales. JRS marketing director Mark Harmon says that with a national ID system coming, the cowhands at JRS will have to pick up the pace.

"Livestock auctions, as a place of first movement, are natural locations to provide this kind of service for customers," says Harmon. "We'll have to see how this all shakes out, but we're looking at all our options." Harmon envisions JRS crews tagging cattle according to customers' premise IDs and entering the data into computers that can link with almost any of today's major data management systems. This will help smaller producers, especially, save money and labor when it comes to tagging efforts.

"Given the nature of our operation, we can be pretty efficient at applying the tags and entering the necessary data," he explains. "We can also buy the tags in bulk, literally by the thousands. Economy of scale should help us reduce costs." Eventually tagging and tracking will become a normal service function for markets—a service livestock auctions will have to become accustomed to providing to keep customers from seeking out other marketing venues. "A lot of producers don't have the desire or ability to deal with tagging and data entry on the farm," adds Harmon. "It's a natural role for us to play."

criticisms

JRS's current plan is to have RFID tagging and scanning capabilities "coming in" and "going out" of the yards, according to Steve Owens, who with Jackie Moore owns the stockyards. Owens's biggest concern is not the cost of setting up tagging and scanning equipment; he's more wary that ID and tagging activities will interfere with the flow of cattle through the yards. "Maintaining an orderly movement of cattle is critical to the operation of any stockyards," he says. "We simply can't afford to adopt any technology that will slow us down."

Owens and Moore believe that there will have to be some RFID standards developed that will allow all livestock tagging systems to "agree" with each other. Whichever system they use, he says, has to be a one-time, one-tag system that is as seamless as possible. The biggest threat to flow comes when tags are missing, misread, or incompatible with reading and scanning systems. "No system is going to be perfect," he admits. "But they've got to be close to 100 percent or it'll create all kinds of problems for us."

JRS management emphasizes the ID numbers associated with the cattle flowing through its facilities will be the only data layer transferred to the next owner or to the next premises. "Even when it's only a number being transferred," Harmon explains, "we want assurances that the numbers will be held in a secure system—one that will only be used when a traceback is required under the authority of the national ID system."

Before JRS invests a lot more time and money in RFID technology, Owens and Moore want to be reasonably certain, at least for the time being, that another technological advancement will not completely replace it. "Is there other technology on the horizon that will make RFID obsolete at some point?" Owens asks.

RFID World Livestock Roundup

The following sections examine use of RFID for livestock in Australia, Brazil, Canada, the European Union, France, Japan, New Zealand, and the United Kingdom.

Australia

In 2002, Australia's National Livestock Identification Scheme (NLIS) initiated a system of permanent animal ID. The system is voluntary, except in Victoria, where the state government introduced legislation that cattle born in Victoria after January 1, 2002, must be identified with a NLIS tag before it leaves their property of birth.

The NLIS uses devices such as ear tags and rumen boluses embedded with an electronic microchip (with matched ear tags). The device is read electronically by readers at sale yards, abattoirs, or farms, and the information is sent to the national database via e-mail, fax, or mail. The database, which is accessed via user names and passwords, can store and provide information such as animal disease and residue status; market eligibility; lost, stolen, and mortgaged cattle; and commercial information.

The Cattle Council of Australia has endorsed a 14-digit, whole-of-life breeder tag that will identify the state, region, herd, year of issue, and individual animal. The program is run by SAFEMEAT, an industry and government partnership, and the program is delivered by Meat and Livestock Australia.

Brazil

Brazil is phasing in a mandatory national cattle ID and traceability system. Starting in June 2002, all beef for export to the European Union had to be enrolled in the program. The deadline for animals destined to other foreign markets was December 2003. Producers located in areas free of foot-and-mouth disease (FMD) must be in the program by the end of 2005. By 2007, all cattle and buffalo in the country must be in the program.

Canada

The Canadian Cattle Identification program was put in place under the Health of Animals Act to improve the traceability of the national cattle herd. This program does not prevent disease but rather improves the turnaround time and efficiency of all tracebacks, trace forwards, and "tracethroughs." In Canada, an ID ear tag must be applied by the time an animal leaves its herd of origin.

As a minimum requirement, the ear tag originally consisted of a visible unique number, bar code, and Canadian Cattle Identification Agency (CCIA) logo. Because of readability problems with the bar code system, however, CCIA moved to RFID on January 1, 2005. This will provide the Canadian cattle industry with further automation of data collection and the ability to easily transfer necessary management information quickly and accurately.

CCIA assigns unique numbers to tag manufacturers, and tags are distributed through authorized service centers and other outlets. The service centers maintain records of which numbers went to which producers. Primary producers are not required to maintain records. At the packing plant, a unique number will be maintained up to and including the point of carcass inspection.

In the event of a health or safety issue involving an animal, the Canadian Food Inspection Agency (CFIA) will be given access by the CCIA to the record of the herd of origin. CFIA will trace from both the herd of origin and the last location of the animal to determine the source of the problem.

European Union

Since January 1, 2000, all livestock in the European Union have been tagged with one ID tag in each ear within 20 days after their birth. The ID code follows the animal through a mandatory meat-labeling system. A "passport" for each head of livestock (cattle, sheep, and goats) is issued within 14 days of notification of its birth. The passport contains ID code, birth date, sex, breed or coat color, ID code of the dam and sire, and ID code of the farm of birth and all farms where the animal has been kept. Animals may be moved only if accompanied by their passports.

France

In France, one sector of private industry has taken cattle ID and meat tracing into its own hands. Soviba Group's 4,500 cattle, 1,200 pig, and 400 sheep producers have developed a computerized, farm-to-consumer traceback system. Soviba is the third largest consumer meats company in France and is recognized as the leader in "quality" initiatives.

In line with a mandatory national ID program, Soviba farmers receive a passport containing herd number, breed, date of birth, and other information issued by the cooperative within eight days after a calf is born. This stays with the calf throughout its lifetime.

In Soviba's packing plant, the cattle passport is recorded and a batch number is allocated to each carcass. This information is updated throughout the disposition of the meat. Thus, each tray of meat, even ground beef, can be traced back to its original farm. A unique traceback protocol allows shoppers to scan a label on a package of meat and access information about the producer that raised the animal. In addition, consumers can visit the Soviba Web site and learn such information as an animal's ID number, breed, sex, and age. They also can access a photo, name, address, and map pinpointing the producer's farm.

Japan

After experiencing eight cases of BSE, Japan initiated legislation in June 2003 to implement a compulsory system of full traceability of cattle from the farm through retail sale. All cattle must be individually ear-tagged, and information, including the ID number, breed, sex, and transportation and production history, must be entered into a national database. In addition, new regulations have been proposed to require producers to maintain records on feed use and feed suppliers.

The system is designed largely to allay food safety fears among Japanese consumers. In fact, one company marketing Wagyu beef offers a computerized system that allows consumers at point of purchase (or on their home computers) to key in a 10-digit number that is carried on the beef product label. Thus, they can access such information as the animal's birth date, breed, and origin as well as a photo of the producer and the results of BSE tests performed on that animal. Japan's Ministry of Agriculture, Forestry, and Fisheries tests every carcass for BSE. The Japanese government also mandates country-of-origin labeling on all imported products at retail but doesn't require full traceability at this time.

New Zealand

As of July 1, 1999, every person who owns or is in charge of cattle or deer must ID each individual animal. A herd number is required to be printed on official tags issued to that person. The ID program will allow for people to use other herd, farm, or business identifiers on official tags. A national herd register will link approved ID numbers to people in charge of a herd. The initial purpose of the program was to trace sources of bovine tuberculosis when infected animals are found at slaughter.

United Kingdom

The current U.K. system follows EU-wide rules on beef labeling. The rules are intended to meet consumers' concerns that cattle and the meat from them should be more easily traceable. The British Cattle Movement Service (BCMS) now operates a system tracking every calf, cow, and bull registered from birth to death. The ID protocol is strict. Each calf must be marked with double ear tags at birth. Producers then apply for a passport with numbers corresponding to the ear tags.

BCMS uses a bar code and optical character recognition system that can decipher hand-written letters and numbers. Reports of cattle movements can also be sent electronically. Passport applications must be accurately completed and sent to the BCMS within 15 days of tagging. Movements of cattle must be registered within 15 days, and deaths must be reported within seven days. BCMS expects to produce more than 3 million new checkbook-style cattle passports every year.

Part III
THREATS

Chapter 16

RFID: THE DOOMSDAY SCENARIO

Katherine Albrecht[1]

Introduction

In December 1085, William the Conqueror commissioned the "Domesday Book," a massive project to record all of England's 13,418 settlements south of the rivers Ribble and Tees (the border with Scotland at the time). It was an exhaustive compilation, the greatest and most exact land survey that the world had ever known. The book included extensive records of landholders, tenants, natural resources, buildings, livestock, and practically all other tangible assets. At the time, an observer wrote, "There was no single hide nor yard of land, nor indeed one ox nor one cow nor one pig which was left out."[2] The collection effort was finished by the summer of 1086.

A valiant effort, to be true. But there was one problem: Despite the all-encamping nature of the book, or perhaps because of it, much of the information in the Domesday Book was out of date before the book was even finished. In fact, by the time William died in September 1087, the project was abandoned.

With modern technology, we can do better. Much better.

For the first time in history, it may soon be possible to keep track of everything—every pencil, sweater, light bulb, car, and even every person—through tiny embedded computer chips hooked up to miniature antennas. Plans are

---

1. Katherine Albrecht is a consumer privacy expert and the founder of CASPIAN.
2. "The Domesday Book Online—Frequently Asked Questions." www.domesdaybook.co.uk /faqs.html (accessed November 23, 2004).

under way to replace the bar code with these devices, called radio frequency identification, or RFID, tags. If this happens, every manufactured object on earth could be assigned its own ID number and tracking tag.

The plan will be devastating to privacy. The information contained on RFID chips can be read at a distance, right through a person's pocket, backpack, or purse. The reader devices that pick up the information can be invisibly embedded in doorways, floors, walls, and shelving to keep track of people and their possessions as they go about their daily business. A linked network of readers could create a system of pervasive surveillance so detailed it could eventually be used to monitor our every move.

This chapter examines the trends that could lead to such a system, including placing the tags onto consumer goods, installing reader devices that would keep track of the tags, and creating the databases that would store vast quantities of information. Because the function of these databases determines how RFID tags and readers will impact privacy, this chapter proposes a new taxonomy for describing the databases that will store unique RFID numbers. Finally, it takes a brief look at some abuse scenarios and calls for restraint.

RFID Tags and the EPC Code

RFID tags can be embedded into or affixed to virtually any physical item, from car tires and aircraft parts to underwear and eyeglasses. If we adopt the RFID visionaries' view of the future,[3] a time will come when RFID tags are cheap and plentiful, readers are tiny and powerful, and RFID tags will have replaced the bar code on all manufactured goods.

An RFID tag consists of a tiny RFID computer chip connected to a miniature antenna that uses radio waves to communicate at a distance with nearby reader devices. An RFID tag typically ranges from the size of a postage stamp to the size of a pager, although some can be as small as the period at the end of this sentence.

Low-cost "passive" tags operate without an independent power source, getting their power wirelessly from the reader that scans them. They can be read from a distance of a few inches to up to 20 or 30 feet away, depending on their frequency, antenna size, and other factors. Once embedded in a protective

---

3. This discussion does not take into account the considerable consumer opposition to item-level RFID tagging. For EPC tags to replace the bar code, widespread consumer opposition will have to be quelled, ignored, or overridden.

housing, they have a theoretical lifetime of decades. Tags with their own power source, called "active" tags, can transmit information up to a mile or more. But these tags have a lifetime of just a few years because of the limited shelf life of their batteries.

Today, RFID tags are used primarily on crates and pallets to aid in supply chain inventory management. The long-term plan, however, is for RFID tags to replace the UPC bar code. Affixing RFID tags to individual consumer items, a process called item-level tagging, is one of the more problematic uses of RFID.

The organization charged with migrating today's bar code to an electronic product code, or EPC, is in a position to make this a reality. EPCglobal is a joint effort of the Uniform Code Council and EAN International, the organizations that manage the U.S. and overseas bar code systems, respectively. In addition, the plan has the backing of some of the world's largest retailers and consumer product manufacturers, including Wal-Mart, Target, Procter & Gamble, Gillette, Kraft, and Nestle.

The EPC consists of a 96-bit string of data (think of 96 zeros and ones, or two to the 96th power). This numbering scheme provides enough number combinations to uniquely number every product manufactured on the planet for the next 1,000 years. As described by EPCglobal, each EPC number will contain the following partitions:[4]

- A *header* that identifies the version of EPC
- A *manager number* that identifies the company associated with the product
- An *object class* number that identifies the product type
- A unique *serial number*

This relationship is illustrated in Figure 16.1.

016	37221	654321	2003004000
HEADER	EPC Manager	Object Class	Serial Number

Figure 16.1   EPC Data Number Partitions

From a privacy perspective, there are several crucial differences between the planned "radio bar code," or EPC tag, and the bar code of today. The first is

---

4. EPCglobal. "Electronic Product Code." www.epcglobalus.org/Network/Electronic%20Product%20Code.html (accessed October 7, 2004).

the unique serial number each EPC tag will contain. This number makes it possible to distinguish a specific item from a sea of similar items and to track it over time. Second, EPC tags can be queried remotely, without an individual's knowledge, by reader devices in the environment. (This concern is addressed in the next section.)

Another crucial difference is the ease with which an RFID tag can be hidden. Because they do not require line of sight, RFID tags are capable of transmitting information from hidden locations in a product or item. RFID tags have been sandwiched between layers of cardboard, incorporated into product labels, encapsulated in plastic, and sewn into the seams of clothing. This is not a theoretical concern; many deployments of item-level RFID in consumer products to date have already involved hidden tags.

At least one major company specializes in hiding RFID tags in goods and querying them at strategic locations. Checkpoint Systems, which touts itself as "the world's largest integrator of RFID technology into consumer product packaging,"[5] specializes in a process called source tagging, which means hiding "invisible,"[6] paper-thin anti-theft tags in consumer products at the point of manufacture. Checkpoint has used source tagging to conceal anti-theft tags in the lining of men's suits and has even sandwiched tags into the soles of shoes.[7]

While Checkpoint's primary line of anti-theft tags, known in the industry as electronic article surveillance (EAS) tags, do not contain unique ID numbers, the company recently purchased 100 million RFID tags[8] to integrate into its anti-theft source-tagging operations. In at least one trade show, Checkpoint showcased this ability with a display of RFID-laced fabric labels from Calvin Klein and Champion athletic wear. Presumably, Checkpoint is already incorporating its RFID tags into a wide variety of consumer products. This means that consumers right now could be unknowingly wearing and carrying items with remotely readable RFID tags in them, long before EPCglobal implements an RFID-based bar code replacement.

5. Checkpoint. "Checkpoint Systems Introduces EPC Solution Center." Checkpoint Press Release, January 12, 2004. www.checkpointsystems.com/content/news/press_releases_archives _display.aspx?news_id=59 (accessed October 7, 2004).

6. Checkpoint's Web site states, "'Invisible' EAS is more effective. Hidden from shoplifters and employees alike, Checkpoint source tags provide tamper-proof protection for profitable high-theft items." Source: Checkpoint. "Retailers reap the rewards of source tagging." www.checkpointsystems.com/content/srctag/partic.aspx (accessed October 7, 2004).

7. Checkpoint. "Source Tagging Shoes Is a Step in the Right Direction." Promotional PDF, Checkpoint. www.checkpointsystems.com/docs/ST_Shoes.pdf (accessed October 7, 2004).

8. Collins, J. "Checkpoint Buys 100 Million Tags," *RFID Journal*. March 30, 2004. www.rfid-journal.com/article/articleview/853/1/1/.

A Ubiquitous RFID Reader Network

The problem with tags in goods, of course, is that they can be read without consumers' knowledge or consent. Someone can do this overtly, by directly pointing a reader at a tag, for instance, or it could be done through readers embedded in the environment. A network of such embedded RFID reader devices may be closer than most people realize. Already, plans are under way to install RFID readers in doorways and floors to identify people and scan their belongings.

IBM, for instance, has developed a product called "Margaret," which uses doorway RFID readers to identify customers as they enter banks and financial institutions. The idea is to identify the more valuable clients to single them out for preferential treatment. IBM describes the program as follows:

> An RFID tag fitted to the customer's bank card or passbook could be used to signal their arrival at a branch. As they pass through the doors, the card would alert a customer information system. Bank staff could personally greet high-net-wealth customers, or customers could be greeted by name by tellers, who would already have their account information on-screen when they arrive at the counter.[9]

A leading industry publication, *RFID Journal*, supports this use of RFID readers at building entrances, suggesting that in addition to their use in banks, "The same system could be used in upscale restaurants or retail boutiques, where a high-degree of personal service is important."[10]

Texas Instruments is encouraging retailers to install doorway RFID readers for "keeping track of the customers walking in the door."[11] Its Web site touts an RFID-enabled frequent shopper card that can be read right through a shopper's purse and describes how consumers "with a TI-RFid tag in their purse, pocket, or wallet can be detected by reader systems at doorways. Readout antennas can also be in counters, walls, and in floors." It also details how "the technology can tell retailers exactly who's in their store at any given moment, while offering full purchase histories for each shopper. In addition, stores will know what the customer bought at their last visit and what they might need for accessories."[12]

9. Ward, V. "Coming Everywhere Near You: RFID." IBM, www-1.ibm.com/industries/financialservices/doc/content/landing/884118103.html (accessed October 7, 2004).
10. "RFID May Boost Service at Banks." *RFID Journal*, April 25, 2003. www.rfidjournal.com/article/articleview/396/1/1/.
11. "Customer Loyalty Mechanism with TI-RFID," Texas Instruments. www.ti.com/tiris/docs/solutions/pos/loyalty.shtml (accessed June 16, 2004). Archived at: http://web.archive.org/web/20040205161015/http://www.ti.com/tiris/docs/solutions/pos/loyalty.shtml (accessed October 7, 2004).
12. Ibid.

On my tour of the RFID industry's flagship Future Store in Rheinberg, Germany, in 2004, I observed that RFID readers had been installed at the store's entrance. Their purpose became clear when I discovered that the Future Store had hidden RFID tracking devices in the loyalty cards issued to over 10,000 of its customers (referred to as "guinea pigs" in an IBM press release[13]) without the shoppers' knowledge or consent.[14] It took a customer protest outside the store to get the practice stopped and the cards recalled.

Alarmingly, the anti-theft portals we pass through every day may be turning into RFID readers. Checkpoint has redesigned a line of doorway portals—the anti-theft gates installed in tens of thousands of retail locations and libraries worldwide—to be EPC compliant.[15] Checkpoint promotes this line (ironically named Liberty readers) as having "the ability to migrate easily to RFID technology."[16] In 2003, a senior Checkpoint executive boasted, "The technology is ready to pilot," and revealed, "We're working with forward-thinking consumer product goods manufacturers and retail clients on pilots."[17] It may not be long before retailers and marketers have the ability to scan us and our belongings every time we enter a store.

RFID readers will appear in more than just building entrances. They are likely to be used on roads and highways to keep track of traffic and record the movements of individual automobiles. The British government has invested over £1 million in a three-year trial of RFID-tagged license plates. Reader devices at roadsides would be capable of reading tags on cars going 200 to 300 miles per hour. A centralized system would link observed tag information with vehicle data such as registration number, owner details, and tax records.[18] In the United States, the Department of Transportation has been quietly working on a massive, multibillion-dollar plan to monitor all vehicular traffic with near-microscopic precision through road sensors, GPS, and cell phone technologies.[19]

13. IBM. "Metro Opens High-Tech Shop and Claudia Approves," IBM, April 28, 2003. http://www-1 .ibm.com/industries/wireless/doc/content/news/pressrelease/872672104.html.

14. For the full story and photographs of the card, including an x-ray of the hidden RFID tag, see "Scandal: The RFID Tag Hidden in METRO's Loyalty Card," part of CASPIAN's 12-page special report on the Metro Future Store. www.spychips.com/metro/overview.html

15. RFID Journal, "Checkpoint Bridges EAS-RFID Gap," *RFID Journal*. January 28, 2003. www.rfidjournal.com/article/articleview/285/1/1/

16. Checkpoint, "Liberty Brochure–Soft Goods," Promotional PDF, Checkpoint, www.checkpointsystems.com/docs/liberty_brochure.pdf (accessed October 7, 2004).

17. "Checkpoint Systems Demonstrates End-to-End RFID Solutions for the Retail Consumer Product Supply Chain." Checkpoint Press Release, November 7, 2003. www.checkpointsystems.com/content/news/press_releases_archives_display.aspx?news_id=58 (accessed October 7, 2004).

18. "RFID-Enabled License Plates to Identify UK Vehicles." *RFID News*, June 10 2004. www.rfidnews.org/news/2004/06/10/rfidenabled-license-plates-to-identify-uk-vehicles/ (accessed October 7, 2004).

19. Servatius, T. "Big Brother in Your Car: Futuristic High-Tech Could Save Your Life—and Raid Your Privacy." *Creative Loafing Charlotte*, September 29, 2004. www.charlotte.creativeloafing.com/2004-09-29/news_cover.html (accessed October 11, 2004).

Of course, a government mandate could speed the deployment of these ubiquitous reader networks. The Department of Homeland Security or the FBI could, for example, claim a pressing security need to identify and monitor everyone and everything entering public and quasipublic spaces. Reader devices could be mandated for use in "high-security" locations first, such as airports and courthouses, then gradually expanded to include other government buildings like schools and post offices, until finally they would encompass office buildings, shopping malls, and apartment buildings. Eventually, the entire nation could be blanketed with RFID readers.

A few years ago, the notion of a government-mandated RFID surveillance network would have sounded preposterous. However, the federal government's recent willingness to sacrifice civil liberties on the altar of post-9-11 security makes such a scenario all too conceivable today.

While the societal route to installing ubiquitous RFID readers in buildings could take a variety of forms, one thing is clear: The technical challenges involved would be relatively straightforward. The hardware infrastructure necessary to wire a reader into a doorway or parking lot entrance requires little more than electricity, an RFID reader, and a network connection (and even the latter is not an absolute requirement).[20]

Although developing the software infrastructure to capture, transmit, and store all of this data will present a more daunting task, it will be comparable to the near-term challenge of tracking billions of individual RFID-tagged items as they move through today's complex supply chains. By the time reader networks capable of tracking broad-scale human movements begin to appear, the groundwork for developing the necessary software will have already been laid.

Watching Everything: RFID and the Four Databases It Will Spawn

> An infinite amount of dynamic data can be associated with the [EPC] serial number in the database.
>
> —EPCglobal, Frequently Asked Questions[21]

---

20. Note that in some applications (e.g., household electrical meters), data is manually collected by a service technician on a periodic basis.
21. "The ID System (Tags and Readers)." EPCglobal. www.epcglobalus.org/Network /ID_System.html (accessed October 7, 2004).

Once RFID tags appear on everything, it will be possible to track items over time and store detailed records on their "activities" in a variety of databases. As those who have had their Social Security or credit card number fall into the wrong hands can attest, a unique serial number can serve as a key to unlock vast amounts of information stored in corporate and government databases. And just as Social Security numbers have strayed from their original purpose to now appear in an ever-spiraling number of record systems, EPC numbers are likely to do the same, finding their way over time into a myriad of applications and databases. While some of these databases will have little impact on privacy, others will be ripe for abuse.

Because it is so crucial to understand how these databases will impact privacy, I've broken them down into four functional categories:

- Database #1 will contain manufacturing and shipping information pertinent to logistics and supply chain management.
- Database #2 will contain product identification information similar to that contained on bar codes today.
- Database #3 will contain records made at the point of sale when the goods are sold to private parties.
- Database #4 will store information about tagged items observed after the point of sale.

Database #1: The "Where-Did-This-Come-From?" Manufacturer's Database

Database #1 will store information about items as they move through the manufacturing process and continue down the supply chain. If the item is a pair of walking shoes, for example, at some point early in the manufacturing process, an RFID tag containing a unique EPC number will be incorporated into the shoe, making all of its subsequent activities uniquely trackable in this database. Though the actual EPC number would be longer, for the sake of simplicity, let's say the shoe is assigned a unique serial number #308247. (Remember that in EPCglobal's numbering scheme, there can be no other item on the planet with this same number.)

The first database entry for tag #308247 would likely record the fact that the tag has been assigned to a walking shoe, along with the time and place the tag and shoe were first linked. At every point in the manufacturer's supply chain where the shoe is detected by a reader, a new entry will be made to the record. For example, as a crate of shoes is loaded onto a truck, a reader in the loading bay might send a command to update every shoe's data record with an identical entry, such as "loaded onto truck #518 at 09:17:08." Many of these entries would functionally resemble time stamps on a toll ticket.

When completed, the Database #1 record for our single shoe might look a little like a travel log recording when it was seen passing critical transfer points along the supply chain. This information could enable the company to pinpoint where things went wrong if a shipment were damaged or lost, for example. By itself, Database #1, containing little more than a log of manufacturing information, batch numbers, transfers, and other details poses little threat to consumer privacy.

Database #2: The "What-Is-This?" EPC Database

Database #2 will be maintained by EPCglobal to replace the bar code. At a retail store, Database #2 will be used to tell a cash register how much to charge for a particular item being rung up. A scan of the tag will return something like this: "That tag identifies a size 8 woman's left walking shoe. And that tag identifies a size 8 woman's right walking shoe. Those items list together at $49.99."

Unlike Database #1, which may be treated as a closely guarded trade secret by the companies involved, Database #2 will be widely available by design. Not only will thousands of retailers need access to the data it contains, but consumers will likely be encouraged to use it, too. As an early sign of this trend, Philips and Nokia have both worked on integrating EPC-compliant RFID readers into their mobile phones, in hopes that consumers will want to use them to look up additional information on products they see in stores or on the street.[22]

Database #2 spells obvious but serious problems for privacy since anyone with access to the "what is it?" database could use an RFID reader to identify other people's possessions—silently, invisibly, and remotely. This means that, theoretically, a passenger sitting near me on the train could aim a cell phone reader at my closed purse, get back a string of EPC numbers, cross reference them in Database #2, and learn that I am carrying a hairbrush, two pens, and a racy novel. Similarly, the government could use a doorway reader to surreptitiously scan passengers for anarchist literature, an employer could hide a reader device in a worker's cubicle to scan for prescription medications, and a stalker could scan a woman's undergarments right through her clothes as she walks unknowingly past.

---

22. Partridge, C. "RFID: More Fun Than You Might Think." *Vnunet*, March 15, 2004. www.vnunet .com/analysis/1153521 (accessed October 7, 2004).

The notion that one's clothes or purse would become transparent in the presence of an RFID reader (or a stranger's cell phone) is deeply disturbing. However, since the trouble is somewhat obvious, I am hopeful that society will devise strategies to protect people from the threat posed by Database #2.

Database #3: The "Who-Bought-It?" Point-of-Sale Database

Database #3 will store transaction information created at the cash register (or at the point-of-sale, or POS, terminal as the industry calls it) when the product's unique ID number is captured from its tag and linked with the purchaser's identifying information. This database will severely undermine privacy for several reasons: The infrastructure to create it is nearly universal; the data capture and linkage will be automatic, impersonal, and invisible; and the data can be easily centralized and redisseminated for other uses. Worst of all, because it will be silent and its implications are hard to grasp, society may not mobilize a response until it's too late.

To fully appreciate the problems with this database, it's important to understand what happens today when a consumer shops at a national retail chain. While many people still think of cash registers as simply adding machines with cash drawers, they have become sophisticated, ubiquitously networked, high-speed computer terminals, feeding purchaser data directly into massive databases.

Unless shoppers make a point of paying with cash (which is anonymous[23]), they communicate their identity with every transaction they make. If they shop at a major chain with a frequent shopper card, credit card, or ATM card, a list of each item purchased will likely be stored in the retailer's database—in a record with their name and card number at the top. This means that the store can view an itemized list of purchases a shopper has made over time. Depending on the retail chain, these records can stretch back ten years or more.

A company called Information Resources, Inc. (IRI) has been consolidating data from retail POS terminals since 1987 and now collects and consolidates data from over 32,000 U.S. food, drug, and mass merchandise retail stores into a single, centralized database. IRI is just one of several POS data "centralizers."

---

23. Although cash is still anonymous at present, digital payment systems may lead to a "cashless society" in which anonymous purchases could be impossible. Even if cash remains available, it may lose its anonymity. Hitachi has developed a tiny RFID tag called the "mu chip," which could be embedded into currency to make it uniquely trackable. See Chai, W. "Radio ID Chips May Track Banknotes." *CNET*, May 22, 2003, http://news.com.com/2100-1017-1009155.html.

Never heard of IRI? That's exactly the problem. While some privacy-conscious customers may wince when they hand their card to the cashier, most people give little thought to where the data goes after that. The multibillion-dollar customer relationship management (CRM) infrastructure that captures people's personal data and traffics it to others is largely invisible.

Since today's POS terminals automatically capture bar code data and record it in the purchaser's data record, by default, we can assume that the same thing will happen with EPC tag data. The difference, however, is that the EPC tags data will include *unique ID numbers*. Just as today's invisible POS databases record *what* we buy, tomorrow's POS databases will record *which one*—unless something proactive is done to prevent it.

As an example of what this might mean, consider again the case of shoes. When I buy a pair of shoes today, the shoe retailer might record the fact that Katherine Albrecht buys size 8 walking shoes. This information could enable someone to make inferences about my age, income, and interests, or it might be sold to outside companies that want to market products to me. And while it may bother me to know that information about my taste in shoes is on the auction block, there is a limit to how that information can be used to invade my privacy. Knowing *what* shoes I wear does not tell you much about *where* I wear them, what I *do* in them, or with *whom*.

Someday, however, a shoe retailer will not only note that I bought a pair of size 8 walking shoes, but it will record the fact that those shoes contain *unique tag number #308247*—and a whole new dimension of surreptitious data gathering opens up. In all the world, there will be no other pair of walking shoes—no other item, period—authorized to transmit that unique ID number but *mine*.

At some point, shoe retailers nationwide are likely to keep records not only on the type of shoes their customers buy but also on the unique ID numbers associated with millions of people's shoes. Once those databases are consolidated (perhaps with the help of companies like IRI), anyone able to obtain them would have the ability to identify people secretly, at any point where they step on a sidewalk, welcome mat, floor tile, or carpet embedded with an RFID reader device.[24]

For the RFID numbers in shoes to serve as de-facto people identifiers, not only will tag data have to be linked with the purchaser ID as described, but the tags

---

24. For images of prototype floor-based RFID readers, see, for example, Manzoor, S. "The Aware Home: Research Initiative by GVU Center, College of Computing, Georgia Institute of Technology." http://w5.cs.uni-sb.de/~butz/teaching/ie-ss03/papers/AwareHome/ (accessed October 7, 2004).

will have to be left "live" after the customer leaves the store, as well. This is a very real possibility, if the corporations backing RFID have their way.

Sandy Hughes of Procter & Gamble acknowledges that customers' "personal information [is] connected to the items they buy through loyalty cards and other programs offered by some retailers" and touts the "tremendous potential benefits to having active [EPC] tags" after items leave the store.[25] NCR, which manufactures POS terminals for retailers and employs a full-time "Technical Evangelist for RFID,"[26] recommends that retailers capture the unique EPC code data at checkout. The company believes, "The real power of this technology for retail results from associating these unique [EPC] identifiers with other information of interest …in a database that pertains to the item."[27] Presumably, this data would include the purchaser's identity. NCR also recommends leaving RFID tags live to facilitate returns[28]—a particularly controversial application because it means that consumers must leave tags intact and transmitting for the duration of the warranty period or presumably forfeit their right to return the items.

Database #4: The "Where-Has-It-Been-Seen?" Post-Sale Surveillance Database

The EPC has been described as a "simple, compact 'license plate' that uniquely identifies objects,"[29] and that's an apt comparison. Just as the license plate on a car enables government agents,[30] marketers,[31] and misguided do-gooders[32] to record people's presence at given locations, the EPC numbers integrated into people's belongings—and perhaps even into people themselves[33]—will render them trackable as they go about their daily business.

---

25. Personal Communication, Sandy Hughes.
26. NCR's Dan White refers to himself by this title.
27. NCR. "RFID in the Store: 50 Ideas for Revolutionizing the Store Through RFID." (NCR White Paper, 2003), 4.
28. Ibid., 23.
29. "Electronic Product Code." EPCglobal. www.epcglobalus.org/Network/Electronic%20Product%20Code.html. (accessed October 7, 2004).
30. "License plate recognition." The New York Surveillance Camera Players. www.not-bored.org/license-plate-recognition.html (accessed October 7, 2004).
31. Safeway once sent employees to two rival grocery stores to copy the license plate numbers from 1,000 cars in their parking lots. For $5,000, it purchased the home address to which each car was registered from the California Department of Motor Vehicles. Source: Greg Lucas, "DMV Information Sold Illegally, State Audit Finds Agency Also Reaped Profits by Overcharging Clients." *San Francisco Chronicle*, July 3, 1997, A19. Mirrored at www.dui.com /old-whatsnew/DMV/dmv.info.sold.html (accessed October 7, 2004).
32. Pastor Jim Norwood, the mayor of Kennedale, Texas, takes photographs of cars parked in porn shop parking lots, then mails them to the cars' registered owners with an invitation to attend his church. Source: "Pastor Brings Porn Fight to Mayor's Office." NBC Channel 5 Dallas, June 1, 2004. www.nbc5i.com/news/3369257/detail.html (accessed October 7, 2004).
33. The VeriChip human ID implant is one such device.

Once people begin carrying live RFID tags in their shoes, on their clothing, in their wallets, and on other items, their identities will become transparent to anyone with a reader device and access to Database #3. Reader devices at building entrances and exits, coupled with this information, will lead to the creation of Database #4, containing detailed logs of people's movement across "checkpoints" in much the same way Database #1 will record the passage of inventory across supply chain checkpoints. Such scans will make it possible to create detailed reports on where and how people spend their time and to make reasonably accurate guesses about whom they spend their time with, too.

At the Global Supply Chain, RFID & GTIN Standards Conference in October 2004, Paul Heino of Sundex Information Systems demonstrated this type of "people-as-inventory" tracking scenario. Promotional materials from the conference describe how attendees were rigged up with RFID tags and tracked— exactly like inventory:

> As a delegate you will have an RFID tag in your badge, and Paul Heino will briefly explain explain [sic] how RFID technology can track the movement of delegates (as "products") by tracking their movements around the conference. This demonstration will illustrate the tremendous potential for greater efficiency through RFID-centric automation. Don't worry; there's NO risk to your privacy.
>
> —Promotional email describing the Global Supply Chain, RFID & GTIN Standards Conference, held October 14, 2004, in Toronto, Ontario, Canada

Heino's example illustrates on a small scale what will be possible on a grander scale down the road.

Corporate Abuse

RFID was developed to make things easier to watch and to simplify the process of putting information about those things into databases. Given its raison d'être, it is not surprising it has already been abused for hidden surveillance of human beings, even at this early stage.

Shelf-mounted RFID readers can be used to monitor shoppers as they interact with tagged inventory. Several highly publicized cases of in-store RFID misuse have already occurred. In June 2003, British retailer Tesco was caught taking close-up photographs of customers as they picked up tagged Gillette razor products containing hidden RFID tags,[34] and a similar trial may have taken place in Massachusetts before being cancelled.[35] The *Chicago Sun Times* reported that Procter & Gamble executives trained a webcam on a cosmetics display rigged with RFID sensors at an Oklahoma Wal-Mart store, then used it to observe women interacting with tagged lipsticks from their offices 750 miles away.[36]

And as mentioned earlier, the RFID industry's Future Store in Germany issued thousands of shopper cards containing hidden tracking devices to the unknowing shoppers the industry referred to as "guinea pigs."

RFID is a new technology, and much of its potential, for both good and evil, has yet to be realized. However, based on incidents that have taken place so far, it appears the stealthy nature of the technology both invites and facilitates secret observation of unwitting subjects. Whenever RFID tags and readers are in use, this risk should be taken seriously. Unfortunately, until laws are passed to require labeling on RFID-tagged goods, the public will have no way to avoid participating in such experiments in the future.

Had it not been for whistleblowers, investigation by activists, and serendipity, the public would never have learned about these trials. Each was hidden from the people being observed, and the companies involved denied their existence to journalists and advocates.[37] Even after evidence revealed that Gillette helped develop the RFID-reader-enabled "smart shelf" to photograph Gillette customers for theft-prevention purposes, for example, Gillette spokesman Paul Fox told a Silicon.com reporter, "We have never [had], nor do we have, any intention to track, photograph, or videotape consumers."[38]

Government Abuse

While corporate abuse of RFID is troublesome, a more worrisome prospect is that the government will someday find RFID an attractive—and powerful—tool for invading privacy and infringing on civil liberties. The Defense Department and other government agencies have already expressed an interest in

34. For details, see CASPIAN's Boycott Gillette Web site: www.boycottgillette.com/spychips.html.
35. Baker, C. "Wal-Mart to forgo tracking chips." *Washington Times,* July 17, 2003. www.washtimes.com/business/20030717-095919-1439r.htm.
36. Wolinsky, H. "Chipping away at your privacy." *Chicago Sun Times,* November 9, 2003. www.suntimes.com/output/lifestyles/cst-nws-spy09.html.
37. I was personally involved with these stories as they broke and can attest to the denials made to journalists and advocates with whom I spoke.
38. McCue, A. "Gillette shrugs off RFID-tracking fears." Silicon.com, August 14, 2003. http://news.com.com/Gillette+shrugs+off+RFID-tracking+fears/2100-1039_3-5063990.html.

obtaining data contained in commercial databases.[39] That desire, coupled with the vastly expanded surveillance powers the government has granted itself since 9-11, mean that Databases #3 and #4 could fall into government hands where they could be used to identify and track citizens engaged in peaceful political activities.

For example, government agents who could not storm into a gun show, peace rally, union meeting, or prayer service demanding to see people's IDs could instead use RFID tags, readers, and databases to obtain the same information, cleanly, efficiently, and secretly. Agents could infiltrate such events with portable RFID readers hidden in their backpacks and use them to scan the EPC numbers associated with people's belongings. The resulting data could be cross-referenced with Database #3 (retailer POS records) to identify everyone present.

Such surreptitious scanning would reveal not only who had attended the event but who the attendees' associates are as well. If I wear a watch my mother bought me for my birthday, carry a pencil I borrowed from a colleague at work, and tuck my husband's winter scarf into my coat pocket, you would know whom to begin questioning about me should you choose to examine my "network of contacts." The prospect is sobering.

Conclusions

William's Domesday team ultimately failed. We can do better. But do we want to?

Once businesses begin putting unique, automatically readable ID numbers into the physical goods we own and carry with us, it will be nearly impossible to prevent the abuses I've described. By working to render the world trackable, supply chain managers may solve their short-term problems, but in the long run they will create tremendous privacy problems for the rest of us.

As its supporters and cheerleaders like to remind us, RFID is a revolutionary technology that promises unprecedented visibility of the physical world. The exciting dream of a transparent supply chain, in which every item and its movements are logged and recorded, could easily develop a nightmarish flip side, where every person, possession, and activity is logged and recorded. Unless we take proactive steps to prevent it, someday our children and grandchildren will be scanned by a reader device every time they enter the town library, cross the threshold of the local elementary school, or set foot in a store.

As industry rushes to embrace RFID, society's response should take its vast potential for abuse into account at every step. The difference between a *transparent supply chain* and a *transparent society* may be far smaller than we realize.

39. The "Total Information Awareness" project was one such effort.

Chapter 17

MULTIPLE SCENARIOS FOR PRIVATE-SECTOR USE OF RFID

Ari Schwartz[1]
Paula Bruening[2]

Introduction

The private sector's rollout of RFID at the item level predictably raises concerns about consumers' ability to protect the privacy of their personal information. This use of RFID represents the introduction of a new method of data collection in an environment already rich with opportunities for business and government to create powerful dossiers on individuals' purchases, preferences, and movement throughout the world.

To the extent that RFID technologies collect information that is not specific or linked to individuals and individual identity, they tend not to sound an alarm about privacy. But as the power of the technology increases so that information collected through RFID can be associated with a specific individual, perceptions of RFID as an invasive technology raise serious concerns.

In public policy discussions about the threats to privacy raised by emerging technologies, experts often make the point that *technologies* do not invade privacy; people use technology to engage in privacy-invading activities. But while the assertion that technologies are policy neutral has become dictum, privacy neutrality is assured only if measures are taken—in law, through technology,

1. Ari Schwartz is the associate director of the Center for Democracy and Technology (CDT).
2. Paula Bruening is the staff counsel for CDT.

and in industry self-governance—to enable consumers to exercise control over the collection of their personal information.

Whether new technologies invade privacy or remain privacy neutral depends on whether privacy issues raised by the technology are examined and addressed early. Ensuring that new technologies are developed and deployed in a manner that makes it possible for consumers to exercise control over if and how much their personal information is collected and used requires a three-pronged approach.

First, the *design of the technology* must incorporate privacy-enhancing technologies such as those that limit the collection of data, anonymize data, or offer users control over the collection of their personal information. Empowering users to consent to or deny the collection of information by a technology, or to disable a technology entirely when appropriate, gives them a critical tool for managing the collection and use of their personal information.

Second, the collection, use, and retention of information with the technology must be guided by *traditional principles of fair information practices incorporated in legislation.* Such baseline legislation would establish consistent expectations for both consumers and businesses about their rights and responsibilities related to the data collected and would impose the force of law.

Third, companies using the new technology to collect information must *engage in self-regulation:* self imposed, industry-wide policies that foster responsible data collection, sharing, and use. When it is enforced, self-regulation can build on the basic requirements set out in law, allowing industry to tailor its approach to privacy in a way that serves both business and consumers and allows industry to respond promptly to emerging technologies, evolving business models, and unanticipated privacy problems.

The appropriate balance of these three elements—technology, government action, and self-regulation—depends on several factors. These include the nature of the information collection technology, the way it is used, the kind of information it collects, and the public's perception of the technology and its concern about possible privacy invasion.

RFID raises unique concerns, in part because it is invisible to consumers; unless consumers are notified, they may be oblivious to its use. These concerns are heightened because of the passive way that information is collected from the RFID chips. Consumers do not engage in any active way to relinquish information or engage in data collection. And the readers are potentially ubiquitous. Current RFID readers have only short-range capabilities, but developers promise that more powerful readers will densely populate public *and* private spaces.

These considerations, specific to RFID technology and data collection, must guide decision making about how technology solutions, law, and self-regulation are implemented.

Failure to properly account for these considerations can result in negative consequences for businesses, consumers, and the development of new technology. Public backlash against surreptitious use of technologies could slow implementation and impede its innovation for beneficial uses. As a result, neither the public nor industry would realize RFID's benefits, and government, spurred by public demand, could step in to enact legislation that would be ineffective at curbing abuses while stifling or skewing technology development.

This chapter describes a series of scenarios that illustrate the best and worst results from the implementation and use of RFID for information collection. They are written from the vantage point of 2015, which is the not-too-distant future. The scenarios speculate about the decisions that might be made in the development of technology, the level of attention paid to consumer concerns and public policy about RFID, industry and government decisions on where and how to use the technology, and the possible consequences of these decisions for privacy. These scenarios are intended not to be predictive but rather to serve as the starting point for thought-provoking discussion about how best to address the privacy concerns raised by this technology.

Scenario 1: "No One Wins"

In mid-2004, industry and government increased their use of item-level RFID tagging with little thought to consumers' perception about the possible invasiveness of the technology. At that time, the chips were used only in manufacturing processes and distribution chains to enhance inventory control and tracking of deliveries. However, plans were in place to implement tags more widely and to deploy more powerful tags that could transmit more sensitive information. Developers of RFID systems and organizations using the tags took no steps to consider the privacy implications of the technology and paid little attention to issues surrounding responsible tag use and the management of the information the tags collect.

To fill the vacuum created by this lack of policy, by 2006, California passed a law that limited the use of RFID chips, such that the chips contained in merchandise purchased by consumers must be deactivated. Massachusetts also passed a law requiring opt-in consent by consumers for use of RFID in any way.

The effect of these laws was to make it nearly impossible for companies to use RFID for even the most innocuous purposes. Companies doing business in

California had used RFID technology for inventory control, but their inability to be sure that the tags were deactivated at the customer checkout raised concerns about liability and led them to end their use entirely. Massachusetts companies found themselves unable to manage the opt-in requirement and also stopped using the tags.

Unwilling to assume the costs and liability of RFID tags, companies sought other measures to monitor inventory. Initially, companies simply increased store and stockroom video surveillance to reduce theft. By 2010, facial recognition cameras had become increasingly common in stores, both on the public storeroom floor and in stockrooms. Capitalizing on the capabilities of this technology, companies soon began matching consumer purchasers with facial ID, all without customer knowledge or consent. Although the purpose of this practice initially was to reduce the incidence of shoplifting, companies eventually used it for behavior-based marketing research.

Data-mining companies began buying the proprietary databases created as a result of this practice. In 2015, two companies announced that they had collected images of over 150 million Americans and tied this information to their purchasing habits. The result: unprecedented consumer concern about privacy.

Scenario 2: "Shangri-La"

While developing plans for broad implementation of RFID in retail stores, companies recognized that, as with other information collection technologies, RFID might raise consumers' concerns about privacy. Moreover, companies learned from the experience they gained from implementing other information collection technologies that it is best to address privacy concerns early. To encourage consumers' acceptance of the technology and to protect the trust relationship, companies decided to directly address consumers' concerns about collection and storage of information through RFID technology and an associated network of databases.

Working with consumer and privacy advocates, technologists, industry coalitions, and academic experts, RFID implementers developed an effective self-regulatory regime to govern information collection through RFID. Under the self-regulatory program, consumers are given clear, effective notice that RFID technology is in use, and in most instances, they have the opportunity to make decisions about the collection of information via the tag and the persistent use of the tag after the product leaves the store. Collectors and custodians of information using RFID employ strong, reliable security measures for their databases, and consumers are provided the opportunity to access information mentioned about them. Robust enforcement, through independent oversight organizations and consumer recourse mechanisms, promote the credibility of self-regulatory measures

To further enhance the effectiveness of these efforts, the business community, working with consumer advocates, initiated a far-reaching public education campaign about how RFID technology is used and how consumers can exercise their privacy rights with regard to information collected through the technology.

To promote broad adoption of self-regulation, industry leaders and trade associations worked closely with companies to highlight its benefits, both to businesses and to the companies developing RFID technology.

Tag manufacturers required companies using the tags to sign agreements saying they would follow the rules. Companies outside the self-regulatory structure soon found doing business much more difficult and eventually complied with the standards. While readers are available for purchase, companies consider the information about individual items proprietary and guard it closely, making it extremely difficult for sensitive information to fall into the wrong hands.

Scenario 3: "The Wild West"

In 2008, businesses and government began deploying item-level RFID tags on a broad scale. Unmoved by expressions of concern about this technology's impact on privacy, they made no effort to address the issue through technology, self-regulation, or law.

Immediately after the first RFID tags were deployed in retail establishments, researchers concerned about consumer privacy and misuse of the tags and the information collected from them published papers on how to clone and destroy the tags. Privacy vigilantes, angered by the lack of protection for information collected through RFID, began to wander through stores killing existing tags and placing cloned tags in the pockets of clothing to render the RFID technology useless.

Tags used by government were treated similarly. The efforts to use RFID for baggage handling and customs control were frustrated, and government agencies were forced to return to twentieth-century, pre-9/11 approaches to securing travelers and borders. Citizens and government became fearful of the ability of bad actors to thwart the tags. In place of RFID, government and law enforcement adopted more onerous and invasive search and questioning procedures for travelers.

By 2010, retailers and government began to use new, slightly more expensive tags that were harder to clone or destroy. However, two years later, information on a low-cost means to jam the new RFID readers was widely distributed. Implementers found that the large investment in the second-generation technology was completely wasted. As a third generation is developed, companies question the wisdom of investing in a continued "Spy vs. Spy" situation, particularly because anti-RFID activists are more organized than ever.

Scenario 4: "Trust but Verify"

In 2006, Congress passed legislation establishing baseline privacy protection for information collected about consumers. The law applied to no particular technology but rather codified in law long-established principles of fair information practices: *notice, choice, security, access,* and *recourse* to guide companies' collection and management of consumer information.

To comply with this general law governing information collection, companies using RFID were required to:

- Provide consumers with notice that RFID technology is being used and disclose the kind of information being collected by the technology
- Obtain the consent of the customer to share any personal information they collect using RFID for any purpose other than completing a transaction and inventory control
- Provide appropriate security for the information collected
- Provide individuals with the ability to access the information retailers maintain about them and correct inaccurate information—similar to what is currently being done with credit reports

The requirements of the law provided technologists and companies implementing RFID with some baseline expectations about privacy as well as the responsibilities attendant to the collection and use of information in general. Armed with this knowledge, companies using RFID were able from the outset to put in place the technological and information management controls to enhance privacy.

Over and above these baseline requirements, the business community, prompted by consumer advocates, recognized that RFID raised some technology-specific questions about information collection. For example, how might a company most effectively offer notice to a consumer?

The flexible environment of the Web to provide notice already tests companies' ability to effectively and clearly communicate complex technical and legal concepts with consumers. However, Web-based notice about the use of an invisible technology that collects information with no active consumer engagement presents even greater challenges.

Similarly, how would companies make it possible for consumers to exercise choice about the collection and sharing of information gained with RFID technology? How could they ensure that their choice would be honored?

To respond to such concerns, the business community developed privacy-respectful best practices for the use of RFID technologies. Building on the basic requirements in law, business was free to develop creative solutions to RFID-specific privacy challenges.

In 2010, state attorneys general began to file lawsuits against companies found not in compliance with the requirements of the baseline privacy law. Meanwhile, business continued to develop and refine best practices in response to the developing technology and relied on self-regulatory regimes to address RFID-specific concerns.

Conclusions

RFID is a technology at the political crossroads. Examining scenarios for implementation of the technology and public policy is helpful to the extent that it urges policymakers—in government and in industry—to consider the potential harm and benefits that might result from a policy about privacy and RFID. It may also prompt them to explore the logical progression of events following the adoption of a policy and the expected and unexpected consequences that might result. Reliance on any one approach to addressing the privacy questions raised by this technology—including taking no action at all—is risky. The outcome could distort or impede the development of a technology that may offer significant benefits for consumers or that so severely compromises trust in the technology that public acceptance becomes impossible. The answer lies in a mix of approaches that provides a foundation of assurances for consumers in law and the flexibility of industry solutions that can respond quickly to rapidly changing technology and applications.

Chapter 18

WOULD MACY'S SCAN GIMBELS?: COMPETITIVE INTELLIGENCE AND RFID

Ross Stapleton-Gray[1]

Introduction

This chapter speculates on how RFID technologies in retail stores could impact competitive intelligence between retail rivals as well as competitive activity further up the supply chain. The scenarios presented are intended more to raise questions than to posit answers, although I suggest one plausible approach—a recoding strategy—for retailer management of RFID, given the risk of disclosure of competitive intelligence.

In-Store Scenarios

Consumer goods companies such as Gillette and Procter & Gamble say they are interested in using "smart shelves" as a tool to help increase sales by ensuring that store shelves are always stocked with their products. With stock levels being continuously monitored by computers receiving wireless signals from the products themselves, retailers would no longer have to rely on employees to monitor their shelves.[2]

---

1. Ross Stapleton-Gray, Ph.D., is president of Stapleton-Gray & Associates, Inc., an information technology and policy consultancy in Albany, CA.
2. "Retailers take stock of 'smart shelves.'" January 8, 2003. http://zdnet.com.com/2100-1103-979710.html.

One retailer is already experimenting with inventory control using RFID tags. By placing RFID readers on its store shelves, the retailer can identify low-stock items, analyze traffic and purchase patterns, and identify potential theft of its products.[3]

In other words, retailers can benefit greatly from RFID as a means for in-store data collection. However, these benefits can be turned on their heads if that same data can be captured surreptitiously by a competitor for the cost of moving an "agent" with a reader through the same retail store. A competitor could even perform readings over time, thus constructing a longitudinal profile of stock flow.

It's true that this same retail intelligence can be performed today; an individual could visually examine shelves, recording product serials. However, the quantitative difference if one uses RFID for this same purpose—for example, the ability to scan a whole aisle merely by walking its length with a reader hidden in a backpack—enormously improves feasibility.[4]

Consumer Technology as a Means of Intelligence Gathering

There are, of course, more imaginative ways to collect RFID data than secreting a complete tag reader in a backpack: passively listening as tags are read by the store's own readers, for example, or perhaps even collecting signals from outside the store. Although read distance is fairly limited today—usually measured in centimeters—innovative use of technology might permit a greater "standoff" distance.[5]

Consumers likely won't be equipped with RFID readers anytime soon. But it's reasonable to expect that reader equipment now available only to industry or science, for instance, could eventually be merged into end-consumer communications equipment. Motorola, Symbol, and Nextel have announced (optical) bar code reader modules for cell phones.[6] Ventures such as Microsoft's AURA

---

3. "The corporate impact of real-time inventory tracking." August 12, 2003. http://techrepublic .com.com/5100-6296_11-5054050.html.
4. These methods also raise questions of legality, which it is not within the scope of this chapter to discuss.
5. Vivato (www.vivato.net) is a WiFi equipment provider whose products use directional antennas based on phased arrays to provide connectivity (normally limited to hundreds of meters, with omnidirectional antennas) out to several kilometers. Similar innovation in RFID interrogation might allow for reading of tags from a sufficient distance to avoid issues of physical trespass in collecting product intelligence.
6. "Nextel, Motorola and Symbol Technologies Offer First Wireless Bar Code Scanner for Mobile Phones." June 11, 2003. www.motorola.com/mediacenter/news/detail /0,1958,2880 _2342_23,00.html.

project are experimenting with end-user annotation of physical spaces via Web logs or scannable tags (e.g., bar codes, including product UPCs) using standard commercial personal digital assistants (PDAs) with attached readers.[7]

Many consumer UPC scanning service ventures have been launched only to falter or fail (e.g., DigitalConvergence, Airclic, Barpoint, IQorder), in the process consuming in excess of half a billion dollars of venture-capital funding. But some companies may eventually succeed. Some of the factors that produced the earlier failures have already changed, such as the pervasive use of Internet-accessible PDAs and cellular phones and the lower cost of add-ons to enable scanning.

Other Sources of Competitive Intelligence

Management of the Object Name Service (ONS) specified in the Electronic Product Code (EPC) architecture could also have a significant impact on retailers' ability to gather competitive intelligence. The ONS provider or providers will be party to a tremendous volume of transactions as manufacturers, retailers, and others up and down the supply chain make product inquiries. These inquiries may be to learn the status of specific items or, at a higher level, to fetch product descriptions for an in-store customer information service or to create content pages for a store Web site. All may be fodder for intelligence gathering and analysis.

To prevent surreptitious data collection, all content-exchanging transactions ideally would be confidential to the parties, with no transactional information retained by the ONS providers (other than what might be required for billing for services). However, ONS providers might attempt to reserve the right to monetize transaction logs, possibly through analysis and sale of aggregated statistics.

If a retailer made inquiries via the Internet, any exchanges would be encrypted or otherwise protected from interception. The truly paranoid user of ONS might employ a proxy to conceal the source of the inquiry.

On the other hand, elements of what EPCglobal terms the EPC Network might more readily surrender competitive intelligence. EPC Discovery Services, announced by VeriSign in late 2004, as well as analogous services from other providers are intended to permit RFID-bearing objects to be "tracked and traced." This is so that supply chain partners can alert each other to shipment location, times and dates shipments are received, and so on. Theoretically, only

---

7. http://aura.research.microsoft.com/aura/AuraPortal/

authorized parties would have access to such information; in actuality, poor security, misconfiguration, laziness, and bad practice may make such services a goldmine of transactional information.

So, Who Wants to Know?

Competitive intelligence on a retailer's inventory can include data on both inventory type and turnover. This data may be of interest to retail competitors, suppliers, manufacturers, and third-party companies collecting data for analysis.

Note: EPC scanning in the store would provide only unique identifiers of tagged items, though they are sufficient to identify the manufacturer and product type; through repeat scans over time, one could gauge product turnover. EPC scanning alone would reveal nothing regarding product pricing.

Some of the discussion on the value of RFID in stores presumes an effective flow of transactional information back to manufacturers, allowing them to make "just-in-time" decisions on production. We ought to question how likely this is to occur, given the complexity of system interaction and the information economy. Will manufacturers really provide incentives to retailers for such reporting?

The Value of Functional Tags on the Shelves

Consumer goods in retail stores might be separated into four categories:

- Items without tags that the retailer has no interest in monitoring
- Items without tags that the retailer has an interest in monitoring
- Items with tags that the retailer has no interest in monitoring
- Items with tags that the retailer has an interest in monitoring[8]

Over time, an increasing number of items will bear tags; an increasing percentage of tags will be more capable and permit reprogramming, beyond "killing"; and the retailer will have a capacity and interest in monitoring a larger percentage of the products on the shelves. "Over time" might constitute decades, however, given considerations of cost and perceived value.

---

8. One could also imagine a fifth category: items surreptitiously tagged by some other party, unbeknownst to the retailer. This might constitute an exotic form of competitive espionage and is mentioned here merely to include all (even remote) possibilities.

Figures 18.1 through 18.3 capture the situation for a hypothetical store over some indeterminate time (clearly dependent on the nature of the goods sold; a retailer of luxury goods would look markedly different from a grocery store). Figure 18.1 represents the present, when there are no tags placed on consumer goods by manufacturers. Although none of the goods bear tags, the retailer may have an interest in monitoring some subset of the products (e.g., through use of tags attached by the retailer to help prevent theft). Figure 18.2 describes the situation at some point in the future when approximately a quarter of all of the items bear tags applied by the manufacturer. In this case, an assumption is made that most of those items are also of interest to the retailer for monitoring purposes (given that these are likely to be the more expensive or interesting items, it is not an unreasonable assumption). By Figure 18.3, tags have achieved even greater penetration, and the store has become more sophisticated in the use of tools to monitor items.

■ No tag; no interest   □ No tag; interest

Figure 18.1   Present Day Scenario: No tags are placed on consumer goods by manufacturers.

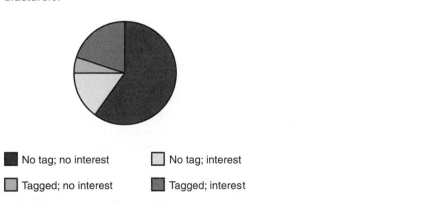

■ No tag; no interest   □ No tag; interest

■ Tagged; no interest   ■ Tagged; interest

Figure 18.2   A Future Scenario 1: Approximately a quarter of all the items bear tags applied by manufacturers.

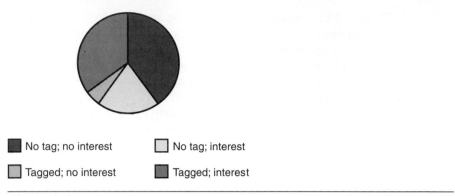

■ No tag; no interest		□ No tag; interest
▨ Tagged; no interest		▨ Tagged; interest

Figure 18.3   Future Scenario 2: Tags have achieved even greater penetration.

The relative sizes of the categories are largely speculative but may fit a particular retailer with a fairly strong interest in monitoring product on the shelves.

In the three scenarios, there is a potential for "outsider" interest in information from tagged items; that interest might extend to both categories of tagged items (those of interest and those not of interest to the retailer).

As discussed at greater length below (regarding a "recoding" strategy), the retailer could consider (1) suppressing potential collection by preemptively killing any tag on an item not of interest in its own monitoring and (2) making use of retailer-applied tags on products not tagged by the manufacturer.

Qui Bono?

Cursory analysis suggests that retailers may see *fewer* benefits than other parties from adoption of RFID at the product level.

It seems plausible that the value of EPC RFID tags at the point of sale will be very low until and unless nearly all products are tagged. All of the information required to easily record and charge for a purchase will be present in the "legacy" product code (UPC, ISBN, etc.). Most stores and most consumers will have little interest in a record of the item's unique serial (an element of the EPC but not provided in the UPC). It may be that manufacturers will also be providing a print rendition of the EPC, whether or not they ever intend to encode it in an RFID tag.[9]

Accommodating consumers' concerns regarding surveillance after the purchase will fall on the retailer: "You are selling me this product, and you must kill its

---

9. The most obvious reason for doing so would be to accommodate the situation in which a tag is destroyed or disabled.

RFID." At this point, and largely as speculation on the potential for consumer surveillance, a few small but vocal consumer advocacy groups have been lobbying for RFID tags on products to be easily (if not always) killed at the point of sale. These groups include Consumers Against Supermarket Privacy Invasion and Numbering (CASPIAN) and the Electronic Frontier Foundation (EFF). The latter's position on RFID tags on consumer products, stated in testimony before a California Senate inquiry on RFID and privacy, is that they should be killed at the point of sale until such time as tags are fully capable of reflecting consumers' desires for their management.[10]

Note: Most of the focus regarding RFID tags on products has been on the major manufacturers and retailers whose buy-in would be necessary to achieve a "critical mass" of demand. However, if point-of-sale killing of RFID tags were widely demanded, it would place a tremendous burden on myriad *small* retailers, many or most of which would have no interest in RFID themselves and presumably have little or no capability to kill tags. It is also difficult to envision a scenario in which tags could be readily killed even by "mom & pop" retailers yet be sufficiently secure against disabling by shoplifters.

Dead Tags Tell No Tales

The value of preserving tags in the store will depend in part on the demand for functioning post-purchase tags; depending on public opinion, this might be an expectation that RFID tags *not* persist after the sale. If there is strong consumer demand that RFID tags be killed at the point of sale, retailers will have an incentive to kill every tag they don't themselves need before they move products onto shelves or areas where they are monitored by others.

A Recoding Strategy

An ideal solution for suppression of "leakage" of information (short of no RFID tags whatsoever) is use of store-specific tags, or tags whose values are understandable only with access to the store's internal information systems.

Recoding RFID tags would include (1) reprogramming reprogrammable tags with "store internal" values mapped to the actual EPCs, (2) killing nonreprogrammable tags, and (3) affixing tags with "store internal" values to items whose tags were killed or that never bore RFID tags where in-store monitoring is desired. The first action could be performed at any of several points—when

---

10. "Privacy advocates call for RFID regulation." August 18, 2003, and author's notes from the California Senate hearing. http://news.com.com/2100-1029_3-5065388.html.

stock is received, in inventory, on the shelves—with minimal effort (assuming some RFID management infrastructure such as a reader capable of rewriting tags). It could also be performed piecemeal and over time. Any time a store reader encounters a reprogrammable tag with an EPC, it can reprogram it to a store-internal value; the store's information systems would hold the two values (original EPC and in-store assignment) as equivalent. If killing tags is required at point-of-sale to address consumer privacy concerns, it could also be done earlier, such as when stock is moved out to the shelves.

Conclusions

Any developments in competitive intelligence based on RFID collection and analysis will depend on EPC's penetration into the retail sales environment; much of the speculation in this chapter could be rendered meaningless by a slow adoption of consumer product tagging.

One overarching hypothesis is that RFID on consumer packaged goods will not be useful to most retailers for the foreseeable future. As a consequence, retailers might adopt a policy of killing RFID tags before moving goods to the shelves, adding efficiency to killing tags (if required, after a sale), and lessening the risk of information leakage to competitors.

The preceding analysis assumes some demand for competitive intelligence by others (e.g., competing retailers or manufacturers attempting to gain insights into their products' markets without reliance on reporting by the retailers). Exactly what demand will arise depends on many factors, including technical and legal.

Chapter 19

HACKING THE PROX CARD

Jonathan Westhues[1]

Introduction

Many companies use proximity cards to control physical access to their facilities. Employees hold their cards within a few inches of the reader; the reader receives a unique ID from each card and transmits it to some central computer that decides whether to open the door. The proximity card works just like a magnetic stripe card or an ordinary metal key, but it doesn't actually have to touch the reader: It sends its identification code over the air. This can seem magical, considering that the tag is credit card-thin.

The principle of operation is the same as for passive RFID tags. The proximity card reader constantly transmits a strong unmodulated carrier: It broadcasts a powerful radio-frequency signal that carries no information. The tag derives its power and clock from this carrier, as a crystal radio does. The tag uses some of this power to operate the digital circuitry integrated on the card. The rest of the power is used to transmit an information-bearing ID signal back at the reader. In this way, it is possible for the cards to operate without an internal power source, which decreases the cost and size of the cards and eliminates the inconvenience of dead batteries.

I happened to have an Indala FlexPass proximity card, and I wanted to know how it worked. I knew the basic theory of operation, but I did not know any of the details of the radio link. At the time I was in my third year of an undergraduate program in electrical engineering, and I had some experience in wireless communications. I did not know how complicated the cards were, but I was fairly confident that I could build an improvised reader and at least determine what security

---

1. Jonathan Westhues is an undergraduate student in electrical engineering at the University of Waterloo. He has experience in a number of fields relating to wireless communications, embedded software, and electronic design.

291

features were present. It turned out that there was no security at all. Once I figured out the low-level radio link, it was trivially easy to "clone" the cards. In a few weeks of spare time, I built a device that could read a proximity card's secret identification code and later replay that code to a legitimate reader.

That means that I can clone a legitimate proximity card. This has a number of implications. Proximity card holders can easily duplicate their cards to give copies to friends or to retain a copy after giving back the legitimate card. This is the same risk that is present with ordinary metal keys (though certain high-security keys make this more difficult) or, to a lesser extent, with magnetic stripe cards. Proximity cards are worse, though, because they can be cloned over the air. My prototype had a read range of inches; commercial long-range readers achieve a read range of feet. An attacker could clone your proximity card without ever removing it from your wallet. Fortunately, this attack can easily be stopped through the use of cryptographic techniques. Cards that use these techniques are available now, but they are only beginning to be adopted in practice.

Reverse-Engineering the Protocol

I had access to a card and reader, but I could not find any credible documentation on the protocol. I did find a datasheet that claimed that the card worked with a 125kHz carrier. (For comparison, AM radio uses signals around 1000kHz. This is a very low-frequency signal to be transmitted over the air. The radio link works more like a transformer than like a typical pair of antennas.) I wound a few dozen turns of magnet wire on a cardboard form, taped it to the legitimate reader, and measured the voltage that the reader induced onto the coil. There was indeed a 125kHz sine wave, large, a few volts peak to peak. The cards did work at 125kHz.

Now I knew the frequency at which I should broadcast my carrier in order to energize the card. I constructed a circuit to force a strong signal through my antenna coil at 125kHz. I set the card on top of my antenna, and I used an oscilloscope to look for information returned from the card. In general, this is a difficult problem. The carrier that the reader transmits is very powerful. Most of this power is wasted, but some of it is received by the card's antenna. Of the power received by the card's antenna, some must go to the digital logic on the card; what is left is used to transmit the card's ID back to the reader. We would therefore expect that the signal returned from the card would be much less powerful than the signal we are transmitting to the card.

This is a problem because we cannot shield ourselves from the signal that we are transmitting. We will always see the sum of the signal that we transmit to the tag and the signal that the tag transmits back to us. We must therefore build some sort of circuit that will distinguish our carrier from the tag's ID signal. The techniques for doing this are well known and discussed extensively in literature published by RFID tag manufacturers.

I built a simple reader, basing my design on a circuit topology described in an application note from Microchip. With my improvised reader, I observed an information-bearing signal from the tag that was over a hundred thousand times less powerful than the carrier that appeared superimposed on top of it. This is actually not very hard to work with; commercial long-range readers deal with much more powerful carriers and still weaker signals from the tag. I used an analog circuit to measure the voltage across the antenna and pick out just the signal from the tag. I then fed the signal from the tag into an off-the-shelf microcontroller, which I programmed with software to detect whether a tag was present and, if a tag was present, record its ID. Figure 19.1 shows my first prototype hardware. The leftmost board contains a microcontroller and some hardware to drive the antenna coil. The smaller board provides the reader functionality; it measures the voltage across the antenna and returns a representation of the information-bearing signal from the tag to the microcontroller. The antenna coil (right) is about a hundred turns of magnet wire on a 2.5-inch-square form.

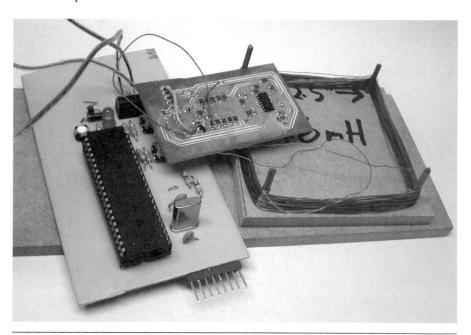

Figure 19.1   My first prototype hardware for a proximity card reader.
(Image reprinted courtesy of Jonathan Westhues.)

At this point, I had most of the functionality of a commercial proximity card reader, the kind that would be bolted to the wall next to a door. Since I could read a legitimate card's ID, the obvious next step was to replay the card's ID to a legitimate reader. This would prove that I had read the card's ID correctly. The hardware that I had built was already capable of transmitting a signal around 125kHz; it had to be in order to transmit the carrier that powered the card while I read it. The replay functionality was therefore a simple matter of software. I wrote a routine to transmit the ID that I had received and stored in memory over the air, using the same antenna that I had earlier used to obtain that ID.

I was now ready to test my device. I held a legitimate proximity card next to the device's antenna, and I pressed the "read" button. The microcontroller indicated that it had stored the card's ID in memory. I then moved my antenna next to a legitimate reader, and I pressed the "replay" button. It worked; the card reader beeped, and the door clicked open. I had cloned the card.

Why It Wasn't Very Hard

The hardware that I built was not particularly expensive. My first prototype cost less than $100 to build; a slightly improved version could be marketed in kit form for under $50. I built my prototype with ordinary hand tools and a soldering iron. Any competent designer, working in a reasonably well-equipped lab, would have no trouble duplicating my work.

This may seem surprising, since proximity cards and other RFID tags appear to be very complex. Commercial RFID tags typically contain full-custom integrated circuits, which represent an investment of hundreds of thousands or millions of dollars. However, the protocol that the tags use over the air is very simple. Practical RFID tags are complex not because of what they do but because of the constraints on how they do it. A commercial RFID tag must operate with as little power as possible. Because it is powered by the reader, every microwatt that the tag consumes must have come in over the air. The signal broadcast by the reader gets weaker as the tag moves away from the reader. The tag's power consumption therefore determines its read range; the tag stops working when it is too far from the reader to receive enough power to operate. A custom integrated circuit gives designers freedom to optimize for minimum required power. Also, commercial tags are designed to fit in extremely small packages and to be produced in large volumes. All of these factors lead manufacturers of RFID tags to make design choices that involve huge costs up front.

However, none of that particularly mattered to me. My "RFID tag" was a printed circuit board several inches square, and it ran off a 9-volt battery. I did not have a commercially marketable product, but my device could still generate a signal

Figure 19.2 My improved proximity card reader/cloner.
(Image reprinted courtesy of Jonathan Westhues.)

that, to the reader, looked identical to one transmitted by a legitimate card. If the cards had incorporated additional security features, this would have been just the first step of my attack. No such features were present, however, so once I had reverse-engineered the protocol used over the air, I was basically done.

Figure 19.2 shows an improved proximity card reader/cloner that I built after verifying that my first prototype worked as designed. The antenna is the coil of red magnet wire that runs along the perimeter of the plastic enclosure. The largest integrated circuit visible (the largest black rectangle) is the microcontroller; the rest of the parts transform the signal from the antenna into something that the microcontroller can deal with.

Security Implications

I can copy a proximity card at least as easily as I can take an impression of a key. This means that it's not a very good idea to reuse visitor cards without changing the ID (and that it doesn't really matter whether you get the physical card back from the employee you just fired). More insidiously, it's quite practical to read people's cards without removing them from their wallets. A bit of deliberate clumsiness, a reader up my sleeve, and I would have little trouble cloning anyone's card. The read range achievable increases as the power of the carrier transmitted by the reader goes up. The power transmitted by commercial readers is, depending on the frequency band, limited by government regulation, by the American Federal Communications Commission (FCC), or an equivalent agency. This probably would not be a major concern for anyone making practical use of a proximity card reader/cloner. There are still constraints, however. As the transmitted power increases, the voltages on the antenna elements climb into the kilovolts and the electrical design becomes increasingly difficult. Also, long-range readers typically must use large-diameter antenna coils; commercial long-range readers use rectangular coils that measure several feet on their longest dimension. Still, a read range of several feet would not be difficult to achieve if we could tolerate a bulky and power-hungry reader. Commercial RFID tag readers designed for inventory tracking in warehouses and similar applications already deliver this kind of range. We expect that an attacker could do at least as well as the commercial reader and, because the attacker would be free to ignore the legal limits on the transmitted power, probably somewhat better.

I could also exploit the fact the distance at which the cards will be powered is less than the distance at which they can be read. The read range of the cards is limited by two factors: The carrier that the reader transmits must be strong enough to power the card, and the information-bearing signal from the card must be strong enough that the reader can distinguish it over the random background noise that is always present. In practice, the first factor dominates: The signal from the card is still easily intelligible at the reader at the point at which the card loses power and shuts down. This means that if somehow the card became powered from something other than our reader, our read range would go up. This situation occurs in practice when another reader is reading the card. For example, the reader that I built can read my Indala FlexPass card from a distance of no more than an inch. However, if I hold the card very close to another reader, my reader can distinguish the card's ID from a distance of more than six inches.

This means that a sniffer concealed somewhere near a legitimate reader could intercept real transactions at a significant distance. The FlexPass signal can easily penetrate drywall; an attacker could find a legitimate reader and then mount a sniffer on the opposite side of the wall. This sort of attack is particularly good because the card repeats its ID over and over as long as it is energized. I could use signal processing techniques to average multiple copies of the pattern, further improving my read range.

In fact, I would not even have to get all of the bits right. If the cards used a 32-bit ID and I thought that I had one of the bits wrong, I could simply try all 32 variations with one bit flipped. If I used a "soft-decision" demodulation algorithm, in which the output is not a 0 or a 1 but a probability that the bit is 0 or 1, I would have a reasonable idea of which bits are most likely to be incorrect. I would first try flipping the bits that are almost as likely to be 0 as they are to be 1. The number of possibilities to try increases sharply with the number of incorrect bits (for a 32-bit ID: 32 for 1 bit wrong, 496 for 2, 4,960 for 3), but I could use the soft decisions to try the most likely error patterns first.

Protecting Against These Types of Attacks

All of the attacks described above can be avoided. They are all simple variations on a classical "replay attack," in which an eavesdropper, after observing a legitimate transaction, learns enough to later masquerade as one of the parties involved. The techniques to stop this are well known. The problem is that the secret ID, which is all that my reader/cloner needs to convince the legitimate reader that it is a legitimate card, is transmitted over the air. Because the secret ID is transmitted over the air, it can be intercepted. We need a method by which the card can prove to the reader that it knows some secret but without sending that secret over the air.

The most obvious approach is to use "rolling codes." Instead of choosing a single secret code, the reader and the tag agree on a list of secret codes. For the first transaction, they use code number one; for the second transaction, they use code number two, and so on. An eavesdropper who captures the first secret code hasn't learned anything of interest because the reader is now expecting the second secret code. This presents some difficulties, however. The reader and the tag must remain in sync: If the tag sends code number three but the reader is expecting code number four, the door will not open. This means that the tag must have some sort of nonvolatile memory in which it can store its "synchronization count" while it is not powered.

This presents a practical problem for devices like proximity cards. It might not be possible to integrate nonvolatile memory on the microchip inside the card, depending on the particular semiconductor process used. Also, the card might lose power at any time as the user moves it away from the reader. If the card loses power between transmitting its ID and incrementing the synchronization count, it will end up out of sync with the reader, which is irrecoverably bad. The techniques to avoid this problem require additional nonvolatile memory, complexity, and time. I do not know of any passive identification systems that use rolling codes. If the identification token that the user carries is battery powered, however, we can guarantee that we won't lose power between transmitting the ID and incrementing our count, so a rolling code scheme becomes practical. Keyless entry devices for cars, for example, often use rolling codes.

We can modify the system slightly so that the tag need not keep track of the synchronization count. Again, the reader and the tag agree on a long list of secret codes. When the reader wishes the tag to authenticate itself, it sends a command to the tag: "Broadcast secret code number 1473." The tag replies with the requested secret code, and the reader checks whether it is correct. As long as the reader requests a different secret code each time, an eavesdropper never learns anything that will be valuable in the future. In the previous transaction, the eavesdropper could have learned the value of secret code number 1473. This is useless, however, if next time the reader asks for secret code number 8962. The command from the reader to the tag ("send me secret code number 1473") is called the challenge; the answer from the tag ("secret code number 1473 is 23854") is the response. The reader must generate the challenges randomly or pseudorandomly. Otherwise, an attacker who can predict which challenge will be issued next could impersonate the reader and obtain the response corresponding to that challenge from the legitimate card. At this point, the attacker could impersonate the card to the reader. The reader will send the challenge that the attacker expects and already knows the response to.

It must also be unlikely that any code will be repeated in a reasonable period of time. (The definition of "a reasonable period of time" will vary depending on how much time we expect that an attacker will spend eavesdropping.) If a challenge is reused, an eavesdropper might have observed the transaction in which the reader sent that challenge to the card. In that transaction, the card would have sent the response back over the air, so the eavesdropper could have intercepted the response as well. If the attacker pretending to be a card receives a challenge that was sent before, the attacker can send the corresponding familiar response and will be indistinguishable from the legitimate card.

For a passive proximity card system, challenge/response will likely be more practical than rolling codes. Because the reader always tells the tag which secret code it should transmit, the tag need not keep track of which code it should transmit next itself, so it does not need any nonvolatile storage. This is good because a passive proximity card might lose power at any time. This makes it difficult for the card to perform atomic operations on nonvolatile memory.

A practical system, whether it uses challenge/response or rolling codes, will not use a huge lookup table of secret codes. It will use a mathematical function: Given the challenge, this function will return the response (or given the synchronization count, it will return the rolling code). This function must be chosen very carefully, so that it is not possible to guess the function by observing a large number of challenge/response pairs. Practically, we do not want just one function; we want to generate an entire family of functions by varying a parameter (the shared secret key) so that instead of inventing a new function for each card, we can just change the key. These "keyed functions" are referred to as message authentication codes (MACs). They are often realized in terms of hash functions like SHA1 or MD5. However, the principle remains the same; this is just an implementation detail.

The particular function chosen and the lengths, in bits, of the challenge and the response determine the security of the system. For example, consider a system with a 3-bit challenge. This gives us eight possible challenges, so the reader cannot perform more than eight transactions without reusing a challenge. With such a system, an eavesdropper would not have to listen for long before seeing every possible challenge and, consequently, every response. At this point, the eavesdropper could masquerade as a legitimate card: For any challenge that the reader might send, the eavesdropper would know the response. The challenge and response must therefore be long enough that an eavesdropper cannot practically observe every possible transaction and build a lookup table. Note that the transactions here need not be legitimate transactions. Instead of intercepting transactions between a legitimate reader and a legitimate card, we could build a malicious reader. This would allow us to send many challenges to the card in a short period of time. This means that an 8-bit challenge still might not be secure, even though it probably would not be practical for an attacker to observe 256 legitimate transactions in a reasonable period of time. A malicious reader could simply send every possible challenge, all 256 of them, and record every possible response.

Challenge/response proximity cards are commercially available now. However, they are more expensive than the simple ID-only cards. As of this writing, ID-only cards retail for about $2 each in small quantities. Cards marketed as using challenge/response currently cost about $10 each. This price difference is to be expected because the computational complexity of calculating the response from the challenge is greater than that involved in reading a fixed ID out of memory. Also, the challenge/response scheme requires bidirectional communication between the reader and the card. With a simple ID-only card, the card transmits its ID and the reader listens. With a challenge/response card, the reader transmits the challenge while the card listens, and then the card transmits the response while the reader listens. This adds complexity not just to the card but also to the reader. However, such a system, if it is implemented correctly, will resist all of the attacks described in this chapter.

Indala has an unusual technology called FlexSecur in which before the card's ID is programmed, the ID is encrypted with a secret key. The reader, which knows the secret key, decrypts it before sending it to the computer that decides whether to open the door. The message sent over the air is encrypted so that an eavesdropper could not determine the unencrypted ID without knowing the secret key. It is difficult to imagine why an eavesdropper would want to do this, though. The legitimate reader is expecting the encrypted ID, and the encrypted ID, which is broadcast over the air, is the same each time. The replay attacks discussed earlier are still entirely practical. An attacker who, like me, blindly duplicated a legitimate card would not even notice that it was there. I have not been able to determine whether FlexSecur was present on the FlexPass that I cloned.

It is possible that this scheme would have some value if the ID were an otherwise valuable piece of information (like a Social Security number, for example);

in such a case, FlexSecur would prevent an attacker from learning that information, although the attacker would still be able to open the door. This would probably still be a bad idea for other reasons, though. Alternatively, this scheme would be useful if the IDs were assigned with some structure—for example, if employees were numbered 0000, 0001, 0002, and so on. If these IDs were programmed directly onto the card, a brute force attack would be much easier: We could start from all zeros and count up, and we would find a legitimate card very quickly (and the janitor's card shortly after that). The encryption step would complicate such an attack. FlexSecur might provide some security benefits in some situations, but the most practical attack on the proximity cards—a replay attack to gain entry using an eavesdropped ID—still works perfectly.

Conclusions

So the FlexPass cards, as designed, are insecure because they can trivially be cloned. This is not necessarily bad. Security is inevitably a question of tradeoffs. Indala could have designed its proximity card system with challenge/response authentication from the beginning. This would have added cost and complexity, however, and most people simply don't need anything that secure.

I live in a house with five pin tumbler locks on the doors; anyone can learn to pick these locks with a few hours of practice. So far, this has not been a problem. In fact, it is a feature—if I lock myself out of the house, I can get in without breaking a window. The FlexPass card that I cloned could, in theory, be more secure, but this does not make it useless. It does not provide absolute mathematical security—in the real world there is no such thing—but it adds another barrier to entry. It is entirely reasonable for us to choose a cheap and insecure solution when a secure alternative exists, as long as we are aware that we are doing so.

The key, of course, is that we should be aware that we are doing so. I first posted a description of my experiments to the Internet in October 2003. Since then, I have received large volumes of e-mail from people who had just always assumed that whatever the cards did, they had to be more secure than *that*. One nameless blogger still refused to believe that the cards were insecure: "Well yes, he might have been able to read the thing, but of course the cards use challenge/response, right, so it's not like he can do anything with it…." The staff in the facilities department at the company where I worked believed me, but they were not impressed. When they learned about my device, they politely asked me to keep it very far away from any of their buildings. (My employer did use Indala FlexPass cards, the same brand that my device could clone.) Later, they requested that I remove either my write-up or my résumé from my Web page to ensure that the company was not publicly associated with my proximity card exploits.

I had not done anything particularly novel, though. The marketing literature that I had seen wasn't very clear about the technical details of the cards, but it never claimed that they provided any kind of cryptographic security. The companies that sell these proximity cards know exactly how secure their products are; I can't imagine that anything I discovered about the FlexPass cards would surprise the engineers who designed them. Yet when I reported what I had found, their customers were surprised. This suggests that many of the organizations installing proximity card systems do not have a clear understanding of the security tradeoffs involved.

RFID tags do offer some inherent security. A bar code can be photocopied. A magnetic stripe is a little bit better, but user-friendly readers and writers are available off the shelf for a few hundred dollars. By comparison, my FlexPass proved inconvenient to copy. However, as RFID technology becomes more prevalent, the incentives to break weak security will increase. Designers of RFID systems must not blindly rely on the complexity of their technology for security. As for any system, they must consider what security is required and, if necessary, use appropriate mathematical and cryptographic tools.

References

Anderson, R. *Security Engineering: A Guide to Building Dependable Distributed Systems*. New York: John Wiley & Sons. 2001.

"HCS360 KeeLoq Code Hopping Encoder." Microchip Technology Inc., 2002. http://ww1.microchip.com/downloads/en/DeviceDoc/40152e.pdf.

Lee, Y. "AN678: RFID Coil Design." Microchip Technology Inc., 1998. http://ww1.microchip.com/downloads/en/AppNotes/00678b.pdf.

"MCRF200 Contactless Programmable Passive RFID Device." Microchip Technology Inc., 1998. http://ww1.microchip.com/downloads/en/DeviceDoc/21219h.pdf.

Sorrells, P. "AN680: Passive RFID Basics." Microchip Technology Inc., 1998. http://ww1.microchip.com/downloads/en/AppNotes/00680b.pdf.

basis for implementing so-called Personal Area Networks (PANs), Bluetooth was originally designed simply as a way to replace cables with radio waves.

Cables, after all, can be quite annoying—too short, too long, wrong gender, wrong connector. Cables become tangled, damaged, and lost. Even worse, they constantly are changing, so a cable that you purchased last year for one phone won't work next year with your new phone.

Bluetooth's creators envisioned a cable-free world in which many types of devices would work together simply because they all implement the shared Bluetooth standard. For example:

- You could use a Bluetooth-enabled cellular telephone to access the Internet from a Bluetooth-enabled laptop or handheld computer.
- You could use a Bluetooth wireless headset one minute with your cell phone in a trans-Atlantic phone call and the next minute with a fancy speech recognition program running on your laptop.
- Your Bluetooth-enabled cell phone could "beam" your business card to the Bluetooth-enabled personal digital assistant (PDA) of someone you met at a conference.
- Best of all, a phone purchased three years ago will interoperate with today's laptop and tomorrow's wireless headset, provided that they all follow the same standard Bluetooth "profiles."

To deliver on this vision, Bluetooth had to do more than deliver reliable, low-power, high-speed connections between devices of different manufacturers: Bluetooth also had to be secure and simple to use. Without security, users would not trust Bluetooth devices with their information. People would not adopt a standard knowing that it could expose their credit card numbers and confidential documents to the world or allow others to eavesdrop on their conversations.

Usability is just as important. Without a usable implementation, the public would shun the technology, rendering Bluetooth a spectacularly well-funded white elephant.

Today Bluetooth is well on its way to becoming a commercial success. The technology is in tens of millions of mobile and handheld devices around the world, including cell phones, PDAs, headsets, and laptops. Bluetooth is also showing up in machines that would connect with these devices—machines like printers, cars,[3] and even refrigerators.[4]

---

3. BMW has a Bluetooth option available for some of is high-end cars.
4. Toshiba sells a Bluetooth-enabled refrigerator, Model #GR-463IT, currently available for sale only in Asian markets. Levine, D. "Mobile Technology: Trend Forecast 2003." Telluride Group, December 24, 2002. Volume VII, No. 12. Available at www.tellgroup.com.

But in many ways, Bluetooth still has not delivered adequate security or usability. While it is a great technology for using wireless headphones with cells phones or for wirelessly beaming a business card from one Palm-based computer to another, Bluetooth can also be used to surreptitiously track a person's movements about town, wirelessly hijack the contents of a person's address book, or even bug a meeting of corporate CEOs.

As is the case with many wireless technologies, Bluetooth's creators spent far more time fine-tuning its over-the-air protocol and supporting applications than thinking about its security infrastructure. For example, a seven-page article appearing in a 2002 *IBM Technical Journal* stated: "Due to the personal/confidential data contained on the different types of client devices (e.g., the mobile computer), the link formed between these devices needed to be as secure as the cable it was replacing."

The article spent five and a half pages discussing wireless data transmission, multislot frames, usage models, and piconets. On the other hand, security issues garnered less than a page. And half of that discussion covered Bluetooth's provisions for using different-sized encryption keys, allowing the single standard to be used under a variety of regulatory regimes! Most of the hard security issues like key management, spoofing, and even the mechanisms of "pairing" devices were simply ignored.[5]

Implying that encryption resolves the security problems by providing for a secure channel between Bluetooth devices is to seriously underestimate the nature of the security concerns: Without proper authentication, high-strength encryption will merely ensure that no third party will be able to eavesdrop as the hacker steals your personal information.

Early Bluetooth proponents claimed that the wireless protocol's frequency-hopping nature provided security against authorized interception of the wireless signal. Even a casual consideration of this statement proves its falsehood: Clearly, the Bluetooth signal is *designed to be intercepted by other Bluetooth radios*. Frequency hopping alone provides for robustness against unintentional interference but offers no real security against a deliberate attack.

Bluetooth's ubiquity *ensures* that the technology will be with us for a long time; what's needed now is to give an open airing to the technology's risks and to start addressing them.

---

5. Kardach, J. "Bluetooth Architecture Overview." *Intel Technology Journal*, Second Quarter, 2002.

Bluetooth's Background

Bluetooth was conceived in 1994, when engineers at Ericsson Mobile Communications looked into the feasibility of using a low-cost radio signal as a replacement for cable between cell phones and accessories. The engineers settled on a low-power, frequency-hopping system operating within the 2.4GHz unlicensed Industrial Scientific Mobile (ISM) band, a radio band available throughout much of the industrial world.

A few years into the project, Ericsson realized that the technology would be far more successful as an industry standard. Thus, in 1998, after a period of negotiation, Ericsson, Nokia, IBM, Toshiba, and Intel all officially formed a so-called Special Interest Group (SIG) to expedite the technology's development.

"Bluetooth," the SIG's name for the new wireless technology, was taken from a page of Danish history. King Harald Blåtand, whose name loosely translates as Harald Bluetooth, was the first king of Denmark. The name Blåtand allegedly came from the stains on his teeth: Harald was a big fan of blueberries. But the SIG chose Blåtand not because of his gastronomic proclivities but for his political conquests: King Bluetooth was responsible for uniting Denmark and Norway and bringing Christianity to Scandinavia. In the same way that Blåtand was responsible for uniting disparate countries, the SIG's members hoped that their Bluetooth wireless technology would be responsible for uniting multinational companies and a myriad of electronic devices.

The SIG's goal was to develop a technology that was low power, highly reliable, easy to use, and low cost—the group predicted that adding Bluetooth to a device like a mouse or a keyboard would ultimately cost no more than $5. Other firms were invited to join and did; by July 2004, the SIG claimed "over 2,000 member companies representing tens of thousands of individuals around the world."[6]

The Wireless Cable

As a cable-replacement technology, Bluetooth suffered an inevitable chicken-and-egg problem: The Bluetooth radio on a Bluetooth-enabled cell phone is useful only for those who have a Bluetooth-enabled headset or laptop. Of course, those Bluetooth headsets and laptops are useful only for those who have a Bluetooth-enabled cell phone. And until Bluetooth was shipping in volume, adding a Bluetooth radio to a cell phone or a computer didn't cost just $5—it cost more like $50. As a result, even once the technology had stabilized, Bluetooth

---

6. "About the SIG," Bluetooth: The official Bluetooth Web site. www.bluetooth.com/about /members.asp. Cited July 4, 2004.

was delivered on only the highest-end cell phones and laptops— both markets that were wowed by new technology (even if that technology couldn't really be used) and were less price sensitive. In Europe, Ericsson delivered Bluetooth on its most expensive GSM cellular phones. In the United States, IBM shipped Bluetooth on its most expensive ThinkPads.

As expected, Bluetooth became more popular and less expensive over time. Bluetooth has also evolved, with each new revision fixing bugs in the previous version and adding new features. Backward compatibility ensured that newer Bluetooth units could fall back to the previous version of the protocol, allowing them to speak with older systems.

In 2002, Apple dropped the ubiquitous infrared-based IrDA port from its PowerBook computers and instead gave customers the option of having a Bluetooth radio installed.[7] That same year, Bluetooth interfaces started showing up in wireless keyboards, mice, and even some digital cameras. By November 2003, more than 1 million Bluetooth-enabled units were shipping per week worldwide.[8] In July 2004, *InfoWorld* magazine estimated that there were 250 million Bluetooth-enabled devices in use.[9]

The Wireless Part

As previously mentioned, Bluetooth devices use a frequency-hopping radio tuned to the 2.4GHz Industrial, Scientific, and Medical (ISM) band to transmit and receive information. This is the same band used by the popular 802.11b and 802.11g wireless standards. But while the 802.11 standards use direct sequence spread spectrum (DSSS, also known as direct sequence code division multiple access or DS-CDMA), the Bluetooth 1.1 standard uses frequency-hopping spread spectrum (FHSS) techniques.

To implement frequency hopping, the Bluetooth 1.1 standard slices the 2.4GHz ISM band into 79 separate 1MHz channels. Bluetooth radios hop to different channels 1,600 times per second (i.e., every 625 microseconds) using a predetermined pattern. The time that the radio spends on each channel can be thought of as a "slot" during which the radio can either transmit or receive data.

The Bluetooth radio can send or receive a million bits per second in any channel. However, because packets may be only one, three, or five "slots" long,

7. "Apple Introduces New Titanium PowerBook G4 with DVD Burning SuperDrive." Apple Computer, 2002. www.apple.com/pr/library/2002/nov/06pbg4.html.
8. Bluetooth Shipments Exceed 1M per Week. www.computing.co.uk/Analysis/1132445.
9. Schwartz, E. "Bluetooth Can Pack a Mean Bite." *InfoWorld*. July 23, 2004. www.infoworld.com/article/04/07/23/30OPreality_1.html.

Bluetooth 1.1 radios have an effective maximum data rate of 720 kilobits per second in one direction at a time.

The Bluetooth standard calls for radios that transmit at three distinct power levels. Class 1 has a maximum power output of 100mW (20dB/m) and has a theoretical line-of-site range of 100 meters (300 feet) in free space (although only half that under typical conditions). Class 2 has a maximum power of 2.5mW (4dB/m) and a corresponding range of 10 meters (30 feet). Class 3 devices have a power of 1mW (0dB/m) and a range of 1 meter or less, as shown in Table 20.1.

Table 20.1   Bluetooth Class Comparison of Power and Range

Bluetooth Class	Power (mW)	Range (Meters)
Class 1	100	100
Class 2	2.5	10
Class 3	1	1

It's important to note that the range in the table is a function of Bluetooth radio's sensitivity, preamplifiers, and the antenna that is used. Most Bluetooth devices have no amplifier to speak of and are equipped with an omnidirectional antenna that has no effective gain. On the other hand, using a 500mW amplifier and a 19dB antenna mounted on the stock of a sniper's rifle, the consulting group Flexilis in Southern California has successfully eavesdropped on Bluetooth devices at the distance of a mile.[10] And there are persistent rumors that various national intelligence organizations can eavesdrop on Bluetooth communications at a range of 40 miles, or even from orbit.

The Bluetooth 1.2 standards, which are under development as this chapter is written in 2004, is expected to have a maximum data transfer rate of 3Mbits/sec. The 2.0 standard will increase that further to three rates: 4, 8 and 12Mbps. Although the range should be similar to that of Bluetooth 1.1, it is expected that Bluetooth 2.0 will require twice as much power to achieve that higher throughput.[11]

Bluetooth is similar to the popular 802.11 WiFi standard in that both use the 2.4GHz unlicensed band to transmit information wirelessly through the air. For example, both Bluetooth and 802.11 radios can be made very small and use

---

10. "Defcon 12's Fear and Hacking in Vegas." Tom's Hardware Guide Business Reports, August 21, 2004. www6.tomshardware.com/business/20040802l/defcon-05.html.
11. Yoshida, J. "Scientists tip features of Bluetooth 2.0." *EE Times*, June 11, 2002. www.eetimes.com/story/OEG20020611S0033.

tiny antennas (since the wavelength of light at 2.4Ghz is approximately 12.3cm). And as with 802.11, every Bluetooth device has a unique 48-bit address, which Bluetooth calls the Bluetooth Device Address (BD_ADDR). A sample BD_ADDR would be 000C3E123456, which could also be written 00:0C:3E:12:34:56. By design, BD_ADDRs should be unique: Manufacturers promise that they will not create two machines with the same address.

Nevertheless, Bluetooth is different from 802.11 in several significant ways: Bluetooth radios are easier to build, they are less prone to interference, and they use dramatically less power. They are also considerably more hostile: A Bluetooth radio can render all but unusable an 802.11 device within range because the Bluetooth radio constantly hopes through the 802.11 channels. On the other hand, an active 802.11 network will interfere with Bluetooth communications, but it will not interrupt them.

Most Bluetooth devices have direct support for user-supplied "friendly names" like "My laptop" or "Kim's Cell Phone." Although the standard says that these user-friendly names may be up to 248 bytes in length, most devices limit these names to between 20 and 40 characters.

For security purposes, each Bluetooth device is assigned a "Bluetooth passkey," better known as the Bluetooth PIN. The Bluetooth PIN can be represented as a 128-bit value or as a string of Unicode characters. Typically, though, many Bluetooth devices will allow PINs to be only four-character numeric strings, like "1234." This limitation, of course, allows for far easier password cracking. Many Bluetooth devices come with preset PINs like "0000" or "5743." Preset PINs are common on devices that are not large enough to have a keypad to enter a PIN, such as a headset. Most of these devices have a special button that must be pressed to initiate the pairing process.

Bluetooth Profiles

Another important difference between 802.11 and Bluetooth is the scope of the two protocols. The 802.11 standard is concerned primarily with how Ethernet frames (or packets) are transmitted and received through the air. Bluetooth's creators, on the other hand, did not want to create yet another wireless LAN standard. Instead, they wanted a detailed standard that addressed high-level technical issues such as encoding voice or exchanging business contact information.

As a result, the Bluetooth standard specifies a variety of elaborate usage scenarios that dictate how two or more Bluetooth devices will interact. These so-called *Bluetooth profiles* make it easier for people to use Bluetooth products: There should be no fiddling with device drivers, configurations, or other items.

Two products should work together if they implement the same Bluetooth profile. Otherwise, they probably won't.

Typical Bluetooth profiles include simple cable replacements between a computer and various peripherals such as keyboards, mice, printers, and speakers. Another profile connects a Bluetooth headset to a cell phone or laptop computer. Bluetooth also allows people to wear a lightweight headset in their ear and keep their bulky cell phone in their pocket.

Table 20.2 shows the profiles supported by a typical Bluetooth-enabled handheld, the HP iPAQ Pocket PC. Table 20.3 is a list of many profiles prepared by German developer Ingo Heinicke.

Table 20.2   Bluetooth Profiles Implemented by the HP iPAQ Pocket PC[a]

Profile	Function
BPP	Basic Printer profile, for printing from a computer or handheld to a printer.
DUN	Dial-Up Network profile lets a computer or handheld use a cell phone for dial-up networking.
FAX	Send and receive faxes.
FTP	File transfer profile, for transferring files from one device to another.
HCRP	Hard Cable Replacement profile looks like a cable connecting two devices.
LAP	LAN Access profile lets one Bluetooth device use another to access a local area network.
OBEX	Object Exchange profile accesses objects on a remote system. (For example, read and write vCard/vCal entries.)
OPP	Object Push profile sends objects to a remote system
PAN	Personal Area Network profile provides for direct communication between devices on a PAN.
SPP	Serial Port Profile allows one Bluetooth device to access the serial port on another.
ActiveSync	Uses the SPP to allow a handheld computer to connect to an ActiveSync server on a computer.
AGP	Audio Gateway profile allows a device to access audio hardware on another device.

a. "HP iPAQ Pocket PC—Using Bluetooth," Hewlett Packard, Business Support Document. http://h20000.www2.hp.com/bizsupport/TechSupport/Document.jsp?objectID=c00031208. (Accessed July 4, 2004.)

Table 20.3 A Detailed List of Bluetooth Profiles[a]

Profile	Short	Usage	Sample Products	Transfer
Advanced Audio Distribution	A2DP	Audiotransfer	Audioplayer, headphones, micro	723 kBit/s
Audio Video Remote Control	AVRCP	Audio/video remote control	PC, VCR, DVD player	723 kBit/s
Basic Imaging	BIP	Image transfer	Camera, PC, scanner	723 kBit/s
Basic Printing	BPP	Simple print jobs	PDA, printer, phone, PC	723 kBit/s
Common ISDN Access	CIP	ISDN over CAPI	ISDN modem, PC	723 kBit/s
Cordless Telephony	CTP	Cordless telephony	Phones and base	64 kBit/s
Dial-up Networking	DUN	Network connection to Internet	Modem, PC, PDA, phone, AP	723 kBit/s
Extended Service Discovery	ESDP	Extended Service Discovery	PDA, PC	723 kBit/s
Fax	FAXP	Faxing	ISDN modem, PC, printer, fax	723 kBit/s
File Transfer	FTP	File transfer	Phone, PDA, PC	723 kBit/s
Generic Access	GAP	Access control	All Bluetooth units	723 kBit/s
Generic AV Distribution	GAVDP	Audio/video transfer	Audioplayer, PC, PDA	723 kBit/s
Generic Object Exchange	GOEP	Object exchange	Phone, PDA, PC, camera	723 kBit/s
Hands Free	HFP	In-car telephony	Phone, hands-free kit	723 kBit/s
Hardcopy Cable Replacement	HCRP	Printing	Printer, scanner, PC, fax	723 kBit/s
Headset	HSP	Headset voice output	Headset	64 kBit/s
Human Interface Design	HID	Inputs	Keyboard, mouse, PC	723 kBit/s
Intercom	INTP	Two-way communications	Intercom, walkie-talkies	64 kBit/s

a. Information about which cell phones support these profiles can be found at www.skyynet.de. Reprinted with permission.

Table 20.3   A Detailed List of Bluetooth Profiles[a] *(Continued)*

Profile	Short	Usage	Sample Products	Transfer
LAN Access	LAP	Network connection via PPP	Access point	723 kBit/s
Object Push	OPP	Address and date exchange	Phone, PDA, PC	723 kBit/s
Personal Area Networking	PAN	Network connection	Access point	723 kBit/s
Serial Port	SPP	Serial data exchange	Modem, PDA, PC, phone	723 kBit/s
Service Discovery Application	SDAP	Discovery of units	All Bluetooth units	723 kBit/s
SIM Access	SAP	Read SIM cards	Phone, car kits	723 kBit/s
Synchronization	SP	Synchronization	Phone, PDA, PC	723 kBit/s

a. Information about which cell phones support these profiles can be found at www.skyynet.de. Reprinted with permission.

Other Bluetooth profiles govern the exchange of contact information (in vCard/vCal format), file transfer, handheld synchronization, and other tasks typical of handheld and remote devices.

Bluetooth's powers of automated data transfer and synchronization, combined with the ability of 2.4GHz waves to penetrate objects like briefcases and backpacks, allow for hidden computing as well as legitimate data transfer. For example, a user can set devices in certain sleep modes that periodically check for information updates. A user also could leave a laptop in a briefcase and have it periodically receive information updates regarding meetings and calls from the owner's mobile phone. This is a really nifty feature—provided that the transfer happens with the proper knowledge and authorization.

Untrusted Versus Trusted Pairing and Discoverability

Different Bluetooth profiles require different levels of security. Receiving somebody's business card doesn't require that you know who the person is—in theory, you can always delete the business card. On the other hand, you wouldn't want someone else to access your cell phone's modem or download the contents of *your* address book without your permission. To handle these different situations, Bluetooth provides for two basic levels of access: untrusted and trusted.

When you buy a new Bluetooth device, every other Bluetooth device is both unknown and "untrusted." But if you want, you can "pair" two devices, causing the devices to trust each other. When you pair two devices, each device's address is entered into the other's Device Database and marked as "trusted." The pairing process also establishes an encryption key that can be used for transmitting confidential information between the two devices.

The Bluetooth SIG's "Wireless Security" document advises Bluetooth users against pairing in public places. "Theoretically, a hacker can monitor and record activities in the frequency spectrum and then use a computer to regenerate the PIN codes being exchanged. This requires specially built hardware and thorough knowledge of Bluetooth systems."[12] Here the SIG is dramatically understating the risk; the "specialized hardware" is really any Bluetooth-equipped laptop or PDA running a "sniffer" program.

Different Bluetooth devices have slightly different procedures for pairing. For example, you can pair a Macintosh laptop with a PalmOS-based computer by telling the Mac to "set up a Bluetooth device." The Mac searches for nearby Bluetooth devices and displays them in a list. When you choose the Bluetooth device that you want to pair with, you are instructed to type the same four-digit number from the Mac onto the Palm device or vice versa. As noted above, many Bluetooth devices have four-digit PINs that can't be changed.

Bluetooth devices can be "discoverable," which allows them to be readily detected by other nearby Bluetooth devices, or can try to hide their whereabouts. So one way to control malicious pairing attempts is by telling your Bluetooth device to "hide." Essentially, any Bluetooth device that is discoverable periodically listens to a fixed set of 32 frequencies to see if there is another Bluetooth device nearby that is looking for neighbors. If the Bluetooth device is discoverable, it sends back a message with its Bluetooth address. Conversely, when a Bluetooth device is in "nondiscoverable" mode, it will not respond to "inquiry" requests from other Bluetooth devices.

Unfortunately, the term nondiscoverable is somewhat misleading. Even so-called nondiscoverable devices respond to queries made specifically to their BD_ADDR. So all you have to do to find a nearby Bluetooth device is to guess that machine's BD_ADDR and then try to send it a message and see if it responds.

---

12. "Bluetooth Wireless—Help—Wireless Security." Bluetooth SIG at www.bluetooth.com/help /security.asp. (Accessed August 11, 2004.)

In theory, searching for a device's BD_ADDR could take a very long time. BD_ADDRs are 48 bits: If devices had randomly-assigned addresses, it would take on average 2^{47} separate attempts—more than 140 billion tries—to find a nearby device. But this number is misleading because Bluetooth addresses are not randomly assigned. The first 24 bits of a device's BD_ADDR are dedicated to a manufacturer-assigned code (see Figure 20.1), all but eliminating the need to consider those bits in a targeted search. This transforms the address space into one whose size is essentially only 2^{24} (16.77 million) per vendor.

LSB   MSB

company_assigned						company_id					
LAP						UAP		NAP			
0000	0001	0000	0000	0000	0000	0001	0010	0111	1011	0011	0101

Figure 20.1 Example showing the format of BD_ADDR. Figure and text reprinted from Bluetooth Specification.

As shown in the figure, the address is divided into three fields: LAP field (lower address part consisting of 24 bits), UAP field (upper address part consisting of 8 bits), and the NAP field (nonsignificant address part consisting of 16 bits).

One Bluetooth search tool, called RedFang,[13] can distribute a search among 127 individual Bluetooth adapters and try all 16.77 million addresses assigned to a single vendor prefix in around 90 minutes.[14] Considering the relatively small number of manufacturers in combination with the fact that many consumers of Bluetooth technology use their devices in situations such as long flights and train rides, 90 minutes is not an unreasonable amount of time to discover a device. On the other hand, a cascading set of USB hubs to support those 127 Bluetooth adapters might gain some attention on a train or flight, and the adapters would probably interfere with each other. But as we shall see below, some Bluetooth devices have implementation bugs that make them vulnerable to more sophisticated attacks that exploit these bugs. A resourceful attacker who has wisely chosen a location or has a particular target in mind could certainly complete the attack quickly enough to be effective.

---

13. www.atstake.com/research/reports/acrobat/atstake_war_nibbling.pdf
14. Self-reported by the tool's creators.

Current and Speculative Bluetooth Implementations

Today Bluetooth is widely deployed on tens of millions of cell phones, PDAs, laptops, and other devices manufactured by a broad range of companies, including Apple, IBM, PalmOne, Toshiba, and Sony. Bluetooth radios can be made as small as a blueberry and powered by a watch battery for more than a month. Wireless synching with Bluetooth can be considerably faster than wired synching using a serial or USB cable.

Automobile makers such as BMW, Ford, and General Motors are embracing the technology to integrate electronic devices in cars. BMW now offers mobile phone compatibility that allows drivers to synchronize phone data with the vehicle's electronic system and display phonebook entries using the onboard monitor. Phone calls can be placed through the steering wheel or voice activation such that the user never has to physically dial the number.[15]

Manufacturers like Apple and Microsoft have embraced the peripheral usage model and offer Bluetooth keyboards and mice. Apple offers affordable Bluetooth-enabled keyboards and mice that go perfectly with the built-in capabilities of their PowerBook G4s. Other third-party vendors such as Ambicom have developed inexpensive USB printer adapters. D-link has developed a stereo USB adapter that allows a PC to stream music directly to computer speakers. Sony also offers Bluetooth-enabled camcorders to transfer digital video to PCs. These Bluetooth peripherals allow for a truly wireless computer system.

Vendors such as NaviPlay used Bluetooth to extend the functionality of portable electronics such as the iPod. They developed a stereo adapter that connects to an iPod docking port. This allows one to use a remote control to command an iPod and wirelessly stream music to speakers.

The Salling Clicker[16] software for Macs embodies another interesting application of Bluetooth. This software allows users with mobile phones or PDAs to remotely control their Macintosh PCs and notebooks—for example, using the PDA to change slides during a presentation.

Video gaming serves as another great forum for Bluetooth technology. Nokia developed a mobile phone/gaming system called N-gage that allows wireless multiplayer games using Bluetooth. Years ago, high school students connected their Nintendo GameBoys together with a cord to play Tetris against one

---

15. BMW pioneers wireless in-vehicle communication. www.bmw.co.za/Products/Bluetooth /default.asp.
16. www.calling.com

another; today people can play baseball and soccer and even virtually skate-board with a friend using Bluetooth technology.

Bluetooth continues to find new uses. Companies like Code Blue Communications are using Bluetooth's cable replacement capability to redesign medical equipment. Baracoda developed a wireless bar code reader that utilizes the technology to track, tag, and secure retail products. Thus, Bluetooth technology fosters ubiquitous computing and electronic device integration.

Bluetooth Security and Privacy Attacks

Despite Bluetooth's security mechanisms in the specification, many Bluetooth devices are susceptible to a variety of attacks that threaten the privacy of Bluetooth users. These attacks can be loosely grouped into five distinct areas:

- Bluetooth security mechanisms can be bypassed to intercept and decode communications.
- An attacker can use the radio interface to gain access directly to a Bluetooth device and steal information, alter it, or implant new information.
- One Bluetooth device can hijack the services provided by another device.
- Since every Bluetooth device has a unique identifier, a network of Bluetooth-equipped receivers can track the movements of a person within a geographical area.
- Bluetooth communications between two devices could be overheard by a third party.

Attacks can be conducted through legitimate application programming interfaces (APIs) or through implementation bugs. Bluetooth devices have the same sort of bugs and security vulnerabilities as those that have been haunting Microsoft since it starting shipping Internet Explorer in the 1990s: Poor programming practices, poor quality assurance, and a lack of attention to security have resulted in exploitable buffer-overflows and other kinds of attacks. One set of vulnerabilities that has been discovered allows an attacker to reach into a phone's address book and retrieve or modify information. Another vulnerability leaves the database of trusted devices open to attack. To be fair, some cell phone vendors have issued "patches" to fix these vulnerabilities. In practice, of course, many phones won't get patched or otherwise upgraded. An excellent list of which phones are vulnerable to which attacks has been assembled by Adam and Ben Laurie.[17]

---

17. Laurie, B. "Serious Flaws in Bluetooth Security Lead to Disclosure of Personal Data." October 14, 2004. www.thebunker.net/security/bluetooth.htm.

Underlying many of these problems is the fact that the Bluetooth specification is concerned primarily with over-the-air communications, whereas security issues are often either optional or poorly specified. For example, implementers can choose the length of PINs and whether or not to use them; encryption is used only when services request it; the random number generator is implementation dependent. A good algorithm with a bad random number generator is really no more secure than a bad algorithm.[18]

To help address these shortcomings the Bluetooth SIG Security Expert Group released a document called the Bluetooth Security White Paper in April 2002,[19] This white paper looks at different "profiles" of anticipated Bluetooth usage. Included are many sample "security architectures" for these profiles, consisting of suggested access policies and security mechanisms for implementers of the Bluetooth specification.

In addition, the document briefly touches on two of what it calls "security shortcomings" in the standard: vulnerabilities associated with PINs and the dangers of unit keys.[20] This discussion is summarized in the two following recommendations taken verbatim from a 1.5-page long section:

1. Avoid the use of unit keys. Use combination keys instead.

2. Perform the bonding [pairing] in an environment that is as secure as possible against eavesdroppers and use long random Bluetooth passkeys.[21]

This advice can be best described as "short but prudent." In the following sections, we dig a bit deeper.

Cracking Bluetooth

A number of theoretical and actual attacks against Bluetooth devices have been identified.

---

18. www.bsi.de/english/brosch/B05_bluetooth.pdf
19. Bluetooth Security Whitepaper, Bluetooth SIG Security Expert Group. www.bluetooth.com /upload/24Security_Paper.PDF.
20. For an in-depth technical discussion of these and other shortcomings in the Bluetooth encryption model and cipher, see M. Jakobsson and S. Wetzel. Security Weaknesses in Bluetooth. RSA Conference 2001, 2001. http://citeseer.ist.psu.edu/jakobsson01security.html.
21. www.dsv.su.se/~matei/bin/ 4%20-%202i1279/L4_Bluetooth_2.pdf

Guess the PIN on the Bluetooth Device

As discussed earlier, Bluetooth's primary tool in preventing unauthorized pairing is a password used to derive a 128-bit string. Sadly, the Bluetooth specification calls this password a PIN—apparently a reference to the four-digit passwords used by automated teller machines (ATMs). Perhaps because of the name, many manufacturers seem to design their systems to use short, four-digit numeric PINs.

Short PINs are problematic because of the method by which the initialization key is calculated. This initialization key is used to protect the secrecy of the combination or unit key—the heart of a Bluetooth data exchange's security mechanism. The PIN is the only secret input to the symmetric key generation algorithms. Thus, even though the encryption key itself is 128 bits long, if PINs are restricted to four numeric digits, there are only 10,000 possible encryption keys that a particular Bluetooth device will use. If the PIN is too short and pairing is done in a public place, an attacker can record all of the communication between the victim device and another device and compute the keys in reverse.

Default PINs tend to be both too short and too trivial. Professor Juha Vainio at Helsinki University estimates that 50 percent of PINs used are the default value "0000."[22] Allowing PINs to be changed is not a solution because users will still pick PINs that are short and easily typed and thus easily guessed. For example, a user initializing an ad hoc PAN with three Bluetooth devices may need to enter the PIN at least four times. While these problems could be mitigated on the application layer if a key agreement scheme is enforced, this is optional and service dependent. That's not to say that no such key agreement schemes are in use on any Bluetooth device that's ever been made, but such systems are not in general use today.

Spoofing

If one or more of the devices in a pairing scenario are configured to accept it, both devices will agree on one of the embedded unit keys to be used as the link key. Recall that the link key is used as the shared secret during authentication and encryption. Deriving this link key from the unit key is a very bad practice because the unit key is essentially permanent and public. This leads to possible spoofing from a third party. Specifically, once one Bluetooth device pairs with a second device, that first device can masquerade as the second device and authenticate to a third.[23]

---

22. Vainio, JT. "Bluetooth Security." www.niksula.cs.hut.fi/~jiitv/bluesec.html.
23. Ibid.

An unresolved question is the security of the Bluetooth cipher itself. In the influential "Security Weaknesses in Bluetooth," Jakobsson and Wetzel revealed significant flaws in the Bluetooth 1.0 cipher. The latest Bluetooth specification has been revised since the publication of this paper, but many still question the validity of the cipher.[24]

Bluesnarfing

The security of Bluetooth devices should be based on the principle of defense-in-depth[25]—that is, security should come from a variety of security mechanisms, any one of which should be able to fail without compromising the user's security. For example, the security of a user's telephone address book could depend on the phone's BD_ADDR being unknown, the PIN being required to pair with the phone, or a confirmation on the phone's user interface being required to allow the pairing to take place.

The reality, though, is that many Bluetooth devices are designed with the non-discoverable assumption as their only protection from intrusion.

Many Bluetooth implementations are set to automatically share sensitive data with any pingable device. This allows unscrupulous users to "snarf" data from the device without the victim's knowledge. In the newsletter *SecurityFocus*, Bruce Potter, a security consultant at the nonprofit information security group Shmoo Group, described the results of installing a Bluetooth adapter on his Compaq iPaq. He discovered that that it shared *all* his files with *any* device that had his BD_ADDR: "The only thing that was preventing people from finding my PDA and accessing all the files on my PDA was that it wasn't in broadcast mode."[26]

Significantly more alarming than this security hole is another apparent flaw in some implementations of Bluetooth applications. Taking advantage of bugs in the protocols, untrusted devices can reach into the Bluetooth databases, access and modify private data, and even add new BD_ADDRs to the trusted database, according to Adam and Ben Laurie of the security company A.L. Digital Ltd. The attacks that made it possible to unlawfully access Bluetooth phone-books, calendars, images, and other data were first published on the Internet

---

24. For a discussion of the problems with the new cipher, see the detailed presentation given by Ollie Whitehouse at the CanSecWest conference in April 2004 (http://cansecwest.com /csw04/csw04-Whitehouse.pdf).
25. Defense-in-depth is the principle of having independent defense mechanisms at different layers of a system to provide more complete protection. For an excellent discussion of this and other system design principles, see Saltzer and Kaashoek, *Topics in the Engineering of Computer Systems*.
26. www.securityfocus.com/news/5896

in November 2003. The Lauries' claims were met with intense skepticism by many because the document's alarmist tone named vulnerable phone models without providing any example code, a conceptual explanation of the exploit, or other proof to back up their claims.

These claims have since been substantiated. In February 2004, mobile phone manufacturers Ericsson and Nokia admitted that some of their Bluetooth devices were indeed susceptible to the Bluesnarfing attack. While Nokia admitted this problem, the company also told the press that it would not be releasing a fix for it, citing that only a few devices were affected and claiming that the attacks would probably not "happen at large."[27] Meanwhile, Ericsson announced that its newest models were not affected by the vulnerability and advised that users with older phones should turn off Bluetooth in public as a preventive measure.[28]

While these problems can generally be fixed with firmware upgrades, exploits tend to exist for a long time and upgrades sometimes introduce new vulnerabilities. On March 30, 2004, an Austrian researcher named Martin Herfurt successfully executed a Bluesnarfing attack on the phones of 46 unsuspecting users at CeBIT 2004, Europe's largest IT-exposition.[29] Herfurt's equipment was by no means formidable: He used two low-cost Bluetooth dongles and a custom implementation of the Bluetooth stack running on a laptop positioned outside the public restrooms. Herfurt further discovered that he had access to the phones' command sets, allowing him to send short message service (SMS) messages and initiate phone calls in addition to reading and writing phone book entries and other personal data.[30] This sort of vulnerability could potentially make some Bluetooth-enabled phones the new open relay for spammers.[31] Alternatively, someone could use it to bug a room or conversation by simply instructing a vulnerable Bluetooth phone to place a call to an answering machine. Given Bluetooth's range, such an attack could be executed by someone standing on the other side of a boardroom door.

27. "Nokia Admits Multiple Bluetooth Security Holes." ZDNet UK, February 9, 2004. http://news.zdnet.co.uk/0,39020330,39145886,00.htm.
28. "Sony Ericsson Advises Users to Turn Off Bluetooth." ZDNet UK, February 11, 2004. http://news.zdnet.co.uk/communications/wireless/0,39020348,39146123,00.htm.
29. Herfurt, M. "Bluesnarfing @ CeBIT 2004." 2004. Available for download at http://trifinite.org.
30. "BlueBug." Salzburg Research, 2004. Available for download at http://trifinite.org.
31. The open relay problem refers to the phenomenon of spammers using insecure mail servers to send unsolicited and anonymous messages to victims. The problem became so widespread that there are now what Harvard Law Professor Jonathan Zittrain calls "private sheriffs" who maintain and sell lists of the IP addresses of open relays to ISPs so that they may effectively filter out mail from these servers. A server added to the most prominent of these lists is said to be "Blackholed." See the MAPS Realtime Blackhole List for examples of this [12].

Exploits in Bluetooth devices can clearly lead to grave privacy risks for the users of the devices. A poorly implemented Bluetooth stack can expose users to the danger of having their identity spoofed to others and their confidential data revealed.

Social Engineering Through "Bluejacking"

The latest fad among malicious Bluetooth users is "bluejacking," which is abusing the Object Exchange (OBEX) protocol to send messages to other users. The OBEX protocol was intended to allow the exchange of objects across Bluetooth or other ad hoc wireless links.[32] The primary use of OBEX is to exchange contact and calendar information via vCard and vCal objects.

Bluejackers generally create an OBEX object such as a vCard and enter arbitrary strings in the name fields and e-mail fields, enabling them to send a message with some level of anonymity. To be sure, most Bluejacking is primarily fun for the sender and, at worst, annoying for the recipient.

Unfortunately, the fun of this seemingly benign "hack" can give way to a potentially potent social engineering tool.[33] Suppose a malicious bluejacker in a coffee shop sends a message to all nearby Bluetooth users proclaiming, "Enter this four-digit PIN to claim your free cappuccino!" Such a gambit could prove very effective in tricking unsuspecting users into inadvertently accepting pairings with other devices. These pairings can lead to the viewing of confidential data as discussed earlier.

A more imminent threat posed by Bluejacking is wireless spam. Bluejacking allows anyone to send anonymous, unsolicited, and potentially commercial messages to those with Bluetooth devices. Indeed, a developer named Collin Mulliner has already written and released a freeware program called BlueSpam, which, although intended for "friendly" use, enables mass Bluejacking.[34] According to Mulliner's Web site:

> BlueSpam searches for all discoverable bluetooth devices and sends a file to them (spams them) if they support OBEX. By default a small text will be send. To customize the message that should be send you need a palm with an SD/MMC card, then you create the directory /PALM/programs/BlueSpam/Send/ and put the file (any type of file will work .jpg is allways fun) you would like to send into this directory.
>
> ....

---

32. Open OBEX Project. Open OBEX Project Homepage, www.ravioli.pasta.cs.uit.no/open-obex/.
33. www.bluejackq.com
34. "BlueSpam." www.mulliner.org/palm/bluespam.php.

BlueSpam also supports backfire, if you put your palm into discoverable and connectable mode, BlueSpam will intercept all connection attempts by other bluetooth devices and starts sending a message back to the sender.

This is for educational purposes only!"[35]

Bluetapping

Another real risk with Bluetooth is that the communications between two devices may be overheard by a third party. We'll call this risk "Bluetapping."

One way to control the risk of Bluetapping might be by controlling physical access. Recall that class 3 devices have a power of 1mW and a range of 1 meter or less. In theory, you could simply ensure that no hostile Bluetooth receivers are within 1 meter of a potentially vulnerable Class 3 device.

The problem with using physical access to control security becomes evident when Class 1 devices are considered because these have a range of 100 meters. In principle, it may be very difficult to ensure that there are no hostile Bluetooth devices within 100 meters of a potentially vulnerable Class 1 device.

Another problem with using physical access to control security is that the 100-meter range often cited for Class 1 devices is a function of many factors, including the antennas, the amplifiers, and the selectivity of the receivers. With the correct equipment, it is possible to receive Bluetooth transmissions from a much greater distance.

For example, in August 2004, a consultant from the security firm Flexilis demonstrated the firm's custom-built BlueSnipper Bluetooth Sniper at the DEFCON 2004 conference in Las Vegas (see Figure 20.2). The BlueSnipper consisted of a 19dB antenna mounted on gunstock, a sniper's scope, a coax cable, a backpack computer and power supply, and a custom-designed Bluetooth application that can eavesdrop on a Bluetooth headset at a distance of a mile.[36] Quite the tool for those interested in corporate espionage! Of course, the use of such equipment may violate the U.S. Electronic Communications Privacy Act (ECPA) if the headset user has an expectation of privacy. On the other hand, U.S. Courts have held that eavesdropping on cordless phones does *not* violate the ECPA because there is no expectation of privacy with these devices!

---

35. http://www.mulliner.org/palm/bluespam.php
36. For more information on the BlueSnipper, see "IMterview with Bluetooth Hacking Flexilis's John Hering" at www.gizmodo.com/archives/imterview-with-bluetooth-hacking-flexiliss-john-hering-019057.php, August 6, 2004. See also Defcon 12's Fear and Hacking in Vegas" at www4.tomshardware.com/business/200408021/defcon-05.html, August 8, 2004.

Figure 20.2   John Hering and the BlueSnipper Bluetooth Sniper.

Locational Surveillance

Organizations have begun developing and deploying Bluetooth-based locational surveillance systems. The most prominent examples of these were developed at a Danish startup called BlueTags. BlueTags "aims at equipping amusement parks, zoological gardens, shopping centers and other places where children are at a potential risk of getting lost, with an intelligent wireless Location System."[37] Two Danish parks—Aalborg Zoo in 2003 and Europe's third largest amusement park, Tivoli Gardens, in 2004—have adopted BlueTags solutions to track children throughout the park.

Parents rent "BodyTags" and painlessly attach them to their children. Upon rental, the parents' cell phone number is recorded and associated with the codes embedded in the BodyTags. The system reports the location of the children in response to SMS[38]-based queries containing the BodyTag codes.[39]

---

37. www.bluetags.com/sw163.asp
38. SMS is Short Messaging Service, a common protocol used in cell phones for sending text messages.
39. "Danish zoo to deploy Bluetooth tracking system." http://eetuk.com//tech/news /OEG20030624S0033.

While such systems are well intentioned and present some clear benefits in many situations, they also open a Pandora's Box of privacy threats. In the short term, there will certainly be nefarious crackers who work to exploit any security holes in tracking systems in order to track users of the system without their knowledge. The first attacks will likely be based on social engineering, in which case the attacker fabricates a story (perhaps about having lost his or her cell phone and forgetting to write down the BodyTag code) that will convince the system operators to reassign the code or otherwise display the location information to an unauthorized user. Depending on the security measures built into the equipment, it may be easily detached and planted on an unsuspecting person, allowing that person's movements to be tracked remotely and thus paving the way for more technically sophisticated attacks on the database and equipment infrastructure.

In the long term, if location tracking systems become more widely deployed, society could see a rapid loss in the expectation of privacy surrounding one's location. Eventually, tracking could become the norm, with government and private sector organizations developing large systems in which the locations of citizens, customers, and employees are systematically logged. The IBM/Steelcase project "BlueSpace" hints at this possibility, allowing employees within an organization to instantly determine the location of fellow employees who are part of the same team.[40] Another take on this idea is the Bluetooth Person Tracker developed by Collin R. Mulliner.[41]

These risks are not necessarily enough to advise that Bluetooth tracking solutions should not be pursued, but they are serious enough that their societal implications ought to be considered, just as ongoing deployment of RFID must be considered. Bluetooth presents unique challenges because it is particularly well suited to tracking uses. The first adopter of the BlueTags system, Aalborg Zoo, chose a Bluetooth solution over an RFID-based solution in part because the Bluetooth solution is easily scalable to hundreds of devices, whereas the available RFID solutions are constrained by the relatively small number of tags that can be read simultaneously by each antenna. In addition, Bluetooth offers more native opportunities for interaction between devices (e.g., PDAs, smartphones) and the location data.[42]

---

40. www.research.ibm.com/bluespace
41. www.betaversion.net/blt
42. Yoshida, J. "Danish Zoo to Deploy Bluetooth Tracking System." *EE Times UK.* June 24, 2003. http://eetuk.com//tech/news/OEG20030624S0033.

Conclusions

Bluetooth has great potential for giving consumers convenient, easy-to-use information sharing and synchronization between devices. Unfortunately, the protocol and many of its implementations are not secure enough to stop a determined adversary from obtaining sensitive data from or otherwise attacking a victim through his or her Bluetooth-enabled devices.

This is not to say that this is solely (or even mostly) a failing of the developers of the Bluetooth protocol. The end-to-end argument[43] for system design implies that substantial protocol-level security measures might not be wise. In fact, certain passages of the Bluetooth Security Whitepaper imply that this principle may have been considered during design:

> The security requirements for Bluetooth applications will vary based on the sensitivity of the information involved, the market, and the needs of the user. There are some applications that do not require any security and others which require extremely high levels of security. Risk analysis and trade studies need to be conducted prior to implementing new applications using Bluetooth wireless technology. [44]

As a result, the document's authors state that Bluetooth intentionally does not specify "application level security." In theory this allows developers to choose "the most appropriate security mechanisms for their particular application." Only time will tell if this decision results in the deployment of Bluetooth systems that actually have an appropriate level of security for the information they carry.

---

43. The end-to-end argument "suggests that functions placed at low levels of a system may be redundant or of little value when compared with the cost of providing them at that low level [17]." See the seminal paper by Saltzer, Reed, and Clark for more information on this topic.
44. Ibid.

Part IV
TECHNICAL SOLUTIONS

Chapter 21

Technological Approaches to the RFID Privacy Problem

Ari Juels[1]

Introduction

We focus in this chapter on technological aids to RFID privacy. Clandestine scanning of RFID tags will constitute a serious privacy concern for consumers. Other chapters in this book have illustrated the range of privacy threats that unchecked, naïve deployment of RFID could pose. RFID tags emit unique static identifiers that can permit secret physical tracking of individuals. Emerging standards also support RFID-tag emission of the data contained today in ordinary bar codes, including a product specification and manufacturer identity. Should personal items come to contain RFID tags, clandestine or simply unregulated scanning would pose a serious threat—not just to civil liberties but also to personal safety. What a boon it would be to thieves to scan prescription medications, luxury wristwatches, and banknotes in secret! (At the same time, as we discuss later in this chapter, it is important to keep the extent and complexity of the real threat in mind. As mentioned in another chapter, some RFID tags are difficult to read in the presence of water and thus the human body. In some cases, if you're worried about scanning of the RFID tag in your sweater, you may simply need to wear it!)

Industrial users of RFID and privacy advocates have largely embraced two solutions to the problem of consumer privacy[2]. The first is labeling. Packaging

---

1. Ari Juels is a principal research scientist at RSA Security.
2. American Civil Liberties Union (ACLU) et al. RFID position statement of consumer privacy and civil liberties organizations, November 20, 2003. Referenced 2004 at www.privacyrights.org/ar/RFIDposition.htm.

for retail items might be required—by law or corporate policy—to indicate the presence and location of attached RFID tags. The second approach is to disable RFID tags at the point of sale, just as anti-theft magnetic strips are disabled in shops today. EPCglobal standards support this approach by prescribing a "kill" function for tags.[3] On receiving a special command, an RFID tag renders itself permanently inoperable. (This function is protected by a tag-specific PIN to prevent malicious disablement.)

Privacy advocates sometimes also proffer *Faraday cages* as a privacy-protecting measure. A Faraday cage is a container lined with metal foil or mesh that obstructs RFID scanning by deflecting reader radio signals. While useful in some cases, Faraday cages are in general of limited utility. Retail shops will not appreciate their use because they defeat theft-control systems. Convenience is another issue: If there is an RFID tag in your hat, for example, a Faraday cage is an inconvenient privacy-enhancing accoutrement.

Labeling is a valuable way to inform consumers of where RFID is deployed and to facilitate physical removal of tags; labeling is also likely to be cost effective. Killing of tags will certainly be an effective means to prevent abuses of the RFID tags in the hands of consumers. (As described in Chapter 26, NCR: RFID in Retail, killing doesn't always work well now, but it will undoubtedly improve as RFID technology evolves.) Neither labeling nor killing nor Faraday cages, however, address a critical problem: Consumers are likely to *want* live, readable RFID tags!

The benefits of RFID for consumers are already clear. Many consumers already carry RFID devices. ExxonMobil Speedpass is a popular wireless payment device that uses RFID; major credit card organizations have plans to follow suit with their own, similar offerings.[4] Proximity cards for building access are also RFID devices. Existing RFID devices are already subject to clandestine scanning, although their short range and newness offer a certain degree of protection.

RFID tags in retail products will engender a broad spectrum of consumer applications. In the short term, consumers might return items to stores without receipts: An RFID tag can point to a database record containing the original price of an item and its terms of sale. Mobile phone manufacturers are beginning to incorporate RFID readers into handsets.[5] Consumers with their own readers of this kind will be able to scan RFID-tagged personal items to register

---

3. EPCglobal Inc. Draft protocol specification for a 900MHz Class 0 radio frequency identification tag. Drafted by MIT Auto-ID Center, February 23, 2003. Available at www.epcglobalinc.org.
4. Radio-fueled credit cards could end swipe. CNN.com. December 13, 2003. Available at www.cnn.com/2003/TECH/ptech/12/13/goodbye.swipe.ap.
5. Nokia unveils RFID phone reader. *RFID Journal*, March 17, 2004. Referenced 2004 at www.rfidjournal.com.

warranties and catalog items at home. RFID-enabled home appliances could help in imaginative ways. Washing machines could automatically calibrate the water temperature for garments, closets could inventory their contents (and seek fashion advice on the Internet), and medicine cabinets could monitor prescription compliance and detect dangerous drug interactions, and so forth.

This is a brief, evocative list of the myriad intriguing possibilities that RFID could introduce for ordinary consumers in the future. Our aim is to justify the position we take in the remainder of this chapter. Because consumers will inevitably carry live RFID tags on a regular basis, we must prepare for the ensuing privacy concerns.

In this chapter, we discuss four technical ideas proposed by the research community for enforcing RFID privacy. We describe *blocker tags*, which may be viewed as a kind of protocol-jamming, privacy-protecting tool. We also treat a variant called *soft blocker tags*, which aim more at cooperative policy enforcement. We explain how *signal-to-noise measurement* can afford privacy protection by detecting the distance of an RFID reader. Finally, we discuss the notion of using *pseudonyms* to protect privacy by changing the digital persona of a tag.

The Technical Challenges of RFID Privacy

Low-cost RFID tags cannot perform standard cryptographic operations, such as encryption, that protect privacy in ordinary computing environments.[6] (Even if tags could perform encryption, the engineering of a privacy-preserving infrastructure would not be straightforward, as chapters in this book on 802.11 and Bluetooth illustrate.) Nor will Moore's Law necessarily come to the rescue. Unremitting industry pricing pressure will probably ensure that basic RFID tags possess only rudimentary resources for some time to come. Development of new cryptographic algorithms could help; but this is mere speculation.

At first blush, the resource constraints of RFID present a technical quagmire. Consumers will want increasingly to use live RFID tags. Live RFID tags require privacy protection. But an RFID tag is essentially just a minimalist five-cent computer with no room for most digital security as we know it!

---

6. Sarma, S.E., Weis, S.A., and Engels, D.W. Radio-Frequency Identification Systems. In Kaliski Jr., B.S, Kaya Koc, C., and Paar, C., eds. *CHES '02*, pp. 454–469. Springer-Verlag, 2002. LNCS no. 2523 and Sarma, E. Towards the Five-Cent Tag. Technical Report MIT-AUTOID-WH-006, MIT Auto-ID Center, 2001. Available from www.autoidcenter.org.

Surprisingly, the limited resources of RFID tags can actually work in favor of the security architect. A full-sized computer like a home PC or a server frequently connects to the Internet and runs a plethora of complex pieces of software. The very flexibility and power of such a machine makes it difficult to secure. Internet connectivity empowers external attackers; a palette of different software applications provides a menu of security vulnerabilities. In contrast, thanks to it simplicity, an RFID tag interacts with external devices in a constrained manner. It transmits and receives information on an infrequent basis (when in the hands of a consumer, at least). Having no software, it draws on a small set of fixed protocols for communication. Thus, despite limited resources and high degree of mobility, RFID tags can support privacy-protecting technologies.

The following sections discuss how.

Blocker Tags

The *blocker tag* is a proposal by Juels, Rivest, and Szydlo for protecting consumer privacy in a world of live RFID tags.[7] A blocker tag is a simple, passive RFID device, similar in cost and form to an ordinary RFID tag. A blocker tag performs a special function, however. When a reader attempts to scan RFID tags that are marked as "private" (in a manner to be discussed below), a blocker tag jams the reader. More precisely, the blocker tag cheats the tag-to-reader communications protocol in such a way that the reader perceives many billions of nonexistent tags and therefore stalls!

Let us sketch a picture of how blocker tags might work in a supermarket. RFID tags possess a special bit designating them either "public" or "private." All unpurchased items on shelves are initially marked public. The readers in the supermarket can scan these items as normal—during inventory taking, for example. At the checkout register, however, the special bit on purchased items is changed from public to private. Shopping bags at the supermarket come with embedded blocker tags. (Being as inexpensive as ordinary tags, they can be as widespread.) When a shopper carries her purchases home in one of these bags, she benefits from the protection of the blocker: If a reader tries to scan her groceries, the blocker tags will cause it to stall. On the other hand, once the shopper removes the groceries from the bags, her RFID-enabled refrigerator, for example, can scan them normally. Her refrigerator can then perform useful

---

7. Juels, A., Rivest, R.L., and Szydlo, M. The Blocker Tag: Selective Blocking of RFID Tags for Consumer Privacy. In V. Atluri, editor, *Eighth ACM Conference on Computer and Communications Security*, pp. 103–111. ACM Press, 2003.

functions like noting which items are depleted, drawing up shopping lists, warning about expired foodstuffs, and so forth.

Let us now briefly examine the technical details behind the blocker. A chief design challenge in RFID systems is the prevention of radio collisions among data transmitted by tags. If all tags were to broadcast their serial numbers simultaneously, the result would be noise: It would be hard for the reader to disentangle the many overlapping signals. To resolve this problem, reader-to-tag RFID communication protocols impose a careful scheduling on tag messages.

As an example, we briefly describe one such protocol known as *tree-walking*.[8] It is helpful to view the space of n-bit tag serial numbers as a binary tree. If we imagine each left branch as being labeled "0" and each right branch labeled "1," a path from the root to a given node at depth k specifies a k-bit serial-number prefix. Hence, each leaf of the tree corresponds to a unique tag serial number. Suppose that tags carry identifiers of 96 bits in length, as in a current EPCglobal standard. The tree representing serial numbers then has depth 96.

To determine which tags are present, a reader performs a kind of depth-first search on the tree. It starts at the root of the tree, asking all tags to broadcast the first bit in their serial numbers. If the reader receives only a 0 transmission, it knows that all tag serial numbers begin with a 0 and recurses on the left subtree. Likewise, if the reader receives only a 1, it recurses on the right subtree. If the reader detects a broadcast collision—that is, both a 0 and a 1—it recurses on both subtrees for the node. At any given internal node of the tree, the reader performs this same operation; first, though, it transmits a command that causes only tags in the corresponding subtree to respond to its query. Once the reader has completed the process of traversing the tree and determined which tags are present, it can communicate individually with tags by addressing them using their serial numbers. (This process of establishing individual reader-to-tag communication is often called *singulation*.)

In brief, then, to determine tag identities, the reader repeatedly asks subsets of tags to broadcast the bit value of their serial numbers in a particular position. A blocker tag exploits this protocol: When the reader asks a subset of tags to transmit the next bit, the blocker transmits both a 0 and a 1, simulating a broadcast collision among tags. As a result, the reader believes that all possible tags are present. If serial numbers are 96 bits in length, this means that a blocker causes a reader to perceive more than a billion billion billion tags!

---

8. EPCglobal Inc. Draft protocol specification for a 900 MHz Class 0 radio frequency identification tag. Drafted by MIT Auto-ID Center, February 23, 2003. Available at www.epcglobalinc.org.

For a blocking system to work productively, the blocking process must be *selective*. A blocker tag should jam a reader only if the reader tries to scan tags marked private. To achieve this, we may employ a system of zoning, in which half of the serial-number tree is regarded as public and the other is marked as private. For example, the left half of the tree, consisting of all serial numbers starting with a 0, might be treated as a private zone, while the other half is treated as a public zone. The first bit of any serial number in this case would indicate the public or private status of a tag. A blocker would naturally simulate collisions only in the private portion of the tree. In other words, a blocker tag would never prevent scanning of public tags in the left half of the tree but would always do so in the right half of the tree. To change the zone of a tag from public to private in, for instance, a supermarket, it would suffice to flip the first bit of the serial number. (Like the "kill" command, this operation would require PIN protection to defend against malicious rezoning.)

It is useful to refine the blocking approach further so that a cooperating reader can refrain from scanning the right half of the tree, the private zone, when a blocker is present. There are a number of techniques whereby a blocker can "politely" inform a reader of its presence. For example, before scanning, a reader might broadcast a special query, to which blocker tags would respond by announcing their presence.

A malicious blocker, one that always jams the reading process, would of course have a deleterious effect on an RFID environment. It would be a straightforward technical matter to construct such a device (although perhaps expensive to fabricate small, chip-sized ones). But the threat of malicious blockers is a poor reason to avoid beneficial blockers. The possibility of malicious blockers will always exist; the use or avoidance of beneficial blockers will have little impact on this threat. Moreover, it is thankfully easy to detect the presence of a blocker. A reader, for instance, can determine whether a random serial number appears to be present; if so, it is highly likely that it is being simulated by a blocker. (There is room for a game of cat-and-mouse to evolve between malicious blocker designers and defenders. We don't discuss this issue here.)

For blocking to be most effective, the idea would require the support of standards. The builders of RFID systems would need to agree on a convention for zoning, for example. It is the hope of the author that EPCglobal and other relevant organizations will embrace the idea.

Blocker tags do have a couple of drawbacks. First, although they are in principle inexpensive to manufacture, this would be true only for large quantities. Additionally, while they can support a good range of privacy policies, they are not always as flexible as might be desired. For example, blocker tags effectively implement an "opt-out" policy. It is incumbent upon the consumer to have a blocker tag in order to benefit from its privacy protection. Consumers may in some cases prefer an "opt-in" policy instead.

Soft Blocking

Soft blocking is an alternative approach to blocking that can achieve privacy policies of almost arbitrary flexibility.[9] The idea is simple: Blocking takes place in a reader or in a software application rather than at the level of the tag-to-reader protocol. As an example, an opt-in soft-blocker system is possible with "unblocker" tags. RFID readers would in this case be programmed only to scan the private zone on detecting the presence of an unblocker tag. Full privacy would be the default.

Soft blocking requires the cooperation of RFID readers, of course. Audit mechanisms to ensure reader compliance would therefore play a vital role in a soft-blocking system. On the other hand, with the right configuration of readers, it is possible for auditing to be an external process, conducted without examination of the internals of readers. If a reader scans the private zone in the presence of an unblocker, the reader's behavior is detectable through passive monitoring of its signals. In principle, one could construct a fairly inexpensive (and even undetectable) auditing device that would test reader compliance.

In essence, soft blocking is much like the Platform for Privacy Preferences (P3P), a Web-browsing enhancement that ensures compatibility between the privacy preferences of a user and the privacy policy of a server before user information is released.[10] A soft blocker tag may be thought of as a physically embodied privacy policy of sorts.

Aside from its benefits of flexible policy support and external auditability, the soft-blocking approach would also permit very inexpensive blocker-tag manufacture. A soft blocker could be just an ordinary RFID tag that emits a serial number expressing a particular privacy policy.

---

9. Juels, A. and Brainard, J. Soft Blocking: Flexible Blocker Tags on the Cheap. In De Capitani di Vimercati, S. and Syverson, P., eds. Wireless Privacy in the Electronic Society (WPES '04). 2004.
10. Platform for privacy preferences (P3P) project, 2003. World Wide Web Consortium. Available at www.w3.org/P3P.

Signal-to-Noise Measurement

Blocking and soft blocking are protocol-level techniques for privacy enforcement. A rather different technique devised by Fishkin and Roy exploits physical distance between a reader and a tag as a measure of trust.[11] They have demonstrated, in particular, that the signal-to-noise ratio of a reader query, as measured on an RFID tag, gives a rough indication of how close the tag is to the reader. It may thus be possible to build inexpensive circuitry into an RFID tag that can measure reader distance.

This concept is useful when the distance of a reader from a tag provides a good gauge of trust. Scanning of tags over long distances naturally carries a whiff of suspicion. Even in a retail environment, consumers would generally feel uncomfortable having the tags in their shopping bags scanned by a reader ten meters away because they might be unable to see the reader and determine its function and ownership.

Fishkin and Roy propose that tags determine their responses to reader queries according to reader distance. A tag might, for instance, never respond to a query transmitted from more than three meters away. It might reveal its serial number when scanned from three meters or less, however, and might respond to the "kill" command only from a distance of a meter or less. Many different policies are possible. A tag might even convert itself into a blocker when scanned from a suspiciously long distance.

A reader can alter its broadcast power in order to spoof a tag, but it appears difficult for a reader to simulate a *shorter* read distance effectively. Simulating a longer distance, of course, is not advantageous for a reader.

Tags with Pseudonyms

Restricting the quantity of information that tags make available to readers is one approach to protecting privacy. An altogether different approach addresses the problem of clandestine tracking. As proposed, tags may change their identities in a dynamic manner. Instead of a unique serial number, a tag might instead store several unlinkable serial numbers—that is, *pseudonyms*.[12]

---

11. Fishkin, K.P. and Roy, S. Enhancing RFID Privacy via Antenna Energy Analysis. Technical Report Technical Memo IRS-TR-03-012, Intel Research Seattle, 2003. Presented at the MIT RFID Privacy Workshop. November 2003.
12. Juels, A. Minimalist Cryptography for Low-Cost RFID Tags. In Blundo, C., ed. Security in Communication Networks (SCN '04). 2004.

Suppose, for example, that a tag contains five pseudonyms. The tag might emit a different pseudonym every time it is scanned. In this case, someone who scans the RFID tags of a person when she is on one end of a street and scans them again when she is at the other end of the street will see two entirely different sets of pseudonymous identifiers. Thus, the identifiers emitted by the tags will conceal the fact that it is the same tags that are being scanned in the two different places. This helps defeat the problem of physical tracking.

There is a hitch in the pseudonym approach as described, though. What if an attacker harvests *all* of the pseudonyms on a tag by performing repeated, rapid-fire scanning? This would entirely defeat the privacy protection of the pseudonym technique. To forestall this type of attack, an RFID tag can be constructed to delay its rotation through pseudonyms. For example, the tag might transmit a new pseudonym only three minutes after it has been scanned. It is fairly straightforward and inexpensive to build a simple delay circuit into a tag.

In a more complicated version of this scheme, pseudonyms on tags containing rewritable memory may be refreshed by trusted readers. This offers a higher degree of protection.

Pseudonyms need not be an impediment to legitimate use of tag identifiers. The owner of a tag—say a supermarket—can keep a record of the full set of associated pseudonyms in a database or refer to a centralized database service such as the Object Name Service (ONS) proposed by EPCglobal.[13] The identity of a pseudonym-bearing tag will then be transparent.

Corporate Privacy

Consumer privacy has been the focus of much of the media attention on RFID, but it is important to keep in mind that privacy is also an issue for corporate users of RFID. A retail shop, for instance, is vulnerable to inventory scanning by competitors. By monitoring the unique serial numbers of items in stock, someone could learn valuable information about turnover rates. Other valuable information might be similarly gleaned if a rival secretly planted an RFID reader in the warehouse of a competitor. These threats are illustrated in Chapter 18, Would Macy's Scan Gimbels?: Competitive Intelligence and RFID.

The privacy aims of businesses still differ somewhat from those of consumers. In general, businesses will perform RFID reading in physical environments

---

13. EPCglobal, Inc. Object Naming Service (ONS). Brief description available at www.epcglobalus .org/Network/ONS.html.

over which they have a high degree of control, such as warehouses or retail shops. They can attempt to prevent corporate espionage through close monitoring of their premises. As already mentioned, mobile phones may soon come equipped with RFID scanners—and possibly with price-comparison tools for ordinary consumers. Once this happens, it is likely to be nearly impossible to prevent competitors from scanning retail shelves. The pseudonym system could help alleviate the problem somewhat. Other protection measures will no doubt need to evolve to meet the threats posed in retail systems.

Technology and Policy

Some privacy advocates have suggested that consumers should shun technological protections of the kind described in this chapter, such as blocker tags.[14] Their argument is that such privacy-protecting technologies may lull consumers into complacency and permit RFID to flourish—at which point, governments or companies might ban their use. One can similarly argue that people should not hang curtains in their living rooms. Curtains, after all, lead homeowners to an ingrained presumption of visual privacy and could at some point be banned by a government hostile to civil liberties. Simply put, badly conceived laws can undermine even well-crafted technologies and privacy measures. This thinking applies equally well to RFID and ordinary privacy-protecting tools and measures. Well-conceived laws, by contrast, can help reinforce the benefits of privacy-protecting tools.

Certainly, without the support of good policies, technological measures for protecting privacy can be subject to neglect and misuse. It is vital that technology and policy work in concert. Legislation, on the other hand, is a slow process, often at pains to keep pace with rapid technological advance. Legislation is often most potent when it avoids specific technological prescriptions and instead specifies policy aims. Technologies, after all, change faster than laws can.

Conclusions

It is important to keep in mind the real and complex contours of the RFID privacy problem. For instance, certain types of RFID tags are very difficult to read in the vicinity of the human body. Thus, not all tags will require protection all

---

14. American Civil Liberties Union (ACLU) et al. RFID position statement of consumer privacy and civil liberties organizations, November 20, 2003. Referenced 2004 at www.privacyrights .org/ar/RFIDposition.htm.

of the time. In contrast, some varieties, such as RFID tags for implantation in human beings, will require strong and careful protection if they are ever widely deployed.[15]

We have discussed the privacy problem as it applies to the tag-to-reader link in RFID systems. Privacy and security problems exist in many other layers in an RFID system and engender many important questions. How, for instance, can a piece of application software be sure that a particular RFID reader is legitimate and not transmitting false data? How can data transmitted by RFID readers be protected from eavesdropping? Will the massive RFID database maintained by manufacturers and retailers be secure against hacking? These are important questions but generally not peculiar to RFID. Therefore, they may often be addressed through use of standard data security tools. Others, however, are hardware specific. Is it possible to identify and track an RFID tag based on the particular physical characteristics of its signal?

We have focused on only the most basic and inexpensive varieties of RFID tags in our discussion here. While these will undoubtedly be the most prevalent, a spectrum of RFID devices with differing capabilities is emerging. More expensive RFID tags can perform cryptographic operations, enabling different privacy-enhancing techniques from those described here.[16]

RFID is just one breed of wireless technology. The problems of physical tracking and other forms of privacy invasion will apply to nearly all new wireless technologies. GPS receivers are becoming standard features on mobile phones, for instance. Once location-based services proliferate, many people will disclose their location on a more or less continuous basis. Such disclosure will be made voluntarily to a single, carefully regulated entity, a service provider. Moreover, mobile phones are increasingly capable of performing computationally intensive operations—even public-key cryptography—and can implement selective disclosure policies. The problem of location privacy for mobile phones is therefore different from the RFID privacy problem. It is not distinct, however. Once mobile phones come equipped with RFID readers, and as the capabilities and uses of other wireless technologies overlap in new and unpredictable ways, it will be even more important to view wireless privacy protection comprehensively, not just in terms of individual technologies like RFID.

---

15. VeriChip Corp. Corporate Web site at www.4verichip.com.
16. Juels, A. Minimalist Cryptography for Low-Cost RFID Tags. In Blundo, C., ed. *Security in Communication Networks* (SCN '04). 2004. To appear. Weis, S.A., Sarma, S., Rivest, R., and Engels, D. Security and Privacy Aspects of Low-Cost Radio Frequency Identification Systems. In *First International Conference on Security in Pervasive Computing*. 2003.

Chapter 22

RANDOMIZATION: ANOTHER APPROACH TO ROBUST RFID SECURITY

Michael R. Arneson[1]
William Bandy[2]

Introduction

Robust RFID security must both protect business against fraud and shield consumers from privacy intrusions. The keys to robust RFID security are simplicity and a fundamentally secure foundation. However, the evolution of RFID product today is moving away from both and is inviting opportunities for fraud and privacy intrusion. This chapter looks at these vulnerabilities and recommends an alternative approach to achieving robust RFID security.

A foundation of the current evolution of RFID product, driven by user demand and culminating in the EPC Global Generation 2 standard, is using a read/write memory on the RFID tag chip to write an EPC ID number that contains manufacturing and product information, as well as a unique ID number, so that items may be uniquely identified.

The Problems in RFID Security

One of the major problems with storing manufacturing, product, and item information in an RFID tag is that anyone with a reader or reader-like device

---

1. Michael R. Arneson is a founder of Matrics.
2. William Bandy is a founder of Matrics.

would be able to determine specific product information. And people intent on illicitly gaining this information wouldn't limit themselves to just off-the-shelf reader technology that implements only FCC-regulated power levels. They would be able to boost the power and use extremely sensitive receivers to read passive RFID tags from hundreds of feet away, if not more. This capability also has disturbing consequences for consumer privacy because tagged items can be tracked from distances greater than currently imagined possible.

Another problem with using read/write memory on RFID tags is that the information stored on the tags can be surreptitiously altered, again at long distances with illicit high-power readers. In the evolution of the Gen 2 standard, such concerns are being addressed with security mechanisms aimed at preventing unauthorized tag "killings" and memory modification, but the mechanisms rely on the assumption that the signal backscattered by the tag is too small to be eavesdropped on. Without this underlying assumption, there is no security against such attacks.

To achieve security for sensitive tag functions, such as writing to memory, killing, and sending passwords, the tag sends a random 16-bit number to the reader, which the reader uses to encode data sent to the tag. The tag then uses the same 16-bit number to decode the data. Such a scheme works, provided the data link from the tag to the reader is secure. However, if a highly sensitive receiver can be employed to pick up the weak backscattered signal from the tags at distances greater than currently assumed, this security is compromised. Such an illicit reader would be able to pick up the 16-bit random number from the tag used by the reader to encode the data and use it to decode the data to determine what data is being sent to the tag. Such receiver technology is expensive and cumbersome but would not be a barrier to focused criminal activity.

Gen 2 provides for the security feature of locking memory, requiring a password to unlock it. This approach prevents unauthorized writing of memory, which is particularly useful when tagged goods are in transit. However, the use of such passwords requires a database management system that links specific passwords to specific tags, and that is cumbersome to administer. Also, since the password is sent by the reader to the tag in the same manner as secure data, the password can be retrieved by an eavesdropper, compromising it.

Finally, the Gen 2 standard will be public knowledge and product will be widely available to anyone for an illicit purpose, such as in the black market. The act of reverse-engineering both readers and tags would be technically feasible with today's advances in technology, even within the confines of small company and university laboratories. Laboratories all over the world will be quickly at work reverse-engineering both tags and readers to devise various attacks and ways to defeat the Gen 2 security features. This level of exposure will invite the kinds of creative attacks seen today with virus, worm, and Trojan horse attacks of Microsoft operating systems. The result is that Gen 2 tags will be vulnerable to a wide range and variety of security attacks and misuse. This vulnerability also closes some approaches to address consumer privacy concerns.

Some of the consumer privacy concerns are being addressed by the Gen 2 "kill" command, which renders the tag inoperable at the point of sale (POS). However, as pointed out elsewhere in this book, there is an interest in being able to "unkill" the tag for item returns and other uses. One simple approach is to have the RFID tags removably attached to items so that instead of killing the tag, a clerk simply removes it at the POS and hands to the customer, who can retain it for item returns. However, removably attaching a Gen 2 tag to items invites fraudulent exploitation. Since the tag is readily obtainable and programmable, a Gen 2 removably attached tag can be detached anywhere along the supply chain, including the store, and a another tag put in its place, which carries, for example, a lower price for the item or a different item identifier. Tags could also be attached to counterfeit goods and introduced undetected into the supply chain as legitimate product. Tags that could not be purchased for such illicit use could easily be counterfeited.

Conclusions

What is the solution to this problem of security with RFID? The most fundamentally secure solution is simply to store a random number in a read-only memory as the tag ID. A 112-bit random number can provide more than 10^{33} different numbers, more than enough to ensure uniqueness of the tag ID. Product information would be associated with its tag ID through a local database under control of the specific business entity selling or otherwise disposing of that product. Today's advances in real-time database management provide systems that are fast enough to handle even the largest of a store's requirements, like those of Wal-Mart.

Why is this more secure? First, people with illicit reader devices would not be able to obtain any useful information from a tag population. All they will see is a string of random numbers. Without access to a specific secure, encrypted database, they could not recover any product information.

Also, since the memory is a write-once read-only—such as accomplished at the time of manufacture by laser cutting, linking, or fusing, for example—it cannot be rewritten to, eliminating that line of security attacks and compromises.

Next, even though the read-only tags would be readily available for illicit use or for reverse-engineering and counterfeiting, nothing useful could be gained. A read-only tag could not be illicitly placed on any product item, legitimate or counterfeit, outside the item supply chain and then introduced into the supply chain because the random number will not be in the database. Therefore, when it is read, the database will flag an error. The only way to introduce counterfeit items into a legitimate supply chain would be to attach counterfeit tags that replicate numbers from tags already in the supply chain. However, when inter-rogated, the database would note the replicated numbers and flag the event as a suspicious activity.

This simple approach reduces vulnerability of the security threats discussed above. First, it dramatically reduces attack exposure or the threat. The only way to compromise a secure system is to compromise the specific secure local data-base that associates tag IDs with product description. Database security can be locally controlled, whereas Gen 2 tags themselves are vulnerable to the uncon-trolled and unbounded problems of a worldwide attack. And with security reli-ant not on layers of complexity but rather on a simple underlying concept, there is nothing for the user to implement to achieve the security and therefore nothing that can be done for the sake of convenience, as with Gen 2 tags.

But what about the kill function, which is essential to address some the privacy concerns? Since the memory is read only, the tags cannot be written to or erased to kill them. The kill function must be achieved through the database, where at the point of sale, the unique tag ID is removed from the active data-base and put into another database for "inactivated" tags. The reason the tag ID is moved into another database instead of just being erased from the active data base is so that items can be returned by a customer.

Therefore, a killed tag would still be readable, responding with its ID, but there would be no way to associate that ID with product information. The tag will basically be ignored. Once the items are purchased and the tags are killed by having their IDs removed from the active database, the customer can con-tinue to browse in the store carrying or wearing those items. The tags will not be noted as those belonging to the active database, and no product information can be obtained. But if the customer returns an item to the store where it was purchased, the tag ID would be retrieved from the secure "inactivated" data-base and moved to the active database for appropriate disposal of that item. A customer could walk into the store with an item to return, but until the tag on the item is specifically unkilled at the return desk, it would not be recognized by the store's active product database.

But most important, read-only random number ID tags will enable item tags to be removably attached to the items they are identified with without the security threat of having legitimate tags exchanged with other tags anywhere in the supply chain, as discussed above. Therefore, if the customer desires, the store can both kill the tag by removing its ID from the active database and physically remove it from the item, handing it to the customer for disposal or retention for item return. This is a fundamentally enabling feature of the read-only random-number ID tag, and it not only provides supply chain security but also addresses the basic privacy concerns of the consumer.

Such a product is available today with EPCglobal Class 0 as well as from a subset of EPCglobal Gen 2. The read/write memory can be replaced by a program-once memory (such as with laser cutting) so that the tag is thereafter read only and not modifiable. The memory would be programmed with a random number, and the Gen 2 ID data structure would be associated with that random number in the secure database.

Chapter 23

KILLING, RECODING, AND BEYOND

David Molnar[1]
Ross Stapleton-Gray[2]
David Wagner[3]

Introduction

"**D**ead men tell no tales," and dead tags don't talk. This is the logic behind RFID tag "killing," a proposal for enhancing consumer privacy that has received wide attention. In tag killing, RFID tags are rendered permanently inoperative by use of a special command. Killing is envisioned as an answer to privacy concerns over "item-level tagging" in the retail setting, in which each item is provided with a unique RFID tag. The logic behind tag killing is simple: if the RFID is destroyed at the point of sale, the item can no longer be tracked via RFID after it has passed to the consumer. At first glance, RFID tag killing appears to be an inexpensive way to address privacy concerns with RFID deployment. Unfortunately, there is more to tag killing than meets the eye.

Tag killing has received so much attention because it has become clear that privacy in item-level tagging will be a hot-button issue in consumer acceptance of RFID. Privacy issues in item-level tagging include the possibility of tracking individuals by a unique tag or a collection of tags.

Today, one of the most influential bodies in supply chain and retail RFID is EPC-global, Inc., a joint venture of the Uniform Code Council and EAN International,

---

1. David Molnar is a graduate student in computer science at the University of California at Berkeley studying cryptography, privacy, and computer security.
2. Ross Stapleton-Gray, Ph.D., is president of Stapleton-Gray & Associates, Inc., an information technology and policy consultancy in Albany, CA.
3. David Wagner is an assistant professor in the computer science department at the University of California at Berkeley with extensive experience in computer security and cryptography.

two primary bodies that administer current commercial bar codes. Supported by Wal-Mart, among others, EPCglobal publishes specifications for RFID tags and defines mechanisms for use of RFID data. Tag killing has been enshrined by EPCglobal in its specifications for RFID tags, all of which support a password-protected kill command.

Unfortunately, there are several issues with kill commands. First, killing tags prevents all post-point-of-sale uses for RFID tag information. These uses are expected to become more important as the use of RFID tags on retail items spreads.

Second, RFIDs used for rental and borrowing, such as in libraries, should not be killed because the RFID must be used when borrowers return the item. This is particularly problematic because these applications pose some of the clearest privacy risks. Video rental records and library patron records are protected by both state and federal law. If it is possible to scan people with an RFID reader and determine what videos or books they are reading, the spirit of these laws can be completely circumvented.

To address these issues, we suggest "recoding" as an additional tool for RFID privacy. In recoding, a tag is overwritten with a new ID number when it changes hands. Without knowledge of the map from the old ID number to the new ID, it is impossible to link sightings of the item from before and after recoding. Recoding may occur at point of sale or within the supply chain when an item passes from one organization to another. For example, a retailer might recode RFID tags on items received from a distributor so that other parties cannot determine how many items were bought of each type; these new RFID tag IDs might also point to a private database of the retailer.

We can use recoding as a tool to build RFID "infomediaries." An infomediary is a trusted third party that mediates requests for information about an RFID tag; for example, the infomediary might allow only requests that match a specified privacy policy. The use of an infomediary makes possible post-point-of-sale RFID applications while lessening privacy concerns.

In addition, rental stores and libraries can act as their own infomediaries and control access to information about their items. Recoding can also be used to remove information from an RFID tag that is not needed for post-point-of-sale applications.

Both killing and recoding raise infrastructure issues that need to be solved before they can become viable privacy protections. In particular, only authorized parties, such as a retailer, should be able to kill or recode tags. How is this restriction enforced? We discuss the "kill passwords" and write passwords in current-generation RFID tags and ways to distribute these passwords to authorized retailers.

In addition, killing and recoding both require an RFID reader, but readers are not currently widespread in retail settings. More important, some retailers will see less benefit from installing RFID readers than will manufacturers or distributors. Therefore, we expect RFID readers to be much less widespread in retail stores, which is a problem because readers are needed at the point of sale to perform killing or recoding. We discuss several approaches to this problem, such as legislating that every retailer install an appropriate RFID reader for killing or recoding tags.

In the end, while both are important tools, neither killing nor recoding is the final answer in RFID privacy. We close by identifying privacy issues not addressed by either killing or recoding and motivate the need to go beyond these two mechanisms.

RFID Recoding and Infomediaries

The post-sale applications prevented by RFID tag killing justify considering other options such as recoding. In this section, we also show how recoding RFID tags can work with the RFID processing framework proposed by EPC-global to create "infomediaries."

Applications Prevented by Killing

Killing RFID tags at point of sale prevents several beneficial applications in the short, medium, and long terms. In the short term, RFID tag killing prevents tags from being used to manage returns and recalls. Many stores would find it easier to manage returns of items by keeping a database of tag IDs from items sold. When an item is presented for a return, the store might find it useful to scan the item and compare the tag's information with what's in the database. Tags could also facilitate product recalls. While these applications could be enabled by optical bar code scanning, it is believed that RFID technology will reduce the overhead needed to gather this data and check items against the database.

Unfortunately, these schemes for product return and recalls are incompatible with killing of RFID tags. We note, however, that many of these applications do not require RFID tags but only unique identifiers for each item. If it were possible to print bar code labels containing EPC codes, which are unique to each item instance, those labels could be used for recall and return.

One of the short- to medium-term applications enabled by RFID item tagging, and not possible with optical bar code scanning, is automatic sorting of items for recycling. Different materials require different recycling processes. Currently, items placed for recycling must be sorted by hand or semiautomatically, which greatly increases the cost of recycling and limits its use. If the composition of an item is encoded onto its RFID tag, the vision is that sorting can be made fully automatic[4]. This vision is possible only if tags remain unkilled at point of sale.

In the longer term, item-level RFID tagging may enable a wide range of applications after the sale. Nokia recently released a kit that allows certain cell phone models to read RFID tags; combined with item-level tagging, this could provide a way for people to scan an item and be automatically directed to further information about that item. Washing machines equipped with RFID readers could read RFID tags on clothes containing wash instructions. Refrigerators could detect spoiled food and warn their owners. An article by Roy Want describes some of these applications.[5] At Microsoft Research, the Advanced User Resource Annotation (AURA) project led by Marc Smith is exploring the space of possible applications enabled by end-user scanning of tags.[6]

Some of these applications are more speculative than others. The privacy risks, however, are not at all speculative. We suggest a principle for evaluating RFID architectures: *We should not allow speculation about the potential applications of tomorrow to justify definite degradations of privacy today.* Put another way, it is better to design architectures that "fail private." We also note that some applications may not need the full information about an item; for example, recycling applications need only the composition of the item, not its specific serial number. Recoding offers one way to limit the amount of information available from an item's RFID tag to only the minimum needed.

Recoding and Electronic Product Codes

Electronic Product Codes (EPCs), like Universal Product Codes (UPCs) before them, are fundamentally two-part codes. The first part of the code is a unique identifier of a manufacturer. This unique identifier is assigned by EPC-global, which is the entity responsible for maintaining the EPC namespace. The second part of the code is an identifier for a product, assigned by the manufacturer. A key innovation of the EPC is that the second part of the code also includes a unique identifier for each instance of each product. Figure 23.1 shows the format of an EPC.

---

4. Saar, S. "RFID System Implementations for Environmental Applications." Online at www.princeton.edu/~vmthomas/recyclebox.html.
5. Want, R. "RFID: A Key to Automating Everything." *Scientific American*, January 2004.
6. Smith, M., Davenport, D., and Howard, H. "AURA: A mobile platform for object and location annotation." *Ubicomp.* 2003.

Manufacturer ID	Item Type ID	Serial Number
Assigned by EPCglobal	Assigned by Manufacturer	

Figure 23.1   The format of an Electronic Product Code (EPC).

Each field of an EPC, however, provides information that might be used to compromise privacy. The first field is the manufacturer's unique ID or, in EPCglobal parlance, the "EPC Manager Number." Knowing this field alone provides only a coarse-grained knowledge (e.g., "This is an item manufactured by Tom's of Maine"). Knowing both the first and second fields gives the manufacturer plus the product identifier, which is enough to determine a specific type of item ("12 oz. can of Coke Classic"). Knowing those two fields plus the unique serial number would allow for tracking over time.

It is important to understand that EPCs will complement and expand on existing product codes such as UPCs currently used in product bar coding; item-level EPCs will in all likelihood be based on previously assigned UPCs. There are numerous commercial sources of information mapping UPCs to product names and other information. Google even offers a free, if crude, equivalent. Product codes—both the EPC and its non-RFID-oriented predecessors—are supposed to be readily used as indices to product information, with little regard for privacy interests.

One could imagine several recoding schemes intended to frustrate or confuse such mappings. For example, one could zero out the unique serial number on an EPC, which reduces the EPC to little more than a UPC: If the tag is read, one will know the manufacturer and the product but cannot make any meaningful inferences that would rely on tracking a specific instantiation of that product.

The recoding scheme with the greatest potential for privacy protection is one in which all the fields are remapped: The original manufacturer ID is changed to that of an entity that administers recoding services, and this administrator then assigns a unique serial number to be contained in the other fields. The administrator retains an association of the new EPC and the original so that knowing the former, one could retrieve the latter, if permitted. We call such an administrator an "infomediary."

An infomediary has an ability to apply access controls and govern who can know what about whom. For example, a consumer might have an item recoded at point of sale with an EPC that lists the infomediary as the "manufacturer ID," together with a serial number assigned by the infomediary. Now, if someone reads the tag and wishes to know what the item is, that person must ask the infomediary. The infomediary, in turn, consults the consumer's privacy policy before responding to the request. For example, the infomediary may allow requests for information on clothing RFID tags from the consumer's washing machine but deny requests from unknown RFID readers.

In rental or borrowing applications, the rental store or library could act as its own infomediary. Before item checkout, the RFID tag contains an EPC that identifies the item. At item checkout, the RFID tag is recoded with a new random identifier and the store as the "Manufacturer ID." Then, when the item is read, any third-party RFID reader must query the store to learn anything useful. Readers belonging to the store, such as those used for item check-in, can be permitted to access the store database. Requests from third-party readers can be denied.

An infomediary could be implemented within the context of the EPC Object Name Service (ONS) proposed by EPCglobal. The ONS offers a service that maps EPC manufacturer IDs to URLs; these URLs in turn lead to Web sites set up by the manufacturer that provide more information about the item given its type ID and unique serial number. The ONS is being built by VeriSign, Inc., a company that has experience running a Certificate Authority for Web public-key infrastructure and managing the Domain Name Service. Once the ONS is built, an infomediary could be implemented simply by registering its specific manufacturer ID with the ONS and creating a Web site to store privacy policies and handle the resulting traffic. Therefore, EPC privacy infomediaries appear feasible in the near term, as long as RFID tags support recoding.

Infrastructure Issues

Protecting the Kill Switch

In architectures that use killing, some mechanism must be used to prevent unauthorized killing of RFID tags. Current EPCglobal specifications state that a password will be used. In Class 1 915MHz tags, this password is 8 bits, while in Class 0 13.56MHz and 915MHz tags, the password is 24 bits. A tag will not honor a kill command without the proper password, and passwords are unique to each tag.[7]

This raises the question of how passwords are provisioned to legitimate RFID equipment at point of sale. Without the passwords, tags cannot be easily killed,

---

7. EPCglobal, Inc. Version 1.0 EPC Tag Specifications. Available online at www.epcglobalinc .org/standards_technology/specifications.html.

so we lose the privacy benefits of tag killing. On the other hand, if passwords are easy to guess or poorly protected, adversaries might abuse the kill feature and kill tags before point of sale.

Perhaps the most straightforward answer is to have a central database mapping RFID tag IDs to kill passwords, perhaps maintained by the RFID tag manufacturer. Unfortunately, this database becomes a single point of failure: If it is ever compromised by an adversary, all tags in the database become vulnerable to malicious killing.

As a simple alternative, we propose "two-part" RFID tags. The first part of the RFID tag reveals the kill command for the entire tag to any reader but can itself be deactivated without a password. When a manufacturer takes delivery of tagged items, it reads the first part to obtain the tag kill command, places that into its own private database, and then deactivates the first part. Later, when the manufacturer passes items to a distributor or when a distributor passes items to a retailer, it also passes a database mapping RFID tag IDs to kill passwords; these databases can be managed by bilateral agreements.

Recoding, Rewritable Tags, and Vandalism

Recoding requires rewritable tags, but the ability to rewrite a tag must be protected. Otherwise, RFID tag "vandalism" becomes possible—a vandal can change the data on an RFID tag to make an item appear to be something it is not or simply erase the tag entirely. Vandalism might be performed to deny service to legitimate users, or there might be some financial motive involved.

Although RFID tag vandalism has not yet been reported, we suspect it is only a matter of time. Environments such as libraries already suffer attacks from fairly sophisticated vandals. With respect to financial motives, scams have already appeared that switch optical bar code labels. For example, Home Depot suffered nearly half a million dollars in losses from a group of thieves that created bar code labels for low-cost items, pasted them on top of high-cost items' labels, bought the items at a discount, and then returned the items for the full price. In the RFID setting, we could expect to see a quick "cloning" of other items found in the same store, in which a thief would read a code off a cheap (but similar) product, and then overwrite the tag of a more expensive product.

Many of today's RFID tags employ a "write then lock" architecture, in which the tag data can be written an unlimited number of times and then irrevocably "locked." After locking, the data on the tag cannot be modified or erased. Unfortunately, this irrevocable lock does not work for recoding because the data on the RFID tag must be modified. Instead, some kind of write password will need to be employed; the password can then be provisioned as we have described for kill passwords.

The "Subthreshold" Retailer

Killing or recoding a tag requires both an RFID reader and the infrastructure to provision it with the appropriate passwords as we have discussed. Both readers and infrastructure cost money. Even though we have discussed ways of avoiding a centralized password repository, creating this infrastructure is still a significant investment.

Not all retail outlets may make the investment necessary to enable killing at point of sale, an observation made independently by Sandy Hughes (see Chapter 27, P&G: RFID and Privacy in the Supply Chain). We call a retail outlet that is unable or unwilling to provide RFID tag killing a "subthreshold" retailer. For example, a small family-owned convenience store may decide that an RFID reader is too expensive for the in-store benefit it provides.

The problem with subthreshold retailers is that they allow for RFID tags to "leak" into the post-sale environment. Because tags are applied at manufacture time, subthreshold retailers may take delivery of items with live RFID tags. Neither the subthreshold retailer nor the ordinary customer is capable of even detecting the presence of tags, let alone of killing them. As a result, items may be sold to a customer with live RFID tags, even if the recommended best practice is that all tags must be killed at point of sale.

Who Pays?

The case of the subthreshold retailer illustrates a problem with both RFID tag killing and recoding infrastructure: Who will pay? A large part of the cost falls on the end retailer, but the retailer has the least incentive to deploy RFID equipment. Consumers are unlikely to have their own RFID readers in the foreseeable future, so it is likely that many goods will be sold without an RFID reader present. Therefore, it becomes difficult to depend on killing or recoding RFID tags at point of sale as a privacy mechanism.

One way to address this problem would be to legislate that all retailers must possess appropriate RFID equipment to perform killing or recoding. One advantage of this approach is that auditing compliance is fairly straightforward. A single visit to a store suffices to check whether the infrastructure is in place. In addition, once a store has bought the necessary equipment, it can be continually used for tag killing or recoding. While some pieces of legislation concerning RFID are under consideration in several states, including California and Utah, we are not aware of any that explicitly treats the issue of readers in the retail setting. Unfortunately, such legislation is likely to be politically problematic, and the cost of such infrastructure would almost certainly be passed directly to consumers.

Another approach to RFID tag killing would be to shift the site of killing to the distributor. Before delivering items to a retailer without the means to kill tags, the distributor could simply kill the RFID tags en masse. This could be required by legislation or codified as part of industry best practices. Again, this can be audited for compliance fairly easily; anyone with an RFID reader could check for the presence of unkilled tags.

As a final alternative for tag killing, we could ask for tags that can be physically destroyed by consumers. Peter de Jager notes that physical destruction has the major advantage that anyone can be convinced that the tag is really destroyed (see Chapter 30, Experimenting on Humans Using Alien Technology). With approaches that require the use of RFID readers to kill or recode tags, it is difficult for most people to verify that the tag is in the correct state—for example, that the tag is "all dead" as opposed to "mostly dead" and possibly able to be awakened later.

Conclusions

There are several take-home points from our analysis. First, killing alone is not enough, and new mechanisms are needed for building privacy-preserving RFID architectures. Killing is not sufficient for applications that involve borrowing or for post-sale applications such as recycling.

Second, recoding is a useful tool for building privacy-protecting RFID architectures. Recoding allows "excess" information to be removed from a tag at point of sale and for the construction of EPC infomediaries. Recoding and infomediaries can produce privacy-friendly architectures for applications that are not well served by tag killing.

Finally, both killing and recoding raise infrastructure issues. While the solutions to these issues may be simple, these issues must still be resolved before these mechanisms can become effective. Finding a satisfactory solution will require both policy tools, such as legislation, and good technical design.

Even after the infrastructure issues have been solved, however, there are still privacy issues that will not be addressed by killing or recoding. Live RFID tags of today's generation have static identifiers between recodings. Therefore, it is possible to track individuals by linking different sightings of the same RFID tag identifier. Until the RFID tag is recoded, the movements of the tag can be registered and correlated by different readers.

Even if individual tags change their identifiers, an individual may carry multiple RFID tags. This "constellation" of RFID tags can uniquely identify an individual. Unless many of the tags change their identifiers at the same time, recording readings of constellations that share many tags may give enough information to track an individual.

In general, static identifiers on RFID tags, combined with no access control (such as a read password) for tags, enable tracking invasions of privacy. In addition, once sightings of these identifiers have been placed in a database, controlling the inferences that may be drawn from that database raises a set of database privacy issues by itself.

Dealing with these privacy issues will require measures that go beyond killing and recoding. Ari Juels outlines current and future technical solutions for preventing tracking attacks (see Chapter 21, Technological Approaches to the RFID Privacy Problem). There is a rich literature on database privacy issues, and these issues are notoriously difficult to deal with. Killing and recoding are just the first steps.

Part V
STAKEHOLDER PERSPECTIVES

Chapter 24

TEXAS INSTRUMENTS: LESSONS FROM SUCCESSFUL RFID APPLICATIONS

Bill Allen[1]

Introduction

There's a lot of uncertainty, concern, and speculation about how new RFID initiatives may affect our lives as well as how the ability to identify and track the assets and products we use every day may affect privacy and personal safeguards.

The questions are certainly valid. Some of the speculation may not be. Assumptions about what this technology can and can't do are often false or just misunderstood. But it's clear that, as with the introduction of any new technology, RFID manufacturers and developers and the companies that deploy these powerful tools have an obligation to understand, explain, and respond to concerns about the path on which RFID technology may lead us.

While RFID has more than a decade-long history of consumer acceptance from highway toll tags, anti-theft devices for automobiles, and wireless payments, it's still viewed as a new technology by many people. As with any new information technology, the success or failure of RFID depends on how well consumers understand not just how the technology works but also the implications and benefits of how their data is being used. Most important, success depends on how well consumers are empowered to control, authorize, and protect that information.

---

1. Bill Allen is an employee of Texas Instruments Incorporated.

Experience with the Internet and the emergence of e-retailing offers a parallel example of this important principle of consumer acceptance. Ten years ago, the technology to conduct Web searches and to make online purchases was readily available. Yet it took the Internet community several more years to understand and respond to consumer concerns about privacy and financial safeguards before e-retailing became mainstream. Certainly, early adopters were buzzing around the "Net" buying and selling with abandon. But until the industry developed strong and secure protections, built financial and transactions safeguards like PayPal, and shifted from an opt-in versus opt-out mentality, consumers did not trust and embrace the Internet as an alternative retail channel. The lesson learned was that retailers won't embrace a new technology until they're confident they have earned their customers' trust.

The same is true with RFID. The industry is at a juncture where market leaders like Wal-Mart and Target want to reshape the retail experience through RFID. Contactless payments will be more and more common. RFID will create new and as yet unimagined value for retailers and consumers alike. But a successful deployment depends on helping consumers understand this technology, assuring them that data and transactions are safe and secure, and showing them that they can control how and where the information collected by RFID tools can be used.

The good news is that this is not new ground for the RFID industry. Over the past decade, Texas Instruments had seen a number of important, mainstream adoptions of RFID that teach us a lot about building trust, educating the public, creating privacy and security safeguards, and empowering consumers.

Toll Tracking: Who Knows Where You Are Going?

One of the early wide-scale adoptions of RFID began more than ten years ago with the introduction of now-common RFID toll-tag highway payment systems. California and New York led this trend in the early 1990s, and state transportation authorities across the country now deploy active (battery-powered) toll tags to help drivers cut their commuting time, reduce highway congestion and pollution, reduce fraud, and create new efficiencies for our existing highway infrastructure.

Yet when these Intelligent Highway Vehicle Systems (IHVS) technologies were first deployed, it was not without some concern over how this transaction information might be used. Might law enforcement officers, tracking the time a car took between tolls be able to calculate a vehicle's speed and issue automatic speeding tickets? Would the advanced sensors and digital cameras that tracked cars and digitally photographed the license plates of "toll-jumpers" provide personal information that could be misused?

These were good questions, and wisely, the designers of early systems and the regulators charged with overseeing the projects anticipated these concerns and addressed them through a series of existing and new consumer privacy protections. For example, California already had a law in place that stated only a car's license plate, not its occupants could be photographed. Even before many of these systems went live, state Department of Transportation offices put in place strong and explicit protections on the use of this data, shielding its use by law enforcement, except under the guidelines of a court subpoena. The result of this forethought and the established regulatory safeguards was the quick and now wide-scale adoption and acceptance of this toll-tag technology by consumers across the country.

The lesson? Anticipate and respond to potential privacy concerns with a combination of technology and regulatory responses that provide assurance and safeguards for consumers. Build privacy protection into the front end of the project, not as an afterthought.

Contactless Payment: Are Safeguards Already in Place?

Perhaps nothing raises more privacy red flags than people's concern about third-party access to their purchase and buying history. There is the debate over who owns your financial records as well as the delicate balance between personal privacy and the enhanced services and benefits that RFID payment and loyalty systems offer.

RFID-based contactless payment systems are widely used today to buy everything from gasoline and convenience store items to fast food and movie rentals. Banks and other financial services companies are moving toward offering RFID contactless credit cards.

In the mid-1990s, Mobil Oil, now ExxonMobil, pioneered the first large-scale use of RFID for its Speedpass payment system. The company recognized early on the value that speed and convenience offered its customers and used an RFID key fob and vehicle transponder to deploy one of the largest RFID applications.

Consumers had a number of questions about RFID, such as, "Can my credit card number be 'captured' by someone with an RFID reader?" and "How do I make sure I'm not paying for someone else's gasoline?" The company wisely addressed these and other questions early in the deployment of the technology.

ExxonMobil's response to consumer questions demonstrates the importance of early education about the use of new technology and offers insight into gaining consumer acceptance and ensuring the protection of financial information. In promotional and enrollment materials and on its Web site, the company anticipated and answered these concerns by explaining that there is never a credit card number on the tag, only an ID number, and that the number couldn't be read except by the pump. They noted an RFID card or key fob is safer than a credit card because there's no number or personal identification printed anywhere on the RFID device.

In addition, what consumers don't see inside the RFID payment tag is the advanced technology being deployed by financial institutions to ensure the authenticity and security of these payment systems. Far more than just an ID tag linked to a credit card number, today's contactless payment systems involve authentication technologies that offer a sophisticated "challenge and response" to ensure the proper RFID tag is linked to the consumer's account. All of this is virtually invisible to the consumer, yet it provides a higher level of security protection than those that have been employed for years in high-value financial transactions and transfers.

ExxonMobil also assured customers that many of the consumer privacy and financial safeguards that have been in place for years for credit cards also apply to RFID. Consumers have limited liability for purchases and can report lost or stolen RFID tags just as they do credit cards. A number of international and U.S. consumer protection laws, such as the European Data Protection Act of 1998, the Federal Code of Fair Information Practices, and the recent Gramm-Leach-Bliley Financial Modernization Act, already provide consumer information and financial liability protections. These regulations restrict the use of consumer data, and the Federal Trade Commission (FTC) is empowered to enforce compliance. In fact, charges have been brought by the FTC against companies that do no comply, and these companies have been substantially fined.

In short, while contactless payment may be a relatively new RFID application, many of the consumer protections and technology safeguards born from years of experience in the credit card industry were already in place. As the market learned about these protections and better understood the technology, the program expanded dramatically to the point today where more than 8 million consumers now rely on Speedpass to make purchases.

As of this writing, virtually every major credit card company is piloting RFID contactless payment solutions based on the ISO/IEC 14443 standard. The ISO/IEC 14443 standard provides increased security and a faster rate of data exchange, as required for financial transactions. Transaction information is stored securely on the radio frequency (RF) chip and securely transmitted over the contactless interface. The security on the chip features National Institute of Standards and Technology (NIST) approved cryptographic algorithms, including Triple DES and SHA-1, developed by the National Security Agency (NSA), guaranteeing a level of financial protection for RFID that consumers expect from their financial services companies.

So while the industry needs to be vigilant about potential issues and abuses and must urge regulatory protection against new threats, a number of laws and processes already in place give us both guidance and assurance that consumer protections exist and are effective.

RFID and Automotive Anti-Theft: Staying Ahead of the Security Curve

Perhaps the widest application of RFID is the least known to consumers. Yet millions of people have saved hundreds of millions of dollars with RFID through the anti-theft devices in their cars and trucks. Today, the majority of vehicles around the world are protected with an RFID-based anti-theft system. A small transponder embedded in the head of the key communicates with a reader near the ignition switch. If the proper code is not read, the car will simply not start.

What is not so simple is the technology that goes into these widely deployed systems. RFID manufacturers have continued to build in the latest security and protection. Although there is no report of any tag being replicated over the years, advances in RFID anti-theft systems now include a rolling encryption algorithm that changes a car's challenge-response code each time the key is used. If a tag was stolen and its ID read and replicated—assuming anyone has the technology to do this—by the time the "new" key ID could be deployed, the ID number would not longer be valid. It is a testament to the security of RFID that there are no reports of any RFID anti-theft system being thwarted.

It is often a challenge to explain the nuances and complexity of the many security technologies built into RFID that can ultimately allay the privacy and security concerns of consumers. But it's an absolute imperative that RFID suppliers address if they want to win the confidence of the public. If consumers are worried about RFID privacy and protection, they can take comfort that many of these issues have been addressed and solved before. RFID has a great history of innovation, and manufacturers are continually looking at advances that stay ahead of any potential threat.

With concerns that RFID tags may be covertly read by retailers or people looking to invade another's privacy, the fact is the RFID tag that millions of people already carry in their pocket every day has yet to be "cracked" or its ID information "intercepted." Yet the industry is responding to these concerns by limiting the functionality of new RFID tags, especially at the item level. The new EPCglobal Inc. Generation 2 UHF standard allows for a 32-bit password function that can be used to disable the tag at the point of purchase should the customer choose that option. That means there are more than 4 billion password options, which makes it difficult to crack and kill the tags without the tag owner's permission. It's a great example of how a consumer concern is being addressed by manufacturers through a technology solution.

So, as the market moves toward wide-scale adoption of RFID for everything from retail logistics and anti-counterfeiting to contactless payment, suppliers, system integrators, application developers, and companies deploying RFID must turn toward their customers to listen to their questions and concerns. The industry needs to respond with information, safeguards, and empowerment.

How and What We Communicate

There's a deluge of information and misinformation in the market that makes it tough for companies to ensure that their communication is accurate, relevant, and reasonable. It's one thing to present a vision of how this technology can be used, but it's another to espouse long-range hypothetical scenarios that may never exist. Talk of the practicality of the widespread acceptance of implanting chips in people, of orbiting satellites that can read tags from space, and of a world where everything, and perhaps everyone, is connected by RFID creates a sense that this technology may reach into our lives in ways that are understandably inappropriate and intrusive. Consumers will tell the industry where and how to use the technology—not the other way around.

With the depth of meaningful benefits that RFID can offer here and now, more concrete than a blue-sky vision, the industry needs to articulate these benefits more clearly. Reducing counterfeit products, protecting the drug and food supply chain, creating new consumer conveniences, making retailers more responsive to individual needs, or building product history information for warranties and repairs are all benefits that consumers value.

Listen to the Consumer

The industry should listen to and understand what consumers want and need and, even more important, what they don't want. Technology can respond with the right protections and safeguards, and processes can create safe and secure environments for these transactions. All this begins when industry listens to the consumer and puts the consumer front and center in every application.

Protect Data

As we've learned from e-retailing, the industry has to ensure that an RFID-enabled world is secure and that information about transactions and people are kept private. RFID, with its capacity for advanced encryption and control over read ranges, inherently offers superior protections. The market must communicate these values to consumers before they will be ready to embrace this technology.

We've seen in the past that the RFID industry can keep ahead of the security curve with new protections and safeguards from hardware, software, and systems perspectives. As RFID is deployed in more and more applications and data is stored and leveraged in new ways, companies entrusted with consumer information will have to be more and more vigilant about the technologies they use. At the same time, these companies need to create and enforce privacy and security policies that consumers can trust if RFID is to be truly accepted by the market.

Empower the Consumer

When consumers understand a technology and the benefits it brings and they trust the companies providing these new services, the adoption curve is steep. Core to this trust is the empowerment of consumers to control, restrict, access, and change the information that drives these applications.

Just as we've seen with Internet news and promotional information, consumers need control over opting into these programs. Do they, for example, want the RFID tag on their recently purchased product to stay active for the convenience of warranty or return programs, or do they want the tag disabled at the point of purchase? Are consumers told how this information is being used to benefit them? As with their own financial records, do consumers have access to reports, and can they change incorrect information? Is there an active or double opt-in process that lets customers choose if and how purchase information can be shared?

Conclusions

Many of the provisions for RFID security are already in place under existing privacy and financial regulatory protections, but the industry needs to reinforce these controls and ensure that customers have an RFID bill of rights that gives them the assurances they need to trust the technology and the companies behind these programs.

There's a lot of heritage in RFID and other consumer-driven information technologies, such as the Internet, that can guide consumers down this new but sometimes uncertain path. As the technology and innovative applications progress, the market needs to ensure that it stays focused on the most important stakeholder in this equation—the consumer.

The industry, including RFID suppliers, retailers, manufacturers, and others implementing the technology, needs to communicate with consumers about RFID and inform them when it is being used. Consumers need to control how and when the tags are used and must be able to disable or remove them. All of us, as consumers, will reject any technology that we find annoying, difficult to use, or intrusive. Yet, we'll readily adopt technology that adds convenience to our lives. RFID is an enabling technology that will bring new benefits to consumers if industry takes the steps to build a bond of trust and understanding with them.

Chapter 25

GEMPLUS: SMART CARDS AND WIRELESS CARDS

Christophe Mourtel[1]

Introduction

Smart cards have the tremendous advantage, over their magnetic stripe ancestors, of being able to execute cryptographic algorithms locally in their internal circuitry. This means that the user's secrets (be these PIN codes or keys) never have to leave the boundaries of the tamper-resistant silicon chip, thus bringing tremendous security to the overall system in which the cards participate.

Smart cards contain special-purpose microcontrollers with built-in self-programmable memory and tamper-resistant features intended to make the cost of a malevolent attack far greater than the benefits. This chapter is both a survey of the existing components and their applications and a description of some of their possible evolutions.

What Is a Smart Card?

In the time scale of the silicon industry, the idea of inserting a chip into a plastic card is rather old: The first patents are now 20 years old! But practical applications emerged only eight years ago because of limitations in storage and processing capacities of past circuit technology. New silicon geometries and processing refinements lead the industry to new generations of cards and more

---

1. Christophe Mourtel is a hardware security expert in the security technology department at Gemplus, one of the world's smart card leaders.

ambitious applications such as wireless communications (GSM), pay TV, loyalty, and physical access control.

Over the last four years, there has been an increasing demand for smart cards from national administrations and large companies such as telephone service providers, banks, and insurance corporations. More recently, another market opened up with the increasing popularity of home networking and the Internet.

The physical support of a conventional smart card is a plastic rectangle on which can be printed information about the application or the issuer (even advertising) as well as readable information about the card holder (for instance, a validity date or a photograph). See Figure 25.1. This support can also carry a magnetic stripe or a bar code label. An array of eight contacts is located on the micromodule in accordance with the ISO 7816 standard, but only six of these contacts are actually connected to the chip, which is (usually) not visible. The contacts are assigned to *power supplies* (Vcc, Vpp), *ground*, *clock*, *reset*, and a *serial data* communication link (commonly called I/O). Their specification part in the standard is being reconsidered because of requests from various parties (suppression of the two useless contacts, creation of a second I/O port, I2C bridging, etc.).

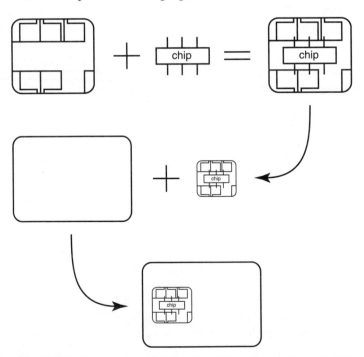

Figure 25.1   Smart Card manufacturing.

For the time being, card CPUs are still 8-bit microcontrollers, and the most common cores are Motorola's 68HC05 and Intel's 80C51, but new 32-bit devices will soon appear. RAM capacities (typically ranging from 76 to 512 bytes) are very limited by the physical constraints of the card. The program executed by the card's microprocessor is written in ROM at the mask-producing stage and cannot be modified in any way. This guarantees that the code is strictly controlled by the manufacturer. For storing user-specific data, individual to each card, the first generation of nonvolatile memories used EPROMs,[2] which required an extra "high" voltage power supply (typically from 15V to 25V). Recent components contain only EEPROM, which requires a single 5V power supply (frequently the same voltage used by the card's microprocessor) and can be written and erased thousands of times. Sometimes, it is possible to import executable programs into the card's EEPROM according to the needs of the card holder. Finally, a communication port (serial via an asynchronous link) is available for exchanging data and controlling information between the card and the external world. A common bit rate is 9600 bits/s, but much faster interfaces are commonly being used (from 19,200 up to 115,200 bits/s) in full accordance with ISO 7816.

EEPROM size is a critical issue in the design of public-key applications, as cryptographic keys must be large in order to be secure. Consequently, smart card programmers frequently adopt typical optimization techniques such as regenerating the public-keys from the secret-keys when needed, regenerating the secret-keys from shorter seeds, avoiding large-key schemes (for instance, Fiat-Shamir), or implementing compression algorithms for redundant data (text, user data, etc.). Some further employ EEPROM garbage collection mechanisms, with several manufacturers having developed real and complete operating systems for this purpose.

The security of smart cards starts with the fact that all of a card's various functions are gathered into a single chip. If this were not done, the external wires linking one chip to another could represent a possible penetration route for unauthorized access (or use) of the card. Complicating this design is the fact that ISO standards specify that the card be able to withstand a specific set of mechanical stresses such as bending and flexing. The size of the chip is consequently limited; many of the constraints on smart card functions—especially their limited memory and cryptographic capabilities—follow from this limitation.

Smart card chips are very reliable; Most manufacturers guarantee the electrical properties of their chips for ten years or more. ISO standards specify how a

---

2. Electrically Programmable Memory (EPROM) and Electrically Erasable Programmable Memory (EEPROM or E²PROM); nonvolatile memory (NVM) means usually provided for data storage.

card must be protected against mechanical, electrical, or chemical aggressions, but for most existing applications, a card is obsolete long before it becomes damaged. For example, the French phone card's failure rate is less than three per 10,000 pieces.

In general, smart cards can help whenever secure portable objects are needed and, in particular, whenever the "external world" needs to work with data without knowing its actual value. The card's tamper-proofness, combined with public-key cryptography (secretless terminals), generally provides adequate solutions to many everyday security problems.

Smart Card Communication and Command Format

Communication with smart cards is ruled by the (previously mentioned) ISO standard 7816/3. Only two protocols are currently defined in this standard (byte-oriented T = 0 and block-oriented T = 1), although up to 14 are available for future expansion. These standards specify the electrical levels, frequency, and details of the protocol used to communicate between the smart card and the "external side"—that is, the rest of the world.

The minimal hardware needed to operate a card consists of:

- A mechanical interface: the *connector*
- An electronic interface: the *coupler*
- A box containing the above two elements: the *smart card reader* (or simply *"reader"*)

The simplest readers are similar to modems and manage only the ISO communication protocol without interacting "intelligently" with the operating system of the card. They are called "transparent readers" and should, at least in theory, operate with any smart card from any vendor that complies with the ISO standard.

The most sophisticated readers can be programmed with parts of the application logic and contain data (for instance, RSA or DSA public keys), files, and programs. They can execute cryptographic functions; completely replace a PC; have keyboards, PIN pads, or displays; and generally use a specific programming language. They do not support all types of smart cards, even if the cards comply with the ISO standard, because these sophisticated readers often use particular commands that are unique to given card designs.

To operate a card, the reader needs to implement the following four functions:

- Power the card on and off
- Reset the card
- Read data from the card (*get commands*)
- Write data to the card (*put commands*)

Get and put commands contain a header (actually a function code consisting of 5 bytes designated by CLA, INS, P1, P2, and LEN) according to which the card processes the incoming data. An acknowledge byte and a couple of status bytes (SW1 and SW2) are sent during (and after) the execution of each command.

Card Life Cycle

Although the card life cycle and manufacturing are described in many different sources, we particularly recommend Fuchsberger, et al.'s excellent overview.[3]

Smart card manufacturing starts with the design of the card operating system and the application software, following the principles applying to any software for use in security applications. This is in itself a nontrivial task, but at least the memory available in smart card chips is relatively small, which limits the eventual size of the software. There have to be checks that the operating system meets its specification and also that no unintended features have been included.

The ROM mask of the operating system is then given to the chip manufacturer, which will return an implementation of the code for cross-checking before manufacturing the batch of chips. This is in itself a useful integrity check, but clearly, one normally requires this code to be kept confidential, so its distribution should be carefully controlled. Furthermore, the manufacturer has to be accountable for all chips made, some of which, because of yield failures, will need to be destroyed. Otherwise, an attacker may obtain raw chips to mount any form of counterfeit operation.

The batch of chips is distributed to the fabricator (smart card manufacturer) whose task it is to embed the chips in the plastic cards. The role of the fabricator varies considerably between customers and their services. At a very minimum, the fabricator must test the complete IC card to ensure its operational state. In some cases, the fabricator completely personalizes the card to the requirements of the issuer.

---

3. Public-Key Cryptography on Smart Cards. Proceedings of the International Conference on Cryptography, Policy and Algorithms, LNCS 1029, pp. 250–269.

Smart Card Applications

New generations of smart cards are becoming available for applications that include pay TV, mobile communications, electronic cash, and a variety of other uses.

Pay TV

One of the first applications of microcontroller-based smart cards was pay TV. The card appears to be both an ideal identification token (associated with the subscriber) and an efficient loyalty support.

In most pay-TV applications (the two best-known European examples are Eurocrypt and Videocrypt), the program provider broadcasts periodically (typically each 100ms to 500ms) an encrypted *control-word* (temporary key) under which the image is encrypted. Only valid cards can extract this control-word from the data stream, decrypt it, and send it to the decoder.

A second interesting marketing model is "pay-per-view." In this setting, the viewer buys a preloaded card and progressively spends the loaded amount (in general, a time coefficient is associated with each program).

Finally, cards also appear to be efficient sponsoring tools. In general, the sponsor issues free cards, valid only during a given event (for instance, a baseball game), and distributes them. The broadcast will then be accessible free only by the card-owners.

Mobile Communications

GSM security is essentially based on the tamper-proofness of the smart card (renamed Subscriber Identity Module, or SIM, in the standard). Each SIM is associated with a set of secret and public parameters (IMSI, Ki, PIN, PUK, etc.) that allow the operator to locate the mobile phone and route calls and digital messages (Short Message Services).

Smart cards present major security and cost advantages over passive code identification. Fraud losses due mainly to card loss or password disclosure are far less frequent than fraud losses due to password eavesdropping in non-tamper-resistant systems.

Electronic Cash

Microcontroller or authenticated-memory cards can be used for storing or representing legal tender in several ways:

- The smart card can be a bidirectional link between the cardholder and his bank account. In such a case, terminals may check the genuineness of the card by diverse cryptographic protocols (depending mainly on the terminal and card's computational powers).
- The card can act as an electronic purse and store in EEPROM a balance that can be converted or transferred from the card to the point-of-sale terminal and the bank.
- Payment protocols can be anonymous (preserve the user's privacy exactly as paper money does) or auditable (as with a regular checking account). The smart card industry considers that the banking sector will be one of the main card application fields during the coming decade.

Other Applications

Smart cards are also used in loyalty applications, electronic copyright (typically software protection), gaming, physical access control, Internet security, and many other areas.

Gemplus considers that, in the long term, the best way of fitting to clients' needs will probably consist of providing end users with a *blank card* whose ROM mask contains a general-purpose high-level operating system. On the top of that, users will add either their own (homemade) applications or ready-to-use programs bought and downloaded from a software editor.In this scenario, the card's natural tamper-resistance, combined with public-key cryptography capabilities, appears to be a natural approach to provide both passive and active software protection.

"Contactless" Cards

The term "contactless product" comprises a broad range of technologies such as infrared, optical radio, or high-frequency products. Some of those products are battery powered, while others derive their energy from the magnetic field they bathe in. In this section, we focus on radio-frequency products powered by a magnetic field.

Up to now, contactless products were used mainly in proprietary applications. This practice led to a severe lack of harmony among the communication protocols. Moreover, the products used were generally memory cards, which further limited the interest in making any studies.

The International Organization for Standardization (ISO) and the International Electrotechnical Commission (IEC) developed a standard for contactless products. This standard, named ISO/IEC 14443, defines the protocol communication between a contactless product and a reader through a magnetic field emitted by a reader. This magnetic field provides power to the contactless products and also carries the data exchanged between the reader and the card through amplitude modulation. This standard permits the development of a range of readers and cards that will be able to work together.

At the beginning, most of the contactless products were memory based—that is, they provided storage but no processing capability. Increasingly, contactless cards will be able to support processing as well

Dual-interface cards are cards that can be communicated with through either a contact or a contactless interface. Moreover, such dual-interface products have expanded the scope of the contactless technology to applications like banking or e-purse, for which the security constraints are more severe.

It is very important to understand the potential weaknesses and the intrinsic strengths of both the contactless and the dual-interface technologies. Some new attack paths or security flaws might have been introduced by the contactless technology itself or by the interoperability between the two modes.

In this scope, it is interesting to conduct a systematic and complete analysis of contactless and dual-interface products. For this reason, the following items are investigated:

- Specificities of contactless standards and protocols
- Constraints linked to the contactless interface
- Comparison of the contactless interface with the contact one
- Cryptography used in contactless products

Protocols and Secure Communication Schemes

For the past eight to ten years, contact smart cards have been thoroughly studied, and experts in physical security, cryptography, embedded O/S, Java security, protocol security, and other areas have spent a huge amount of energy assessing the security of existing applications and products. One important point related to the security of contact applications is the physical connection between the reader and the card. In many applications, physical constraints force and guarantee a one-to-one communication; that is , the reader can initiate communication with only one card at a time and a given card can respond to only one reader.

That basic property is no longer valid for the contactless and dual-interface applications, and the risk analysis has to be conducted with this point in mind. In contactless and dual products, there is no physical link between the reader and the card, and the reader is designed to communicate with several cards at a time.

Since there is no physical link between the reader and the cards, it is simple to introduce a malicious probe, a malicious card, or a malicious reader without anybody being aware of it. One could imagine substituting a card for another; deleting some reader commands in order to shunt parts of the application, or forcing cards to perform malevolent transactions. All these configurations and scenarios have to be carefully analyzed when one is trying to build secure and trustworthy communication schemes.

Contactless applications are designed to allow data exchange between one reader and several cards at a time (the reader in fact communicates with only one card at a time, but the presence of several cards is managed through time-multiplexing). From the reader's point of view, it is therefore important to manage in a secure manner the context switch from one card to the other.

With the latest generation of dual-interface cards, the contact and the contactless applications share a core, RAM, and nonvolatile memory. Applications' sharing is something already tackled in the contact technology, but it is worth checking whether some additional protections have to be introduced when dual-interface products are involved.

Another specificity of the contactless technology relates to the high probability of having cuts in communication and power. Of course, antitearing mechanisms are implemented, even for contact cards, but the high occurrence of such events might have some impact on the design of the supported applications.

Constraints of Contactless Products

Contactless applications often have requirements that differ from those of the contact applications. The contactless interface is used mainly for its rapidity and user friendliness. Some parameters, like working distance, speed, environmental sensitivity, or interoperability, are very restrictive for contactless applications. In the following sections, we focus on those different items and analyze their impact on the secure design of contactless and dual products.

Speed and Working Distance

The feature governing speed and working distance is a key element to the design of the contactless products. In fact, the contactless power supply is assumed by the magnetic field provided by the reader. The effective power available on the card's side is linked to the distance between the card and the reader. Increasing the distance between card and reader decreases the available power; roughly 1 centimeter corresponds to a power of 1mA. The power required for a cryptographic execution, for example—which is the highest-consuming function—is available between 0 and 7cm. When a card's chip has less power, it could not run at the maximum working frequency. The frequency's adaptation has must be finely tuned to find a compromise between speed and working distance. No limitation, except time or working distance requirements, exists for the use of cryptography on contactless products. Today, contactless products allow symmetric cryptography as well as asymmetric cryptography.

Transport applications are good examples of time-constrained applications for which the transaction time is upper-bounded to 150ms. Depending on the application, the cryptographic part is variable; it could be necessary to limit the working distance to increase speed for reaching this constraint.

Other constraints are defined in the standard ISO/IEC 14443. For example, the smart card has to work between 0 and 10cm. In that particular example, the standard does not specify if a working distance of 10cm has to be maintained even during cryptographic operations. (It is commonly admitted that 10cm cannot be maintained on these kinds of executions using today's technology.) Nevertheless, an application designer will have to choose between speed and working distance when developing the card's operating system.

Interoperability

This notion of interoperability became relevant only after pilot applications were deployed in mass volume. Problems arose because of the analog interface between the reader and the card. This interface is very sensitive to the physical parameters of the reader and the card (reader's demodulator, card's modulator, card's resonance frequency, quality factor of the card, and so on). Depending on the variation of these parameters, a card could operate or not with a specific reader. When an application is widely deployed, there are often many manufacturers of cards and readers involved; this large number of possible configurations implies that some of them are not functional. Finding the test-table's parameters that guarantee that a card or a reader will be "interoperable" is a big issue for the deployment of contactless applications.

Contactless Products and the Contact Interface

Contactless applications have some specificity that could be summarized under three headings: communication, physical security, and software security.

Communication

A contactless product communicates with the reader without any physical link. This communication channel could be a potential weakness in terms of security; it will be interesting to identify the adequate countermeasures.

Lack of Physical Link

The absence of physical link between the card and the reader allows a "user-friendly" utilization of the smart card; cardholders can keep their cards in their wallets, for example, when they use them. This characteristic also requires a lower cost of maintenance for the reader, but it has its own weaknesses. The absence of any physical link forces the communication between the card and the reader to be secure and trustworthy.

Some contactless applications are designed for a possible communication between a reader and several cards at the same time. This means that reader can alternatively talk with one of the cards in front of it—cards cannot talk to each other, even through the reader. The parts must be able to trust each other and be sure that no part has been perverted. Well-known countermeasures, like mutual authentication, have to be applied. A mutual authentication permits the card and the readers to prove that they are authorized to speak to one another. The exchange of a shared secret, for instance, shows that the card and the reader are what they claim to be.

In contactless communications, the card could be (in)voluntarily removed from the magnetic field. For example, the "moving" card in front of a reader antenna could generate this natural "instability" of chip power supply. From the card operating system's point of view, this characteristic has to be included during the development. For example, some backup mechanisms could be implemented to restore the context after tearing.

The lack of any physical link also allows a malicious system to hide some commands sent by the reader to the card, with the aim of blocking an action in the card; for example, the malicious system could try to block a decrement command sent to the card with intent to undecrement an electronic purse. Blocking this command would prevent the amount of money in the card from being decremented after a purchase! From the reader's point of view, the command to decrement the counter would have been sent, but from the card's point of view, no money would be removed. Some systems try to detect this kind of attack by querying the card to make sure that the decrement command has actually been executed—for example, by reading the card's value a second time to make sure that the card's value has actually been decremented.

Spying

Because contactless communication is done through the magnetic field, it is easy to catch and spy on the exchange of data between the card and the reader. No countermeasure can block this spying. On the other end, some countermeasures like data ciphering can block the capacity to interpret the data in a way to use it in some command reply scenarios.

Use of a Smart Card Without the Cardholder's Consent

Contactless communication allows a card to initiate communication without a clear engagement of the cardholder. We could envision that a malicious reader could be put in front of a smart card without the knowledge of the cardholder and collect some information from the card. This privacy issue is the main threat that inhibits the acceptance of the contactless communication. Fortunately, some simple countermeasures, as already explained (mutual authentication between the card and the reader, PIN code, etc.), are efficient against this risk. Some other solutions exist, like a push button that stops the card from functioning until the cardholder takes the card in hand or some specialized encasings that shield the card from the magnetic field of a malicious reader.

Card Holder's Privacy

The ability to read a contactless card's content without the explicit agreement of the cardholder can be a serious threat to the owner's privacy. This point deserves to be mentioned even if its social and legal impacts may vary from one country to the other. The countermeasures already mentioned limit this possibility, but it is important to say that the low-level commands in the ISO 14443 standard require that a card always replies to a command from the reader. The first response sent back by the card to a reader command is a serial number. This information could present, with some cross-checking method, sufficient information to outline a person's movements.

ISO standards limit that threat, allowing the card to send back a random serial number in a countermeasure that blocks the link between a card's serial number and a "named" cardholder. We could also imagine that the card is put in a shield case.

Denial of Service

We saw that it is possible for a malicious organization to collect some information without the cardholder's consent. Another effect of a malicious use could be a card malfunction. Imagine that a malicious reader is designed not to collect information but to block the card by physically destroying it through and electromagnetic spike or presenting the wrong PIN code many times, blocking the correct PIN code presentation attempt. This attack could have a big effect in an airport or on a subway, for example. A denial of service could damage all mass transit systems, forcing them to switch to a backup system with less security or transit flow speed.

Physical Security

We saw previously that almost all attacks could be blocked with well-known countermeasures if the threat is correctly identified. From an application point of view, the contactless communication is as secure as a contact one. We now have to look at security from a physical point of view. For contact products, some attacks using the card's leakage are well known (such as Simple Power Analysis and Differential Power Analysis). The literature mentions a lot of possible attacks that use power analysis or fault analysis. Many software countermeasures were developed against these threats, and their efficiency is independent from the communication channel. On the other hand, some chip manufacturers developed hardware countermeasures to blur the chip's current consumption. These countermeasures have to be correctly studied and evaluated to determine their efficiency in the contactless mode.

For dual-interface products in particular, we need to study the security of the contactless interface to ensure that this interface does not bring in new paths of attacks. It may be that additional design countermeasures have to be implemented by chip manufacturers to guarantee a high level of resistance against fault attack.

Software Security

We already spoke about the possible compromise in performance with respect to working distance and speed. From the cryptographic point of view, it is the same stake. All known cryptographic algorithms could be performed on contactless products; technically there is no limit on contactless products. Chip manufacturers choose to clock the chip with low-frequency values. This choice allows the cryptographic algorithms' computation with an acceptable working distance by lowering the amount of power required, but it simultaneously increases the length of time required for computation. Other technical choices could reduce the time of computation. This time is often the cause of the assumption saying that cryptography is not possible in contactless applications.

When one is considering the range of available security mechanisms, the primary factor determining whether or not they can be adapted to contactless cards is the amount of electrical power that is required to implement them.

Conclusions

The number of contactless applications is rapidly growing. However, some customers are hesitant to use them because of concerns about security and the limited knowledge regarding the specifics of contactless technology. The good news is that adequate security measures do exist; concerns over security should not be an impediment to deploying this promising technology.

Of course the recent introduction of dual-interface smart cards and the use of this kind of products in high-level applications increase the level of confidence needed in this technology. A good identification of particularities shows that contactless is as secure as the contact technology. We think that dual-interface products represent an opportunity to combine the strengths of both contact and contactless cards with technology that is available today.

Chapter 26

NCR: RFID IN RETAIL

Dan White[1]

Introduction

RFID has come into the market with great fanfare and excitement over the last couple of years. Companies promoting their products have made astounding claims about what the future holds and the capabilities of their merchandise. Some of their visions, such as a refrigerator talking to food and automatically reordering when the milk carton is empty,[2] seem to come directly from a sci-fi thriller.

Weeding through the marketing and hype can be a daunting task, especially for those not close to the technology. As an integrator of the technology, NCR has done extensive testing with various RFID systems to separate fact from fiction, particularly in retail store environments. This chapter details the results of these experiments and highlights some of the potential uses for RFID. It also reveals the inherent limitations of the technology.

Payment Applications

RFID has been in use for years in many common applications. Keeping track of lost pets and farm animals,[3] collecting tolls automatically as cars speed past,[4]

---

1. Dan White is the technical evangelist for RFID and emerging technologies in NCR's Retail System Division.
2. "Merloni Unveils RFID Appliances." *RFID Journal* article at www.rfidjournal.com/article /view/369/1/1.
3. Oxley Web site, www.oxley.co.uk/animal-id.
4. Fastrak Web site, www.511.org/fastrak.

providing building security access,[5] and checking out library books[6] are just a few of the widespread uses for RFID already in the market today.

Current Installations

Payment systems such as Exxon/Mobil Speedpass[7] have millions of users speeding up their payment at the gas pump. Mastercard has issued large quantities of Paypass credit cards and has embedded tags in the back covers of cell phones. Consumers can "tap and go"[8] using their cell phones, making the RFID interface faster and more convenient than traditional magnetic stripe credit cards.

Food Ordering

RFID payment systems can be leveraged for many other uses. Imagine that your spouse calls you at work and says, "Honey, I just ordered dinner at our favorite restaurant for the kids and me. Would you add what you would like and pick it up on your way home?" You log in to the restaurant's Web site using your Speedpass or other payment token. The order your spouse just placed comes up, and you add your selection.

When you get to the drive-through window at the restaurant, a kiosk is waiting for your Speedpass token to pull up the order and send it directly to the kitchen. Because Speedpass is a payment system, cash back can be added to the food order and charged to your account.

This online ordering system has several inherent advantages. First, you don't have to remember the entire order or wait for the kids in the back seat to decide what they want at the drive-through window. Second, you don't have to rely on a microphone that makes speech hard to understand. You can be sure the order is entered correctly. An example of a kiosk for ordering food is shown in Figure 26.1.

Of course, getting the correct order to the kitchen has solved only half the problem. NCR is still working on how to ensure that the order is filled correctly. Perhaps placing RFID chips in the food packaging is an option. Then each item can be verified against the order as the bag goes through the drive-through window. These tags would have only information such as "large fry" and "hamburger" with no unique identity, alleviating privacy concerns.

---

5. HID Web site, www.hidcorp.com.
6. Vernon RFID Web site, www.vernlib.com/vernrfid.asp.
7. Speedpass Web site, www.speedpass.com.
8. "Just tap and go!" Paypass Web site, www.paypass.com.

Figure 26.1   A kiosk provides cash back before sending a food order directly to the kitchen. (Image © 2004 NCR; reprinted with permission.)

All of the basic technologies to implement a food-ordering and payment solution are readily available today and work very well. Any type of RFID payment token can be used to identify and pay for the order. Although most of the industry interest is in supply chain uses, one should not overlook the other potential uses for RFID that are available in the short term.

Inventory Management Applications

Most of the industry interest has been in logistics, managing inventory and moving pallets and cases from a manufacturing plant to various distribution warehouses. While there are advantages in the supply chain, RFID also provides the ability to locate items within a store. One key issue retailers face is if they cannot find a product, they cannot sell it. The focus of this chapter is on managing inventory at the store.

Out-of-Stocks

Active inventory management on store shelves is a well-documented[9] and often cited example of using RFID within a store. In this scenario, a consumer might take the last two boxes of bandages from the shelf. The system recognizes that there are no more bandages and sends an alert to store personnel to restock the shelf. The alert can be through a beeper, an e-mail to a cell phone, or a message to a PDA. This is called an out-of-stock condition, and it is a major concern for both retailers and consumer goods manufacturers.

When an out-of-stock occurs, the retailer loses business approximately half the time[10] because consumers came in with the intent to buy a specific product. Most consumers who cannot find what they are looking for simply leave the store to find the product elsewhere rather than ask for help. When consumers do not have a preference about a specific brand, they purchase a competitive product, and the manufacturer of the out-of-stock item loses the business. In some cases, consumers may determine they like the competitive product better, and the manufacturer has lost not only that day's sale but also future sales.

Research shows 7 percent to 8 percent of items are out-of-stock at any one time.[11] Solving this problem could provide big returns for both retailers and consumer goods manufacturers.

Theft Prevention

Active inventory management could also assist in preventing theft before items leave the store. Gillette Mach3 razors are small, high-cost items that are easy to resell. They are among the most stolen items in the world. One simply needs to go to eBay or a flea market to see the availability of "hot" razor blades.

With an active inventory management system in place, the system could detect potentially abnormal behavior[12] such as ten razor packages being removed at once. A security camera strategically placed in the store could alert store security to watch for the individual who removed the razors and make sure the razors are paid for before the shopper leaves the store. This could be done in a real-time

---

9. MeadWestvaco Intelligent Systems Web site, www.mwvis.com.
10. "An out of stock typically will be a lost sale to the retailer 49% of the time and a lost sale to the consumer goods manufacturer 37% of the time." From Gillette presentation at Retail Systems 2003.
11. McGarvey, R. "Trouble tracking inventory? Tag it like a wild animal." www.entrepreneur .com/article/0,4621,294559,00.html.
12. Forcinio, H. "Prevent Losses with RFID." www.managingautomation.com/maonline/magazine /read.jspx?id=3176.

store environment, and action would be taken only if the person attempted to leave the store without purchasing the items.

Electronic Shelf Labels

RFID inventory shelf systems can be tied into electronic shelf labels. Electronic shelf labels are small tags with a display that can be updated remotely from a computer. An example is shown in Figure 26.2. As items are moved around in the store, the RFID systems can automatically determine what product has been moved and update the electronic shelf label with pricing and product information.

Technical Limitations

Many hurdles need to be overcome before active shelf inventory is adopted across the industry. Reading RFID-tagged items on a shelf is difficult for a number of reasons. Various materials differ in how friendly they are to radio frequencies. In the UHF frequency band (900–930MHz for the United States),

Figure 26.2   NCR RealPrice electronic shelf label provides real-time updates as inventory is relocated. (Image © 2004 NCR; reprinted with permission.)

any product containing lots of water absorbs RF energy. This is the basic principle behind how a microwave oven works. Microwave ovens operate at the resonant frequency of water, 2.4GHz. RF waves cause the water to vibrate,[13] which heats the food. UHF systems operate close enough to water's resonant frequency to be greatly impacted by liquid products. Depending on the proximity of the tag to the liquid, the read performance is significantly degraded and may cause the tag not to respond at all. Metal reflects RF energy and has an equally detrimental impact on read rates.

It is likely that product packaging will have to change to accommodate RFID tags. The tags will need to be separated from metals or liquids to operate properly. Products currently in metal cans may change to plastic containers, as seen in Proctor & Gamble's recent move to plastic packaging for Folger's AromaSeal coffee. Besides the packaging and product constraints, the metal shelves and close stacking of products are challenges in this environment.

Cost and Installation Limitations

System costs and installation of active inventory systems are also a concern. Each shelf will likely require a separate antenna, costing retailers a few hundred dollars. Each RFID reader accepts two to four antennas and typically costs over a thousand dollars today. With all the shelves in a typical store, the investment can be overwhelming. Of course, a store might install readers only in critical areas where they tend to have a larger issue with maintaining stock.

Over time, reader costs will come down as volume increases, but the wiring of antennas is a long-term problem. Fragile coaxial cables are not welcome in the hostile retail shelf environment. Stores are constantly moving inventory, shelves, and gondolas and would have to carefully route antennas and readers as well as provide A/C power. All of these factors create major installation problems. A more robust method to implement wiring in shelves is required.

Misplaced Inventory

Out-of-stocks don't always occur because customers remove items for purchase. Items are often put in the wrong place by consumers or store personnel. This is a problem for all retailers, but it is especially problematic in the clothing industry. Have you ever gone through a rack of clothing only to

---

13. Brain, M. "How Microwave Cooking Works." http://home.howstuffworks.com/microwave.htm.

determine your size and style are not in stock? Could the item have been put somewhere else?

Some retail employees spend a significant amount of time putting items back where they belong. RFID can provide an automated means of quickly allowing store personnel to locate misplaced items and put them in the correct location. Whether it is clothes or DVDs, mixing of products is a chronic, time-consuming issue.

In the clothing or shoe area, active RFID tags may be a better solution. Since these items typically carry a higher cost, NCR's RealPrice electronic shelf tags can be deployed as an active RFID solution to alleviate many store issues at once. Running power and wiring to each shelf or rack is not necessary because the RealPrice tags contain a battery. A few antennas strategically placed in the ceiling can cover an entire store, dramatically improving the infrastructure costs and reliability. Each garment would have its own active tag with pricing information, providing real-time price updates.

Rather than have store personnel manually update pricing, retailers could update the tag from a central server in the store as sales or closeouts occur. This system ensures that the price on the garment matches the price at checkout. The store could have "Happy Hour" promotions to get more traffic during slow times and provide consumers with discounts. Additionally, because the system provides accurate inventory counts, the store could be updating pricing in real time and provide discounts on particular sizes and styles that are overstocked. Providing this feature in an active computer-based pricing system could reduce the overall cost of labor, driving prices down for the consumer.

Product Locator

There are additional advantages to having a battery-powered tag. Rather than wade through an entire rack of shirts or stack of jeans, consumers could go to a kiosk that lists the styles and sizes available in the store. They could then choose their style and size, prompting the system to send a message to the active tag to light up and beep helping them quickly locate the item. An example of this is shown in Figure 26.3.

By reusing the tag, the retailer minimizes the costs of a battery and display. The store personnel would remove the active tag and reuse it on new items as they come into the store for restocking. Because the tag is removed before the clothing leaves the store, any personal privacy concerns for having RFID tags on clothing are also eliminated.

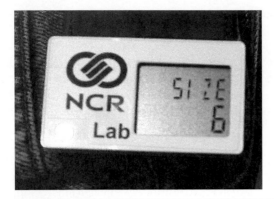

Figure 26.3   NCR RealPrice tag lights up an LED to help a consumer locate an item. (Image © 2004 NCR; reprinted with permission.)

Back Room

Another related inventory location problem is back-room stock location. Many retailers have a harder time finding inventory in the back room than on the store floor. In fact, sometimes at shoe stores, finding a particular size and style is so hard, store personnel will simply tell a customer that the shoe is out of stock rather than look for it in the back storage room. If the back room were automated to track all items and provide the exact location, restocking would be greatly simplified and reduce the number of out-of-stocks in the store selling area.

Having accurate information about store stock can also reduce overall inventory levels. Many times when a partial case of items can't be found, the store will order more, only to find the partial case later and end up with too much of an item.

Mobile Systems

A mobile inventory management system is an alternative to wiring all the shelves and installing a large number of readers throughout the store. A store employee would use a mobile RFID reader that reads all items and shelf locations. The shelves would have their own RFID tags to provide the location information. One day, a robot could automatically go down the aisles and take inventory. Utilizing currently available consumer technology, a Roomba robotic vacuum could clean the floors and take inventory at the same time!

Hybrid Scanners

As products in the store are enabled with RFID tags, point-of-sale checkout systems will have to change to take advantage of the additional information that will be available. Retailers have a huge investment in checkout systems and want to keep equipment as long as possible. Doing so requires migrating existing systems to accommodate new technologies such as RFID.

Use of hybrid scanners will be one solution to migrating a current checkout system. A hybrid scanner is a standard bar code scanner with an RFID reader and antenna embedded. With it, retailers can begin using the data from RFID-tagged items during the transition period when everything in the store is not tagged.

RFID tags provide unique identities for individual items, unlike today's bar code. For example, every bottle of water may have the exact same bar code, but each bottle would have a different RFID tag number so that RFID technology will function properly. With a bar code, the scanner must "see" the bar code directly in its line of sight, so the cashier must manually pass each item over the scanner to get a proper read. RFID does not have a line-of-sight requirement. An RFID reader has an invisible field that allows it to read multiple tags at once. If every bottle of water had the same tag, it could not tell if it was reading one bottle of water or many.

Traceability

A unique identity can provide some very useful information. Tracking goods from the manufacturer to the consumer is important for pharmaceutical and specific food items. Certain drugs are counterfeited because of their value. It is critical that cancer patients know for sure the drugs they are taking are genuine. RFID can provide a complete audit trail from the manufacturer to ensure that the drug is not counterfeit.[14]

Of course, other manufacturers are interested in reducing counterfeiting[15] also. Imitation shampoos and nonauthentic clothing end up on store shelves throughout the world. It does not take much of an investment for someone to mix up some imitation shampoo in a bathtub and sell it as a branded product. Not only does the manufacturer lose profit on counterfeit items, since it did

---

14. www.eweek.com/article2/0,1759,1608448,00.asp.
15. Forcinio, H. "Prevent Losses with RFID." www.managingautomation.com/maonline/magazine/read.jspx?id=3176.

not provide the goods, but it may also lose customers when they buy the inferior product and are dissatisfied.

Certain foods also need to be tracked through the supply chain. Beef has been a major source of controversy with the outbreak of "mad cow" disease. Knowing where all beef from a particular herd ended up will help reduce consumers' concern and industry waste. Large quantities of meat would not have to be destroyed to ensure safety; only the meat in question would need to be traced and eliminated.

Perishable Products

A unique identity can also provide direct benefit to consumers. As dated items approach expiration, the store could provide automated discounts to customers at the time of purchase. For example, a bottle of orange juice might be discounted 50% when it is within two days of expiration. Instead of having store personnel manually apply discount stickers, grocers would use the hybrid scanner to read the RFID tag, look up the expiration date, and automatically provide the discount.

Recalls

Recalls could also be automated. Companies that make baby products and pharmaceuticals spend a great deal on recalling items that are defective or tainted. The RFID tag can flag items at checkout, and recalled products can be replaced before they leave the store. For baby products or other items that tend to have a high rate of recalls related to safety issues, RFID-enabled automatic registration could provide consumers with information if a recall occurs after purchase.

No More Receipts

One of the most obvious benefits to consumers for item-level RFID tagging is eliminating the need for keeping receipts. The unique code in an RFID tag allows the store to know the actual date, location, and cost of the item purchased. Therefore, if the product needs to be returned for a warranty or refund, no receipt is needed. Gift returns would provide full refund of purchase price rather than the lowest sales price over the last year. Hybrid self-checkout systems (as shown in Figure 26.4) could be turned into hybrid self-return stations for the rush after Christmas.

Figure 26.4 NCR hybrid FastLane reads RFID tags while scanning bar codes. (Image © 2004 NCR; reprinted with permission.)

Technology Analysis

A hybrid scanner will allow the retailer to test RFID technology performance while the bar code provides accurate pricing details. Percentage of RFID reads, number of defective tags, antenna placement, and other technical details can be analyzed without impacting current operations in the store.

NCR announced the first RealScan hybrid scanner in 2002, and a hybrid Fast-Lane self-checkout system in 2004 (Figure 26.5). Labs and pilots to utilize hybrid systems are planned for the future.

Figure 26.5 NCR hybrid scanner migrates existing POS systems to gather RFID information at checkout. (Image © 2004 NCR; reprinted with permission.)

Privacy Concerns

Consumer advocacy groups are concerned about personal privacy with individually tagged items. They fear that RFID technology may be abused because tags can be read by a third party without the individual's knowledge. Clothing and items that are regularly carried by a consumer would be of particular concern.

Telemarketers, identity theft, and the onslaught of spam have raised the public awareness of personal privacy issues and have impacted public attitude and opinion. Providing accurate information about RFID technology and its benefits to the consumer will help alleviate these concerns.

Ultimately, giving consumers a choice will be important in helping the general population become comfortable with the technology. Since only a few products will be tagged at the item level initially, a kiosk could disable the tags before consumers leave the store.

Given the current state of RFID technology, disabling one tag at a time is the only reliable option available. Obviously, putting one item at a time in a kiosk is not ideal. As the technology matures, disabling of tags will move to checkout. Depending on the consumer's wishes, all or some tags may be disabled. For example, a tag on clothing might be disabled, but one on a filled prescription would not. In the long term, consumers may be more concerned about recalls, drug interactions, warranties, automated returns, and other after-purchase benefits of RFID than about privacy.

RFID Portal

Of course, when most people think of the long-term goal of using RFID at checkout, they picture consumer pushing a shopping basket full of groceries past a portal, watching it being rung up automatically, and immediately walking out of the store. The technology available today can provide this type of space-age demonstration, taking checkout time from minutes to seconds!

Several key events must take place before the vision of portal checkout can become a reality (see Figure 26.6). First, every item in the store has to be individually tagged. Given current costs of 20 to 50 cents per tag,[16] it will likely take some time for a 50-cent candy bar to get an RFID tag. Second, all items in the basket must be read consistently. If a consumer purchases a can of green beans, a bag of aluminum wrapped potato chips, or a jar of apple sauce, the current RFID systems will have difficulty reading every item. Finally, RF fields are difficult to contain, and it is hard to keep the RFID reader from picking up stray tags in a nearby aisle or cart.

To show what the future might be like, NCR demonstrates a shopping cart full of groceries passing by a portal that flawlessly reads every item. The portal reads every item every time because the products have been carefully chosen and placed in the cart.

To highlight the realities of the current technology, a small hand basket then passes through the portal with eight items that are very hard to read (see Figure 26.7). The portal typically reads four items from the hand basket. NCR has demonstrated the portal to almost 100 retailers, and every one stated that a

---

16. Schwartz, E. "Wal-Mart Promises RFID Will Benefit Suppliers." June 17, 2004. www.infoworld
   .com/article/04/06/17/HNwalmart_1.html.

Figure 26.6   RFID portal reads every item as a grocery cart passes through.
(Image © 2004 NCR; reprinted with permission.)

50 percent read rate was not acceptable for checkout. They want consumers to pay for all of their groceries!

Given the current levels of theft and potential labor savings, the technology probably does not need to be 100 percent accurate, but it will need to reliably read all items most of the time to be accepted in the industry. Actual percentage rates will likely be retailer specific and be driven by internal efficiencies and costs.

In the hand basket demonstration, the portal picks up three items from the grocery cart full of items that passed through earlier, even though it is sitting several feet away! For consumers, not knowing if the portal picked up items in the next aisle, the impulse items located near the checkout, or the HDTV the customer behind them is buying is a great concern. Consumers need to have confidence that they will not be charged for items they did not receive. Limiting the RFID read zone to only those items in a certain area is difficult.

Figure 26.7   Basket with RFID items that are hard to read.
(Image © 2004 NCR; reprinted with permission.)

Conclusions

RFID is currently being used in many applications and is providing convenience and benefits to consumers today. Payment applications will continue to expand and provide faster ways to pay and order items. Tagging pallets and cases will improve logistics efficiencies and lower costs in the supply chain. Benefits in the store will grow as the cost of RFID tags drops so that individual items can be marked. Once item-level tagging is available, tracking items in the back room and on the store floor will become feasible. Ultimately, RFID tags will make it to checkout to provide direct benefits to the consumer with automated discounts on expiring items, no-receipt refunds, information on recalls, and simplified warranty registration. Obviously, there are some technical hurdles on the way to the portal self-checkout system, but technology will continue to improve. In the not-too-distant future, maybe you will pass through a portal, simply walk out with your groceries, and have your receipt e-mailed to you.

Chapter 27

P&G: RFID AND PRIVACY IN THE SUPPLY CHAIN

Sandy Hughes[1]

Introduction

Consumers' concern about RFID is an old sentiment applied to a new technology. The introduction of the Internet decades ago opened the floodgates for businesses to market directly to consumers via e-mail and Web sites.

Some companies, like Procter & Gamble, one of the world's largest advertisers of consumer goods, called the Internet a "New Media" channel. Some consumer groups called it "Big Brother." Claims of individual profiling "*they* will know all that I do and buy" have been heard since the early 1990s. A study conducted in the United States in 2000 showed that 95 percent of consumers were at least somewhat concerned about the possible misuse of their personal information.[2] Today, 71 percent of U.S. consumers feel that protection of their personal information and privacy is more of a concern today than it was several years ago.[3] In other words, the "privacy issue" is not going away, but applying Fair Information Practices and sound privacy principles to any new technology as it is introduced can address it. Procter & Gamble's experience with Internet marketing and commitment to ensuring consumer trust is an example of how a company can make money and continue to do excellent marketing while still respecting and protecting an individual's personal information and privacy. This chapter highlights how the same principles can be applied to the use of RFID in the supply chain as well.

---

1. Sandy Hughes is the Global Privacy Executive (CPO) at The Procter & Gamble Company.
2. Lou Harris & Associates, 2000.
3. Yankelovich, 2004 State of Consumer Trust.

Procter & Gamble's Position

P&G markets over 300 brands in more than 140 countries worldwide, with 2003–2004 sales over $50 billion. Such brands as Tide/Ariel, Pampers, Pantene, Bounty, Pringles, Crest, and Olay are used over 2 million times a day. Our corporate purpose is:

> We will provide branded products and services of superior quality and value that improve the lives of the world's consumers. As a result, consumers will reward us with leadership sales, profit, and value creation, allowing our people, our shareholders, and the communities in which we live and work to prosper.[4]

The P & G employee mantra is "The Consumer is Boss". We like to think that there are two key moments when we must win with consumers to make them continue to purchase our products. The first moment of truth (FMOT) is when the shopper decides which product to select off the shelf. The second moment of truth (SMOT) is when the shopper uses the product and decides whether that was a good purchase or not and whether to purchase it again. Accordingly, the objective of our Global Privacy program is to "create an environment of trust where consumers willingly share information so that we can better meet their needs for products and services." These objectives have served us well— P&G sales continue to grow steadily in the double digits each year, and P&G brands were chosen number 1 in consumer trust among consumer product good companies in the United States in 2004.[5]

Our Privacy Policy[6] is built not just on individual country privacy laws but also on internationally accepted privacy principles, or "fair information practices" established by the Organization for Economic Co-operation and Development (OECD), the European Union Data Protection Directive, and the U.S. Department of Commerce's/European Union Safe Harbor Privacy Principles. Our overriding principles are that:

- We protect an individual's personal information as if it were our own.
  - Security controls and guidelines for handling the data are continually refreshed, assessed, and audited.
  - We do not trade, sell, or lease personal information entrusted to us.

4. www.pg.com/company/who_we_are/ppv.jhtml
5. Ponemon & TrustE, Most Trusted Companies for Privacy, June 2004.
6. www.pg.com/company/our_commitment/privacy_epc/index.jhtml

- We inform or provide notice to consumers about:
  - How we will use their data and resultant benefits to them
  - Choices they have for further interaction or communication with us
  - How they can contact us to stop using their data or correct data they have provided to us

Successful companies know that protecting consumer privacy is more than just compliance with laws; it is plain old good business. An example at P&G is our Pampers Parenting Web site[7] and Newsletter (see Figure 27.1), launched in 1996. Over 2 million parents trust us with personal information like their names and addresses, children's ages, due date for expectant moms, and household income in addition to answers to occasional product surveys. In exchange, we provide them with monthly newsletters customized to the age of their babies, children, or month of pregnancy. Included in the newsletter are questions and answers from leading practitioners, tips and techniques, games and activities to do with children, and a paragraph for dads. In our privacy statement online, we talk about how we protect the security of their data, how they can contact us to view or change it, and how they can "opt out" from future newsletters and contacts. Our experience has shown that our brand loyalty is very high (we can measure this through coupons or offers made only through our newsletter), and that the opt-out rate is very low.

Applying the same principles and guidelines across all types of data, businesses, and geographies allows P&G to manage our Global Privacy Program most efficiently. And even if RFID tags will not contain personally identifiable information, the perception of consumers is that they *do*; therefore, P&G includes the use of RFID within the scope of our program.

RFID Technology and the Supply Chain

P&G was one of the early proponents of using RFID to improve the supply chain. The supply chain for the consumer product goods industry consists of the flow of goods between manufacturers and their suppliers. Included are exchanges between manufacturers' warehouses and distribution centers, between distribution centers and retailers' warehouses, and then at individual retail stores and eventually out of their back rooms onto shelves for purchase by consumers.

Over the years, computer systems and electronic data networks have enabled the tracking of product throughout the supply chain, with checks and balances along the way, to make sure what leaves one location arrives at the next. But it doesn't always balance: Product can be stolen, diverted, damaged, inaccurately counted, and so on—and the "checking" can take a lot of time and resources if every pallet

---

7. http://us.pampers.com/en_US/home.do

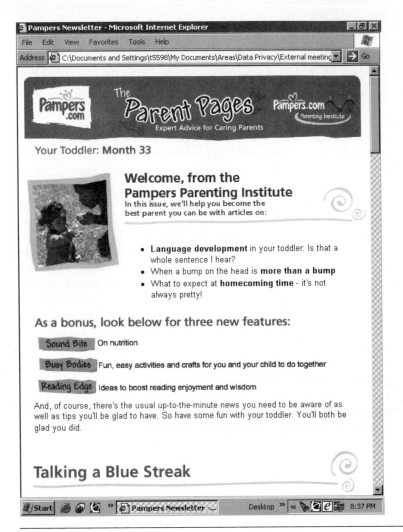

Figure 27.1   Pampers parenting web site and newsletter.
(Image © 2004 Procter & Gamble; reprinted with permission.)

of cases and every case must be counted. The advent of the bar code decades ago greatly improved supply-chain efficiency: Machines or devices can scan a bar code and electronically communicate a unique item and its manufacturer code to the computer systems and data network, which will then translate it and process the information. Bar code scanners are found throughout the supply chain, including the last stop at the cash register when a product is purchased.

Despite the advantages of bar codes and their reader devices, there are still weak points in the supply chain because each bar code must be physically seen and scanned. If a case on a conveyor belt is not facing in the direction of an automatic scanner or if a clerk accidentally skips the scan of a product, accuracy is compromised. People who must track down "lost" product or physically scan it can be better utilized in higher-value tasks like providing better customer service.

RFID technology, combined with an Electronic Product Code (EPC), takes the bar code to a new level of speed and accuracy. Unlike the bar code, which requires line of sight by the device that reads it, radio waves can detect, read, and transmit the information from many "electronic bar codes" at once. P&G is very interested in this technology because our key objective is to "win at the first moment of truth" with consumers: We want our products to be "at the right place at the right time at the right price." If consumers want an out-of-stock product, as is the case 8 to 12 percent of the time today, they will be unhappy and we may lose a sale. We keep over 65 days of inventory, costing us over $3 billion annually, because we are not able to see consumer demand fast enough from retailers. Thus, we are adding unnecessary cost to the supply chain. This is the main reason P&G opened the door when the MIT Auto-ID Center came knocking with the concept of the EPC network.

The Auto-ID Center[8] was a global research organization headquartered at the Massachusetts Institute of Technology (MIT). Founded in 1999, the Center was created in response to the Uniform Code Council's (UCC's) vision of building a next-generation universal bar code. Further, the Center's mission was to design the infrastructure and develop the standards to create a universal, open network for identifying individual products and for tracking them as they flow through the global supply chain. The UCC recognized that to achieve its goal, it would need to garner support from others. Accordingly, it enlisted P&G and the Gillette Company. Together, the three organizations provided seed funding to establish the Center, and over the next two years brought together over 100 retailers, manufacturers, technology providers, and trade associations.

As mentioned in earlier chapters, RFID technology has been used for decades in the military, transportation, and animal tracking sectors, to name a few. The concept of the Electronic Product Code network uses much less powerful radio frequencies that work only at short distances. These frequencies read very "dumb" tags with an antenna and an EPC that only "speaks when spoken to" with no battery.

Like many current numbering schemes used in commerce, the EPC is divided into numbers that identify the manufacturer and product type. But the EPC uses an extra set of digits—a serial number—to identify unique items. The EPC is the key to the information about the product it identifies that exists in the EPCglobal Network.

---

8. http://archive.epcglobalinc.org/aboutthecenter.asp

These very simple tags make them much less expensive than traditional RFID, therefore providing an opportunity for use in physical identification of objects such as within the consumer product supply chain. EPC as a solution to improve supply chain inefficiencies also requires a complete integration of technologies in a secure network to interpret the reading of the tags and transmit the information to the appropriate applications of inventory and order management between retailers and their suppliers.[9]

Once the technology had been tested and the process deemed feasible, the Auto-ID Center coalition transferred ownership for commercialization and ongoing administration of standards to the "parents" of the universal bar code, UCC/EAN. UCC/EAN spawned a joint venture called EPCglobal to manage the program. The transition of ownership to EPCglobal was effective in November 2003. Although the Auto-ID Center is no longer in existence, the Auto-ID labs continue to provide upstream technical research and development, including solutions for public policy concerns. I will talk more about EPCglobal and Public Policy later in this chapter.

Because P&G was one of the early sponsors of the Auto-ID Center, even lending Kevin Ashton from our marketing business to serve as executive director, we anticipated public policy issues for the technology. The Auto-ID Center began discussing how to approach it as early as 2000, conducting online research using P&G research tools in 2001, followed by more extensive research in 2002.[10] The results showed that over 70 percent of consumers did have concerns about the technology related primarily to privacy, followed by health and safety and then the environment. One key conclusion from this work was that the Auto-ID Center needed a panel of independent expert policy advisors from around the world, and as a result, the Center's Independent Policy Advisory Council was formed in the summer of 2002. The Council met for the first time in fall 2002.[11] In parallel, development of the EPC technology was proceeding rapidly to the point where it had to "come out of the lab" at MIT Auto-ID Center and into "the field"—a live environment to test the feasibility and benefits. Field tests were run on a small scale, beginning with pallets of cases, then on cases of products, and finally on individual products or items.

At P&G, our current focus for implementation of EPC is on pallets of goods and cases. At the time that this book goes to the publisher, we have no plans for implementing the technology on individual items. However, we continue to run our EPC program with the objective to test and learn. Two elements of the EPC program, the pallets and the wired dock doors, are shown in Figures 27.2 and 27.3, respectively.

9. www.epcglobalinc.org
10. Duce, H. "Auto-ID Center Public Policy...Consumer Opinion." May 2003.
11. Auto-ID Center Independent Advisory Council make-up.

EPC tag and Barcode

Figure 27.2 Pallets of bounty loaded 2 wide × 2 high into truck.
(Image © 2004 Procter & Gamble; reprinted with permission.)

Reader

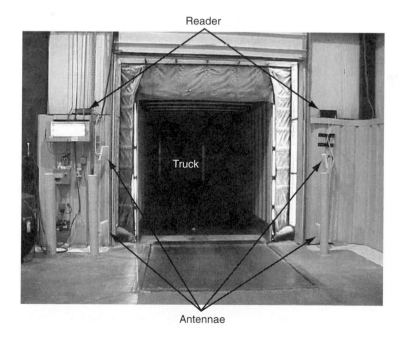

Truck

Antennae

Figure 27.3 Wired 1 outbound dock door: two antennae per side.
(Image © 2004 Procter & Gamble; reprinted with permission.)

One of our first tests, with the Metro Future Store in Germany,[12] continues to this day. This store uses many state-of-the art technologies, which is highly publicized and known by consumers, who encounter knowledgeable floor clerks to help with questions. We have tested pallets, cases, and even items with the FutureStore to learn about the technology—its benefits and short-comings. Even today a consumer may find a Pantene shampoo bottle with a clearly identifiable EPC tag. The tag can be peeled off the product and dis-carded as the customer leaves the store, and full shelf notice and information about "smart chips" are available. Metro recently quantified the results of the tests to find process efficiency rose by 12 percent to 17 percent with RFID. Losses and theft were down 11 percent to 18 percent, and merchandise avail-ability increased 9 percent to 14 percent. Does that mean that the pilot was flawless? Of course not. According to Dr. Gerd Wolfram, Metro Project Manager, FutureStore Initiative:

> "We had some technology problems with item-level tagging. Not every item was read on the shelf. There were so-called blind spots (on the on-shelf RFID readers)," he said, with metal and liquid products presenting problems. "There's also a cost factor," he added. The cost of the tags and readers, as well as the engineering and cabling needed to install full supply chain RFID tracking, is prohibitive, even for the bigger retail chains. Item-level tagging—in contrast to case and pallet level—is still a long way off for retailers, Wolfram said—10 to 20 years before individual products will carry the chips.[13]

Another early test conducted by P&G was with Max Factor Lipfinity Lipstick at a Wal-Mart store in Broken Arrow, Oklahoma, for four months in spring 2003. Items and shipping totes were tagged and read as they left P&G and then at key points of the supply chain: Wal-Mart's distribution center, the store's receiving dock, the back room, and finally the shelf. The Intellishelf, built by International Paper, is an RFID/EPC enabled six-shelf application that held all 39 colors of Max Factor Lipfinity lipstick. The shelf was connected to a com-puter software system that included a Web site and handheld computer device (PDA) that notified key Wal-Mart and P&G personnel when:

- The shelf was out of stock, or almost out of stock, so action could be taken to keep it in stock

12. http://www.future-store.org/servlet/PB/-s/o3ltyu1mjmkz1o421k56lr14ti0v0k7/menu/1000154/index.html
13. Best, J. "Metro Retailer to Follow RFID Test with Full Rollout." *CINet news*, September 2, 2004.

- Products were in the wrong place, allowing associates to quickly reorganize the shelf with the products in the right places for the consumer
- A potential theft was in progress, enabling a response before it happened

The test showed that, similar to the results reported by Metro, tagging pallets and cases was much more reliable and accurate than what was experienced at the item level on the shelf. In addition, because of the costs for the tags and the shelf readers, item-level tagging would have a long development cycle before it would be feasible for rollout. After this and other tests at the item level, the industry decided that it should focus solely on pallet- and case-level tagging while continuing to work the issues of technology, benefits definition, and public policy related to item-level tagging.

P&G and Wal-Mart were unfairly represented in a news article as conducting a "secret" test in which we "spied on consumers." Facts missing from those articles were:

- EPC tags were glued to the inside flap of the lipstick packaging so that when the lipstick was removed from the packaging, the tag was discarded as well.
- Wal-Mart gave notice to consumers at the shelf that "electronic merchandise systems" were in place, and during the four-month test, Wal-Mart received no consumer comments or questions.
- Web cameras were in full view and focused on the shelf for remote transmission to P&G and Wal-Mart offices for the purpose of comparing technology "reads" with what could be physically viewed. Any consumer who may have come in view of the camera would have shown us the back of her head or her hand. Even if the consumer had turned around with her back to the shelf and stared directly into the camera, there would be no way to know her identify.
- There were no other EPC readers on the store floor, including none at the cash register, to reveal consumer identity or consumer activity.

Unfortunately, this article had wide distribution without the facts, and one consumer advocacy group requested that consumers boycott Wal-Mart and P&G products. Fortunately, P&G had fewer than 50 consumer complaints about our use of RFID/EPC and the boycott request.

Given this early information, beginning with the research of the Auto-ID Center, P&G has taken a leadership role in the industry to address consumer concerns for public policy. We do this in two ways:

- *Internally* to serve as a role model for other companies
- *Externally* via the EPCglobal Public Policy Steering Committee

Even though P&G and other members of the EPCglobal membership have no plans for item-level implementation for the next five to ten years, we feel consumer concerns for the technology must be addressed *today* so that there will be no reason for concern later when the technology and costs are ready to support item-level EPC.

Internal P&G Protocols

P&G has published and approved from the highest levels the "P&G Position on EPC Usage." We publish this statement on our public Web site,[14] along with questions and answers about the technology and our use of it. What's most important is that we list our test locations, including dates, volumes, and whether use of the technology is at the pallet, case, or item level. Consumers can use a "Contact Us" electronic link to ask additional questions. In addition, procedures and examples have been created for use by project teams that more specifically outline P&G requirements for partnering with retailers in tests that could involve items or cases that might be sold as consumer units.

External P&G Protocols

P&G founded and led the EPC Privacy Officers Forum of manufacturers and retailers, beginning in May 2003. This work culminated in the first set of Guidelines for EPC Usage on Consumer Products being approved by the Auto-ID Center in October 2003.[15] In November 2003, as mentioned earlier, the ownership for commercial rollout of EPC and ongoing administration was transitioned to EPCglobal, a joint venture of the UCC (the originator of Auto-ID Center) and EAN international (equivalent to UCC outside the United States). EPCglobal describes itself as follows:

> EPCglobal is leading the development of industry-driven standards for the Electronic Product Code (EPC) to support the use of Radio Frequency Identification (RFID) in today's fast-moving, information rich trading networks. We are a member-driven organization comprised of leading firms and industries focused on creating global standards for the EPCglobal Network. Our goal is increased visibility and efficiency throughout the supply chain and higher quality information flow between your company and its key trading partners.[16]

14. www.pg.com
15. www.epcglobalinc.com
16. www.epcglobalinc.org

P&G Committee Work

Under the auspices of EPCglobal, Inc., and picking up from the EPC Privacy Officers forum mentioned previously, an EPCglobal Public Policy Steering Committee was formed in March 2004. This is a team focused on the consumer products industry, with 25 members representing major manufacturers, retailers, and trade associations in Europe and North America. The committee is actively recruiting members from Asia and Latin America as well. The mission of the EPCglobal Public Policy Steering Committee is to manage critical EPC public policy issues around the world. I am a member of the EPCglobal Public Policy Steering Committee.

The formation of this team is important because unlike with Internet marketing direct to consumers, one company on its own cannot solve the privacy and public policy issues of EPC implementation. Effective use of RFID in the supply chain is—and must be—a team effort to meet the objectives of retailers and manufacturers to optimize the process. In addition, each party has a role to play in earning consumers' trust of the technology so that everybody wins. If consumers don't trust the technology, they may not buy the product, may not even shop at that store, and the whole premise of improving the supply chain to make consumers happy and sell more product is compromised!

Supply Chain Dependencies

After we look at the general dependency manufacturers and retailers have on each other within the supply chain, I will describe the team effort required to protect consumer privacy. For the EPC network to be efficient, the industry must set standards so that a manufacturer's tag can be recognized and read at all touch points by all retailers with which it does business. Otherwise, manufacturers would have to have separate systems for each retailer, which would be very expensive to maintain. Similarly, a retailer cannot cost effectively manage different tag numbering schemes for various manufacturers and would theoretically have to have various types of reader protocols and internal systems to accommodate nonstandard tags.

Geography presents another challenge for global company operations. Besides unique tag numbering, radio frequency spectrum varies by country. In some cases, governments want to regulate the use of RFID radio wave usage. A lot of work still needs to be done to collaborate and compromise on workable standards across all businesses and countries in the world. It would be inefficient for multinational companies that source product globally (produce in one country and export to many) to have to manage different tag protocols because of differing radio wave frequencies.

Just as standards and solutions for EPC numbering and RFID spectrum are required for optimizing the supply chain, common standards and guidelines for protecting consumer privacy are also required to maintain consumer trust. Manufacturers and retailers are dependent on each other to implement good privacy practices and therefore receive the trust (and continued business) of our common consumers. The Guidelines for EPC Usage were approved by the Auto-ID Center board in November 2003 and adopted by EPCglobal.

Global Guidelines for EPC Usage

The following section includes portions of the currently published (2005) EPCglobal guidelines for EPC usage, which follow the basic privacy tenets of notice, choice, and security. These Guidelines are available in their entirety in Appendix E. We also look at the role and issues EPCglobal, manufacturers, and retailers have and their dependency on each other to protect privacy for consumer items using RFID and EPC tags.

Consumer Notice

> Consumers will be given clear notice of the presence of EPC on products or their packaging. This notice will be given through the use of an EPC logo or identifier on the products or packaging.
> —EPCglobal

The implication of this guideline is that consumers will come to recognize a logo or identifier, signifying that an EPC tag exists, and then know what it means. The challenge to educate consumers to recognize this identifier is stated in a subsequent guideline. The EPCglobal Public Policy Steering Committee has begun to set the notice standards and inform consumers with specific wording on labels attached to packages.

Manufacturers are at the beginning of the supply chain and apply the tags, so it is most logical that they provide the notice on the product (or case packaging if a case could be purchased by a consumer) because they know where it is located. If manufacturers do not provide a notice on the product that a tag exists, then to meet the guidelines, retailers would be obligated to apply labels or stickers on every product as it is put on the shelf. This would take even more time than handling the product with bar codes today, which goes against the objective to optimize the supply chain. Therefore, retailers become dependent on manufacturers to provide the notice on consumer items.

Major issues for manufacturers are size and location of the identifier. It is very important that the identifier be recognizable; however, on some very small products, space on product labeling and graphics is at a premium. For example, ingredient lists, directions, and warnings are also important and required by law in some countries and cannot be shortened or eliminated. For globally sourced product, wording must be in multiple languages—which presents even more of an issue. Managing package "real estate," as it is called, will continue to be an issue as long as the bar code remains in parallel with its EPC cousin. It may take decades until EPC replaces the bar code.

Retailers, being the first "face" to the consumer, are in the best position to protect consumer privacy but also have the largest burden for doing so. As mentioned previously, retailers depend on manufacturers to apply the tag and provide notice that a tag is present. To address consumer issues for health and safety in regard to readers throughout the store, the retailer may have to inform consumers that RFID readers are present. Even if retailers will not be reading EPC tags on the shelf floor, some manufacturers' products will have tags and therefore identifiers because they are required by other retailers. (At some point, after RFID has expanded to the majority of items throughout the supply chain, it will not be cost efficient for a manufacturer to separate product with tags between retailers that are using the technology and those that aren't. To do so would require duplicate inventory of products and therefore higher cost to all.)

Consumer Education

> Consumers will have the opportunity easily to obtain accurate information about EPC and its applications, as well as information about advances in the technology. Companies using EPC tags at the consumer level will cooperate in appropriate ways to familiarise consumers with the EPC logo and to help consumers understand the technology and its benefits. EPCglobal would also act as a forum for both companies and consumers to learn of and address any uses of EPC technology in a manner inconsistent with these Guidelines.
> —EPCglobal

Educating consumers to recognize products with EPC tags will take time and requires a multimedia campaign similar to what was done with ingredient labels. The transition to widespread understanding of this new symbol is being addressed by shelf notices, stickers on cases, and/or customer service notices. Retailers have an added burden to educate their employees about RFID and EPC tags in case a consumer has questions at the store. General education about the technology itself is required to mitigate fears the media has propagated among consumers and other public and governmental bodies. This education campaign is a top priority for the EPCglobal Public Policy Steering Committee—manufacturers, retailers, trade associations, and consumer advocacy groups share responsibility for the education campaign.

Consumer Choice

> Consumers will be informed of the choices that are available to discard or remove or disable EPC tags from the products they acquire. It is anticipated that for most products, the EPC tags would be part of disposable packaging or would be otherwise discardable. EPCglobal, among other supporters of this technology, is committed to finding additional efficient, cost effective and reliable alternatives to further enable consumer choice.
> —EPCglobal

There are really only two feasible choices, given today's technology, that a manufacturer alone can give to a consumer: discard the tag by throwing away the package or don't buy the product. A consumer can discard the tag if a product has secondary packaging that will be removed and thrown away. Examples of secondary packaging are boxes that contain computer printers or lipsticks, plastic and cardboard containers protecting razors, or plastic wrap on DVDs or paper towels. However, many products do not have secondary packaging, so to meet this guideline with today's technology would require either applying a tag that could be "peeled off" the product or not putting a tag on the product. These choices are not sufficient when optimization of the entire supply chain is considered, so other solutions must be created.

Manufacturers' tags that can be easily peeled off by consumers run the risk of premature removal—accidentally in adverse environmental conditions, through heavy handling to put them on the shelf, or by children running through the store aisles, all of which defeat the purpose of efficient supply chain management to track products to the shelf. But the biggest issue is that making a tag large enough to peel off presents the same issue with package real estate mentioned before—something else important to the consumer could be hidden, like instructions or ingredients. In summary, manufacturers alone can provide notice that a tag is present but can offer very limited choices to consumers for disabling, discarding, or deactivating it.

Retailers, with the current state of technology, can offer no other 100 percent satisfactory solutions to consumers beyond that consumers remove or discard the tags themselves, enabled by the manufacturer. While tag protocol has coding to allow the tags to be deactivated or disabled, RFID readers that can both read and deactivate tags are very expensive and are not 100 percent effective. One two-way reader in 2004 cost several thousand dollars; when the cost is multiplied by the number of checkout counters in a store across a country, it can amount to millions of dollar, once again going against the objective of RFID to optimize the supply chain. On the latter point, a retailer that promises to "disable" or deactivate a tag that later is found not to have been deactivated risks losing the trust of the consumer. Making a promise and then reneging on it is worse than not offering it in the first place. The technical community continues to suggest solutions to protect consumers' privacy. However, the solutions must also be transparent—to add even a couple of seconds per item during the checkout process to get consumer consent can add frustration to consumers who want to get quickly in and out of the store. Good solutions will require the collaboration of technology providers, consumer groups, *and* manufacturers and retailers.

Record Use, Retention, and Security

> The Electronic Product Code does not contain, collect or store any personally identifiable information. As with conventional bar code technology, data that is associated with EPC will be collected, used, maintained, stored and protected by the EPCglobal member companies in compliance with all applicable laws. Companies will publish, in compliance with all applicable laws, information on their policies regarding the retention, use and protection of any personally identifiable information associated with EPC use.
> —EPCglobal

In the future, as applications of benefits for consumers that require linking EPC numbers with personally identifiable information go beyond what is done today with bar codes, new forms of notice will be required to tell consumers the choices available to them regarding benefits and deactivation of the EPC tag. For example, the clerk at the cash register may ask if a consumer would like to register for a warranty program for a product. With EPC, the "serial number" or unique identifier for the product is embedded in the EPC numbering scheme, along with the item code and manufacturer's code. All of the consumer's personal information could come from a loyalty card, so by pushing a key on the register, the clerk could register the consumer for the warranty, without filling out a card or form, as is the norm today.

If either manufacturer or retailer does not do its part to protect consumer privacy and consumers believe their privacy has been violated, it reflects poorly on both manufacturer and retailer. This dependency will continue as future benefits provide reasons to combine EPC-tagged purchases with personal information and give consumers a reason to choose to leave the store with active EPC tags.

Because retailers are the ones that scan, collect, and store the final information on purchases, they will also control what data is collected on consumers and is then distributed to the manufacturer. Responsible stewards of the data will ensure that it is properly protected in a secure environment and transferred to manufacturers or other suppliers only with consumer permission.

Conclusions

The Guidelines for EPC Usage were designed for use by EPCglobal members in the consumer products industry. However, sometimes they have been publicly interpreted as applicable for other uses of RFID, which is not always realistic and so will require modifications by other parties outside EPCglobal. For example, choices available to consumers for products bought for individual use can be different from those choices available in the automotive industry or medical/hospital environment. Automobile tires are required by law in the United States to have lot-control tracking, and RFID makes this much more feasible and cost effective. However, a tire tag is not a product a consumer could logically "discard, disable, or remove"—the choices currently given to consumers in a retail environment. In addition, in a hospital, it would not be safe for patients to have the option to remove an identification or locator RFID tag because doing so might allow harm to come to the patients or allow them to harm others. Choices will continue to evolve as the technology advances, but it will take people who can see the positive vision *as well as* be committed to ensuring individual privacy protection to make the use of RFID a win-win proposition. This is a team effort that takes all of us to win.

Although full implementation of item-level tagging is quite a few years off, consumer perception today is that the technology must be controlled before it becomes widespread. However, it is the free use and thinking of the technology that will identify the most benefits for consumers. We need inventors and technologists to continue development so that more choices are available to consumers as well as to manufacturers and retailers in providing those choices.

The EPCglobal Public Policy Committee is chartered with addressing all of these issues and working with technology providers to deal with consumer concerns. RFID technology is the way of the future; therefore, we must and will find solutions to protect consumer privacy throughout the supply chain and still reap the benefits. P&G will continue to play an active role in this endeavor because we believe in the future of the technology for the benefit of consumers, and earning their trust is one key to success.

Chapter 28

CITIZENS: GETTING AT OUR REAL CONCERNS

Robert Ellis Smith[1]
Mikhail Zolikoff[2]

Introduction

Although some concerns about privacy have arisen in the public debate on RFID technology, there are a number of more subtle issues regarding privacy that must still be examined. To understand these possible threats to personal privacy from RFID technology, it is essential to understand privacy itself.

Privacy is not simply the right to keep secrets. If it were, it would be a hollow concept indeed. Nor is privacy synonymous with security. Although safeguarding information—what we know as "security"—is an essential component of protecting privacy, it is not the only part. Security, the set of precautions for protecting systems, is actually one-fifth of what is generally called "privacy" in today's world. Specifically, no laws protect this data, and just because data "is in general not accessible to the general public," as some people claim, that doesn't mean it isn't disclosed occasionally or that it can't be accessed (or linked) by those in authorized positions or by persons with subpoena power.

Privacy includes an expectation that information will be accurate and fair and used for the purposes for which it was originally gathered. Privacy promotes *transparency* of information collection—that is, a means for individuals to know what information is gathered and how it is used. Contemporary concepts of privacy also give people the right to inspect and correct information about themselves and to prevent secondary uses of personal information as well as to

---

1. Robert Ellis Smith is the publisher of *Privacy Journal*.
2. Mikhail Zolikoff is a graduate student at the Gerald R. Ford School of Public Policy, University of Michigan.

expect that the data will be kept secure.[3] With respect to ensuring transparency and a right of access, privacy actually makes security *more* challenging than it would otherwise be. After all, it is easier to secure systems whose existence is kept secret and to which outsiders have no access. Security involves *closing in* systems. Privacy involves *opening up* systems.

In the RFID debate, it is important also to remember that the concept of privacy it is properly applied only to individuals. Privacy is a human right. Individuals, not organizations, have privacy rights.[4] Organizations may want to keep secrets, but that is different from having a right to privacy.

Security is important for protecting data and assets of all kinds, whether or not they pertain to identifiable persons. By contrast, privacy pertains only to data about individuals.

With these definitions of personal privacy in mind, we can narrow the concerns about privacy and RFID technology.

Prior to the Point of Sale

It is difficult to imagine threats to personal privacy from the use of RFID tags before the point of sale. The only interest that citizens have in use of RFID in manufacturing and distribution is realizing cost reductions or increased convenience. The advantages of using the technology to expedite shipment of raw materials; to assemble materials in production; to control inventory during production, distribution, and marketing; to stock retail shelves; and to measure aggregated (anonymous) consumer choices are clear. The advantages here—at least at this point in the development of this innovative technology—seem to outweigh any conceivable privacy threat to individuals. This point should be made clear: Protecting privacy does not require doing away with RFID technology altogether.

After the Point of Sale: Nonconsumer Goods

The potential for misuse of consumer interests occurs after the point of sale. But even in the case of nonconsumer goods, consumers' interests are not

---

3. Smith, R.E. "The Law of Privacy Explained." *Privacy Journal.* 1993. p. 50. These principles constitute what since 1973 has been called the "Code of Fair Information Practice." The discussion in this chapter is confined to the use of RFID in tangible goods.
4. *The Law of Privacy Explained*, p. 48. See also Elder, D.A. *The Law of Privacy.* New York: Clark Boardman. 1991. p. 12. "The almost universal, accepted doctrine," according to David A. Elder, *Privacy Torts.* Eagan MN: West Group. 2002. Secs. 1:3 and 1:4.

threatened by all applications of RFID technology. In fact, the majority of applications foreseeable for the next decade may not threaten individual rights. These applications involve nonconsumer goods, those millions of tangible items made for, sold to, and used by businesses, organizations, and governmental entities. These items might include office equipment, construction materials, industrial and heavy machinery, weaponry, vehicles, or common office supplies. RFID chips offer institutional users the benefits of more efficient tracking and locating of items. Deterioration or aging of items could be monitored. Losses and thefts could potentially be reduced. Institutions could keep track of dangerous or regulated substances in the items that they use and dispose of.

It is hard to imagine a threat to privacy posed by an active RFID chip embedded in a brick. That is true even if the brick is part of a personal residence or purchased by an individual. The identity of the item is not tied to a particular individual, and even if it were, no harm would result.

After the Point of Sale: Consumer Goods

But how about products sold directly to individuals?

Products in this category of "consumer items" are normally used every day, are highly personalized, and often are portable. They include personal hygiene products, food and beverages, apparel, mobile and landline telephones, personal computers, recreation equipment, and reading materials. Even here, use of RFID in some consumer goods will not raise major concerns about privacy. These include products that are temporary or disposable; any possible tracking of their use will be short-lived. Should a lot of energy be expended worrying about a technology that can track the life cycle of a disposable razor? A similar category includes products whose use is innocuous or routine, even if known to strangers. Should a lot of energy be expended worrying about RFID tracking of baby powder or a light bulb or a teapot?

Still for many categories of items, privacy is threatened. The best example of these is clothing. Individuals purchase clothing in the marketplace, they wear it on their persons, it reflects their tastes and their physical size, they leave it behind (or traces of it) as they come and go, and they often possess it for many years. Apparel is as intimate to some persons as their bodies themselves. It reflects their gender and their economic status; it may reflect ethnic group or religious affiliation; it often contains documents identifying the person; it is a matter of personal choice supposedly beyond the reach of government regulation. Any technology that permits remote identification of particular items of clothing and the potential linking of that information to the identity of the individual has huge implications for personal privacy. To understand why, it is necessary to return to definitions of privacy and to understand more sophisticated notions of privacy.

After the Point of Sale: Privacy Interests

Privacy involves far more than the ability to keep personal secrets. It involves the right to make decisions about one's own life without interference from the state or coercive commercial forces. These decisions include selecting the name by which you will be known or the means by which your children will be reared and educated. They include the freedom to jog in a community park or travel to another state, to select recorded music in a shopping mall or attend a political rally. These amenities of life include choice of house of worship or vacation plans, medications and periodicals, family size, and sexual partnerships. They involve a right of autonomy, the right to move freely in our society, the right to come and go. Some judges and privacy specialists have called this personhood.[5]

Three justices of the U.S. Supreme Court recognized this in a 1992 opinion preserving the pro-choice rights in Roe v. Wade. "At the heart of liberty," Associate Justices Sandra Day O'Connor, Anthony Kennedy, and David Souter wrote, "is the right to define one's own concept of existence, of meaning, of the universe, and of the mystery of life. Beliefs about these matters could not define the attributes of personhood were they formed under compulsion of the State."[6]

Actually, this point of view has been part of Supreme Court precedents since 1890, when the court declared, "No right is held more sacred, or is more carefully guarded, by the common law, than the right of every individual to the possession and control of his own person, free from all restraint or interference of others, unless by clear and unquestionable authority of law."[7]

Confidentiality, access to and control of information about oneself, a right to move freely, and a right to make crucial decisions about one's own life—all are implicated by the right to privacy, whether we are speaking of the constitutional

---

5. Smith, R.E. "Ben Franklin's Web Site, Privacy and Curiosity From Plymouth Rock to the Internet." *Privacy Journal*. 2000, 2004. pp. 258, 279.
6. Planned Parenthood of Southeastern Pennsylvania v. Casey, 505 U.S. 833 (1992). We're not implying that use of RFID by a private organization, or even by a governmental body, necessarily constitutes a violation of the Constitution. We are arguing that use of RFID falls within threats to recognized principles of privacy. Some of those principles stem from tort law, others from Constitutional law, and still others from the "Code of Fair Information Practices."
7. Union Pacific Railway Co. v. Botsford, 141 U.S. 250 (1891).

right as recognized by the Supreme Court or of the expectation of privacy that we as citizens take for granted every day.

Justice Harry Blackmun, in a 1986 dissent that three other members of the court agreed with, described these "somewhat distinct, albeit complementary, lines" in the right to privacy: one is "decisional" and the other is "spatial."[8]

First, he said, "[the court] has recognized a privacy interest with reference to certain decisions that are properly for the individual to make. Second, it has recognized a privacy interest with reference to certain places without regard for the particular activities in which the individuals who occupy them are engaged."

"The case before us implicates both the decisional and the spatial aspects of the right to privacy," said Blackmun. So do RFID applications. The right to privacy includes the right to make certain decisions about one's life *and* the right to keep secret certain places where we come and go. RFID applications, to the extent that they include any tracking of the identity of a purchaser and the whereabouts of products, threaten both the decisional and the locational aspects of privacy.

It is the potential for RFID-generated signals to locate items (and therefore to locate users of these items) in which the greatest danger lurks.

Much of the attention on the privacy threats in RFID technology currently focus on the potential for it to amass information about the individuals who purchase or possess certain items. But if we think about it, the greater threat is the probability that this new technology will permit businesses or governmental agencies to monitor uses of products and the physical movements of individuals who possess tagged items.

By the same token, the possibility that the application of RFID technology will result in a massive system for keeping track of the movements of masses of individuals, day in and day out, is not the greatest threat. That is an unlikely scenario, in part because of the business priorities of the corporations fostering RFID development and in part because of the limits of the transmitting technology itself.

What is most threatening about the use of RFID in consumer goods, especially apparel, is that it permits anyone with a reading device to trace the origin of the product—not of the whole population but of targeted individuals. Tracing a product back to its origin, or simply back to the point of purchase, will in most cases permit the linking of that item to the identity of the individual who purchased it.

---

8. Bowers v. Hardwick, 478 U.S. 186 (1986).

"Anyone with a reading device" could be a police investigator examining evidence at a crime scene. It could be an Internal Revenue Service auditor. It could be a misguided market researcher. It could be an obsessed potential father-in-law or a political opponent. It could be a twenty-first-century identity thief. Most threatening, perhaps, it could be a stalker.

Possible Scenarios

One advocate says that RFID chips are "like three-year-olds. All they can say over and over is, 'I'm here,' 'I'm here.'" This will be a stagnant technological revolution if in five years RFID tags can contain no more than locator information! There is every reason to expect, given the investment in this technology and its potential, that the tags will serve several sophisticated functions.

Other advocates insist that the technology has no potential for surveillance because tags cannot be read at long range or because businesses are too competitive and cost conscious to engage in such nastiness. That is only part of the story. RFID will be used by governmental agencies and other users outside the for-profit sector.

Further, the short range does not prevent several forms of tracking. There was an excellent example of this in April 2004. Hewlett-Packard sponsored RFID chips in the shoelaces of all runners in the Boston Marathon—in their shoelaces! As the runners stepped on special mats with transponders along the 26-mile marathon route, their times and places in the race were immediately recorded so that news reporters and spectators could follow their progress on a Web site. This was a voluntary use of RFID but it should demonstrate the potential for surveillance and stalking through RFID, regardless of the limited range of RFID signals and the competitive concerns of businesses using the technology. Voluntary, benign applications of technology like this easily become habitual. Habitual acceptance of tracking like this soon leads to acceptance of less benign applications because we have been conditioned to believe that all RFID applications are harmless.

Here is an example of the distortions that can happen with tracking technologies: A motorist who moved from New York State turned in his E-ZPass, which automatically deducts tolls from his bank account when his vehicle passes through a toll booth. He returned it via UPS.

"Two weeks passed and I received my normal E-ZPass e-mail statement," he told the *New York Times*. "My recently surrendered pass had been used by someone to go from Newark to Exit 18 on the New Jersey Turnpike. I immediately called E-ZPass and informed them that someone had stolen my pass.

"Very calmly, the E-ZPass representative said, 'Sir, your E-ZPass was not stolen; it is in the UPS truck, and every time that truck goes through an E-ZPass toll booth, it is going to register another toll.'"

The same can happen with other forms of RFID and inevitably will. Is it no more than a relatively harmless unintended consequence of technology? Or is it absolutely predictable that aberrations of this kind will occur if RFID chips implanted in clothing, personal computers, recreation equipment, and certain other personal items remain activated once the items are in the hands of end users? As this becomes commonplace, so will the unintended aberrations. This example also shows the damage that can result if law enforcement investigators come to think that an RFID tag automatically can be linked to the person who currently possesses the item.

To the extent that the identity of an item can be linked to the identity of a purchaser, the consequences can affect the welfare of that individual. Imagine if the purchase was made by check, credit card, or debit card. It is easy to make a link. If the purchaser paid by cash but left identifying information for delivery or for warranty protection, it is also easy to make a link. If only the date and place of purchase is determined from the RFID chip, current technology will permit a link to the identity of the individual purchaser with a little sleuthing: There may well be a preserved videotape of the transaction, a fingerprint, or a DNA sample left on transaction documents. This link is possible because RFID technology, unlike bar code and other technologies, permits the electronic labeling *of each unique item*.

That is why the average person will find wearing certain apparel or possessing certain products with an embedded identifying chip a threat to freedom of movement and sense of autonomy. Not because people have something to hide, but because they value their personal liberty.

These are examples of the simple sleuthing that a retail employee, database operator, law enforcement officer, or anyone else with authorized access to the database can accomplish. It is important to remember that no laws on the books prohibit anyone from accessing retail customer data or disallow the public disclosure of that information.

Eliminating the RFID Threats to Privacy

The way to eliminate these fears is simply to deactivate the chips at the point of sale. Manufacturers and retailers, by the time a product moves across the checkout counter, will have realized virtually all of the benefits that they claim for RFID technology. And by deactivating the RFID tag at this point, they will have immediately diffused virtually all of the privacy concerns.

The fact that supporters of RFID technology have not readily agreed to total deactivation is enough to raise suspicions. The claims that after-sale RFID chips will accelerate the processing of returns, warranties, recalls, and consumer research ring hollow. Existing technology, like bar codes, makes these tasks manageable today. When was the last time a hard-nosed businessperson approved the investment of millions of dollars in new technology to make it easier for a customer to return an item or get it repaired?

At this point, all of the perceived advantages of RFID activation after the point of sale, taken together, do not outweigh the actual privacy concerns or even the *potential* privacy concerns. Do the math: Continuing activation diminishes peace of mind and trust in the technology. It limits freedom of action by citizens. It creates fears of tracking and massive data collection.

On the other hand, continuing activation potentially accelerates returns and warranty servicing. It permits tracking of consumers for the life of the product, both by those with a constructive purpose, like law enforcement officers and consumer researchers, and by those with evil intent, like stalkers, terrorists, or curious idlers. The privacy concerns outweigh the values of continuing activation.

Mitigating the Threats: "Continue Activation" as the Default for Nonconsumer Goods

Despite this weighing of the values, there will be manufacturers and retailers that insist on continuing activation. With regard to many products, including those for individual use, continued activation is innocuous, even throughout the life of the product. A private-sector standards-setting body for RFID technology, like EPCglobal, could classify these products.

There are precedents for standards-setting bodies in the private sector: The Uniform Code Council sets standards and classifications for Universal Product Codes (bar codes) on thousands of consumer and nonconsumer products. The International Standard Book Number Agency manages a system of enumerating and classifying millions of book titles; the International Center for the Registration of Serials does the same for periodicals. The National Institute for Standards and Technology within the U.S. government does this in several areas and could be assigned this task. The U.S. Department of Labor classifies the North American Industry Classification System for thousands of job titles and subspecialties (formerly SIC codes).

Right now, EPCglobal, a joint venture of EAN International and the Uniform Code Council, could be designing a process for granting a license to use RFID technology and for classifying consumer and nonconsumer products. This classification could include subcategories of products indicating whether they bear a "continue activation" or "deactivation" default.

It is important to remember that in this proposed system, the designations are *a default only*. A default can be changed, under certain conditions. The standards-setting body could make exceptions when they were warranted. In most categories of products, a consumer should be able to deactivate the RFID chip regardless of the default.

Continued activation as a default is appropriate for all nonconsumer goods. At least that appears to be the case at present. As we learn more about the likely capabilities of the technology, this may change. We may learn in the future, for instance, that a chip embedded in a brick may tell too much about a homeowner. In that case, interested persons could petition the standards-setting body for a change in the default for bricks.

Mitigating the Threats: "Continue Activation" as the Default for Certain Consumer Goods

Continued activation is appropriate, or at least harmless, in consumer products that (1) are temporary or disposable, like razors, milk containers, or pencils; (2) are already regulated or for which registration is currently required, like tobacco, alcoholic beverages, toxic substances, prescription drugs, motor vehicles, and some firearms; (3) are commonly used as weapons or have proven to be the instrumentalities of crimes; (4) have characteristics that create general agreement that the dangers of an identifying tag that includes place and date of purchase is minuscule. Items like garden tools, appliances, hardware, and perhaps furniture fit this category.

Many users of prescription drugs will argue that even though the drugs are currently regulated, the privacy interest is so obvious as to warrant deactivation as the default. In fact, the privacy interest is so obvious that it warrants mandatory deactivation, not merely a default. On the other hand, medical specialists may parry by demonstrating the need for permanent activation. An active chip could potentially be programmed to alert the user to overdoses or conflicting medications; it could aid in returns and renewals. We have to learn more before deciding.

Mitigating the Threats: "Deactivation" as the Default for Sensitive Products

There is an important category of items for which continued activation is inappropriate. The potential threat to personal autonomy and freedom is great enough to warrant deactivation. This category should include any type of garment or footwear because these items are personal to the individual and worn on an individual's person. Any system of identifying the uniqueness of such an item, whether with the knowledge of the individual or not, is so threatening to personal autonomy that it makes deactivation essential, unless the individual for some reason requests activation.

Included in this category in addition to garments should be personal items that people commonly carry on them or that tell something about their health condition, personal tastes, or lifestyle or that tend to lead to identification of an individual. Kosher foods are an example because they tend to tell something about an individual, something that an individual ought to be entitled to reveal only voluntarily. Luggage is an example because an individual commonly carries it from place to place. Over-the-counter medicines or low-sugar foods are examples for a different reason; they tend to reveal health conditions.

Cosmetics and jewelry are still other examples, not because they reveal lifestyle or can lead to identifying a person, but simply because they are commonly carried on one's person. To permit a system of electronic reading of signals from jewelry would have a chilling effect on individuals' freedom of movement. This could lead to abuse. Therefore, consumers are entitled not to have active chips imbedded in jewelry after the point of sale. The same is true of all of the items in this category.

Hybrid Products

As in any classification system, certain products will fail to fit neatly into a category because they may be used for different purposes or have multiple characteristics. The standards-setting body would arbitrate classifications of these hybrids. If the manufacturer or retailer chose not to accept deactivation as the default, it would have to present evidence to the standards-setting group that the value of lifelong activation outweighs the possible threat to privacy and autonomy.

The Baseball Bat Dilemma

But what about products that may defy classification? A baseball bat is a good example. On one level, it is disposable. On another, it is an innocuous product that tells nothing especially revealing about the person who possesses it. On still another level, it has the potential of being used as a deadly weapon.

A police investigator who finds a bloody baseball bat in the vicinity of a homicide will find value in the presence of an embedded chip, in determining the time and place of purchase and the history of manufacturing. There may be a high value in perpetually identifying the item. This reality does not mean that the chips in *all* baseball bats should remain activated forever. The purpose of RFID technology, we are told, is to keep track of manufacturing, marketing, inventory, and consumer usage, not to create footprints in products that aid law enforcement.

Other products fit the "baseball bat" dilemma: rope, belts, fertilizer, toxic substances. A standards-setting body could arbitrate these issues. One effect of this process is that manufacturers and retailers would tend to kill the tags at the point of sale rather than exert the effort to get permission for after-sale activation. After all, what manufacturer of baseball bats wants to argue before a public body that its product is commonly used as a weapon? This process alone would tend to lessen the number of items with permanent activation chips.

Enforcing This Scheme by Law

It is tempting to say that this system of licensing and activation defaults can be enforced by law. Surely, the system can be created by a federal law and made mandatory by a federal law. The law would set up the classifications and perhaps require that individuals have a means to deactivate RFID tags themselves by using handheld devices purchased from electronics stores or by using the deactivation technology made available to them at retail stores. The law would deny governmental access to RFID identifying information except when an agency secured a court order based on probable cause or could show exigent circumstances.

But a law is not the sole means for protecting citizens from potential RFID abuses.

The CALEA Experience

The experience with federal regulation of electronic surveillance—wiretaps—in the 1990s shows also that laws alone are no guarantee of protection. Laws can be changed.

The electronics-surveillance law carefully drafted in 1968 created a scheme for making wiretaps the exception not the rule and provided procedural safeguards for a very small number of wiretaps to be employed by law enforcement for good reasons. The law said that wiretaps could be used in crime investigations only as a last resort and that any extraneous monitoring of innocent phone conversations must be minimized. Both requirements remain part of the law today.[9]

Even with their very limited authority to intercept phone conversations, federal and state investigators discovered how useful wiretaps can be. But by the 1990s, new technologies had made it very difficult for law enforcement to install taps, even if they had court approval to do so. Digital signals, as opposed to the old analog method, were difficult to intercept. More than half the telephone communications traffic by then was data, not human voices.

For two years, the Federal Bureau of Investigation made it one of its highest priorities to get Congress to require telephone companies to redesign their systems to make telephone intercepts feasible. In 1994, it succeeded. Congress approved language that apparently for the first time in American history requires private businesses to redesign their technology to make life easier for law enforcement. The Communications Assistance for Law Enforcement Act of 1994 (CALEA) says: "A telecommunications carrier shall ensure that its equipment, facilities, or services ... are capable of expeditiously isolating and enabling the government, pursuant to a court order or other lawful authorizations, to intercept, to the exclusion of other communications, all wire and electronic communications carried by the carrier..."[10] Telecommunications providers must bear most of the cost of this.

Law enforcement will soon realize the potential of RFID tags in criminal investigations, much as fingerprints, DNA samples, and serial numbers are used today. It is one of the mysteries of the current privacy debate that law enforcement agencies, which would seem to be the great beneficiaries of permanent activation, have been absent from the debate. Have industry advocates told them to lay low? Are they unaware of the capabilities of this new technology?

When law enforcement agencies wake up to this bonanza of potential evidence, it is easy to imagine "the Radio Frequency Identification Assistance for Law Enforcement Act." That would create a requirement that RFID chip manufacturers alter their technology to make it useful to law enforcement, presumably to kill the "kill" capability and perhaps to add useful data to the chips.

Then we will see the lobbying muscle of the RFID crowd. The airline lobbyists succeeded in 2004 in getting the House of Representatives actually to defeat a

---

9. 18 U.S.C. §2510.
10. 18 U.S.C. §2522.

bill that would have required inspection of cargo on passenger airlines.[11] Since the terrorist bombing of the federal building in Oklahoma City in 1995, lobbyists for fertilizer companies have persuaded Congress that they shouldn't be required to include taggants,[12] which act much like rudimentary RFID chips, in fertilizer, even though it is generally agreed that fertilizer is the ingredient of choice for terrorist bombers and the taggants will trace the substance to the place of purchase.

The risk is too great that a law intended to protect citizens' rights can be altered later if law enforcement interests are persuasive or persistent enough or if the shock of a terrorist attack or major crime leads voters to accept almost any limit on their liberties.

On the Other Hand: The Electronic-Funds Experience

In the early 1970s, a group of academics and futurists were given the assignment of assuming that they were data processing advisors to the Soviet secret police (KGB) and then designing a system for maintaining surveillance of all citizens and visitors.[13]

After some study, what was their solution? Devise a real-time system for the electronic transfer of funds, both among financial institutions and between banks and their customers. They found this the cheapest and easiest way to monitor citizens' behavior. (It also permits the custodians of the system to alter their behavior *and* to prevent any or all transactions.) Such a system knows where a participating customer is at any time a transaction is conducted as well as what he or she is buying and the restaurants and hotels that person is patronizing. One of the participants in the study noted, "You can't alleviate any misgivings with legislation against using the system in that fashion."

The scholars had created a scheme identical to our debit card-ATM-credit card system. Yet the system is not employed in the United States as a surveillance system for the government. It is true that law enforcement agencies have used

---

11. The House voted 211–191 on June 18, 2004, to defeat an amendment to the Homeland Security appropriation bill that would have required any cargo security plans to include the inspection of cargo transported on passenger airplanes.
12. Taggants are microscopic substances, such as tiny pieces of multilayered colored plastic, added to a product to indicate its source of manufacture. Fertilizer manufacturers complained that a requirement to add tiny taggants would add weight and expense to their product and perhaps lead to liability if their product were traced to a crime.
13. Recounted by Paul Armer of the Center for Advanced Study in the Behavioral Sciences, Stanford, CA, in *Privacy Journal*, March 1975.

data from automated teller machines and from debit-card transactions to investigate specific crimes, *after the fact*, but they have not been permitted to use the system in real time or to use it for generalized searches. Remarkably, the debit-card network is not even used as a source for individualized marketing data.

There are at least two reasons:

- Government and industry people came to believe that customers would not have agreed to participate in the ATM system if they had suspected that it would be used for law enforcement purposes. Once discovering its secondary uses, bank customers would cease using the debit-card network, according to the common wisdom.
- The efficiencies of the electronic funds transfer system are too important to the industry to risk losing them by allowing the funds system to also be used as a law-enforcement tracking system.

There are two federal laws on the books, both predating the universal acceptance of ATM technology, that would be an impediment to use of the ATM network for surveillance.[14] But standing alone, the laws would not prevent this kind of secondary use. What prevents it is a culture of primary use that the industry and consumers alike have created around the system. Consumers simply came to expect that the debit-card system would be used only to move funds for their convenience, not to track their movements and their use of money.

If that kind of culture of protection grows around RFID technology, consumers will be persuaded to accept the technology. However, that culture will grow only if consumers know about the technology and see benefits to it.

The industry must create the common wisdom that RFID technology will not be a system for surveillance. And it must do so not by saying so, over and over. It must do so by insisting on safeguards in the technology and limitations on applications of the technology.

Mitigating the Threats: Different Frequencies

There is a third way to ensure protections in this cutting-edge technology: devoting research and development to creating two separate frequencies for RFID transponders, one before the point of sale and one after. Already, software supporting RFID chips and permitting different frequencies has been

---

14. The Right to Financial Privacy Act of 1978, 12 U.S.C. §3401. Electronic Funds Transfer Act, 15 U.S.C. §1693c(a)(9).

developed.[15] Regardless of the type of product or the "default," the transmitting frequency of all RFID tags would have to be switched to an alternative frequency when the item is sold in the consumer market. This could be as automatic in cash registers and in credit card sales as the assessment of sales tax. No sale could be complete with this step. It would be illegal to sell an item without changing the frequency.

This technological fix would then permit making fine distinctions in the capabilities of RFID after the point of sale. All post-sale tags would operate on a designated frequency. Deactivating certain tags would then be easier. Reactivating tags, if that is to be an option, would be more feasible. This fix may motivate a third-party market for devices that deactivate tags, either by retailers, individuals, or intermediaries.

The post-sale frequency, by definition, would have a vastly diminished range. There is no justification, after the sale of an item, for the tag to be read electronically from more than a few feet. The post-sale frequency could perhaps be deactivated by inexpensive "zappers" available in the consumer market. But the frequency pre-sale, because of additional layers of protection when it is made, could be deactivated only with expensive, highly sophisticated devices. This scheme overcomes legitimate concerns that the availability of individual deactivators would create a nightmare in the manufacturing cycle. Imagine the havoc wrought by a disgruntled employee running through a manufacturing plant with a handheld zapper. Making the pre-sale frequency or characteristics of the chip highly difficult to sabotage diminishes that risk. Making the post-sale frequency or characteristics of the chip easy to deactivate ("to sabotage") empowers the consumer without disrupting production.

An Additional Consideration: Chip Security

Guaranteeing the security of RFID chips in tangible items is an issue, but it is a security issue, not a privacy issue. By the same token, it is true that you cannot guarantee privacy without first guaranteeing security. Shockingly little attention has been given to the possibilities of counterfeiting chips or altering the data in chips through devious and clever forms of hacking.

Advocates for the technology continue to repeat the mantra: "It's impossible to modify an RFID chip once it is programmed." But the same has been said about computer databases, about electronic mail and automated highway toll systems, about debit cards and credit cards, and about the Internet itself. These claims

---

15. See announcement September 15, 2003, by ThingMagic, Cambridge, MA. See also www.rfid-journal.com, Frequently Asked Questions, "RFID systems use many different frequencies…"

turned out not to be true. "There is no technology that cannot be compromised or subverted," observed the Privacy Commissioner of Canada in 2003."[16]

Can a person with a reader take identifying data from a legitimate RFID tag and then mimic it or re-create a counterfeit version of it? Could a hacker, for instance, alter the tag in a high-price consumer item to persuade a retail store that the item was still covered by a warranty? Someone will find a way.

Since 1991, strangers have co-opted individuals' identities in order to purchase products in their names or gain legitimacy as immigrants. This is called identity theft. We can imagine a new form of identity theft in which a stranger mimics or re-creates the identity of *an object* to frame an individual or to realize financial gain by manipulating the data in an RFID chip.

Too little attention has been given to these security concerns as RFID advocates race to assure us that the new technology is cost effective *and* unassailable to criminal attack or accidental alteration.

There can be no guarantee of privacy protection in RFID development if these security threats are not resolved. On the other hand, privacy precautions that take into account only security will miss the point entirely.

Conclusions

We have proposed a number of strategies related to privacy and RFID technology. They include making deactivation of tags mandatory for a certain category of products, deactivating tags on certain products as a default, enacting a law mandating different levels of deactivation, having a private-sector standards-setting body create the different levels, creating a culture of tolerating only primary uses for RFID tags, creating different frequencies before and after sale, and assuring security of the chips themselves, These are not alternative strategies. To assure confidence in the RFID applications of the future, there will need to be legal protections, a culture of protection, *and* privacy-enhancing innovations in the technology itself.

Principles of privacy ought to be wielded as scalpels, not meat axes. In an age of high technology, it is possible to make fine distinctions both in pubic policy and in the employment of technology, especially in technology that directly

---

16. Testimony of George Radwanski, Privacy Commissioner of Canada, March 18, 2003, before the Parliament Committee on Citizenship and Immigration, Ottawa, quoted in *Privacy Journal*, April 2003, p. 6.

affects individuals. The time is now, when RFID technology is in its infancy, to design systems that make fine distinctions, protecting privacy where it is most threatened and ignoring alarmist scenarios in which privacy is not actually threatened. The time is now to design systems that have enough flexibility to be adapted in the decades ahead to accommodate changing attitudes about personal privacy, about terrorism and crime, and about consumer marketing. Experience shows that today's alarmist scenarios can become tomorrow's reality.

Chapter 29

ACTIVISTS: COMMUNICATING WITH CONSUMERS, SPEAKING TRUTH TO POLICY MAKERS

Beth Givens[1]

Introduction

Radio frequency identification (RFID) is a technology with potentially profound societal implications. Used improperly, RFID has the potential to jeopardize consumer privacy, reduce or eliminate anonymity in situations where anonymity is appropriate, and threaten civil liberties. Yet its development by a worldwide consortium of industry players has proceeded with a minimum of public policy consideration, either by industry itself or by legislative and regulatory bodies.

In this chapter, I summarize the characteristics of RFID that have the potential to threaten privacy and civil liberties and discuss the shortcomings of some of the technology- and education-based solutions that have been proposed. I conclude with a call for a formal technology assessment of RFID, similar in scope to the assessments conducted by the now defunct Congressional Office of Technology Assessment (OTA).

---

1. Beth Givens is founder and director of the Privacy Rights Clearinghouse, a nonprofit consumer information and advocacy organization based in San Diego, California, and established in 1992. www.privacyrights.org.

RFID Characteristics That Threaten Privacy

RFID proponents have described numerous benefits of RFID, from enhancing the shopping experience of consumers to ridding landfills of toxic materials. But RFID is a classic information technology, with respect to its potential downsides. If the technology is implemented irresponsibly, we as a society could experience it not as a wonderful convenience with many social benefits but as a tool for consumer profiling and tracking—in other words, as one part of a larger surveillance infrastructure.

The key question we face is how to shape the implementation of RFID to ensure its socially beneficial aspects and to prevent the negative ones.

RFID has several characteristics that, working together, could threaten privacy and civil liberties:

- The capacity of the Electronic Product Code (EPC) tags, currently at 96 bits, is sufficient to uniquely identify all objects around the globe. We surround ourselves with a huge number of objects—clothes, furniture, appliances, food, automobiles, movie tickets, public transportation passes, credit cards, driver's licenses, passports, and birth certificates. It is conceivable that tagged objects will ultimately be tied to personal identity, thereby enabling the development of a tracking and profiling infrastructure.
- The fact that both tags and their readers can be installed invisibly means that tags can be read from a distance without the individual's knowledge or consent.
- Enormous databases will be developed to track RFID tags from factory floor to point of sale and even beyond.

It is the "beyond" that is of concern to privacy and civil liberties advocates—the item-level data on the tag could be combined with personally identifiable information, either in databases or, when read-write capabilities are more sophisticated and less expensive, on the tags themselves.

When these characteristics are combined, there is the potential to create a comprehensive infrastructure for individual tracking and profiling, resulting in widespread privacy intrusion and the loss of civil liberties.

Proposed Technology-Based Solutions

A variety of technology-based "fixes" have been proposed to mitigate the potential threats. One is to "kill," or permanently deactivate, tags at point of sale. Another is to provide consumers with tag-blocking devices.

However appealing these proposed solutions appear upon first glance, they are not satisfying from a consumer rights perspective. Killing or blocking tags does not address in-store tracking, for example. And some of the strategies for tag killing are inconvenient and are likely to be used by only a small percentage of shoppers.

One proposal is to place tag-deactivation kiosks in stores. Shoppers can visit these kiosks to deactivate tags after paying for goods. However, I question the effectiveness of this approach. How many supermarket shoppers with $100 worth of groceries in the cart and two young children in tow will stop by the kiosk to deactivate their tags? Probably very few.

Another proposal is to offer consumers the choice to kill tags at the point of sale. But merchants could offer incentives or disincentives to encourage their customers to not deactivate tags; for example, they might make it more difficult to return or exchange items that do not have working tags. While some might think this is unlikely, we have only to look at the present-day situation around product returns to realize that it is a real possibility.

One of the top ten complaints we have received at the Privacy Rights Clearinghouse over our 12-year history is about merchants that do not enable shoppers to return items *unless* they provide name, address, phone number, and driver's license number—and that's when the customer *has* the receipt. We have received such complaints for all the top-name retailers, too numerous to list here. Such a scenario could evolve for RFID tags as well.

Disadvantages that I foresee for blocker devices are that they, like killer-kiosks and voluntary deactivation at point of sale, add a burden to consumers. Furthermore, blocker tags fail to protect consumers when products are separated from the tag. And like the kill choice, they create two categories of consumers: Those who take the time and energy to use the blocking device and the larger number for whom deactivation is inconvenient or meaningless.

Is Consumer Education the Answer?

Industry representatives are touting consumer education as an important way to mitigate consumer concerns and instruct individuals on the choices they have to protect their privacy. For me as a consumer educator, this recommendation strikes close to home.

I think it's important to differentiate between a true consumer education campaign and an industry-sponsored public relations campaign. Let me give you one example of the former:

In 1996, I participated in a comprehensive consumer education program for the implementation of Caller ID in California. The message of consumer choice revolved around complete phone number blocking versus selective blocking. The message was developed by a committee composed of representatives of all stakeholders, including consumers, phone industry representatives, and regulatory agency officials (California Public Utilities Commission).

The message was ultimately conveyed via many media outlets (radio, TV, and newspaper public service announcements) and in many languages. By the time Caller ID was launched, a survey found that two-thirds of consumers were aware of their choices. The effort was guided by an academician and communications scholar. Her area of expertise was in the field of public information campaigns.

If a consumer education campaign is launched for RFID, I strongly recommend the adoption of strategies borrowed from such efforts rather than from the realm of public relations campaigns.[2]

Calling for a Technology Assessment

In August 2003, I testified on RFID before a California legislative committee. During my presentation, I characterized the development of RFID as occurring in a "public policy void."[3] To the best of my knowledge, that hearing, convened by California State Senator Debra Bowen, was the first such public policy forum. Since then, a handful of state legislatures have debated bills to partially regulate the implementation of RFID; a U.S. Senator has called for

---

2. To learn more about this consumer education campaign, read Givens, B. "Caller ID: The Case for Consumer Education" (June 18, 1996). www.privacyrights.org/ar/callerid.htm.
3. Givens, B. "RFID and the Public Policy Void." Testimony presented at Joint Committee on Preparing California for the 21st Century, California Legislature, Aug. 18, 2003. www.privacyrights.org/ar/rfidhearing.htm.

Congressional hearings, and the Federal Trade Commission has convened a wide-ranging day-long workshop to hear testimony from industry, government, and consumer representatives. In addition, academic institutions have launched research projects to address the societal implications of RFID.[4]

Further, the industry consortium behind the development of the EPC standard adopted a set of privacy principles in late 2003 to guide the implementation of RFID. This document calls for industry players to voluntarily adopt the principles of consumer notice, consumer choice, consumer education, and record use, retention, and security.[5]

But can these disparate approaches provide sufficient protection, given the potentially profound implications of RFID on privacy and civil liberties? Leaders from privacy and civil liberties organizations from around the world say "No."

In November 2003, nearly 50 consumer, privacy, and civil liberties organizations issued a position statement on RFID. The effort was led by CASPIAN and the Privacy Rights Clearinghouse, joined by EPIC, EFF, the ACLU, and other consumer-oriented organizations.[6]

The position statement calls for the implementation of RFID to be guided by a robust set of Principles of Fair Information Practices, based on the principles adopted in 1980 by the Organisation for Economic Co-operation and Development.[7] We focused on the principles of openness (transparency), purpose specification, collection limitation, accountability, and security safeguards.

---

4. According to the National Conference of State Legislatures, interviewed by Beth Givens in June 2004, the following state legislatures considered RFID legislation in 2003: California, Maryland, Missouri, Utah, and Virginia. In March 2004, U.S. Senator Patrick Leahy called for Congress to hold hearings on RFID. In: Bacheldor, B. "Sen. Leahy Calls on Congress to Study RFID," *Information Week*, March 25, 2004. http://informationweek.securitypipeline .com/news/18402730.

The Federal Trade Commission held a workshop on June 21, 2004. Presentations of the panelists are available at www.ftc.gov/bcp/workshops/rfid/index.htm.

For example, academic research is under way at the University of California Los Angeles (UCLA) and University of California, Berkeley (UCB). See the Web site of the UCLA Center for Embedded Network Sensing at www.cens.ucla.edu. For UCB research, see www.sortingdoor.com. This list is not comprehensive.

5. EPCglobal (www.epcglobalinc.org) was formerly the Auto-ID Center, based at the Massachusetts Institute of Technology. Its "Guidelines on EPC for Consumer Products" are at www.epcglobalinc.org/public_policy/public_policy_guidelines.html.

6. CASPIAN is Consumers Against Supermarket Privacy Invasion and Numbering, founded and directed by Katherine Albrecht. Its Web site is www.nocards.org. The RFID Position Statement appears in Appendix A of this volume and can be found online at www.privacyrights.org/ar /rfidposition.htm.

7. Organisation for Economic Co-operation and Development. www.oecd.org.

The position statement also called for a comprehensive "technology assessment" to be conducted by an impartial body, akin to the assessments conducted by the now-defunct Congressional Office of Technology Assessment. The OTA existed from 1972 to 1995.[8]

Even though industry is moving full-speed ahead with RFID, I continue to believe that such an assessment is vitally important for the responsible implementation of this technology.

Ideally, a technology assessment of RFID would consist of a multidisciplinary analysis covering its expected benefits as well as its adverse impacts. The assessment would include impacts on labor and the economy, environmental and health implications, and of course threats to privacy and civil liberties. It would be overseen by an impartial body. Representatives of all stakeholders including consumers would be involved.

Here are examples of questions that could be addressed by a technology assessment:

- What are RFID's technical strengths? What are its technical limitations? Is RFID effective on all materials? Do its limitations, if any, suggest that it is more appropriate for certain applications than others?
- Are there other technologies that can accomplish much the same benefits as RFID but that are less intrusive? (One alternative technology could be, for example, 2-D bar codes.)
- What are some potential unintended consequences of item-level tagging that could present risk to individuals' privacy and civil liberties? Would law enforcement, for example, adopt surveillance strategies that take advantage of the unique RFID identifiers and their concomitant data base records?

The following questions go to the heart of RFID, particularly the 96-bit standard developed by the industry consortium EPCglobal:

- Can manufacturers and retailers realize many of benefits of RFID without resorting to the placement of a *unique* 96-bit identifier, the EPC, on every consumer product that is released into the marketplace?
- Can a generic RF tag, similar to the standard bar code today, accomplish the same benefits?

---

8. To learn more about the now-defunct U.S. Congressional Office of Technology Assessment and its many studies, visit the archives housed at the Web site of Princeton University: www.wws.princeton.edu/~ota.

For example, one benefit of RFID that has been touted is labeling toxic materials found inside computer products, such as components containing lead and nickel-cadmium. The placement of RFID tags on these components could make it easier to detect and remove them before they are deposited in landfills. Yet such materials do not need the fully unique identifier; they need only a generic tag that emits the code for lead or for nickel-cadmium.

Likewise, there may be many other ways to benefit from the RFID technology without embedding unique identifiers in every product.

The overall goal of an RFID technology assessment would be to enable all concerned, from industry leaders to policymakers, to make informed decisions about the best ways to implement the technology and to maximize the social and economic benefits and prevent or minimize the harmful ones.

One aspect of Congress's former technology assessment process that I find particularly worthy of replication is that each study posed multiple policy scenarios, not just one. Stakeholders could, for example, consider a rollout of the technology with high, moderate, or low amounts of government oversight—and consider the long-term ramifications for each approach.

Conclusions

I strongly recommend that the FTC—or perhaps the National Academies of Science, an academic institution, or even a consortium of several impartial bodies working together—oversee a technology assessment for RFID. It is not too late, and several pieces are already under way separately among industry groups, academic institutions, and consumer organizations.

With that in mind, I close with a statement from U.S. Senator Patrick Leahy who in March 2004 called for Congressional hearings on RFID:

> We need clear communications about the goals, plans, and uses of the technology, so that we can think in advance about the best ways to encourage innovation, while conserving the public's right to privacy.[9]

---

9. Bacheldor, B. "Sen. Leahy Calls on Congress to Study RFID." *Information Week*, March 25, 2004. http://informationweek.securitypipeline.com/news/18402730.

Chapter 30

EXPERIMENTING ON HUMANS USING ALIEN TECHNOLOGY

Peter de Jager[1]

Introduction

The title of this chapter is a 100 percent accurate description of some current RFID implementation strategies. In the following pages, we'll see why it's accurate, why it's a bad approach, and what we can do about it. The problem the RFID industry faces is that there is some strong resistance to a technology that is seen to further invade our privacy. To solve this problem we need to understand what feeds this resistance to change.

I once worked for six months inside a retail clothing store of a major company. I was one of the firm's technologists, and my manager and I decided that I could gain a better understanding of the business and the logistical chain by working at the blunt end for a while.

Every few months we would close down the store to do inventory: just me, my coworkers, 10,000 items, and a handful or two of bar code readers. It was monotonous work: Pull the dress out, scan it, put it back in the rack. Pull the next dress out, scan it, put it back in the rack. And so on until the wee hours of the morning.

---

1. Peter de Jager is a speaker/writer/consultant focused on how we assimilate the change brought about by technology.

After that painful experience, putting RFID in the retail chain sounds like a fine idea to me. Push a button, scan the store. Bingo. Everything counted, inventory done. With that scenario, albeit a simplistic one, RFID has obvious and immediate benefits, but there is a fly in the ointment. RFID technology has the potential to be a double-edged sword.

The Surveillance Society: It's Already Here

RFID privacy activists state that RFID technology can be dangerous. RFID tags can be used for much more than tracking merchandise; specifically, they can track customers once they've bought the merchandise. The activists tell me that I should be concerned about RFID chips in tires because these tires would allow my car to be tracked anywhere in the world.

I live in Toronto where the local toll road, Highway 407, has adopted E-ZPass technology to let people automatically pay their tolls. I have a transponder in my car, so the toll company is already tracking me wherever I drive on the 407. My Electronic Toll Collection (ETC) records are linked to my driver's license and therefore to my address. The company can, through the help of the Canadian government, bill me for driving on the Queen's highway.

What happens if I choose not to carry a transponder in my car? At each on-ramp and exit, there is a camera hooked up to an Optical Character Recognition (OCR) system that can read my license plate as I drive by, and again with the help of government databases, the toll company sends me a bill in the mail.

Hundreds of thousands of people worldwide have decided that the convenience of this type of RFID-based toll system far outweighs the loss of anonymity while they are driving—an anonymity that they really didn't have to begin with.

Despite the benefits of RFID, the perceived ability to "identify at a great distance" raises the hackles of a vocal percentage of the population. They will resist, with all their might, the creation of a society in which instant, pervasive identification is the norm—unless, of course, we make it our business to solve the real problem. That problem, I believe, is resistance based on ignorance and misconceptions. To accomplish that goal, we need to stop making things worse with hyped-up marketing claims and faulty implementation methodologies.

A Trick to Overcome Resistance

What is at the core of resistance to RFID technologies? To answer that question we need a better understanding of what we mean by "resisting change."

In the mid-1990s, I gave up my job as a technologist and started the year2000.com Web site. I became a full-time public speaker, taking it upon myself to warn the civilized world about the dangers of the so-called millennium bug. In some ways, I was to Y2K what Katherine Albrecht (author of Chapter 16, RFID: The Doomsday Scenario) is to RFID and privacy.

As I traveled around the world giving lectures and being interviewed by every conceivable kind of news organization, it became clear to me that the millennium bug was not a technical problem; it, like most problems, was a people problem. The real issue was people's reluctance to accept that a problem existed. In other words, companies were not very good when it came to implementation change.

I met with many managers who realized that while they were responsible for the implementation of the technical change, they lacked the financial support of upper management. They began to realize that their problem wasn't with implementing a technical change but in convincing management that this change was necessary.

Likewise, with RFID, there are the technical challenges of making RFID work and the totally separate challenges of getting people to embrace a new technology. The first is easy; just throw techies, deadlines, and money at the problem. The second is far more difficult and most commonly ignored.

When people implement change in the corporate world, they often fail, and when they fail, they almost always make the same statement: "I would have been able to implement the change if only *they* hadn't resisted.

Alas, resistance to forced change is a part of the change process. If I try to change you, you *will* push back.

We already have RFID examples of this phenomenon. Key chain tags for purchasing gas are encountering very little resistance. The benefits are obvious: fast checkout at the gas station. Consumers are deciding for themselves that RFID in this situation is okay. On the other hand, Wal-Mart's attempts to attach RFID tags to consumer products offer no visible benefit to the consumer, some misconceived downsides, and no discussion with the consumer. Not surprisingly, some consumers are actively resisting the introduction of RFIDs in this situation.

Most books about change management tell us that if we resist change, we are part of the problem. That's utter nonsense. Resisting change that is forced upon us is a survival mechanism. It is one of the most natural things in the world. If you try to sell me something, I had better have a well-developed skill of "resistance" or I'll end up buying everything you offer.

Resistance *is* good. And this is what his happening with the deployment of RFID. The privacy advocates are resisting, and RFID manufacturers and potential users are crying in their beer. They see the privacy advocates as obstacles to the deployment of this glorious RFID technology. They wish that the privacy vanguard would just go away. You can hear their plaintive echoes of "I'd be able to implement RFID, if only *they* didn't resist!" If RFID advocates wish to achieve successful RFID implementations, they must accept that resistance to RFID is an integral part of their implementation problem.

Constituents to Change—and to Stasis

Any proposed change in an organization creates at least two constituencies: one is composed of those who want the change and are poised to benefit from it. The other is that group threatened by change, the people who push back.

In the case of RFID, there are many constituencies. The first are the inventors, creators, and manufacturers of this technology. These are the organizations making the RFID chips and writing RFID middleware and even the marketing consultants who are selling plans on how to deploy RFID within an organization.

The second major constituency is the users. This is Wal-Mart, the U.S. Department of Defense, ExxonMobil, and any other large organization that perceives that it might benefit from deploying this technology.

Then there is the constituency of RFID privacy advocates. They are the key constituents of stasis—perhaps even reversal. They see RFID technology as enabling further attacks on privacy. They're determined to stop it if at all possible or at least to craft the deployment of the technology so that it presents the smallest possible threat to personal privacy.

Besides sparring with each other, these constituencies are engaged in an elaborate courtship for the attention of perhaps the most important major constituency: members of the Fourth Estate, or the media. All of the messages from the first three constituencies get funneled through the media and affect the perceptions of consumers in general.

Consumers are the key. If consumers in general reject RFID technology, the companies that can profit from RFID will have to halt their implementations. The fate of RFID depends on whether the average consumer embraces or rejects the technology.

The manufacturers and the users obviously want consumers who will accept this new technology and won't be overly concerned with privacy issues. The privacy advocates, on the other hand, want the consumers to reject RFID technology because of privacy concerns. RFID isn't just a technical issue; it's a battle for control over how people perceive the technology.

Acceptance of RFID is ultimately in the hands of consumers. If every consumer focused on the threat to personal privacy, real or imagined, posed by RFID, we would never see RFID tags in a supermarket. An example of this resistance based on perception is the vehement and successful rejection of genetically engineered foods in Europe.

Fundamentally, the battle for consumer perception is played out in the media. If RFID is a non-story, consumers will likely accept it. If privacy advocates can persuade the media that RFID is the last step toward the plunge of society into an Orwellian future, consumer RFID technology is dead on arrival.

Right now, because of dreadful marketing on the part of the RFID advocates, the privacy advocates own this story. The reasons for this are simple. The speculation that companies and governments could track individuals via satellite, that a mugger could scan the amount of cash in your pocket, or that I might be able to scan the medications in your medicine cabinet all make for tasty news items. That companies are "secretly" experimenting with RFID technologies makes the news items even juicer.

It is dangerous to make sweeping generalizations about any industry sector, but it is possible to make some generally accurate observations about the media. If your message is newsworthy, the media will relay some variation of it to the public. In general, they will frame your message to suit their needs, not yours.

Journalists share a common basic goal: to write good copy. Whatever appears, be it in a newspaper, on the radio, or on TV, the story must catch the attention of the reader. Otherwise the game is lost, and the public goes elsewhere.

This is why the privacy advocates have been so successful to date with RFID— especially Katherine Albrecht and CASPIAN. They have set the language and created the public agenda. And they have done so incredibly well. Calling RFID tags "spy chips" was a stroke of brilliance. When they labeled Wal-Mart's test of

Lipfinity in Broken Arrow, Oklahoma[2], the "Broken Arrow Affair," they demonstrated their genius in coining a memorable phrase.

These phrases work because they are attention getting and technically accurate. The media embraces these phrases because they contribute directly to good copy and make perfect headlines.

Meanwhile, the RFID industry keeps putting out press releases and having trade shows that inadvertently aid the privacy advocate's agenda. The RFID industry presents a single consistent message: "RFID tags can be read anywhere. We will produce trillions of them. And we will tag everything on the planet."

Every time the privacy advocates read one of these RFID press releases, they are receiving a gift from their opponents. It's like playing chess against somebody who places his queen alone in the middle of the board. You wouldn't warn your opponent that he's making a stupid move and potentially damaging his long-term interests. No, you're thinking, "Goody, goody, goody! Do it again!"

The RFID controversy is an easy story to spin. The lipstick trail was a trial of technology. Procter & Gamble wanted to see how the technology would work. Well, a test is also an experiment, and this test involved human beings. And those humans weren't exactly properly informed about the trial. So it is very easy, and even accurate, to say that this company was "conducting secret experiments on human guinea pigs." It's called hype, and it's the mainstay of any good press release or news headline.

Do you think that a media person, a journalist, would turn away from anything that has to do with a large corporation conducting secret experiments on an unsuspecting consumer? Especially when Procter & Gamble offers nothing to counter it? Is it any wonder we have a growing consumer resistance to RFID?

Privacy Advocates Own This Story

Unless the RFID manufacturers and users adopt a more consumer-friendly approach, they will not be able to roll out RFID. Although we might disagree with some of the privacy concerns, to those holding those concerns, they are legitimate enough to have them protesting and picketing against any company experimenting with RFID.

---

2. For a discussion of the Lipfinity trial in Broken Arrow from the other side, see Chapter 27, P&G: RFID and Privacy in the Supply Chain.

Privacy, Change, and Language

I disagree with the concerns of the anti-RFID privacy advocates because I think their concerns are misplaced. When I am told that somebody might be able to scan me and figure out what kind of underwear I am wearing, my response is, so what? In a society like ours in North America, we consciously go out and buy knock-off Gucci items so that people think we're carrying a Gucci hand-bag. Why should I care if people think I am wearing a particular kind of underwear, a Nike swoosh, or anything else?

But I recognize that my feelings are not universal. In a series of surveys throughout the 1990s, Columbia University Professor of Public Law Alan Westin discovered that American attitudes on privacy fell into three distinct categories:

> These are *Privacy Fundamentalists*, who reject offers of benefits, want only opt-in, and seek legislative privacy rules; *Privacy Uncon-cerned*, who are comfortable giving their information for almost any consumer value; and … *Privacy Pragmatists*. Privacy Pragmatists ask what's the benefit to them, what privacy risks arise, what protections are offered, and do they trust the company or industry to apply those safeguards and to respect their individual choice.[3]

In 2001, Westin reported that the Privacy Fundamentalists made up 25 percent of the population, the Pragmatists made up 63 percent of the population, and the Privacy Unconcerned had dropped from 20 percent in the 1990s to 12 percent. I haven't taken Westin's test, so I don't know if I'm genuinely uncon-cerned or if I'm simply a very pragmatic pragmatist.

Even though I am not a Privacy Fundamentalist, I accept that people who resist change are entitled to their concerns and that unless those concerns are addressed, they will act on them. For example, if I am attempting to bring about a change in an organization such as implementing a new accounting sys-tem and there are concerns about how this change will work, I must address those concerns. If I don't, the resistance against the implementation will increase. I can't ignore these concerns, even if they are totally irrational or based on false assumptions.

---

3. Westin, A. "Opinion Surveys: What Consumers Have To Say About Information Privacy," testimony before the Subcommittee on Commerce, Trade, and Consumer Protection, May 8, 2001, 3:00 pm. Washington, D.C. http://energycommerce.house.gov/107/hearings /05082001Hearing209/Westin309.htm.

This is the key to successful change management. The change advocate is responsible for addressing the resistance to the proposed change. Ignoring, demeaning, or showing disrespect to those resisting the change will *always increase* their determination to resist.

The RFID manufacturers and advocates like Wal-Mart have not only chosen to ignore the privacy advocates and hope their concerns will go away, they have also inadvertently made their position worse by conducting field tests in secret. Secrecy has never succeeded in reducing public concern about any technology. The RFID industry also seems to be totally unaware of the power of a word or a phrase.

Wal-Mart and Proctor & Gamble chose to run the Lipfinity trial in a town named Broken Arrow. Clearly, there was a desire to have the trial in an out-of-the-way place, but Broken Arrow? The phrase Broken Arrow has a preestablished meaning, one already capitalized on by Hollywood. Remember the movie of the same name about nuclear terrorists? When the media found out about the trial, and the media *always* finds out, it was a certainty that they would run with the story. The companies did not have control over the media running the story, but they did have control over the term Broken Arrow. The trial could have—should have—been run somewhere else.

For an even more powerful example of lexigraphical bungling, look to Alien Technology, one of the leading RFID chip manufacturers.

Alien Technology makes the joke on its Web site that the company is "bringing RFID down to earth." But the term "alien" also dangerously ties into the cultural psychosis in North America about alien abductions and embedded chips. While obviously a joke, and amusing to the technologists, the poor choice of the company name makes it far too easy for the media to make sly connections to conspiracy theorists.

RFID technology treads dangerously close in some people's minds to the area of scripture, Revelations, and the "Mark of the Beast." There is a legitimate segment of the consumer base that believes in the mark of the beast. There is no point in disrespecting their perspective. We have to take them into account if we want RFID implementations to succeed.

With these PR gaffs documented, you can now see the source of the title of this chapter. You probably laughed when you first read my choice of title, but the fact that you laughed suggests that the media would latch on to the same connections and have fun with it, to the detriment of RFID implementations. The title is not just good copy: it's accurate.

The RFID industry needs to recognize it has a PR problem on its hands. There are technical and organizational problems associated with any implementation of a new technology. This isn't news. It's also not news that how people react to change is crucial to the success or failure of any technical implementation, yet the RFID industry has both ignored and aggravated those concerns.

How to Make Consumers Demand Change (and RFID)

Every product-level RFID trial to date has had the same problem: there has been no benefit to the consumer. Why shouldn't consumers feel apprehensive about a new technology if the privacy advocates are saying that it's bad news and the consumers themselves get no tangible benefit?

If you are a government policy maker, RFID offers opportunities for you to ingratiate yourself with your constituency. As a result, we're seeing some fairly aggressive anti-RFID legislation beginning to appear. Senator Jarrett Barrios of Massachusetts drafted legislation (SB1834) designed to regulate the use of radio frequency identification technology.

His proposed legislation attempted to implement three core concepts, saying consumers have the right to:

- Know RFID is being used
- Opt out of using the technology at the point of purchase
- Deactivate RFID at the point of purchase

While the RFID industry seems to aggravate the privacy advocates at every turn, it doesn't have to be this way. It could implement relatively easy techniques that would not only decrease resistance but also increase sales at stores that experiment with RFID. If RFID is marketed properly, consumers will demand it. The best proof of this statement is that automatic toll booths and gasoline tags (Speedpass) have been rolled out with little public resistance.

First, a company attempting to implement RFID must offer a discount to consumers willing to purchase RFID-enabled products. Next, it must be absolutely and totally transparent about how it will use the information gained from the RFID technology. It must explain what the technology is, what it can do, and what it can't do. People will line up to see a new technology in action, especially if there is a visible benefit to them.

The best defense against militant privacy advocates is to gain consumer trust. Gain the trust of consumers and they won't feel that they need privacy legislation to protect them from the use of RFID.

Arthur C. Clark said, "Any sufficiently advanced technology is indistinguishable from magic." With this quote in mind, to most people, an RFID tag is magic. While I consider myself a "techie," I lack the detailed knowledge necessary to build an RFID tag. I cannot see how an RFID tag works, so even to a reasonably knowledgeable techie, an RFID is magical. This magic factor poses a real problem for RFID proponents.

Until now, the primary weapon the RFID industry has had to counter the concerns of the privacy advocates is the notion that we can "kill" the tag at the point of purchase. Consumers don't need to worry about chips being embedded in shoes, clothes, or goods, the industry says, because any consumer who doesn't want the chip there can have it killed.

Aside from the time it takes to kill a chip, there's a bigger, more fundamental and nontechnical problem with kill: Consumers cannot determine for themselves if the chip is dead. Remember, the reason consumers have a privacy concern is that they don't trust those trying to distribute RFID chips. So when we tell consumers that we've killed a chip, how do they know that it's really dead? If they don't trust us in the first place, why should they trust us when we say the chip is dead?

Kill technology doesn't work. You can't kill the image of the RFID chip that's in my head. I can't see that the RFID chip in my sneaker is killed. Could it be just sleeping? Perhaps it's waiting for a password to be sent to it after I exit the store?

Kill technology is a dead end because it solves the wrong problem. The problem is trust.

There is a good way to kill an RFID chip: Throw it in a microwave and wait until you see the sparks. Throwing these chips in the microwave, as dangerous as it might be, does work. When I *see* the fireworks inside my microwave, I know that tag is dead.

An alternative to the kill solution is to place all chips on pull-tabs—pull the tab and the chip is physically removed from the consumer product. Or rip off the antenna, if you can convince the consumer public that removing the antenna permanently and irrevocably kills the chip. I want to be able to pull that tab and physically destroy the RFID chip at my leisure—or not. But it should be my choice. And if I pull that tab, I know that the tag is dead.

This is a trust issue. If you are going to kill something, it has to be either a physically visible kill or a simple removal.

Conclusions

Rolling out a new technology means we will encounter resistance. Resistance is normal. But if we choose to ignore the concerns, we are courting disaster. We are courting failed trials. We are courting lost sales. And ultimately, we are courting legislation that will place restrictions on how we can deploy a beneficial technology. Leaving how we can best use a new technology to politicians will guarantee that we shackle the benefits of future innovation.

Placing unique IDs on consumer products readable invisibly at a distance opens up a can of worms that we don't need to open. If we must have an RFID on a product, it should be visible, it should be removable, and it should be breakable.

RFID is not that big a deal. My cats are tagged. My dog is tagged. I have two different gas tags in my pocket. I have a transponder in my car. Who knows what else I have on underneath. It doesn't bother me. It doesn't bother most people.

I'm a member of the Privacy Unconcerned. If you told me that I'm gong to get a discount every time I use a particular credit card, I'm going to use that credit card, even if it is imprinted on my thumb. It doesn't bother me in the least.

I am not the typical consumer. The typical consumer is concerned with the perceived loss of privacy. Address that issue and RFID becomes a corporate asset; ignore that issue and it'll become an albatross around your neck.

Chapter 31

ASIA: BILLIONS AWAKEN TO RFID

Bimal Sareen[1]

Introduction

Asia, home to more than 50 percent of humankind, is waking up to RFID. The continent contains lands of diverse people, cultures, and political systems. India, the world's most populous democracy, is flanked by dictatorships, military states, and kingdoms. China, the world's largest Communist country, has successfully managed to sustain a trade surplus in excess of $100 billion and is rapidly emerging as the world's manufacturing hub.

But the very fact of Asia's cultural, political, and economic diversity makes it unlikely that RFID privacy issues will emerge here as they have in the West. More likely, RFID will be accepted for the value it offers, even as Asian countries learn practical lessons from the U.S. and European experience with the technology.

Factors Separating Western and Asian RFID Experience

The free press in the United States and Europe has played a critical role in shaping the public perception that RFID is a technology with significant privacy implications. Things are very different across Asia, where press freedom is

---

1. Bimal Sareen is passionate about the responsible use and adoption of RFID technology. He is the founder and CEO of AVAANA; an RFID-based technology, innovation, and integration services company. He also serves in a voluntary capacity as the founding president of the RFID Association of India.

not uniform and is generally less free and the concept of social privacy is neither pervasive nor uniform.

Asian culture holds many varying definitions of morality and ethics: What may be morally unacceptable in the United States may not be an issue in many Asian countries and vice versa. Similarly, the definition of business ethics varies by country and, in many cases, within different parts of the same country.

Most Asian countries are part of the developing world. In developing countries, other factors—like basic infrastructural necessities such as clean drinking water, power, affordable communications, housing, and three meals per day—dominate governmental agendas; privacy-related issues are often of secondary concern.

Many Asian governments are not full democracies and have varying levels of freedom. In many cases, governmental sensitivity to personal privacy is lacking. To add to this, a number of governments are "omniscient" and, if they desire, have access to and control of most aspects of private life. This lack of privacy is less of an issue, especially where other important factors like food for the family, clean drinking water, and a good infrastructure for conducting business dominate the priorities.

Privacy: Western Luxury or Western Construct?

On the surface, Western technology seems to keep personal privacy to a minimum. Sophisticated credit card databases follow the effects of U.S. consumers' buying power. Citizens have their purchases tracked while they establish purchasing identities that then become salable public property. Consumer movement could be examined via locatable automated purchases, tollbooths, and even cellular location systems indexed against phone and credit card records.

Meanwhile, privacy-aware consumers fight to protect and keep private their own data: Social Security and credit card numbers, date of birth, mothers' maiden names, biometric data, and other means of personal identification.

In the United States, the government attempts to balance citizens' privacy concerns with the sophisticated lobbying of the credit-card-related industries. Privacy laws have emerged that attempt to limit the information dissemination from these sophisticated databases. However, a nagging insecurity about the lack of privacy, although an acknowledged part of life in the United States, is disconcerting to many.

RFID as the Lightning Rod of Privacy Activists

RFID has come to the forefront during a period of heightened political and economic insecurity. The brilliant minds that conceived and propagated the vision of ubiquitous RFID probably did not anticipate the backlash that this insecurity could muster. The fragmented nature of the RFID industry does not help matters, either. Because of their inability to create a high-profile, sustained media campaign, RFID industry proponents have been unable to provide influential voices of calm.

The U.S. media's sensationalistic portrayal of RFID has resulted in actions unfortunate for responsible RFID industry proponents. Key regulations in various U.S. states are now being proposed as prophylactic measures, without necessarily giving the industry sufficient time to educate and respond effectively.

The Indian Perspective on Personal Privacy

India has been discussing a privacy law for some time now. Currently, items typically associated with an individual's privacy profile—Social Security number, mother's maiden name, date of birth, or fingerprints—are freely handed out by local citizens. In India, many less educated people use a thumbprint in lieu of a signature, and all fingers are printed when people register a land deed at the registrar. Mothers' maiden names are known by most and dates of births are freely provided and are required by most commercial organizations. In fact, those who resist giving their birth date or fingerprint attract glaring stares.

However, as the citizens of this rapidly growing economy are also rapidly increasing in buying power, marketing companies, many of which are unscrupulous in their techniques, are easily extracting information from unsuspecting consumers to build Western-style databases.

In India, the adoption of credit and smart cards is raising awareness today of confidentiality and secure access rather than of privacy. Indians seem to commonly believe that information about oneself is not truly confidential. In a society where personal information in known by many, Indian citizens would like confidential and secure access for their financial transactions first. Personal privacy, although desirable, is usually of lower priority.

India's closest attempt at pro-privacy legislation is The Information Technology Act of 2000. This Act includes provisions that cover unauthorized access and data theft from computers and networks, with a violation penalty of approximately $200,000. At the same time, however, the Act does not have specific provisions for privacy of data.

India's success in the outsourcing business seems to have hastened consideration of an amendment to the Information Technology Act. New clauses will be added that will conform to the European Union's Data Protection Directive and the U.S. Safe Haven privacy norms. Customers in the United States and Europe are having a positive effect and are primary drivers of adopting strict security and confidentiality norms.

Other Asian Countries' Views on Privacy

China has its own concepts of privacy. Although it is likely to consider data protection laws for its global clients through a Personal Data Protection Bill, the personal privacy concerns of Chinese citizens are not expected to emerge as major issues in the near future.

Japan's primary pro-privacy legislation is the 1998 Act for the Protection of Computer Processed Personal Data. The Personal Data Protection Bill, passed in 2003, may also have some applicability to RFID technology deployments. Overall, however, the perception of many in Japan is that privacy laws are discussed mostly in theory but have less impact on actual practice.

South Korea is unique in Asia in that it has a seemingly comprehensive privacy and data protection law. A current (2004) bill aims to ensure that government at all levels can collect private information only with an individual's consent. This bill also specifies that reasons for the collection of personal information must be stated clearly on relevant documents and Web sites. Further, Korea's Ministry of Information and Communication intends to develop regulations targeted to mobile service providers, which have thus far avoided privacy laws for tracking users.

Malaysia has no clear laws that address data privacy, nor does it adhere to international privacy agreements. The situation is similar in countries such as *Indonesia*, *Pakistan*, and *Bangladesh*.

It is important to acknowledge that privacy continues to evolve and is a dynamic concept across Asian countries.

The Extant Paper Database and Electronic Credit Card Systems

In many ways, today's Asian governments and corporations have a level of automation that has not been seen in the United States for more than 25 years. Throughout Asia, there is still an enormous installed base of paper records.

On the other hand, many Asian governments are rushing ahead and could soon surpass the United States in their adoption of information technology and so-called E-governance initiatives, For example, the Indian and Chinese governments are planning to create huge databases to provide smart electronic identity cards to all citizens. When they do, hundreds of millions, if not billions, of consumers will instantly be using RFID-based technology via smart cards on a daily basis.

A Cultural Predisposition to Technology Adoption?

Unlike the United States and its counterparts, most developing countries have not experienced decades of widespread technology adoption and thus lack a comparative "installed base" of technology adoption experience.

Rather, technology adoption has been associated with form, function, and consumer status or "fashion"; more practically, technology is popularly associated with the *application* that it leverages rather than the *technology itself*. As an example, many Asians have adopted cell phones for status, form, and function more rapidly than Americans have. Not only are cell phones "cool," they also provide the voice-to-voice communication that is so important to the cultures of many countries in the region. The status-conscious Asian has also begun to associate adoption of new technologies as a key status differentiator. The actual technology behind the phones is vastly secondary.

Establishment of National Identities

Countries are increasingly using specialized technology as a means to establish and leverage competitive national identities. A recent example is India's unprecedented leadership in outsourcing. This industry, now the talk of the international business world, was nonexistent in the region a few years ago. China has successfully taken a leadership role in low-cost manufacturing. The

Philippines is also aggressively pursuing outsourcing, as are other countries attempting to establish national identities in this space.

The World Trade Organization (WTO), with its combined threat and opportunity for global competition, has also proven to be a strong catalyst for nations to search for and establish new areas of globally competitive differentiation.

A Complex Interplay of Social Systems and Technology

In Asia, the following societal predispositions may assist the rapid adoption of RFID:

- Frequent absence of governmental regulation over new types of technologies and industries
- Lack of a historical installed base around technology
- Cultures that don't necessarily view emerging technologies with suspicion
- Lack of widespread public and governmental debate around adoption of new technologies
- An abundance of nondemocratic governments
- The absence of a prevalent unfettered press

It is fair to assume that the need for identity-based personal privacy is not only a Western privilege but perhaps also a Western construct. Thus, the Asian adoption of RFID technologies will be conditional not on privacy issues but rather on practicality of the applications that RFID enables.

RFID in India

The Asian continent is home to many of the factories and processing plants that assemble the products moving around in the supply chains of Western economies. As a result, many Asian countries are gearing up at the national level to adopt and promote RFID. Thus, it is almost a *fait accompli* that RFID will be successful in the Asian countries that promote it.

India's largest software and outsourcing services companies have established RFID solution departments. RFID startups are emerging. Awareness of RFID technology is increasing, aided by India's unfettered media. Enjoying the global success of its software industry, the government is becoming predisposed to new technologies where India can establish a potential leadership position.

Leading names in outsourcing and software such as Wipro, Infosys, and TCS have established RFID solutions departments, initially to help their retail customers in the United States adopt RFID at the application level. These companies are focusing largely on the software layer and are hoping RFID enables opportunities for enterprise application development similar to the Y2K and the SAP conversions that put the Indian software industry on the global map.

The "insourcing" business is beginning to touch RFID as well. Oat Systems, an RFID middleware provider, has established its software development group in India. AVAANA, a solutions and services provider, has established a unique focus on the hardware layer related to both innovation and integration services.

Currently, India's software-dominant companies are focusing primarily on RFID software and integration services layers. AVAANA is the notable exception at this time, with its focus on hardware and implementation. Multinationals like HP and Sun are beginning to focus on local RFID opportunities, and their international marketing initiatives have begun to reflect that attempt. These multinationals currently perceive their local RFID business as an extension of their professional services businesses and thus are focused on software service. HP recently established a preferred relationship with AVAANA for RFID solutions and expertise.

Increasingly, RFID startups that target the local and global market have begun to emerge. However, because India's venture capital community has yet to wake up to leveraging India's potential in RFID, it has a noticeable dearth of early-stage venture money. Such financial constraints will drive down the number of pure RFID startups, at least for a while.

Local Deployments of RFID in India

Chitale Dairy, a leading dairy in the Indian state of Maharashtra, was an early adopter of RFID-based animal tracking for its cattle. AVAANA is working on locally based solutions for Wal-Mart compliance support, warehouse management, retail, and manufacturing. Other companies are beginning to focus on identifying and developing solutions related to electronic security and access control.

India-based multinational corporations are actively ramping up on RFID technology. They realize that to cater to the global market in any sector, as they do in the software development area, Indian companies need to adopt technologies like RFID that improve efficiency and security . This adoption needs to be done now to be timely.

A Positive Outlook for Retail and Industry

India's retail sector is still closed to foreign investment, which it needs to flourish. However, in anticipation of loosening restrictions in this area, an estimated 300 malls are in various stages of development around the country. With improved infrastructure and premium brands entering these malls, local retail is likely to become a cautious customer of RFID for automated inventory and store management.

Specialty retailers such as Meena Bazaar, which deals in saris, the women's national dress, are considering RFID for point of sale, inventory, and security. Indeed, some industry leaders are beginning to recognize that the benefits of RFID technology are not limited to complying with the Wal-Mart mandate. Practical applications and the ability of the technology to address previously unaddressed pain points are emerging as key drivers of adoption.

For example, a large conglomerate with interests in textiles, paper, and chemicals decided to adopt RFID for its manufacturing enterprise after determining that this technology allowed it to address previously unsolvable issues. At the same time, the conglomerate is now positioned to comply with the Wal-Mart mandate.

E-Governance Applications

Enormous projects related to e-governance applications are now under way and are focused largely on the contactless RFID smart card industry.

The World Bank and the Asian Development Bank (ADB) have recently targeted funding for projects that enable improved governance. The Indian Government is pursuing e-governance as a national agenda item. The goal and belief is that overall economic and social development is enabled by better governance, enabled by technology. With an abundance of technology resources, India is an attractive destination of funds for e-governance. Additional impetus is provided by the political leadership that offers a platform of development to its constituents. The e-governance projects offer an early deployment for RFID across the states of India.

India had over 50 million smart card users by mid-2003. The majority of them were related to e-governance projects regarding welfare, municipal works, and transportation. Other plans in development will require political power to begin implementation. These include the 26 million Employee Provident Fund (EPF) implementations. Indeed, government at the state and local levels is already thinking out of the box to improve efficiencies.

The Delhi Metro uses smart cards in a more traditional manner, but some atypical usage examples exist throughout India. For example, the police department in the southern city of Hyderabad is installing RFID equipment at preselected homes and other locations. The system is designed to track the movement of officers as they perform their patrols by recording each officer's identity and time of arrival at specified locations. The goal of the system is both to monitor the current location of the officers and to enforce discipline. This is in contrast to the earlier system, which was prone to tampering: Police had to get local residents' signatures to prove they were patrolling as planned.

A Strategic Position

At the time of this writing, India is still the preferred destination for business process outsourcing. It is also increasingly becoming a preferred destination for research and development. IBM, Texas Instruments, and Intel have research labs in India that are expanding in scope and presence. The vaunted Indian Institutes of Technology (the IITs), an acknowledged source of some of the best tech brains in the world, are also beginning to take interest in RFID. And attracted to the idea of returning to family in a plentiful job market, Indians working abroad are now starting to return home.

Government Adoption, Not Regulation, for RFID

India's high-growth software and services industry has conformed with and exceeded world-class standards, making it one of the highest-growth industries as a noticeable contributor to the nation's gross domestic product. Many credit this rapid expansion to the "absence" of government regulation and backing of the industry. India's high-growth cable TV industry had operated in the absence of government regulation and assistance. India now has one of the largest cable TV industries in the world, growing from zero to well over 50 million subscribers in just a few years.

The government's awareness of RFID applications is increasing. Recently, the press carried the first noticed public tender for RFID equipment for the transportation industry. Government departments are now evaluating whether they should leverage RFID technology for tracking the enormous number of government paper files. The media also reported that the government is considering adding an RFID tag to Parliament's visitor identification cards.

Overall, if the Indian government stays out and does not regulate the RFID industry—rather, if it becomes a widespread adopter and customer of this technology, as some hope—it could help India establish a leadership worldwide position in this space.

India-Specific RFID Deployment Concerns

RFID initiatives by leading software companies in India is, to a large extent, focused on solving the RFID software application and migration problems of the West. Privacy issues are expected be temporal and will be distractions that reflect Western, rather than any native, concerns. Indian officials wishing to deploy RFID will be far more concerned with cost than with privacy. Additionally, Indian citizens' privacy concerns may well be rapidly overcome as RFID success stories are captured by the press and shared with all.

Affordability, UHF Expectations, and HF Deployment Realities

It is the culture of India to be extremely cost conscious. Most multinationals have had to accept this characteristic and adjust their expectations on pricing and margins. Indian product pricing and margin norms are often different from those in other countries. The affordability of existing RFID solutions will initially limit the size of the available market in India. But once domestic companies offer local, lower-cost RFID solutions, deployment constraints related to affordability should be alleviated.

Another Indian concern about RFID affordability is the price of the tags themselves. For example, the head of the retail premium sari chain is considering deploying RFID in his stores but is disappointed with current pricing. Having been caught up with the highly publicized prospect of the 5-cent tag, or even the 25-cent tag available today, he is now frustrated because he must use a higher-cost tag for his particular merchandise.

The reason is this: Saris are dielectrically complex for RFID. Many saris are intricate and made from diverse materials that include gold, silver, or other metallic threads; glass; precious and semiprecious stones; silks; cotton; and other natural and artificial materials. The lowercost UHF Electronic Product Code tags will not work reliably under these conditions, so a more expensive HF RFID solution had to be developed.

This retail chain owner doesn't care about what RFID frequency is required for his solution, but he does care about the cost. The incremental cost of using HF over standard EPC solutions is quite painful. As a result, the retailer is planning to reuse RFID tags. Such reuse is being designed into the RFID system to make it work properly. (This is not tremendously surprising, as many Indian retailers often reuse disposable EAS [Electronic Article Surveillance] tags, something Western merchants probably would not consider.).

RFIDAI: Enhanced Focus at the National Level

EPCglobal's local arm in India is beginning to take an active role in highlighting RFID and is attempting to highlight the value of EPC. A few software industry leaders and other entrepreneurs have recently established a national association, the RFID Association of India (RFIDAI). RFIDAI is not a standards body like EPC, but a pan-industry association that intends to promote the responsible adoption of RFID in India. In addition to using EPC UHF, RFIDAI recognizes and supports ISO and other frequencies that are ready for more immediate deployment.

RFID in India: Summary

RFID is poised for successful mass deployment in the world's largest democracy. India has the unfettered press, entrepreneurial experience, and technical resources necessary to create a potential powerhouse in RFID technology software and services. The success of the software and cable TV industry notwithstanding, RFID's success in India is likely to be inversely proportional to the regulatory interest of the government. The ideal situation may emerge in which the government acts as a positive catalyst as a promoter and customer without any regulation.

RFID Across Asia

The following sections look at the status of RFID in China, Hong Kong, Japan, South Korea, Malaysia, and Singapore.

China

Government as Driver

China is likely to emerge as a notable RFID player, both in Asia and worldwide. Among other factors, China is a centrally planned Community society, so it seems natural for the Chinese government to use RFID to expand its already deep control over its populace and economy. China has established the

National RFID Tags Standards Working Group, which is dedicated to studying RFID on a national scale.

China also plans to issue its billion-plus citizens a single identification card to be used as a bank card, driver's license, and credit card. This smart card may utilize RFID technology, allowing the government to keep even more data on its citizens. For example, the government is expected to provide a few million scanners so that it can scan the IDs of its citizens. RFID may also be used in healthcare, presumably with the intention of avoiding a reoccurrence of the unfortunate SARS trauma faced by the world. All in all, RFID and related technologies will make it considerably easier for China to automate its records.

The Chinese Manufacturing Advantage

As the world's low-cost manufacturing center, China is the origin of a large number of global supply chains. Two-thirds of the world's top retailers have purchase centers in China. Driven by the Wal-Mart mandate to bring all of its top U.S. suppliers into RFID compliance many companies are pursuing the adoption of RFID in the logistics value chain. And if other nations are not responsive to RFID manufacturing, China may leverage its existing strength in manufacturing and establish a leadership position in manufacturing RFID components.

In general, China is taking RFID very seriously. RFID forums are being held, and national conferences are planned to discuss RFID standards and the industry at large. Many hope that this will hasten China's progress toward broader deployment.

Hong Kong

The Hong Kong Special Administrative Region of China (HKSAR) recently announced a major RFID deployment at the new Hong Kong International Airport: RFID-tagging airport baggage. As a commercial hub and one of the largest regional ports, Hong Kong is a significant window of world trade and logistics to mainland China. HKSAR is poised to establish itself as a leading implementer of RFID. It is already a participant in the U.S. Homeland Security plan for secure shipments to the United States and is implementing RFID as part of this.

Home to many international distribution centers (DCs), HKSAR is a logical environment for rapid RFID adoption. Philips is testing RFID at its HKSAR DC. In addition, the local Retail Technology Industry Association has petitioned the government's Communication and Technology branch to collaborate with EPCglobal to review the importance of RFID for its retail and logistics industries.

Japan

Japan is a leading adopter and driver of new technologies. Currently, the Japanese government and national industries have partnered to promote RFID. The government has already opened the UHF band for unlicensed used by RFID technology as well. Although in Japan UHF has traditionally been used by mobile phones, taxis, and truck communications, the Japanese government has recognized the need for international compliance and has taken this step ahead of other Asian countries. Using the same frequencies as Western markets also spurs the R&D and manufacture of products used in those Western markets. With smart national ID cards issued, Japan's postal department also is proceeding toward adoption.

A Surprising Consumer Pull

As Japan already has efficient supply chains with low shrinkage rates, the benefits offered by RFID are not expected to be as substantial as in countries with less efficient supply chains. On the other hand, because Japanese consumers already use RFID technology via the contactless smart cards prevalent in railway transportation and have had a positive experience, they are surprisingly aware of RFID and seem eager to expand their usage.

The Japanese population is already predisposed to leverage RFID technology in the food industry, with Internet refrigerators and home networks. Tagging food items with information on origin, allergens, freshness, and cooking instructions is a likely outcome of this interest. This initiative fits in well in a country where sushi is automatically replaced if it is out on the table for more than 30 minutes.

RFID usage in Japanese libraries is well established. In addition, booksellers are leveraging RFID to keep track of books and map in-store buying behavior.

An Industry Poised for Expansion

Japanese technology leaders, including Hitachi—inventor of the mu chip that can be embedded in a piece of paper—NEC, and Fujitsu, are already in the RFID business. Their expertise, combined with the momentum provided by Japan's re-emergent economy, indicates that this industry is poised to leverage

RFID technology as a global industry provider. In an age of standardization, however, the question will be whether Japanese industry will follow and drive international standards or continue its historical record of pursuing proprietary standards.

South Korea

South Korea wishes to establish a leadership position in RFID. An industry–government partnership that includes the famous Electronics and Telecommunications Research Institute (ETRI), the Korea Electronics Institute, and the Korea Electronic Payment Forum has also motivated Korea's Ministry of Information and Communication to commit approximately 163 billion won (approximately $163 million) until 2010 to develop and commercialize RFID technology nationwide via its Ubiquitous Sensor Network Plan.

Korean conglomerates such as Samsung and LG are now committed to RFID. Korea is a manufacturing powerhouse, and industry officials anticipate that business associated with the plan will generate 18 trillion won (approximately $18 billion) by 2010 in additional production.

Not to be outdone by Japan, Korea's Ministry of Information and Communication is considering allocating 910–914MHz—traditionally also used for mobile phone service—for RFID, in addition to the 433MHz frequency. This will encourage manufacturers to pursue the expanded markets in the West.

Malaysia

Malaysia is not exempt from the regional competition of the so-called Asian Tigers. Kuala Lumpur Airport is now considering RFID-enabling its baggage system. Following the lead of the EU initiative, the Malaysian government may embed RFID tags in its currency notes and select government documents such as the passport. The Japanese research firm FEC has apparently licensed its intellectual property to the Malaysian government, which in turn has redubbed it the Malaysian Microchip. The Universiti Terbuka Malaysia at Kuala Lumpur (UNITEM) is also using RFID in its library.

Singapore

Singapore already uses RFID technology. Its National Library Board was the first library system adopter of RFID for use with its collection of 10 million books. It also experimented with RFID during the SARS outbreak, and a few hospitals still use the technology to track staff and patients.

Singapore's government has established RFID as a national technology priority and as the next growth area for its ICT industry. It is preparing to take a leadership role in the region. For example, Singapore's Infocom Development Authority (IDA) has devised a S$10 million (about US$6 million) plan for RFID development and deployment. The IDA intends to build five RFID-based supply clusters by 2006 and attract and bring together a variety of providers, including those in logistics, manufacturing, retail, pharmaceutical, and consumer goods, along with infrastructure and technology solution providers.

The IDA has established the Singapore RFID Alliance, with intended links to other similar bodies across Asia. This network will promote continental adoption of RFID and its standards. It will leverage experts in academia, industry, and government to promote RFID and share best practices.

Conclusions

The Asian continent has awakened to the possibilities of RFID. National plans are being devised and national battle lines are being drawn to establish a leadership position in RFID software, applications, services, manufacturing, and policy. Each country seems to want to establish a global leadership position based on its inherent strengths. Because of the state of the technology and the industry's present fragmentation, competitive forays and the creation and consolidation of RFID companies will take place simultaneously as new market and technology leaders emerge.

RFID has become an economic imperative for Asian nations: Asian companies that do business with companies in the West or compete with them will soon have no choice but to understand and adopt RFID for their enterprise. Once Asian countries become adopters, however, it is entirely possible that Asia will enjoy a higher growth rate for the adoption of RFID applications and systems than Western nations will.

Within Asia, RFID growth and development will be focused on its two most populous countries, China and India. Both countries are likely to establish regional, if not worldwide, leadership positions coming from their natural areas of strength: China in hardware and India in software applications and services.

Asia's rate of RFID adoption may be much quicker than some people anticipate. Asian nations, because of their particular cultural and industrial circumstances, will almost certainly make the transition of RFID-based systems far more quickly and with less conflict than will their counterparts in the West. In so doing, they will almost surely create an RFID technology base that takes into account Asian sensibilities and cultural norms rather than Western ones.

Chapter 32

Latin America: Wireless Privacy, Corporations, and the Struggle for Development

Jennifer Torres-Wernicke[1]

Introduction

Privacy, particularly personal privacy as it relates to technology is not an issue in Central America. Privacy issues seem trivial compared with the extreme poverty faced by many people in this part of the world. Talking about privacy in data is a luxury . . . except for large telecom providers.

In the newly deregulated environments of many Central American countries, the privately held large corporation reigns supreme. Telecom providers, unlike their customers, are well hidden behind the "corporate veil." Central America has no legislation that forces telecommunication companies to give out information about usage and traffic statistics, services offered, or any other aspect of wireless technologies. These technologies use the free spectrum to operate, and government agencies—like the Superintendence of Electricity and Telecommunications[2] (SIGET) in El Salvador and the other "Superintendencias" in the Central American region—have no legal right to require the companies to provide that kind of information.

---

1. Jennifer Torres-Wernicke holds a master's degree in Information Systems Management from Carnegie Mellon University and is the CISO of an important Central American financial institution.
2. SIGET is la Superintendencia General de Electricidad y Telecomunicaciones. www.siget.gob.sv

These superintendencies regulate the bandwidth that a company uses and the power it uses for transmission. But they do not regulate the *services* offered in that bandwidth or the *technology* used to provide them. Thus, official data available publicly is very scarce. Various superintendence personnel have told me that for years, efforts have been made to change the law, with little success.

This chapter explains in detail the status of wireless technology in individual Central American countries as it relates to penetration, types of usage, and trends, and it assesses the social implications of all these areas.

An Overview of Wireless Services Penetration into Central America

One could say that wireless services are taking "baby steps" into Central America. Panama, El Salvador, and Costa Rica are the countries where wireless services have developed most widely.

Overall, the use of WiFi technology in public places is very scarce; home usage is increasing more rapidly. Bluetooth has been introduced mainly via mobile phones but still has very low penetration. No projects of significant scale have been done with RFID.

Spread Spectrum

Services using Spread Spectrum have been available since the early 1990s, when the Internet began to penetrate the region. Licensed companies give dedicated access to their clients via any of the three bands designated for the Spread Spectrum. Companies like GBM (an IBM Alliance company), CyTec, and Salnet, as well as many others, provide dedicated connections for clients, a lower-cost solution than laying a fiber optic or cable infrastructure.

Important Central American users of spread spectrum technology are electrical energy generators and meteorology stations, which use this spectrum for measurements and control systems. Some financial-services kiosks and ATMs communicate to their banks via radio antennas, especially those located in remote areas. However, these developments have led rapidly to a saturation of the electromagnetic airwaves in these bandwidths, thus forcing spread spectrum into a technically nonviable solution.

WiFi

Central American WiFi services are in only very early development. In El Salvador, the country with the greatest WiFi penetration, the biggest providers are the Spanish Telefonica and Telemovil, a Salvadorian/U.S. company.

Since 2001, Telemovil has provided WiFi service, via the 802.11b protocol, in public venues. These "hot spots" include the Salvadorian International Airport as well as some malls, hotels, restaurants, coffee shops, and universities. This Salvadorian WiFi service is branded as "e-spots."[3] It is commercialized via pre-paid cards, which have connection time and date limits.

A newer offer in the Salvadorian wireless market is Telefonica's free *Integra para Llevar*[4] (Integra to Go) hotspots service, which began in February 2004. This service is also available in public places like coffee shops, restaurants, malls, hotels, and universities.

RFID

As of this writing, Central America has no significant commercial implementations of RFID. However, the subject is being introduced at important conferences about supply chain logistics. Local industry players are just learning about RFID technology, and some larger companies are beginning to experiment with it.

Wal-Mart has been one of the drivers for the adoption of RFID technology. The retailer required its suppliers to place RFID tags on their merchandise by January 2005. In this region, several manufacturing plants produce products sold at Wal-Mart, so the decision to use RFID tags was already made for them.

The regional bodies in charge of RFID implementation are the EAN[5] organizations in each country (called DIESCO[6] in El Salvador). According to DIESCO, RFID is being used in El Salvador for inventory management by the International Airport and by two of the nation's major retail companies. Similar implementations are being experimented with in other Central American countries.

---

3. http://espot.telemovil.com
4. www.telefonica.com.sv/integra_llevar.html
5. www.ean-int.org
6. DIESCO EAN El Salvador. www.diescoean.com.sv

Pervasiveness of Telecommunications in Central America

This section provides more context on the status of telecommunications technologies in the countries of Central America. Panama is currently the most advanced Central American country in terms of telecommunications infrastructure, probably because of Panama's robust financial industry's requirements for telecommunications services. Panama is followed by El Salvador, Costa Rica, and Guatemala. At the lower end are Honduras and Nicaragua, but this order might change soon as the significant modernization initiatives that are under way take hold.

The following analyzed and summarized information was gathered from the reports "Communications Markets,"[7] "Country Forecasts and Outlooks,"[8] "Latin American Mobile Market: Trends and Developments,"[9] "Links for Comparing the Leading 802.11 Wireless ISPs/WiFi HotSpot Networks & WiMAX Broadband Wireless ISPs in Central America & the Caribbean Islands,"[10] "2004 Telecoms in Latin America—Mexico, Central America and the Caribbean,"[11] and interviews with employees at SIGET.

Panama

In January 2003, Panama opened its telecom industry to competition, which ended Cable & Wireless (C&W) Panama's long monopoly. In May 2004, 19 concessions were awarded for local fixed-line, 28 for domestic long-distance, and 58 for international long-distance services. Sixteen companies are now authorized to offer international long-distance services.

The mobile market is still dominated by BellSouth, the market leader, and by C&W. Both have exclusive concessionary rights to cellular phone services until 2007.

Panama's telecom infrastructure is modern and dependable; it relies on five global submarine fiber optic cables that cross from ocean to ocean through the Panama Canal.

7. "Communications Markets." Pyramid Research, Inc. June 2004.
8. "Country Forecasts and Outlooks." Pyramid Research, Inc. 2004.
9. "Latin American Mobile Market: Trends and Developments" Telecom Trends International (TTI). July 2003. www.researchandmarkets.com/reportinfo.asp?report_id=28381
10. Zelenka, T. "Links for Comparing the Leading 802.11 Wireless ISPs / WiFi HotSpot Networks & WiMAX Broadband Wireless ISPs in Central America & the Caribbean Islands." 2004. www.onelasvegas.com/wireless/Central_America_and_the_Caribbean_wireless_ISPs.html
11. "2004 Telecoms in Latin America - Mexico, Central America and the Caribbean." Published by Paul Budde Communication Pty Ltd., distributed by Global Information Inc. June 2004. www.gii.co.jp/english/pa20454_telecoms_latin_america.html

El Salvador

El Salvador has one of the most liberalized telecom markets in Central America. In 1998, the state-owned telecommunications institution was privatized and opened for competition. Since then, foreign and local operators have invested millions of dollars in the country's telecom infrastructure, which has vastly accelerated its development. Investment has permitted diversity in telecom services. In 2003, a 51 percent equity stake of CTE Telecom was sold to América Móvil; in that same year, the telecommunications industry accounted for 3.09 percent of the Salvadorian GDP.

The Salvadorian fixed-line density is about 11 percent. Mobile telephony overtook fixed-line use in 2002 and had reached over 17 percent penetration by early 2004. The Salvadorian mobile communications market has benefited from the entrance of two new competitors: América Móvil's Personal and Digicel. In addition, this highly deregulated market has promoted speedy introduction of new technologies and services.

Internet usage has grown steadily as well. Coverage is concentrated mostly in the capital, San Salvador, and a few of the bigger cities.

Costa Rica

With its modern and sophisticated telecommunications infrastructure, Costa Rica is the Central American leader in Internet penetration. Oddly, its telecommunications monopoly, the Instituto Costarricense de Electricidad (ICE), is state owned and controls the country's energy and telecommunications markets, making Costa Rica one of the least liberalized telecom markets in Latin America.

This situation will change in the near future, however. Costa Rica's entry into a regional free trade agreement will provide for a free market of data networks and Internet services by January 2006 and free-market cellular services by January 2007.

Guatemala

Guatemala has the largest communications market in Central America, generating over $700 million in communications service revenues in 2001. But unlike the markets in most other countries in the region, Guatemala's fixed communications market has continued to expand impressively in recent years, fueled by the entrance of three companies: TELGUA's SERCOM, Telefonica, and BellSouth. Overall, however, Guatemala has a very low fixed-line density partly because a high percentage of its population lives in rural areas.

With one of the most liberal radio spectrum regulatory models in the world, the Guatemalan mobile telephony market has grown fast. Mobile phones overtook fixed lines in 2001, and today there are more than two mobile customers for every fixed-line customer. In 2003, the leading mobile companies started overlaying their Time Division/Demand Multiple Access (TDMA) networks with Global System for Mobile Communications (GSM) technology.

Honduras

Honduras has the fourth-lowest fixed-line penetration in Latin America, after Haiti, Nicaragua, and Paraguay. While fixed-line services are a state-owned monopoly called Hondutel—full liberalization is scheduled for December 2005—some services and mobile telephony are already open to competition. In 2003, the government began a program called *Telefonía para Todos* (Telephony for All) in order to bring telephony services to all Hondurans. This program has allowed over 30 suboperators to offer fixed service to begin the market's liberalization.

Millicom/Celtel held a monopoly over the Honduran mobile market for eight years, until April 2003, when Megatel entered the market. Hondutel has also received a license that allows it to offer mobile services in 2005.

The Internet has been slow to develop because over half of the population lives below the poverty level, and large areas of the country have no telephone connection at all.

Nicaragua

Nicaragua has the second-lowest fixed-line density in Latin America. However, Enitel Movil and PCS Digital (América Móvil)— launched GSM services in 2002, breaking TCN BellSouth's monopoly . Privatization of the telecom market was completed in January 2004, when the government sold its remaining 49 percent share in the incumbent fixed-line operator Enitel to América Móvil. Local and long-distance markets were slated to be opened for competition by December 2004, but the opening was again postponed and the new target date isunlikely to be met because of a new mandate to establish a replacement regulatory body to manage the segment's liberalization.

It is worthwhile to recognize that in Nicaragua, one of the world's most advanced frequency spectrum management systems is currently in use.

Internet uptake is increasing at a rapid rate, going from 1.3 percent of the population in December 2002 to 3.9 percent in mid-2004, but it is currently restricted by Nicaragua's low fixed-line density.

Privacy Concerns

According to SIGET, no indigenous Central American organizations or groups focus on technology's impact on individual privacy. Personally, I have found that the great majority of Central American citizens, even the highly educated ones, have very little concern about data privacy. Identity theft is virtually unheard of, and people give away sensitive information easily.

However, slowly, the public seems to take information security issues more seriously, particularly as they relate to the financial industry. This increased awareness of security has been fueled by the regulation of some industries, including the financial sector. As part of the security discussion, privacy concerns are just now beginning to have an audience.

Large Central American companies routinely sell their customer information, and nobody seems to complain. Considering that more than half of the region's population lives at extremely low income levels and the other half struggles to have a merely decent living, it's easy to understand why someone might give away private information eagerly in exchange for small benefits.

Old Assumptions in a New World

The ability to violate personal privacy increases with the power and speed of information technologies. Phenomena that contribute to privacy invasion include globalization, compatible information systems, and data that are easily transmissible into different formats. Central American nations are in the early stages of building information systems, and most people are in favor of a unique, government-provided ID number that can identify one individual everywhere. The advantages created through that kind of information link are so impressive and economically attractive that discussing the dangers is frowned upon. Additionally, the cultural assumption is that a person who does not want to share his or her "public" information must be hiding something evil.

In the work environment, an employee would never question an employer's request for personal information. Nor would tracking systems be questioned. Within the business community, there is a growing desire to track mobile computing devices such as laptops with RFID tags throughout the company. The relationship between employee and employer in these countries is such that it generally leaves no room to question the employer's guidelines.

The Author's Experience Living in El Salvador

In El Salvador, it is customary to write your phone number when you sign the vouchers of your purchases. I seldom get away with "forgetting" to write down my number. Sometimes, cashiers ask for some ID as well. This is when attempting to keep private information private becomes a total nightmare: your ID number is written on that same piece of paper, which of course contains your account number instead of asterisks and your phone number. A sophisticated store will even put all your data in a database, right in front of you.

Periodically, I have vowed to move back to paying cash only. But the convenience of plastic is just as alluring in El Salvador as it is in the United States, and I end up using my highly unprivate credit cards again.

My Salvadorian friends, most of whom are engineers with master's degrees obtained in the United States and Europe, often joke with me about privacy issues. The first time I talked to them about the ease of identity theft in El Salvador was when I was trying to stop them from giving away their personal information to the cigarette or liquor commercial campaigns that go from bar to bar gathering personal data.

My friends laughed. They said that identity theft required a level of sophistication far too high for the education level of the average Salvadorian criminal and that any of our thieves, after trying to come up with an identity theft plan, would prefer to take a rifle and steal from some rich family the old fashioned way.

I am sure that some of this is true. But as much as I would like to believe that "our thieves" are old school, unsophisticated, and uneducated, I wonder how long it will take for sophisticated criminal minds to emerge in this privacy-naive place and seize the opportunity. Did I mention that El Salvador and the region have no comprehensive privacy legislation? This region could be heaven for identity theft and similar crimes.

An Overview of Privacy Across Latin America

In 1965, the Organization of American States called for protecting privacy as a human right in the "American Declaration of the Rights and Duties of Man." One would expect to see legislation covering privacy issues in all American countries by now, but the reality varies greatly.

I don't know of any local organization that is worried particularly about privacy issues in the Central American region, but one international organization that is concerned about this issue globally is Privacy International. A survey of Privacy Laws and Developments worldwide[12] revealed that none of the Central American countries seems to have privacy legislation. According to the map[13] published on this report, only Nicaragua has a pending effort to enact a privacy law. However, some South American countries are adopting laws to combat privacy violations that occurred under previous authoritarian regimes. For example, Argentina, Chile, Peru, Colombia, and Brazil now have privacy-protecting legislation.

Without appropriate legislation, international transfer of personal information is prohibited. Argentina was the first Latin American country to obtain this approval from the European Union. Argentina passed the Law for the Protection of Personal Data (LPPD) in 2000 and the Regulation of Privacy Law in 2001. This legislation, however, is primarily a result of Argentina's strong economic and business relations with Europe.[14]

In 1996, Brazil passed a bill promoting privacy of personal data in conformance with the OECD's "Guidelines for the Protection of Privacy and the Transborder Flows of Personal Data,"[15] which affects both public and private records. In addition to the standard prohibitions against unfair gathering and use of personal data, the bill entitles every citizen to access his or her data; correct, supplement or eliminate it; and even be informed that such data exists. Brazil also punishes insertion of false data into information systems with a prison sentence of two to 12 years and detention from three months to two years[16] for those who make unauthorized alterations of information systems data.

---

12. "Privacy and Human Rights, 2003." Electronic Privacy Information Center and Privacy International, First edition 2003. www.privacyinternational.org/survey/phr2003
13. www.privacyinternational.org/survey/dpmap.jpg
14. www.privacyinternational.org/survey/phr2003/countries/argentina.htm
15. OECD "Guidelines for the Protection of Privacy and the Transborder Flows of Personal Data" 23 September 1980. www.oecd.org/document/18/0,2340,en_2649_34255_1815186_1_1_1_1,00.html
16. www.privacyinternational.org/survey/phr2003/countries/brazil.htm

The Colombian government, because of terrorism concerns, is trying to restrict privacy rights in terrorist cases so that it can intercept or record communications without a court order. The private sector has neither a law nor a legal framework to protect data. However, initiatives now exist to create legislation that complies with international data protection principles. Although Colombia signed both the American Convention on Human Rights and the United Nations International Covenant on Civil and Political Rights,[17] as in the Central American countries, Colombian legislation hasn't kept up with technology advances.

In Peru, the president has the authority to remove privacy rights in a "state of emergency." This tactic has been used frequently in the past, most recently in May 2003, during widespread strikes by farmers, judiciary workers, and teachers. Peru has also signed the American Convention on Human Rights.[18]

A Word on the U.S.-Mexican Border

The U.S.-Mexican border is an area of increased surveillance these days. Mexican authorities regularly perform security inspections of the homes in areas bordering the United States. In the United States, a biometric facial features recognition system is being used to identify the commuters who are allowed entrance to the country. This system records driver's licenses, vehicle registration numbers, and passport status. Every time a commuter crosses the border, this information goes to a database and checks the immigration status of this individual. Mexico has not adopted the OECD.[19]

In May 2003, after the FOIA requests initiated by the Electronic Privacy Information Center (EPIC, www.epic.org), it was brought to light that ChoicePoint, the leading provider of public record information for law enforcement and other government agencies, was selling public registries of Latin American countries (e.g., Argentina, Brazil, Colombia, Costa Rica, and Mexico) to the American immigration law enforcement agency. The transfer of personal information is strictly legislated in Argentina, and according to Privacy International, it is about to be legislated in Colombia, Costa Rica, and Mexico. As a result, several Latin American countries started investigations into the legality of the transfer of such information.

---

17. www.privacyinternational.org/survey/phr2003/countries/colombia.htm
18. www.privacyinternational.org/survey/phr2003/countries/peru.htm
19. www.privacyinternational.org/survey/phr2003/countries/mexico.htm

What About the United States?

Many sophisticated readers of this chapter may shake their heads at the short-sightedness and naiveté of Central Americans. But look closer: Many Americans are beginning to give out more information to the government in the interests of national security. While I believe that the critics of this trend in the United States are beginning to carry a larger influence, many U.S. citizens follow the same line of thought as their Central American counterparts. It's not a small amount of money they're after, but a perceived small amount of security after 9/11. Americans often accept privacy violation for safety or other benefits in return.

Conclusions: Privacy, Poverty, and the Future

Recently, I heard that there are still families in Central America surviving on less than $1 per day. Those families, usually with five or more members, live in huts made out of cardboard and leaves. When this is your reality and the reality of many of your compatriots, your priorities are bound to be different. Gaining something, however small, in exchange for giving away your personal information negates any risk to personal privacy. What is privacy, anyway, if you own nothing and have no power? Only through economic and social progress will this cycle change.

I believe the Central American people must be educated about how to protect their privacy. They must acknowledge that technology is becoming more and more ubiquitous in their lives and that today, and increasingly in the coming decade, information and communications technologies are a major force that drives development and social progress worldwide.

I want to end by emphasizing how important it is for Central American countries to watch and learn about privacy legislation from their more developed neighbors. Third-world nations replicate to a large extent from first-world nations, and the United States and the countries of Europe must serve as a firm model for privacy legislation, mechanism of oversight, and enforcement to provide necessary privacy protection for all.

APPENDIXES

POSITION STATEMENT ON THE USE OF RFID ON CONSUMER PRODUCTS

November 20, 2003
Available at www.spychips.com and www.privacyrights.org

Issued by:
Consumers Against Supermarket Privacy Invasion and Numbering (CASPIAN)
Privacy Rights Clearinghouse
American Civil Liberties Union (ACLU)
Electronic Frontier Foundation (EFF)
Electronic Privacy Information Center (EPIC)
Junkbusters
Meyda Online
PrivacyActivism

Endorsed by:
American Council on Consumer Awareness, Inc.
Association Electronique Libre (AEL)
Austrian Association for Internet Users
Grayson Barber, First Amendment Attorney and Privacy Advocate
British Columbia Civil Liberties Association
Canadian Internet Policy and Public Interest Clinic (CIPPIC)
Center for Democracy and Technology (CDT)
Citizens' Council on Health Care
Computer Professionals for Social Responsibility (CPSR)
Consumer Action
Consumer Assistance Council
Consumer Project on Technology

Deutsche Vereinigung für Datenschutz e.V. (DVD)
Electronic Frontier Canada
Electronic Frontier Finland
Electronic Frontiers Australia
European Digital Rights
FoeBuD e.V., Big Brother Awards Germany
Forum Computer Professionals for Peace and Social Responsibility (FIfF)
Foundation for Information Policy Research
Simson Garfinkel, Author, Database Nation
Edward Hasbrouck, Author, The Practical Nomad
Kriptopolis
Liberty U.K.
Massachusetts Consumers' Coalition
National Association of Consumer Agency Associates (NACAA)
NoTags.co.uk
Option Consommateurs
Privacy International
Privacy Times
Private Citizen, Inc.
Privaterra
Public Interest Advocacy Centre
Quintessenz
Statewatch
Virginia Rezmierski, Ph.D.
World Privacy Forum

Introduction

Radio frequency identification (RFID) is an item-tagging technology with profound societal implications. Used improperly, RFID has the potential to jeopardize consumer privacy, reduce or eliminate purchasing anonymity, and threaten civil liberties.

As organizations and individuals committed to the protection of privacy and civil liberties, we have come together to issue this statement on the deployment of RFID in the consumer environment. In the following pages, we describe the technology and its uses, define the risks, and discuss potential public policy approaches to mitigate the problems we raise.

RFID tags are tiny computer chips connected to miniature antennae that can be affixed to physical objects. In the most commonly touted applications of RFID, the microchip contains an Electronic Product Code (EPC) with sufficient capacity to provide unique identifiers for all items produced worldwide.

When an RFID reader emits a radio signal, tags in the vicinity respond by transmitting their stored data to the reader. With passive (batteryless) RFID tags, read range can vary from less than an inch to 20–30 feet, while active (self-powered) tags can have a much longer read range. Typically, the data is sent to a distributed computing system involved in, perhaps, supply chain management or inventory control.

Threats to Privacy and Civil Liberties

While there are beneficial uses of RFID, some attributes of the technology could be deployed in ways that threaten privacy and civil liberties:

- Hidden placement of tags. RFID tags can be embedded into or onto objects and documents without the knowledge of the individual who obtains those items. As radio waves travel easily and silently through fabric, plastic, and other materials, it is possible to read RFID tags sewn into clothing or affixed to objects contained in purses, shopping bags, suitcases, and more.
- Unique identifiers for all objects worldwide. The Electronic Product Code potentially enables every object on earth to have its own unique ID. The use of unique ID numbers could lead to the creation of a global item registration system in which every physical object is identified and linked to its purchaser or owner at the point of sale or transfer.
- Massive data aggregation. RFID deployment requires the creation of massive databases containing unique tag data. These records could be linked with personal identifying data, especially as computer memory and processing capacities expand.
- Hidden readers. Tags can be read from a distance, not restricted to line of sight, by readers that can be incorporated invisibly into nearly any environment where human beings or items congregate. RFID readers have already been experimentally embedded into floor tiles, woven into carpeting and floor mats, hidden in doorways, and seamlessly incorporated into retail shelving and counters, making it virtually impossible for a consumer to know when or if he or she was being "scanned."
- Individual tracking and profiling. If personal identity were linked with unique RFID tag numbers, individuals could be profiled and tracked without their knowledge or consent. For example, a tag embedded in a shoe could serve as a de facto identifier for the person wearing it. Even if item-level information remains generic, identifying items people wear or carry could associate them with, for example, particular events like political rallies.

Framework of RFID Rights and Responsibilities

This framework respects businesses' interest in tracking products in the supply chain, but emphasizes individuals' rights to not be tracked within stores and after products are purchased. To mitigate the potential harmful consequences of RFID to individuals and to society, we recommend a three-part framework. First, RFID must undergo a formal technology assessment, and RFID tags should not be affixed to individual consumer products until such assessment takes place. Second, RFID implementation must be guided by Principles of Fair Information Practice. Third, certain uses of RFID should be flatly prohibited.

Technology assessment

RFID must be subject to a formal technology assessment process, sponsored by a neutral entity, perhaps similar to the model established by the now defunct Congressional Office of Technology Assessment. The process must be multi-disciplinary, involving all stakeholders, including consumers.

Principles of Fair Information Practice

RFID technology and its implementation must be guided by strong principles of fair information practices (FIPs). The eight-part Privacy Guidelines of the Organisation for Economic Co-operation and Development (OECD) provides a useful model (www.oecd.org). We agree that the following minimum guidelines, based in part on these principles, must be adhered to while the larger assessment of RFID's societal implications takes place:

- Openness, or transparency. RFID users must make public their policies and practices involving the use and maintenance of RFID systems, and there should be no secret databases. Individuals have a right to know when products or items in the retail environment contain RFID tags or readers. They also have the right to know the technical specifications of those devices. Labeling must be clearly displayed and easily understood. Any tag reading that occurs in the retail environment must be transparent to all parties. There should be no tag reading in secret.
- Purpose specification. RFID users must give notice of the purposes for which tags and readers are used.
- Collection limitation. The collection of information should be limited to that which is necessary for the purpose at hand.

- Accountability. RFID users are responsible for implementation of this technology and the associated data. RFID users should be legally responsible for complying with the principles. An accountability mechanism must be established. There must be entities in both industry and government to whom individuals can complain when these provisions have been violated
- Security Safeguards. There must be security and integrity in transmission, databases, and system access. These should be verified by outside, third-party, publicly disclosed assessment.

RFID Practices That Should Be Flatly Prohibited:

- Merchants must be prohibited from forcing or coercing customers into accepting live or dormant RFID tags in the products they buy.
- There should be no prohibition on individuals to detect RFID tags and readers and disable tags on items in their possession.
- RFID must not be used to track individuals absent informed and written consent of the data subject. Human tracking is inappropriate, either directly or indirectly, through clothing, consumer goods, or other items.
- RFID should never be employed in a fashion to eliminate or reduce anonymity. For instance, RFID should not be incorporated into currency.

Acceptable Uses of RFID

We have identified several examples of "acceptable" uses of RFID in which consumer-citizens are not subjected to "live" RFID tags and their attendant risks:

- Tracking of pharmaceuticals from the point of manufacture to the point of dispensing. RFID tags could help ensure that these critical goods are not counterfeit, that they are handled properly, and that they are dispensed appropriately. RFID tags contained on or in the pharmaceutical containers should be physically removed or permanently disabled before being sold to consumers.
- Tracking of manufactured goods from the point of manufacture to the location where they will be shelved for sale. RFID tags could help ensure that products are not lost or stolen as they move through the supply chain. The tags could also ensure that the goods are handled

appropriately. Tags should be confined to the outside of product packaging (not embedded in the packaging) and be permanently destroyed before consumers interact with them in the store.

▪ Detection of items containing toxic substances when they are delivered to the landfill. For example, when a personal computer is brought to the landfill, a short-range RFID tag could communicate toxic content to a reader at the landfill. It is important to underscore that uses such as the landfill example do not require—and should not entail—item-level unique identifiers. Rather, the RFID tag would emit a generic recycling or waste disposal message.

Conclusions

We are requesting manufacturers and retailers to agree to a voluntary moratorium on the item-level RFID tagging of consumer items until a formal technology assessment process involving all stakeholders, including consumers, can take place. Further, the development of this technology must be guided by a strong set of Principles of Fair Information Practice, ensuring that meaningful consumer control is built into the implementation of RFID. Finally, some uses of RFID technology are inappropriate in a free society and should be flatly prohibited. Society should not wait for a crisis involving RFID before exerting oversight.

Although not examined in this position paper, we must also grapple with the civil liberties implications of governmental adoption of RFID. The Department of Defense has issued an RFID mandate to its suppliers, schools, and libraries that have begun implementing RFID, the European Union and the Japanese government have considered the use of RFID in currency, and British law enforcement has expressed an interest in using RFID as an investigative tool. As an open democratic society, we must adopt a strong policy framework based on Principles of Fair Information Practice to guide governmental implementation of RFID.

###

RFID Position Paper

Attachment 1
November 14, 2003

Limitations of RFID Technology: Myths Debunked

The following technological limitations have been proposed as reasons why consumers should not be concerned about RFID deployment at this time. We address each perceived limitation in turn, and explain why, in themselves, these limitations cannot be relied upon as adequate consumer protection from the risks outlined above.

1. Read-Range Distances Are Not Sufficient to Allow for Consumer Surveillance

RFID tags have varying read ranges depending on their antenna size, transmission frequency, and whether they are passive or active. Some passive RFID tags have read ranges of less than one inch. Other RFID tags can be read at distances of 20 feet or more. Active RFID tags theoretically have very long ranges. Currently, most RFID tags envisioned for consumer products are passive with read ranges of under 5 feet.

Contrary to some assertions, tags with shorter read ranges are not necessarily less effective for tracking human beings or items associated with them. In fact, in some cases, a shorter read range can be more powerful. For example, if there were an interest in tracking individuals through their shoes as they come within range of a floor reader, a two-inch read range would be preferable to a two-foot read range. Such a short range would help minimize interference with other tags in the vicinity and help ensure the capture of only the pertinent tag positioned directly on the reader.

2. Reader Devices Not Prevalent Enough to Enable Seamless Human Tracking

The developers of RFID technology envision a world where RFID readers form a "pervasive global network" It does not take a ubiquitous reader network to track objects or the people associated with them. For example, automobiles traveling up and down Interstate 95 can be tracked without placing RFID readers every few feet. They need only be positioned at the entrance and exit ramps. Similarly, to track an individual's whereabouts in a given town, it is not necessary to position a reader device every ten feet in that town as long as readers are present at strategic locations such as building entrances.

3. Limited Information Contained on Tags

Some RFID proponents defend the technology by pointing out that the tags associated with most consumer products will contain only a serial number. However, the number can actually be used as a reference number that corresponds to information contained on one or more Internet-connected databases. This means that the data associated with that number is theoretically unlimited and can be augmented as new information is collected.

For example, when a consumer purchases a product with an EPC-compliant RFID tag, information about the consumer who purchased it could be added to the database automatically. Additional information could be logged in the file as the consumer goes about her business: "Entered the Atlanta courthouse at 12:32 PM." "At Mobil gas station at 2:14 PM." Such data could be accessed by anyone with access to such a database, whether authorized or not.

4. Passive Tags Cannot Be Tracked by Satellite

The passive RFID tags envisioned for most consumer products do not have their own power, meaning they must be activated and queried by nearby reader devices. Thus, by themselves, passive tags do not have the ability to communicate via satellites.

However, the information contained on passive RFID tags could be picked up by ambient reader devices that in turn transmit their presence and location to satellites. Such technology has already been used to track the real-time location of products being shipped on moving vehicles through the North American supply chain.

In addition, active RFID tags with their own power source can be enabled with direct satellite transmitting capability. At the present time, such tags are far too expensive to be used on most consumer products, but this use is not inconceivable as technology advances and prices fall.

5. High Cost of Tags Makes Them Prohibitive for Wide-Scale Deployment

RFID developers point to the "high cost" of RFID tags as a way to assuage consumer fears about the power of such tags. However, as technology improves and prices fall, we predict that more and more consumer products will carry tags and that those tags will become smaller and more sophisticated. We predict that the trend will follow the trends of other technical products like computers and calculators.

###

RFID Position Paper

Attachment 2
November 14, 2003

A Critique of Proposed Industry Solutions

The RFID industry has suggested a variety of solutions to address the dangers posed by RFID tagging of consumer products. Among them are killing the tags at point of sale, the use of "blocker tags," and the "closed system." We examine each strategy in turn.

Killing Tags at Point of Sale

Some have proposed that the RFID tag problem could be solved by killing the tags at the point of sale, rendering them inoperable. There are several reasons we do not believe this approach alone and without other protections will adequately protect consumer privacy:

Killing tags after purchase does not address in-store tracking of consumers.

To date, nearly all consumer privacy invasion associated with RFID tagging of consumer products has occurred in the retail environment, long before consumers reached the checkout counter where chips could be killed. Examples include:

- Close-up photographs were taken of consumers as they picked up RFID-tagged packages of Gillette razor products from store shelves equipped with Auto-ID Center "smart shelf" technology.[1]
- A video camera trained on a Wal-Mart cosmetics shelf in Oklahoma enabled distant Procter & Gamble executives to observe unknowing customers as they interacted with RFID-tagged lipsticks.[2]
- Plans are under way to tag books and magazines with RFID devices to allow detailed in-store observation of people browsing reading materials.[3] This potential was demonstrated at the Tokyo International Book Fair 2003. According to Japan's *Nikkei Electronic News*, "By placing tag

---

1. Gilbert, A. "Cutting edge 'smart shelf' test ends." *CNET News*. August 22, 2003. Available online at http://news.com.com/2100-1008_3-5067253.html.
2. Wolinsky, H. "P&G, Wal-Mart store did secret test of RFID." The *Chicago Sun Times*. November 10, 2003. Available online at www.suntimes.com/output/lifestyles/cst-nws-spy09.html.
3. Chai, W. "Tags track Japanese shoppers." *CNET News*. May 8, 2003. Available online at http://news.zdnet.co.uk/business/0,39020645,2134438,00.htm.

readers on the shelves of bookstores, the new system allows booksellers to gain information such as the range of books a shopper has browsed, how many times a particular title was picked up and even the length of time spent flipping through each book."

We recognize the need for stores to control shoplifting and make general assessments to enhance operations. However, monitoring and recording the detailed behaviors of consumers without their consent, even if only within the store, violates Principles of Fair Information Practice.

Tags can appear to be "killed" when they are really "asleep" and can be reactivated.

Some RFID tags have a "dormant" or "sleep" state that could be set, making it appear to the average consumer that the tag had been killed. It would be possible for retailers and others to claim to have killed a tag when in reality they had simply rendered it dormant. It would be possible to later reactivate and read such a dormant tag.

The tag killing option could be easily halted by government directive.

It would take very little for a security threat or a change in governmental policies to remove the kill-tag option. If RFID tags are allowed to become ubiquitous in consumer products, removing the kill option could enable the instant creation of a surveillance society.

Retailers might offer incentives or disincentives to consumers to encourage them to leave tags active.

Consumers wishing to kill tags could be required to perform additional steps or undergo burdensome procedures, such as waiting in line for a "killer kiosk"[4] and then being required to kill the tags themselves. Consumers who choose to kill the tags might not enjoy the same discounts or benefits as other consumers or might not be allowed the same return policies. In many areas of privacy law, this retailer incentive is recognized, and there are legislative prohibitions against inducing the consumer to waive their privacy rights.[5]

The creation of two classes of consumers.

If killing tags requires conscious effort on the part of consumers, many will fail to do so out of fear, ignorance, or lack of time. Many will choose not to kill the tags if

---

4. "NCR Prototype Kiosk Kills Rfid Tags." *RFID Journal*, September 25, 2003.
   Available online at http://www.rfidjournal.com/article/articleview/585/1/1/.
5. See, for example, California SB 27, codified at 1798.84 (a).

doing so is inconvenient. (The current killer kiosk requires loading one item at a time, a lengthy and time consuming process.) This would create two classes of consumers: those who "care enough" to kill the RFID tags in their products and those who don't. Being a member of either class could have negative ramifications.

Blocker Tags

RFID blocker tags are electronic devices that should theoretically disrupt the transmission of all or select information contained on RFID tags. The proposed blocker tag might be embedded in a shopping bag, purse, or watch that is carried or worn near tags with information consumers want blocked.[6]

Blocker tags are still theoretical.

According to our understanding, the blocker tag does not yet exist. Until a blocker tag is built and tested, there is no way to know how effective it will be and whether it can be technically defeated.

The presence of blocker tags could encourage the widespread deployment of RFID tags.

The blocker tag might encourage the proliferation of RFID devices by giving consumers a false sense of security. While the proposed invention is an ingenious idea, it's one that could be banned or be underutilized if consumers become complacent. It's also possible that such an electronic device could be technically defeated either purposefully or because it stops functioning naturally.

The blocker tag could be banned by government directive or store policy.

Consumers could lose the right to use blocker tag devices if the government deems that knowing what people are wearing or carrying is necessary for national security. They might disallow the devices altogether or name selective spaces in which blocker tags would be disallowed. It is not inconceivable to imagine a ban on such devices in airports or public buildings, for example.

Retail stores might ban blocker tags if they believe the tags might be used to circumvent security measures or if they believe knowing details about consumers is valuable in their marketing efforts.

Once RFID tags and readers are ubiquitous in the environment, a full or partial ban on a privacy device like the blocker tag would leave consumers exposed and vulnerable to privacy invasion.

---

6. "RFID Blocker Tags Developed." Silicon.com. August 28, 2003. Available online at www.silicon .com/software/applications/0,39024653,10005771,00.htm.

Blocker devices add a burden to consumers.

A blocker tag shifts the burden of protecting privacy away from the manufacturers and retailers and places it on the shoulders of consumers. In addition,
busy consumers might forget to carry blocker devices or forget to implement
them, especially if additional steps are required to make them effective.

A blocker tag fails to protect consumers once products are separated from the blocker tag.

Blocker tags theoretically work only when they are close to the items they are
designed to "conceal" from RFID reader devices. Once items are out of the
range of the blocking device, consumers would be exposed and vulnerable to
privacy invasion. For example, a consumer might buy a sweater and feel that
the information on the embedded RFID tag is unexposed because she is carrying it home in a bag impregnated with a blocker device. However, once she
removes that sweater from the bag and wears it in range of a reader device,
information from that tag could be gleaned.

The creation of two classes of consumers.

Like the kill tag feature, blocker tags will also likely create two classes of consumers: those who block tags and those who do not.

Closed System

Industry proponents argue that when RFID applications are confined to closed
systems, the data is only accessible to those within the system and those with a
government mandate (perhaps via legislation such as the Communications
Access to Law Enforcement Act (CALEA)). Therefore, they argue, society-
wide profiling and tracking are not likely. An example of a current closed application is RFID in libraries. *The Grapes of Wrath* in Library X has a different
code than the same book in Library Y.

Whereas today RFID applications are confined to closed systems, there will be
great incentives to standardize product-level tagging. Publishers, for example,
may someday ship books to libraries and bookstores with writable tags. Each
copy of *The Grapes of Wrath* will contain a portion of its EPC code that is the
same on every other copy. The library will be able to customize the remainder
of the code to suit its own inventory control purposes.

Even if closed systems remain closed, their lack of transparency makes them
troubling from a privacy perspective. Because details about closed systems

might not be readily available, consumers could have difficulty obtaining the information necessary to assess privacy risks and protect themselves.

Conclusion

We appreciate that industry proponents are making an effort to address consumer privacy and civil liberties concerns associated with RFID technology. However, while we believe the proposed solutions are offered in the proper spirit, they provide inadequate protection. Until appropriate solutions are developed and agreed upon, we believe it is improper to subject consumers to the dangers of RFID technology through item-level consumer product tagging.

###

Signers
Katherine Albrecht, Director, CASPIAN, www.spychips.com
    Media Inquiries: (877) 287-5854, kma@nocards.org
Liz McIntyre, Director of Communications, CASPIAN, www.nocards.org
    Media Inquiries: (877) 287-5854, liz@nocards.org
Beth Givens, Director, Privacy Rights Clearinghouse, www.privacyrights.org
    Media Inquiries: (619) 298-3396, bgivens@privacyrights.org
Lee Tien, Senior Staff Attorney, Electronic Frontier Foundation, www.eff.org
    Media Inquiries: (415) 436-9333 x 102, tien@eff.org
Jason Catlett, President and Founder, Junkbusters Corp., www.junkbusters.com
    Media Inquiries: catlett@junkbusters.com
Deborah Pierce, Executive Director, PrivacyActivism, www.privacyactivism.org
    Media Inquiries: (415) 225-1730
Barry Steinhardt, Director of the Technology and Liberty Program, American Civil
    Liberties Union (ACLU), www.aclu.org
Kenneth J. Benner, President, American Council on Consumer Awareness, Inc.,
    accaus@aol.com
Alexandre Dulaunoy, President, Association Electronique Libre (AEL), www.ael.be
Peter Kuhm, International Relations, Austrian Alliance for Internet Users (VIBE!AT),
    www.vibe.at
Grayson Barber, First Amendment Attorney and Privacy Advocate,
    www.graysonbarber.com
Murray Mollard, Executive Director, British Columbia Civil Liberties Association,
    www.bccla.org
Philippa Lawson, Executive Director, Canadian Internet Policy and Public Interest
    Clinic (CIPPIC)
Paula Bruening, Staff Counsel, Center for Democracy and Technology, www.cdt.org
Twila Brase, President, Citizens' Council on Health Care, www.cchconline.org
Susan Evoy, Managing Director, Computer Professionals for Social Responsibility,
    www.cpsr.org
Ken McEldowney, Executive Director, Consumer Action, www.consumer-action.org

Paul Schrader, Executive Director, Consumer Assistance Council,
   www.consumercouncil.com
James Love, Director, Consumer Project on Technology, www.cptech.org
Dr. Thilo Weichert, President, Deutsche Vereinigung für Datenschutz e.V. (DVD),
   www.aktiv.org/DVD/
Richard S. Rosenberg, Vice-president, Electronic Frontier Canada, www.efc.ca
Ville Oksanen, Vice Chairman, Electronic Frontier Finland, www.effi.org
Irene Graham, Executive Director, Electronic Frontiers Australia, www.efa.org.au
Chris Hoofnagle, Associate Director, Electronic Privacy Information Center (EPIC),
   www.epic.org
Maurice Wessling, President, European Digital Rights, www.edri.org
Rena Tangens & padeluun, FoeBuD e.V., Big Brother Awards Germany,
   www.foebud.org, www.bigbrotherawards.de
Hans-Joerg Kreowski, Chair, Forum Computer Professionals for Peace and Social
   Responsibility (FIfF), http://iug.uni-paderborn.de/fiff
Ian Brown, Director, Foundation for Information Policy Research, www.fipr.org
Simson Garfinkel, Author, Database Nation
Edward Hasbrouck, Author, The Practical Nomad, travel writer and consumer advocate
   www.hasbrouck.org
Jose Manuel Gomez, Editor, KRIPTOPOLIS, www.kriptopolis.com
Caoilfhionn Gallagher, Senior Researcher, Liberty U.K.,
   www.liberty-human-rights.org.uk
Paul J. Schlaver, Chair, Massachusetts Consumers' Coalition, www.massconsumers.org
Jonathan D. Abolins, Author, "Meyda Online: Info Security, Privacy, and Liberties
   Studies," www.meydaonline.com
Kathleen Thuner, President, National Association of Consumer Agency Associates
   (NACAA), www.nacaanet.org
Chris McDermott, Director, NoTags.co.uk, www.NoTags.co.uk
Jacques St Amant, Privacy Analyst, Option Consommateurs,
   www.option-consommateurs.org
Simon Davies, Director, Privacy International, www.privacyinternational.org
Evan Hendricks, Editor, Privacy Times, www.privacytimes.com
Robert Bulmash, President & Founder, Private Citizen, Inc., www.privatecitizen.com
Robert Guerra, Managing Director, Privaterra, www.privaterra.org
John Lawford, Research Analyst, Public Interest Advocacy Centre, www.piac.ca
Rene Pfeiffer, Board Member, Quintessenz, www.quintessenz.org
Tony Bunyan, Director, Statewatch, www.statewatch.org
Virginia Rezmierski, Ph.D., Ann Arbor, Michigan
Pam Dixon, Executive Director, World Privacy Forum,
   www.worldprivacyforum.org

###

RFID and the Construction of Privacy: Why Mandatory Kill Is Necessary

Position Paper: The Electronic Frontier Foundation

Social norms are the unwritten rules of society. They're an important prompt for taking such ordinary privacy precautions as putting a personal letter in an envelope or closing the door to a telephone booth. No law, placard, or label warns us to seal the envelope or close the door; it's clear that our privacy is in peril, and our experience in society tells us exactly what to do about it.

Equally important, our legal norms of privacy are often built on the foundation of these same privacy precautions. It's no accident that Katz v. United States, the Supreme Court case holding that telephone conversations are constitutionally private, expressly referred to the fact that Mr. Katz had closed the phone booth door.[1]

But what happens to privacy in the absence of social norms? More specifically, what happens when technology outpaces the development of the precautions and norms necessary to protect privacy?

---

1. Katz v. United States, 389 U.S. 347, 352 (1967) ("One who occupies [a telephone booth], shuts the door behind him, and pays the toll that permits him to place a call is surely entitled to assume that the words he utters into the mouthpiece will not be broadcast to the world. To read the Constitution more narrowly is to ignore the vital role that the public telephone has come to play in private communication.").

Below, we argue that technologies that threaten privacy should be designed and deployed with a substantial buffer zone—a meaningful "breathing space"[2] to ensure that rapid technological advances do not overtake the development of privacy norms. To establish such a breathing space for radio frequency identification (RFID) technology, EFF advocates at this initial stage of deployment mandatory "kill" for RFIDs in consumer goods at the point of sale. Other proposed solutions, however well-intended, place too much of a knowledge and resource burden on an uninformed public and run the risk of building social norms around the technology that do not protect privacy.

How RFIDs Threaten Privacy

Imagine a world where your every possession—clothes, books, cash—could be precisely and invisibly tracked. In this world, your purchases, movements, and activities could be monitored in real time or recorded for posterity by marketers or the government, all without your knowledge or consent. This is the world that pervasive RFID technology could lead to.

Touted as the new bar code, RFID technology uses tiny computer chips and antennas integrated into "tags" that hold data—at the very least, a *unique* ID number—and report that data when triggered by an electronic scanner, thus enabling the automatic identification and tracking of tagged goods. RFIDs the size of a grain of rice can be near-invisibly embedded in the sweater you're wearing, the disposable razor you've bought, or the book you've just checked out of the library.

But RFID tags are far more than bar codes. Depending on the radio frequency being used, they can be read from up to 25 feet away, even through packaging, and multiple tags can be read simultaneously. Also, bar codes only identify a class of products. To an RFID scanner, every "tagged" bottle of Coke is different. It's no surprise that one U.S. senator has called RFIDs "barcodes on steroids."[3]

This makes RFIDs a convenient way to track inventory.[4] It also makes them a convenient way to do something less benign: track people and their activities through their RFID-tagged belongings.

---

2. The notion of "breathing space" for rights comes from free speech jurisprudence. Because First Amendment freedoms are "delicate and vulnerable, as well as supremely precious in our society," they "need breathing space to survive." NAACP v. Button, 371 U.S. 415, 433 (1963). The same is true for privacy rights in an age of rapid technological change.
3. Remarks of Senator Patrick Leahy, The Dawn of Micro Monitoring: Its Promise and Its Challenges to Privacy and Security, Conference on Video Surveillance: Legal and Technological Challenges, Georgetown University Law Center, Mar. 23, 2004, <http://leahy.senate.gov /press/200403/032304.html>.

The obvious problem is that most current RFID tags are promiscuous and stealthy. They'll talk to any compatible scanner, and you won't even know about it. Thus, unless RFIDs are killed or removed when you buy something, you're as easily tracked as the things you buy. It won't happen right away, because neither RFIDs nor RFID sensors are socially pervasive today. But we shouldn't wait until it happens before we act to protect our privacy.

Privacy Is Socially Constructed

Privacy isn't simply something we have; we normally produce privacy by taking physical actions like closing a door. Thinking about privacy as something we construct or produce makes it clear that having the necessary knowledge and resources is critical. We won't take steps to protect our privacy unless we're aware that it is at risk. Once we've decided to take these steps, we need the resources to do it.

We take for granted the availability of envelopes for sending snail mail. But encryption for email isn't nearly as readily available. To make matters worse, most people aren't even aware that encryption is necessary for safeguarding email privacy, and relatively few know how to use it. As such, the technology is out of step with contemporary privacy norms as codified by law; we may have a legal "reasonable expectation" that email is private, but in fact it is not.

In the case of RFID technology, the problem is greatly exacerbated. But few people know that RFID tags exist, much less pose an imminent threat to personal privacy. There is no requirement to warn people that items they have purchased are embedded with RFIDs, and no currently available resources, technical or otherwise, for dealing with them. Moreover, the law doesn't yet recognize much of an expectation of privacy in our daily movements.[5]

---

4. Wal-Mart has set a January 2005 deadline for its top product suppliers to ship RFID-tagged pallets and cases to some RFID-savvy distribution centers. See Carol Sliwa and Bob Brewin, RFID Tests Wal-Mart Suppliers, *Computerworld* (Apr. 5, 2004), http://www.computerworld.com/softwaretopics/erp/story/0,10801,91913,00.html>. The U.S. Department of Defense has announced that it wants all of its suppliers to put RFID tags on "the lowest possible part, case or pallet packaging" by January 2005. Matthew French, For DOD logistics, tags are it!, *Federal Computer Week* (Nov. 3, 2003), http://www.fcw.com/fcw/articles/2003/1103/pol-dod-11-03-03.asp.

5. A recent Washington state case involving GPS tracking bucks this trend. In State v. Jackson, 76 P.3d 217 (2003), the state supreme court found that police need a search warrant to install a tracking device on a suspect's car, noting that "the device can provide a detailed record of travel to doctors' offices, banks, gambling casinos, tanning salons, places of worship, political party meetings, bars, grocery stores, exercise gyms, places where children are dropped off for school, play, or day care, the upper scale restaurant and the fast food restaurant, the strip club, the opera, the baseball game, the 'wrong' side of town, the family planning clinic, the labor rally. In this age, vehicles are used to take people to a vast number of places that can reveal preferences, alignments, associations, personal ails and foibles. The GPS tracking devices record all of these travels, and thus can provide a detailed picture of one's life." Id. at 223.

In the complete absence of a common pool of knowledge about RFID technology, the privacy-invasive practices it enables, and the resources necessary to combat abuse, the only effective stopgap measure for protecting privacy is a "default setting," or architecture, that supports it.

The architecture or design of a system or device is enormously powerful; a single design choice can automatically make it easier or more difficult for you to protect privacy. Even a "soft" default has the power to shift significant knowledge and resource burdens to the user. For this reason, an email program with built-in encryption is infinitely more congenial to privacy production than an email program that will encrypt only if the user adds an encryption plug-in.

Given this reality, the appropriate default for RFID tags right now is mandatory kill. A set of fair information practices that includes the option to kill is merely a soft default. Only when people have a reasonable basis for making such a decision will the choice be meaningful.

Privacy Is Hard to Protect

Privacy violations aren't like most other harms for the simple reason that they're usually invisible. There's no way to know that your phone is being tapped, or that a federal agent is looking at your bank records. Even if you do discover that your privacy has been invaded, as in a case of identity theft, you may never find out precisely how, when, or where the breach occurred. This makes privacy very hard to protect.

On the Internet, protecting privacy is even harder. The technical architecture is such that people regularly and unknowingly shed information about themselves. Surfing the Web feels anonymous, but unless you take specific steps to mask your computer's Internet Protocol (IP) address, each visit to a new website announces your unique address to whomever is "listening."

RFID technology recreates this architecture in the physical world. Today's RFID tags are "dumb," indiscriminately broadcasting whatever information they contain to any compatible sensor. And just as on the Internet, all of this happens without your knowledge or consent. There is no way for you to know when a stranger is reading the title of the book in your briefcase, or, for that matter, a mugger taking silent inventory of your shopping bag to see whether it's worth stealing.

By requiring that RFIDs are disabled or removed at the point of sale, we can build a wall between the back rooms of inventory control and the world of everyday life, where none of us can yet contemplate the full scope and range of potential privacy abuses. Otherwise, we adopt an architecture that heavily favors those "in-the-know," who will be free to develop ways to exploit it at the expense of an unwitting public.

Technologies Have Careers, or Trajectories

One major difficulty with assessing the privacy risks of a particular technology is that technology evolves. And in the age of computers and the Internet, technology evolves quickly, and, often, unpredictably.

We can reasonably expect RFIDs to get smaller, cheaper, smarter, and more flexible. We can also expect the unexpected—that people will find uses for RFID technology that we cannot now imagine. Its current capabilities are just that—current. Privacy safeguards based on these capabilities are therefore likely to become obsolete, and this makes the RFID industry's argument that the technology is privacy-safe especially flimsy.

An FAQ by the Auto-ID Center claims that RFIDs are safe because they (currently) have three privacy-protective characteristics: "physical protection," provided by a short read-range; "data protection," relying on the fact that an RFID tag's unique code is meaningless without access to a back-end database; and "personal protection," afforded because RFID data identifies only objects, not the people who carry them.[6]

But none of these so-called protections holds up under scrutiny. Read-range is a red herring; we pass through doorways all the time, and RFID sensors can be built into gates and doorways. There's no reason why a dedicated attacker wouldn't get physically close to a target; surveillance using RFID scanners is stealthy. And the RFID industry is already working on extending read-range.

The fact that an attacker needs access to a back-end database to make sense of RFID data is of equally small comfort. The implicit assumption is that outsiders pose the privacy threat. But the attacker could be an insider with ready access to the database, such as a store employee. Whether or not that's the case, no computer system is completely secure. If the information in the database

---

6. See "Auto-ID Center Q&A," <http://www.eff.org/Privacy/Surveillance/RFID/autoidfaq.php>.

will unlock the value of RFID data, we should expect that intruders will find security holes or develop the tools to bypass security.[7]

Finally, the Auto-ID Center's promise of "personal protection" is carefully qualified, and for good reason. While associating individuals with RFID-embedded objects isn't an explicit function of the system linking RFID codes to product information, it "may be done"—and, in all likelihood, will be done— "by other computer systems." The data aggregation industry is a multi-billion dollar business, and there is nothing special about RFID data that would prevent interested parties from combining it with other pieces of information to build personal profiles or determine identity.[8]

It's a waste of time and energy to try to counter the industry's disingenuous arguments that RFID tracking systems are already safe-by-design. They're not. The architecture was designed specifically to favor the tracker, not the object (or person) tracked. Until the industry develops smarter tags and systems that allow us easily and reliably to know what information our RFID-tagged items are broadcasting to the world, and to control that broadcasting as we see fit, mandatory kill is the only safe option.

Technologies Cannot Be Evaluated in Isolation

Combining technologies with one another, or combining them in the context of other social changes, can create privacy-hostile synergies. Direct marketing, for example, took off only after the U.S. Post Office introduced the zip code.[9] Marketers simply combined census data that had been stripped of identifying details with directory information, creating massive databases of nuanced information about American households. Data-mining techniques, meanwhile, only became truly useful and widespread with increased capacity for data storage and processing.

The RFID industry asks us to believe that the information that today's RFID tags indiscriminately broadcast will stay within some fictional closed universe

---

7. For example, in early 2003 hackers got the names, social security numbers, and email addresses of about 59,000 people from a computer system at the University of Texas. The breach could have been prevented with basic precautions. Associated Press, "University Social Security numbers stolen online," *USA Today* (Mar. 9, 2003) <http://www.usatoday.com /tech/news/computersecurity/2003-03-06-texas-hack_x.htm>.

8. For instance, Experian maintains a database of credit information on about 205 million people and demographic information on about 215 million consumers in 110 million U.S. households. [http://www.experian.com/corporate/factsheet.html] ChoicePoint, Inc. has 14 billion records on individuals and businesses. ChoicePoint Online [http://www.choicepointonline.com].

9. See Daniel J. Solove, Privacy and Power: Computer Databases and Metaphors for Information Privacy, 53 Stan. L. Rev. 1393, 1406 (2001) (footnotes omitted).

of data, and will therefore never be combined with personally identifiable information. But we've already seen a German supermarket chain experiment with inserting RFIDs into store loyalty cards, making it possible to link the card with a customer's personal information.[10] Combining RFIDs with video surveillance could enable even more intrusive tracking.[11]

The danger goes well beyond invasive marketing techniques. It's not likely that you would give a total stranger permission to examine the contents of your backpack, but with live RFID tags embedded in your belongings, you wouldn't have to. RFIDs can and will enable passive, involuntary surveillance in a variety of different contexts for a broad range of purposes, including ones we can't yet envision. The reason is simple: there is nothing to prevent it.

Technologies Are Political, Not Neutral

The way that a technology develops is always the function of different variables. It's not just "the market" that guides development—there are also social, political, and legal forces at work. Due to the strong demand for improved emergency services, we have a push for location-tracking technologies in cars and cell phones. The technical architecture of our modern telecommunications system, meanwhile, has been modified specifically to make it easy for the FBI to secretly tap phone calls.[12] In each instance, the design of the technology is political, embodying a set of values that reflects a process of negotiation among stakeholders.

The development of privacy norms is likewise a process of negotiation. Yet the public, often lacking the information or organizational clout necessary to negotiate effectively, is susceptible to "spin" by other players with agendas that do not serve the public interest. In today's cluttered consumer landscape, where we have things like PDAs, cell phones, or car keys to keep track of, we are eager to adopt technology to make our lives more manageable. At the same time, corporations and the government have a powerful incentive to gather and analyze the details of our lives. It isn't in their interest to warn us of the privacy invasions that RFIDs invite.

---

10. Thomas Claburn, The closer RFID gets to consumers, the hotter privacy issues become, *Information Week* (Feb. 16, 2004) <http://www.informationweek.com/story/showArticle.jhtml?articleID=17603415>.

11. "Wal-Mart Stores and Procter & Gamble quietly tested a controversial new retail technology earlier this year that allowed P&G employees to observe shoppers via a Webcam as they removed cosmetics from shelves." Alorie Gilbert, "Smart shelf" test triggers fresh criticism, CNET News.com (Nov. 14, 2003) <http://news.com.com/2100-1017-5107918.html>.

12. See Electronic Frontier Foundation: CALEA Archive <http://www.eff.org/Privacy/CALEA/archive.php>.

The message we hear from the RFID industry is "We will gladly provide consumer-beneficial, privacy-respecting RFID applications tomorrow, for sacrifice of consumer privacy today." Its current strategy for addressing privacy concerns isn't to focus on making RFIDs more secure but, rather, to convince the public that RFID adoption is inevitable and that the privacy issues will take care of themselves. Unfortunately, there is little reason to believe that the public will correctly interpret these efforts as spin.

The idea of an "Internet for things" is seductive—and not just for businesses or the government. The ability to take instant inventory of one's moving boxes, closets, or bookshelves, for example, is appealing. Who wouldn't want to "Google" for a pair of lost eyeglasses? But there is no reason why we should have to sacrifice our privacy in order to enjoy these kinds of benefits. The RFID industry's rhetoric suggests a false dichotomy: that we must either embrace today's privacy-corroding RFID systems, or forego using them at all. But the true choice is between developing and deploying RFID systems that recognize our legitimate interest in protecting privacy and developing and doing RFID systems that don't.

The promise of consumer-friendly and privacy-safe RFIDs is being used to justify the premature commercial release of a technology that currently benefits only business and government stakeholders, while degrading our ability to go about our daily lives in private. Those seduced by this potential or vulnerable to spin are likely to sign away their right to privacy without even knowing it. Mandatory kill is the only effective way to avoid this scenario. When RFID technology realizes its potential and the architecture is truly safe-by-design, we can reconsider the mandatory kill policy—but no sooner.

Privacy Norms Develop Poorly During Rapid Technological Change

If the development of new technology presents a challenge for protecting privacy, the challenge is even greater when it develops rapidly. New computer viruses propagate much faster than we can develop the means to combat them. Often, we're unaware that our computer systems have been infected. Once we recognize the problem, we need access to the antidote and the technical know-how to administer it.

The demand for faster toll payment has spurred the rapid, widespread adoption of RFID systems for tracking cars. But the ability to protect your privacy when using these systems hasn't developed beyond the laughable option of placing a Mylar bag over your automobile's RFID tag. It goes without saying that "bagging the tag," as the California Metropolitan Transit Commission calls it, would not scale with RFIDs the size of rice grains flooding the environment. Even if you're told that your belongings are embedded with live RFIDs and are aware that your privacy is at risk, there are no commonly known or readily available ways for you to prevent anyone from secretly scanning them.

We all know to close the door to a telephone booth or seal the envelope to a private letter. Very few of us know to encrypt our email. Fewer still know that RFID tags exist, pose a privacy threat, and can and should be disabled. We need time, or "breathing space," to develop appropriate privacy norms and precautions around RFIDs. In the interim, mandatory kill is the simplest and most efficient solution to the problem.

Conclusion: Mandatory Kill Is Necessary

Some argue that mandatory kill is a Draconian solution and that we should instead push for a set for fair information practices for RFIDs. While EFF supports the principles behind such proposals as Simson Garfinkel's "RFID Bill of Rights," they place too much of a burden on individuals to act on their own behalf with respect to RFID use, especially in the absence of common, public knowledge about its risks.

A set of information practices alone has shown to be a poor protector of privacy, as demonstrated by the relative ineffectiveness of the Privacy Act. Furthermore, some rights carry ancillary costs. We do not yet have RFID systems that enable people to read and edit the information on their RFID tags, or that notify people that their RFIDs are being scanned. Administering and enforcing such a complex system of rights and responsibilities would probably be economically infeasible today. But prohibiting supply-side use of RFID tags until those systems are widely deployed seems unreasonable.

Mandatory kill avoids all of this. The simple requirement that RFIDs be disabled at the point of sale is both relatively inexpensive and possible using current technology. Rather than putting faith in a set of rules that must be understood by the public, individually applied during every transaction, and administered by some as-yet-undefined enforcement authority, mandatory kill builds the necessary breathing room for privacy directly into the architecture. It does so with small transaction, enforcement, and administrative costs, and with great benefit to privacy.[13] Businesses could still benefit from RFID use, while people could have much less fear of being tracked.

It won't be long before RFIDs are implanted into every corner of our everyday lives. We need a realistic way to protect ourselves right now. When RFID technology that empowers us rather than threatens our privacy is inexpensive and widely available, and we have the requisite knowledge to use that technology sensibly, mandatory kill should certainly be re-evaluated. But until that day, RFIDs must be permanently disabled before they reach the customer.

---

13. Admittedly, point-of-sale kill doesn't address the threat of in-store tracking. See, e.g., Winston Chai, Tags track Japanese shoppers, *CNET News.com* (May 8, 2003) < http://news.zdnet.co.uk /business/0,39020645,2134438,00.htm> ("By placing tag readers on the shelves of bookstores, the new system allows booksellers to gain information such as the range of books a shopper has browsed, how many times a particular title was picked up and even the length of time spent flipping through each book").

GUIDELINES FOR PRIVACY PROTECTION ON ELECTRONIC TAGS OF JAPAN

Takato Natsui[1]

Introduction

This appendix provides a short history and a private translation of the Guidelines for Privacy Protection on Electronic Tags by the Ministry of Inner Affairs and Telecommunication (MIT) and the Ministry of Economy, Trade and Industry (METI) in Japan (June 8, 2004).

Short History of the Guidelines

To improve technologies by using radio frequency identification and at the same time address concerns about the privacy intrusion that may be caused by such technologies, the relevant Ministries of Japan have been discussing the issue over the past few years.

The METI and its committees and study groups examined RFID and have held many meetings and hearings. Examinations by the METI, which governs the IT industry and privacy protection issues related to technologies, were

---

1. Takato Natsui is a professor at Meiji University Law Facultyin Tokyo and an attorney with the Asuka-Kyowa Law Firm, Tokyo, Japan.

performed by authorities from the information technology industry in Japan. Many IT corporations believe that the technologies related to RFID tags have the potential to boost the IT industry. At the same time, privacy protection advocates severely criticize deployment of RFID because of privacy concerns.

After its research and examinations, the Committee published "The Committee Interim Report on the Improvement in Products Traceability" in April 2003. Based on the results of the report and other research on relevant foreign legislations or guidelines such as the EPC Guidelines (EPCglobal), the METI drafted and published "The Draft Guidelines for Privacy Protection on Electronic Tags." The METI solicited public comments on the draft guidelines in January 2004 and completed and published the final version of Guidelines of the METI in March 2004.

The MIT was also interested in RFID because it governs telecommunication matters, and in general, radio frequency or wireless transmissions as a communication measure can be interpreted inside the telecommunication area. MIT's committee and some study groups provided the results of their examination. The Committee published "The Committee on Examination of Advanced Utilization of Electronic Tags in the Ubiquitous Era; Final Report" in February 2004.[2] Also, the MIT solicited public comments on the final report. It had originally planned to prepare different guidelines on RFID tags at the time.

Many Japanese people and IT companies were afraid of the confusion that could result if there were multiple sets of guidelines on privacy protection concerning RFID tags. They thought that the might be too complicated both politically and practically.

Consequently, the METI, MIT, and other relevant agencies of the Japanese government agreed on an integrated and final version of the guidelines on RFID tags that was published in of June 2004.

---

2. www.soumu.go.jp/s-news/2004/040223_2.html

Private Translation

Guidelines for Privacy Protection on Electronic Tags

8th of June 2004

The Ministry of Internal Affairs and Telecommunication (MIT)
The Ministry of Economy, Trade and Industry (METI)

Part I. Introduction: The Need for Consumer Privacy Protection on Electronic Tags

Regarding the problem of personal information protection, when an electronic tag (this means a device that consist of an IC chip with antenna; which is used to be attached to some industrial products; in which some information can be stored to identify an identification of the product to be distinguished from other products; and the information stored onto the device can be read by means of radio frequency) is used, naturally, "the personal information protection law" (Law No.57-2003) shall be applied. Personal information is information about an "individual who exists and from which a specific individual can be distinguished by the description of the name, date of birth and so on contained in the information concerned (including descriptions which can be compared with other information easily and by which a specific individual can be identified)" (Article 2 paragraph 1), and information which isn't related to the identification of a specific individual doesn't correspond to personal information. Therefore, the law doesn't cover such information which has no relation to specific individuals.

However, even if such information isn't deemed to be personal information, generally the problem of privacy protection can take place. As for the protection of privacy, it is a problem generally to discuss as itself, and of course it isn't suitable to discuss that whole argument in this Committee.

Some points of an argument which takes place from the peculiar character of electronic tags can be presumed. In other words, due to the conditions where the nature of electronic tags hasn't been fully recognized by a consumer, the consumer has no recognition that an electronic tag is still attached to the item which they possess, or possesses an item without any recognition that an electronic tag is still attached to the item and move. Furthermore, it seems that the identification number and attribute data of the item which he/she possesses can be read in a form which is outside his/her recognition.

The fear that an electronic tag is removed at the time when an item is exchanged by hand to a consumer in the store doesn't grow. But in the future, after an item has been exchanged by hand to a consumer, the case that an electronic tag will be attached to secure some consumer profits or for a social need can be presumed. For example, there are some cases where for the purpose of the preservation of the environment electronic tags will be attached for recycling, cases where for the purpose of increasing the safety of used cars the repair history will be stored in electronic tags attached to such used cars, or the use of electronic tags to avoid a misuse or wrong instruction of medical drags. These may not be to the advantage or convenience of the individual consumer concerned.

"The Committee interim report on the improvement in products traceability" by the Ministry of Economy, Trade and Industry (April 2003) concluded that storing personal information onto such an economical and cheap electronic tag as that may be attached to broadly deliverable consumer goods for the purpose of a tracing of consumer goods or a supply chains management and so on, shall be stopped until better technology is developed.

However, if we can recognize the existence of every type of electronic tags, then such a case will be able to take place as that personal information may be stored onto an electronic tag or electronic tags.

In the case where personal information should be stored onto an electronic tag, even if the personal information protection law may be not applied, it is necessary that we have to take account of the due handling of the electronic tags. Because the electronic tags have a characteristic that information stored onto them can be retrievable remotely, and this characteristic may cause such a case as that personal information of an individual consumer can be read by other people without any awareness of the consumer.

As mentioned above, due to that issues can be caused by the peculiar characteristics of an electronic tag, even if the personal information protection law shall not be applied directly to the information relating to electronic tags, a preference of consuming of an individual or family can be presumed by using of the information stored onto electronic tags. Therefore, it is very important to make electronic tags be accepted smoothly in our society by adopting adequate measures from the viewpoint of the privacy protection.

For the purpose of these, we decided to draft the Guidelines under a consensus that it is very significant to clarify fundamental policies and to specify the details of the policies, as long as acceptance can be found by relevant parties (including relevant business entities or consumer protection activity groups, and so forth). Under these considerations, the MIT and METI made the

Guidelines, notify this broadly to the relevant business entities or consumer protection activity groups and so on.

Also, every business entity would be expected to address adequately the handling of electronic tags based on fundamental policies in the guidelines and having a good concern for their relationship with consumers depending on their types of business.

In addition, because the conception of privacy protection may be modified in response to a change of social environment, recognition by consumer or technological developments, these guidelines shall be amended based on such changes in the future. Also, when new consensus for privacy protection policy on electronic tags is reached between concerned people, more guidelines will be able to be added.

Part II. Guidelines for Privacy Protection on Electronic Tags

1. Purpose

The purpose of these guidelines is to clarify fundamental policies for consumer privacy protection on electronic tags for every category of business through which the introduction of electronic tags into our society can be prompted while taking account of the usefulness of electronic tags.

2. Scope of Guidelines

These Guidelines provide some rules preferably to be adopted by business entities which may handle electronic tags and any items using electronic tags after the acquisition of such items by a consumer.

3. Indication of Electronic Tags Attachment

Every business entity which wishes to continue to attach electronic tags to any items after the acquisition of such items by a consumer shall explain or post up the fact of electronic tags attachment to the item and the characteristics and contents of information stored in such electronic tags to the consumer ("information of electronic tags" and so forth), or shall indicate the fact of electronic tags attachment to the item and the characteristics and contents of information stored in such electronic tags on the item or on its packaging so as to be recognized thereof by the consumer. The explanation and posting up shall be recognizable for consumers, for instance, by means of posting up at the shops.

4. Ultimate Right of Choice

If a consumer wishes to de-activate any electronic tags on any items which he/she acquired while well understanding the characteristics of the electronic tags, they can do so. Every business entity which wishes to continue to attach electronic tags to the items after the acquisition of such items by the consumer shall explain or post up measures for de-activating, or indicate thereof on the item or on its packaging providing a choice to the consumer whether to de-activate such electronic tags prior to finishing such an acquisition.

Examples: measures to de-activate electronic tags:

1. Wrapping up electronic tags by aluminum foils, to block off a communication between the electronic tags and readers of them;
2. Removing electromagnetically all or a part selected by a consumer of information (including an identification number of the electronic tags) stored onto electronic tags, or making unable to read them; or,
3. Detaching electronic tags.

5. Information on Social Merits of Electronic Tags

Including the case in which environmental issues would be caused by lost information on the recycling of commercial goods or the case in which safety would be affected by lost information on the history of car repair due to de-activating the electronic tags. If any consumer interests or social interests can be injured then every business entity shall provide such information to the consumer by indication or other similar measure.

6. Data Matching in Database Systems

If a business entity may operate a data match of some personal information stored in any database systems with any information stored in electronic tags, even if such electronic tags don't involve any personal information at all, such stored information in the electronic tags shall be deemed to be personal information which the Personal Information Protection Law of Japan protects.

Examples: Obligations for business entities under the Personal Information Protection Law:

1. Purpose of use
   Obligation to specify of personal information;
   The consent of the data subject shall be acquired when personal information may be used against the purpose of use.

2. Collection of personal information
   Inadequate collection of personal information shall be prohibited;
   Immediately notice or publication of the purpose of collection is necessary when personal information is collected.
3. Management of personal data
   Personal data shall be kept as a correct and updated data;
   Adequate protection measures to prevent illegal disclosure, loss or damage of personal data shall be performed;
   The consent of the subject shall be acquired when personal information is transmitted to other person.

7. Limitation on Collection or Use of Information in the Case Where Personal Information Is Stored onto Electronic Tags

The business entities which handle personal information by means of storing them onto electronic tags shall make best effort to notify or publicize the purpose of use in relation to the collected personal information onto electronic tags to the data subject, notwithstanding the number of personal information, at the time when the personal information is collected or used. The consent of the data subject shall be acquired when personal information may be used against the purpose of use.

8. Ensuring of the Integrity of Information in the Case Where Personal Information Is Stored onto Electronic Tags

The business entities which handle personal information by means of storing them onto electronic tags shall make best effort to perform following matters, notwithstanding the number of personal information, at the time when the personal information is recorded:

The business entities shall have the

1. Personal data shall be kept as a correct and updated data so as to fit for the purpose of use;
2. Under claims given from consumers, business entities shall disclose information concerning the consumer and stored onto the electronic tag as well as the personal information of the consumer that is linked with identification information stored onto the electronic tag. Also business entities shall correct any errors involved in the information under claims given from consumers;
3. Adequate protection measures to prevent illegal disclosure, loss or damage of personal data shall be performed.

9. Information Manager

Business entities shall settle an information manager, and publicize the contact points, so as to ensure an adequate management of information in accordance with privacy protection concerning electronic tags, and to ensure adequate and quick response to any claims on them.

10. Education

Every business entity, business organization and department or agency of the Japanese Government ought to make their efforts to help consumers' understanding of electronic tags, by means of providing adequate information, so as to let consumers have accurate knowledge of the purposes of deployment, characteristics, merits and demerits of electronic tags, and to let consumers be able to decide by themselves how to handle the electronic tags.

Adapting Fair Information Practices to Low-Cost RFID Systems

Simson Garfinkel

Introduction

This paper was originally presented at the Ubiquitous Computing 2002 Privacy Workshop, Göteborg, Sweden.

Abstract

Within the coming years, low-cost radio frequency identification (RFID) systems are expected to become commonplace throughout the business-to-business and business-to-consumer marketplace. Much of the work to date on these systems pertains to systems engineering and electronic product code issues. This paper discusses ways to ensure personal privacy and presents policies and technologies that could limit abuse.

Introduction to RFID

"Automatic Identification" (Auto-ID) describes a wide class of technologies used for automatically identifying objects, individuals, and locations. Typical Auto-ID systems assign a code to a product model or type. This code can then be automatically read and manipulated by an information processing system. The Universal Product Code (UPC)/ European Article Number (EAN) bar code present on most consumer items sold in the world is one of the most widely used Auto-ID systems. Today more than 5 billion UPC/EAN codes are scanned worldwide on a daily basis [EAN02].

Auto-ID systems are expected to undergo two fundamental changes within the coming years. The first change will be the way that these codes are read and automatically processed; the second change involves the codes themselves. These issues must be addressed in the design, implementation, and deployment of the system to protect the privacy of individuals.

From Optical Scanning to RFID

Instead of printed-on optical patterns that are read with an optical scanner, the next generation of Auto-ID systems will be based on electronic tags that are "read" using a wireless transceiver. These systems, collectively known as Radio Frequency Identification (RFID), have been increasingly used throughout the world in recent years.

RFID systems typically operate in the ISM and other free bands (9–135kHz; 13.56MHz; 868–870MHz in Europe; 902–928MHz in the United States.) Tags can be *active*, which means that they are equipped with a power source for sending their responses, or *passive*, in which case they are powered by the reader. Active tags are more expensive, are generally more reliable, and can be read over distances of several tens of meters. Passive tags are cheaper, are less reliable, and can be read over distances ranging from a few centimeters to a few meters.[1]

RFID tags offer many advantages over traditional optically scanned tags:

- Optical bar codes need to be in plain view to be read; RFID tags can be read through fabric, paper, cardboard, and other materials that are transparent to the frequency of operation.

---

1. The power consumption of the passive tag's electronics determines the range at which the tag can be read. For this reason, the industry has also developed *semi-active* tags that use an embedded battery to power the electronics but still employ passive response such as RF backscatter for uplink from the tag to the reader.

- Traditional optical bar codes are limited to 13 digits of information, and two-dimensional bar codes are limited to several hundred; RFID tags can store hundreds or thousands of bytes of information.
- Only a single optical bar code can be read at a time; dozens of RFID tags can be read at the same time with a single reader. For example, an RFID reader could be used to read all of the individually tagged items within a case of merchandise.
- Optical bar codes are read-only; advanced RFID tags can store information and perform limited processing.
- Optical bar codes are *promiscuous*, in that any reader can read any compatible optical bar code that comes in range; RFID tags can be assigned a password, limiting who has the ability to read them.
- The only way to deactivate an optical bar code is by obliterating or obscuring it; RFID tags can be electronically deactivated.

From Product Codes to Serial Numbers

Each UPC/EAN code is assigned by a manufacturer to a particular class of product. For example, the UPC 041508 800822 refers to a case of a dozen 750ml bottles of San Pellegrino sparkling natural mineral water. Each bottle inside the case has a UPC with the code 041508 800129. A shipping container might contain a thousand cases, all with the same code.

Each RFID tag, by contrast, can have its own unique identifying code. A shipping container of RFID-tagged San Pellegrino cases would have thousands of separate unique codes. One way of assigning these could be to use a standard UPC/EAN code as a prefix and to append a unique serial number. Such a system would allow easy integration with existing inventory systems while simultaneously allowing new applications that make use of the unique ID.

RFID Today

RFID systems are now used for a variety of industrial and consumer applications, including access control, asset management, and warehouse automation.

Electronic toll collection and road pricing are typical uses of active and semi-active tags.[2] Automobiles are equipped with an active tag that can be read as they move through a toll booth or drive along the road. Each tag has a unique serial number; a database correlates the serial number with an account number that is automatically debited each time the tag is read [EZP02].

---

2. Passive tags can also be used for Electronic Toll Collection and road pricing.

Implantable passive tags have seen significant use for tagging household pets. Stray animals that are brought to shelters are scanned for a tag. If the shelter finds a tag, it can find the name of the owner by looking up the tag's serial number in a database [AVI02] [HAM02].

RFID Tomorrow

It is widely believed that RFID tags will migrate into consumer items as the price of tags drops to US$0.05 and below. For example, individually serialized RFID tags could be embedded in packages of high-value razor blades when the blades are manufactured. These tags could then be used to track the packages of blades as they are shipped from the factory through distribution and ultimately to retail shelves.

By giving each package a unique serial number, RFID would allow the manufacturer to:

- Keep track of material and assets in the supply chain, thereby reducing inventory.
- Pinpoint the location of theft (by determining that 1,000 packages in 30 cases of razors that were scanned leaving a shipping dock were not subsequently scanned when the cases were loaded onto a truck).
- Stop product diversion (when a shipping container of individually serialized batteries that were manufactured and labeled for sale in Hong Kong is scanned at the Port Authority in New York City).
- Stop importation of counterfeit consumer goods (even if the counterfeit goods contain an RFID tag, the serial number in the tag will not be registered as a genuine article.)
- Have more control over product recalls. Grocers could use an RFID scanner to rapidly locate tainted goods on store shelves; suspect serial numbers could be programmed into cash registers to prevent consumers from purchasing items that are blacklisted.

For consumers, some examples of the benefits of Auto-ID technology include:

- Compliance monitoring of medication dosage in elderly patients (An RFID reader could note if a medicine bottle is taken out of the cabinet.)
- Alerts to the consumer about product recalls (especially if there is a networked RFID reader at the door to the consumer's house)
- Automatic replenishment of refrigerators and pantries
- Ovens that can adjust themselves to properly cook prepackaged foods by reading their tags

Amusingly enough, the application of finding lost keys in a cluttered house or apartment—an application that has frequently appeared in popular accounts of RFID technology—will probably *not* be a near-term application. Finding lost keys would require not only equipping a keychain with an RFID tag but also equipping each room in a house with multiple RFID readers to allow for triangulation. Even then, the system might not be able to find keys that had fallen behind or into a couch or similar RF shields, unless the keys were equipped with active or semi-active tags.

Privacy Issues

Ubiquitous deployment of RFID tags in consumer products could pose several challenges to consumer privacy:

- Tags could be read by unauthorized readers. (Although 13.56MHz tags cannot be read from more than a meter away, unshielded passive 915MHz tags can be read from many meters.)
- Since human beings are not sensitive to radio signals, RFID tags could be read covertly.
- A database could be used to build long-term tracking associations between tags and holders. Alternatively, such a database could simply be created at the checkout counter by correlating RFID tags with payment information. (Today this can be done with item info to track purchases made by an individual, but it is not currently possible to identify *which* consumer purchased *which* box of milk.)
- The communication between the reader and the tag could be covertly monitored.

We can imagine several scenarios in which these properties could be exploited:

- A practical joker could covertly inventory, say, the undergarments of nearby pedestrians.
- Household electronics and other kinds of products might covertly inventory which other products are in the consumer's house and then report this information back to a central repository—assuming that these "moles" have network access. Such information might be used to target the consumer for special offers or to deny the consumer offers that he or she might otherwise receive.
- Additional unique identifiers could be stored into programmable RFID tags.
- A store could use a covert RFID reader to inventory the contents of a shopper's bags as the shopper enters the store—or even window shops.

(In practice, such an application with a passive tag would be difficult, since paper can be an effective shield to some frequencies used by passive RFID systems.)

[SAR02] presents several technical measures for protecting the privacy of users, including:

- At time of purchase, the tag could be either completely deactivated or else the unique serial number could erased, leaving only the prefix.
- Passwords could be assigned to the tags by the purchaser; this would prevent tags from being read without the owner's permission.

These measures depend on the consumer being aware of the existence of the tag and having the technical ability and the necessary patience to deactivate or reprogram an RFID tag. A lingering concern is that consumers might not exercise these technical measures for any of a number of reasons:

- The manufacturer or merchandiser might wish to make future use of the tag.
- The consumer might not be informed of the tag's existence.
- Sufficient hurdles might be placed before consumers wishing to have a tag deactivated that, practically speaking, no consumers will exercise this option. (For example, consumers might be forced to purchase special equipment or be required to call a phone number that is frequently busy to obtain an unlock code.)
- The manufacturer might not wish to go to the expense of purchasing tags that are reprogrammable or that have a "self-destruct" feature.

I believe that these problems can be solved through the use of policy and licensing requirements.

Fair Information Practices and the RFID Bill of Rights

Much current thinking on informational privacy issues is based on the Code of Fair Information Practice ([HEW73]), developed by the U.S. Department of Health, Education and Welfare in 1973.[3] The code has been subsequently expanded in [OEC80] [EU95] and [CAN99].

We propose an "RFID Bill of Rights" that brings Fair Information Practice to deployment of RFID systems. The Bill of Rights consists of five guiding principles for the creation and deployment of RFID systems:

Users of RFID systems and purchasers of products containing RFID tags have:

1. The right to know if a product contains an RFID tag.
2. The right to have embedded RFID tags removed, deactivated, or destroyed when a product is purchased.
3. The right to first class RFID alternatives: consumers should not lose other rights (e.g., the right to return a product or to travel on a particular road) if they decide to opt out of RIFD or exercise an RFID tag's "kill" feature.
4. The right to know what information is stored inside their RFID tags. If this information is incorrect, there must be a means to correct or amend it.
5. The right to know when, where, and why an RFID tag is being read.

Together, items #1 and #5 mandate that there should be no covert RFID systems. One approach is to have a logo that must be prominently displayed on any product that contains an RFID tag and in any area that is under surveillance by RFID readers. Likewise, organizations that wish to declare a space "free" of RFID readers could have similar placards; freedom could be assured through the use of RFID reader detectors or RFID jammers.

Item #2 overcomes the fear that stores might find it inconvenient to provide consumers with a means for deactivating their tags. Tags that comply with the Auto-ID Center's standard will be required to incorporate a password-protected "kill" feature. Rather than forcing consumers to find their passwords, a more consumer-friendly approach would be for manufacturers to use standardized kill passwords or else to either kill tags or erase unique serial numbers as part of the checkout process.[4]

---

3. The Code of Fair Information Practice is based on five principles:

    There must be no personal data record-keeping systems whose very existence is secret.

    There must be a way for a person to find out what information about the person is in a record and how it is used.

    There must be a way for a person to prevent information about the person that was obtained for one purpose from being used or made available for other purposes without the person's consent.

    There must be a way for a person to correct or amend a record of identifiable information about the person.

    Any organization creating, maintaining, using, or disseminating records of identifiable personal data must assure the reliability of the data for their intended use and must take precautions to prevent misuses of the data. [HEW73]

4. One potential problem with a widely known "kill" password is the notion that a saboteur might enter a store for the purpose of killing all of the store's RFID tags. To protect against such actions, stores could be equipped with RFID sensing systems that will quickly report any such activity. Killing an RFID tag requires exercising anti-collision algorithms to find a particular tag, addressing the tag, and finally sending the "kill" command with sufficient power to affect a kill. Because of this involved procedure, even a high-speed RFID tag-killing system would not be able to kill more than five tags per second. Such a system would have a distinct radio signature and would be easily found by a store with RFID readers in every aisle.

Item #3 seeks to avoid penalizing consumers who decline to partake in RFID-enabled services. It is easy to imagine how poorly designed RFID system could be coercively deployed if consumers are not given a choice regarding its use. For example, if the only way to ride on a particular highway is by paying the toll with an RFID tag, then even consumers who are opposed to the tag might nevertheless use it if there is no other way for them to commute to work.

Item #4 is a straightforward application of fair information practices to RFID systems similar to the application of these principles to smart cards in [GAR99].

Item #5 is likely to be the most controversial. There are many ways that consumers can be informed that their RFID tags are being read. For example, a prominent placard could be placed in the vicinity of a reader. Readers could emit a tone or flash a light when a reading takes place. Alternatively, the tag itself could emit a tone or flash a light. In addition, a tag equipped with memory could count the *number of times* that it has been read. Of course, a passive tag would not have an accurate time source to remember *when* the reading took place, and a simple count may not by itself add enough information. In general, though, most of these options would add cost to the tag, either in the form of a battery or in the form of increased functionality.

Yet another alternative is providing concerned consumers with RFID reader detectors. Such detectors could be cheaply made and equipped with real time clocks and position-aware technology such as GPS. Although such detectors might not be a primary means for enforcing item #5, they could prove to be a powerful means for finding organizations that do not comply with these principles.

These principles could be legislated or could be adopted on a voluntary basis. If voluntary, conformance with the principles could be ensured through licensing of logos, protocols, or intellectual property required for proper RFID operation.

Conclusions

RFID is a powerful technology, and it is a technology that is likely to see worldwide deployment within the coming years. Attention to Fair Information Practices and related public-policy issues today will ensure that these systems are designed and deployed in a manner that is compatible with evolving privacy principles.

References

[AVI02]   Avid   Microchip   Identification   systems   for   animals, www.avidmicrochip.com/.

[CAN99] The House of Commons of Canada, 2nd Session, 36th Parliament, 48 Elizabeth II, 1999, Bill C-6, "Personal Information Protection and Electronic Documents Act."

[EAN02] "Note to Editors," EAN International and the Uniform Code Council, www.ean-int.org/index800.html.

[EU95] European Union Directive 95/46/EC of the European Parliament and of the Council of 24 October 1995 on the protection of individuals with regard to the processing of personal data and on the free movement of such data. http://europa.eu.int/comm/internal_market/en/dataprot/law/.

[EZP02] E-ZPass Regional Consortium Service Center, www.ezpass.com/.

[GAR99] Garfinkel, S. "Smartcard holder's bill of rights." www.simson.net /smartrights.html.

[HEW73] U.S. Department of Health, Education and Welfare, Secretary's Advisory Committee on Automated Personal Data Systems, Records, computers, and the Rights of Citizens (1973).

[HAM02]   Home   Again   Microchip   Identification   System,   www .homeagainid.com/.

[MAL02] Mallory Sonalert Products, "Introduction to Sonalert Audible Signal Devices," www.mallory-sonalert.com/sonalert_audible_intro.htm.

[OEC80] Organisation for Economic Co-operation and Development, Guidelines on the Protection of Privacy and Transborder Flows of Personal Data, 1980.

[SAR02] "Low Cost RFID and the Electronic Product Code," Sarma, S.E., Weis, S.A., Engels, D.W., Auto-ID Center, Massachusetts Institute of Technology, Cambridge, MA 02139. 2002.

GUIDELINES ON EPC FOR CONSUMER PRODUCTS

EPCglobal, Inc.[1]

Introduction

Electronic Product Code (EPC) is an emerging system that uses Radio Frequency Identification (RFID) for the automatic identification of consumer products. RFID is now being used in everything from automobiles to security pass cards, and it serves a variety of purposes. One of its widespread uses is in devices such as EZ Pass in the US and Liber T in France that speed the passage of autos through highway toll booths.

Benefits

EPC has the potential to be used on many everyday consumer products as they move through the supply chain – from factories through distribution centres and into retail stores. As EPC evolves, it promises to offer significant benefits to consumers and companies. The improved information in the supply chain will help speed products to the shelf and insure they are available when consumers want and in the quantities they need. Removal of expired products will be easier, and prompt removal of any recalled product will be facilitated. In addition, checkout times for customers could be significantly shortened.

---

1. Guidelines are property of EPCglobal, Inc. Reprinted with permission.

Privacy

To allow EPC to realise its potential for consumers, retailers and suppliers, it is important to address privacy concerns prompted by the current state of the technology while establishing principles for dealing with its evolution and implementation. Accordingly, the sponsors of EPC have adopted the following Guidelines for use by all companies engaged in the large-scale deployment of EPC. These Guidelines are intended to complement compliance with the substantive and comprehensive body of national and international legislation and regulation that deals with consumer protection, consumer privacy and related issues. They are based, and will continue to be based, on industry responsibility, providing accurate information to consumers and ensuring consumer choice.

Evolution

As new developments in EPC and its deployment occur, these Guidelines will evolve while continuing to represent the fundamental commitments of industry to consumers. It is hoped that further developments, including advances in technology, new applications and enhanced post-purchase benefits, will provide even more choices to both consumers and companies on the use of EPC tags. The sponsors of EPCglobal support continuing their focused efforts in these development areas to assure responsible and effective development of both the EPC technology and these Guidelines.

Administration

These Guidelines will be administered by EPCglobal, a joint venture between EAN International and the Uniform Code Council. The EAN.UCC also sets and maintains standards for the product code now used on consumer products. EPCglobal also will be responsible for updating these Guidelines. For EPC to gain broad acceptance, consumers must have confidence in its value and benefits. . . and the integrity of its use. EPC participants are committed to gaining and retaining this public confidence. EPCglobal will monitor the proper use of these Guidelines and be responsible for updating them.

Because EPC is an emerging technology in an early development stage, usage Guidelines supplementing or modifying those below will evolve as applications are developed and implemented. For example, if developments in the technology or its use provide consumers added flexibility in controlling EPC tags or record personal consumer information beyond that provided by conventional bar code technology, changes to notices required to consumers or to the Guidelines themselves may be appropriate. Given the current state of the technology and the relatively early stage of its deployment at the consumer unit level and to allow participants appropriate time to implement the Guidelines, EPCglobal has established January 1, 2005 as the expected date by which companies will follow the Guidelines below.

Guidelines

1. Consumer Notice
   Consumers will be given clear notice of the presence of EPC on products or their packaging. This notice will be given through the use of an EPC logo or identifier on the products or packaging.
2. Consumer Choice
   Consumers will be informed of the choices that are available to discard or remove or in the future disable EPC tags from the products they acquire. It is anticipated that for most products, the EPC tags would be part of disposable packaging or would be otherwise discardable. EPCglobal, among other supporters of the technology, is committed to finding additional efficient, cost effective and reliable alternatives to further enable customer choice.
3. Consumer Education
   Consumers will have the opportunity easily to obtain accurate information about EPC and its applications, as well as information about advances in the technology. Companies using EPC tags at the consumer level will cooperate in appropriate ways to familiarise consumers with the EPC logo and to help consumers understand the technology and its benefits. EPCglobal would also act as a forum for both companies and consumers to learn of and address any uses of EPC technology in a manner inconsistent with these Guidelines.
4. Record Use, Retention and Security
   The Electronic Product Code does not contain, collect or store any personally identifiable information. As with conventional barcode technology, data which is associated with EPC will be collected, used, maintained, stored and protected by the EPCglobal member companies in compliance with applicable laws. Companies will publish, in compliance with all applicable laws, information on their policies regarding the retention, use and protection of any personally identifiable information associated with EPC use.

Summary

The purpose of these Guidelines is to provide a responsible basis for the use of EPC tags on consumer items. Under the auspices of EPCglobal, these Guidelines will continue to evolve as advances in EPC and its applications are made and consumer research is conducted. As EPC evolves, so too will new issues. EPC participants are committed to addressing these issues and engaging in a dialogue about them with interested parties.

Realizing the Mandate: RFID at Wal-Mart

Gus Whitcomb, interviewed by Simson Garfinkel[1]

Wal-Mart, the nation's largest retailer, is moving full-speed ahead with its plans to incorporate RFID into its business process. In 2003, Wal-Mart announced that its top 100 suppliers would be required to put an RFID tracking device inside every pallet or case delivered to a Wal-Mart warehouse by January 2005. RFID chips, Wal-Mart said, would allow the company to track the movement of inventory as it moves through the supply chain, making it possible to monitor the flow of merchandise, reduce theft and product diversion, increase product awareness, and directly feed the company's existing inventory control systems.

In November 2003, Wal-Mart detailed its plans for RFID deployment at a meeting of its top 100 suppliers in Bentonville, Arkansas. Linda Dillman, the company's CIO, said that Wal-Mart was working with 2 suppliers, wanted to expand to 12 suppliers soon, and wanted to have a 100 percent read rate of items coming through its dock doors, according to an article in the *RFID Journal*.[2]

In April 2004, Wal-Mart announced that its initial deployments of RFID were well under way. Eight early adopters—Gillette, Hewlett Packard, Johnson & Johnson, Kimberly-Clark, Kraft, Nestle Purina PetCare, Procter & Gamble, and Unilever—were delivering 21 products with RFID tags to the Wal-Mart regional distribution center in Sanger, Texas. Test readers are also installed at seven pilot stores in the Dallas/Fort Worth metroplex.

---

1. A version of this article originally appeared on the Technologyreview.com Web site; we are grateful to TR for granting permission to reprint it here. Garfinkel, S.L. "RFID Rights." *Technology Review* November 2004. April 6, 2005. www.technologyreview.com/articles/04/11/wo_garfinkel110304.asp.

2. "Wal-Mart Details RFID Requirement." *RFID Journal*, November 6, 2003. www.rfidjournal.com/article/articleview/642/1/1/.

At the same time, the company's press release[3] took pains to note that tagged cases and pallets may be distributed to stores throughout North Texas and South Central Oklahoma—or even elsewhere. "It is possible that tagged cases and pallets will arrive at Wal-Mart stores around the country." The company said that since readers will not be installed at other stores, the cases will be handled as normal.

Wal-Mart has said that right now its tags are for internal use, not for the checkout aisle. But three of the items in the test, two HP Photosmart photo printers and an HP ScanJet scanner, will have RFID tags built into product boxes. Wal-Mart has promised that the "outer packaging will be marked with an EPCglobal symbol" so that customers understand that the products they are purchasing contain an RFID tag.

Should consumers be worried? Katherine Albrecht, founder and director of CASPIAN (Consumers Against Supermarket Privacy Invasion and Numbering), is one of the privacy activists who has been leading the charge against RFID. In November 2003, Albrecht received international media attention[4] when she revealed that Wal-Mart and Procter & Gamble had conducted a test of RFID-tagged Max Factor Lipfinity lipstick at a Wal-Mart store in Broken Arrow, Oklahoma. Albrecht and others claimed that, despite the company's promises, consumers had not been properly notified that the lipstick boxes contained RFID tags. And earlier that year, Wal-Mart had canceled plans to test Gillette's RFID-enabled "smart shelf" in Brockton, Massachusetts, after Albrecht had publicized the retailing giant's plans.[5]

"Wal-Mart is blatantly ignoring the research and recommendations of dozens of privacy experts," said Albrecht when Wal-Mart announced its early success with RFID. "When the world's largest retailer adopts a technology with chilling societal implications, and does so irresponsibly, we should all be deeply concerned."

Every story has two sides, of course. Representatives from Wal-Mart and Procter & Gamble repeatedly said that there was adequate notification inside the Broken Arrow store. And even though Wal-Mart admitted to canceling the trial in Brockton, the company insisted that Albrecht had nothing to do with it.

---

3. www.walmartstores.com/wmstore/wmstores/Mainnews.jsp?BV_SessionID=@@@@1016643452.1 098297641@@@@&BV_EngineID=ccccadcmilmfdfdcfkfcfkjdgoodglg.0&pagetype=news&cont entOID=13794&year=2004&prevPage=NewsShelf.jsp&template=NewsArticle.jsp&category-OID=-8300&.

4. For example, Vance, A. "Wal-Mart turns customers into RFID Lab Rats." *The Register*, November 13, 2003. www.theregister.co.uk/2003/11/13/walmart_turns_customers_into_rfid/.

5. Bray, H. "Gillette, Wal-Mart drop plan for radio ID chips." *Boston Globe*, July 10, 2003. www.massconsumers.org/Press-Release/BostonGlobeOnline-Business-GilletteWalMart-dropIDchips.htm.

To get to the bottom of this controversy—and to find out how the company's RFID deployment is going—I spoke with Gus Whitcomb, whom at the time was Wal-Mart's director of Corporate Communications, asking how Wal-Mart and its suppliers were handling the company's RFID deployment and mandate.

Q: When did Wal-Mart start with RFID?

A: We joined MIT's Auto-ID Lab in 1999. We've been moving forward with advancing the technology in a retail setting ever since.

Q: Is the Wal-Mart mandate on-track? Will your top suppliers really be able to provide the chips?

A: We'll have more than 100 suppliers participating come January 2005, which exceeds our original goal of 100.

Q: What has the reaction been from your suppliers?

A: All suppliers have endorsed the idea of improving supply chain visibility. As with any technology being used in a new setting, RFID has its champions and its critics. We believe that companies that really explore RFID and what it can do for them internally will actually find participating in the Wal-Mart initiative a by-product of their adoption rather than the reason for it. We also believe having more than 30 volunteers for the January 2005 milestone demonstrates that suppliers believe RFID can add value to their organizations.

Q: Is Wal-Mart going to be using the Object Naming Service (ONS) for looking up tag serial numbers to find out what they mean, or is Wal-Mart going to be getting EPC codes directly from its suppliers?

A: The EPCglobal network is still being developed, but we have been huge advocates of its development and anticipate using it in the future.

Q: In your April 30, 2004 press release, you said you would be having readers at dock doors and on conveyer belts. Have you tested any of the technology yet? If so, how did the test go?

A: On April 30, we launched a pilot that remains ongoing. This pilot will actually grow until it "morphs" into the actual January 2005 milestone.

During the pilot to date, we have worked with eight suppliers shipping tagged cases and pallets of 21 different products. The pilot has gone well. We've learned a lot, which was its purpose. You want to get any minor bugs out of the way before your broad implementation date.

Q: Is the North Texas project a demonstration, or are you really, going to be using RFID in the business process? That is, will you be running the RFID system in parallel with the existing system, or using it without a safety net?

A: Remember, RFID is not being rolled out to every store immediately. We are taking a measured approach. That said, RFID is a strategic, complementary system designed to enhance supply chain visibility.

We are currently validating system enhancements to some of our current applications, which will improve our process at store level for products that are tagged. The aim of this will be to drive improved in-stock for our customers and improved sales for our suppliers and Wal-Mart.

Q: What do you do if a tag doesn't read?

A: During the pilot we have really worked hard to understand why. Sometimes it might have to do with placement, or with the materials that are tagged. Or the size of the antenna selected. All of this information is shared back with technology companies and suppliers.

We do appreciate that from time-to-time a tag may get damaged; however, this is no different than a bar code getting damaged today. We have found that if a tag is verified as it is applied at the manufacturer, they are very robust and last the lifecycle of the product.

Q: What sort of read rates or failure rates have you seen with tags in your pilot?

A: We're seeing an average of around 90 percent read rates right now at store level. This is fantastic when you consider that includes product stacked on stocking carts going out to the sales floor. Other read points are seeing higher rates.

It is extremely important for people to understand that a 100 percent read rate is not required to see an immediate and impactful benefit from RFID. A 90 percent read rate is giving us 90 percent more information that we had before.

Q: Where are you going to deploy the actual readers? In portals, on fork lifts, on shelves, or hand-held?

A: Readers are deployed at distribution centers on select dock doors and conveyor systems. They are also deployed at stores on dock doors, strategically throughout the backroom and at the entrance to the sales floor. Handheld readers and readers on forklifts are definitely in the plans.

Q: What sort of training do you anticipate that RFID will require?

A: For our associates it will be minimal if we do our jobs correctly. The system will be there to support their efforts to take care of the customer. We're working to make it as useful and user friendly as possible.

Q: What kind of hurdles and glitches have you come across in deploying to date?

A: Typical things that you encounter when you bring a technology into a new working environment. We discussed this a little earlier on in the question about reads.

Q: When does Wal-Mart intend to move from pallet-level tagging to item-level tagging?

A: There is no timetable to do that. We have a lot to learn at the case and pallet level.

Q: CVS is deploying item-level tags in the pharmacy as part of the jumpstart project. Do you have similar plans for your stores, or your pharmacies?

A: We are participating in a pharmaceutical trial that we don't discuss for security reasons.

Q: Do you think that there is any value for RFID within the consumer's home?

A: Our interest focuses around in-store usage.

Q: For some objects that Wal-Mart sells—for example, large TVs—the case is the unit that the consumer purchases and takes home. Will these cases have RFID tags in them? If so, will consumers have the option of having the tags removed or killed prior to their leaving the store?

A: The consumer has three choices:

1. Buy the product and keep the tag;
2. Buy the product and remove the tag anytime post-purchase; or,
3. Don't buy the product.

Q: Is Wal-Mart concerned about competitive intelligence issues, such as competitors scanning Wal-Mart RFID tags en-route or in the store?

A: No.

Q: Is Wal-Mart concerned about consumer backlash?

A: We have seen a very thoughtful approach to the new technology by consumers during our pilot. They understand its applications and potential and seem ready to embrace it for companies that comply with

1. EPCglobal guidelines and
2. The company's own privacy policies.

Q: Katherine Albrecht of CASPIAN takes credit for causing Wal-Mart to cancel its Brockton, Massachusetts trial after she publicly revealed it. Can you give me Wal-Mart's side of the story?

A: There was no secret test. We discussed the concept with the supplier. We worked with the supplier to set up a prototype. But we pulled the plug before it ever went live. I'm not sure you can publicly "reveal" something that never took place.

Q: So why was the Brockton trial pulled?

A: Because we weren't going to pursue item-level tagging. We participated in the Broken Arrow trial just to test our theory that you needed to start at the case and pallet level. The test confirmed it.

Q: Katherine Albrecht said that the Lipfinity trial with Procter & Gamble in Broken Arrow was a "secret trial" that was done without consumer notification. Was the trial actually secret, or did the consumers that Katherine spoke with just not see the signs and placards?

A: There were signs up at the store.

Albrecht states that RFID trials are conducted in secret. Not True. You can look at media in the Dallas/Fort Worth area for the past six months and see how much effort we've put into informing consumers of the pilot. A tear off sheet has been available to consumers during this testing period. It has been placed at the shelf level of the HP printers and scanners that have tags on the outer packaging. The "holding tests in secret" argument simply doesn't hold water.

INDEX

Register
Your Book

at www.awprofessional.com/register

You may be eligible to receive:
- Advance notice of forthcoming editions of the book
- Related book recommendations
- Chapter excerpts and supplements of forthcoming titles
- Information about special contests and promotions throughout the year
- Notices and reminders about author appearances, tradeshows, and online chats with special guests

Contact us

If you are interested in writing a book or reviewing manuscripts prior to publication, please write to us at:

Editorial Department
Addison-Wesley Professional
75 Arlington Street, Suite 300
Boston, MA 02116 USA
Email: AWPro@aw.com

Addison-Wesley

Visit us on the Web: http://www.awprofessional.com